VISUAL DATA INSIGHTS USING SAS ODS GRAPHICS

A GUIDE TO COMMUNICATION-EFFECTIVE DATA VISUALIZATION

LeRoy Bessler

Apress®

Visual Data Insights Using SAS ODS Graphics: A Guide to Communication-Effective Data Visualization

LeRoy Bessler
Mequon, WI, USA

ISBN-13 (pbk): 978-1-4842-8608-1   ISBN-13 (electronic): 978-1-4842-8609-8
https://doi.org/10.1007/978-1-4842-8609-8

Managing Director, Apress Media LLC: Welmoed Spahr
Acquisitions Editor: Susan McDermott
Development Editor: Laura Berendson
Coordinating Editor: Jessica Vakili

Distributed to the book trade worldwide by Springer Science+Business Media New York, 233 Spring Street, 6th Floor, New York, NY 10013. Phone 1-800-SPRINGER, fax (201) 348-4505, e-mail orders-ny@springer-sbm.com, or visit www.springeronline.com. Apress Media, LLC is a California LLC and the sole member (owner) is Springer Science + Business Media Finance Inc (SSBM Finance Inc). SSBM Finance Inc is a **Delaware** corporation.

For information on translations, please e-mail booktranslations@springernature.com; for reprint, paperback, or audio rights, please e-mail bookpermissions@springernature.com.

Apress titles may be purchased in bulk for academic, corporate, or promotional use. eBook versions and licenses are also available for most titles. For more information, reference our Print and eBook Bulk Sales web page at http://www.apress.com/bulk-sales.

Any source code or other supplementary material referenced by the author in this book is available to readers on the Github repository: https://github.com/Apress/Visual-Data-Insights-Using-SAS-ODS-Graphics. For more detailed information, please visit http://www.apress.com/source-code.

Printed on acid-free paper

To creators of data visualization, the intended readers,

and

to William S. Playfair, Philippe Buache, and Guillaume de L'Isle

whose graphic innovations in the late 1700's in England and in France

remain the most widely used and frequently used ways to provide and find visual data insights

Let your computer draw a picture
to let viewers see the data
with image for an easy, immediate impression
of what's larger, what's smaller
of what the trend is
of what the relationship is
of what the distribution is
including geographically
and with precise numbers for correct, reliable understanding.

Let it paint a picture
that shows the viewer what's important.

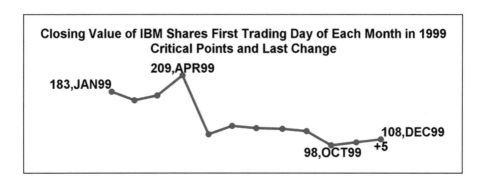

Contents

About the Author

LeRoy Bessler is a data analyst, a SAS software expert, a data visualization aficionado since 1981, and an advocate for and demonstrator of his graphic design principles since 1991. He earned a Ph.D. in physics with a minor in mathematics from the University of Wisconsin-Milwaukee. He served as Assistant Professor of Mathematics at Milwaukee School of Engineering and later was appointed Senior Fellow in Theoretical Physics at Queen Mary College, University of London. When finding the theory of submicroscopic elementary particles becoming, to his taste, increasingly unphysical, LeRoy returned to the United States to devote his interest and energy to the macroscopic needs of American business using computers and networks, working for employers and clients in finance, health insurance, property and casualty insurance, manufacturing, energy, and retail.

After a variety of roles, responsibilities, and accomplishments in information technology, he decided to concentrate on using SAS software as his IT tool. LeRoy has supported SAS servers, SAS software, SAS data, and the users of those facilities, as well as working as a data analyst and SAS programmer. His distinguishing expertise with SAS software has been communication-effective data visualization, and software-intelligent application development for reliability, reusability, maintainability, extendability, and flexibility—to deliver Visual Data Insights™ and Strong Smart Systems™.

Still a professor at heart, LeRoy has shared his ideas, knowledge, and experience at conferences for SAS users throughout the United States and in Europe. With the help of volunteers, he has enjoyed creating SAS user mutual education opportunities. LeRoy is a How To contributor to VIEWS News, the online quarterly for SAS users.

He has served as an elected and appointed local government official and on the boards of social services, cultural, and civic nonprofit organizations.

About the Technical Reviewer

Philip R. Holland has over 30 years of experience of working with SAS software. In 1992, he formed his own consultancy company, Holland Numerics Ltd. Since then, he has provided SAS technical consultancy and training in the financial, retail, and pharmaceutical sectors in the UK, Belgium, Holland, Germany, and the United States. Since 1995, he has presented papers on a wide range of SAS-related topics at SAS user conferences and seminars in the UK, Europe, and the United States and has published four SAS-related books and eight SAS-related courses.

While writing his thesis for a doctorate in chemistry in the 1980s, he gave an early draft to a colleague to read, and they found 60 errors in spelling and grammar in the first chapter! This made him realize that no one can proofread their own work, because you read what you think is there, rather than what you have actually written. Since then, he has helped other book and SAS program writers avoid his own proofreading embarrassment.

Acknowledgments

I am immensely grateful to executive editor Susan McDermott for engaging me to write this book, to Apress editors Jessica Vakili, Rita Fernando, and Laura C. Berendson, to Apress production coordinator Krishnan Sathyamurthy, to Apress project manager Angel Michael Dhanaraj, and to Philip R. Holland who did the technical review. It was Phil who got me connected to Apress. Without these people, and the rest of the Apress team, there would have been no book.

I am indebted to Marcia Surratt, Lelia McConnell, Martin Mincey, Kathryn McLawhorn, Amber Elam, Cyrus Bradford, and Liz Edwards at SAS Technical Support who handled my problems and questions during this project.

Alan Paller, an analyst in the early days of the computer graphics industry, encouraged me to become the advocate for graphics at Miller Brewing Company. There, at my suggestion, Thomas S. Cain added support of all three graphics software products to my workplace responsibilities. Atis Purins commissioned me do a makeover of the monthly report to Miller management on usage, capacity, and performance for all of the information technology facilities. That project not only engaged my graphic design principles, but also inspired me to implement what I call Software-Intelligent Application Development. SIAD assures that the code can auto-adapt to changes in the run-time environment to maintain the design objectives. Chris Potter, the 1990 SAS Users Group International Conference Graphics Section Chair, liked what he saw in one of my presentations and encouraged me to promote my design principles at future conferences. That is how my journey of developing and sharing my ideas, knowledge, and experience with SAS software for data visualization began.

Over decades, numerous conference organizers kindly provided me so many opportunities to write and speak about SAS topics, including data visualization. That engendered my development of an ever-growing list of design guidelines for graphics and color use, and a portfolio of examples to illustrate application of those guidelines.

I thank David V. Evans of J.C. Penney who hired a repatriated computer know-nothing as an information technology trainee, starting me on a new career. That career ultimately got me to this book.

Carol Bessler gets me through life. Thank you.

Introduction

The visual data insight provided by graphics is essential to understand data. Statistics alone clearly are not sufficient, as demonstrated with Anscombe's quartet of data sets, for which regressions are plotted in Figure 1. All four very different images have statistics that are nearly identical. See the four tables in Table 1 and further remarks there.

This book is an experience-based, practical handbook for applying communication-effective design principles (48 for graphs and 23 for color), as demonstrated in 327 examples.

The data visualization tool used is SAS ODS Graphics, but the principles are software independent, relevant for *any* tool.

Graphs can make it unnecessarily difficult to understand the data, can confuse the viewer, or can mislead the viewer. If a graph needs an explanation, it has failed to communicate.

Misuse of color (or colour in some countries) likewise has adverse visual consequences. I've seen—no, I struggled to see—yellow text or yellow markers on a white background and black text on dark blue. The only options worse could be white on white and black on black. Another common problem is the use of continuous color gradients for color coding. Determining exactly which colored areas are the same color is impossible, and matching an area color with its corresponding color along a continuous color gradient legend is likewise. Those are not the only or the worst unwise uses of color.

This book explains and demonstrates how to get the best out of ODS Graphics, relying on numerous guidelines. Three deserve special emphasis.

First, though images are for quick, easy inference, the associated precise numbers are needed for correct, reliable inference. The book shows all of the ways to make them part of the image. Moving the eye from a graphic element (bar end or plot point) to axis tick mark values and estimating is not a solution.

Let your data talk. Show and Tell. Data can *show* its behavior with the visual—which category is bigger/smaller or where it's going over time—and it can *tell* the viewer its values with annotation, an axis table, or web-enabled mouseover text.

Second, avoid information overload. *Show the Viewer What's Important.* Use ranking and subsetting. Three ways of subsetting are shown in Figure 4-7. Another way is via sparse presentation, as in Figures 1-18 and 1-15. Ranking is a huge help, is used in numerous examples, and requires little code.

Third, both readability of the text and usability of any color coding are usually taken for granted, but must be assured. See the recommendations.

The principles in this book are application independent, and the examples can be adapted to any data for any industry, enterprise, or organization.

Code for all of the examples can be downloaded at `https://github.com/Apress/Visual-Data-Insights-Using-SAS-ODS-Graphics`. Some examples use %INCLUDE statements to retrieve macros or included code blocks. A zip file of includables must be downloaded. If your site does not have SAS/ETS, a zip file of needed ETS data sets can be downloaded. The overwhelming majority of examples use SASHELP data sets that all sites have.

You can re-create *any* example, and experiment with options, or apply the example code to your own data, adapting the code however desired.

The book's scope is anything that ODS Graphics can do. Though the examples cannot show you everything, they do span that range.

As I traveled through the range, applying recommended principles to representative examples, I also built alternatives that are unexpected, but improved. The improvements are too many to enumerate here. An old and frequently repeated (not by me) criticism of pie charts is refuted—three ways. And the simplest possible pie chart is demonstrated as a very powerful visual.

You will see innovations. For statistics, there are new ways to create distributions, box plots, and histograms. For categorical data, there is the Tree Chart, Flag Chart, CrossRoads SignPost Chart, and bar chart with no bars. For time series data, there is the Sparse (not spark) Line—alone, in tables, in panels, and web enabled—and also a trend line with no line.

Three different ODS Graphics features to create composites of graphs and/or tables are covered. One way is web enabled, with the added benefit of pop-up mouseover text, which is indispensable in cases where permanent annotation of plot points is infeasible.

This book is the culmination and, in effect, an illustrated biography of my working, learning, and discovery with SAS graphics software since 1981. My conclusions about best design with graphics and color gradually grew longer and longer. I have applied them with the benefit of experience, now using SAS ODS Graphics to create images, illuminations, and insights for data, which are correct, clear, concise but complete, convincing, compelling, and, when needed or otherwise appropriate, colorful. Join me in the quest.

LeRoy Bessler

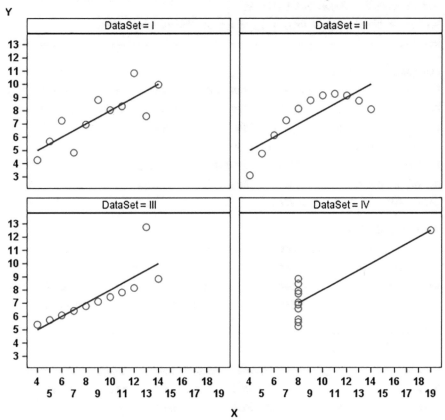

Scatter Plots & Regression Lines for Anscombe's Quartet of Data Sets for Which Statistics Are Nearly Identical

Figure 1. Demonstration of the need for and value of data visualization

I learned about the four data sets from an article by Philip R. Holland in Issue 54 (2nd/3rd Quarter 2011) of VIEWS News. For more information about Francis J. Anscombe's data sets, see https://en.wikipedia.org/wiki/Anscombe's_quartet. For the example of The Datasaurus Dozen, see www.autodesk.com/research/publications/same-stats-different-graphs.

Table 1. SAS REG procedure statistics for the Anscombe quartet data

```
Model: MODEL1   Dependent Variable: y
Number of Observations Read 11, Number of Observations Used 11
DataSet=I ------------------------------------------------------------
```

Analysis of Variance

Source	DF	Sum of Squares	Mean Square	F Value	Pr > F
Model	1	27.51000	27.51000	17.99	0.0022
Error	9	13.76269	1.52919		
Corrected Total	10	41.27269			

Root MSE	1.23660	R-Square	0.6665
Dependent Mean	7.50091	Adj R-Sq	0.6295
Coeff Var	16.48605		

Parameter Estimates

Variable	DF	Parameter Estimate	Standard Error	t Value	Pr > |t|
Intercept	1	3.00009	1.12475	2.67	0.0257
x	1	0.50009	0.11791	4.24	0.0022

```
DataSet=II ---------------------------------------------------
```

Analysis of Variance

Source	DF	Sum of Squares	Mean Square	F Value	Pr > F
Model	1	27.50000	27.50000	17.97	0.0022
Error	9	13.77629	1.53070		
Corrected Total	10	41.27629			

Root MSE	1.23721	R-Square	0.6662
Dependent Mean	7.50091	Adj R-Sq	0.6292
Coeff Var	16.49419		

Parameter Estimates

Variable	DF	Parameter Estimate	Standard Error	t Value	Pr > |t|
Intercept	1	3.00091	1.12530	2.67	0.0258
x	1	0.50000	0.11796	4.24	0.0022

(continued)

Table 1. (*continued*)

```
DataSet=III --------------------------------------------------------------
Analysis of Variance
Source             DF    Sum of Squares  Mean Square   F Value    Pr > F
Mode                1           27.47001     27.47001     17.97    0.0022
Error               9           13.75619      1.52847
Corrected Total    10        41.22620
Root MSE               1.23631    R-Square      0.6663
Dependent Mean         7.50000    Adj R-Sq      0.6292
Coeff Var             16.48415

Parameter Estimates
                       Parameter      Standard
Variable    DF         Estimate         Error    t Value   Pr > |t|
Intercept    1          3.00245       1.12448       2.67     0.0256
x            1          0.49973       0.11788       4.24     0.0022

DataSet=IV ---------------------------------------------------------------
Analysis of Variance
Source             DF    Sum of Squares  Mean Square   F Value    Pr > F
Model               1           27.49000     27.49000     18.00    0.0022
Error               9           13.74249      1.52694
Corrected Total    10        41.23249
Root MSE               1.23570    R-Square      0.6667
Dependent Mean         7.50091    Adj R-Sq      0.6297
Coeff Var             16.47394

Parameter Estimates
                       Parameter      Standard
Variable    DF         Estimate         Error    t Value   Pr > |t|
Intercept    1          3.00173       1.12392       2.67     0.0256
x            1          0.49991       0.11782       4.24     0.0022
```

Design
Principles

Principles of Communication-Effective Graphic Design

The principles presented here are actually software independent, but the mission of this book is to help you implement them with SAS ODS Graphics. Among the numerous principles presented here, three key design objectives that deserve special emphasis and should always guide your graphic design are as follows:

- Provide precise numbers whenever possible, rather than force the graph viewer to estimate them, such as the Y and X values for plot points. A graph enables quick, easy inference, but the precise numbers are needed for correct inference.

- Show the viewer what's important.

- Assure readability. It is not automatic.

© LeRoy Bessler 2023
LeR. Bessler, *Visual Data Insights Using SAS ODS Graphics*,
https://doi.org/10.1007/978-1-4842-8609-8_1

Be Brief, Clear, Picturesque, and Accurate

I try to always be guided by the following quote from Joseph Pulitzer:

> *Put it before them briefly so they will read it,*
>
> *clearly so they will appreciate it,*
>
> *picturesquely so they will remember it,*
>
> *and, above all, accurately so they will be guided by its light.*

Though not about graphic communication, this quote by the famous newspaper publisher (known for the Pulitzer Prizes, which were established in 1917 as a result of his endowment to Columbia University) is wise advice for any communication. A graph is inherently picturesque, but is not automatically clear nor devoid of superfluous content. If the source data is accurate, the graph will be an accurate representation of information—if its design does not distort it.

3D Pie Charts Are *Always* Misleading

Look at Figure 1-1, an illuminating and convincing example that 3D pie charts are always misleading (unless they consist of only two or four slices). The slices are laid out in this fortuitous way only because the slices are really ordered alphabetically by the slice names that I have chosen to omit. I did not deliberately create this proof that 3D pie charts distort and falsely communicate. The inherently dangerous 3D pie chart did it *for* me.

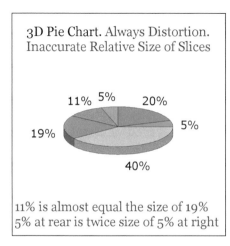
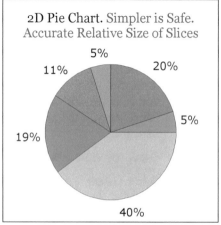

Figure 1-1. 3D pie chart *versus* 2D pie chart

3D Bar Charts Are Anticommunicative

The subtitles in the bar charts in Figure 1-2 explain how and why 3D bar charts are anticommunicative. For the 2D example, I suppress the really not very helpful X axis and display the precise values in a column adjacent to the bars—a communication-effective graph needs to display precise numbers, not just an image with axis values to estimate numbers.

ODS Graphics cannot create 3D bar charts, but there is the option to fill bars with what are called "data skins" instead of uniform solid fill color. A data skin can produce bars that look puffy, like long buttons, and can produce a puffy pie. The data skin adds no communication value. It is nothing more than a 3D-like effect that can be used, if desired, for decoration.

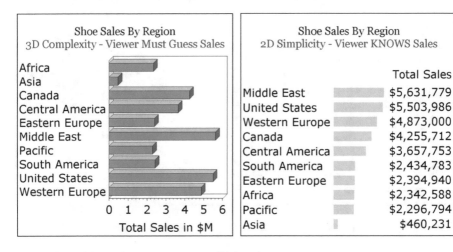

Figure 1-2. 3D bar chart versus custom 2D bar chart

Graphs Need Image *and* Precise Numbers

Provide image plus precise numbers:

- *Image* for quick and easy inference
- *Precise numbers* for accurate and reliable inference

Consider the pair of bar charts that were presented in Figure 1-2. It is *impossible* to reliably determine precise numbers by comparing bar ends (or point locations for a scatter plot or trend line) to axis values. Moving your eye from a bar end (or a plot point) to an axis and mentally interpolating the approximate corresponding point on the axis to estimate a number based on the framing tick mark values is a futile, unreliable, unacceptable way to try to get the precise number and certainty.

In Figure 1-3 are two ways to present a scatter plot of data. In the right-hand-side plot, there is no guesswork required to get the precise Y and X values. Then in Figure 1-4, drop lines are used. They can get the viewer's eye to the correct place on the axis, but the viewer still needs to estimate, based on the "enclosing" tick mark values. But drop lines are helpful when you do not have annotation of the Y and X values. In Figure 1-4, annotation is instead used to deliver information other than the scatter plot coordinates. That scatter plot could have been made more informative by including Age in the data labels and by color-coding the markers based on Sex which is a variable in the input data set.

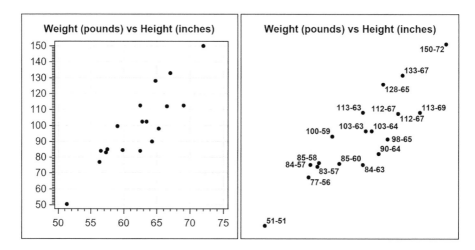

Figure 1-3. Scatter plot with grid and tick mark values versus annotated scatter plot

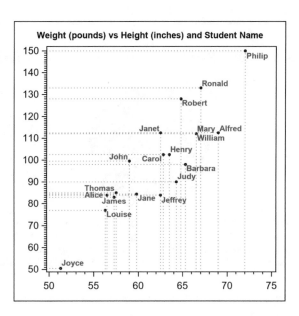

Figure 1-4. Using drop lines makes axis values and tick marks more helpful

When neither annotation nor drop lines are sufficient to get numbers for a scatter plot, the only solution is a companion table, on the same page, or as an Excel table that is linked to a web-deployed scatter plot.

A pie chart should include descriptions, values, and percents of the whole. When labels overlap or (for tiny slices) disappear, use a legend instead of labels as in Figure 1-5.

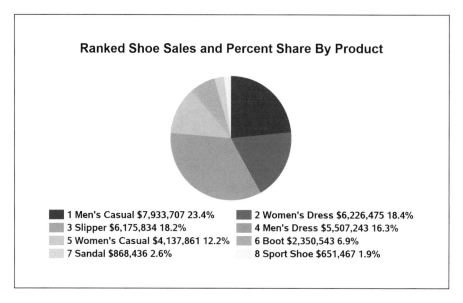

Figure 1-5. Fully informative ranked pie chart with legend

A legend requires moving the eyes from each slice to its legend entry. A good alternative is the ODS Graphics CALLOUT option shown in Figure 1-6, where there is a dashed line from each slice to its label. An extra benefit is avoiding the preprocessing to prepare the fully informative legend entries.

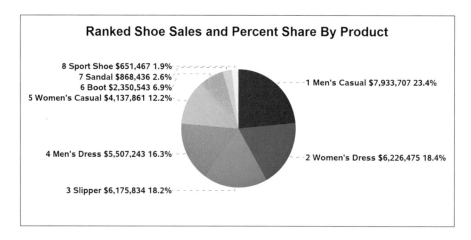

Figure 1-6. Fully informative ranked pie chart with callout labels

A bar chart can have its numbers in a column next to its bars, as in the 2D bar chart in Figure 1-2. Another way to provide those numbers, and more, is to use Y axis tables as columns next to the bar category labels. In Figure 1-7, three Y axis tables are used to create what is a ranked and rank-labeled bar chart alternative to a pie chart.

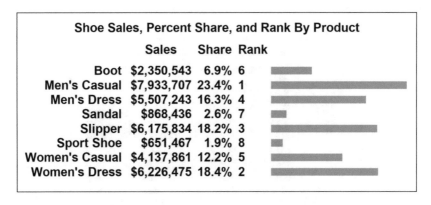

Ranked Shoe Sales and Percent Share By Product

Rank		Sales	Share	
1	Men's Casual	$7,933,707	23.4%	
2	Women's Dress	$6,226,475	18.4%	
3	Slipper	$6,175,834	18.2%	
4	Men's Dress	$5,507,243	16.3%	
5	Women's Casual	$4,137,861	12.2%	
6	Boot	$2,350,543	6.9%	
7	Sandal	$868,436	2.6%	
8	Sport Shoe	$651,467	1.9%	

Figure 1-7. A ranked order rank-labeled fully informative horizontal bar chart

For a large number of categories, you can provide them in alphabetical order for easy lookup, but still can provide Rank as shown in Figure 1-8.

Shoe Sales, Percent Share, and Rank By Product

	Sales	Share	Rank	
Boot	$2,350,543	6.9%	6	
Men's Casual	$7,933,707	23.4%	1	
Men's Dress	$5,507,243	16.3%	4	
Sandal	$868,436	2.6%	7	
Slipper	$6,175,834	18.2%	3	
Sport Shoe	$651,467	1.9%	8	
Women's Casual	$4,137,861	12.2%	5	
Women's Dress	$6,226,475	18.4%	2	

Figure 1-8. An alphabetical order rank-labeled fully informative horizontal bar chart

A Usable Stacked Bar Chart Requires an Axis Table to Deliver the Precise Values

A usable stacked bar chart must have an axis table to deliver the precise values. For Figure 1-9, the only thing you can do is visually compare the sizes of bar segments, but with no accurate knowledge of the Sales values.

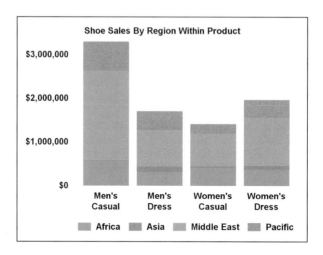

Figure 1-9. This typical stacked bar chart is unable to provide precise values of sales

In a bar chart with more segments, moving your eye from bar segments to the X axis table is not easy or efficient, but Figure 1-10 is truly informative and allows a viewer to quickly and easily identify Product-Region combinations with larger sales.

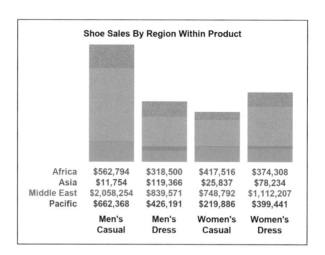

Figure 1-10. Usable stacked bar chart with precise values for the bar segments

The red segments in two of the stacked bars in Figures 1-9 and 1-10 is a good demonstration that color with insufficient mass is difficult to distinguish. Color distinguishability is discussed further in Chapter 2.

A Clustered Horizontal Bar Chart Is Better Than a Stacked Bar Chart

When there are two categorical key variables, Figure 1-11 is a better solution. The precise values are adjacent to their bars.

Figure 1-11. A clustered horizontal bar chart

With no legend, the color is not needed for legend purposes, but it allows the viewer to more quickly visually compare the sales in any region across all products. Rather than have to find the bar label in the list of region bars for each product.

For Bar Charts, Horizontal Is Usually Better

On a vertical bar chart, the bar labels along the X axis or the values that you want to display at the bar ends might be too wide. On a horizontal bar chart, space problems are less likely.

For a Line Plot with Discrete X Values, an X Axis Table Is an Alternative to Annotation

An X axis table can be color-coded so that no legend is necessary (see Figure 1-12). Instead of relying on going to look for a legend, the identity of any plot point is already in the row label for Y values in the color that corresponds to the color of the line. This color-coded plot is an efficient and effective way to find all of the information needed to interpret a multi-line plot.

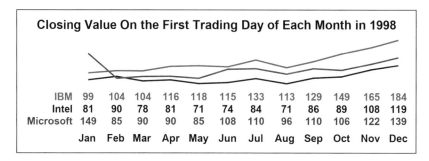

Figure 1-12. Multi-line overlay plot with X axis table

Furthermore, *unlike* the case in Figure 1-13, on a multi-line plot, even if the plot points within a line are sufficiently separated to make annotation in principle possible, collisions between annotation and other lines or between annotation for one line with annotation for another line are always likely, unless the lines happen to be well separated throughout their extent, which is not the case in Figure 1-12.

Curve Labels Eliminate the Need for a Legend

On a multi-line plot, the effect of collisions between annotation and lines can be mitigated by using a lighter shade for each line's color. The curve labels in Figure 1-13 provide an easier and faster way for a viewer to identify lines than a legend.

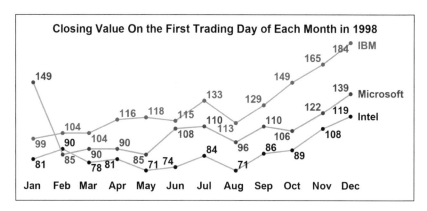

Figure 1-13. Multi-line overlay plot with data labels and curve labels, no Y axis needed and no legend needed

Show Them What's Important

Suppressing superfluous graphic paraphernalia, as is discussed later in this chapter (and demonstrated with coding in Chapter 3), limits what the viewers look at and is consistent with the principle of Showing Them What's Important. But showing what's important is very easy to implement for bar charts and pie charts with ranking and for bar charts with subsetting. The discussion here pertains to data with a categorical key, such as Sales by Region.

Show Them What's Important with Ranking

Order the bars in a bar chart or slices in a pie chart by the value of the measurement of interest, from largest to smallest. *Show* the Rank as part of the bar or pie slice labeling.

If you have a chart where a small value is desirable, instead order the bars or slices from smallest to largest.

In a case where the number of bars in a chart is large, such as the 50 states of America plus the District of Columbia, you might instead order the bars alphabetically for easy lookup. Perhaps better, you could present the bar chart twice, both alphabetically and by magnitude of the measurement.

Show Them What's Important with Subsetting

By subsetting I mean limit the data presented, rather than delivering all of it. If you have ranked the data, this increases the focus on what's important. For example, instead of creating a bar chart of the population of every one of the 195 countries in the world, you might present a subset of only the Top 25, Top 10, or Top Whatever. There are the familiar Top 10 lists. For music, there are the Top 40 lists.

There is also the concept called the Pareto Principle, or "The 80-20 Rule." It says that in many situations, about 80% of the results come from 20% of the causes. For example, 80% of an enterprise's sales might come from 20% of its customers. Since they have shown themselves to be more heavily interested, that 20% might be the ones to be more frequently solicited for additional purchases. Another variation of this phenomenon could be that 80% of an enterprise's problem reports might come from 20% of its customers. There is nothing magical or inevitable about 80 and 20. The percentages might be, say, 90 and 10. The key concept, for graphic design, is that not every category is equally important, and it is useful to focus on the most important for enterprise operation.

Another way to think about subsetting is the idea of limiting the message. Always remember Pulitzer's advice from the beginning of this chapter: "Put it before them briefly." I once received the same advice from my assistant Kenneth J. Wesley when I was agonizing over a report to executive management. He said, "LeRoy, put it on one page. If you make it longer, they won't read it."

Some time later, at the suggestion of Atis Purins, I was doing a design and construction makeover for reports on the performance, capacity, and usage of all of Miller Brewing Company's computer resources. One report was on disk capacity consumption and ran to numerous pages. By limiting the number of consumption purpose categories ordered by size to one page, attention was drawn to a much shorter list, and it accounted for a huge percent of the total consumption burden, thus showing the information that was most important. What had been unwieldy became readable, and when any new report features were added, I was directed to adhere to the new design concept. The decision to use subsetting and ranking limited the volume of information, and kept the focus where appropriate.

When subsetting the input categories for a bar chart, it is essential to inform the viewer as to the relative significance of what's in versus what's out. As demonstrated in Figure 1-14, use the title and subtitles to give the viewer of the graph these facts:

- The total number of categories
- The grand total of the measurement over all categories
- The number of categories shown
- The subtotal of the measurement for the categories shown
- What percent of the grand total is that subtotal

Three Ways to Do Ranked Subsetting

An extremely popular way, anywhere, to do ranking and subsetting is with, for example, a Top Ten List. From this first way that I thought of, the title of a report was "Top 20 Cities Account for Subtotal Shoe Sales of $24,402,060 which is 72.09% of the Grand Total." And in that case, the subtitle was "All 53 Cities Have Grand Total Shoes Sales $33,851,566." That pair of statements embodies the design and information principles for titles that I presented in the preceding section.

A second obvious solution is to use a cutoff, in which case a possible title could be something like "Ranked X Cities with Sales of At Least $1,000,000 Account for…," where X would be the number that pass the test and where the end of the title would be analogous to that of the Top 20 Cities report.

A third way of subsetting that I particularly like is to limit the ranked categories to only enough to account for a specified percent of the grand total of the measurement of interest, as in Enough Ranked Cities to Account for At Least 90% of Grand Total Shoe Sales. This avoids picking an arbitrary N for Top N or an arbitrary cutoff for the measure of interest (see Figure 1-14).

In Chapter 4, all three ways to do subsetting are shown in Figure 4-7.

Figure 1-14. Ranked and subsetted bar chart, selecting subtotal percent of grand total

If you like, you could web-deploy multiple subsets and allow the viewer to navigate among them with links. You could even include a link to a complete list of all of the categories. How to web-deploy interlinked graphs with ODS HTML5 will be shown in Chapter 14.

Simplicity Accelerates and Facilitates Visual Insights into Data

Simplicity accelerates and facilitates visual insights into data. Needless complexity impedes and/or obstructs communication. Simplicity is powerful. Simplicity is elegant.

Elegance (like in an elegant mathematical proof) consists of

- Everything necessary
- Only the necessary

Let's take a look at the simplest graph I've ever created. At first glance, the pie charts in Figure 1-15 look trivial, but they really are not. I *usually* advocate against consolidating very small slices in a pie chart or very small bars in a bar chart into an "Other" category. It prompts the question, "What is in 'Other'?" Your graph design should anticipate and answer all questions, not create them.

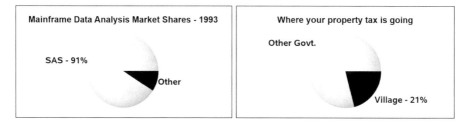

Figure 1-15. The Extremes of Other with "The Pac-Man Pie Chart"

Here, the smallness of "Other" in the chart on the left dramatizes the fact that the sum of all of the competitive products' market shares was insignificant. The sizes and values for their tiny market shares were deemed by me as not worth showing.

Conversely, the chart on the right is expressly meant to prompt interest in what is in "Other." I created it during my time as a local elected official, to emphasize to residents that the bulk of their real estate property tax payment went to other public bodies which were also getting a share (in some cases, a much larger share). Since the tax was paid to the office of our Village Treasurer, he would receive letters of concern about the size of the bill. To anticipate and address questions and concerns, the pie chart was included in a cover letter that went out with the annual tax bill. There also was a table of supporting detail, which compared the current amounts and growth of all of the shares of tax bill total. We did explain what was in "Other," but *after* graphically emphasizing the smallness of Village government's share of the bill.

I call this design "The Pac-Man Pie Chart," and I call these examples "The Extremes of Other." Why "Pac-Man"? Who is that guy? *Pac-Man* is a video game that was introduced in 1980. It features a little creature who looks like a yellow pie with a slice missing.

A Sparse Graph Is Easily and Quickly Interpreted

Two examples of this arose back in 1990, when I developed a way of sometimes presenting trend data (also known as "time series" data) that I called "Sparse Line Annotation." Of course, either Pac-Man pie chart in Figure 1-15 also qualifies as a "sparse graph" because of its simplicity.

I was working at Miller Brewing Company and wanted to graphically compare two historical data sets, one for Miller Lite and the other for all beer in America. For both plots, knowing *every* precise Y value was not important. The interesting feature is the *behavior* of each trend and an apparent correlation in their behaviors. However, that correlation is not the focus of this discussion.

What is sparse on this pair of graphs is my choice of which Y values to annotate and which X values to show on the axis. In later chapters, you will see a more compact and even sparser way to present the essential data for a trend line.

From Figure 1-16, I concluded that the most interesting data in a trend might usually be the values of Y (the measure of interest) and X (the date) for

- The start

- The end

- Any intermediate maximum

- Any intermediate minimum

- The size and direction of change since the date previous to the end date (not shown in the examples created then and presented here)

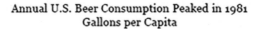

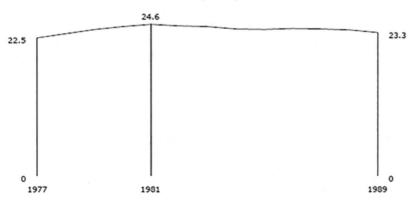

Figure 1-16. Sparse Line Annotation case 1: start, end, and maximum

From Figure 1-17, I realized that an additional point of interest could be a point, not a minimum or maximum, where the trend permanently changes in any of these ways:

- From rapidly increasing to slowly increasing

- From slowly increasing to rapidly increasing

- From rapidly decreasing to slowly decreasing
- From slowly decreasing to rapidly decreasing

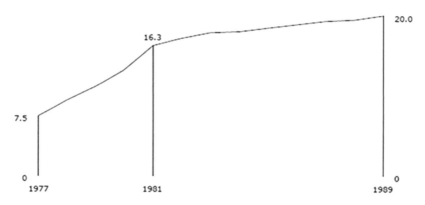

Figure 1-17. Sparse Line Annotation case 2: start, end, and trend change

Sparse Line Annotation has been updated and significantly enhanced as is shown in Figure 1-18, which is taken up as Figure 8-9. As an alternative to an overlay plot, see also Sparse Line Tables and Sparse Line Panels in Figures 9-9, 9-11, 9-12, and 9-13 and the web-enabled Sparse Line Table in Figure 14-15. The new Sparse Lines remove the X axis entirely and provide X values as part of the data point annotation, not just the Y values. An important new feature in the new Sparse Line, standalone or in any of the composites, is to provide, as additional annotation for the last data point, the change since the second last data point, which is always of interest when looking at the last data point.

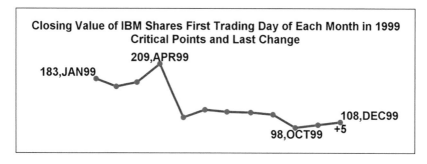

Figure 1-18. The updated and enhanced Sparse Line, using different data

Inform the Viewer About the Key Data Points of a Multi-line Overlay Plot

As I previously explained, the most interesting Y values on any trend line are usually the start, end, and any intermediate minimum or maximum. Picking those out visually is easy on a single-line plot or when the number of X values is small on a multi-line plot. A kinder alternative for any multi-line overlay plot is to *deliver* the information to the viewer, rather than require it to be discovered by scrutiny. The viewer of your output will appreciate convenience, completeness, and certainty in the information delivery.

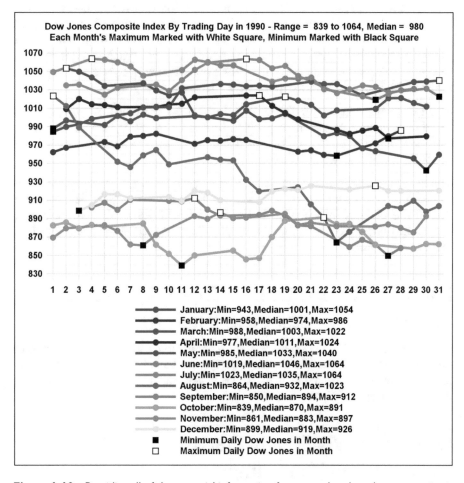

Figure 1-19. Providing all of the essential information for an overlay plot when annotation is infeasible

For a Trend, Usually Start the Y Axis at Zero

In Figure 1-16, I started the Y axis at zero. That happened to make the trend line for the first plot look nearly flat. It is interesting and appropriate that industry observers described this range of American beer consumption history as flat.

SAS ODS Graphics, like other software, by default will take the range of the Y variable and allow it to use all of the vertical space. If you have a need or desire to see the trend with maximum variation, that is the right design.

However, the disadvantage is that it can cause a trend viewer unnecessary anxiety about unfavorable slope in the trend or unjustified elation about favorable slope. Rather than react to the most recent slope of the trend, the latest value on a trend line should be evaluated based on the magnitude of the change or based on whether or not the latest value has reached a desired goal or crossed a dangerous threshold. **If there is a desired goal or a dangerous threshold, include a reference line for it on the graph.**

If you use web delivery for the trend line, you can present both views of the trend hyperlinked together, to provide both an unexciting view of the trend and the ability to see it with the *maximum* variation. An alternative option is to stack the two views in a document page.

The recommendation to start the Y axis at zero is always practical for a single-line plot. However, for an overlay plot, it can be impractical. For example, even if the table of information at the bottom of Figure 1-19 were omitted, the already crowded and crisscrossing plot lines would be squashed together in a useless mess.

For a Bar Chart, Unless There Are Negative Values, Always Start the Value Axis at Zero

This avoids distorting apparent relative magnitude of the bars. From time to time, I see the unfortunate decision to start a bar chart somewhere above zero. Presumably, the reason is to save vertical space, but the result is deceptive, intentionally or not.

Use Maximally Simple Design to Focus on What's Important

We can put a graph "before them briefly" and maximize focus where it's needed by keeping the layout simple as possible. Here, my concern is not limiting the information or the graphic elements, but on omitting and suppressing non-information and superfluous graphic artifacts.

Before computer graphics software became available, we manually plotted our data with a pen or pencil on graph paper. If you have never seen it, you can find pictures online. Graph paper was usually a grid of green lines on white paper. ODS Graphics can emulate it. That is, as shown in the left-hand-side plot in Figure 1-3, it can provide grid lines, axis lines, tick marks, minor tick marks, axis values, and a border around the plot area. In the right-hand-side plot in Figure 1-3, I suppressed the traditional graphic framework and added annotation for the plot points, using ODS Graphics data labels.

Feasibility of annotation of a scatter plot depends on plot point density. With fewer, I could have included the names of the people. The annotated plot delivers the information briefly (i.e., without superfluous graphic paraphernalia), clearly, picturesquely, and accurately—there is no guesswork required to get the precise Y and X values. With annotation, the viewer gains information, and the image loses the superfluous axis lines, axis values, axis tick marks, and grid lines. In Chapter 3, you will see, among other things, the code used to create the annotated scatter plot with its maximally simple framework.

Another example of suppressing the superfluous graphic paraphernalia is the 2D bar chart in Figure 1-2. It briefly delivers the bars, the categories, and the values, the only things that the viewer needs to see and needs to know. There are no axes, no axis labels, no tick marks, and no tick mark values—which would need to be used to guess the precise values for each category if the column of values had not been provided instead.

I saw a recommendation to display the minimum of traditional graphics paraphernalia in Edward Tufte's presentation at a Computer Measurement Group conference in the 1980s.

Tell Them What's Important with a Headline

The typical title of a graph tells the viewer what is being shown. If that is not self-evident from the graph, such information can instead be put in the second title line when devoting the first line to a headline. If there is something especially significant in the graph, or some inference that can be drawn from the graph, or the graph shows a very encouraging result or implicitly carries a cautionary message, do not leave it to the viewer to discover it. *Just come right out and SAY IT*, in a headline.

A Graph Footnote Does Not Need to Be Small

If the information is important, do not undersize it. A footnote that is merely identifying a data source, or providing some boilerplate statement(s), could reasonably be in a small font size, to save vertical display space and to avoid distraction from important information or the image.

When the footnote contains important information, make it the same size as the title. ODS Graphics title lines are always Bold by default. Consider making your footnote(s) Bold as a standard, unless a footnote is better diminished for cases mentioned in the preceding paragraph.

Assure Text Readability

This seems like an obvious design guideline. Readability is always important, but it is not automatic. You should not assume it.

Text readability is essential since the letters and numbers on a graph are as important as the graphic elements. Image accelerates and facilitates inference from, and understanding of, the data, but precise data (the labels and numbers) assure reliable and correct inference and understanding. I emphasized that at the opening of this chapter. In Chapter 2, we will see that color "readability" also matters, whether it is color of text or color of graphic elements.

If you are satisfied with how the software defaults format the text for a specific graph without your specifying text characteristics, that's the simplest solution. If not, adjust the software's options to deliver text and numbers you deem most readable.

Font Size and Font Weight Affect Readability

The main determinants of readability are font size and font weight. Thicker letters and numbers (i.e., those with **Bold** weight) are always more readable.

Despite best intentions, actual font size used might sometimes have to be dictated by getting text to fit without overlap of adjacent text items, such as plot point annotations. In that case, sparse annotation might be a useful workaround. In the situations demonstrated in Figures 1-16 and 1-17, sparse annotation is a benefit, not a deprivation of important information.

It is believed that sans serif fonts, such as Arial, are better for visually impaired readers. If sans serif fonts benefit visually impaired readers, then I contend that they can benefit *all* readers. An advantage of sans serif fonts is that they are drawn with a uniform thickness throughout the contour of the character, rather than with thin and thick points around their contour. Thick is always easier to see. There is a counterargument in favor of serif fonts, but it pertains to reading large amounts of text, such as in a novel. For a graph, serif fonts are not an advantage for any viewer.

Keep Text Horizontal

Use horizontal text whenever possible. That is the way that we read most languages. One often sees vertical text used as the label for a vertical axis. Forcing it to be horizontal might force the displayed graph area to be narrower. A simple alternative is to put the axis labels in a subtitle, if they are not already in the graph title, either explicitly or implicitly.

If the horizontal axis is obviously the date, there is no value in labeling it. Use the space available to maximize the vertical display space for the graph. This is a more efficient use of the graph viewer's time and attention. Tell them what's important, not what they can know at a glance, without explicitly being told.

Another place where one sometimes sees vertical text or tilted text is as the tick mark values on the horizontal axis. When some horizontal axis tick mark values are automatically omitted by software (in ODS Graphics, this is called "thinning"), if the omitted ones can be inferred from adjacent displayed values to the left and the right of where there would be a tick mark value, then no harm is done. Apart from options to control the characteristics of the tick mark values (font face, font size, font weight, font color), ODS Graphics provides controls on thinning, as will be shown later. There is also an option to use STAGGER on the X values, by displaying them in two rows below the X axis. As you move from left to right, the X value is in the top row, then in the bottom, then back in the top, and so on. If you cannot turn off the thinning with an option, and thinning causes a problem, then reducing font size is the obvious solution.

Never Use Backgrounds—They Impair Readability

The readability of text is too often diminished or even obstructed by decorative features such as textured backgrounds, color gradient backgrounds, and, what can easily be the worst, photographs. The graphic part of your image should not have to compete for the attention of the viewer. The graph and the text in your ODS Graphic image needs a *plain* solid color background, preferably white, but in any case definitely a background color of high contrast with the text color.

The use of colored text or text on colored backgrounds is discussed in Chapter 2. The simplest and most important principle for color is: use color to communicate, not to decorate.

Readability Depends on Display Situation

If your audience will receive hardcopy of your graph or might print your graph, be sure to evaluate your graphic output as printed. **Print it!** Verify that what you get is what you expected, what you intended. The image and text on your monitor screen are shining light at your eyes. Hardcopy is viewed with reflected light which presents a weaker image to your eyes, with the consequence that text, thin lines, small plot point markers, and legend color swatches can be difficult to read or to interpret as to precise color.

If creating color output that is expected to be printed by somebody, try to assure that they have access to a color printer.

A Graph Can Have a Companion Table

When you cannot provide the precise numbers *inside* the graphic image, a companion table is the solution. You can deliver a graph and its companion table on the same page, or on separate pages in the same file, if delivering as a PDF or Microsoft Word document. In Excel, you can deliver a graph and its companion table on the same worksheet or in separate worksheets in the same workbook. In HTML, they can be on the same web page or on interlinked web pages.

Web Graphs

There are special considerations and capability to consider when presenting your graphs with HTML packaging.

Include Data Tips (a.k.a. Mouseover Text)

Whenever permanent annotation does not fit, include data tips via mouseover text. This displays the precise numbers, but, of course, they disappear when the mouse moves on. Besides displaying the values being graphed, you can optionally display additional information related to the graphic element as in Figure 1-20.

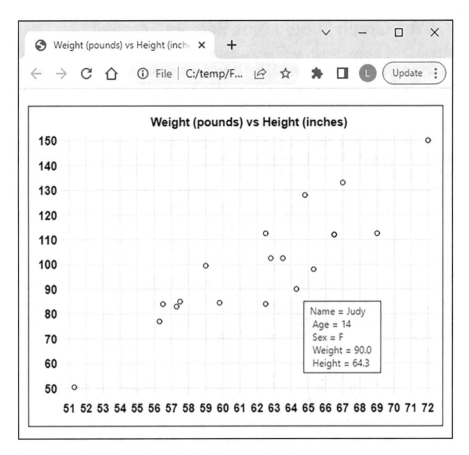

Figure 1-20. Web plot with maximally informative data tips

A Web Graph Can Have a Companion Hyperlinked Excel Table

Consider providing the web graph viewer the opportunity to inspect, using Excel, all of the data statically (unlike data tips, which are temporary). This is a good solution for a scatter plot or a trend line that is too dense for annotation to provide precise numbers. (You can instead put the table on the same or another web page.)

A recipient of your web graph is likely to have Excel on their computer and the knowledge of how to use it. How to deliver a web graph with a linked Excel table companion will be explained later. The Excel table can be hyperlinked back to the web graph.

You can deliver not just the values of the variables being graphed, but any additional data elements that might be in the input data set used for the graph.

A Web Graph Should Not Require Scrolling

A trend line, or any graph, is best viewed in its entirety. It must never require horizontal scrolling. A horizontal bar chart with very many bars, if designed as shown earlier, that does not require comparing bars with an X axis could be usefully viewed with vertical scrolling.

Optimize the size of the image file to fill, but not exceed, what you expect to be the probable size and shape of the screens used to view the web page— **Show Them the Entire Picture**. If in doubt as to the best size, it would be better to err in the direction of smaller, within the limits of readability. If necessary, the web page viewer should be able to use the browser's zoom feature to enlarge or shrink the displayed material.

Summary

This is a review of the Principles of Communication-Effective Graphic Design.

These reminders are what I like to call my Principia Graphika, a title inspired by *Principia Mathematica* by Sir Isaac Newton (1687). That title was reused for three volumes by Alfred North Whitehead and Bertrand Russell (1910, 1912, 1913):

- Effective communication is brief, clear, picturesque, and accurate so that it is read, understood, remembered, and reliable.

- Provide image plus precise numbers: image for quick and easy inference and precise numbers for accurate and correct inference. Estimates based on axis tick mark values are unreliable.

- A scatter plot or a trend (a.k.a. time series) plot, if not too dense, can be annotated.

- For plots which cannot be annotated, an X axis table might be able to deliver the Y values.

- For a plot where neither annotation nor an X axis table is feasible, drop lines can show the correct locations on the axes, but the viewer of your plot will still need to estimate the value.

- On a multi-line plot, if full annotation is infeasible due to label-label or label-line collisions, a color-coded X axis table can deliver the Y values and can identify each plot line without a legend.

- On a multi-line plot without such a color-coded X axis table to serve, in effect, as a legend, curve labels could be used instead.

- If you have a multi-line plot that cannot be annotated, and an X axis table is infeasible, you can augment its legend entries by appending to each of them that line's values for start, end, minimum, and maximum (and maybe statistics, such as average).

- For a dense plot, when neither annotation nor an X axis table is feasible, you can supply the precise values, using a web graph, to provide not only mouseover data tips but also the input data as a web table or an Excel spreadsheet hyperlinked from and back to the web graph.

- If you cannot embed precise numbers in a graph image, whether a plot or any other type, you can create a same-page package of graph and companion table with ODS PDF or ODS Word, or use ODS Excel to put the graph and table on the same worksheet or in separate worksheets in the same workbook

- A simple and sparse graph is easily and quickly interpreted.

- Often, the only Y values of significant interest for a trend line (time series plot) are start, end, and any intermediate maximum, minimum, or point where a persistent change of trend occurs. For that, you can use what I call an Annotated Sparse Line. Another item of interest is the change since the second latest plot point, which can be included in the annotation for the end plot point. I call this graph interchangeably Sparse Line and Annotated Sparse Line. A sparse plot line without annotation would be useless. So, "Annotated" should always be understood when referring to a Sparse Line.

- A pie chart should include slice descriptions, values, and percents of the whole as slice labels. When needed, use the CALLOUT label option, which is less likely to suffer label overlap, or move all label information to a legend.

- Arrange the slices in a pie chart in order of decreasing size. Show them what's important.

- For a pie chart, usually avoid the use of an "Other" pie slice. A graph should anticipate and answer questions, not prompt them, such as "What's in 'Other'?" However, in some cases what I call "The Pac-Man Pie Chart" can be an effective communication tool for The Extremes of Other (see the examples).

- The guidelines for pie charts also apply to donut charts.

- A bar chart can have the values as data labels at either end of its bars, or in axis tables, rather than forcing the viewer of your graph to guess them using axis tick mark values.

- Use horizontal bar charts, rather than vertical, whenever possible. Fitting the descriptive labels or optional data labels for the bars then is less likely to be a problem.

- With input data preprocessing, you can create horizontal bar chart labels that concatenate rank, description, value, and percent of the total. Without such preprocessing to concatenate it, you can instead deliver all of this information with simple category description labels and with three Y axis tables to provide columns of the other information.

- Normally, you should arrange the bars in order of decreasing importance (i.e., rank). Show them what's important. For a large number of bars, include the numeric rank.

- For a very long list, you can arrange bars alphabetically by category to facilitate finding any category quickly, but include a column of the rank values to show importance.

- Show them what's important with a horizontal bar chart:
  - With ranking—Order the bars by size.
  - With subsetting—Subset the data whenever sufficient, with three alternative methods:
    - Top N (e.g., Top 10)
    - Top P% (i.e., enough of the ranked values to account for P percent of the grand total)
    - All of the ranked values above (or below) a cutoff

- To inform the viewer as to the significance of what's in versus what's out, if subsetting the input data for a bar chart, use title and subtitles to inform the viewer of the graph about five facts:

  - The total number of categories

  - The grand total of the measurement over all categories

  - The number of categories shown

  - The subtotal of the measurement for the categories shown

  - What percent of the grand total is that subtotal

- The only usable stacked vertical bar chart is one with an X axis table, to deliver the precise values for bar segments.

- A clustered horizontal bar chart is a better alternative than a stacked bar chart.

- Simplicity is powerful. Simplicity is elegant.

- An elegant graph presents

  - Everything necessary

  - Only the necessary

- Simplicity accelerates and facilitates visual insights.

- Needless complexity impedes and/or obstructs communication.

- 3D pie charts always distort the relative size of shares.

- 3D bar charts are needlessly complex and more difficult to use than 2D.

- Use simple design to focus on what's important. Omit graph frame and axis lines. Use tick mark values and grid lines only to aid communication or interpretation when it is impossible to provide precise numbers on the graph using techniques in this book.

- If possible, make your graph title a headline—announce the conclusion/revelation. (Describe *what* is graphed in a subtitle.)

- If a footnote contains important information, make its text size the same as that of the title. If the title is bold, consider making the footnote bold, unless there is some reason to diminish it.

- Keep all text horizontal.

- Anything that might be in an axis label can instead be put into the graph's subtitle or title.

- Make all text and numbers readable:

  - Use sufficient size.

  - Assure high color contrast on a plain background.

  - Bold face always enhances readability.

  - Sans serif text is more readable.

- Never use background images, textured backgrounds, and color gradient backgrounds. They impair graph and text readability.

- If your audience is going to receive hardcopy of your graph or print your graph, be sure to evaluate your graphic output as printed.

- Unless it includes negative numbers, normally start your vertical axis at zero.

- On a trend plot, if there is a desired goal or a dangerous threshold for the measurement being monitored and tracked, include a reference line for it on the graph.

- When delivering a graph via HTML/web page:

  - *Always* provide mouseover data tips.

  - If you cannot annotate precise numbers in the graph image, deliver them with a companion Excel spreadsheet, linked from and back to the web page. You could instead put the table on the same web page or on an interlinked web page.

  - Size the image file to fill, but not exceed, what you expect to be the probable size and shape of the screens used to view the web page—***Show Them the Entire Picture***.

Principles of Communication-Effective Use of Color

The guidelines discussed in this chapter will apply not only to graphs, plots, and charts but also to tabular reports, spreadsheets, web pages, maps, and text. One of the commonest visual communication design problems I see is the misuse of color. This chapter can help you to avoid that. All of the guidelines are intended to help you accomplish this simply stated goal: *use color to communicate, not to decorate.*

Avoid Red and Green for "Bad Versus Good"

Color blindness affects about 1 in 12 men and 1 out of 200 women in the world. That's about 350 million people who are unable to correctly see color. Since it affects so many people, it's important to be careful as to how you use

© LeRoy Bessler 2023
LeR. Bessler, *Visual Data Insights Using SAS ODS Graphics*,
https://doi.org/10.1007/978-1-4842-8609-8_2

color in your communication materials if you want to be confident that you will successfully communicate with anyone who looks at your images.

Though there are different types of color blindness, the most common is red-green color blindness. This means that the person is unable to tell the difference between red and green. Consider how this could affect someone viewing a graph with red and green color coding (the so-called "traffic lighting"). Color blindness is a widely and regrettably underappreciated problem.

Figure 2-1 shows safe alternatives to red and green, which include red and blue and orange and green. (For the use of orange and green, see the population density change map of Ireland in Figure 2-15.) The five color-coding options in Figure 2-1 can apply not only to signed data but also to cases of very bad, bad, neutral, good, and very good. In the examples, the color blocks with dark or very strong color fill would be more readable if the text were white instead of black. I will come back to this matter later.

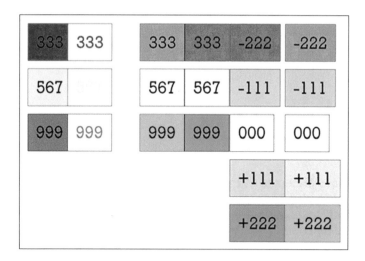

Figure 2-1. "Traffic lighting" at the left to color-code bad and good versus alternatives at the right that are distinguishable by persons with the commonest form of color blindness. (The text and background color combinations were **not** chosen for readability.)

Color-Coding Data with a Multiple Shades of the Same Hue

One frequently sees the use of a single hue with varying shades, sometimes using a continuous color gradient legend. A common example is a contour plot of the depth of a body of water. However, it is important to respect the fact that **the eye can have difficulty distinguishing color when confronted with numerous shades of the same hue, even when they are not in a continuous color gradient**.

Consider, for example, the challenge posed by Figure 2-2. Knowing exactly where the color fill from one of the cells is on the legend is impossible. (If you knew where it was on the legend, you then would need to estimate its value. For that, more values on the legend would be helpful. The best solution is annotation of the cells.)

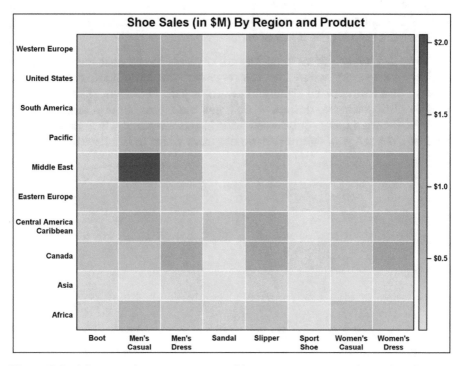

Figure 2-2. A heat map for a continuous variable, using a continuous color gradient legend

So, when color-coding a graph, how many shades of a single hue can be reliably distinguished?

Many years ago, I was told that the human eye cannot reliably distinguish more than five shades (degrees of lightness/darkness) of a single hue. From time to time, I have seen examples where more than five colors were used for color coding that confirmed that assertion. It was somewhere between difficult and impossible to distinguish all of the shades.

Out of respect for the alleged five-shade limit, I respected it when I created the by-county membership map in Figure 2-15. The color palette used is definitely distinguishable.

If desired, one can add white, the lightest shade of any hue, and black, the darkest shade of any hue, to increase the size of any single-hue palette. These extreme shades of the hue are always distinguishable from the nonextreme.

This issue of distinguishability has nothing to do with *seeing* the shade. The eye can see all shades of any hue. However, with a color-coded graph, you need to compare a colored item—a bar, a pie chart slice, a plot marker, a map geographic area—with a legend of color swatches. Also, when you compare one of the colored items with another, it's useful to know, with certainty, whether the color is the same or different.

In Figure 2-3, where there is no legend, the cells in the heat map are coded with the same color when the cells represent the same numeric value. The values range from one to eight, and my color palette of eight shades of red is reliably distinguishable, despite what I was once told about a limit of five. I used RGB-coded colors (discussed later in this chapter), which make it easy to divide the range of lightness/darkness from white to black within any hue.

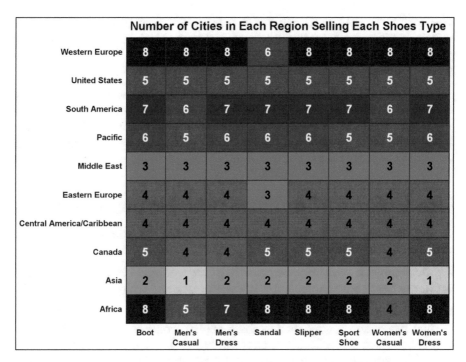

Number of Cities in Each Region Selling Each Shoes Type								
Western Europe	8	8	8	6	8	8	8	8
United States	5	5	5	5	5	5	5	5
South America	7	6	7	7	7	7	6	7
Pacific	6	5	6	6	6	5	5	6
Middle East	3	3	3	3	3	3	3	3
Eastern Europe	4	4	4	3	4	4	4	4
Central America/Caribbean	4	4	4	4	4	4	4	4
Canada	5	4	4	5	5	5	4	5
Asia	2	1	2	2	2	2	2	1
Africa	8	5	7	8	8	8	4	8
	Boot	Men's Casual	Men's Dress	Sandal	Slipper	Sport Shoe	Women's Casual	Women's Dress

Figure 2-3. A heat map for a discrete variable, using eight distinguishable shades of red, omitting the legend—unneeded due to data labels

"True red," or whatever you might want to call it, falls right in the middle of the white to black range. I selected four equally separated color steps between the middle and each of the extremes. That gave me nine reds. In Figure 2-3, I only need eight. The darkest red, not used, looks almost like black.

The net of this is that five is not the maximum, and I am not certain what *is* a universally applicable maximum number of shades, if any, when holding the hue constant. It might depend on the choice of hue. The keys to distinguishability are (a) that the shades are sufficiently separated and (b) that you visually evaluate the result of your selection.

The heat map example in Figure 2-2 involves sales data that is continuous, not discrete. In Figure 2-3, the number of cities where a product is sold in a region is in all cases a number in the range one to eight. However, the sales dollars for each product-region category in Figure 2-2 are widely variable.

In principle, the dollar amounts could be annotated inside each cell for Figure 2-2 by using a small enough font, but a small number of color codes would not suffice, and the colors could not be equally separated because the increments between sales dollars are widely variable. So, the natural choice is a continuous color gradient, but matching the cell color to a level on the gradient is *very* difficult.

The secret to distinguishability of a palette of color codes of one hue is sufficient differences in the lightness/darkness. With a continuous color gradient, those differences are infinitesimal, which makes colors on the gradient indistinguishable unless they are for values sufficiently far apart.

However, even if some colors on a continuous color gradient, such as the one in Figure 2-2, are sufficiently distinguishable, it is impossible to reliably associate any one of those colors with the specific area fill in the graph, if any, that is actually the same color. A continuous color gradient is *never* a practical tool to identify precise values.

Use Color to Communicate, Not to Decorate

To decide how or whether to use color, always ask yourself what is the purpose of using color.

If your graph does not require color (e.g., for a legend or to color-code the data), the best color combination is always black and white.

If your legend is to identify different area fills on a chart, and the number of distinct fills is small, gray shades could suffice. For four easily distinguished gray shades, see the RGB color codes in Figure 2-11, where CX000000 and CXFFFFFF are the color codes for black and white. If you would need more than four gray shades plus black and white, then a palette of colors should be considered instead for the sake of easier distinguishability. As I look again, I notice that, though the four gray shades are easily distinguishable, the darkest gray is troublesomely close to black, at least for my eye. A better fifth shade of gray would be white, not black.

Use of Color Can Confuse

Viewers attribute significance/meaning to your use of color, even if you intend none. The use of color without a communication objective can disorient, confuse, or even mislead the viewer. Here's a real-life example.

In an article that I once read, there was a bar chart analogous in design to that in Figure 2-4. My simulation here compares the sales of six brands. (This simulation uses real sales data for a consumer product, but the actual brand names have been "anonymized.") Analogous to the situation for that real bar chart for other data, there is no relationship between Brand F and Brand A and none between Brand B and Brand C, despite the pairs having the same colors. This use of color in the article had me puzzled. However, upon looking at other charts in the article, I saw that all of them used that same limited palette of four colors. My conclusion was that the *available* palette was limited to the four colors, and when color fill was applied to the bar chart, the creator reused the first two colors. Regardless of the reason for the strange use of color, that bar chart was confusing. All bars in that chart could have instead been just one color or empty with a black contour. Either choice would have been unambiguous and communication-effective. It is always best to use color to communicate rather than to decorate. Decoration can confuse.

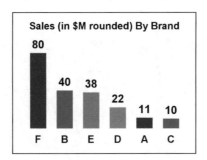

Figure 2-4. Confusing color use prompts a question when viewed. What is the relationship between brands with the same fill color?

Establish and Use a Personal Color Palette for Consistency

Use color consistently throughout a collection of graphs. To make that easier, establish a personal palette and rules for use of color for various purposes.

To establish a palette, you need to get acquainted with the colors available. There are multiple color naming schemes supported by ODS Graphics. The simplest choice is to use the SAS "Predefined Colors." *However, make no assumptions about what a SAS Predefined Color name will deliver.*

The best way to get to know the Predefined Colors is to look at them. (There are, in a few cases, multiple names for the same color.) If you open a web browser and search for "SAS Predefined Colors," you will be able to find an illustrated list of the Predefined Color names.

Alternatively, so that you can create a permanent, easily accessed reference display, in Listing A2-5 in Appendix A is a SAS program to generate an Excel worksheet of samples of the SAS Predefined Colors. **(You can also go to www.apress.com/ISBN and click the "Download source code" button.)** In the worksheet, you can delete rows for colors of no interest and save a subset of colors worksheet as a personal easy-to-look-up palette of SAS Predefined Colors. (The Excel workbook includes a second worksheet to display samples of 360 HLS Colors, without and with embedded text, and a column for their SAS HLS color codes.)

An excerpt from the program's output worksheet is shown in Figure 2-5. Column E which contains the SAS RGB color codes was omitted in the screen capture for Figure 2-5. Columns C and D enable you to evaluate whether Black or White is the better choice for text color when the SAS Predefined Color is the background color. If the chart shows that Black text on Brown background is hard to read, then Brown text on Black background is also unacceptable. The same is true for the color pair White and Chartreuse.

	A	B	C	D
17	Brown		Brown	Brown
18	Burlywood		Burlywood	Burlywood
19	CadetBlue		CadetBlue	CadetBlue
20	Chartreuse		Chartreuse	Chartreuse
21	Chocolate		Chocolate	Chocolate
22	Coral		Coral	Coral
23	CornFlowerBlue		CornFlowerBlue	CornFlowerBlue
24	CornSilk		CornSilk	
25	Crimson		Crimson	Crimson
26	Cyan		Cyan	Cyan

Figure 2-5. Ten of the SAS Predefined Colors with demonstration of readability (or not) for black text and white text when using each color as a background

See the "Color Systems" section for alternatives to the SAS Predefined Colors.

Beware of Color Names

SAS Predefined Colors are the easiest to specify and to understand (except for some color names being what I think is misleading, or at least names that I would not choose for them).

Nominally, there are 151 colors. Of those, four of them are one- or two-character abbreviations for also-present full color names. Besides that, six shades of gray (US English) are the same as six shades of grey (UK English), *and* Cyan and Aqua are the same color, as are Magenta and Fuchsia (elsewhere often, but acceptably, spelled as Fuschia—I cannot explain the existence of two different spellings). There are only 139 distinct SAS Predefined Colors and 145 color names, of which six are alternate names (greys instead of grays).

Rather than relying on a color name when choosing, see the color first. The spreadsheet that you can create with the SAS program in Listing A2-5 in Appendix A *shows* you the color. See Figure 2-5. Is what you find in row 21, for example, *your* idea of what Chocolate looks like?

RGB and HLS color systems are discussed near the end of this chapter.

Benefits of Boring Black and White

Technology to print black and shades of gray is faster, cheaper, and more reliable.

Black, white, and shades of gray are easier to use. Not only is the equipment simpler, but also these "boring" colors require no agonizing over color selection.

Finally, such output is more copyable. Regardless of the proliferation of cheap color printers, the copiers that you find in abundance in the workplace are still mostly black and white. Why does that matter? Well, good graphs, maps, and tables—if hardcopy—will get copied when people want to share them.

I always recall a colleague coming back to the office excited about a presentation that he had attended and from which he decided to share the handouts. Unfortunately, the slide prints were in color, but the copies that he gave us were black, white, and gray shades.

Having said all that, my mission is to help you achieve communication-effective use of color, not black and white.

Color Requires Sufficient Mass to Be Distinguishable

Avoid text that is too small or too thinly drawn. Color requires sufficient mass to be distinguishable:

- Make colored text big enough and thick enough.
- Make colored lines thick enough.
- Make colored plot point markers big enough and use solid filled markers.
- Make legend color swatches big enough.

See Figure 1-10 for an example of color text that is thick enough to be easily visually associated with the color filled bar segment.

See Figure 1-19 for an example of color used for plot lines and plot markers that are thick enough and big enough to make it easy to distinguish the different colors and to connect the legend entries with plot elements.

In ODS Graphics, the best way to control the size of legend color swatches is with FILLHEIGHT set to the height of the legend entry text descriptions and with FILLASPECT=GOLDEN, which delivers a rectangle, rather than a square for the swatch. "GOLDEN" means that the width of the rectangle will be approximately 1.618 times the height, which is called The Golden Ratio. See Figures 1-5, 1-9, or 1-11 for examples of a legend with Golden Ratio color swatches.

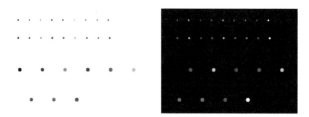

Figure 2-6. *Plot point marker size determines its color distinguishability*

Never Use Background Images or Textured or Color Gradient Backgrounds

They *always* impair or actually obstruct text and/or graph readability.

Use a Plain Solid Color Background

Text and graphs display most readably on a plain solid color background, preferably white. If not white, try cream or another sufficiently light color.

Provide High Contrast Between Text Color and Background Color

On a white or light color background, text must be sufficiently dark. On a dark background, such as dark area fills for a pie chart or map, use white text.

Bad examples I have seen include black text on blue and yellow text on white. The only worse combinations that I can think of are black on black or white on white, or any other color on itself as a background.

I am always puzzled about the creator's objective when I receive an email blast with gray text or visit a web page that uses gray text. I once had the nighttime experience of seeing an office building which had its resident/owner company name in a lighted sign at the top. The sign used (nonlight) blue text on a black background, providing an unintended nonidentification. You can have that same visual noncommunication experience, in simulation, by looking at the lower-right corner of the right-hand illustration in Figure 2-7. That office building was demolished and replaced, mercifully without that signage color pair.

Figure 2-7. Colored text on white and black backgrounds. Insufficient contrast provides an uninvited vision test, too often with an unsuccessful communication result

Pie Charts and Color

If you can actually fit labels of readable size inside a pie chart's slices, assure that the contrast between label color and slice color is sufficient. Dark backgrounds require white labels. Varying the label color between black and white, depending on slice fill color, requires the use of an ODS Graphics Attribute Map (more coding). To avoid extra work, choose a palette of all light fills or all dark fills.

Better alternatives are outside labels or a legend. For outside labels, the CALLOUT option (see Figure 1-8) has the added benefit of lessening the probability of label overlap between adjacent slices.

Another solution is a legend (see Figure 1-5) that contains all of the labels for each pie slice. Assure that the color swatches are big enough to be easily distinguishable, as discussed earlier.

For any pie slices that are tiny, use a color bright and strong enough to be distinguishable, especially if using a legend.

If, for any reason, you are dissatisfied with a pie chart, consider a bar chart like the one shown in Figure 1-7. It delivers the category and precise numbers for value and percent of total. It provides a visible comparison of the size of the values, but does lack the pie chart's way of visually presenting the size of the share of the whole.

Emphasis Options for Colorless Text

For emphasizing text without depending on color, consider Bold, *Italics*, ***Bold Italics***, <u>Underline</u> (if not in a web page context, where underlined text might be misconstrued as the label of a hyperlink), or ALL CAPS (use sparingly).

Choosing the Right Colors

The decision to *use* color imposes the requirement to *choose* colors, unless you are willing to live with the software's default color decisions, regardless of the consequences for your visual communication mission. Consider the color use options explained as follows.

A Light Color Can Be the Right Color

On a bar chart, especially with many bars, a dark color will create an overwhelming visual mass, and empty bars can create visual confusion between bars and spaces. A light color is best.

In Figure 2-8, three bar charts have BARWIDTH=0.5, which means that bars take up half the vertical width made available for the bars' part of the overall image. With the default bar width used in the first example, the impact of full-strength color becomes absolutely overwhelming.

Figure 2-8. Gray bars are visible without being overwhelming like black or causing confusion between bars and spaces like white—confusion more likely when there are many more bars

With light color bars, the graph title, the categories, and the values dominate the image, with the bars there as an easy and quick way to assess the relative magnitude of the values for the categories.

Uncolor Might Be the Right Color

Use color or uncolor as follows:

- If no data levels or categories, use black and white.
- If few levels or categories, gray shades can suffice.
- If many levels or categories, color is necessary.

"Transparent" Color As the Right Color

Transparent colors are helpful for graphs that have overlapping elements, as in Figure 2-9. Transparency can range from 0 (opaque color) to 1 (no color). The use of TRANSPARENCY=0.5 makes the band that overlays part of the plot light blue, which is 50% of the way from white to "true blue" or the "undiminished" shade of blue.

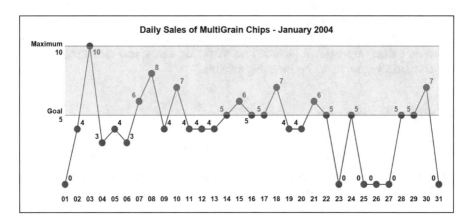

Figure 2-9. Time series plot with a band, with transparency = 0.5. A good way to dramatize achieving (or not achieving) the goal with this easily created unobtrusive highlight

Color Differs on Different Media

A computer screen uses RGB colors; a printer uses CMYK colors. Screen displayed color and printed color look different. A computer screen's colored text and colored graph elements shine at your eyes, but on paper you see them with reflected light, which makes the colors and the image less impactful. If you expect your output to be printed, be sure to verify that what gets printed will look how you would like it to look. Print it.

If preparing a presentation, test the result on the projector to be used whenever possible. The color on your computer screen may differ from that projected. If possible, change your color(s) to something that displays as you wish. If not, at least you will be able to deliver your presentation with no surprises. I always remember my projector versus computer screen color discrepancy experiences.

In one case, every speaker at the conference had the same problem, so it was not a personal embarrassment to any of us. Red and blue projected as orange and purple. The other case was a conference presentation by me on the use of color. I had included a slide to demonstrate that color name "light pink" was unreliable. Using it in the software involved yielded a color darker than pink. I was astonished to see, instead, projected colors of light gray and gray. Fortunately, this on-site pretest had alerted me to what would happen at presentation time.

Two different monitors are the same medium, but it was disconcerting to notice that colors on my laptop were different from the same colors on my auxiliary monitor. Though they are two different devices from the standpoint of details of the technology used, it *did* surprise me. The lesson demonstrated is that use of color can introduce uncertainty as to the outcome when somebody else views your visual production. The always safest color palette is black and white, if it suffices. Gray shades are a harmless addition to that palette, unless the palette includes so many, or some too close together in lightness/darkness, as to be indistinguishable.

Color Systems

Here, we look at RGB colors and HLS colors. Besides these and the SAS Predefined Colors, there are *other* color systems supported by ODS Graphics. Feel free to investigate them, if desired. These three systems have served me well and could be adequate to your needs.

RGB Colors

RGB colors are blended from red, green, and blue. Before discussing RGB colors in the context of SAS ODS Graphics, let me explain them in a domain that might be familiar to users of Microsoft Office tools. In, for example, Microsoft Word, if you wish to change the color of text, the Font Color dropdown presents you with four choices: Theme Colors, Standard Colors, More Colors, and Gradient. If you select More Colors, you are presented with two tabs, Standard and Custom. The Standard tab offers you lots of color buttons. Custom permits you to blend or mix any color from a palette (for RGB) of 16,777,216 colors.

If you select the Custom tab, you can pick a color with a mouse click in a band of all available colors. Instead, you can pick a color model, either RGB or HSL (for hue, saturation, lightness). RGB is the default model. There you select the amounts of red, green, and blue by typing in any number between 0 and 255 for each of the three colors (giving you 256 X 256 X 256 possible colors). Red is 255, 0, 0 for the three numbers. White is 255, 255, 255, while black is 0, 0, 0. You can get lighter shades of red by adding equal parts of green and blue (e.g., 255, 102, 102). This is shown in Figure 2-10.

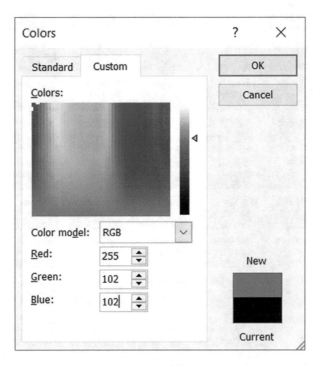

Figure 2-10. RGB color controls in Microsoft Office

To programmatically specify RGB colors in SAS ODS Graphics, you must use the SAS RGB color codes, which are eight-character strings of the form CXrrggbb, where rr, gg, and bb are hexadecimal numbers for the amount of red, green, and blue. Each r, g, and b can be anything among the values 0, 1, 2, 3, 4, 5, 6, 7, 8, 9, A, B, C, D, E, F, where A, B, C, D, E, and F are the hexadecimal equivalents of 10, 11, 12, 13, 14, and 15. I will not try to explain the hexadecimal number system here, but will simply mention that, for example, decimal 255 and 102 are FF and 66 in hexadecimal. So, the preceding Microsoft Office color selection is SAS RGB color code CXFF6666.

Figure 2-11 is a display created using SAS software to show shades of RGB primary and secondary colors and shades of gray, including white and black. In the second, fourth, and sixth columns are secondary colors yellow, cyan (turquoise), and magenta. In the fifth row are the "true" colors. As you add green and blue to red, it gets lighter. Here, I show four lightening steps 3333,

6666, 9999, CCCC, adding 20%, 40%, 60%, and 80% of green and blue to red. When reducing the red, while omitting green and blue (i.e., setting each of them to 00), the red gets darker. The darkening steps are CC, 99, 66, 33, reducing red to 80%, 60%, 40%, and 20%. Setting red to 0% produces black.

Figure 2-11. Color samples for some RGB color codes, with distinguishable lightness/darkness spacing

HLS Colors

The HLS color-coding system uses hue (what we might simply call "color"), lightness, and saturation. For any hue, lightness can vary from 0%, which is black, to 100%, which is white. 50% lightness is the color as we normally see it. Saturation varies from 100%, which is the color as we normally see it, to 0%, which is gray. Decreasing saturation from 100% adds progressively more gray to the basic hue.

Figure 2-11 shows you various lightness and darkness for the six RGB primary and secondary colors, four shades of gray, black (CX000000), and the color that is invisible on white paper, white (CXFFFFFF).

With the HLS color codes, you can select *any* of the 360 hues and vary the value ll to make the color lighter or darker. The values of hhh for 24 of those colors are shown with the corresponding color sample wedges in Figure 2-12. Set ss to FF for a fully saturated color. You can use any value for ll between 00 and FF. The illustrations in Figure 2-14 show you the lightening and darkening effect of using ll greater than 7F and less than 7F and the effect of decreasing the saturation.

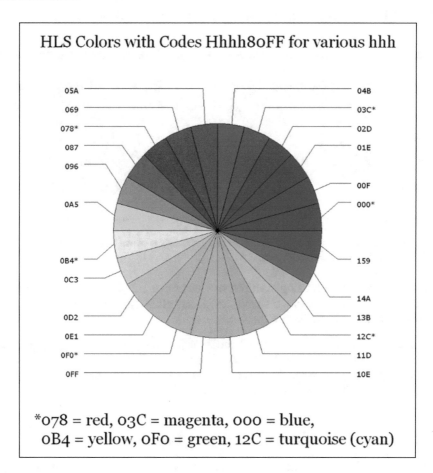

Figure 2-12. Twenty-four of the 360 possible hues in the SAS HLS color-coding system

Figure 2-13. A denser, "linearized" version of the full range of 360 HLS hues

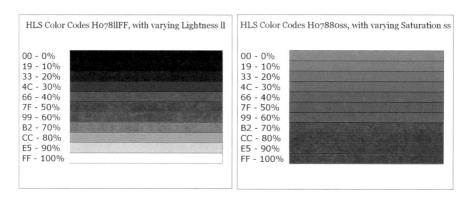

HLS Color Codes H078llFF, with varying Lightness ll	HLS Color Codes H07880ss, with varying Saturation ss
00 - 0%	00 - 0%
19 - 10%	19 - 10%
33 - 20%	33 - 20%
4C - 30%	4C - 30%
66 - 40%	66 - 40%
7F - 50%	7F - 50%
99 - 60%	99 - 60%
B2 - 70%	B2 - 70%
CC - 80%	CC - 80%
E5 - 90%	E5 - 90%
FF - 100%	FF - 100%

Figure 2-14. Demonstration of the hue red as the lightness or saturation is varied while holding the other parameter constant

Remember that when using multiple shades of one hue in a graph, select ones that are sufficiently distinguishable. You can also use white and black, the extreme shades of every hue.

For a tool to create an Excel worksheet of the 360 HLS colors analogous to that shown (as an excerpt) for SAS Predefined Colors in Figure 2-5, see Listing A2-5 in Appendix A. **(You can also go to www.apress.com/ISBN and click the "Download source code" button.)**

Examples of Good Color Use

After all of this *talk* about communication-effective use of color, let's *see* examples.

Figure 2-15 at the left uses five easily distinguished shades of green, plus white for the counties with no information, that is, no members.

Figure 2-15 at the right uses two shades of green and two shades of orange for two levels each of increasing and decreasing population density, with gray for No Change. White would have been a satisfactory alternative to gray.

Figure 2-15. Two by-county maps: at the left, an organization's membership in the United Kingdom; at the right, population density change in Ireland

Figure 2-16 relies on a color-coded X axis table to not only deliver the Y values with accuracy and precision (making a would-have-been less communicative Y axis and Y values superfluous) but also provide delivering the plot line identities available via the row labels for the axis table.

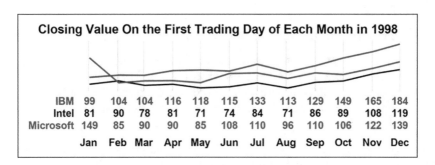

Figure 2-16. Closing value of three stocks by month in 1998. Color-coded X axis table makes annotation and legend unnecessary

Figure 2-17 adds a block plot to a grouped needle plot which is annotated with a text plot. The needle plot grouping distinguishes and identifies Male versus Female with color. The block plot groups all students of the same age with color. *A needle plot is, in effect, a vertical bar chart with the narrowest possible bars.*

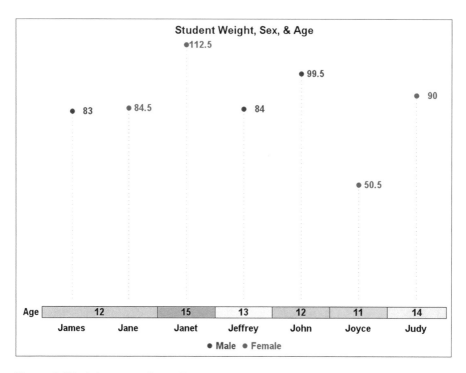

Figure 2-17. Information about all students whose first name initial is "J." Grouping gender with color-coded markers and weight data labels, grouping age with color-coded blocks for the age labels

Summary

This is a review of the Principles of Communication-Effective Use of Color.

These reminders are what I like to call my Principia Color, a title inspired by *Principia Mathematica* by Sir Isaac Newton (1687). That title was reused for three volumes by Alfred North Whitehead and Bertrand Russell (1910, 1912, 1913). Note that *color* is the Latin word for *color* (American English) and *colour* (British English).

These guidelines apply not only to graphs, plots, and charts but also to tabular reports, spreadsheets, web pages, maps, and text.

- You can use red and blue, or orange and green, as communication-effective alternatives to "traffic lighting." The commonest form of color blindness cannot distinguish between red and green. Either gray or white is a good choice for neither bad nor good.

- When using multiple shades of one hue, assure that they are truly distinguishable. If uncertain, have another person evaluate the image as to the distinguishability of the hues chosen. Color gradient legends are the most extreme example of using too many shades of one hue to be distinguishable.

- Use color to communicate, not to decorate.

- How or whether to use color: What communication purpose would it serve?

- Use of color can confuse, rather than communicate.

- Use color consistently. A personal color palette can help.

- Beware of SAS Predefined Color names. They can be misleading. Test them. There is the option of using RGB or HLS colors instead, as well as other systems also supported by ODS Graphics.

- "Boring" black and white, if printed, has benefits:

  - Black and white printers are faster, cheaper, and more reliable.

  - More copyable (there are more, cheaper, faster monochrome copiers in the typical workplace)— useful documents get copied.

  - Black, white, and gray shades require no color selection decisions.

- Color requires sufficient mass to be distinguishable (especially if printed).

  - Text must be big enough and thick enough.

  - Plot lines must be thick enough.

  - Plot point markers must be big enough and solid filled.

  - Legend color swatches must be big enough.

- Never use background images or textured or color gradient backgrounds.

- Use a plain solid color background.

- Maximize color contrast between text and background.

- When pie chart labels overlap, use colored slices and a legend.

- Consider emphasis options for colorless text:
  - **Bold**
  - ***Bold Italics***
  - *Italics*
  - <u>Underline</u> (if not on a web page)
  - ALL CAPS (use sparingly)
- A light color might be the right color for a bar chart with many bars:
  - A dark color will create an overwhelming visual mass.
  - Empty bars can create visual confusion between bars and spaces.
- Uncolor might be the right color for graphs:
  - If no data levels or categories, use black and white.
  - If few levels or categories, gray shades might suffice.
  - If many levels or categories, color is necessary.
- "Transparent" color can be useful for graphs with overlapping elements.
- Color differs on different media (verify your satisfaction with the results):
  - A monitor uses RGB colors; a printer uses CMYK colors.
  - Color shining at you (monitor) versus reflected color (paper).
  - Your computer screen versus a presentation projector.

Widely Applicable Examples You Can Use

Introduction to SAS ODS Graphics

First is some general coding information that applies to all of the examples here and in the following chapters. Then there are examples to get you acquainted with ODS Graphics coding syntax.

The approach here and in the remainder of the book is to present syntax by example, rather than to try to present every possible option. That is covered best in the *SAS 9.4 ODS Graphics Procedures Guide*, which is available online and is readily found with an Internet search. At the time of writing this book, the latest version of the guide was the Sixth Edition, last updated July 30, 2020.

In the code, bold face is used to highlight parts that are newly introduced for the example, to emphasize preprocessing DATA and PROC steps needed to prepare any input, or to connect related parts of the code.

Code listings for examples in this and all chapters (as well as macros and code blocks accessed with the %INCLUDE statement in the code) can be downloaded by readers at https://github.com/Apress/Visual-Data-Insights-Using-SAS-ODS-Graphics.

© LeRoy Bessler 2023
LeR. Bessler, *Visual Data Insights Using SAS ODS Graphics*,
https://doi.org/10.1007/978-1-4842-8609-8_3

Outer Structure of ODS Graphics Code in Examples

Some of this code is optional. This code, and the code for the examples, always includes explicit controls for image dimensions. You can instead take the default image sizing and, if necessary, manually resize it in the context where you use it—such as after insertion in a Microsoft Word document. However, if you take the default dimensions, your output will look different from what you see here. You can customize other aspects of the code, if needed, to suit the default dimensions.

In Chapter 14, you will see how to programmatically deliver ODS Graphics output as web pages. In this introduction, and in most of the examples, the coding used routes the output to a disk file with a specified filename.

SAS can be used on a variety of computer platforms, Windows, UNIX, and mainframe. For this book, all of the examples were created with Windows.

The code in Listing 3-1 and in some of the examples in later chapters includes comments between /* and */. They are ignored by processing of the code. You can delete them with no effect on processing and can add your own comments in your code.

Listing 3-1. *Outer code for all of the examples, even when some of it is not shown*

```
/* Submitting this code in a SAS session
   will do nothing unless you include an SG PROC step */

/* SHORT FORM: */

ods results off; /* optional */
ods _all_ close; /* recommended */
ods listing style=listing /* custom styles can instead be used */
  gpath='C:\temp' dpi=300;
ods graphics on / reset=all scale=off width=5.7in height=4.275in
  imagename='YourImageName';
/* your graph creation code here */
/* As an example, you could try
   title 'Test Image from Short Form Code';
   proc sgplot data=sashelp.class;
   scatter x=height y=weight;
   run;
   This is a non-executable COMMENT. */
ods _all_ close; /* recommended */

/* THE FULLER STORY: */
```

title; footnote; /* Set them back to null to prevent previous ones
used during the SAS session from being reused for the current
intended output. A prior title is likely to be overridden by a
current TITLE statement. Since FOOTNOTE statements are much less
frequently used, it is easy to inherit a prior footnote unless it
is set back to null. */

ods results off; /* No output to the Results window. The output is
viewable and accessible only from the disk location at gpath.
For RESULTS ON, your graphic output will go to the SAS Results
window, so that you can view it from inside your SAS session.
This option works the same way with the = sign, as in
ods results=off;
ON is the default. Use it if you prefer.
OFF is a preference of the author.
This statement will appear in any source code for the book
that you download. You may delete the statement with no adverse
result for the image. */

ods _all_ close; /* This is recommended as standard practice.
No results to any ODS destination unless requested below.
This assures that no other ODS destination is still open
from a prior code submission during the same SAS session
(or open by default if one is, e.g., using SAS Enterprise Guide).
Another destination being open could have adverse consequences,
or at least unexpected consequences and unnecessary output. */

ods listing

dpi=300 /* this was used for images for this book,
but is not required in the general case. Increasing DPI,
the DotsPerInch resolution, improves the image quality. */

/* style=listing This default style can be sufficient.
In this chapter, it is used for most of the examples.
Any default text attributes (font family, font size,
font weight) that are not to your satisfaction must be
specified with overrides, using ATTRS options for graph parts
and FONT= and HEIGHT= for titles and footnotes.
However, most of the examples in later chapters use a custom
ODS style, usually as an easy, concise way to control text
characteristics, to make ALL text, except that for which direct
overrides are used, to be displayed with the same font face,
font size, and font weight (in this book, always Bold).
A frequent example is STYLE=GraphTextFontArial11ptBold. */

gpath='C:\temp'; /* disk location for output. It can be a
permanent location instead. If no gpath is specified, the image
file is placed in a work folder identified in the SAS log. */

```
/* possible data preprocessing code here,
   or prior to the beginning */

ods graphics on /

  reset=all /* best practice, to prevent inheriting settings
  from a prior ODS GRAPHICS statement submitted during the
  same SAS session.*/

  /* width=10in height=7.5in
     These are dimensions of a non-wide-screen PowerPoint slide.
     If you specify only width,
     height is automatically 0.75 X width.
     Default dimensions are 640px by 480px (pixels).
     Inserted in Word, the default size is 6.67 inches by 5 inches,
     unless the available page width automatically shrinks it. */

  width=5.7in /* compatible with page width in this book */

  imagename='BeAsVerboseAsYouLike'
          /* It is probably best to not exceed 64 characters,
             which is the Windows limit if you would copy the file.
             If no imagename is specified, it is automatically
             assigned a filename identified in the SAS log. */

/* border=on This is the default.
   Maybe turn it off if creating the image for a slide,
   unless you prefer that frame. */

  scale=off /* If you want to try scale=on,
               please read the SAS documentation.
               I do not use it here. When I tried it,
               the results never were what I preferred.
               NOSCALE is equivalent alternative syntax. */

/* imagefmt=png
   Always the default for the LISTING destination */

  ; /* semi-colon for end of the ODS GRAPHICS statement */

/* your graph creation code here */
/* As an example, you could try
   title 'Test Image from Long Form Code';
   proc sgplot data=sashelp.class;
   scatter x=height y=weight;
   run;
   This is a non-executable COMMENT. */
```

```
ods listing close; /* This is recommended as standard practice.
  For the LISTING destination, it is not mandatory.
  In most examples in this book, it is omitted for brevity.
  The output image file is created without it,
  not only available in the GPATH folder,
  but also viewable in the OUTPUT window.
  However, for some destinations, it is mandatory.
  If so, without the close no output file is created,
  and it is not viewable in the OUTPUT window.
  An alternative is ODS _ALL_ CLOSE; */

title; footnote; /* Set them back to null to prevent current ones
  being reused for next output during the same SAS session if you do
  not specify new ones. Of course, if this current code block does
  not include a FOOTNOTE statement, then nullification is
  superfluous, but harmless.
  Most subsequent code submissions are likely to include
  their own TITLE statement(s), in which case, nullification is
  superfluous, but harmless.
  In most examples in this book, nullification is omitted. */
```

In the example code shown in this book, some of the framing is omitted. That saves page space and avoids taking up the time of the reader with standard code that is always present and not customized to the example. Typically omitted are

title; footnote;
ods results off;
ods _all_ close;
< Example-Specific Code Goes Here >
ods listing close;
title; footnote;

In the code available for download for the examples, the statements highlighted in bold are always included.

Also, note that ODS GRAPHICS is a synonym for ODS GRAPHICS ON.

Inner Structure of ODS Graphics Code

There will always be an SG procedure (PROC) statement, such as PROC SGPLOT. (SG is for "Statistical Graphics.")

The PROC statement has its own required parameters and some options. It has various subordinate statements, such as the SCATTER statement to create a scatter plot with PROC SGPLOT.

In addition, there typically are supporting statements, for example, to control axis content and format with XAXIS and YAXIS statements. To control the legend when one is required, there is a KEYLEGEND statement if the default is not what I recommend for the example. In some cases, you can use one or more XAXISTABLE or YAXISTABLE statements, for which examples will be shown. You might want to add one or more reference lines with the REFLINE statement(s).

For supporting text, there are TITLEn and FOOTNOTEn statements, where n can be 1 to 10 (where TITLE1 is the same as TITLE). Title and footnote text will never overlay the graph. The INSET statement allows you to place text at eight different places around the periphery of the graph (optionally formatting it with line breaks, a border, and background color), but there is no protection from overlaying parts of the graph.

For various features of the ODS Graphics output, a COLOR= option is available. Black is always the default, unless the GROUP= option is used to distinguish the graphic elements for different values of the GROUP variable, such as the color of the markers at the points for Female versus Male in a plot of Weight versus Height.

Rather than try to enumerate all of the available options for various ODS Graphics statements and parameters, the focus in the examples will be to present only the features needed and to comment on them if appropriate. Available options not used are left to the reader to discover in documentation. Those possibilities will inevitably increase over time with enhancements to the software, so software documentation will always be the up-to-date and most comprehensive source for finding what's available.

Text Attributes Control in ODS Graphics

The text parts of ODS Graphics output include titles, footnotes, text that is placed at any of eight positions inside the graph area with the INSET statement, text that is placed at X and Y coordinates with the TEXT statement, or text displayed by using other ODS Graphics statements or with their options.

Besides TITLEn, FOOTNOTEn, and INSET statements with their own format controls, there are also controls for text associated with parts of a graph, with controls like DATALABELATTRS, TEXTATTRS (for the TEXT and INSET statements), VALUEATTRS (for values on axes, in legends, etc.), LABELATTRS (for the labels of axes, a legend, etc.), TITLEATTRS (for the title of a legend, etc.), CURVELABELATTRS (for the curves on a multi-line plot), and SEGLABELATTRS (for the chunks of a stacked bar chart).

This section is a discussion of *direct* controls for text format, which can override the controls that are specified by the ODS style. For ODS LISTING, the default style is LISTING. The explanation of the creation and use of custom styles is later in this chapter in the section "Control of Text Attributes with a Custom ODS Style."

Some of the format controls for TITLE and FOOTNOTE statements are shown in Table 3-1.

Table 3-1. Format controls for TITLE and FOOTNOTE statements

Format Controls	Notes
justify=	Left, right, and center are the choices, where center is the default
font=	
height=	Various possible units, but here only point size (pt) is used
color=	BLACK is the default; see Chapter 2 for more about colors
link=	Used to create hyperlinks (as will be shown later)

Footnotes are centered by default. The default centering of titles is not in the center of the overall image. Unless you explicitly code justify=center, the title is centered over the plot area, excluding the vertical axis area with its tick mark values and excluding the space for any legend that might be placed at the side of the plot.

Additional options are BOLD and ITALIC. Here, you will usually see the use of, for example, font='Arial/Bold' rather than font='Arial' BOLD. In the later chapters, you might see the use of Arial Black with NORMAL weight as default. Arial Black is thicker than Arial bold face. It can be used to make very small text more readable.

In all of the examples in this book, I try to use the same SIZE or HEIGHT for all of the text in the image. Exceptions occur when some text aspect of the image will not fit unless made smaller. Some titles are larger than the body text of the image.

For the various graph text attribute options (such as those mentioned earlier—DATALABELATTRS, etc., the use of which will be demonstrated by example), the controls are shown in Table 3-2.

Table 3-2. Format controls for various graph text attribute options

Format Control	Notes
family=	For font family
size=	For font height
color=	
style=	Choices are ITALIC and the default NORMAL
weight=	Choices are BOLD and the default NORMAL

Note the following: Conventions for size= are the same as those for TITLE/ FOOTNOTE height=. Arial/Bold is not a font family. For graph text attributes, use family=Arial weight=bold.

See some of the text capabilities and controls in action in Figure 3-1.

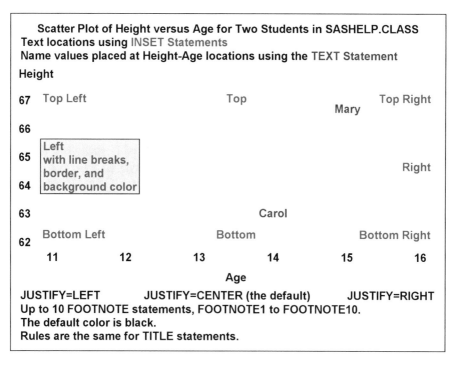

Figure 3-1. Eight places where you can inset text in the graph display area, and demonstration and comments about FOOTNOTE and TITLE controls

SAS provides sample data sets in the SASHELP data library. The CLASS data set contains name, sex, age, height, and weight for 19 students. Carol is the name of my wife, and Mary is the name of one of her friends. Neither of them was a student in SASHELP.CLASS.

Listing A3-1 in Appendix A has the code to create Figure 3-1. **(You can also go to www.apress.com/ISBN and click the "Download source code" button.)** The code in the appendix looks complicated only because there are lots of INSET, TITLE, and FOOTNOTE statements. Conceptually, it is simple. In Listing 3-2 some of the essential statements for this example are shown.

Note that you can change color, font, height, and justification for the segments of a title or footnote. See the TITLE2, TITLE3, and FOOTNOTE1 statements for examples of such color and justification changes.

Listing 3-2. *Code to control characteristics of segments of titles and footnotes*

```
title1 font='Arial/Bold' height=10pt justify=CENTER
  'Scatter Plot of Height versus Age for Two Students in SASHELP.CLASS';
title2 font='Arial/Bold' height=10pt justify=LEFT
  'Text locations using ' color=blue
  'INSET Statements';
title3 font='Arial/Bold' height=10pt justify=LEFT
  'Name values placed at Height-Age locations using the ' color=red 'TEXT
  Statement';
footnote1 font='Arial/Bold' height=10pt
  justify=left 'JUSTIFY=LEFT'
  justify=center 'JUSTIFY=CENTER (the default)'
  justify=right 'JUSTIFY=RIGHT';
```

Listing 3-3 shows the code for the only complicated INSET statement. Besides POSITION Left, there are seven more locations, such as TopLeft, Top, and Bottom. For them, the INSET statements used in this example include only a single quoted description of the location, the POSITION option to assign the location, and the same TEXTATTRS assignment as shown.

Listing 3-3. *Controls for text display using the INSET statement*

```
/* separating the assigned INSET string into quoted pieces
   produces a line break in between each quoted piece */
inset 'Left' 'with line breaks,' 'border, and' 'background color' /
  position=Left
  border
  backcolor=yellow
  textattrs=(color=blue family=Arial size=10pt weight=Bold);
```

Measurement Units

For sizing text (wherever it is—titles, footnotes, INSET strings, etc.), for sizing plot markers, or assigning plot line thickness, the units available are listed in Table 3-3. *Default units are pixels.*

Table 3-3. Measurement units for text when using HEIGHT= or SIZE=

Unit	Description
PT	Point size, at 72 dots per inch
PX	Pixels
PCT or %	Percentage of the graphics output area
CM	Centimeters
IN	Inches
MM	Millimeters

Do not assume that, for example, 50 PCT means the height of the text will be 50% of the height of the image.

Borders

The outer border of the image is controlled by the ODS GRAPHICS statement, and the inner border is controlled on the SG PROC statement. It is easier to show than to describe what/where is the inner border. (On slides, you might wish to omit outer borders.) **Borders, both outer and inner, are turned on by default.**

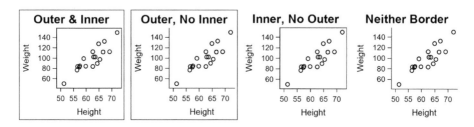

Figure 3-2. Image borders (outer) and graph area borders (inner)

Listing 3-4. Code used to create the four parts of Figure 3-2

```
ods listing style=GraphFontArial5ptBold
  /* use of custom style requires Listing 3-13
     to have been previously run to create it */
    gpath="C:\temp" dpi=300;

ods graphics / reset=all scale=off width=2.7in height=2.7in;
  /* the dimensions persist for all subsequent outputs
     unless they are changed or reset to the defaults. */
```

```
ods graphics / imagename="Fig3-2_Outer_Inner";
title font='Arial/Bold' height=12pt
  'Outer & Inner Borders';
proc sgplot data=sashelp.class;
scatter x=height y=weight; run;

ods graphics / imagename="Fig3-2_Yes_Outer_No_Inner";
title font='Arial/Bold' height=12pt
  'Outer But No Inner Border';
proc sgplot data=sashelp.class noborder;
scatter x=height y=weight; run;

ods graphics / imagename="Fig3-2_No_Outer_Yes_Inner" noborder;
title font='Arial/Bold' height=12pt
  'Inner But No Outer Border';
proc sgplot data=sashelp.class;
scatter x=height y=weight; run;

ods graphics / imagename="Fig3-2_No_Outer_No_Inner" noborder;
title font='Arial/Bold' height=12pt
  'No Outer And No Inner Border';
proc sgplot data=sashelp.class noborder;
scatter x=height y=weight; run;
```

From Defaults Through Customization for a Simple Scatter Plot

In this and subsequent chapters, some of what I described in the first section of this chapter as "outer code" is omitted. Also, in the code, any syntax that is essential to the result, and is not the same as that used in a preceding example, is often (but not always) displayed with **bold** text.

We will explore several ways to customize a simple scatter plot. The scatter plot is inherently simple in that it consists of only 19 plot points. It uses the SASHELP.CLASS data set for information about students: name, age, sex, height, and weight. Some of the capabilities demonstrated are infeasible on a scatter plot with much denser points.

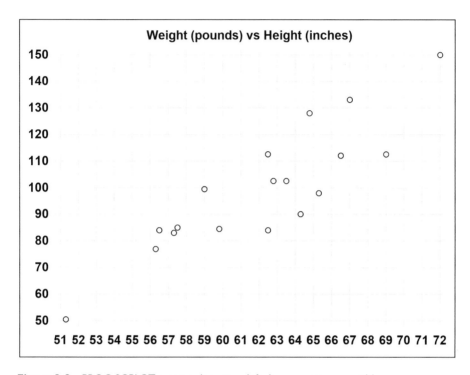

Figure 3-3. PROC SGPLOT scatter plot using defaults, except image width

Listing 3-5. *Code used to create Figure 3-3*

```
ods listing style=listing gpath="C:\temp" dpi=300;
ods graphics on / reset=all scale=off
  width=5.7in /* Fit on this page without shrinking.
  Let height default to 3/4 of width. */
  imagename="Fig3-3_Scatter_Plot_Using_Defaults";
title1 "Notice the off-center position of this title by default";
proc sgplot data=sashelp.class;
scatter y=weight x=height;
run;
```

Now let's try to make the plot more informative, even if suboptimally.

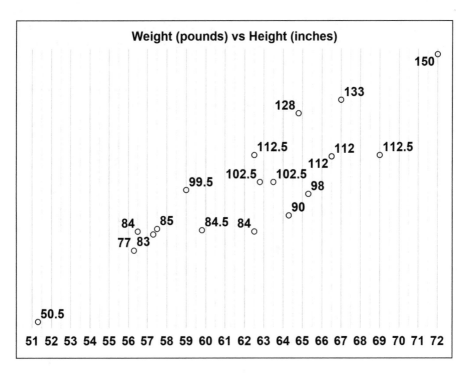

Figure 3-4. Moving labels to the title to make more usable plot space. Providing more axis values. Adding grid and minor grid lines

Listing 3-6. *Code used to create Figure 3-4*

```
ods listing style=listing gpath="C:\temp" dpi=300;
ods graphics on / reset=all scale=off width=5.7in
  imagename="Fig3-4_Scatter_Plot_Custom_Title_And_Axes";
title font='Arial/Bold' height=11pt
  'Weight (pounds) vs Height (inches)';
proc sgplot data=sashelp.class noborder;
scatter y=weight x=height;
yaxis
  grid /* line at each tick mark value */
  minorgrid /* lighter lines between grid lines */
  display=(noline noticks nolabel)
          /* suppressing superfluous graphic paraphernalia
             that have no communication value */
  values=(50 to 150 by 10)
  valueattrs=(family=Arial size=11pt weight=Bold);
xaxis grid minorgrid
  display=(noline noticks nolabel)
  values=(51 to 72 by 1)
  valueattrs=(family=Arial size=11pt weight=Bold);
run;
```

Figure 3-4 still requires guessing what the actual values might be. Let's look at ways to *tell* the viewer the values. It's easy to annotate values for the Y variable.

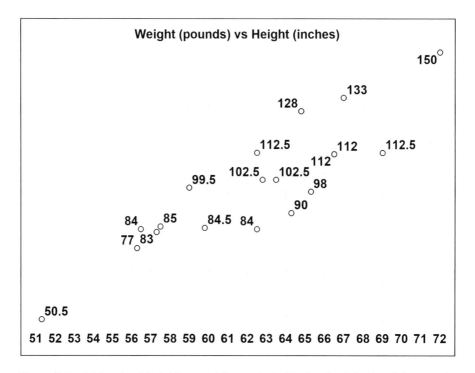

Figure 3-5. Adding data labels (that can deliver only the Y values by default) and dropping the unneeded Y axis

Listing 3-7. *Code used to create Figure 3-5*

```
ods listing style=listing gpath="C:\temp" dpi=300;
ods graphics on / reset=all scale=off width=5.7in
  imagename="Fig3-5_Scatter_Plot_Yvalue_DataLabels_Yaxis_Omitted";
title font='Arial/Bold' height=11pt
  'Weight (pounds) vs Height (inches)';
proc sgplot data=sashelp.class noborder;
scatter y=weight x=height /
  datalabel=weight /* It could be ANY variable in the input data.
  The Y variable is actually the default datalabel variable.
  So, DATALABEL=WEIGHT is superfluous, but harmless. */
  datalabelattrs=(family=Arial size=11pt weight=Bold);
yaxis display=none; /* There is no use for the axis here. */
```

```
xaxis grid minorgrid
  display=(noline noticks nolabel)
  values=(51 to 72 by 1)
  valueattrs=(family=Arial size=11pt weight=Bold);
run;
```

We can do better in Figure 3-6, because plot points are not too dense. The values are rounded to integer to require less space without reducing font size. This prevents collisions between the data labels.

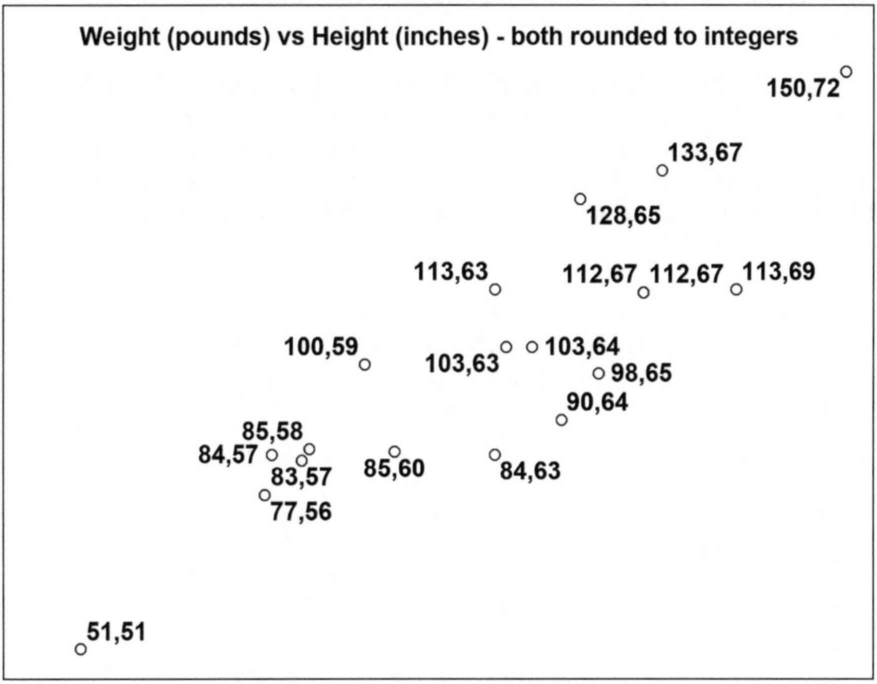

Figure 3-6. No axes needed

Listing 3-8. Code used to create Figure 3-6

```
data work.ToPlot;
length YcommaX $ 6;
set SASHELP.CLASS;
YcommaX = trim(left(round(weight,1))) || ',' ||
         trim(left(round(height,1)));
run;
```

```
ods listing style=listing gpath="C:\temp" dpi=300;
ods graphics on / reset=all scale=off width=5.7in
  imagename=
  "Fig3-6_Scatter_Plot_X_and_Y_Data_Labels_Both_Axes_Omitted";
title font='Arial/Bold' height=11pt
  'Weight (pounds) vs Height (inches) - both rounded to integers';
proc sgplot data=work.ToPlot noborder;
scatter y=weight x=height / datalabel=YcommaX
  datalabelattrs=(family=Arial size=11pt weight=Bold);
yaxis display=none;
xaxis display=none; /* There is no use for the axis here. */
run;
```

The SASHELP.CLASS data set also contains name, age, and sex for each student. Let's look at ways to deliver more information on one graph. There is a trade-off of precise Y and X values for delivery of other information at the plot point. The incremental benefit of minor grid lines is omitted. Visual display of the value of the sex variable is provided via color coding, which requires a legend.

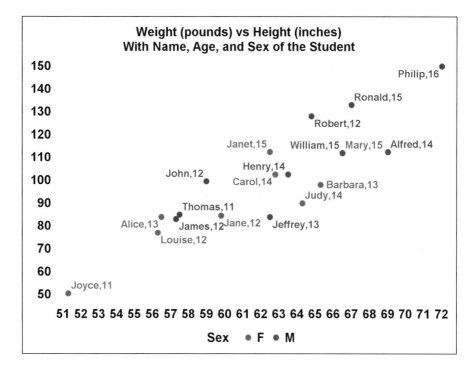

Figure 3-7. More information provided, but exact values of weight and height must be estimated—cannot be precise

Figure 3-7 provides information other than X or Y as data labels and via color-coding the plot point marker and using a legend.

Listing 3-9. *Code used to create Figure 3-7*

```
data work.ToPlot;
length DataLabelText $ 11;
set SASHELP.CLASS;
DataLabelText= trim(left(name)) || ',' ||
               trim(left(put(age,2.)));
run;

proc sort data=Work.ToPlot;
by sex;
run;

ods listing style=listing gpath="C:\temp" dpi=300;
ods graphics on / reset=all scale=off width=5.7in
  imagename=
  "Fig3-7_Scatter_Plot_ColorCoded_Markers_and_DataLabels_Not_XorY";
title1 font='Arial/Bold' height=11pt justify=center
  'Weight (pounds) vs Height (inches)';
title2 font='Arial/Bold' height=11pt justify=center
  'With Name, Age, and Sex of the Student';
proc sgplot data=work.ToPlot noborder;
styleattrs datacontrastcolors=(blue red);
  /* Colors are applied to markers, datalabels, and legend color swatches in
     the order of the values of the group variable in the input data set. That's
     why the sort is done. */
scatter y=weight x=height /
  group=sex
  datalabel=DataLabelText
  datalabelattrs=(family=Arial size=9pt weight=Bold)
  markerattrs=(symbol=CircleFilled);
  /* default empty circle would have less evident color */
yaxis grid /* minorgrid NOT USED */
  display=(noline noticks nolabel)
  values=(50 to 150 by 10)
  valueattrs=(family=Arial size=11pt weight=Bold);
xaxis grid /* minorgrid NOT USED */
  display=(noline noticks nolabel)
  values=(51 to 72 by 1)
  valueattrs=(family=Arial size=11pt weight=Bold);
keylegend / noborder
  titleattrs=(family=Arial size=11pt weight=Bold)
  valueattrs=(family=Arial size=11pt weight=Bold);
run;
```

As shown in Figure 3-8, drop lines and minor tick marks can make reliable estimates of weight and height possible to the first decimal place. The result is a very "busy" image, but it is usable and communicative. Not shown here, but the DROPLINE statement can be used selectively for any one or more plot points, rather than all of them, and can be used to provide a drop line to the X axis (the default), the Y axis, or to both axes.

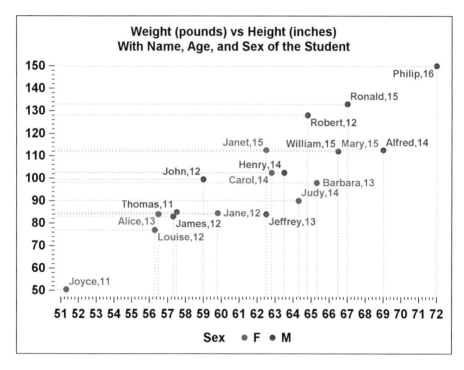

Figure 3-8. Here, you can know weight and height nearly with precision and certainty, but it is a very busy plot. With enough additional data points, collisions would be inevitable

Figure 3-8 adds drop lines and major and minor tick marks to the plot of Figure 3-7.

Listing 3-10. *Code used to create Figure 3-8, additions and changes to code for Figure 3-7*

```
ods graphics on / reset=all scale=off width=5.7in
  imagename=
  "Fig3-8_Scatter_Plot_DropLines_and_Major_and_Minor_TickMarks";
  dropline y=weight x=height /
    dropto=both /* default is =x */
    lineattrs=(pattern=Dot color=Gray
    thickness=1px); /* pixels, other units are available */
```

```
yaxis
  minor minorcount=4
  display=(noline nolabel)
  values=(50 to 150 by 10)
  valueattrs=(family=Arial size=11pt weight=Bold);
xaxis
  minor minorcount=4
  display=(noline nolabel)
  values=(51 to 72 by 1)
  valueattrs=(family=Arial size=11pt weight=Bold);
```

See Figure 3-9. When the X variable is discrete, a feasible option is the use of an X axis table to deliver the Y values. No Y axis is needed then. Drop lines are probably not really needed to determine the X values in this case, but they do no harm and do accelerate the identification of the X values. More than one X axis table can be created on the same graph, and X axis tables can be located above or below the X axis values and its label. In this context, with the color-coding tie to the identification in the title, the X axis label is really superfluous. Visually, and functionally, this image looks like, and serves as, an alternative to a vertical bar chart, with big-dot-headed pins replacing the bars.

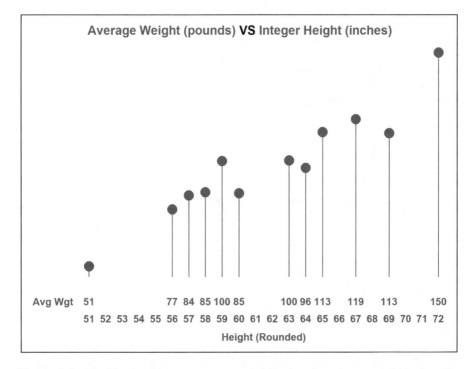

Figure 3-9. The X axis table puts every rounded Y value above its rounded X value. The viewer has precise knowledge (at integer level), and there is no chance of data label collisions

Figure 3-9 uses a color-coded title instead of a legend, drop lines for X values, and an X axis table to deliver the Y values, which makes a Y axis unnecessary.

Listing 3-11. *Code used to create Figure 3-9*

```
data ToSummary;
set sashelp.class;
IntegerHeight = put(height,2.);
run;

proc summary data=ToSummary nway;
class IntegerHeight;
var weight;
output out=ToPlot mean=MeanWgt;
run;

ods listing style=listing gpath="C:\temp" dpi=300;
ods graphics on / reset=all scale=off width=5.7in
  imagename=
  "Fig3-9_Scatter_Plot_ColorCoded_DropLines_and_Xaxistable";
title font='Arial/Bold' height=11pt justify=center
   color=red "Average Weight (pounds) "
   color=black "VS "
   color=blue "Integer Height (inches)";
proc sgplot data=ToPlot noborder;
scatter y=MeanWgt x=IntegerHeight /
  markerattrs=(symbol=circlefilled size=9pt color=red);
dropline x=IntegerHeight y=MeanWgt / dropto=x lineattrs=(color=red);
yaxis display=none;
xaxistable MeanWgt /
  location=inside
  position=bottom
  title=' '
  label='Avg Wgt'
  labelattrs=(family=Arial size=9pt weight=Bold color=red)
  valueattrs=(family=Arial size=9pt weight=Bold color=red);
xaxis
  display=(noline noticks)
  values=(51 to 72 by 1)
  valueattrs=(family=Arial size=9pt weight=Bold color=blue)
  label='Height (Rounded)'
  labelattrs=(family=Arial size=9pt weight=Bold color=blue);
format MeanWgt 3.;
run;
```

Since PROC SUMMARY delivers, as an always included extra, the frequency of each value of the CLASS variable, it is easy to add some value with data labels as shown in Figure 3-10.

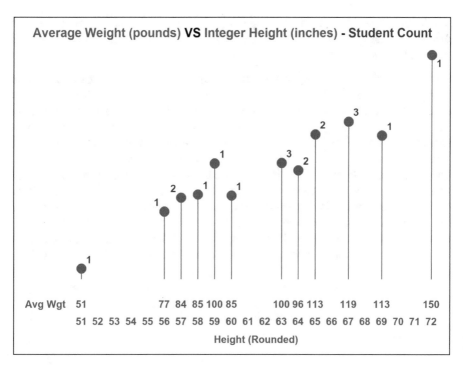

Figure 3-10. Adding more information with a data label

Listing 3-12. *Changes to the code for Figure 3-9 used to create Figure 3-10*

```
ods graphics on / reset=all scale=off width=5.7in
  imagename=
  "Fig3-10_Scatter_Plot_Added_DataLabel_Mentioned_in_the_Title";
title font='Arial/Bold' height=11pt justify=center
  color=red "Average Weight (pounds) "
  color=black "VS "
  color=blue "Integer Height (inches) "
  color=black "- "
  color=purple "Student Count";
scatter y=MeanWgt x=IntegerHeight /
  markerattrs=(symbol=circlefilled size=9pt color=red)
  datalabel=_freq_
  datalabelattrs=(family=Arial size=9pt weight=Bold color=purple);
```

You could add DATALABELPOS=TOP to assure that the data label is always directly above the marker. Accepting the default, as done here, allows the software to position each data label as it thinks best, based on the situation as it assesses it. Since, as has been mentioned earlier, multiple X axis tables are permitted, the Student Count for each Age could instead have been put in a second X axis table, rather than using the DATALABEL option. That would put Age, Weight, and Height for the data point all adjacent to each other in a stack at each X axis value, the quickest and most efficient way to discover the information.

Figure 3-11 shows a more ambitious use of X axis tables. As the number of distinct Y values for the most Y value–rich X value increases for a different input data set, the vertical size of the image would need to increase. If you are not interested in tying each Y value to its plot point with color coding, the X axis table for the height values could be rendered in the default color black. The benefit of this X axis table is to prevent any identification problem due to collisions between data labels in the "plot point stack" for each X value. Later, you will see how an X axis table is used for multi-line overlay plots, where on-image annotation is impossible without collisions between label and label or between label and some other line. The code to create this more complex example is in   Listing A3-11 in Appendix A. **(You can also go to www. apress.com/ISBN and click the "Download source code" button.)**

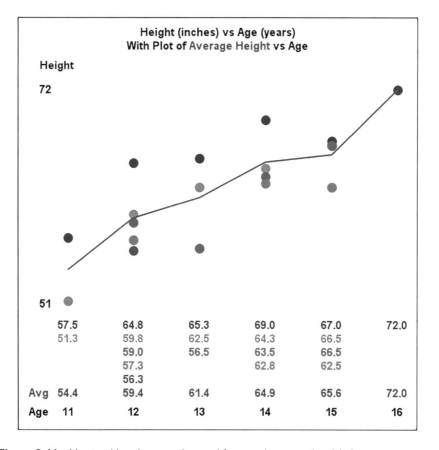

Figure 3-11. X axis tables eliminate the need for any plot point data labels

Control of Text Attributes with a Custom ODS Style

The ODS style is a powerful method to simplify the control of text attributes and at the same time to deliver graphs with consistent use of text attributes.

To make all of the text in an ODS graph 11pt Arial Bold, if you have created the required ODS style, you need only add a simple option to your ODS LISTING statement, as in

```
ods listing gpath="C:\temp" dpi=300 style=GraphFont11ptArialBold;
```

Instead, in some cases, the text characteristics are directly controlled with FAMILY=, SIZE=, WEIGHT=BOLD for graph elements and FONT='Arial\ Bold' and HEIGHT= for TITLEs and FOOTNOTES. In most cases, however, the font/family, size/height, and weight can be defined for all graphic text using a custom ODS style. That reduces coding for the examples, and the style can be selectively overridden for specific text. A uniform style for all of the text in a graph is efficient and consistent. There is no communication benefit from a variety of text characteristics in an image. The only purpose of overriding a style with direct text controls is either to get everything to fit without collisions due to limited space or to achieve some particular communication objective.

Color cannot be specified in a custom style used for text attributes. You can specify text color directly with COLOR= in whatever is the relevant ATTRS option for the graph feature of interest and on TITLE and FOOTNOTE statements.

There are several custom styles used in this book. All of them use font family Arial and font weight Bold. This maximizes readability, regardless of font size. The custom font size varies between 5pt, 6pt, 7pt, 8pt, 9pt, 10pt, 12pt, and, the most frequent, 11pt. In some examples, the size of certain text parts of the graph is overridden using the relevant attribute option, as in, for example, DATALABELATTRS=(SIZE=8pt) for a case in which the custom style's font size for all other text parts is 11pt.

Before running the code for the examples that use ODS styles, on a one-time basis you must run the custom style setup code which stores them permanently in your SASUSER template store. The setup code uses a macro. You can use that same macro to create any custom style that you wish.

For the ODS LISTING destination, the default style is LISTING. On the ODS LISTING statement, if you omit the STYLE= option, or include STYLE=LISTING, the consequences are identical. But most often, a typical example in a chapter will use ODS LISTING STYLE=GraphFontArial11ptBold. In some cases, a smaller font size is used in order to get everything to fit without collisions.

The one-time ODS style creation code that you must run is in Listing 3-13. The AllGraphTextSetUp macro controls the text characteristics of ALL text in the graph with the font Family, Size, and Weight specified. It affects axis values and labels, axistable values and labels, keylegend and gradlegend values and titles, datalabel values, curve labels, stacked bar segment labels, and donut hole labels.

Any of those characteristics, including the font Family, for text parts of the graph can be overridden, if necessary with VALUEATTRS, LABELATTRS, TITLEATTRS, DATALABELATTRS, CURVELABELATTRS, SEGLABELATTRS, HOLELABELATTRS, or, in the case of titles or footnotes, with FONT= or HEIGHT=.

If using one of these ODS styles, there is no way for TITLE or FOOTNOTE statements to UNBOLD the text that has been bolded by the default value for WEIGHT in this macro. You would need to run the macro with WEIGHT=NORMAL to create a style for text with Normal, rather than Bold, weight.

For your use outside of the setup code in Listing 3-13, you can change the macro defaults to whatever are your preferences in an altered version of the macro if you choose to create one, or you can simply override them upon your invocation of this macro.

Listing 3-13. *Run this one time to store eight custom ODS styles permanently in your SASUSER template store, so the styles can be used in examples later in the book*

```
%macro AllGraphTextSetup(Size,Family=Arial,Weight=Bold);

/* If stored, this macro fileName must be AllGraphTextSetup.sas */
/* The other option for Weight is Normal. */
/* The number N specified for Size is used as Point size, Npt.
   This number is the macro's positional parameter. A macro may have
   at most one positional parameter, and it must be first in the
   invocation of the macro, when other parameters are used. */

/* Family may be used for font names with embedded blanks,
   such as Times New Roman, but the style created omits blanks,
   as in style name GraphFontTimesNewRoman10ptBold.
   Blanks are removed with the %LET statement below. */
%let FamilyForStyle = %sysfunc(compress(&Family,' '));

proc template;
  define style GraphFont&FamilyForStyle.&Size.pt&Weight;
  parent=styles.listing;
  class GraphFonts /
```

```
      'GraphValueFont' = ("&Family",&Size.pt,&Weight)
      'GraphLabelFont' = ("&Family",&Size.pt,&Weight)
      'GraphDataFont'  = ("&Family",&Size.pt,&Weight)
      'GraphTitleFont' = ("&Family",&Size.pt,&Weight)
      'GraphFootnoteFont' = ("&Family",&Size.pt,&Weight);
end;
run;

%mend AllGraphTextSetup;

%AllGraphTextSetup(5);
%AllGraphTextSetup(6);
%AllGraphTextSetup(7);
%AllGraphTextSetup(8);
%AllGraphTextSetup(9);
%AllGraphTextSetup(10);
%AllGraphTextSetup(11);
%AllGraphTextSetup(12);
```

Because of macro defaults, these invocations are equivalent to, for example:

```
%AllGraphTextSetup(11,Family=Arial,Weight=Bold);
```

If using a font family name with embedded blanks, it must be enclosed in quotes as in

```
%AllGraphTextSetup(11,Family='Arial Narrow',Weight=Bold);
```

for which the ODS style created would be GraphFontArialNarrow11ptBold.

After running the preceding code block, your SAS log includes eight NOTEs of the form

NOTE: STYLE 'GraphFontArial11ptBold' has been saved to:
SASUSER.TEMPLAT

for 5pt, 6pt, 7pt, 8pt, 9pt, 10pt, 11pt, and 12pt.

SASUSER.TEMPLAT is your default permanent template store. Styles are written there by default. Whenever you reference a style, SASUSER.TEMPLAT is where ODS Graphics will look for it by default. SASUSER.TEMPLAT is part of your SASUSER profile. If you delete the profile in the SASUSER data library, you will lose SASUSER.TEMPLAT. If not, the styles will be there permanently.

You can define template stores at other locations than SASUSER, but that is not necessary here and is outside the scope of this chapter. If interested, please consult SAS documentation.

You can list all of the styles in SASUSER.TEMPLAT with the code in Listing 3-15. With the code in Listing 3-16, in the SAS log you can list the source code that was used to create a style in SASUSER.TEMPLAT.

The eight styles will be permanently available in your SASUSER template store. If you never run the setup code, but use a LISTING statement such as

```
ods listing style=GraphFontArial11ptBold gpath="C:\temp" dpi=300;
```

then your SAS log will contain this message:

WARNING: Style GRAPHFONTARIAL11PTBOLD not found; Listing style will be used instead.

You can, of course, create other custom styles. You can permanently store the preceding macro source code, %MACRO statement through %MEND statement, in any convenient location. For example, on Windows, you can create a folder such as C:\SharedCode. The filename must be AllGraphTextSetup, and the filetype must be sas. The other option is to simply paste the macro source code into your SAS code creation and submission window.

To use a stored macro, if in C:\SharedCode, your application program must start with

%include "C:\SharedCode\AllGraphTextSetup.sas";

If using Arial 12pt Bold, before your SG PROC step, you must use two statements:

```
%AllGraphTextSetup(12);
/* Note the coordinated use of 12 above and below */
ods listing style=GraphFontArial12ptBold gpath="C:\temp" dpi=300;
/* For macro invocation without overrides for Family and Weight,
   the style created will be for Arial and Bold, as done here. */
< example-specific code here >
ods listing close;
```

If you wish to use, for example, Verdana 10pt Normal, your macro invocation and your ODS LISTING statement must be

```
%AllGraphTextSetup(10,Family=Verdana,Weight=Normal);
ods listing style=GraphFontVerdana10ptNormal
    gpath="C:\temp" dpi=300;
```

If you wish to use instead Verdana 10pt Bold, you can omit Weight= from the macro invocation since Bold is the default.

When a custom style is not being used, the ODS LISTING statement can omit the STYLE= option, which produces the same result as the default, STYLE=LISTING.

The code in Listing 3-9 was used to create Figure 3-7 with the default style. The code in Listing 3-14 can create an identical Figure 3-7 by using a custom style created and stored with a prior one-time run of the code in Listing 3-13. The required STYLE= option is highlighted in Listing 3-14, as are the statements that have been simplified by omitting text attribute specifications. The SCATTER statement includes an override for the data label font size.

Listing 3-14. *Code used to creating Figure 3-7 with a custom style, but overriding font size for data labels*

```
data work.ToPlot;
length DataLabelText $ 11;
set SASHELP.CLASS;
DataLabelText= trim(left(name))||','||trim(left(put(age,2.)));
run;

proc sort data=Work.ToPlot;
by sex;
run;

ods listing style=GraphFontArial11ptBold
  /* use of custom style requires Listing 3-13
      to have been previously run to create it */
  gpath="C:\temp" dpi=300;
ods graphics on / reset=all scale=off width=5.7in
  imagename="Fig3-7Duplicate_CustomStyleAndDataLabelSizeOverride";
title1 justify=center 'Weight (pounds) vs Height (inches)';
title2 justify=center 'With Name, Age, and Sex of the Student';
proc sgplot data=work.ToPlot noborder;
styleattrs datacontrastcolors=(red blue);
scatter y=weight x=height /
  group=sex
  datalabel=DataLabelText
  datalabelattrs=(size=9pt)
  markerattrs=(symbol=CircleFilled);
yaxis grid
  display=(noline noticks nolabel)
  values=(50 to 150 by 10);
xaxis grid
  display=(noline noticks nolabel)
  values=(51 to 72 by 1);
keylegend / noborder;
run;
```

In Listings 3-15 and 3-16 and their outputs are two ways to investigate what is in the SASUSER.TEMPLAT default template store.

Listing 3-15. *Code to list all of the styles in default template store SASUSER.TEMPLAT*

```
ods listing
  file="C:\temp\Listing3-15_ContentsOfSASUSERdotTEMPLAT.txt";
options nocenter nonumber linesize=max pagesize=max;
 title 'Contents of the Default Template Store SASUSER.TEMPLAT';
proc template;
 list / store=sasuser.templat;
run;
```

Output 3-15. Content listing (this is an excerpt of only three styles from the full list)

```
Contents of Default Template Store SASUSER.TEMPLAT
14:31 Saturday, August 20, 2022

Listing of: SASUSER.TEMPLAT
Path Filter is: *
Sort by: PATH/ASCENDING

Obs    Path                                      Type

56     GraphFontArial10ptBold                    Style
61     GraphFontArial11ptBold                    Style
80     GraphFontArial9ptBold                     Style
```

Listing 3-16. *Code to display the source code in the SAS log that was used to create a style in SASUSER.TEMPLAT, in this case the GraphFontArial7ptBold style*

```
/* PROC PRINTTO routes the SAS log to the TXT file. */
/* TITLE statement text cannot be displayed in the SAS log */
/* OPTIONS NOSOURCE suppresses display of the %PUT statements,
   but not their output to the SAS log. */
/* OPTIONS NONOTES suppresses display of SAS NOTEs in the log. */
options nosource nonotes;
proc printto new log=
  "C:\temp\Listing3-16_SASlogForPROCTEMPLATEsourceCodeDisplay.txt";
run;
%put Display in the SAS LOG of SASUSER.TEMPLAT PROC TEMPLATE;
%put Source Code used to create the GraphFontArial7ptBold Style;
%put SASUSER.TEMPLAT is the default template store;
%put %str( ); /* blank line */
proc template;
 source GraphFontArial7ptBold;
run;
proc printto;
```

```
run;
options source notes; /* restore normal conditions */
```

Output 3-16. TXT file for the SAS log

```
Display in the SAS LOG of SASUSER.TEMPLAT PROC TEMPLATE
Source Code used to create the GraphFontArial7ptBold Style
SASUSER.TEMPLAT is the default template store

define style GraphFontArial7ptBold;
    parent = styles.listing;
    class GraphFonts /
        'GraphFootnoteFont' = ("Arial",7pt,bold)
        'GraphTitleFont' = ("Arial",7pt,bold)
        'GraphDataFont' = ("Arial",7pt,bold)
        'GraphLabelFont' = ("Arial",7pt,bold)
        'GraphValueFont' = ("Arial",7pt,bold);
end;
```

For More Introduction and Added Information

There are several resources that you might find helpful, especially for first-time users or for more information. See the purpose-annotated section at the end of book, For Further Information on SAS ODS Graphics. None of those additional resources are devoted to demonstrating and implementing the design principles presented in my Chapters 1 and 2.

Summary

This introductory chapter demonstrated concepts and capabilities to prepare you for learning, in subsequent chapters, the broad range of what else you can do with ODS Graphics. In this chapter and the others, the emphasis is on the communication-effective use of ODS Graphics.

To display more than titles and footnotes, INSET and TEXT statements can place text, or even numbers, in places other than the top and bottom of a graph.

Grid lines, minor grid lines, tick marks, minor tick marks, and drop lines can help the viewer of your graph to *estimate* the values of X and Y variables with some eye-roving. Data labels and axis tables *deliver* precise, not estimated, values with minimal viewing and interpretation effort.

When a third variable, called a GROUP variable, is available, color coding and a legend allow you to provide additional information unambiguously.

There is an optional border for the perimeter of the image, as well as an optional border for the edges of the "inner" display area for the graph. Those edges are the axes and top and left-side boundaries. Turning off the inner border does not turn off the axes.

There are options to suppress or customize axis lines, axis values, tick marks, and axis labels. For the text in labels, data labels, a legend, etc., there are attribute options to control the font (its "family"), the size, the color (black is the default), and whether it is Bold and/or Italic instead of the default (Normal). You might have noticed that all examples here use **Bold** text, to maximize readability.

With plot marker attribute options, you can control the symbol, the size, and the color. The default is unfortunately an open circle. When using color-coded symbols, a filled marker is essential for easy color distinguishability.

For lines, the attribute options are pattern, thickness, and color. There are 46 different line patterns available, but the only ones used here and suggested are Solid (the default), Dot, ThinDot (more widely separated dots, not smaller ones), Dash, and ShortDash. If using color-coded lines, it is essential to assure a thickness which makes the color easy to identify.

Since any colored text in the examples is in a bold face font and not tiny in size, those text colors are unambiguous.

Bar Charts, Butterfly Charts, Waterfall Charts, Dot Plots, Needle Plots, Area Bar Charts, Text Graphs, and Line Charts: Charts for Categorical Data

Bar charts and their functional equivalents are used for categorical data. The data of an enterprise, organization, government, or researcher has keys or qualifiers that are categories, such as product, service, customer, area (e.g., region), etc. There is also data with variables that are dates, times, or datetimes, also known as time series data, trend data, or temporal data, but that is a subject of Chapter 8.

© LeRoy Bessler 2023
LeR. Bessler, *Visual Data Insights Using SAS ODS Graphics*,
https://doi.org/10.1007/978-1-4842-8609-8_4

Data with one categorical key or category variable can be visually presented with horizontal or vertical bar charts, dot plots, needle plots, butterfly charts, a novel text-only ranked graphic, and innovative derivatives of overlay needle plots that I have called a Tree Chart, a Flag Chart, and a CrossRoads SignPost Chart. Based on function, not structure, the latter three charts can serve as alternatives to pie charts and bar charts.

Waterfall charts are a special case of vertical bar charts. They are intended to present temporal data as plus and minus changes between (and with) start value and end value of the response variable. Butterfly charts are a special case of horizontal bar charts. A butterfly chart could instead be rendered as a vertical bar chart, in which case you might see (and say) the butterfly as (is) flying.

Pie charts and donut charts are also frequently used for categorical data, but they are the subject of Chapter 5.

Data with two categorical variables can be visually presented with more complicated versions of horizontal bar charts, vertical bar charts, dot plots, and needle plots, as well as with heat maps (Chapter 6), bubble plots (Chapter 7), and panels or lattices of charts (Chapter 9). Data with even more than two category variables can be handled as well, with PROC SGPANEL as covered in Chapter 9. (There is a simple example of using PROC SGPANEL in this chapter in Figure 4-17.)

Here, the focus is on PROC SGPLOT, which supports several different ODS Graphics statements that create plots suited to categorical data. We will explore all of them, for cases some of which are common, others that are not, and new chart designs nowhere else available.

Also included at the close of the chapter are area bar charts, which are *not* currently supported with an AREABAR statement in PROC SGPLOT and require special means to create them.

Present the Categories in Your Charts and Plots in Ranked Order

When presenting categorical data, usually rank the categories in order of importance. If large is important, present from largest value of the response to the smallest.

If small is important, present from smallest to largest.

If the number of categories is large (like all of the countries in the world, or the 50 states in the United States and the District of Columbia, or all of the counties in an American state or in the United Kingdom, or all of the administrative divisions of any other country), you can present the categories alphabetically in a horizontal bar chart. If rank is also important to emphasize, consider presenting categories both ways, alphabetically and ranked, in two separate charts. In any case, you can include rank number in a Y axis table as a companion to the category in an alphabetic-order chart of the information.

In every case possible and appropriate, the charts and plots in this chapter present the categories in ranked order.

Provide Precise Numbers for Your Charts and Plots for Categorical Data

You can present the precise numbers with data labels, axis tables, segment labels (for stacked charts), and the TEXT statement. In this chapter, in only three cases are precise numbers not delivered in the examples. Two are default bar charts, and the third is a demonstration of an effort to make the best of a suboptimal situation—the omission of precise numbers in these three examples is a choice, not a requirement of the software.

Present the precise numbers whenever possible. They are the alternative to uncertainty, ambiguity, and ignorance.

Bar Charts

Bar charts and pie charts are the commonest ways to present categorical data. That is not an accident. Both types of charts are easy to understand.

Bar charts are easier to label than pie charts—where tiny slices are hard or impossible to label and where label collisions between adjacent slices can happen. There are solutions to these pie chart problems, but they are shown in Chapter 5.

William Playfair is often credited with inventing the bar chart. He was one of its earliest users. His first was a clustered and ranked horizontal bar chart of Scotland's imports and exports to and from 17 places during the period Christmas 1780 to Christmas 1781.

There were at least two bar charts earlier than Playfair's.

As explained in the book by Michael Friendly and Howard Wainer, *A History of Data Visualization and Graphic Communication*, Philippe Buache and Guillaume de L'Isle published an overlaid vertical bar chart for the semiannual high and low water levels of the Seine River from 1732 to 1766. Above that bar chart was a table of information.

In "One for the History Books: An Early Time-Line Bar Graph" by Ronald K. Smeltzer (CHANCE, 23:2, 54–56, DOI: 10.1080/09332480.2010.10739807) is an overlaid vertical bar chart without any table. The chart overlays the monthly high and low water levels of the Seine River from 1760 to 1766. It was published in 1770 by Philippe Buache.

None of these early bar charts is the very simple bar chart that one sees most often today.

Bar Chart Types

Bar Charts for One Category Variable and One Response Variable

After showing what you can get with the defaults, better solutions will be covered. Also, there will be non-bar charts—dot plots and needle plots—which function equally well as and analogously to bar charts, even if they look different. One of their benefits is that the function of comparing magnitude of the response is delivered with less visual mass in the image, which emphasizes the numbers and text—which convey the always essential information. A unique example is a graph with text and numbers only, but still functionally and structurally a graph, as you will see and be able to agree.

Bar Charts for One Category Variable and Multiple Response Variables

In the easiest way to do this, the second and any additional response variables are not delivered in graphical form, but as axis tables, which you have previously seen, for example, in the fully informative horizontal bar chart of Chapter 1. The limitation of axis tables is that they are only a lookup, with no companion graphic comparison of those values, but a graphic companion is not always necessary—which, for example, is the case for the fully informative horizontal bar chart.

A second solution is an "overlay" bar chart, where bars are not overlaid, but drawn side by side.

A third solution is an overlay bar chart that indeed has the bars for one response variable overlaid on the bars for a second response variable.

A fourth solution is an area bar chart. Each bar is drawn using one response value for its height and the other response value for its width. This is best understood by looking at an example such as Figure 4-61.

A fifth solution entails preprocessing the input data to convert each of the different response variables into values of a second categorical variable. Such preprocessing is used in Listing 4-0 for creation of the data set for the Dollars of Sales and Profits by Product Line, which is input for, among others, Figures 4-8 to 4-11.

Charts for Two Category Variables and One Response Variable

For bar charts, there are two common ways to handle this: stacked bar segments (if a horizontal bar chart, really concatenated and not stacked bar segments) and clustered bars. For dot plots and needle plots, the options are clusters or overlays.

With two categorical variables, one serves as the CATEGORY variable and the other as the GROUP variable. For bar charts, the GROUPDISPLAY option can be CLUSTER or STACK. For dot plots and needle plots, the GROUPDISPLAY option can be CLUSTER or OVERLAY.

Charts for More Complicated Categorical Data

PROC SGPANEL, discussed in Chapter 9, enables you to visually present more complicated situations, such as ones with more than two category variables.

General Remarks About Code Used

Several examples have %INCLUDE statements for code or macros from folder C:\SharedCode, which could instead be any folder or location of your choice.

The following framing code has been more expansively discussed in Chapter 3 in the section "Outer Structure of ODS Graphics Code in Examples." The framing code for all examples in this chapter and others is

```
ods results off; /* verify results by opening the image file,
                    rather than using the SAS Output window */
ods _all_ close; /* avoid unintended consequences
                    and superfluous concurrent output */
< ODS LISTING statement here >
< example-specific code here >
ods listing close; /* ALWAYS Best Practice */
```

For brevity, the example code in listings omits the first two lines and the last one. It is best to add them back at your runtime. (Source code files include them.)

The ODS LISTING statement can vary. All of the examples in this chapter use a statement of the following form to specify the text characteristics:

```
ods listing style=GraphFontArial11ptBold gpath="C:\temp" dpi=300;
```

but often with a font size other than 11pt. The statement assumes that the ODS style GraphFontArial11ptBold has been created. To assure that all of the styles needed in this chapter are available, use this code:

```
%include "C:\SharedCode\AllGraphTextSetup.sas";
%AllGraphTextSetup(7);
%AllGraphTextSetup(8);
%AllGraphTextSetup(9);
%AllGraphTextSetup(10);
%AllGraphTextSetup(11);
```

For more information about ODS custom styles, as well as the source code for the AllGraphTextSetup macro, see the section "Control of Text Attributes with a Custom ODS Style" in Chapter 3. For information about options for direct control of text attributes, which can override the default text attributes that are set up by an ODS style, see the section "Text Attributes Control in ODS Graphics" in Chapter 3.

Input Data and Discrete Attribute Map for the Examples

In some examples, a custom data set is built with a DATA step. For many examples, the input data is either SASHELP.SHOES or SASHELP.ORSALES. In other examples, data from SASHELP.SHOES or SASHELP.ORSALES must be preprocessed for the SGPLOT PROC step.

With the same discrete attribute map, several examples use the same color palette as color coding in bar charts, dot plots, or needle plots for values of the category variable Product_Line in the ORSALES data set (green for Outdoors, blue for Sports, etc.). The color is applied to bars, markers, lines, and text.

With one-time setup processing in Listing 4-0, you can avoid running the same code over and over. This non-graphics code need not be repeated in every example that needs its output for input.

Listing 4-0. *Code used to prepare data used in several examples*

```
/* The following code creates a data set for multiple examples
   that use data derived from the SASHELP.ORSALES data:
   sasuser.OR_SalesProfitByProdLineAndTotal */

proc summary data=sashelp.orsales;
class Product_Line;
var Profit Total_Retail_Price;
output out=work.ORsalesSummary sum=;
run;

data sasuser.OR_SalesProfitByProdLineAndTotal;
keep SalesOrProfit Product_Line Dollars DollarsInM;
```

```
length SalesOrProfit $ 6;
format Dollars dollar12.;
set work.ORsalesSummary;
if _type_ EQ 0
then Product_Line = 'Total';
SalesOrProfit = 'Sales';
Dollars = Total_Retail_Price;
DollarsInM = Total_Retail_Price / 1000000;
output;
SalesOrProfit = 'Profit';
Dollars = Profit;
DollarsInM = Profit / 1000000;
output;
run;

/* The following code creates data set sasuser.CityTotals
   used in multiple examples that use SASHELP.SHOES data */

proc summary data=sashelp.shoes nway;
class Subsidiary;
var Sales;
output out=work.Summary sum=;
run;

proc sort data=work.Summary out=work.Sorted;
by descending Sales;
run;

data sasuser.CityTotals;
set work.Sorted;
Rank = put(_N_,2.);
run;

/* The following code creates data set sasuser.ORsalesDattrMap
   used in multiple examples that use SASHELP.ORSALES data
   or its derivative sasuser.OR_SalesProfitByProdLineAndTotal.
   In those examples, the PROC SGPLOT statement includes
   DATTRMAP=sasuser.ORsalesDattrMap
   and the HBAR, VBAR, DOT, or NEEDLE statement includes
   ATTRID='GroupColors' */

data sasuser.ORsalesDattrMap;
retain ID 'GroupColors';
length ID $ 11 Value $ 15
  FillColor TextColor /* hbar & vbar charts */
  MarkerColor /* dot plots & needle plots */
  LineColor /* needle plots */
  $ 6;
```

```
Value='Total'; FillColor='Orange';
TextColor=FillColor; MarkerColor=FillColor; LineColor=FillColor; output;
Value='Sports'; FillColor='Blue';
TextColor=FillColor; MarkerColor=FillColor; LineColor=FillColor; output;
Value='Outdoors'; FillColor='Green';
TextColor=FillColor; MarkerColor=FillColor; LineColor=FillColor; output;
Value='Clothes & Shoes'; FillColor='Black';
TextColor=FillColor; MarkerColor=FillColor; LineColor=FillColor; output;
Value='Children'; FillColor='Purple';
TextColor=FillColor; MarkerColor=FillColor; LineColor=FillColor; output;
run;
```

Horizontal Bar Charts

Horizontal bar charts, rather than vertical bar charts, are usually the better way to present categorical data in a bar chart. They are easy to label—no label fitting problems, which happen when labels for vertical bars, or data labels for the ends of the vertical bars, are too wide. Their interpretation is straightforward. The only common practitioner foible is to require the viewer to compare bar ends with axis values, which is forced reliance on, at best, what is only an estimate of the actual value for each category. We can easily cure that problem. But first let's show you the ODS Graphics default.

Default Horizontal Bar Chart

Notice that the title is centered over the axis area, rather than being centered in the image. If you wish the title to be centered within the full width of the image, always include JUSTIFY=CENTER in your TITLE statement. As previously explained in Chapter 3, in any graph with an axis area, titles and footnotes are by default centered over the axis area.

The default font is Arial. The default size for the title is 11pt. The default size for axis values and labels is 9pt. The default weight for titles is Bold.

The input data set for Figure 4-1 is SASHELP.SHOES, which includes Sales, Returns, and Inventory, Numbers of Stores, all by Region, by Subsidiary (City), and by Product.

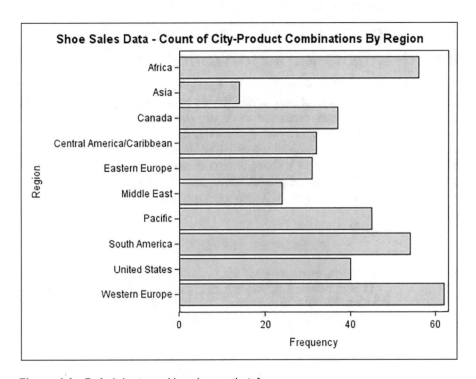

Figure 4-1. Default horizontal bar chart underinforms

Listing 4-1. *Code used to create Figure 4-1*

```
ods listing style=listing gpath="C:\temp";
ods graphics on / reset=all scale=off
      width=5.7in /* actual default is 640px
                      default height is always 3/4 of width */
      imagename="Fig4-1_ObsCountsByRegion_DefaultHbarChart";
title justify=center
  'Shoe Sales Data - Count of City-Product Combinations By Region';
  /* This long title is automatically centered in the image.
     By default, a short title would be centered above the plot
     area. Use of JUSTIFY=CENTER would prevent that. Including it as
     a matter of routine can do no harm.*/
proc sgplot data=sashelp.shoes;
hbar Region; /* with no RESPONSE variable, the statistic charted is
        the Frequency Count for values of the Category variable */
run;
```

Easy Communication Effectiveness Improvements for a Horizontal Bar Chart

Figure 4-2 is the ODS Graphics alternative to implement one of the commonest solutions during the days of only SAS/GRAPH to display precise values at the ends of the bars. An easier method to display the values was as a table at the right margin. With a bar chart with many bars, the distance between bars and values could create ambiguity about which value was for which bar, especially in the case of short bars in a chart where there are much longer bars also present. The ODS Graphics HBAR statement DATALABELS option is an always reliable solution. Figure 4-2 also uses ranking.

Figure 4-2. Ranked horizontal bar chart with data labels

Listing 4-2. *Code used to create Figure 4-2*

```
ods listing style=listing gpath="C:\temp";
ods graphics on / reset=all scale=off width=5.7in height=2.5in
  imagename="Fig4-2_RankedWithDataLabels_EasilyImprovedHbarChart";
title font='Arial/Bold' height=11pt
      /* same as default font and height */
  justify=center /* center of the image
                      instead of center of the bars area */
  'Ranked Shoe Sales By Region';
proc sgplot data=sashelp.shoes noborder;
hbar Region / response=Sales
  stat=sum /* total sales for all products by region
               across all cities in region
               SUM is the default for STAT when RESPONSE is used */
  categoryorder=respdesc /* turn on ranking */
  datalabel /* turn on data labels */
  datalabelattrs=(family=Arial size=11pt weight=Bold)
```

```
  datalabelfitpolicy=none /* SAS log calls for this, to prevent
    data label suppreession, when image height is reduced
    from the default. This option is also used in other examples. */
  fillattrs=(color=CX009900)
  barwidth=0.6 /* width close to height of bar labels & data labels
                 0.5 bars are too thin
                 0.7 bars dominate the image */
  nooutline /* no outline on bars */
  displaybaseline=off; /* NOLINE for the YAXIS
                          does not turn BASELINE off */
yaxis display=(nolabel noline noticks)
  fitpolicy=none /* to prevent axis value thinning when
                    image height is reduced to 2.5 inches*/
  valueattrs=(family=Arial size=11pt weight=Bold);
xaxis display=none; /* X axis is unneeded due to data labels */
run;
```

Figure 4-3 is an easy further improvement, putting Category and Response values adjacent to each other, by use of the option DATALABELPOS=LEFT.

Figure 4-3. Ranked horizontal bar chart with data labels at left end of bars so that category and value are immediately adjacent—uncertainty as to association is impossible

Listing 4-3. Code used to create Figure 4-3, changes from Figure 4-2 in bold

```
ods listing style=GraphFontArial11ptBold /* using a custom style */
  gpath="C:\temp" dpi=300;
ods graphics on / reset=all scale=off width=5.7in height=2.5in
  imagename="Fig4-3_Ranked_CatAndValAdjacent_DataLabelPosEQleft";
title justify=center 'Ranked Shoe Sales By Region';
proc sgplot data=sashelp.shoes noborder;
hbar Region / response=Sales
```

```
stat=sum /* same as default when RESPONSE= is used */
categoryorder=respdesc
datalabel
/* DATALABELATTRS now come from custom style */
datalabelfitpolicy=none
datalabelpos=left /* at the left end of the bar */
fillattrs=(color=Green)
barwidth=0.6
nooutline
displaybaseline=off;
yaxis display=(nolabel noline noticks) fitpolicy=none;
/* VALUEATTRS now come from custom style */
xaxis display=none;
run;
```

In Figure 4-4, the left-end data labels used in Figured 4-3 are replaced with a Y axis table, and a second Y axis table is added to display the Percent of Total. Though the shapes in the visual part of the image are different, this is the functional equivalent of a pie chart, where there can be the problem of collisions between the labels for the slices, especially with a ranked pie chart where all of the smaller pie slices are brought together.

Figure 4-4. Ranked horizontal bar chart with two Y axis tables; from an information standpoint, this can serve as an alternative to a pie chart, but is visually different

Listing 4-4. Code used to create Figure 4-4

```
ods listing style=GraphFontArial11ptBold gpath="C:\temp" dpi=300;
ods graphics on / reset=all scale=off width=5.7in height=2.5in
  imagename="Fig4-4_Ranked_TwoYaxisTables_CategoryValuePctAdjacent";
```

```
title justify=center 'Ranked Shoe Sales By Region';
proc sgplot data=sashelp.shoes noborder;
hbar Region / response=Sales
  stat=sum /* same as default */
  categoryorder=respdesc
  fillattrs=(color=Green)
  displaybaseline=off nooutline barwidth=0.6;;
/* VALUEATTRS & LABELATTRS for Y Axis Tables
   are controlled by the STYLE */
yaxistable Sales / stat=sum
  position=left   /* to the left of the bars */
  location=inside /* to the right of the category column */
  label='Sales';
yaxistable Sales / stat=percent
  position=left   /* to the left of the bars */
  location=inside /* to the right of the category column AND */
      /* to the right of any previously defined Y axis table */
  label='Share';
yaxis display=(nolabel noline noticks) fitpolicy=none;
xaxis display=none;
run;
```

Maximally Informative Horizontal Bar Chart—Ranked by Measure of Interest

This is a bar chart design that I developed and constructed decades ago with SAS/GRAPH before the availability of Y axis tables in ODS Graphics. Then I did it by preprocessing the input data for the graph creation step. I combined Rank, Category, Value, and Percent Share of the Total into a very long category value, which then, of course, served as the bar label. Figure 1-14 is an example of these prebuilt multi-component bar labels. In Figure 4-5, Rank, Value, and Share are all provided automatically via Y axis tables from raw data using ODS Graphics.

Capturing the numeric rank for its Y axis table requires input data preprocessing. Adding the Rank number to the graph as follows would be unnecessary for a small set of bars, but it's valuable with a large set of bars or if the bar categories are displayed in alphabetical order.

In a way, the result is, in effect, a table with the bars there only as an easy-and-quick-to-use visual tool to compare the Sales values. Also, since the graph has category, value, and percent, it can serve as a pie chart alternative, especially when the number of categories or multiple tiny slices makes a pie chart impractical.

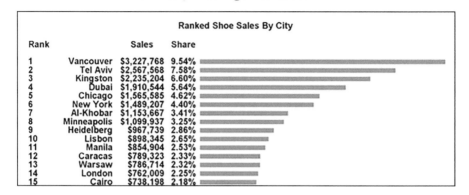

Figure 4-5. Ranked fully informative horizontal bar chart (image physically truncated here). The precision of the percent share is automatically determined by the software

Listing 4-5. *Code used to create Figure 4-5*

```
ods listing style=GraphFontArial8ptBold gpath="C:\temp" dpi=300;
ods graphics on / reset=all scale=off width=5.7in height=6.5in
  imagename="Fig4-5_Ranked_YaxisTablesForRankCategoryValuePercent";
title justify=center "Ranked Shoe Sales By City";
proc sgplot data=sasuser.CityTotals noborder;
  /* Subsidiary is City */
hbar Subsidiary / response=Sales categoryorder=respdesc
  fillattrs=(color=CX009900) barwidth=0.5 nooutline
  displaybaseline=off;
yaxistable Rank / label='Rank' /* stat=sum is default,
  but one observation per city, so SUM is same as Rank */
  position=left     /* to the left of the bars */
  location=outside; /* to the left of the category column */
yaxistable Sales / label='Sales'
                    position=left location=inside;
yaxistable Sales / stat=percent
                    position=left location=inside label='Share';
yaxis display=(nolabel noline noticks) fitpolicy=none;
xaxis display=none;
run;
```

With such a long list of categories, presenting them in alphabetical order, as in Figure 4-6, can be more convenient for lookup of a category.

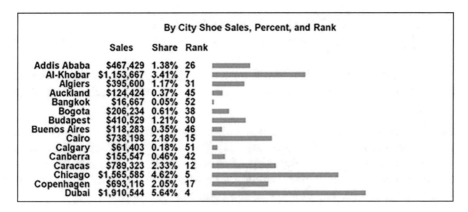

Figure 4-6. Alphabetical description order for the fully informative horizontal bar chart including the rank (image physically truncated here)

The YAXISTABLE statement for Rank now has LOCATION=INSIDE and is the last YAXISTABLE statement in the PROC SGPLOT step.

Listing 4-6. *Code used to create Figure 4-6*

```
proc sort data=sasuser.CityTotals out=work.ToChart;
by Subsidiary;
run;

ods listing style=GraphFontArial8ptBold gpath="C:\temp" dpi=300;
ods graphics on / reset=all scale=off width=5.7in height=6.5in
  imagename="Fig4-6_AlphaOrderBarChart_CategoryValuePercentRank";
title justify=center "By City Shoe Sales, Percent, and Rank";
proc sgplot data=work.ToChart noborder;
hbar Subsidiary / response=Sales
  fillattrs=(color=CX009900) barwidth=0.5 nooutline
  displaybaseline=off;
yaxistable Sales / position=left location=inside label='Sales';
yaxistable Sales / stat=percent
                   position=left location=inside label='Share';
yaxistable Rank  / location=inside position=left label='Rank';
yaxis display=(nolabel noline noticks) fitpolicy=none;
xaxis display=none;
run;
```

Subsetted Ranked Fully Informative Horizontal Bar Charts

As discussed in Chapter 1, if you want to put the focus on what's important and definitely of interest, you can present a ranked subset, rather than *all* of the data.

Not only is not all of the data equally interesting, but not all of the data is a priori important. Possible cases are: (a) Top 10 (or some other number); (b) all categories with the measure of interest above or at some minimum; and (c) enough of the higher ranked categories to account for at least, say, 80% of the total (or any percent of the total that you prefer).

Unlike the preceding examples, where all of the shares of the whole are presented, the next three examples each present a subset of the shares.

There is preprocessing of input data to create the same derivative input for all three cases. It captures all totals needed as macro or symbolic variables and prepares totals by city in rank order for use in the case-specific image creation steps. The remaining code for all three cases is largely the same, except for three sections: (1) a control statement at the top; (2) a DATA step in the middle to do the selection of the subset and to prepare the Ranks, the Shares, and macro variables; and (3) those TITLE statements which, in part, retrieve macro variables to display case-specific information. The PROC SGPLOT step is always the same.

Figure 4-7 is a stacked display of examples for the three ways to present subsets of the categories. Note that all three display analogous text for TITLE3 and the same text for TITLE4. Listing 4-7 is only the code for the third of the examples.

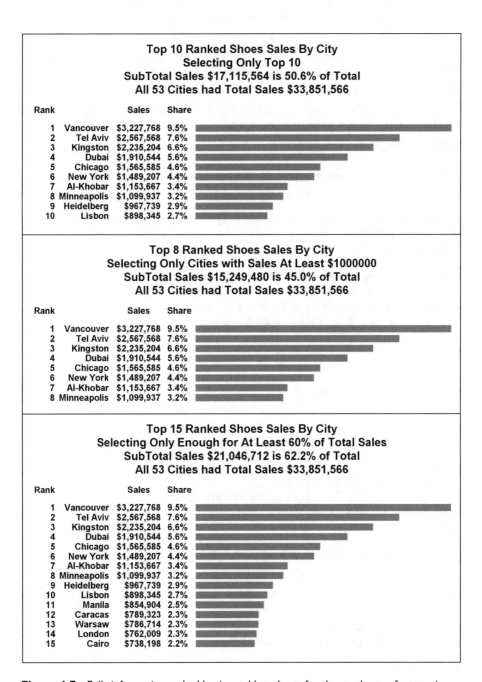

Figure 4-7. Fully informative ranked horizontal bar charts for three subsets of categories

Listing A4-7 in Appendix A contains the code for *all three* cases, as well as further discussion (in section "About These Three Images") related to creating graphs like these. The code for examples Figure 4-8 and beyond is less complex.

The code used to create the bar chart for the subset that is a percent of the total response is the least obvious code, as compared to that for the other two subsets.

Listing 4-7. *Code used to create the bottom image in Figure 4-7, with three statements and one DATA step highlighted that change for the other two cases*

```
/* Data selection criterion and image height for the bottom image */
%let SubtotalPercentSelected = 60;
%let HeightForBottomImage = 3.14in;

/* Pre-processing of input data for all three cases,
   to capture all totals needed as macro or symbolic variables,
   and to present totals by city in rank order
   for use in the image creation steps */

proc summary data=sashelp.shoes;
class Subsidiary;
var Sales;
output out=work.Totals sum=;
run;

data _null_;
set work.Totals nobs=CityCountPlusOne;
where _type_ EQ 0;
call symput('TotalSales',Sales);
call symput('TotalDollars',trim(left(put(Sales,dollar11.))));
call symput('CityCount',trim(left(CityCountPlusOne - 1)));
run;

proc sort data=work.Totals out=work.CityTotals;
where _type_ NE 0;
by descending Sales;
run;

data work.ToBottomChart;
retain SubTotalSales SubTotalPercent 0;
set work.CityTotals;
Rank = _N_;
Percent = 100 * (Sales / &TotalSales);
Share = trim(left(put(Percent,4.1))) || '%';
SubTotalSales + Sales;
SubTotalPercent + Percent;
output;
```

```
if SubTotalPercent GE &SubtotalPercentSelected
then do;
  call symput('TopPercentCount',trim(left(_N_)));
  call symput('SubTotalSales',
              trim(left(put(SubTotalSales,dollar12.))));
  call symput('SubTotalPercent',
              trim(left(put(SubTotalPercent,4.1))) || '%');
  stop;
end;
run;

ods listing style=GraphFontArial8ptBold gpath="C:\temp" dpi=300;
ods graphics on / reset=all scale=off width=5.7in
  height=&HeightForBottomImage
  imagename="Fig4-7Bottom_RankedSubsetHBarChart_SubtotalPercent";
title1 font='Arial/Bold' height=10pt justify=center
  "Top &TopPercentCount Ranked Shoes Sales By City";
title2 font='Arial/Bold' height=10pt justify=center
  "Selecting Only Enough for At Least &SubtotalPercentSelected.% of
  Total Sales";
title3 height=10pt justify=center
  "SubTotal Sales &SubTotalSales is &SubTotalPercent of Total";
title4 height=10pt justify=center
  "All &CityCount Cities had Total Sales &TotalDollars";
proc sgplot data=work.ToBottomChart noborder;
hbar Subsidiary / response=Sales categoryorder=respdesc
  fillattrs=(color=Green)
  displaybaseline=off nooutline barwidth=0.7;
yaxistable Rank  / location=outside position=left label='Rank';
yaxistable Sales / location=inside  position=left stat=sum label='Sales';
yaxistable Share / location=inside  position=left label='Share';
yaxis display=(nolabel noline noticks) fitpolicy=none;
xaxis display=none;
run;
```

After this powerful example which requires complicated preprocessing for the SGPLOT procedure code step, we can lighten up the code load considerably and look at other examples that deliver important communication value with simpler code.

Horizontal Charts for One Category Variable and Two Response Variables

These first examples are feasible when the two response variables have common units (say dollars or counts) and have a range such that the response with the largest values does not dwarf the bars for the response with smaller values.

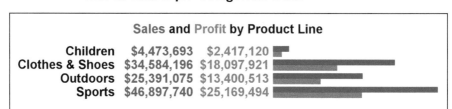

Figure 4-8. One category and two responses side by side, two Y axis tables, and a color-coded title instead of a legend

Listing 4-8. Code used to create Figure 4-8

```
ods listing style=GraphFontArial11ptBold gpath="C:\temp" dpi=300;
ods graphics on / reset=all scale=off width=5.7in height=1.25in
  imagename="Fig4-8_OneCategoryTwoMeasures_HBarsSideBySide";
title justify=center color=Blue  'Sales' color=Black ' and '
  color=Green 'Profit' color=Black ' by Product Line';
proc sgplot data=sashelp.orsales noborder noautolegend;
hbar Product_Line / response=Total_Retail_Price stat=sum
  displaybaseline=off nooutline fillattrs=(color=Blue)
  barwidth=0.4 discreteoffset=-0.2;
hbar Product_Line / response=Profit stat=sum
  displaybaseline=off nooutline fillattrs=(color=Green)
  barwidth=0.4 discreteoffset=+0.2;
yaxistable Total_Retail_Price / location=inside position=left
  nolabel valueattrs=(color=Blue);
yaxistable Profit / location=inside position=left
  nolabel valueattrs=(color=Green);
yaxis display=(nolabel noline noticks) fitpolicy=none;
xaxis display=none;
format Total_Retail_Price dollar12. Profit dollar11.;
run;
```

The use of a legend as in Figure 4-9 is the more traditional solution.

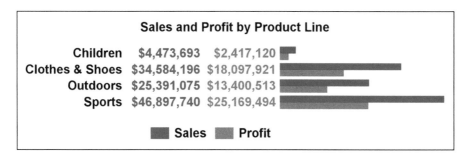

Figure 4-9. Same side-by-side hbar chart, but with a legend, not a color-coded title

Listing 4-9. *Code used to create Figure 4-9, changes from Figure 4-8 in bold*

```
ods listing style=GraphFontArial11ptBold gpath="C:\temp" dpi=300;
ods graphics on / reset=all scale=off width=5.7in height=1.75in
  imagename="Fig4-9_OneCategoryTwoMeasures_HBarsSideBySide_Legend";
title justify=center 'Sales and Profit by Product Line';
proc sgplot data=sashelp.orsales noborder; /* remove NOAUTOLEGEND
                          option to permit the legend to be created */
hbar Product_Line / response=Total_Retail_Price stat=sum
  displaybaseline=off nooutline fillattrs=(color=Blue)
  barwidth=0.4 discreteoffset=-0.2;
hbar Product_Line / response=Profit stat=sum
  displaybaseline=off nooutline fillattrs=(color=Green)
  barwidth=0.4 discreteoffset=+0.2;
yaxistable Total_Retail_Price / location=inside position=left
  nolabel valueattrs=(color=Blue);
yaxistable Profit / location=inside position=left
  nolabel valueattrs=(color=Green);
yaxis display=(nolabel noline noticks) fitpolicy=none;
xaxis display=none;
format Total_Retail_Price dollar12. Profit dollar11.;
label Total_Retail_Price='Sales' Profit='Profit';
  /* replace the default labels for the legend */
keylegend / noborder title=' '
  position=BottomLeft /* improves the location of the legend */
  autooutline /* match OUTLINE or NOOUTLINE
                  on HBAR or VBAR statement */
  fillheight=11pt /* FILLHEIGHT should match legend values' SIZE */
  fillaspect=GOLDEN; /* length and height of rectangular
                        color swatches in "Divine Proportion" */
run;
```

Using data labels in Figure 4-10 looks better with the bars split.

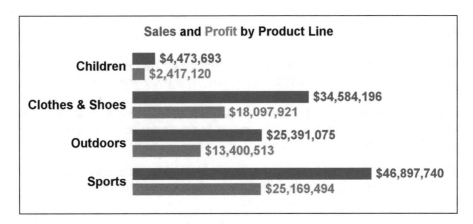

Figure 4-10. Attaching the response values directly to the bars with data labels

Listing 4-10. *Code used to create Figure 4-10*

```
ods listing style=GraphFontArial11ptBold gpath="C:\temp" dpi=300;
ods graphics on / reset=all scale=off width=5.7in height=2.5in
  imagename="Fig4-10_OneCatTwoMeasures_HBarsSideBySide_DataLabels";
title font='Arial/Bold' height=11pt justify=center
  color=Blue  'Sales' color=Black ' and '
  color=Green 'Profit' color=Black ' by Product Line';
proc sgplot data=sashelp.orsales noborder noautolegend;
hbar Product_Line / response=Total_Retail_Price stat=sum
  displaybaseline=off nooutline fillattrs=(color=Blue)
  barwidth=0.3 discreteoffset=-0.2
  datalabel datalabelattrs=(color=Blue)
  datalabelfitpolicy=none;
hbar Product_Line / response=Profit stat=sum
  displaybaseline=off nooutline fillattrs=(color=Green)
  barwidth=0.3 discreteoffset=+0.2
  datalabel datalabelattrs=(color=Green)
  datalabelfitpolicy=none;
/* YAXISTABLE statements removed */
yaxis display=(nolabel noline noticks) fitpolicy=none;
xaxis display=none;
format Total_Retail_Price dollar12. Profit dollar11.;
run;
```

Figure 4-11 is a bona fide overlay, not a lay-beside.

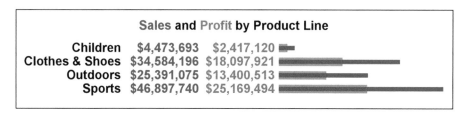

Figure 4-11. Like Figure 4-9, but overlaying Profit bars on top of Sales bars

Since Sales always exceed profits, this graph could be successfully rendered with both the Sales and the Profit bars being the same width. In that case, it would be analogous to the first bar charts ever created, which compared high and low water marks of the Seine River over time, using gray shades, not color. So they were, in effect, time series bar charts, similar to, but simpler than, Figure 4-38.

The chart in Figure 4-11 looks somewhat like the bullet graph designed by Stephen Few, but his construct is more complex than this and is not taken up here.

Listing 4-11. *Code used to create Figure 4-11*

```
ods listing style=GraphFontArial11ptBold gpath="C:\temp" dpi=300;
ods graphics on / reset=all scale=off width=5.7in height=1.25in
  imagename="Fig4-11_OneCatTwoResp_OneBarSetOverlaysTheOtherBarSet";
title justify=center color=Blue  'Sales' color=Black ' and '
  color=Green 'Profit' color=Black ' by Product Line';
proc sgplot data=sashelp.orsales noborder noautolegend;
/* omit the Figure 4-10 offsets in the HBAR statements */
hbar Product_Line / response=Total_Retail_Price
  stat=sum displaybaseline=off
  nooutline fillattrs=(color=Blue) barwidth=0.3;
/* bars from the second HBAR statement overlay those from first */
hbar Product_Line / response=Profit
  stat=sum displaybaseline=off
  nooutline fillattrs=(color=Green) barwidth=0.6
  transparency=0.2; /* let the blue bar underneath
                       partially show through */
yaxistable Total_Retail_Price / location=inside position=left
  nolabel valueattrs=(color=Blue);
yaxistable Profit / location=inside position=left
  nolabel valueattrs=(color=Green);
yaxis display=(nolabel noline noticks) fitpolicy=none;
xaxis display=none;
format Total_Retail_Price dollar12. Profit dollar11.;
run;
```

Adding total bars as in Figure 4-12 could also have been done for prior examples.

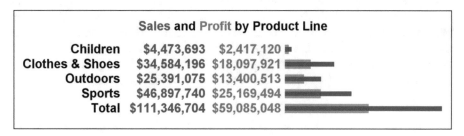

	Sales	and Profit by Product Line	
Children	$4,473,693	$2,417,120	
Clothes & Shoes	$34,584,196	$18,097,921	
Outdoors	$25,391,075	$13,400,513	
Sports	$46,897,740	$25,169,494	
Total	$111,346,704	$59,085,048	

Figure 4-12. Adding total bars to Figure 4-11

Listing 4-12. *Code used to create Figure 4-12, changes from Figure 4-11 in bold*

```
proc summary data=sashelp.orsales;
class Product_Line;
var Profit Total_Retail_Price;
output out=work.ORsalesSummary sum=;
run;
```

```
data work.ToChart;
set work.ORsalesSummary;
if _type_ EQ 0 then Product_Line = 'Total';
run;

ods listing style=GraphFontArial11ptBold gpath="C:\temp" dpi=300;
ods graphics on / reset=all scale=off width=5.7in height=1.5in
  imagename="Fig4-12_OneBarSetOverlaysTheOtherBarSet_WithTotalBars";
title justify=center color=Blue  'Sales' color=Black ' and '
  color=Green 'Profit' color=Black ' by Product Line';
proc sgplot data=work.ToChart noborder noautolegend;
hbar Product_Line / response=Total_Retail_Price
  displaybaseline=off
  nooutline fillattrs=(color=Blue) barwidth=0.3;
hbar Product_Line / response=Profit
  displaybaseline=off
  nooutline fillattrs=(color=Green) barwidth=0.6
  transparency=0.2;
yaxistable Total_Retail_Price / location=inside position=left
  nolabel valueattrs=(color=Blue);
yaxistable Profit / location=inside position=left
  nolabel valueattrs=(color=Green);
yaxis display=(nolabel noline noticks) fitpolicy=none;
xaxis display=none;
format Total_Retail_Price dollar12. Profit dollar11.;
run;
```

In Figure 4-13, the overlaying bar is replaced with what is called an I-beam symbol displayed with a DOT statement instead of a second HBAR statement. Since Sales always exceed Profits, there is no chance of the symbol being somewhat obscured by being on top of the bar. To protect against that problem in the case of other data, one could reduce the bar width, increase the I-beam size, or choose a pair of colors with higher contrast. With the last choice of solution, it would be important to make the bar lighter to achieve contrast. Making the I-beam lighter would make it harder to see on the white background.

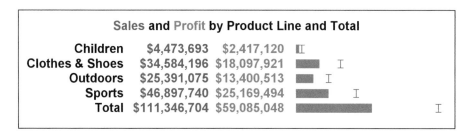

Figure 4-13. Presenting the sales data as an underlaid dot plot, but with I-beam symbols instead of dots

Might this be called a chart of bullets chasing I-beams?

Listing 4-13. *Code used to create Figure 4-13, changes from Figure 4-12 in bold*

```
proc summary data=sashelp.orsales;
class Product_Line;
var Profit Total_Retail_Price;
output out=work.ORsalesSummary sum=;
run;

data work.ToChart;
set work.ORsalesSummary;
if _type_ EQ 0 then Product_Line = 'Total';
run;

ods listing style=GraphFontArial11ptBold gpath="C:\temp" dpi=300;
ods graphics on / reset=all scale=off width=5.7in height=1.5in
   imagename="Fig4-13_HbarAndDotPlotOverLaid_YaxisTables";
title justify=center color=Blue 'Sales' color=Black ' and '
   color=Green 'Profit' color=Black ' by Product Line and Total';
proc sgplot data=work.ToChart noborder noautolegend;
hbar Product_Line / response=Profit
   displaybaseline=off
   nooutline fillattrs=(color=Green) barwidth=0.6;
dot Product_Line / response=Total_Retail_Price
   markerattrs=(symbol=IBeam color=Blue size=8pt);
yaxistable Total_Retail_Price / location=inside position=left
   nolabel valueattrs=(color=Blue);
yaxistable Profit / location=inside position=left
   nolabel valueattrs=(color=Green);
yaxis display=(nolabel noline noticks) fitpolicy=none;
xaxis display=none;
format Total_Retail_Price dollar12. Profit dollar11.;
run;
```

Figures 4-8 through 4-13 are bar chart overlays of various types, some side by side, others actually overlaid in the true sense of the word. If the examples with Total bars had Total bars that dwarfed the Product Line bars, the better solution would be to supply the totals in a subtitle.

The purpose of Figure 4-14 is to permit comparison of the Product Line response values both with each other and with their physically rendered total. It is, in effect, a pie chart alternative, but a linear one, rather than a solid-filled circle.

Chapter 4 | Bar Charts, Butterfly Charts, Waterfall Charts, Dot Plots, Needle Plots, Area Bar Charts, Text Graphs, and Line Charts: Charts for Categorical Data

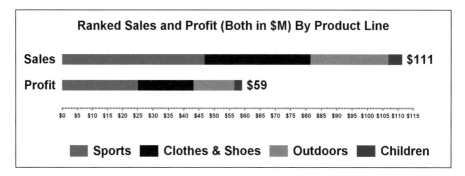

Figure 4-14. Stacked ranked horizontal bar chart. No precise values available, except for all product totals as data labels

Listing 4-14. *Code used to create Figure 4-14*

```
ods listing style=GraphFontArial11ptBold gpath="C:\temp" dpi=300;
ods graphics on / reset=all scale=off width=5.7in height=2in
  maxlegendarea=25
  /* if the default value is accepted instead,
     legend is omitted by the software, with this NOTE in SAS log:
     Some graph legends have been dropped due to size constraints.
     Try adjusting the MAXLEGENDAREA=, WIDTH= and HEIGHT= options
     in the ODS GRAPHICS statement. */
  imagename=
  "Fig4-14_StackedRankedHbarChart_TotalDataLabelsAndDetailedXaxis";
title justify=center
  'Ranked Sales and Profit (Both in $M) By Product Line';
proc sgplot data=sasuser.OR_SalesProfitByProdLineAndTotal noborder
  dattrmap=sasuser.ORsalesDattrMap;
where Product_Line NE 'Total';
hbar SalesOrProfit / response=DollarsInM
  categoryorder=respdesc
  group=Product_Line
  groupdisplay=stack /* default layout when using GROUP= */
  attrid=GroupColors
  displaybaseline=off nooutline barwidth=0.4
  datalabel; /* data label only for each bar's total of responses */
yaxis display=(nolabel noline noticks)
  values=('Sales' 'Profit');
xaxis display=(nolabel noline) fitpolicy=none
  grid minor minorcount=9
  values=(0 to 115 by 5) valueattrs=(size=5pt);
keylegend / noborder title=' ' autooutline
  fillheight=11pt fillaspect=golden;
format DollarsInM dollar4.;
run;
```

The SEGLABEL option can, space permitting, present the precise values as in Figure 4-15. If using sufficiently dark (light) fills, the segment label can be reliably rendered readably in white (black).

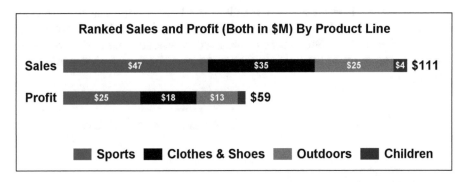

Figure 4-15. Stacked ranked horizontal bar chart with precise values as segment labels, where space permits (note the missing label)

A possible solution to the problem of the missing segment label would be to include a footnote like the one used in Figure 4-31. But there is the better alternative of using the clustered horizontal bar chart in Figure 4-16, which comes with the added benefit of space to display precise dollar values rather than millions.

Listing 4-15. *Code used to create Figure 4-15, changes from Figure 4-14 in bold*

```
ods listing style=GraphFontArial11ptBold gpath="C:\temp" dpi=300;
ods graphics on / reset=all scale=off width=5.7in height=2in
  maxlegendarea=25 /* if default used instead, legend is omitted */
  imagename=
  "Fig4-15_StackedRankedHbarChart_SegLabels_TotalDataLabels";
title justify=center
  'Ranked Sales and Profit (Both in $M) By Product Line';
proc sgplot data=sasuser.OR_SalesProfitByProdLineAndTotal noborder
  dattrmap=sasuser.ORsalesDattrMap;
where Product_Line NE 'Total';
hbar SalesOrProfit / response=DollarsInM
  categoryorder=respdesc
  group=Product_Line
  groupdisplay=stack /* default */
  attrid=GroupColors
  displaybaseline=off nooutline barwidth=0.4
  datalabel
  seglabel seglabelattrs=(size=8pt color=White);
yaxis display=(nolabel noline noticks) values=('Sales' 'Profit');
xaxis display=none;
keylegend / noborder title=' ' autooutline
```

```
   fillheight=11pt fillaspect=golden;
   format DollarsInM dollar4.;
run;
```

A clustered bar chart always delivers all of the benefits of a stacked bar chart with segment labels, but with no space constraints for the bar data labels, as shown in Figure 4-16. Short bars cannot accommodate segment labels when they are instead concatenated in a stacked bar chart. See that problem in Figure 4-15.

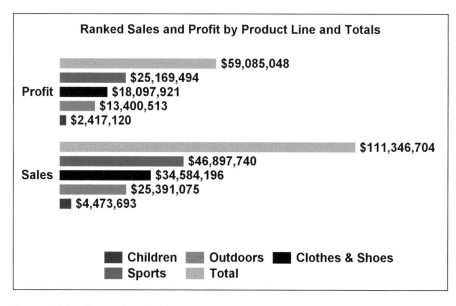

Figure 4-16. Clustered ranked horizontal bar chart with total bars

Listing 4-16. *Code used to create Figure 4-16*

```
ods listing style=GraphFontArial11ptBold gpath="C:\temp" dpi=300;
ods graphics on / reset=all scale=off width=5.7in height=3.5in
   imagename="Fig4-16_ClusteredRankedHbarChartWithDataLabels";
title justify=center
   'Ranked Sales and Profit by Product Line and Totals';
proc sgplot data=sasuser.OR_SalesProfitByProdLineAndTotal noborder
   dattrmap=sasuser.ORsalesDattrMap;
hbar SalesOrProfit / response=Dollars
   categoryorder=respasc /* Clustered bar chart is filled from the
   bottom. Use Response Ascending to get largest bar at the top. */
   group=Product_Line
   groupdisplay=cluster
   attrid=GroupColors
   displaybaseline=off nooutline barwidth=0.7
```

```
datalabelfitpolicy=none
datalabel;
yaxis display=(nolabel noline noticks);
xaxis display=none;
keylegend / noborder title=' ' autooutline
  fillheight=11pt fillaspect=golden;
run;
```

If you prefer, you can eliminate the legend in Figure 4-16 and use a color-coded title. That provides a more immediate association between the datalabel values and their response variable name than does a legend. The viewer always reads the title and then moves the view to the bars and their data labels. To find how to make the change, compare the code for Figures 4-8 (color-coded title) and 4-9 (legend). With a legend, the viewer must view three areas to interpret the chart.

Figure 4-17 uses a panel with a heading to present the category as a heading for each cluster, and there is no need for a legend.

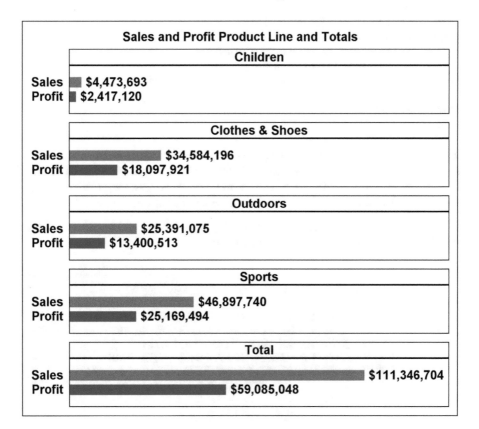

Figure 4-17. A panel of horizontal bar charts moves the values for one of the category variables to headings. This saves horizontal space. Here, the chart is created at full width of the available page space, but could be narrower without reducing the readability (font size)

Because each section of the panel is its own separate hbar chart, the use of CATEGORYORDER=RESPDESC can have no effect on the order of the sections.

Listing 4-17. *Code used to create Figure 4-17*

```
ods listing style=GraphFontArial11ptBold gpath="C:\temp" dpi=300;
ods graphics on / reset=all scale=off width=5.7in height=5in
  imagename="Fig4-17_Panel_TwoCatVarsOneRespVar_HeadersBorders";
title justify=center 'Sales and Profit Product Line and Totals';
proc sgpanel data=sasuser.OR_SalesProfitByProdLineAndTotal
  noautolegend;
styleattrs datacolors=(Green Blue);
panelby Product_Line /
  onepanel
  columns=1
  novarname
  spacing=10;
hbar SalesOrProfit / response=Dollars
  group=SalesOrProfit
  displaybaseline=off nooutline barwidth=0.7
  datalabel datalabelfitpolicy=none;
rowaxis display=(nolabel noline noticks) fitpolicy=none
  discreteorder=data;
colaxis display=none;
run;
```

The PROC SGPANEL solution requires more vertical space than the clustered bar chart. PROC SGPANEL has a lot of capabilities demonstrated in Chapter 9. If the Totals were eliminated, this panel could be reconfigured in a fully symmetric 2 X 2 panel, of one Product Line per quadrant.

In Figure 4-18, the horizontal bar chart for one categorical variable and two response variables is called a butterfly chart.

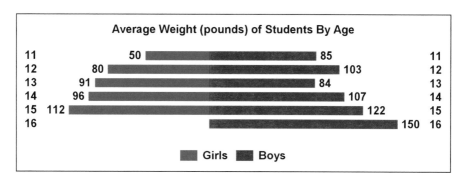

Figure 4-18. Horizontal bar chart known as a butterfly chart

I was unable to find anybody as inventor of the butterfly chart. However, in *A History of Data Visualization and Graphic Communication* by Michael Friendly and Howard Wainer, in the section "US Census Atlases," there are Bilateral Histograms from the 1870 United States Census that look like butterfly charts.

Listing 4-18. *Code used to create Figure 4-18*

```
proc format;
picture AbsoluteValue_ThreeDigits
  low-<0 = '000'
  0<-high = '000';
run;

data work.ToChart(keep=Age GirlWgt BoyWgt);
set sashelp.class;
if Sex EQ 'F' then GirlWgt = 0 - Weight;
else BoyWgt  = Weight;
run;

ods listing style=GraphFontArial10ptBold gpath="C:\temp" dpi=300;
ods graphics on / reset=all scale=off width=5.7in height=2in
  imagename="Fig4-18_OneCatTwoSimilarRespVars_ButterFlyHbarChart";
title1 justify=center "Average Weight (pounds) of Students By Age";
proc sgplot data=work.ToChart noborder;
hbar age / response=BoyWgt stat=mean
  y2axis /* Y axis located to the right of the bars */
  name='BoyWgts' legendlabel="Boys"
  displaybaseline=off nooutline barwidth=0.65
  fillattrs=(color=red) datalabel;
hbar age / response=GirlWgt stat=mean
  name='GirlWgts' legendlabel="Girls"
  displaybaseline=off nooutline barwidth=0.65
  fillattrs=(color=blue) datalabel;
format Age 2. BoyWgt GirlWgt AbsoluteValue_ThreeDigits.;
xaxis display=none;
yaxis display=(noticks noline nolabel);
y2axis display=(noticks noline nolabel);
keylegend 'GirlWgts' 'BoyWgts' /
  noborder title='' autooutline
  fillheight=10pt fillaspect=golden;
run;
```

In Figure 4-19, the butterfly chart presents two pairs of response variables.

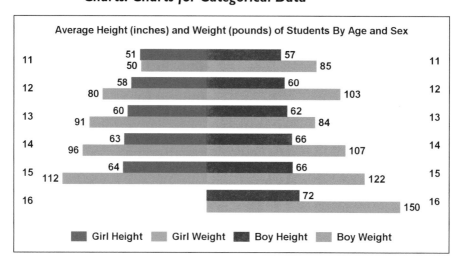

Figure 4-19. Butterfly chart with side-by-side bars for two response variables

Listing 4-19. *Code used to create Figure 4-19, changes from Figure 4-18 in bold*

```
proc format;
picture AbsoluteValue_TwoDigits
  low-<0='00' 0<-high='00';
picture AbsoluteValue_ThreeDigits
  low-<0='000' 0<-high='000';
run;

data work.ToChart(keep=Age GirlHgt BoyHgt GirlWgt BoyWgt);
set sashelp.class;
if Sex EQ 'F' then do;
  GirlHgt = 0 - Height; GirlWgt = 0 - Weight;
end;
else do;
  BoyHgt = Height; BoyWgt = Weight;
end;
run;

ods listing style=GraphFontArial9ptBold gpath="C:\temp" dpi=300;
ods graphics on / reset=all scale=off width=5.7in height=3in
  imagename="Fig4-19_OneCatVarFourRespVars_OverlayButterFlyChart";
title justify=center
  "Average Height (inches) and Weight (pounds) of Students By Age and Sex";
proc sgplot data=work.ToChart noborder;
hbar age / response=BoyHgt y2axis stat=mean discreteoffset=-0.2
  name='BoyHgts' legendlabel="Boy Height"
  displaybaseline=off nooutline barwidth=0.4
  fillattrs=(color=red) datalabel;
```

```
hbar age / response=BoyWgt y2axis stat=mean discreteoffset=+0.2
  name='BoyWgts' legendlabel="Boy Weight"
  displaybaseline=off nooutline barwidth=0.4
  fillattrs=(color=CXFF9999) datalabel;
hbar age / response=GirlHgt stat=mean discreteoffset=-0.2
  name='GirlHgts' legendlabel="Girl Height"
  displaybaseline=off nooutline barwidth=0.4
  fillattrs=(color=blue) datalabel;
hbar age / response=GirlWgt stat=mean discreteoffset=+0.2
  name='GirlWgts' legendlabel="Girl Weight"
  displaybaseline=off nooutline barwidth=0.4
  fillattrs=(color=CX9999FF) datalabel;
format Age 2. BoyHgt GirlHgt AbsoluteValue_TwoDigits.
            BoyWgt GirlWgt AbsoluteValue_ThreeDigits.;
xaxis display=none;
yaxis display=(noticks noline nolabel);
y2axis display=(noticks noline nolabel);
keylegend 'GirlHgts' 'GirlWgts' 'BoyHgts' 'BoyWgts' /
  noborder title='' autooutline fillheight=9pt fillaspect=golden;
run;
```

Dot Plots

Dot plots are horizontal only and can serve as a horizontal bar chart alternative. They were invented by William S. Cleveland in 1981 and suggested as a replacement for pie charts and bar charts.

There had been criticism of pie charts, but it can be overcome by following pie chart design and construction principles presented in Chapter 5.

I see *no* communication advantage for dot plots over bar charts or well-designed pie charts.

Some possibilities with horizontal bar charts are *not available* with dot plots. For example, the options to position data labels are limited to (a) the default location, which might not be to your satisfaction or the best presentation to your viewer, or (b) a column of data labels at the left or right end of the dot plot lines, not immediately adjacent to the dots. The column of response values at the left of the dot plot lines *is* an advantage since it puts them adjacent to their category values.

The only apparent advantage of a dot plot is as choice for a graph creator who does not like bar charts and pie charts.

However, I did use a dot plot as a bar chart companion in Figure 4-13, but, it was as an alternative to equally communication-effective example in Figure 4-12.

Later, in a comparison of certain types of dot plots and needle plots, you will see that needle plots are better than dot plots.

Figure 4-20. Best ranked dot plot (DATALABELPOS=LEFT), the equivalent of the bar chart in Figure 4-3

Listing 4-20. Code used to create Figure 4-20, changes from Figure 4-3 in bold

```
ods listing style=GraphFontArial11ptBold gpath="C:\temp" dpi=300;
ods graphics on / reset=all scale=off width=5.7in height=2.5in
  imagename="Fig4-20_RankedRegionsDotChartDataLabelPosEQleft";
title justify=center 'Ranked Shoe Sales By Region';
proc sgplot data=sashelp.shoes noborder;
dot Region / response=Sales categoryorder=respdesc
  /* all HBAR options removed */
  markerattrs=(color=Green symbol=CircleFilled size=11pt)
  datalabel
  datalabelpos=left; /* left end of the dot line,
                        adjacent to category values.
  Other options are RIGHT (too far from category values),
  and DATA (default) can create confusion as to
  association between data labels and markers. */
yaxis display=(nolabel noline noticks) fitpolicy=none;
xaxis display=none;
run;
```

As noted in the code comments for Listing 4-20, the other choices for DATALABELPOS are unacceptable. Figure 4-21 shows the result with DATALABELPOS=RIGHT, and Figure 4-22 shows the default result for using DATALABELPOS=DATA. All other code for these two examples, except IMAGENAME, is identical to the code in Listing 4-20.

Figure 4-21. DATALABELPOS=RIGHT needlessly maximizes the visual distance between category and response values, a worse disadvantage when there are many categories

Figure 4-22. DATALABELPOS=DATA (the default) can create confusion as to the association between data labels and markers (response value and category value)

With dot plots, you can also create bar chart alternatives that are clusters or are overlays, as shown in Figures 4-23 through 4-26.

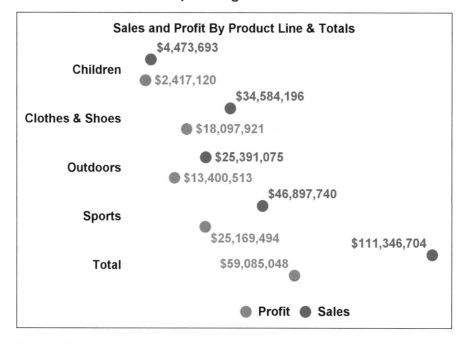

Figure 4-23. Clustered dot plot with grouping by SalesOrProfit

Listing 4-23. Code used to create Figure 4-23

```
ods listing style=GraphFontArial11ptBold gpath="C:\temp" dpi=300;
ods graphics on / reset=all scale=off width=5.7in height=4in
  imagename=
  "Fig4-23_ORsales_ClusteredDotPlot_GroupBySalesProfit";
title justify=center "Sales and Profit By Product Line & Totals";
proc sgplot data=sasuser.OR_SalesProfitByProdLineAndTotal noborder;
styleattrs datacontrastcolors=(Green Blue);
dot Product_Line / response=Dollars
  group=SalesOrProfit groupdisplay=cluster
  markerattrs=(symbol=CircleFilled size=11pt)
  datalabel;
yaxis display=(nolabel noline noticks);
xaxis display=none;
keylegend / noborder title=' ' fillheight=11pt;
run;
```

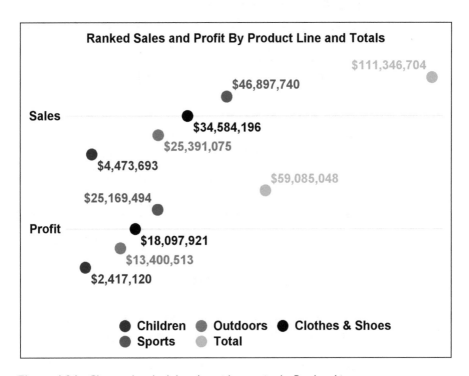

Figure 4-24. Clustered ranked dot plot with grouping by Product Line

Listing 4-24. *Code used to create Figure 4-24, changes from Figure 4-23 in bold*

```
ods listing style=GraphFontArial11ptBold gpath="C:\temp" dpi=300;
ods graphics on / reset=all scale=off width=5.7in height=4.25in
  imagename=
  "Fig4-24_ORsales_ClusteredRankedDotPlot_GroupByProdLineAndTotal";
title justify=center
  "Ranked Sales and Profit By Product Line and Totals";
proc sgplot data=sasuser.OR_SalesProfitByProdLineAndTotal noborder
  dattrmap=sasuser.ORsalesDattrMap;
dot SalesOrProfit / response=Dollars
  categoryorder=respasc /* dots are laid down by increasing response
                          from bottom to top of the plot */
  group=Product_Line
  groupdisplay=cluster
  attrid=GroupColors
  markerattrs=(symbol=CircleFilled size=11pt)
  datalabel;
yaxis display=(nolabel noline noticks) values=('Sales' 'Profit');
xaxis display=none;
keylegend / noborder title=' ' fillheight=11pt;
run;
```

A dot plot, as in Figure 4-25, can be an alternative to an overlay bar chart.

Figure 4-25. Overlay dot plot with grouping by SalesOrProfit. Increasing the image height would not alleviate vertically squashed positioning of the two data labels for each Product Line

Listing 4-25. *Code used to create Figure 4-25, changes from Figure 4-23 in bold*

```
ods listing style=GraphFontArial11ptBold gpath="C:\temp" dpi=300;
ods graphics on / reset=all scale=off width=5.7in height=3in
  /* increasing height would NOT relieve vertical squashing
  of the data label pairs for each Product Line */
  imagename=
  "Fig4-25_ORsales_OverlayDotPlot_GroupBySalesProfit";
title justify=center "Sales and Profit By Product Line and Totals";
proc sgplot data=sasuser.OR_SalesProfitByProdLineAndTotal noborder;
styleattrs datacontrastcolors=(Green Blue);
dot Product_Line / response=Dollars
  group=SalesOrProfit
  groupdisplay=overlay /* this is the default when GROUP= is used */
  markerattrs=(symbol=CircleFilled size=11pt)
  datalabel;
yaxis display=(nolabel noline noticks);
xaxis display=none;
keylegend / noborder title=' ' fillheight=11pt;
run;
```

In Figure 4-26, using Product_Line as the Group variable for the dot plot provides a pie chart functional equivalent to compare portions with each other and with the Total.

Figure 4-26. Overlay dot plot with grouping by Product Line. The relative magnitude and position of the values of the response for each Group variable value "ranks" the data

Listing 4-26. *Code used to create Figure 4-26, changes from Figure 4-24 in bold*

```
ods listing style=GraphFontArial11ptBold gpath="C:\temp" dpi=300;
ods graphics on / reset=all scale=off width=5.7in height=2.25in
  imagename="Fig4-26_ORsales_OverlayDotPlot_GroupByProdLine";
title1 justify=center
  'Sales and Profit (Both in $M) By Product Line and Totals';
title2 height=1pt ' '; /* white space */
proc sgplot data=sasuser.OR_SalesProfitByProdLineAndTotal noborder;
styleattrs datacontrastcolors=(DarkOrange Purple Green Blue Black);
dot SalesOrProfit / response=DollarsInM
  group=Product_Line groupdisplay=overlay
  markerattrs=(symbol=CircleFilled size=11pt)
  datalabel;
yaxis display=(nolabel noline noticks) values=('Sales' 'Profit');
xaxis display=none;
keylegend / noborder title=' ' fillheight=11pt;
format DollarsInM dollar6.1;
run;
```

Vertical Bar Charts

Vertical bar charts are probably nearly as common as horizontal bar charts. They have no inherent superiority or advantage. If the bar category values or bar data labels are too long, there can be a space problem, or, if text is shrunk to accommodate the space limitation, a readability problem.

There are only three applications that I can think of that vertical bar charts can serve, but horizontal bar charts cannot. They are often used for time series with few enough date, time, or datetime intervals, as in Figure 4-38 or 4-39. Waterfall charts, like that in Figure 4-40, are inherently vertical bar charts.

In a third application, a line chart for one response variable is overlaid on a vertical bar chart for another response variable, and the X variable is a common variable with discrete values, as in Figure 4-37. For me the obvious solution would use vertical bars for *both* response variables, as in Figure 4-36.

Figure 4-27, a default vertical bar chart, demonstrates the very common problem that I mentioned in the opening of this section—horizontal space limitations for bar labels. I am a staunch advocate for horizontal text. Tilted text is not horizontal. Viewers normally do not read with their heads tilted to the right.

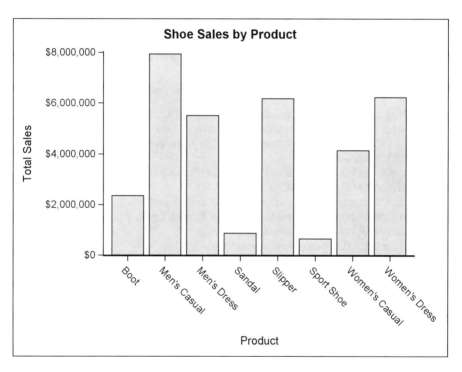

Figure 4-27. Default vertical bar chart, but specifying a response variable, which gets automatically summed by default

Listing 4-27. *Code used to create Figure 4-27*

```
ods listing style=listing gpath="C:\temp" dpi=300;
ods graphics on / reset=all scale=off width=5.7in
                /* actual default is 640px
                   default height is always 3/4 of any width */
  imagename="Fig4-27_VbarChartDefault";
title justify=center "Shoe Sales by Product";
  /* use of JUSTIFY=CENTER yields a result different
     from the true default of omitting JUSTIFY= */
```

```
proc sgplot data=sashelp.shoes noborder;
vbar Product / response=Sales;
  /* When response var is specified,
     response value is summarized by category,
     which is same as STAT=SUM option.
     If no response var is specified,
     default is frequency count by category,
     which is same as STAT=FREQ option.
     Other STAT options are
     MEAN, MEDIAN, and PERCENT. */
run;
```

The ranked and data-labeled vertical bar chart in Figure 4-28 is much better than the default.

Figure 4-28. Ranked vertical bar chart with data labels at the top (the default location)

Listing 4-28. Code used to create Figure 4-28, changes from Figure 4-27 in bold

```
ods listing style=listing gpath="C:\temp" dpi=300;
ods graphics on / reset=all scale=off width=5.7in height=2in
  imagename="Fig4-28_RankedVbarChartWithDataLabels";
title justify=center "Ranked Shoe Sales by Product";
proc sgplot data=sashelp.shoes noborder;
vbar Product / response=Sales
  categoryorder=respdesc
  displaybaseline=off nooutline barwidth=0.8
  datalabel datalabelattrs=(family=Arial size=7pt weight=bold);
xaxis display=(noticks noline nolabel)
  valueattrs=(family=Arial size=7pt weight=bold)
  splitchar=' ' /* so that the values can fit */
  fitpolicy=splitalways;
yaxis display=none;
format Sales dollar11.;
run;
```

▓ **Note**   When using the SPLITCHAR option, as in SPLITCHAR=' ', on an XAXIS statement to split the axis values at any embedded blank (in, e.g., "Sport Shoe"), as in Figure 4-28, it is important to include the option FITPOLICY=SPLITALWAYS. I have observed that the omission of the FITPOLICY admonition can sometimes result in the values not being split, and instead being rendered as tilted values, rather than horizontal. If you omit the recommended option in the code for Figure 4-36, tilted values *will* result.

Figure 4-29 moves the data label to the bottom to put each response value immediately adjacent to its category value. This is the *best* solution for a vertical bar chart for one category variable and one response variable.

Figure 4-29. Ranked vertical bar chart with data labels at the bottom of the bars, easier coding than the equivalent result that is possible with the XAXISTABLE option

Listing 4-29. *Code used to create Figure 4-29, changes from Figure 4-28 in bold*

```
ods listing style=listing gpath="C:\temp" dpi=300;
ods graphics on / reset=all scale=off width=5.7in height=2in
  imagename="Fig4-29_RankedVbarChartWithDataLabelsAtBottomOfBars";
title justify=center "Ranked Shoe Sales by Product";
proc sgplot data=sashelp.shoes noborder;
vbar Product / response=Sales
  categoryorder=respdesc
  displaybaseline=off nooutline barwidth=0.8
  datalabel datalabelattrs=(family=Arial size=7pt weight=bold)
  datalabelpos=bottom;
xaxis display=(noticks noline nolabel)
  valueattrs=(family=Arial size=7pt weight=bold)
  splitchar=' ' /* so that the values can fit */
  fitpolicy=splitalways;
yaxis display=none;
format Sales dollar11.;
run;
```

Figure 4-30 demonstrates the best way to deal with too long labels in a vertical bar chart, other than converting it to a horizontal bar chart.

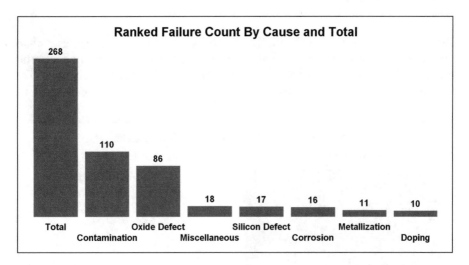

Figure 4-30. Vertical bar chart with total bar, data labels, and XAXIS option FITPOLICY=STAGGER to avoid otherwise necessary choice of either using smaller size of text for axis values or axis values being tilted by software

Listing 4-30. *Code used to create Figure 4-30*

```
proc sql noprint;
select sum(count) into :Total
  from sashelp.failure;
quit;

data work.ToChart; /* add a Total observation */
set sashelp.failure end=lastone;
output;
if lastone;
cause='Total';
count = &Total;
output;
run;

ods listing style=listing gpath="C:\temp" dpi=300;
ods graphics on / reset=all scale=off width=5.7in height=3in
  imagename="Fig4-30_RankedVbarChartWithDataLabelsAndTotalBar";
title "Ranked Failure Count By Cause and Total";
proc sgplot data=work.ToChart noborder;
vbar cause / displaybaseline=off nooutline fillattrs=(color=Red)
  response=count
  categoryorder=respdesc
  datalabel datalabelattrs=(family=Arial size=8pt weight=Bold);
```

```
xaxis display=(nolabel noline noticks) fitpolicy=stagger
  valueattrs=(family=Arial size=8pt weight=Bold);
yaxis display=none;
run;
```

Figure 4-31 is default GROUPDISPLAY=STACKED for a vertical bar chart with two categorical variables. The Y axis is optionally omitted since it would not permit the viewer to get precise numbers for the response values. The SEGLABEL option is used instead.

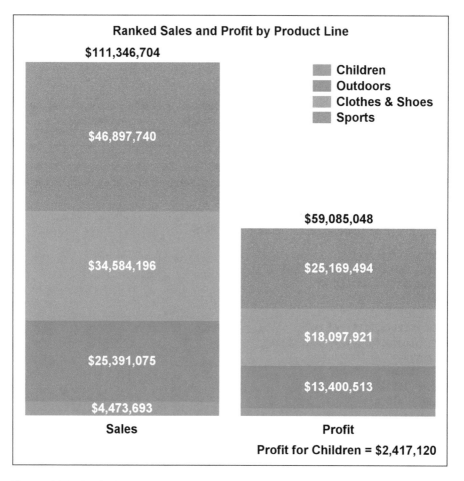

Figure 4-31. Stacked ranked vertical bar chart with segment labels and default color palette (labels are customized as white for readability). Missing segment label is provided with a footnote

Here, the common problem of insufficient space is addressed with a footnote and extra code. To see what the typical solution would look like, in the code from Listing 4-31 you can omit the FOOTNOTE, omit SEGLABEL and SEGLABELATTRS options, delete the YAXIS statement which turns off the Y axis, change the IMAGENAME, and run that instead. The result in Figure 4-31 requires some preprocessing, but is better than the default stacked bar chart. The problem was discovered and the solution was implementable only because this is an ad hoc, iterative experiment, not a production application. A graph that is created by a periodic computer-scheduled job, or in response to an online query, must get the result right the first time, every time. For that situation, a stacked bar chart is infeasible if you want to be certain of always reliably delivering precise numbers, not just a hard-to-interpret image.

Listing 4-31. *Code used to create Figure 4-31*

```
data _null_; /* extract missing segment label data for footnote */
set sasuser.OR_SalesProfitByProdLineAndTotal;
where Product_Line EQ 'Children' and SalesOrProfit EQ 'Profit';
call symput('ForFootNote',trim(left(put(Dollars,dollar12.))));
run;

ods listing style=GraphFontArial11ptBold gpath="C:\temp" dpi=300;
ods graphics on / reset=all scale=off width=5.7in height=5.7in
imagename="Fig4-31_StackedVBarChart_WithSegLabelsAndFootnote";
title justify=center 'Ranked Sales and Profit by Product Line';
footnote justify=right "Profit for Children = &ForFootNote";
proc sgplot data=sasuser.OR_SalesProfitByProdLineAndTotal noborder;
where Product_Line NE 'Total';
vbar SalesOrProfit / response=Dollars
  categoryorder=respasc /* Bar segments are drawn starting at the
  bottom. So, to get the largest segment at the top it is necessary
  to use Ascending category order */
  group=Product_Line groupdisplay=stack
  displaybaseline=off nooutline barwidth=0.9
  seglabel seglabelattrs=(color=white)
  datalabel;
xaxis display=(noline noticks nolabel) values=('Sales' 'Profit');
yaxis display=none;
/* First version WITHOUT SEGLABEL
   omitted the footnote
   and used this YAXIS statement:
yaxis display=(nolabel noline)
  grid minorgrid minor minorcount=4
  fitpolicy=none
  values=(0 to 115000000 by 5000000); */
format Dollars dollar12.;
keylegend / noborder title=' ' autooutline
  across=1 location=inside position=topright
  fillheight=11pt fillaspect=golden;
run;
```

Figure 4-32 is the best way to present a stacked vertical bar chart. The segment response values are disconnected from their bar segments, but color coding connects the segments, their response values, and their Product_Line category values. Even if the segment value did not disappear in Figure 4-31, it would still have the disadvantage of requiring the viewer to consult a legend to find the Product_Line value.

Figure 4-32. Stacked ranked vertical bar chart with color-coded X axis table for precise values knowledge with an image one-fourth the size of Figure 4-31

Replacing segment labels and the regrettably necessary footnote with an X axis table delivers the precise values with a nondisastrous, but actual, loss of immediacy of association. However, the color coding preserves the ability to make associations.

Listing 4-32. *Code used to create Figure 4-32, changes from Figure 4-31 in bold, and SEGLABEL option and KEYLEGEND statement removed*

```
ods listing style=GraphFontArial8ptBold gpath="C:\temp" dpi=300;
ods graphics on / reset=all scale=off width=2.8in height=2.8in
  imagename=
"Fig4-32_StackedRankedVBarChartColorCodedXAxisTableTotalDataLabels";
title justify=center 'Ranked Sales and Profit By Product Line';
proc sgplot data=sasuser.OR_SalesProfitByProdLineAndTotal noborder
  noautolegend dattrmap=sasuser.ORsalesDattrMap;
where Product_Line NE 'Total';
```

```
vbar SalesOrProfit / response=Dollars
  categoryorder=respasc
  group=Product_Line
  groupdisplay=stack
  attrid=GroupColors
  displaybaseline=off nooutline barwidth=0.9
  datalabel;
xaxis display=(noline noticks nolabel) values=('Sales' 'Profit');
yaxis display=none;
xaxistable Dollars / title=''
  colorgroup=Product_Line
  attrid=GroupColors
  location=inside position=bottom labelpos=left;
format Dollars dollar12.;
run;
```

Figure 4-33, using GROUPDISPLAY=CLUSTER, is the better alternative than a stacked bar chart.

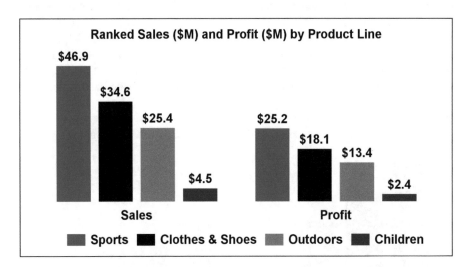

Figure 4-33. Clustered ranked vertical bar chart with data labels and legend

Listing 4-33. Code used to create Figure 4-33

```
ods listing style=GraphFontArial11ptBold gpath="C:\temp" dpi=300;
ods graphics on / reset=all scale=off width=5.7in height=3in
  imagename="Fig4-33_ClusteredRankedVBarChartWithDataLabelsAndLegend";
title 'Ranked Sales ($M) and Profit ($M) by Product Line';
proc sgplot data=sasuser.OR_SalesProfitByProdLineAndTotal noborder
  dattrmap=sasuser.ORsalesDattrMap;
where Product_Line NE 'Total';
vbar SalesOrProfit / response=DollarsInM
```

```
categoryorder=respdesc
group=Product_Line
groupdisplay=cluster
attrid=GroupColors
displaybaseline=off nooutline barwidth=0.8
datalabelfitpolicy=none
datalabel;
xaxis display=(noline noticks nolabel) values=('Sales' 'Profit');
yaxis display=none;
format DollarsInM dollar5.1;
keylegend / title=' ' noborder autooutline
  fillheight=11pt fillaspect=golden;
run;
```

Figure 4-34 is the best vertical bar chart alternative to a stacked vertical bar chart. Everything that the viewer needs to know for the Sales or Profit for any Product Line is adjacent or close together: response value, the Product Line category, and whether the category is Sales or Profit. Its only disadvantage is the constraint on any vertical bar chart of too limited space for horizontal text, whether it is bar labels, data labels, or X axis table content. On a horizontal bar chart, space is unlikely to be a problem for bar labels, data labels, and Y axis tables, and the text is always and only horizontal. The software never tries to tilt it or display vertically as is the case for axis values on a vertical bar chart with too many bars or with very long bar labels.

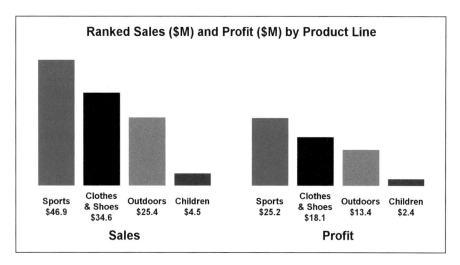

Figure 4-34. Clustered ranked bar chart with response values for group variable combined with the group variable values and used as bottom-of-bar data labels

Listing 4-34. *Code used to create Figure 4-34, changes from Figure 4-33 in bold*

```
data work.ToChart;
length ProductAndDollars $ 26;
set sasuser.OR_SalesProfitByProdLineAndTotal;
where Product_Line NE 'Total';
ProductAndDollars = trim(left(Product_Line)) || ' ' ||
                    put(DollarsInM,dollar5.1);
run;

ods listing style=GraphFontArial11ptBold gpath="C:\temp" dpi=300;
ods graphics on / reset=all scale=off width=5.7in height=3in
  imagename=
  "Fig4-34_ClusteredRankedVBarCustomDataLabelsAtBottomNoLegend";
title1 'Ranked Sales ($M) and Profit ($M) by Product Line';
title2 ' '; /* white space */
proc sgplot data=work.ToChart noborder noautolegend
  dattrmap=sasuser.ORsalesDattrMap;
vbar SalesOrProfit / response=Dollars
  categoryorder=respdesc
  group=Product_Line
  groupdisplay=cluster
  attrid=GroupColors
  displaybaseline=off nooutline barwidth=0.8
  datalabel=ProductAndDollars
  /* datalabelfitpolicy=none */
  datalabelattrs=(size=8pt)
  datalabelpos=bottom;
xaxis display=(noline noticks nolabel) values=('Sales' 'Profit');
yaxis display=none;
label ProductAndDollars='00'X; /* Shrink & hide the unexpected label
  to the left of the row of data labels.
  The useless label, when present, squashes the bars,
  and, unless a smaller font, causes data label collisions. */
run;
```

Like the case of horizontal bar charts, besides the options of stacked and clustered bar charts, one can create a side-by-side overlay chart, as in Figure 4-35.

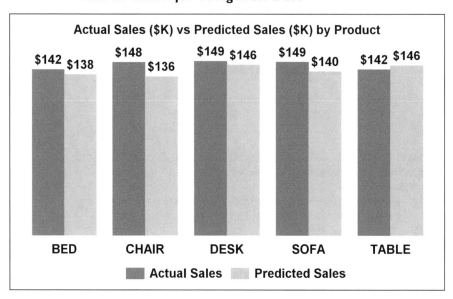

Figure 4-35. Vertical bar chart side-by-side overlay with data labels (a vertical bar chart analogue of the horizontal bar chart in Figure 4-10, but with a legend rather than using a color-coded title)

Listing 4-35. *Code used to create Figure 4-35*

```
data work.ToChart;
set sashelp.prdsale;
Actual  = Actual  / 1000;
Predict = Predict / 1000;
run;

ods listing style=GraphFontArial11ptBold gpath="C:\temp" dpi=300;
ods graphics on / reset=all scale=off width=5.7in height=3.5in
imagename="Fig4-35_OneCatVarTwoRespVars_VBarsSideBySide_WithLegend";
title "Actual Sales ($K) vs Predicted Sales ($K) by Product";
proc sgplot data=work.ToChart noborder;
styleattrs datacolors=(Green LightGreen);
vbar Product / response=Actual
  discreteoffset=-0.2
  displaybaseline=off nooutline barwidth=0.4
  datalabel;
vbar Product /  response=Predict
  discreteoffset=+0.2
  displaybaseline=off nooutline barwidth=0.4
  datalabel;
xaxis display=(noticks noline nolabel);
yaxis display=none;
keylegend / title=' ' noborder autooutline
```

```
    fillheight=11pt fillaspect=golden;
format Actual Predict dollar4.;
run;
```

In Figure 4-36, not only are the units of the response variables different but also their values are disparate, millions versus tens. The problem of that disparate sizing is solved by rescaling the large-valued variable. Also, the responses require different Y axes (which need not be visibly present, due to use of data labels).

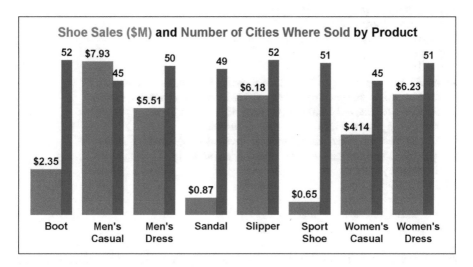

Figure 4-36. Vertical bar chart side-by-side overlay with data labels, but with response variables with different measurement units and color-coded title instead of a legend

Listing 4-36. Code used to create Figure 4-36

```
proc summary data=sashelp.shoes;
class product subsidiary;
var Sales;
output out=work.ToChart sum=;
run;

data work.ToChart; /* rescale the large values so that their bars do not dwarf
the values of the response variable with smaller values */
set work.ToChart;
Sales = Sales / 1000000;
run;
```

```
ods listing style=GraphFontArial9ptBold gpath="C:\temp" dpi=300;
ods graphics on / reset=all scale=off width=5.7in height=3in
  imagename="Fig4-36_OneCatVarTwoRespVars_DiffVbarsSideBySide";
```

```
title height=11pt color=Green 'Shoe Sales ($M)'
  color=Black ' and ' color=Blue  'Number of Cities Where Sold '
  color=Black 'by Product';
proc sgplot data=work.ToChart(where=(_type_ EQ 2))
  noborder noautolegend;
styleattrs datacolors=(Green Blue);
vbar Product / response=Sales
  discreteoffset=-0.2
  displaybaseline=off nooutline barwidth=0.6
  datalabel;
vbar Product / response=_freq_
  discreteoffset=+0.2
  displaybaseline=off nooutline barwidth=0.2
  y2axis
  datalabel;
/* After the rescaling of the Sales data, the Sales values are
  in the units scale. The _freq_ values are in the tens scale.
  If the two response variables were to share the same Y axis,
  the _freq_ bars would dwarf the Sales vars.
  So the two response variables are provided separate Y axes. */
y2axis display=(noticks noline nolabel novalues);
yaxis display=none;
xaxis display=(noticks noline nolabel)
  splitchar=' ' fitpolicy=splitalways;
format Sales dollar5.2 _freq_ 2.;
run;
```

Another way to accomplish the objective of Figure 4-36 is to replace the bars for _freq_ (the Number of Cities) with a VLINE chart. Using different chart types for different and disparate response variables in this way is an excellent use of this type of composite chart for which, until I contrived this example, I had never previously recognized the benefit. Nevertheless, despite the benefit of the option of such use for a line, for me, graphs with lines are "reflexively" in my mind and to my eye for date/time (temporal) data, not categorical data.

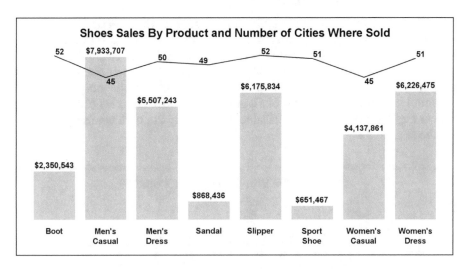

Figure 4-37. Same data as Figure 4-36, but dollars, not $M, using bar chart with a line chart

Listing 4-37. Code used to create Figure 4-37

```
proc summary data=sashelp.shoes;
class product subsidiary;
var Sales;
output out=work.ToChart sum=;
run;

ods listing style=GraphFontArial7ptBold gpath="C:\temp" dpi=300;
ods graphics on / reset=all scale=off width=5.7in height=3in
  imagename="Fig4-37_VbarChartVlineChartOverLay";
title height=10pt
  "Shoes Sales By Product and Number of Cities Where Sold";
proc sgplot data=work.ToChart(where=(_type_ EQ 2))
  noborder noautolegend;
vbar Product / response=Sales
  displaybaseline=off nooutline barwidth=0.8
  datalabel;
vline Product / response=_freq_
  y2axis
  datalabel;
xaxis display=(noticks noline nolabel)
  splitchar=' ' fitpolicy=splitalways;
yaxis display=none;
y2axis display=(noticks noline nolabel novalues)
  min=0; /* Otherwise the range of the _freq_ values fills the
  Y axis area with wild oscillations of no great significance. */
format Sales dollar11. _freq_ 2.;
run;
```

Time series data is sometimes visually presented with vertical bar charts, rather than the customary choice of line plots. The example in Figure 4-38 clearly is a more impactful way to present the data than lines would be. Multi-color multi-line charts are sometimes drawn with lines that are so thin that the color distinguishability is impaired, which defeats the purpose of any legend. However, the method of Figure 4-38 is most effective only when the number of bars versus space available is such that the data labels will actually fit above each bar.

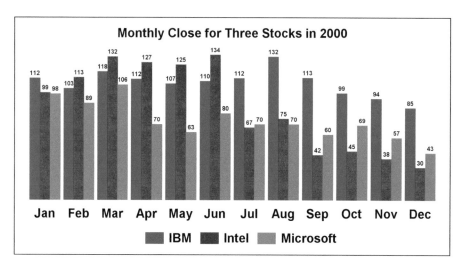

Figure 4-38. Vertical bar chart side-by-side triple overlay with data labels, used to present time series data rather than typical categorical data

A vertical bar chart for time series data is more visually exciting than a multi-line overlay plot. Comparing the values at any time point is more immediate, and the trend across any category's time span is equally discernable as it would be for a line.

Listing 4-38. *Code used to create Figure 4-38*

```
data work.ToChart;
set sashelp.stocks;
if Stock EQ 'IBM' then IBM = Close;
else if Stock EQ 'Intel' then Intel = Close;
else Microsoft = Close;
run;

ods listing style=GraphFontArial11ptBold gpath="C:\temp" dpi=300;
ods graphics on / reset=all scale=off width=5.7in height=3in
   imagename="Fig4-38_VbarChart3BarsOverlayForTimeSeries";
```

```
title "Monthly Close for Three Stocks in 2000";
proc sgplot data=work.ToChart(where=(year(Date) EQ 2000)) noborder;
styleattrs datacolors=(Blue Red Gray);
vbar Date / response=IBM
  discreteoffset=-0.3
  displaybaseline=off nooutline barwidth=0.3
  datalabel datalabelattrs=(family=Arial size=5pt weight=bold);
vbar Date / response=Intel
  displaybaseline=off nooutline barwidth=0.3
  datalabel datalabelattrs=(family=Arial size=5pt weight=bold);
vbar Date / response=Microsoft
  discreteoffset=+0.3
  displaybaseline=off nooutline barwidth=0.3
  datalabel datalabelattrs=(family=Arial size=5pt weight=bold);
xaxis display=(noticks noline nolabel);
yaxis display=none;
keylegend / title=' ' noborder autooutline
  fillheight=11pt fillaspect=golden;
format IBM Intel Microsoft 3. Date monname3.;
label IBM='IBM' Intel='Intel' Microsoft='Microsoft';
run;
```

In annual reports for corporations, I have frequently seen the latest year's data highlighted, understandably so—it's a report with a focus on that year. Figure 4-39 is an example of how to do that, using a discrete attribute map. The use of an attribute map makes the code deliver the intended result regardless of the possibly changing number of years in the report, unlike the use of a STYLEATTRS statement which would require code revision.

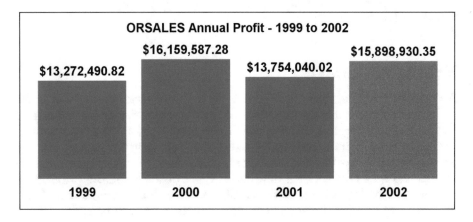

Figure 4-39. Time series vertical bar chart, highlighting the latest response value

With few enough bars, a vertical bar chart *can* accommodate long, very precise data labels, which is typically not the case.

Listing 4-39. *Code used to create Figure 4-39*

```
proc sort data=sashelp.orsales(keep=Year)
  out=work.ForAttrMap nodupkey;
by Year;
run;

data work.YearDattrMap;
keep ID Value FillColor;
set work.ForAttrMap end=LastOne;
length ID $ 8 Value $ 4 FillColor $ 8;
retain ID 'Years';
if LastOne
then FillColor='Green';
else FillColor='CX6666FF';
Value = Year;
run;

ods listing style=GraphFontArial11ptBold gpath="C:\temp" dpi=300;
ods graphics on / reset=all scale=off width=5.7in height=2.5in
  imagename="Fig4-39_TemporalVbarChart_LastIntervalColorHighlight";
title "ORSALES Annual Profit - 1999 to 2002";
proc sgplot data=sashelp.orsales noborder noautolegend
  dattrmap=work.YearDattrMap;
vbar Year / response=Profit
  group=Year
  attrid=Years
  displaybaseline=off nooutline
  datalabel;
xaxis display=(nolabel noline noticks); yaxis display=none;
format Profit dollar13.2;
run;
```

Waterfall Chart

A waterfall chart, as shown in Figure 4-40, is a time series vertical bar chart for presentation of the starting value of the response, the ending value, and the positive and negative changes in between those points. It is a report about change by time interval, rather than value at time interval, except at the end points. As in the case of Figure 4-38, it is a more visually impactful presentation than would be a conventional time series chart of the response, rather than change in response. It is easier to visually compare those changes than if one were instead viewing the actual response points. With a time series plot, if you are interested in the change point to point, you must do the math in your head. In the waterfall chart, as implemented in Figure 4-40, the precise values of those changes are displayed with data labels. A communication-effective graph *informs* the viewer and does not assign work to the viewer. It provides maximum information and maximum value with minimum viewer effort.

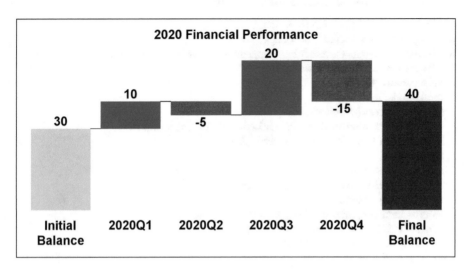

Figure 4-40. Waterfall chart with color coding and data labels

Listing 4-40. *Code used to create Figure 4-40*

```
data dataInput;
length YearAndQtr $ 6 PlurOrMinusDollars 3;
YearAndQtr = '2020Q1';
PlurOrMinusDollars = 10;
output;
YearAndQtr = '2020Q2';
PlurOrMinusDollars = -5;
output;
YearAndQtr = '2020Q3';
PlurOrMinusDollars = 20;
output;
YearAndQtr = '2020Q4';
PlurOrMinusDollars = -15;
output;
run;

data ToChart;
length MinusOneOrPlusOne 3;
set dataInput;
if PlurOrMinusDollars LT 0
then MinusOneOrPlusOne = '-1';
else MinusOneOrPlusOne = '+1';
run;

ods listing style=GraphFontArial11ptBold gpath="C:\temp" dpi=300;
ods graphics on / reset=all scale=off width=5.7in height=3in
  imagename="Fig4-40_WaterfallChart";
```

```
title "2020 Financial Performance";
proc sgplot data=ToChart noborder noautolegend;
waterfall category=YearAndQtr  response=PlurOrMinusDollars /
  colorresponse=MinusOneOrPlusOne
  colormodel=(Red Blue)
  datalabel
  baselineattrs=(color=white)
  /* Bar Chart option displaybaseline=off is not available.
     Hide the base line as a white line. */
  nooutline
  initialbarattrs=(color=CXCCCCCC) /* light gray */
  initialbartickvalue="Initial Balance"
  initialbarvalue=30
  finalbarattrs=(color=CX333333) /* dark gray */
  finalbartickvalue="Final Balance";
xaxis display=(nolabel noline noticks);
yaxis display=none;
run;
```

Needle Plots

Needle plots are vertical only and can serve as an alternative to vertical bar charts. I think of them as extremely narrow vertical bar charts.

Needle plots that are drawn with the circular markers at the top, as in Figure 4-41, are sometimes called lollipop charts, but not by me. The needles in ODS Graphics are not automatically drawn with markers, and a needle plot, as is shown in several examples, can be communication-effective *without* them.

The main advantage of needle plots is as an alternative to dot plots. If you compare dot plots in Figures 4-23 through 4-26 with corresponding function needle plots in Figures 4-45 through 4-48, you will see that the only case where the dot plot is not less visually convenient than the needle plot is for the overlay plots for Product_Line as the group variable. In that case, the dot plot is equally visually convenient, but in all other cases, it is more difficult to interpret. When carrying markers, needle plots are the vertical equivalents of dot plots, but usually better.

There is a coding disadvantage of needle plots compared to bar charts and dot plots. If you want a ranked needle plot, you must sort the input to be used by the NEEDLE statement. It has no ordering option analogous to CATEGORYORDER. The statement does not have CATEGORY and RESPONSE variables. The Y variable serves as the response variable, and the X variable is what it is. So, a sort "BY DESCENDING Y-variable" arranges the X values as desired, and the needle plot will be drawn as desired.

Figure 4-41. Ranked needle plot with data labels—maybe this could be called "the vertical bar chart with the narrowest bars," especially if the optional markers were omitted

Listing 4-41. *Code used to create Figure 4-41*

```
proc summary data=sashelp.shoes nway;
class Product;
var Sales;
output out=work.Summed(drop=_freq_ _type_) sum=;
run;

proc sort data=work.Summed out=work.Sorted;
by descending Sales;
run;

data work.ToPlot;
set work.Sorted;
Sales = Sales / 1000000;
run;

ods listing style=GraphFontArial9ptBold gpath="C:\temp" dpi=300;
ods graphics on / reset=all scale=off width=5.7in height=2.5in
  imagename="Fig4-41_RankedNeedlePlot";
title justify=center 'Ranked Shoe Sales ($M) By Product';
proc sgplot data=work.ToPlot noborder;
needle x=Product y=Sales / datalabel datalabelpos=top
  markers markerattrs=(color=Blue symbol=CircleFilled size=9pt)
  displaybaseline=off;
xaxis display=(noline noticks nolabel)
  splitchar=' ' fitpolicy=splitalways;
yaxis display=none;
format Sales dollar6.3;
run;
```

In Figure 4-42, a block chart is added to deliver a second response variable for the category variable, but with the added benefit of same color coding for all values that are identical. An X axis table could have delivered those values, but not with color coding to identify values that are the same.

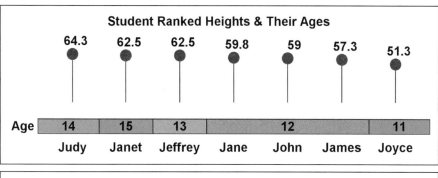

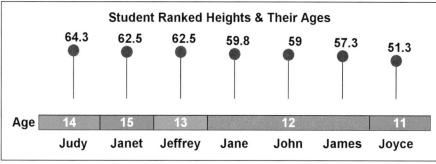

Figure 4-42. Ranked needle plots with data labels plus block chart for second response variable and color-coded grouping of those response values: the upper example uses a default block variable value color; the lower example uses custom color white for improved readability

The block area fills are first five in the ODS Graphics default color palette. For those colors, white values are clearly much more readable. In both cases, the font is Arial Bold. One can make the values more readable with option VALUEATTRS=(family='Arial Black'). You can also make the values more readable with the VALUEATTRS SIZE= control. If you increase the size of the values, you should also use LABELATTRS to match the size of the label to that of the values. However, once you increase the size of the font for the block chart, you should assure that all other text in the composite plot is at least the same size as that in the block chart. There is no benefit in having the block chart text dominate the image.

Listing 4-42. *Code used to create the lower example in Figure 4-42 (this code includes a direction on how to create the upper example, which requires a different imagename)*

```
proc sort data=sashelp.class out=work.ToPlot;
where Name =: 'J'; /* Name must start with 'J' */
by descending height;
run;

ods listing style=GraphFontArial11ptBold gpath="C:\temp" dpi=300;
ods graphics on / reset=all scale=off width=5.7in height=2in
  imagename="Fig4-42Lower_NeedlePlotWithBlockChart";
title justify=center 'Student Ranked Heights & Their Ages';
proc sgplot data= work.ToPlot noborder;
needle x=name y=height / datalabel
  datalabelpos=top /* default as in Figure 4-41 is UpperRight */
  markers markerattrs=(color=red symbol=CircleFilled size=11pt)
  displaybaseline=off;
block x=name block=age / position=bottom
  valueattrs=(color=white); /* To create the upper example
  in Figure 4-42, omit this VALUEATTRS option.
  Black is the default color for this case */
xaxis display=(nolabel noline noticks);
yaxis display=none;
run;
```

The markers can be eliminated as in Figure 4-43, with no loss in communication. It is marginally more difficult to compare lengths of the needles, but with response values sitting right above them, comparison can be done numerically easily and with certainty. In any case, a smaller marker than that in Figures 4-41 and 4-42 would be sufficient.

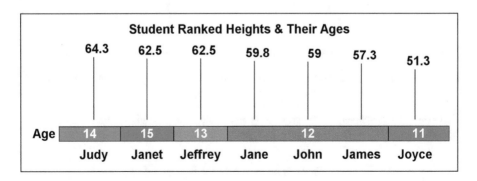

Figure 4-43. A sparse version of the lower example in Figure 4-42

Listing 4-43. *Code used to create Figure 4-43, changes from Figure 4-42 in bold*

```
proc sort data=sashelp.class out=work.ToPlot;
where Name =: 'J'; /* Name must start with 'J' */
by descending height;
run;

ods listing style=GraphFontArial11ptBold gpath="C:\temp" dpi=300;
ods graphics on / reset=all scale=off width=5.7in height=2in
   imagename="Fig4-43_SparseNeedlePlotOrBarChart_WithBlockChart";
title justify=center 'Student Ranked Heights & Ages';
proc sgplot data=work.ToPlot noborder;
needle x=name y=height / datalabel datalabelpos=top
   /* No MARKERS and MARKERSATTRS options */
   displaybaseline=off;
block x=name block=age / position=bottom
   valueattrs=(color=white);
xaxis display=(nolabel noline noticks);
yaxis display=none;
run;
```

In the SASHELP.CLASS data set are several identical ages, since the entire class of nineteen students is between the ages of 11 and 16. With more typical data, identical response values might be less frequent or perhaps not a focus of interest. If so, one can replace the block chart with an X axis table and create an image that is sparser, like the image shown in Figure 4-44.

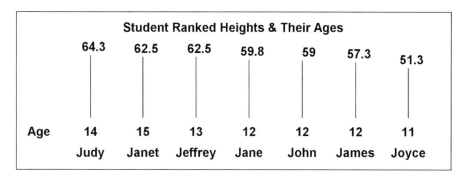

Figure 4-44. A sparser needle plot, using an X axis table instead of a block chart for the age data

Listing 4-44. *The only changes to the code for Figure 4-43 to create Figure 4-44 are to use*

imagename="Fig4-44_VerySparseNeedlePlotOrBarChart"

and to replace the BLOCK statement with

Analogous to the CLUSTER and OVERLAY options for GROUPDISPLAY on dot plots, the same capabilities are available for needle plots, with results that should be compared with Figures 4-23 through 4-26 for dot plots. For me, the needle plots are more conveniently interpreted than their dot plot counterparts.

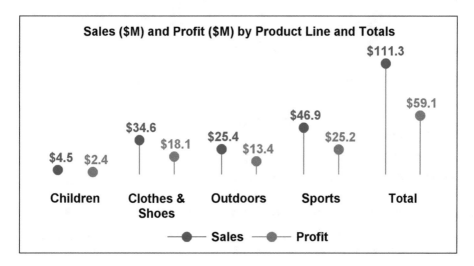

Figure 4-45. Clustered needle plot with grouping by SalesOrProfit

Listing 4-45. Code used to create Figure 4-45

```
ods listing style=GraphFontArial11ptBold gpath="C:\temp" dpi=300;
ods graphics on / reset=all scale=off width=5.7in height=3in
  imagename="Fig4-45_ORsales_ClusterNeedlePlot_GroupBySalesProfit";
title1 'Sales ($M) and Profit ($M) Product Line & Totals';
proc sgplot data=sasuser.OR_SalesProfitByProdLineAndTotal noborder;
styleattrs datacontrastcolors=(Blue Green);
needle x=Product_Line y=DollarsInM / displaybaseline=off
  group=SalesOrProfit groupdisplay=cluster
  markers markerattrs=(symbol=CircleFilled size=9pt)
  lineattrs=(pattern=Solid)
  datalabel datalabelpos=top;
xaxis display=(noline noticks nolabel)
  values=('Children' 'Clothes & Shoes' 'Outdoors' 'Sports' 'Total');
yaxis display=none;
format DollarsInM dollar6.1;
keylegend / title=' ' noborder fillheight=11pt;
run;
```

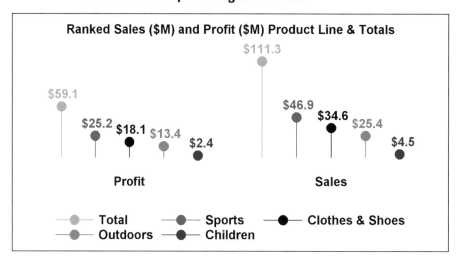

Figure 4-46. Clustered ranked needle plot with grouping by Product Line

Listing 4-46. *Code used to create Figure 4-46, changes from Figure 4-45 in bold*

```
proc sort data=sasuser.OR_SalesProfitByProdLineAndTotal out=work.ToPlot;
by SalesOrProfit descending DollarsInM;
run;

ods listing style=GraphFontArial11ptBold gpath="C:\temp" dpi=300;
ods graphics on / reset=all scale=off width=5.7in height=3in
  imagename=
  "Fig4-46_ORsales_ClusteredRankedNeedlePlot_GroupByProdLine";
title1 'Ranked Sales ($M) and Profit ($M) Product Line & Totals';
proc sgplot data=work.ToPlot noborder
  dattrmap=sasuser.ORsalesDattrMap;
needle x=SalesOrProfit y=DollarsInM / displaybaseline=off
  group=Product_Line groupdisplay=cluster
  attrid=GroupColors
  markers markerattrs=(symbol=CircleFilled size=9pt)
  lineattrs=(pattern=Solid)
  datalabel datalabelpos=top;
xaxis display=(noline noticks nolabel);
yaxis display=none;
format DollarsInM dollar6.1;
keylegend / title=' ' noborder fillheight=11pt;
run;
```

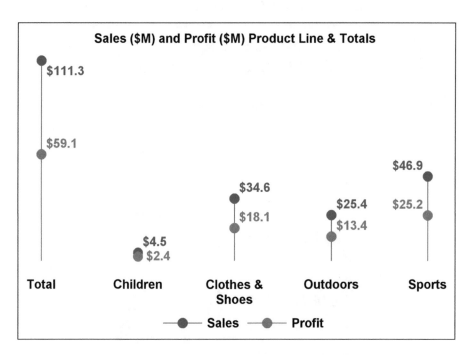

Figure 4-47. Overlay needle plot with grouping by SalesOrProfit

Listing 4-47. *Code used to create Figure 4-47, changes from Figure 4-45 in bold*

```
ods listing style=GraphFontArial11ptBold gpath="C:\temp" dpi=300;
ods graphics on / reset=all scale=off width=5.7in height=4in
   imagename="Fig4-47_ORsales_OverlayNeedlePlot_GroupBySalesProfit";
title1 'Sales ($M) and Profit ($M) Product Line & Totals';
proc sgplot data=sasuser.OR_SalesProfitByProdLineAndTotal noborder;
styleattrs datacontrastcolors=(Blue Green);
needle x=Product_Line y=DollarsInM / displaybaseline=off
  group=SalesOrProfit
  groupdisplay=overlay /* this is default when GROUP= is used */
  markers markerattrs=(symbol=CircleFilled size=9pt)
  lineattrs=(pattern=Solid)
  datalabel; /* taking default DATALABELPOS */
xaxis display=(noline noticks nolabel);
yaxis display=none;
format DollarsInM dollar6.1;
keylegend / title=' ' noborder fillheight=11pt;
run;
```

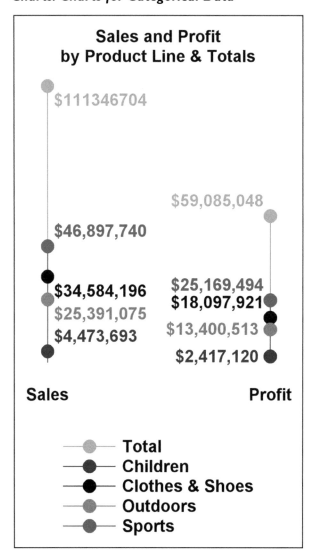

Figure 4-48. Overlay needle plot with grouping by Product Line

Listing 4-48. *Code used to create Figure 4-48, changes from Figure 4-46 in bold*

```
ods listing style=GraphFontArial11ptBold gpath="C:\temp" dpi=300;
ods graphics on / reset=all scale=off width=2.8in height=5in
  imagename="Fig4-48_ORsales_OverlayNeedlePlot_GroupByProdLine";
title1 justify=center 'Sales and Profit';
title2 justify=center 'by Product Line & Totals';
proc sgplot data=sasuser.OR_SalesProfitByProdLineAndTotal noborder
  dattrmap=sasuser.ORsalesDattrMap;
```

```
needle x=SalesOrProfit y=Dollars / displaybaseline=off
  group=Product_Line groupdisplay=overlay
  attrid=GroupColors
  markers markerattrs=(symbol=CircleFilled size=9pt)
  lineattrs=(pattern=Solid)
  datalabel; /* taking default DATALABELPOS */
xaxis display=(noline noticks nolabel);
yaxis display=none;
format Dollars dollar11.;
keylegend / title=' ' noborder fillheight=11pt;
run;
```

Figure 4-49 is contending to be the sparsest ranked vertical bar chart alternative. The needles are rendered barely visible with TRANSPARENCY=0.9 (1.0 would render the needles invisible).

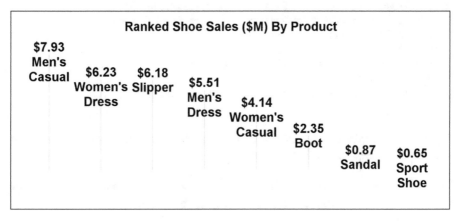

Figure 4-49. Needle plot with 90% transparent needles annotated with two TEXT charts to provide a ranked vertical bar chart equivalent with category values and response values adjacent for maximum focus and immediate association

Two TEXT statements used for Figure 4-49 make it possible to display more information at the needle ends than would the DATALABEL option.

Listing 4-49. *Code used to create Figure 4-49*

```
proc summary data=sashelp.shoes nway;
class product;
var Sales;
output out=work.ToChart sum=;
run;
```

```
proc sort data=work.ToChart;
by descending Sales;
run;

data work.ToChart;
length SalesDollars $ 5;
set work.ToChart;
SalesDollars = put(Sales / 1000000,dollar5.2);
run;

ods listing style=GraphFontArial11ptBold gpath="C:\temp" dpi=300;
ods graphics on / reset=all scale=off width=5.7in height=2.5in
  imagename=
  "Fig4-49_NeedlesAndTextChart_SparserVbarChartAlternative";
title 'Ranked Shoe Sales ($M) By Product';
proc sgplot data=work.ToChart noborder noautolegend;
text x=Product y=Sales text=SalesDollars / position=top;
text x=Product y=Sales text=Product      / position=bottom
  splitpolicy=splitalways splitwidth=7
  splitchar=' ' splitjustify=center;
needle x=Product y=Sales / displaybaseline=off
  transparency=0.9;
xaxis display=none; yaxis display=none; /* no axes needed */
run;
```

Figure 4-50 eliminates the pseudo and super-thin vertical bars (i.e., the super-transparent needles used in Figure 4-49).

Figure 4-50. You cannot get more minimal than this. The use of only text charts provides a ranked vertical bar chart equivalent with category values and response values adjacent for maximum focus and immediate association—without any bars. Is this really a diagonal table masquerading as a graph?

Code used to create Figure 4-50 is identical to that used for Figure 4-49 except for omitting the NEEDLE statement, changing the imagename to Fig4-50_TextChartsAsSparsestVbarChartAlternative, and changing two statements:

```
title color=Black 'Ranked ' color=Blue 'Shoe Sales ($M)'
      color=Black ' By Product';
text x=Product y=Sales text=SalesDollars / position=top
      textattrs=(color=Blue);
```

This is the most unusual layout for a table that I have ever seen or created. This book emphasizes the importance and value of providing precise numbers as a companion to the image. Here, any traditional graphic elements are absent. Instead, the numbers deliver the numbers *and become the image*. It's a very simple, but communication-effective, act of data artistry.

Though I usually abstain from use of color in a graph purely for the sake of decoration, in this case I am deviating from my usual policy. The design is very austere and sparse, and I make the excuse that I am just following Pulitzer's recommendation to make one's communication picturesque, so that people will remember it. Perhaps the little bit of color makes this unusual and unfamiliar way to compose a graphic acceptable to the viewer, more interesting, and more memorable.

Single-Needle Needle Plots

I recently developed several interesting single-needle needle plots. Some can serve as maximally informative pie chart alternatives. In cases where the total response does not dwarf the constituent responses, they can also provide a visual comparison of each constituent with the total, not just a comparison of the constituent category values with each other. Since the needle point labels always include percent of total, *that* important comparison is always available as a precise number even when visual comparison of each constituent with the total is impractical due to dwarfing avoidance requiring that no total needle be shown.

The first example, Figure 4-51, is what I call the Tree Chart.

Figure 4-51. The Tree Chart. A ranked maximally informative pie chart alternative

This marvelous chart will work only if the response values are sufficiently separated in magnitude so that a font and image height can be found that prevent label overlap.

The Tree Chart uses a NEEDLE statement with the OVERLAY option to draw the trunk of the tree, and data labels, using DATALABELPOS=CENTER to display the text strings as two-sided branches that span the trunk. (Yes, I realize that a real tree branch projects from the trunk and does not span it. I am unabashedly taking a "data artistic" liberty.) Though the branches collide with the trunk, they overlay it, which does mitigate the diminished readability.

Let me discuss the Tree Chart, and other single-needle charts to be shown here, versus vertical bar charts. Vertical bar charts require the viewer's eye and mind to move both sideways and up and down. The advantage of the single-needle charts is that they require the viewer's eye and mind to move only up and down—a more efficient and quicker visual interpretation. My eye and my mind like the experience of "climbing" the tree, or a single needle, to see and find rising values. Also, ranking is inherent and automatic by the nature of how the graphic elements are laid down in relation to each other.

Though Figures 4-51, 4-52, and 4-53 are described as pie chart alternatives, the four parts of the total are not displayed as "additive" visual parts, but only comparatively to each other and to the total. In Figure 4-55A, ten parts of a total are displayed "additively" to the whole and are ranked with respect to each other, thus functioning like what I call "the ranked maximally informative pie chart," but linearly, rather than "circularly."

Listing 4-51. Code used to create Figure 4-51

```
/* Start of Common Code used to create Figures 4-51 to 4-55A */

/* This code is used at start of Listings 4-51 to 4-55A. */
/* In Listings 4-52 and 4-53,
the %INCLUDE statement for this code is also preceded by:
%let WHERE = %str(
where Region IN ('Asia' 'Africa' 'Middle East' 'Pacific')
  AND
      Product IN ('Boot' 'Sandal' 'Slipper' 'Sport Shoe');
               );
In Listings 4-54 and 4-55A,
the %INCLUDE statement for this code is preceded by
%let WHERE = %str(); */

%let WHERE = %str(
where Region IN ('Asia' 'Africa' 'Middle East' 'Pacific')
  AND
      Product IN ('Boot' 'Sandal' 'Slipper' 'Sport Shoe');
               );

proc summary data=sashelp.shoes;
&WHERE
class Region;
var Sales;
output out=work.Subset sum=Sales;
run;

data work.FromPrep;
length RegionPercent $ 6 DataLabel $ 48;
retain Invisible 'X' GrandTotal 0;
set work.Subset end=LastOne;
if _type_ EQ 0
then do;
  Region = 'Total';
```

```
RegionPercent = '100%';
GrandTotal = Sales;
call symput('GrandTotal',GrandTotal);
call symput('GrandTotalDisplay',
            trim(left(put(GrandTotal,dollar11.))));
/* two macro variables for use
    in some examples other than Fig4-51 */
end;
else RegionPercent =
  trim(left(put(((Sales / GrandTotal) * 100),5.1))) || '%';
DataLabel =
  trim(left(substr(Region,1,15)))  || ' - ' ||
  trim(left(put(Sales,dollar11.))) || ' - ' ||
  trim(left(RegionPercent));
if LastOne then call symput('Count',_N_); /* not used in Fig4-51
                                             to Fig4-54 */
run;

/* End of Common Code used to create Figures 4-51 to 4-55A */

ods listing style=GraphFontArial10ptBold gpath="C:\temp" dpi=300;
ods graphics on / reset=all scale=off width=5.7in height=5.5in
  imagename=
  "Fig4-51_TreeChart_NeedlePlot_DataLabelsWithCenterAtNeedle";
title1 justify=center
  'Ranked Shoe Sales and Percent Share By Region and Total';
title2 justify=center
  'for Boots, Sandals, Slippers, and Sport Shoes (in Four Regions)';
proc sgplot data=work.FromPrep noborder noautolegend;
needle x=Invisible y=Sales / displaybaseline=off
  group=Region groupdisplay=overlay
  lineattrs=(pattern=Solid color=brown)
  datalabel=DataLabel
  datalabelpos=center
  datalabelattrs=(color=green);
xaxis display=none;
yaxis display=none;
format Sales dollar10.;
run;
```

Figure 4-52 is the easiest and most obvious way to remove the collisions between the trunk and branches (needle and data labels).

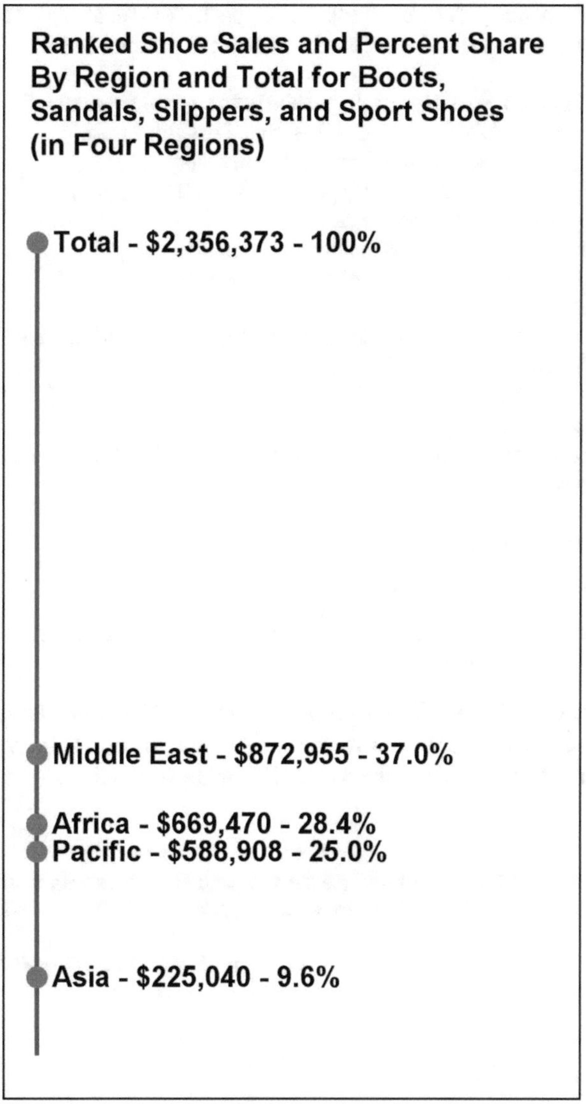

Figure 4-52. The Flag Chart. Another ranked and maximally informative pie chart alternative

Listing 4-52. *Code used to create Figure 4-52*

```
%let WHERE = %str(
where Region IN ('Asia' 'Africa' 'Middle East' 'Pacific')
  AND
      Product IN ('Boot' 'Sandal' 'Slipper' 'Sport Shoe');
            );
%include "C:\SharedCode\CommonPrepForFigures4-51to4-55A.sas";
```

```
ods listing style=GraphFontArial10ptBold gpath="C:\temp" dpi=300;
ods graphics on / reset=all scale=off width=3in height=5.5in
  imagename=
  "Fig4-52_FlagChart_NeedlePlot_DataLabelsAtRightOfNeedle";
title1 justify=left 'Ranked Shoe Sales and Percent Share';
title2 justify=left 'By Region and Total for Boots,';
title3 justify=left 'Sandals, Slippers, and Sport Shoes';
title4 justify=left '(in Four Regions)';
proc sgplot data=work.FromPrep noborder noautolegend;
needle x=Invisible y=Sales / displaybaseline=off
  group=Region groupdisplay=overlay
  markers markerattrs=(symbol=CircleFilled size=8pt color=green)
  lineattrs=(pattern=Solid color=blue thickness=2)
  datalabel=DataLabel
  datalabelpos=right
  datalabelattrs=(color=black); /* would inherit LINEATTRS color */
xaxis display=none;
yaxis display=none;
format Sales dollar10.;
run;
```

Figure 4-53 is the way to reduce the probability of data labels colliding when any response values are close.

This CrossRoads SignPost Chart relies on two NEEDLE statements. Each lays out its Y value positions with a marker. One statement displays the left-side data labels, and the other displays the right-side data labels.

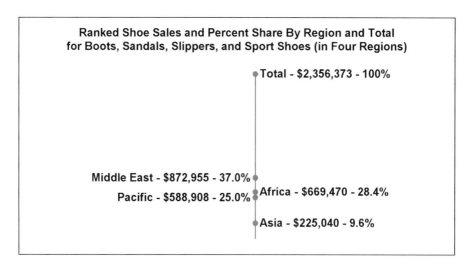

Figure 4-53. The CrossRoads SignPost Chart. Yet another ranked maximally informative pie chart alternative

With the benefit of putting data labels on alternate sides, it is possible to reduce the image height. At three inches, the markers for Africa and Pacific would touch, but the marker size of 8pt in Figure 4-52 was reduced to 5pt for Figure 4-53. Any touching or overlap of markers can be alleviated by reducing marker size, which has no detrimental consequences. The markers could be suppressed entirely. The vertical position of the data labels provides sufficient visual comparability of the relative response values and is in the conceptual spirit of, for example, Figure 4-49, which is a vertical "bar chart" without bars.

The sign posts at a crossroads often point in more than two directions, but CrossRoads SignPost Chart is the best name that I was able to think of.

Listing 4-53. *Code used to create Figure 4-53*

```
%let WHERE = %str(
where Region IN ('Asia' 'Africa' 'Middle East' 'Pacific')
   AND
       Product IN ('Boot' 'Sandal' 'Slipper' 'Sport Shoe');
                 );
%include "C:\SharedCode\CommonPrepForFigures4-51to4-55A.sas";

/* The work.FromPrep data set used for Figures 4-51 and 4-52
   needs further processing to create a needle plot
   with data labels that alternate from side to side. */

proc sort data=work.FromPrep out=work.Sorted;
by descending Sales;
run;

data work.ToTwoSidedNeedlePlot;
length DataLabelLeft DataLabelRight $ 48;
set work.Sorted;
if mod(_N_,2) EQ 0
then DataLabelLeft  = DataLabel;
else DataLabelRight = DataLabel;
run;

ods listing style=GraphFontArial10ptBold gpath="C:\temp" dpi=300;
ods graphics on / reset=all scale=off width=5.7in height=3in
   imagename=
   "Fig4-53_CrossRoadsSignPost_NeedlePlot_AlternateSideDataLabels";
title1 justify=center
   'Ranked Shoe Sales and Percent Share By Region and Total';
title2 justify=center
   'for Boots, Sandals, Slippers, and Sport Shoes (in Four Regions)';
proc sgplot data=work.ToTwoSidedNeedlePlot noborder noautolegend;
needle x=Invisible y=Sales / displaybaseline=off
  group=Region groupdisplay=overlay
```

```
  markers markerattrs=(symbol=CircleFilled size=5pt color=green)
  lineattrs=(pattern=Solid color=blue)
  datalabel=DataLabelRight datalabelpos=Right
  datalabelattrs=(color=black);
needle x=Invisible y=Sales / displaybaseline=off
  group=Region groupdisplay=overlay
  markers markerattrs=(symbol=CircleFilled size=5pt color=green)
  lineattrs=(pattern=Solid color=blue)
  datalabel=DataLabelLeft datalabelpos=Left
  datalabelattrs=(color=black);
xaxis display=none;
yaxis display=none;
format Sales dollar10.;
run;
```

Figure 4-54, a CrossRoads SignPost Chart for all eight regions (and all ten products) but no total label, is a vertical bar chart alternative, but not a pie chart alternative—there is no way to visually compare each region with the total. If the Total label were displayed, the comparative large size of its Sales value would force all of the Region labels to be squashed together toward the bottom of the pole.

With the four regions that have sales values so close together, it was necessary to increase the image height to as much of the page space as possible and to reduce marker size and data label size to prevent collisions.

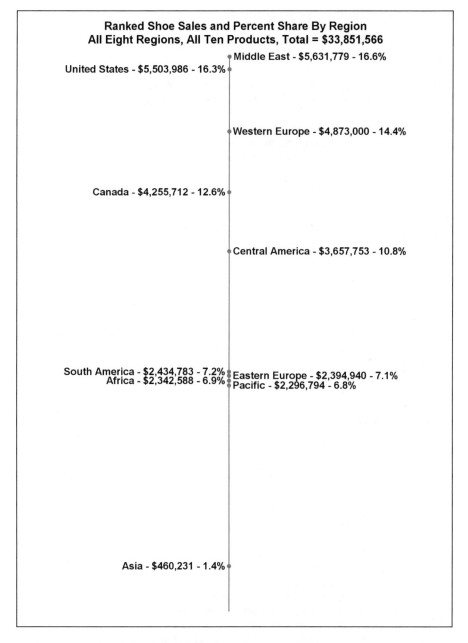

Figure 4-54. A CrossRoads SignPost Chart without the total sign. A maximally informative vertical bar chart alternative, with overlapping very thin "bars"

Listing 4-54. *Code used to create Figure 4-54*

```
/* Differences from code used for Figure 4-53
   are noted with comments */


%let WHERE = %str(); /* keep all regions and products */
%include "C:\SharedCode\CommonPrepForFigures4-51to4-55A.sas";

proc sort data=work.FromPrep out=work.Sorted;
where _type_ NE 0; /* Omit the Grand Total needle.
          It would dwarf the constituent needles. */
by descending Sales;
run;

data work.ToTwoSidedNeedlePlot;
length DataLabelLeft DataLabelRight $ 48;
set work.Sorted;
if mod(_N_,2) EQ 0
then DataLabelLeft  = DataLabel;
else DataLabelRight = DataLabel;
run;

ods listing style=GraphFontArial10ptBold gpath="C:\temp" dpi=300;
ods graphics on / reset=all scale=off width=5.7in height=7.8in
  imagename= /* changed: */
  "Fig4-54_CrossRoadsSignPost_NoTotal_VbarChartAlternative";
title1 justify=center /* changed: */
  "Ranked Shoe Sales and Percent Share By Region";
title2 justify=center /* changed: */
  "All Eight Regions, All Ten Products, Total = &GrandTotalDisplay";
/* The four regions with sales of approximately $2Million
   need separation of their markers and data labels. */
proc sgplot data=work.ToTwoSidedNeedlePlot noborder noautolegend;
needle x=Invisible y=Sales / displaybaseline=off
  group=Region groupdisplay=overlay
  markers markerattrs=(symbol=CircleFilled size=3pt color=green)
  /* make the markers smaller to separate them */
  lineattrs=(pattern=Solid color=blue)
  datalabel=DataLabelRight datalabelpos=Right
  datalabelattrs=(color=black size=9pt);
  /* make the data labels smaller to separate them */
needle x=Invisible y=Sales / displaybaseline=off
  group=Region groupdisplay=overlay
  markers markerattrs=(symbol=CircleFilled size=3pt color=green)
```

```
/* make the markers smaller to separate them */
lineattrs=(pattern=Solid color=blue)
datalabel=DataLabelLeft datalabelpos=Left
datalabelattrs=(color=black size=9pt);
/* make the data labels smaller to separate them */
xaxis display=none;
yaxis display=none;
format Sales dollar10.;
run;
```

Figure 4-54 cannot serve as a pie chart alternative since a visual for the grand total is nowhere in evidence in the image itself, only in the subtitle. It serves as an alternative to a vertical bar chart. However, Figure 4-55A is like a stacked vertical bar chart. Usually, a stacked bar chart consists of multiple segmented bars where each composite bar contains the subcategories (or group values) for a different value of the category variable. However, in Figure 4-55A, each bar segment—actually, needle segment—is for a different value of the category variable.

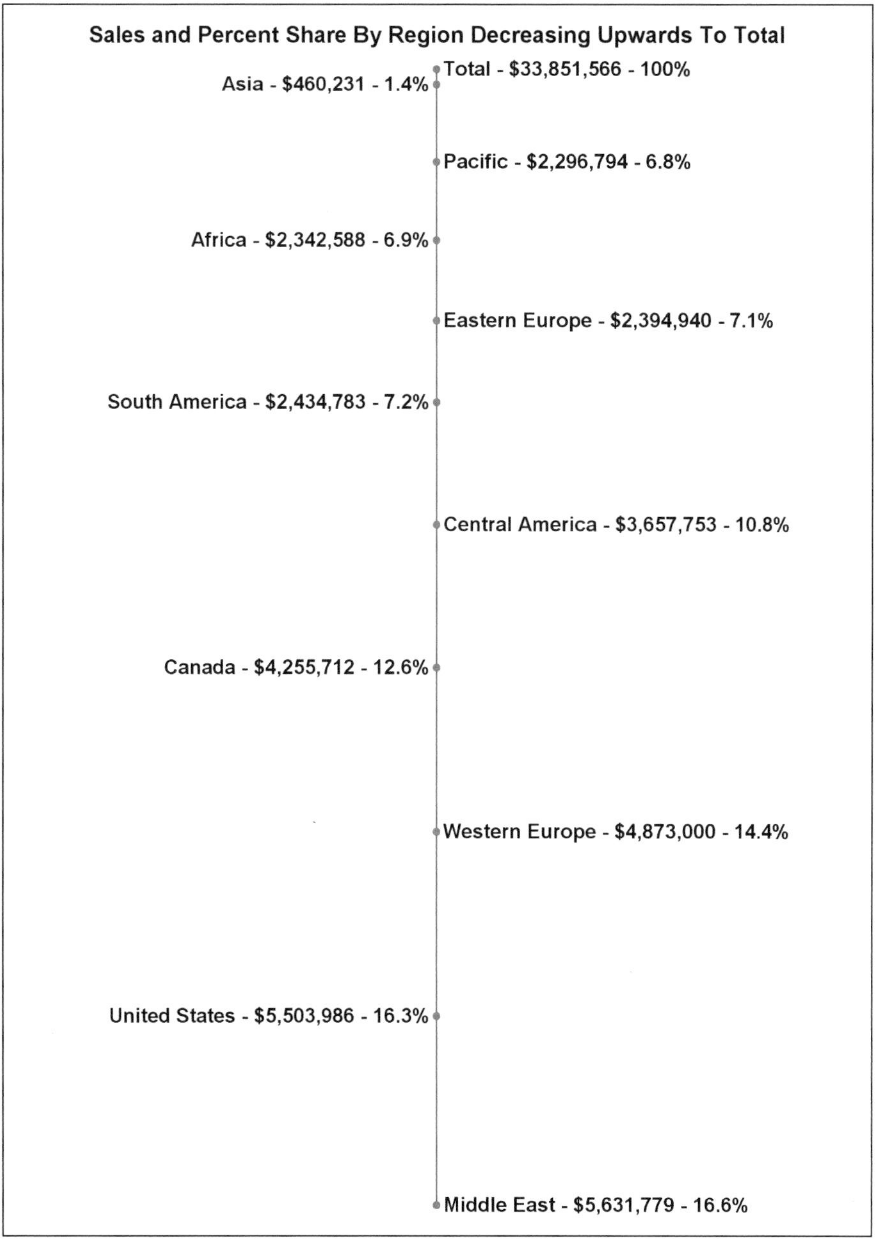

Figure 4-55A. Stacked needle chart. Stacking rather than overlapping to create another ranked maximally informative pie chart alternative

The total is delivered as the combined length of all of the region segments, as the sum of the constituent needles, presented "additively" rather than comparatively as in Figures 4-51 through 4-54.

Figure 4-55A does accomplish its intended objective, but a casual viewer might not immediately understand that each label pertains to the needle segment above. Since I was unable to find a way to color-code a wider version of each needle segment to its datalabel, I developed the fully informative ranked stacked vertical bar chart in Figure 4-55B.

Listing 4-55A. *Code used to create Figure 4-55A*

```
%let WHERE = %str(); /* keep all regions and products */
%include "C:\SharedCode\CommonPrepForFigures4-51to4-55A.sas";

proc sort data=work.FromPrep out=work.Sorted;
by Sales;
run;

data work.ForStackedNeedles;
retain TopOfSegment &GrandTotal;
set work.Sorted end=LastOne;
OrderForApparentSegment = _N_ + 1;
TopOfSegment = TopOfSegment - Sales;
if LastOne then do;
  OrderForApparentSegment = 1;
  TopOfSegment = &GrandTotal;
end;
run;

proc sort data= work.ForStackedNeedles out=work.ReSorted;
by OrderForApparentSegment;
run;

%macro DefineNeedles(Count);
data work.DataWithNeedles;
retain
%do i = 1 %to &Count %by 1;
  Needle&i
%end;
  .;
set work.ReSorted;
if _N_ EQ 1
then Needle1 = TopOfSegment;
%do i = 2 %to &Count %by 1;
  %let j = %eval(&i - 1);
else
if _N_ EQ &i then do;
```

Chapter 4 | Bar Charts, Butterfly Charts, Waterfall Charts, Dot Plots, Needle Plots, Area Bar Charts, Text Graphs, and Line Charts: Charts for Categorical Data

```
  Needle&j = .;
  Needle&i = TopOfSegment;
end;
%end;
%mend  DefineNeedles;

options mprint;


%DefineNeedles(&Count);


%macro CreateNeedles(Count);
%do i = 1 %to &Count %by 1;
needle x=Invisible y=Needle&i / displaybaseline=off
  group=OrderForApparentSegment groupdisplay=overlay
  markers markerattrs=(symbol=CircleFilled size=3pt color=green)
  lineattrs=(pattern=Solid color=blue)
  datalabel=DataLabel
  %if %sysfunc(mod(&i,2)) EQ 0 %then %do;
  datalabelpos=left
  %end;
  %else %do;
  datalabelpos=right
  %end;
  datalabelattrs=(color=black size=9pt);
%end;
%mend  CreateNeedles;

ods listing style=GraphFontArial10ptBold gpath="C:\temp" dpi=300;
ods graphics on / reset=all scale=off width=5.7in height=7.8in
  imagename="Fig4-55A_CrossRoadsSignPostChartWithStackedNeedles";
title1 justify=center
  'Sales and Percent Share By Region Decreasing Upwards To Total';
proc sgplot data=work.DataWithNeedles noborder noautolegend;
%CreateNeedles(&Count);
xaxis display=none;
yaxis display=none;
format Sales dollar11.;
run;
```

Figure 4-55B is a fully informative stacked ranked vertical bar chart with a legend that makes it an alternative to the ranked maximally informative pie chart. The stacked bar looks like one stacked bar from, for example, Figure 4-32. My first attempt to create Figure 4-55B had the bar segments and the legend entries in opposite order. To match the order of the bar segments in Figure 4-55B with the order of the legend entries requires use of GROUPORDER=DESCENDING on the VBAR statement and SORTORDER=ASCENDING on the KEYLEGEND statement. Descending is the numeric order of the response values for each segment as the segments go down the stack. Ascending is the alphabetic order of the legend entries.

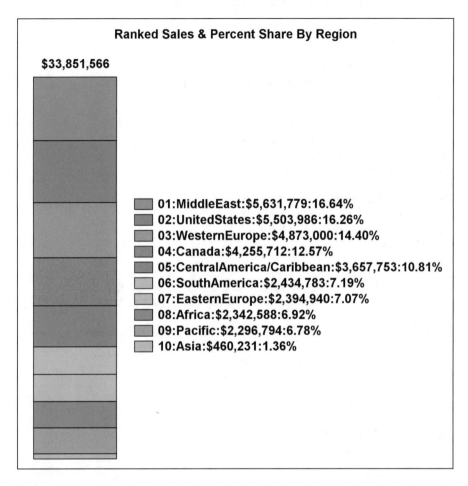

Figure 4-55B. Fully informative stacked ranked vertical bar chart, another alternative to the ranked maximally informative pie chart

Listing 4-55B. *Code used to create Figure 4-55B*

```
proc summary data=sashelp.shoes;
class Region;
var Sales;
output out=work.Summed sum=;
run;

proc sort data=work.Summed out=work.Sorted;
by descending Sales;
run;
```

```
data _null_;
set work.Sorted;
if _N_ EQ 1;
call symput('GrandTotal',Sales);
call symput('GrandTotalForTITLE3',compress(put(Sales,dollar12.)));
run;

data work.ToPlot(keep=RankedRegionWithPctShare Dollars Sales);
retain GrandTotal &GrandTotal;
length RankedRegionWithPctShare $ 64;
set work.Sorted;
if _N_ NE 1;
RankedRegionWithPctShare = compress(put(_N_-1,Z2.) || ':' ||
  Region || ':' || put(Sales,dollar12.) || ':' ||
  put((Sales / GrandTotal) * 100,5.2) || '%');
Dollars = 'Sales';
run;

ods listing style=GraphFontArial11ptBold gpath="C:\temp" dpi=300;
ods graphics on / reset=all scale=off width=5.7in height=5.7in
maxlegendarea=50
imagename="Fig4-55B_FullyInformativeStackedRankedVerticalBarChart";
title1 justify=center
  'Ranked Sales & Percent Share By Region';
title2 " ";
title3 justify=left "    &GrandTotalForTITLE3";
proc sgplot data=work.ToPlot noborder;
vbar Dollars / response=Sales
  group=RankedRegionWithPctShare
  groupdisplay=stack
  grouporder=descending
  displaybaseline=off
  outlineattrs=(color=black);
xaxis display=none offsetmin=0 offsetmax=0;
yaxis display=none;
keylegend / noborder title=' ' position=right
  sortorder=ascending autooutline
  fillheight=11pt fillaspect=golden;
run;
```

A traditional pie chart, whether it has fully informative labels at the perimeter outside each slice, or in callout labels, or in a legend, is more compact than either Figure 4-55A or 4-55B. Only a pie chart with a legend shares the disadvantage of Figure 4-55B with the lack of immediate association between the color-filled graphic element with its description, response, and percent share.

This section is about needle plots, but Figure 4-55B has diverted the discussion to vertical bar charts. The needle plot in Figure 4-54 is posited as a vertical bar chart alternative. Figure 4-56 *is* a ranked fully informative vertical bar chart, which, in effect, takes apart the stack in Figure 4-55B. In the case of both Figures 4-55B and 4-56, the total must be displayed in a subtitle. In the same way that a total needle in Figure 4-54 would have dwarfed all of the other needles, a total bar in Figure 4-56 would have dwarfed all of the other bars. Figure 4-56 is not a pie chart alternative, because there is no visual comparability of each of the parts with the total, but it delivers the category, the response, and the percent of total all in immediate proximity.

Figure 4-56. Vertical bar chart with total in the subtitle, an alternative to Figure 4-54

Note that the Central America/Caribbean region label was truncated to fit. For a horizontal bar chart, category label lengths would not need truncation.

Listing 4-56. *Code used to create Figure 4-56*

```
proc summary data=sashelp.shoes nway;
class Region;
var Sales;
output out=work.AllTotalsToSort sum=Sales;
run;

proc sort data=work.AllTotalsToSort out=work.AllTotalsToPrep;
by descending Sales;
run;

data work.ToChart;
retain GrandTotal 0;
length Region $ 15;
/* LENGTH statement causes harmless WARNING message
   about multiple lengths for a variable */
set work.AllTotalsToPrep end=LastOne;
GrandTotal + Sales;
Sales = Sales / 1000000;
```

```
output;
if LastOne;
call symput('GrandTotal',put(GrandTotal,dollar11.));
run;


ods listing style=GraphFontArial8ptBold gpath="C:\temp" dpi=300;
ods graphics on / reset=all scale=off width=5.7in height=2.5in
  imagename=
  "Fig4-56_RankedVbarWithSalesAndPercentAxisTablesNoTotal";
title1 justify=center
  'Ranked Shoe Sales ($M) and Percent Share By Region';
title2 justify=center
  "All Eight Regions, All Ten Products, Total = &GrandTotal";
proc sgplot data=work.ToChart noborder;
vbar Region / response=Sales
  categoryorder=respdesc fillattrs=(color=Green)
  displaybaseline=off nooutline barwidth=0.65;
xaxistable Sales / stat=sum
  position=bottom /* below the bars */
  location=inside /* above the category axis values */
  label='Sales';
xaxistable Sales / stat=percent
  position=bottom /* below the bars */
  location=inside /* above the category axis values AND */
      /* below any previously defined X axis table */
  label='Share';
xaxis display=(nolabel noline noticks) fitpolicy=stagger;
yaxis display=none;
format Sales dollar5.2;
run;
```

Review of Tree Chart, Flag Chart, and CrossRoads SignPost Chart and the Alternatives of Pie Chart, Vertical Bar Chart, and Horizontal Bar Chart

Innovations in this chapter include the Tree Chart in Figure 4-51; the Flag Chart in Figure 4-52; two uses of the CrossRoads SignPost Chart in Figures 4-53 and 4-54, one used for a subset of the input data and the other used for the complete input data set; and a stacked needle plot in Figure 4-55A.

Figures 4-51, 4-52, and 4-53 can be used as alternatives to a fully informative pie chart. They provide the precise numbers by category for value and percent of a whole and visually depict the parts for direct comparison with the total, with the total value listed. The visual is an inherent, simple, easy-to-interpret comparison of each part with the total and each part with each other. The viewer's eye takes a shorter and direct trip to do comparison and precise number discovery. It's a much simpler visual structure than a bar chart or pie chart.

However, these alternatives can be infeasible if parts of the total have values that are too close together. The Tree Chart and Flag Chart could have an overlap problem. A smaller, but readable, font and/or increasing the height might eliminate that. The CrossRoads SignPost Chart reduces the probability of overlap problems by displaying successive labels on alternating sides of the post. When overlap is not a problem, both the Tree Chart and the Flag Chart have the advantage of requiring less image width.

Figure 4-54 can be used as an alternative to a vertical bar chart. Instead of scanning bars and their category values and datalabels or axis tables for value and percent of total from left to right, the viewer can scan the fully labeled points up and down the CrossRoads SignPost. Since a labeled total point at the top is infeasible due to the fact that its presence would squash the parts points down to the bottom, the total value is displayed in a subtitle. Even without the total present on the post, four of the points are very close together. By displaying Region data labels on alternate sides of the post, overlap is avoided.

Figure 4-56 is the vertical bar chart version of Figure 4-54, but exhibits the vulnerability of bar labels being too wide for the image width available. This bar chart that used the FITPOLICY=STAGGER option for the X axis values is actually incomplete. The X axis value for Central America/Caribbean was truncated as a desperate remedy, and the result suffers. The XAXIS option of SPLITCHAR='/' could have been used, but the result would have been awkward-looking and ugly. Accuracy is always more important than pretty, but this example is only a demonstration, not a recommended solution. Figure 4-56 is the "rotated" version of the elegant and accurate fully informative ranked horizontal bar chart solution in Figure 4-4. That solution can be enhanced by explicitly including the rank number, which is helpful when there are more bars, as is the case for Figure 4-5, ordered by rank number, or Figure 4-6 which orders the same long list of information alphabetically by category for easier lookup of any specific category, but includes Rank Number for reference.

Area Bar Chart

An area bar chart provides a way to compare two response variables for the values of a category variable.

The examples provided here make use of a derivative of a macro that can be downloaded from a site given in Dan Heath's SAS blog "Area Bar Charts using SGPLOT" found at `https://blogs.sas.com/content/graphicallyspeaking/2022/04/30/area-bar-charts-using-sgplot/`.

The source code for that derivative macro and common prep code to create Figures 4-57 through 4-61 are in Listing A4-57 in Appendix A. (The macro and prep code are %INCLUDEd in each of the five listings for the figures.)

That blog also provides a test data set and various code examples using three different macros. The blog content was the inspiration for this section. The blog also includes a macro to create a subgrouped area bar chart, to create areas for values of a subgroup variable within each composite area for the values of the category variable. That is outside the scope of this section.

Also, at the blog the reader can find code to "rotate" the area bars by 90 degrees—that is, to convert what might be called a vertical area bar chart, which is shown in this section, into a horizontal area bar chart.

In the five area bar charts in this section, the area bars are in all cases color-filled. However, in the cases where no legend is used to identify the values of the category variable, the FILL option on the POLYGON statement, and the STYLEATTRS statement used to define the color palette, could be omitted, with no loss in communication effectiveness.

In common prep code for the five examples, a data set and four macro variables are created for use in all five cases.

An AREABAR statement might be provided as an enhancement for the SGPLOT procedure, but until then the examples available in this section and the SAS blog can enable you to create area bar charts.

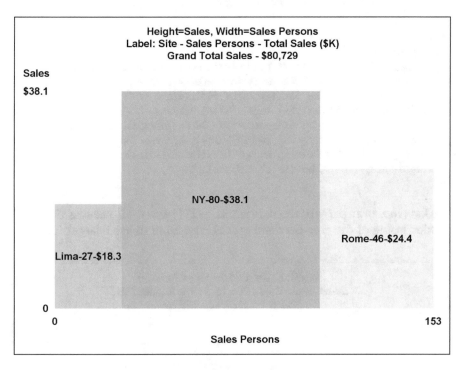

Figure 4-57. Area bar chart with data label parts in a concatenated string

The source code for Modified_genAreaBarDataBasic macro and common prep code to create Figures 4-57 through 4-61 are in Listing A4-57 in Appendix A.

Listing 4-57. *Code used to create Figure 4-57*

```
%include "C:\SharedCode\CommonPrepForFigures4-57to4-61.sas";
%include "C:\SharedCode\Modified_genAreaBarDataBasic.sas";
options mprint;
%Modified_genAreaBarDataBasic(SiteTotalsAndAreasAndYperX,poly_data,
  SiteWithNumbers,SiteTotalSales,SiteSalespersons);
ods listing style=GraphFontArial9ptBold gpath="C:\temp" dpi=300;
/* 9pt for this example in order to fit Lima data label
   within the width of its area bar */
ods graphics on / reset=all scale=off width=5.7in
  imagename=
  "Fig4-57_BasicVerticalAreaBarChart_DataLabelsConcatenated";
title1 justify=center "Height=Sales, Width=Sales Persons";
title2 justify=center
  "Label: Site - Sales Persons - Total Sales ($K)";
title3 justify=center "Grand Total Sales - &GrandTotalSales";
proc sgplot data=poly_data noautolegend noborder;
styleattrs datacolors=(CXCCCCFF CX99FF99 CXFFFF99);
```

```
yaxis offsetmin=0;
polygon x=x y=y id=ID / fill
  group=ID label=ID
  labelattrs=(color=Black); /* The default would use a label color
  for each area that contrasts with that area's fill color. Black is
  more reliably readable, for any light fill color. */
xaxis display=(noline noticks) label='Sales Persons'
  values=(0 to &GrandTotalSalespersons by &GrandTotalSalespersons);
yaxis display=(noline noticks) label='Sales' labelpos=Top
  values=(0 to &MaxSiteTotalSales by &MaxSiteTotalSales)
  valuesdisplay=('0' "&MaxSiteTotalSalesDisplay");
run;
```

Stacking the three parts of the data labels, as in Figure 4-58, reduces the width needed inside of the area bars and makes it possible to use a larger font.

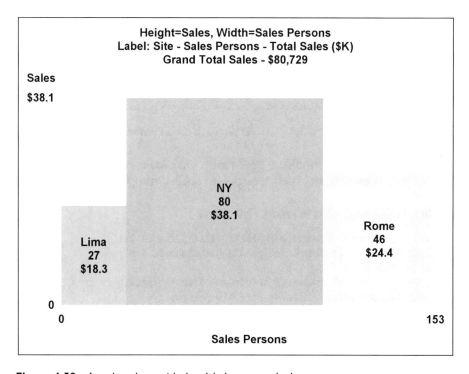

Figure 4-58. Area bar chart with data label parts stacked

Listing 4-58. *Code used to create Figure 4-58*

```
%include "C:\SharedCode\CommonPrepForFigures4-57to4-61.sas";
%include "C:\SharedCode\Modified_genAreaBarDataBasic.sas";
options mprint;
%Modified_genAreaBarDataBasic(SiteTotalsAndAreasAndYperX,poly_data,
  SiteWithNumbers,SiteTotalSales,SiteSalespersons);
ods listing style=GraphFontArial10ptBold gpath="C:\temp" dpi=300;
/* 10pt for this example since data label split eliminates
   the width constraint for Lima data label in its area bar */
ods graphics on / reset=all scale=off width=5.7in
  imagename=
  "Fig4-58_BasicVerticalAreaBarChart_DataLabelsSplit";
title1 justify=center
  "Height=Sales, Width=Sales Persons";
title2 justify=center
  "Label: Site - Sales Persons - Total Sales ($K)";
title3 justify=center "Grand Total Sales - &GrandTotalSales";
proc sgplot data=poly_data noautolegend noborder;
styleattrs datacolors=(CXCCCCFF CX99FF99 CXFFFF99);
yaxis offsetmin=0;
polygon x=x y=y id=ID / fill
  group=ID label=ID
  labelattrs=(color=Black)
  splitchar='-'
  splitjustify=center;
xaxis display=(noline noticks) label='Sales Persons'
  values=(0 to &GrandTotalSalespersons by &GrandTotalSalespersons);
yaxis display=(noline noticks) label='Sales' labelpos=Top
  values=(0 to &MaxSiteTotalSales by &MaxSiteTotalSales)
  valuesdisplay=('0' "&MaxSiteTotalSalesDisplay");
run;
```

A legend for the values of the category variable, as in Figure 4-59, reduces the space needed inside of the areas for their data labels.

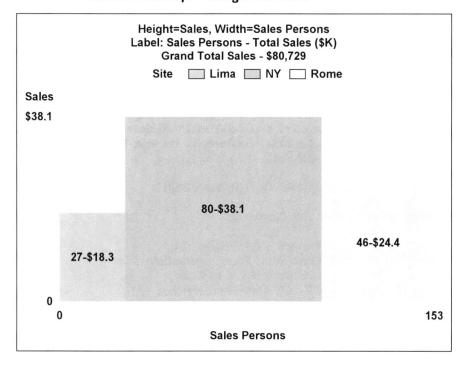

Figure 4-59. Area bar chart with legend for category values and data labels for values of the height and width response variables

Listing 4-59. Code used to create Figure 4-59

```
%include "C:\SharedCode\CommonPrepForFigures4-57to4-61.sas";
%include "C:\SharedCode\Modified_genAreaBarDataBasic.sas";
options mprint;
%Modified_genAreaBarDataBasic(SiteTotalsAndAreasAndYperX,poly_data,
  Site,SiteTotalSales,SiteSalespersons,NumbersForSite);
ods listing style=GraphFontArial10ptBold gpath="C:\temp" dpi=300;
/* 10pt for this example since Site values in legend eliminates
   the width constraint for Lima data label in its area bar */
ods graphics on / reset=all scale=off width=5.7in
  imagename=
  "Fig4-59_BasicVerticalAreaBarChart_WithDataLabelsAndSiteLegend";
title1 justify=center
  "Height=Sales, Width=Sales Persons";
title2 justify=center
  "Label: Sales Persons - Total Sales ($K)";
title3 justify=center "Grand Total Sales - &GrandTotalSales";
proc sgplot data=poly_data noautolegend noborder;
styleattrs datacolors=(CXCCCCFF CX99FF99 CXFFFF99);
yaxis offsetmin=0;
polygon x=x y=y id=ID / fill
```

```
  group=ID label=NumbersForSite
  labelattrs=(color=Black);
xaxis display=(noline noticks) label='Sales Persons'
  values=(0 to &GrandTotalSalespersons by &GrandTotalSalespersons);
yaxis display=(noline noticks) label='Sales' labelpos=Top
  values=(0 to &MaxSiteTotalSales by &MaxSiteTotalSales)
  valuesdisplay=('0' "&MaxSiteTotalSalesDisplay");
format y dollar5.1;
keylegend / noborder title='Site'
  position=top /* make Site identification immediate */
  fillheight=9pt fillaspect=golden;
run;
```

In the preceding three cases, the color palette in the STYLEATTRS
DATACOLORS list is applied in alphabetical order by category variable value.
In the remaining two cases, the color palette is applied in ranking order. Since
the ranking order in each case differs from the alphabetical order, the
STYLEATTRS DATACOLORS assignment changes to assure that each Site
value has its area filled with the same color in all five cases. In any collection
of related graphs, it is important to use color consistently, not seemingly
randomly. The viewer will expect consistency and might find deviations
confusing or mystifying.

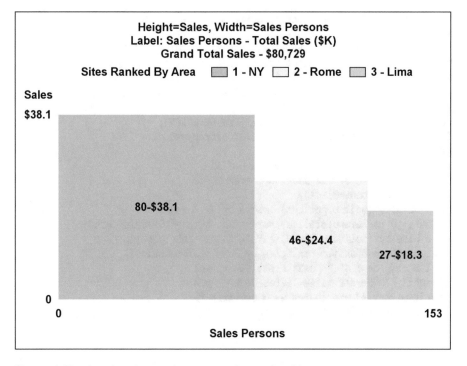

Figure 4-60. Area bar chart with category values ordered by area

In a different context, that is, different data, ranking by the product of the height and width variables might be based on a data-related rationale. Here, the ranking is only a demonstration of the possibility and of how to do it.

Listing 4-60. *Code used to create Figure 4-60*

```
%include "C:\SharedCode\CommonPrepForFigures4-57to4-61.sas";
%include "C:\SharedCode\Modified_genAreaBarDataBasic.sas";

proc sort data=SiteTotalsAndAreasAndYperX out=SitesSortedByArea;
by descending Area;
run;

data ForPolyByArea(keep=SiteRankedByArea SiteTotalSales
                   SiteSalespersons NumbersForSite);
length SiteRankedByArea $ 8;
set SitesSortedByArea;
SiteRankedByArea = trim(left(_N_)) || ' - ' || trim(left(Site));
run;

options mprint;
%Modified_genAreaBarDataBasic(ForPolyByArea,poly_data,
  SiteRankedByArea,SiteTotalSales,SiteSalespersons,NumbersForSite);

ods listing style=GraphFontArial10ptBold gpath="C:\temp" dpi=300;
ods graphics on / reset=all scale=off width=5.7in
  imagename="Fig4-60_BasicVerticalAreaBarChart_OrderedByArea";
title1 justify=center "Height=Sales, Width=Sales Persons";
title2 justify=center "Label: Sales Persons - Total Sales ($K)";
title3 justify=center "Grand Total Sales - &GrandTotalSales";
proc sgplot data=poly_data noborder;
styleattrs datacolors=(CX99FF99 CXFFFF99 CXCCCCFF);
/* change order to preserve site-color correspondence */
yaxis offsetmin=0;
polygon x=x y=y id=SiteRankedByArea / fill
  group=SiteRankedByArea label=NumbersForSite
  labelattrs=(color=Black);
xaxis display=(noline noticks) label='Sales Persons'
  values=(0 to &GrandTotalSalespersons by &GrandTotalSalespersons);
yaxis display=(noline noticks) label='Sales' labelpos=Top
  values=(0 to &MaxSiteTotalSales by &MaxSiteTotalSales)
  valuesdisplay=('0' "&MaxSiteTotalSalesDisplay");
keylegend / noborder title='Sites Ranked By Area'
  position=top /* use legend as a subtitle */
  fillheight=9pt fillaspect=golden;
run;
```

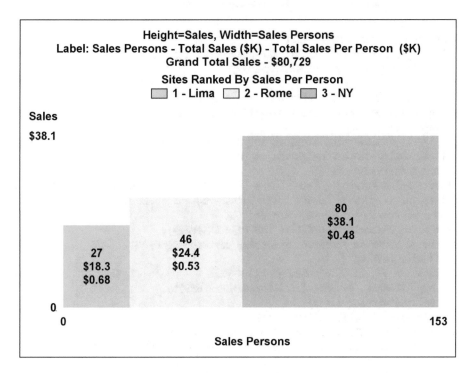

Figure 4-61. Area bar chart with category values ordered by value of Y per value of X

This ranking is based on an obviously important rationale.

Listing 4-61. *Code used to create Figure 4-61*

```
%include "C:\SharedCode\CommonPrepForFigures4-57to4-61.sas";
%include "C:\SharedCode\Modified_genAreaBarDataBasic.sas";

proc sort data=SiteTotalsAndAreasAndYperX out=SitesSortedByYperX;
by descending YperX;
run;

data ForPolyByYperX(keep=SiteRankedByYperX SiteTotalSales
                    SiteSalespersons MoreNumbersForSite);
length SiteRankedByYperX $ 8 MoreNumbersForSite $ 19;
set SitesSortedByYperX;
SiteRankedByYperX = trim(left(_N_)) || ' - ' || trim(left(Site));
MoreNumbersForSite = trim(left(NumbersForSite)) || '-' || trim(left(put((YperX
/ 1000),dollar5.2)));
run;
```

```
options mprint;
%Modified_genAreaBarDataBasic(
  ForPolyByYperX,poly_data,SiteRankedByYperX,SiteTotalSales,
  SiteSalespersons,MoreNumbersForSite);

ods listing style=GraphFontArial10ptBold gpath="C:\temp" dpi=300;
ods graphics on / reset=all scale=off width=5.7in
  imagename=
  "Fig4-61_BasicVerticalAreaBarChart_OrderedYvaluePerXvalue";
title1 justify=center "Height=Sales, Width=Sales Persons";
title2 justify=center
"Label: Sales Persons - Total Sales ($K) - Total Sales Per Person   ($K)";
title3 justify=center "Grand Total Sales - &GrandTotalSales";
proc sgplot data=poly_data noborder;
styleattrs datacolors=(CXCCCCFF CXFFFF99 CX99FF99);
/* change order to preserve site-color correspondence */
yaxis offsetmin=0;
polygon x=x y=y id=SiteRankedByYperX / fill
  group=SiteRankedByYperX label=MoreNumbersForSite
  labelattrs=(color=Black)
  splitchar='-' splitjustify=center;
xaxis display=(noline noticks) label='Sales Persons'
  values=(0 to &GrandTotalSalespersons by &GrandTotalSalespersons);
yaxis display=(noline noticks) label='Sales' labelpos=Top
  values=(0 to &MaxSiteTotalSales by &MaxSiteTotalSales)
  valuesdisplay=('0' "&MaxSiteTotalSalesDisplay");
keylegend / noborder title='Sites Ranked By Sales Per Person'
  position=top /* use legend as a subtitle */
  fillheight=9pt fillaspect=golden;
run;
```

The vertical area bar chart is an alternative to the vertical side-by-side overlay chart demonstrated in Figure 4-36. As an exercise, the reader might find it useful to adapt the CommonPrep code used with this data to the data for Figure 4-36 and then adapt the code for Figure 4-59 to that prepared input. With eight products rather than three sites, it might be necessary to use the SPLITCHAR option to fit the data labels.

Summary

Several ways were shown to communication-effectively present images and precise numbers for categorical data and to rank the categories. You have seen a variety of ways to present data with one or two categorical variables and with one or more response variables. Horizontal and vertical bar charts, dot plots, needle plots, butterfly charts, waterfall charts, and new charts in Figure 4-36 and Figures 4-49 through 4-55A and 4-55B provide many alternative ways to present categorical data visually.

Data labels, axis tables, segment labels (for stacked charts), and the TEXT statement are the available ways to deliver the precise numbers.

For data with only one categorical variable, it is straightforward in bar charts and dot plots to present the categories in ranked order. For data with many categories, it can be useful to present it in alphabetical order in addition or instead. However, for alphabetical ordered categories, with some data preprocessing to prepare a derivative data set, one can include the rank of each category in an axis table to provide both lookup convenience and the rank order of importance.

Another way to emphasize what's important is to subset the data, rather than present all of it. Of course, one can also present all of it, in another graph. This concept is implemented best with a horizontal bar chart, such as the trio of subsetting options in Figure 4-7. For that specific data set, the alternative deliverables are the Top Ten Cities for Shoe Sales, All Cities with Shoes Sales of At Least $1,000,000 (8 cities), and Enough Highest Ranked Cities to Account for 60% of Shoe Sales World-wide (15 cities). Those are subsets of 53 cities.

When presenting a subset of the categories, it is important to include subtitles to report (a) how many categories there are altogether and what their total response is and (b) the count of categories in the subset, their subtotal response, and what percent of the total that subtotal is. This accessory information permits the viewer of a subset chart to assess the relative significance of what has been left out versus what has been reported.

Often, though not always, the proportion of total response for which the details are not reported with subsetting is small. The Pareto 80/20 Rule suggests that 80% of some outcome originates from 20% of the possible sources/causes. Of course, 80 and 20 are not some magical, always applicable numbers, but the "rule" describes a common approximate reality. That's why there are a variety of applicable options for subsetting your data. Subsetting your bar chart can put the focus where it best belongs and show the viewer what's important.

Using a color-coded title where the color used for variable names matches the area fill for their corresponding bars can eliminate the need for a legend. Though only demonstrated for bar charts, the concept could be applied for dot plots and needle plots where applicable. The viewer of a graph always, or one would think so, reads the title first. If one can get the rest of the information by looking at the graphic elements and associated text information, the extra step of looking at a legend to get full understanding can be avoided.

In the examples, the base text characteristics for charts and plots were usually established by specification of a custom style such as GraphFontArial11ptBold on the ODS LISTING statement. As needed, some parts of the images had text characteristics (specifically, the font size) overridden from the custom style base by using SIZE= in the appropriate ATTRS option. Except when space constraints on text dictate otherwise, it is best to render all of a graph's text with the same font size (and, of course, font family and font weight). It's simple and consistent to use only one size. All of the text information should be equally important (if not, for some, then why is it there?) and equally easy to read. Using font WEIGHT=BOLD (as in the prebuilt styles) maximizes readability and does no harm. If some text in your graph needs special emphasis, color can provide that. Unless when color coding, the text in your graph should be black if the background is white or some light color. (I can't think of a compelling reason to not make your graph background white.)

JUSTIFY=CENTER was used on most titles, for reasons already explained in Chapter 3 and again here in this chapter. But here is the story again.

The default justification of titles and footnotes in ODS Graphics is not always in the center of the full width of the image. If the graph is one with an axis area, in order to center a title or footnote in the full width of the image, JUSTIFY=CENTER must be specified on the TITLE or FOOTNOTE statement. Otherwise, the default centering is over the axis area, which is typically shifted to the right by the column of Y axis values.

The only ODS graphs without an axis area—pie charts, donut charts, and maps—have titles and footnotes with traditional centering by default.

For the graphs with axis areas, if the length of the title or footnote exceeds the width of the axis area, then it is centered in the width of the image, as what one usually would expect.

For the situation of a RESPONSE variable that is classifiable with two categorical variables, one variable is chosen as CATEGORY, and the other is chosen as GROUP. It does not matter which is which.

For the GROUP variable, a KeyLegend can be provided. On the PROC SGPLOT statement, you can suppress the legend with the NOAUTOLEGEND option. If you do that, then you can make the color fills of bars or markers decodable with a color-coded title.

When you use a GROUP variable, you must select a GROUPDISPLAY option. For bar charts, the choices are STACKED (the default) and CLUSTER. If you want to know the precise value of the RESPONSE variable for each segment in a stack, it's best to use axis tables, one for each segment. Segment labels deliver the value in an immediate manner with a data label embedded in each segment. However, this solution works completely only if the segments are big enough and the labels are small enough. The benefit of a stacked bar chart is that the viewer sees the size of each segment with respect to each of the others, and with respect to the total, which is the length of the stack. The precise value of that total can be a data label at the end of the bar (if horizontal) or the top of the bar (if vertical). For a vertical bar chart, if the data labels are long they might collide. The benefit of horizontal bar charts is that there is no possibility of collisions between bar labels or data labels.

The CLUSTER option presents what could have been stack segments as a cluster of bars side by side, with one cluster for each distinct value of the CATEGORY variable.

DOT plots are an HBAR chart alternative, and NEEDLE plots are a VBAR chart alternative. For DOT plots, the most useful and unambiguous result for data label position comes from DATALABELPOS=LEFT, which puts the response values adjacent to the category values. For NEEDLE plots, the choices for DATALABELPOS are locations around the end of the needle. The default location is TopRight. Use DATALABELPOS=TOP. Using DATALABELPOS=BOTTOM puts the data label at the bottom of the marker, if present. If no marker is present, the data label overlays the top of the bare needle.

For DOT plots and NEEDLE plots, the GROUPDISPLAY options are OVERLAY (the default) and CLUSTER. When using GROUP, whether GROUPDISPLAY is OVERLAY or CLUSTER, I find NEEDLE plots easier to interpret than DOT plots.

For ungrouped or GROUPDISPLAY=CLUSTER NEEDLE plots, DATALABELPOS=TOP is the best choice. For ungrouped DOT plots, DATALABELPOS=LEFT is the best choice. For grouped DOT plots, it is best to accept the default data label position.

OVERLAY charts can be created for bar charts, by using the BARWIDTH and DISCRETEOFFSET options for the HBAR and VBAR statements. Let me call this Programmatic Overlay, as distinguished from Option Overlay, which is available only for DOT plots and NEEDLE plots. With Programmatic Overlay, you have absolute control over the result. There are at least three types of Programmatic Overlay: (a) bars side by side and touching, as in Figures 4-8 and 4-9 with two sets of bars or Figure 4-38 with three sets of bars; (b) bars side by side, but with gaps between them as in Figure 4-10, or the default outcome with GROUPDISPLAY=CLUSTER as in Figure 4-16; and (c) one set of bars actually drawn on top of the other, as in Figure 4-11. Case (c) does not use the DISCRETEOFFSET option, only two different values of BARWIDTH so that narrow bars can be drawn on top of wide bars.

An interesting variation on Case (c) is to overlay a DOT plot over the base set of bars as in Figure 4-13. In that case, the "IBeams" are all past the ends of the bars. If one or more were on top of the bars, their visibility can be assured by increasing the SIZE in the MARKERATTRS option. Another way to assure visibility is to use a light color for the bars and a dark enough color for the IBeams and draw them last.

A special case of Programmatic Overlay is a "composite" butterfly chart as in Figure 4-19. It expands the concept of the traditional butterfly chart in Figure 4-18, by using BARWIDTH and DISCRETEOFFSET. Just as Figure 4-38 shows that you can do a three-bar-set overlay, one can expand the butterfly chart with any number of sets of bars desired. It is just a matter of adjusting BARWIDTH and DISCRETEOFFSET appropriately.

Almost all of the Programmatic Overlay examples are for the situation of two categorical variables and one response value, such as Dollars for SalesOrProfit by Product Line. The example in Figure 4-36 is a vertical side-by-side overlay without a gap between bars for one categorical variable, but two different response variables. To fit the two sets of bars rather commensurately (i.e., without one set of bars being much larger than all of the bars in the other set), the higher value variable had to be rescaled. A simpler way to deal with this would be to use an X axis table for one of the variables. Another alternative is that in Figure 4-37 which uses the VLINE statement for one response variable and a VBAR statement for the other. The VLINE uses a Y2AXIS so that it can be drawn with its own scale.

Another way to handle two categorical variables and one response variable is with PROC SGPANEL and the PANELBY statement as in Figure 4-17, which is just a more visually complicated way to do the clustered bar chart in Figure 4-16. PROC SGPANEL, discussed in Chapter 9, enables you to visually present additional complicated situations, such as ones with more than two category variables.

The waterfall chart is for applications where the trend shown is the starting value, the ending value, and the intermediate changes, plus and minus, of the response variable for time period to time period, rather than showing the value itself.

Figure 4-50 shows how to create what looks like a table, but visually functions as a ranked vertical bar chart with no bars. The data points are represented with a text stack of response value over category value, for each category along a non-drawn X axis. It only uses TEXT statements.

This chapter includes innovative derivatives of the needle plot (with apparently only one needle because all of the needles are overlaid). I call them the Tree Chart (Figure 4-51), the Flag Chart (Figure 4-52), and the CrossRoads SignPost Charts, in three variations. Figures 4-53 and 4-54 consist of overlaid needle plots, one including a total needle and the other with the total listed in a subtitle, since the size of the total versus its constituents would dwarf them in an overlay. A different design to show the total needle size versus constituent needle sizes is given in Figure 4-55A by overlaying needles as a stack of constituent segments that build the total needle "under" them or with them. In the earlier cases, the total needle and its constituent needles are overlaid, with all needles starting at Y=0. Figure 4-55B, a ranked stacked vertical bar chart, is a better solution than Figure 4-55A.

After that section, there is an expansive analysis of the benefits and uses of the "single-needle charts" and how they compare with pie charts and bar charts, as well as a short reprise on vertical versus horizontal bar charts. A horizontal bar chart is always feasible in situations where a vertical bar chart has category values that are too wide to fit in the image width.

The chapter closed with showing the use of area bar charts as an alternative to overlaid bar charts to present two response variables for one category variable.

Pie Charts and Donut Charts

Pie charts don't need an introduction. Everybody already knows them. They are very, very popular. You see them often, even in the media. They are easy to understand. "Who has the biggest share of the pie?" More broadly, how do the shares of a total compare? Those are questions that a pie chart easily and vividly answers.

The distinguishing inherent power of pie charts and donut charts is that they, if created as appropriate (which is very easy to do), automatically deliver both image for quick, easy inference and precise numbers—response and percent of whole—for reliable, accurate inference. There is *no* guessing, *no* estimating, *no* interpolating. You see and *know* the full truth of the matter at a glance.

Nevertheless, some people sniff and turn up their noses at pie charts. On the Internet, you can find many postings which assert that pie charts are bad. It is a tiresome repetition of obsolete criticism. Pie charts were given a bad name decades ago in academe before there were the current data visualization tools. If one still needed to draw a pie chart by hand as was the case at the time of their invention, THAT would be something I would not want to do. I would appreciate *any* excuse not to have to do it.

© LeRoy Bessler 2023
LeR. Bessler, *Visual Data Insights Using SAS ODS Graphics*,
https://doi.org/10.1007/978-1-4842-8609-8_5

The conclusion of a study was that it's easier to assess with certainty the comparative lengths of bars in a bar chart than the sizes of slices in a pie chart. But that is *irrelevant* if one applies the three key design principles applicable to *all* graphs, including pie charts:

> Show them what's important—in this case, with slice ordering.

> Provide the precise numbers—in this case, both slice values and percents of the whole.

> Assure that all text, character and numeric, is readable—that is not automatic.

With these key principles, which are easy to implement, as you will see, any basis for that criticism about difficulty in pie slice comparability is inapplicable.

There is one defect in pie charts that persists, but not with ODS Graphics. As shown in Figure 1-1, 3D pie charts are always misleading. With ODS Graphics, you cannot stray down that path. In its early years, SAS/GRAPH did not support 3D. After years of SAS users finding ways to create 3D pie charts with the SAS/GRAPH ANNOTATE facility (which can do much more than text annotation), the PIE3D statement was added to SAS/GRAPH PROC GCHART. It can be used to create the bad example in Figure 1-1.

We will see the *good* pie charts that we can create with ODS Graphics. Before we get to that, let me digress into history.

Pie charts were invented by William Playfair in 1801. The first ones appeared in his book *The Statistical Breviary: Shewing, on a Principle Entirely New, The Resources of Every State and Kingdom in Europe.* A breviary is a book of the prayers, hymns, psalms, and readings for the canonical hours. There are seven daytime canonical hours of lauds (dawn), prime (sunrise), terce (mid-morning), sext (midday), none (mid-afternoon), vespers (sunset), compline (retiring) and the one nighttime canonical hour of night watch. There is no doubt that the *Statistical Breviary* was very interesting, but I would not want to read it seven times a day and during night watch.

Donut charts, or doughnut charts, are a latecomer to data visualization. Unlike the case with the pie chart, an Internet search yielded no answer to my questions as to who invented the donut chart and when it was invented. It did turn up a claim that donut charts are superior to pie charts because one's visual brain can more easily and fairly assess the comparative length, around the perimeter, of donut bites than the area of pie slices. However, ordering pie chart slices or donut chart bites, as I like to call the segments, and providing labels with precise numbers for response and percent provide effective, complete, certain visual communication. Such design eliminates any alleged impediments for reliable inference with pie or donut charts.

Donut charts are popular in infographics. An advantage of the donut chart is its hole in the middle where some people like to put big numbers or brief text messages, as you will see demonstrated in this chapter.

As of the time of writing for this book, PROC SGPIE was in Preproduction status. The eventually available Production version's output might differ in some respects from what is shown here.

General Remarks About Code Used

The following framing code has been more expansively discussed in Chapter 3 in the section "Outer Structure of ODS Graphics Code in Examples." The framing code for all examples in this chapter and others is

```
ods results off; /* verify results by opening the image file,
                    rather than using the SAS Output window */
ods _all_ close; /* avoid unintended consequences
                    and superfluous concurrent output */
< ODS LISTING statement here >
< example-specific code here >
ods listing close; /* ALWAYS Best Practice */
```

For brevity, the example code in listings omits the first two lines and the last one. It is best to add them back at your runtime. (Source code files include them.)

The ODS LISTING statement can vary. All of the examples in this chapter use a statement of the following form to specify the text characteristics:

```
ods listing style=GraphFontArial11ptBold gpath="C:\temp" dpi=300;
```

but a few times with font sizes other than 11pt. The statement assumes that the ODS style GraphFontArial11ptBold has been created. To assure that all of the styles needed in this chapter are available, use this code:

```
%include "C:\SharedCode\AllGraphTextSetup.sas";
%AllGraphTextSetup(6);
%AllGraphTextSetup(9);
%AllGraphTextSetup(11);
```

For more information about ODS custom styles, as well as the source code for the AllGraphTextSetup macro, see the section "Control of Text Attributes with a Custom ODS Style" in Chapter 3. For information about options for direct control of text attributes, which can override the default text attributes that are set up by an ODS style, see the section "Text Attributes Control in ODS Graphics" in Chapter 3.

Examples and Methods for Pie Charts

The perils of pie charts have always been with the labels—possible collisions between outside labels that are too close together or inside labels that can't fit in their slices. Here, you will learn methods for peril avoidance or remediation. The objective is to always deliver both graphic image and readable precise numbers.

For a pie chart, the labels should always include three things: category (description), value, and percent. Because there are three labels for each slice, there is a greater chance of collision. The chance for collision increases when you order the slices as I recommend, whether largest to smallest or smallest to largest (whichever size is most important). The ordering inevitably brings the small slices together. And when you have three pieces for each label, the natural configuration used that is the software default stacks them, which even more increases the chance of collision.

From time to time, I see pie chart examples with a few approximately equal slices, often as a demonstration of how to create a pie chart, not one using real-life data. It's a great way to avoid the ugly problem of label collisions.

A believed-to-be solution that prevents collisions is to lump all of the small slices into "Other." Though you have seen me extol the benefit of "The Extremes of Other," that is for special situations, and I explained that the content of Other can be delivered, if desired, with a supplemental vehicle. (See Figure 1-15 and the discussion there for "The Extremes of Other" and "The Pac-Man Pie Chart.") The problem with the convenient solution of using Other is that it prompts the question, "What's in Other?" Your pie chart, or any graph, plot, or chart that you create, should by itself answer *all* relevant questions, not create questions. Here, you will see an example of an *Informative* Other. It's not necessarily feasible in *all* cases that might use an Other slice, but might work in some cases for you.

In some examples, you will see the Category label moved to a legend. This does reduce the collision probability since the label stack for each slice is only two items but imposes a responsibility on the viewer to visually connect the category with its slice and its two numbers. The Fully Informative Legend solution that you will see consolidates *all* of the information in the legend entries, including the rank for each slice. The legend becomes a table of all of the information of interest, with the pie as a visual companion graphic comparator of the shares of the whole.

The Fully Informative Legend solution requires preprocessing the input to prepare the expanded category values. A simpler solution, which also delivers the strings of Category, Response, and Percent, but as labels, is the CALLOUT option for labels. It moves them out of the slices, to assure easy readability, but connects them with their slices, to assure easy association. These labels do lack the Rank that is provided in a Fully Informative Legend, but since the callout labels are connected to the physically ordered slices, the Ranks can be discovered visually.

An important, and for me surprising, feature of PROC SGPIE is that the software automatically decides what color to use for labels that are inside the slices. Some will be black, some will be white, and you might not agree that the color chosen is sufficiently readable. With the DATALABELATTRS statement, you can specify only one color for all of the labels. You can use the STYLEATTRS statement to specify a color palette for the slices that is readability-friendly for your label color.

So let's look at the ways to use a pie chart to answer all of the questions about the data with image and precise numbers, readably, and how to show the viewer what's important.

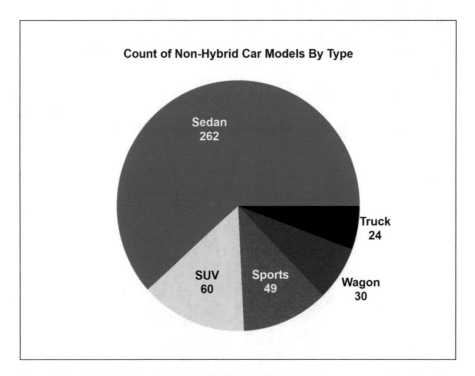

Figure 5-1. Default labels, default label position, default label colors, custom fill colors, slices in descending order

Listing 5-1. *Code used to create Figure 5-1*

```
ods listing style=GraphFontArial11ptBold gpath="C:\temp" dpi=300;
ods graphics / reset=all noscale width=5.7in height=4.3in
  imagename='Fig5-1_DefaultLabelsDisplay_DefaultLabelsLoc';
title1 'Count of Non-Hybrid Car Models By Type';
title2 color=white 'INVISIBLE Text to create white space';
  /* white space is added in several examples */
proc sgpie data=sashelp.cars;
where Type NE 'Hybrid';
styleattrs /* datacolors here are pie slice fill colors */
  datacolors=(blue LightGray red purple black);
pie type / /* type is the CATEGORY variable */
  /* Since RESPONSE= is NOT used. Pie Chart uses frequency counts
     of Category variable, i.e., TYPE */
  otherpercent=0 /* display ALL slices, regardless of how small */
  sliceorder=respdesc /* Order slices by size, largest first.
    Default is ascending order of unformatted Category variable. */
  direction=counterclockwise /* same as default */
  startangle=0 /* same as default, Three O'Clock position */
  startpos=edge; /* default is center, as shown in Figure 5-6 */
run;
```

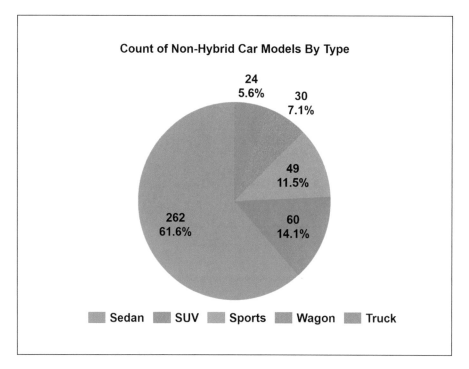

Figure 5-2. Response labels and percent labels requested, software-provided category legend at the bottom, response and percent locations and label colors all assigned by software, position and direction of slices chosen to "match" legend, defaults for slice colors

Listing 5-2. *Code used to create Figure 5-2, changes from Figure 5-1 in bold*

```
ods listing style=GraphFontArial11ptBold gpath="C:\temp" dpi=300;
ods graphics / reset=all noscale width=5.7in height=4.3in
  imagename=
  'Fig5-2_RespAndPct_CatLegend_DefaultLabelsLoc_DefaultColors';
title1 'Count of Non-Hybrid Car Models By Type';
title2 color=white 'INVISIBLE Text to create white space';
proc sgpie data=sashelp.cars;
where Type NE 'Hybrid';
pie type / otherpercent=0
  sliceorder=respdesc direction=counterclockwise
  startangle=90 startpos=edge
  datalabeldisplay=(response percent);
keylegend / noborder title=' ' fillaspect=golden
  fillheight=11pt; /* match the height of the legend values */
  /* KEYLEGEND statement only needed to CUSTOMIZE. Legend is
     automatic if only RESPONSE and PERCENT labels requested. */
run;
```

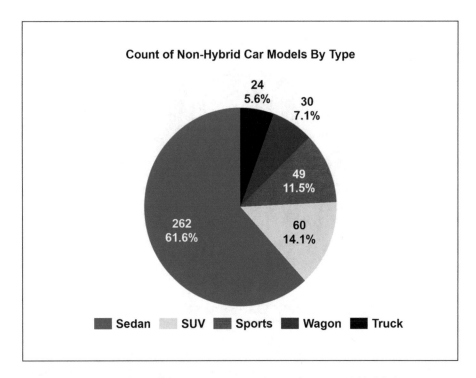

Figure 5-3. Same as Figure 5-2, except custom colors and more readable labels

Listing 5-3. *Code used to create Figure 5-3, changes from Figure 5-2 in bold*

```
ods listing style=GraphFontArial11ptBold gpath="C:\temp" dpi=300;
ods graphics / reset=all noscale width=5.7in height=4.3in
  imagename=
  'Fig5-3_RespAndPct_CatLegend_DefaultLabelsLoc_CustomColors';
title1 'Count of Non-Hybrid Car Models By Type';
title2 color=white 'INVISIBLE Text to create white space';
proc sgpie data=sashelp.cars;
where Type NE 'Hybrid';
styleattrs datacolors=(blue LightGray red purple black);
pie type / otherpercent=0
  sliceorder=respdesc direction=counterclockwise
  startangle=90 startpos=edge
  datalabeldisplay=(response percent);
keylegend / noborder title=' '
  fillaspect=golden fillheight=11pt;
run;
```

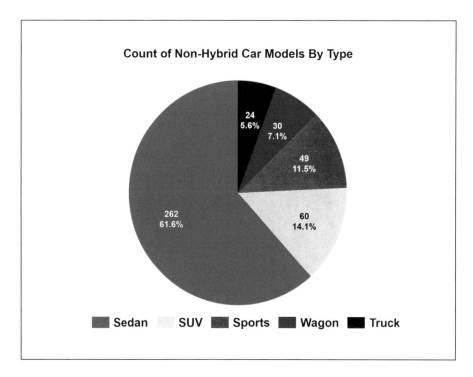

Figure 5-4. Same as Figure 5-3, except all labels inside, which creates room for a slightly larger pie

Listing 5-4. *Code used to create Figure 5-4, changes from Figure 5-3 in bold*

```
ods listing style=GraphFontArial11ptBold gpath="C:\temp" dpi=300;
ods graphics / reset=all noscale width=5.7in height=4.3in
  imagename='Fig5-4_RespAndPct_CatLegend_InsideLabels';
title1 'Count of Non-Hybrid Car Models By Type';
title2 color=white 'INVISIBLE Text to create white space';
proc sgpie data=sashelp.cars;
where Type NE 'Hybrid';
styleattrs datacolors=(blue LightGray red purple black);
pie type / otherpercent=0
  sliceorder=respdesc direction=counterclockwise
  startangle=90 startpos=edge
  datalabeldisplay=(response percent)
  datalabelattrs=(size=8pt) /* so labels fit inside small slices */
  datalabelloc=inside;
keylegend / noborder title=' '
  fillaspect=golden fillheight=11pt;
run;
```

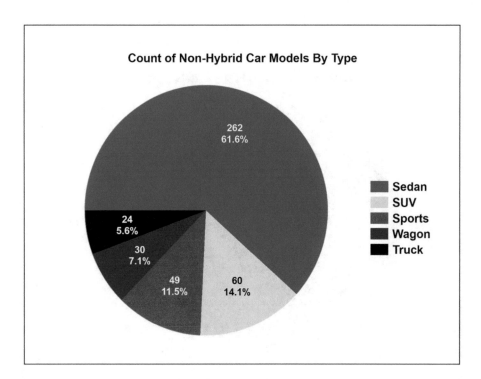

Figure 5-5. Same as Figure 5-4, except legend at the side. Position and direction of slices intended to "match" that of legend

Listing 5-5. *Code used to create Figure 5-5, changes from Figure 5-4 in bold*

```
ods listing style=GraphFontArial11ptBold gpath="C:\temp" dpi=300;
ods graphics / reset=all noscale width=5.7in height=4.3in
  imagename=
  'Fig5-5_RespAndPct_CatLegend_InsideLabels_LegendRightSide';
title1 'Count of Non-Hybrid Car Models By Type';
title2 color=white 'INVISIBLE Text to create white space';
proc sgpie data=sashelp.cars; where Type NE 'Hybrid';
styleattrs datacolors=(blue LightGray red purple black);
pie type / otherpercent=0
  sliceorder=respdesc direction=clockwise
  startangle=180 startpos=edge
  datalabelattrs=(size=9pt) /* changed small slice locations
                             permit a larger font size */
  datalabeldisplay=(response percent) datalabelloc=inside;
keylegend / noborder title=' '
  position=right across=1
  fillaspect=golden fillheight=11pt;
run;
```

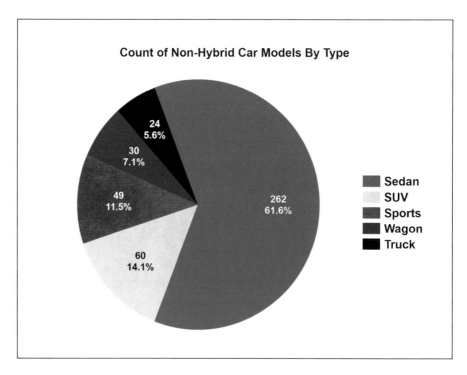

Figure 5-6. Same as Figure 5-5, except software-default starting slice orientation

Listing 5-6. *Code used to create Figure 5-6, changes from Figure 5-5 in bold*

```
ods listing style=GraphFontArial11ptBold gpath="C:\temp" dpi=300;
ods graphics / reset=all noscale width=5.7in height=4.3in
  imagename=
'Fig5-6_RespAndPct_CatLegend_InsideLabels_DefaultSlicing';
title1 'Count of Non-Hybrid Car Models By Type';
title2 color=white 'INVISIBLE Text to create white space';
proc sgpie data=sashelp.cars;
where Type NE 'Hybrid';
styleattrs datacolors=(blue LightGray red purple black);
pie type / otherpercent=0
  sliceorder=respdesc direction=clockwise
  /* startangle=180 startpos=edge These options are removed.
     Accept the defaults instead. */
  datalabelattrs=(size=9pt)
  datalabeldisplay=(response percent) datalabelloc=inside;
keylegend / noborder title=' '
  position=right across=1
  fillaspect=golden fillheight=11pt;
run;
```

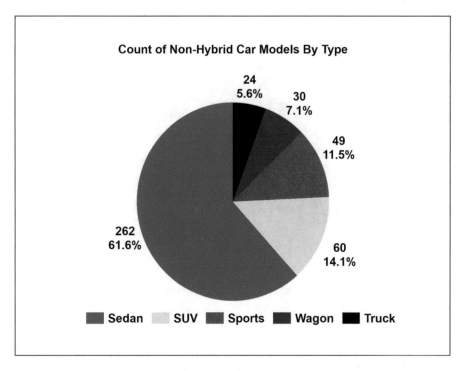

Figure 5-7. Response labels and percent labels outside, legend at the bottom, position and direction of slices intended to "match" that of legend

Listing 5-7. *Code used to create Figure 5-7, changes from Figure 5-6 in bold*

```
ods listing style=GraphFontArial11ptBold gpath="C:\temp" dpi=300;
ods graphics / reset=all noscale width=5.7in height=4.3in
  imagename='Fig5-7_RespAndPct_CatLegend_OutsideLabels';
title1 'Count of Non-Hybrid Car Models By Type';
title2 color=white 'INVISIBLE Text to create white space';
proc sgpie data=sashelp.cars;
where Type NE 'Hybrid';
styleattrs datacolors=(blue LightGray red purple black);
pie type / otherpercent=0
  sliceorder=respdesc direction=counterclockwise
  startangle=90 startpos=edge
  /* datalabelattrs=(size=9pt) Unneeded. No space constraint now. */
  datalabeldisplay=(response percent)
  datalabelloc=outside;
keylegend / noborder title=' '
  /* position=right across=1 defaults now instead */
  fillaspect=golden fillheight=11pt;
run;
```

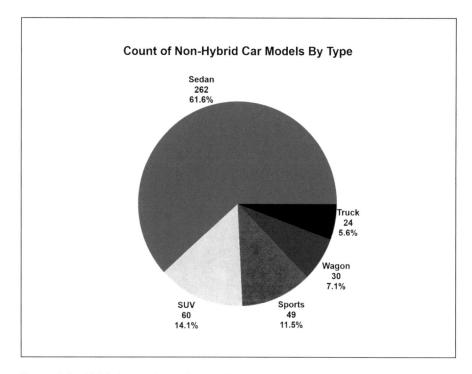

Figure 5-8. All labels outside, easily readable

Listing 5-8. *Code used to create Figure 5-8, changes from Figure 5-7 in bold*

```
ods listing style=GraphFontArial11ptBold gpath="C:\temp" dpi=300;
ods graphics / reset=all noscale width=5.7in height=4.3in
  imagename='Fig5-8_CategoryAndRespAndPct_OutsideLabels';
title1 'Count of Non-Hybrid Car Models By Type';
title2 color=white 'INVISIBLE Text to create white space';
proc sgpie data=sashelp.cars;
where Type NE 'Hybrid';
styleattrs datacolors=(blue LightGray red purple black);
pie type / otherpercent=0
  sliceorder=respdesc direction=counterclockwise
  startangle=0 startpos=edge
  datalabelattrs=(size=8pt) /* appropriate for smallest slice */
  datalabeldisplay=(category response percent)
  datalabelloc=outside;
/* KEYLEGEND statement not applicable */
run;
```

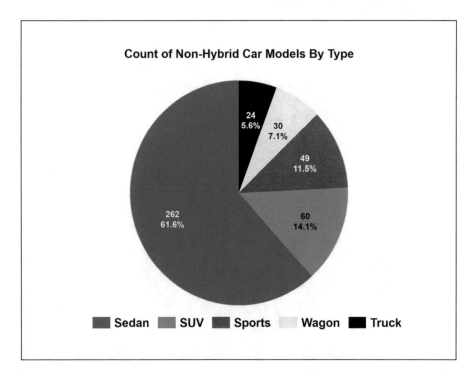

Figure 5-9. Response and percent inside, label colors automatically selected by ODS Graphics, black label somewhat hard to read on darker gray, yellow area fill replaced purple

Listing 5-9. *Code used to create Figure 5-9, changes from Figure 5-8 in bold*

```
ods listing style=GraphFontArial11ptBold gpath="C:\temp" dpi=300;
ods graphics / reset=all noscale width=5.7in height=4.3in
  imagename=
  'Fig5-9_ProblemWithGray_RespAndPct_CatLegend_InsideLabels';
title1 'Count of Non-Hybrid Car Models By Type';
title2 color=white 'INVISIBLE Text to create white space';
proc sgpie data=sashelp.cars;
where Type NE 'Hybrid';
styleattrs datacolors=(blue gray red yellow black);
pie type / otherpercent=0
  sliceorder=respdesc direction=counterclockwise
  startangle=90 startpos=edge
  datalabelattrs=(size=8pt)
  datalabeldisplay=( /* category not in labels */ response percent)
  datalabelloc=inside;
keylegend / noborder title=' '
  fillaspect=golden fillheight=11pt;
run;
```

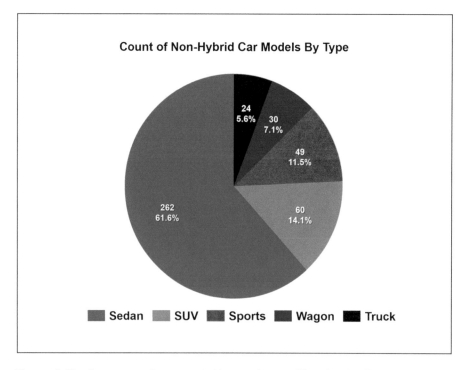

Figure 5-10. Response and percent inside, purple area fill replaced yellow, user-selected white labels, more readable labels on gray

Listing 5-10. *Code used to create Figure 5-10, changes from Figure 5-9 in bold*

```
ods listing style=GraphFontArial11ptBold gpath="C:\temp" dpi=300;
ods graphics / reset=all noscale width=5.7in height=4.3in
  imagename=
  'Fig5-10_YellowToPurple_AllLabelsWhite_ElseSameAsFig5-9';
title1 'Count of Non-Hybrid Car Models By Type';
title2 color=white 'INVISIBLE Text to create white space';
proc sgpie data=sashelp.cars;
where Type NE 'Hybrid';
styleattrs datacolors=(blue gray red purple black);
pie type / otherpercent=0
  sliceorder=respdesc direction=counterclockwise
  startangle=90 startpos=edge
  datalabelattrs=(size=8pt color=white)
  datalabeldisplay=(response percent)
  datalabelloc=inside;
keylegend / noborder title=' '
  fillaspect=golden fillheight=11pt;
run;
```

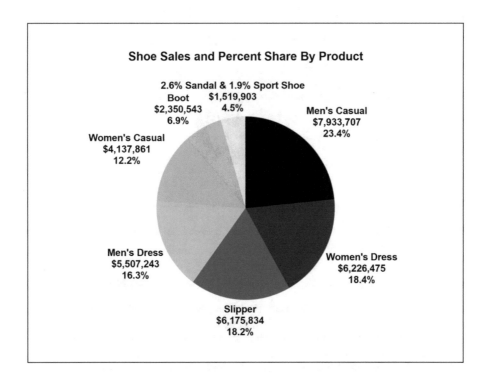

Figure 5-11. Outside labels; informative "Other" slice prevents label collisions

Listing 5-11. *Code used to create Figure 5-11, changes from Figure 5-10 in bold*

```
ods listing style=GraphFontArial11ptBold gpath="C:\temp" dpi=300;
ods graphics / reset=all scale=off width=5.7in height=4.3in
  imagename='Fig5-11_PieOutsideCatRespPctLabels_InformativeOTHER';
title1 'Shoe Sales and Percent Share By Product';
title2 color=white 'INVISIBLE Text to create white space';
proc sgpie data=sashelp.shoes;
styleattrs datacolors=(
BLACK PURPLE CX3333FF CX00FFFF CX00FF00 ORANGE CXFFCC66 CXFFFF00 );
pie Product / response=Sales /* RESPONSE is automatically summed */
  sliceorder=respdesc direction=clockwise
  startangle=90 startpos=edge
  otherpercent=5 /* Use OTHERPERCENT=0 for why OTHER slice needed */
  otherlabel='2.6% Sandal & 1.9% Sport Shoe'
  datalabeldisplay=all /* also includes CATEGORY */
  datalabelattrs=(size=9pt)
  datalabelloc=outside;
run;
```

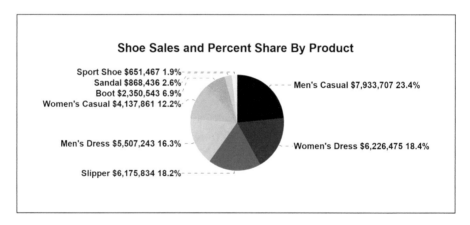

Figure 5-12. Fully informative callout data labels, avoids label collisions without consolidation of small slices into an OTHER slice

Listing 5-12. *Code used to create Figure 5-12, changes from Figure 5-11 in bold*

```
ods listing style=GraphFontArial11ptBold gpath="C:\temp" dpi=300;
ods graphics / reset=all scale=off width=5.7in height=2.5in
  /* My chosen Optimum Height for this width is 2.5 inches.
     Experiment if you wish to arrive at a height you prefer. */
  imagename='Fig5-12_PieWithCallOutLabelsForCatRespPct';
title1 'Shoe Sales and Percent Share By Product';
proc sgpie data=sashelp.shoes;
styleattrs datacolors=(
```

```
BLACK PURPLE CX3333FF CX00FFFF CX00FF00 ORANGE CXFFCC66 CXFFFF00);
pie Product / response=Sales otherpercent=0
  sliceorder=respdesc direction=clockwise
  startangle=90 startpos=edge
  datalabeldisplay=all
  datalabelattrs=(size=8pt)
  datalabelloc=callout;
run;
```

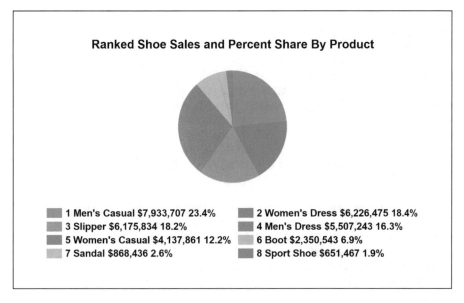

Figure 5-13. Two-across Fully Informative Legend at the bottom, slice rank included in legend, default colors; absence of labels makes collisions impossible, but with necessity to visually connect legend entries with their slices

Listing 5-13. *Code used to create Figure 5-13, changes from Figure 5-12 in bold*

```
/* Prepare a custom CATEGORY variable that includes the real
   category with RESPONSE and PERCENT appended and embedded */

proc summary data=sashelp.shoes;
class Product;
var Sales;
output out=work.Totals sum=;
run;

proc sort data=Totals;
by descending Sales;
run;
```

```
data work.Rank_Product_Sales_Percent;
keep Rank_Product_Sales_Percent Ranked_Product Product Sales;
retain TotalSales 0;
length Rank_Product_Sales_Percent $ 34 Ranked_Product $ 16;
set work.Totals;
if _type_ EQ 0
then do;
  TotalSales = Sales;
  delete;
end;
Rank_Product_Sales_Percent =
  put(_N_ - 1,1.)                            || ' ' ||
  trim(left(put(Product,$14.)))              || ' ' ||
  trim(left(put(Sales,dollar10.)))           || ' ' ||
  trim(left(put((Sales/TotalSales)*100,4.1))) || '%';
Ranked_Product = substr(Rank_Product_Sales_Percent,1,16);
run;

ods listing style=GraphFontArial11ptBold gpath="C:\temp" dpi=300;
ods graphics / reset=all noscale width=5.7in height=3.5in
  maxlegendarea=50
  imagename=
  'Fig5-13_RankedSales_TwoAcrossBottomFullInfoLegend_DefaultColors';
title1 'Ranked Shoe Sales and Percent Share By Product';
title2 color=white 'INVISIBLE Text to create white space';
proc sgpie data=work.Rank_Product_Sales_Percent;
/* no STYLEATTRS statement. Taking default colors. */
pie Rank_Product_Sales_Percent / otherpercent=0
  response=Sales
  sliceorder=respdesc direction=clockwise
  startangle=90 startpos=edge
  /* DATALABELLOC is not needed. No labels to display. */
  datalabeldisplay=none;
keylegend / noborder
  title='White Space' titleattrs=(color=white)
  /* default space between pie and border looks too small */
  across=2 position=bottom
  valueattrs=(size=9pt)
  fillaspect=golden fillheight=9pt;
run;
```

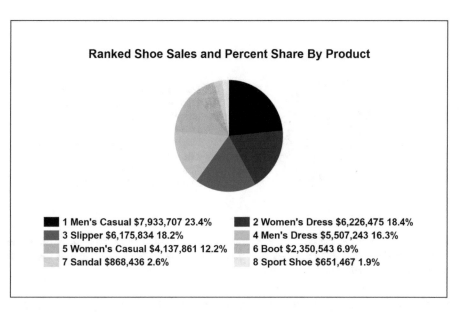

Figure 5-14. Same as Figure 5-13 except custom colors

Listing 5-14. *Code used to create Figure 5-14, changes from Figure 5-13 in bold*

```
/* requires the data preprocessing from Listing 5-13 to have created
   input data set work.Rank_Product_Sales_Percent */

ods listing style=GraphFontArial11ptBold gpath="C:\temp" dpi=300;
ods graphics / reset=all noscale width=5.7in height=3.5in
  maxlegendarea=50
  imagename=
  'Fig5-14_RankedSales_TwoAcrossBottomFullInfoLegend_CustomColors';
title1 'Ranked Shoe Sales and Percent Share By Product';
title2 color=white 'INVISIBLE Text to create white space';
proc sgpie data=work.Rank_Product_Sales_Percent;
styleattrs datacolors=(
BLACK PURPLE CX3333FF CX00FFFF CX00FF00 ORANGE CXFFCC66 CXFFFF00 );
pie Rank_Product_Sales_Percent / otherpercent=0
  response=Sales
  sliceorder=respdesc direction=clockwise
  startangle=90 startpos=edge
  datalabeldisplay=none;
keylegend / noborder
  title='White Space' titleattrs=(color=white)
  across=2 position=bottom
  valueattrs=(size=9pt)
  fillaspect=golden fillheight=9pt;
run;
```

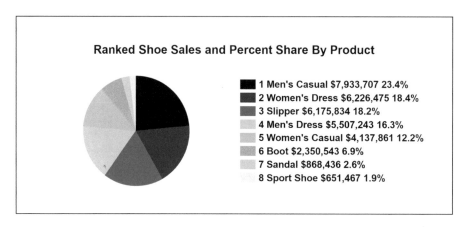

Figure 5-15. Same as Figure 5-14 except one-across legend at the side. Now position and direction of slices "match" that of legend—easier to visually connect legend entries with their slices, and pie "height" is comparable to legend height

Listing 5-15. *Code used to create Figure 5-15, changes from Figure 5-14 in bold*

```
/* requires the data preprocessing from Listing 5-13 to have created
   input data set work.Rank_Product_Sales_Percent */

ods listing style=GraphFontArial11ptBold gpath="C:\temp" dpi=300;
ods graphics / reset=all noscale width=5.7in maxlegendarea=50
  height=2.5in /* height=2.5in for the specified width and font size
                  is the minimum height needed to fit the legend.
                  It also is chosen to provide pie and legend with
                  matching heights. */
  imagename=
'Fig5-15_RankedPie_OneAcrossRightSideFullInfoLegend_CustomColors';
title1 'Ranked Shoe Sales and Percent Share By Product';
title2 color=white 'INVISIBLE Text to create white space';
proc sgpie data=work.Rank_Product_Sales_Percent;
styleattrs datacolors=(
BLACK PURPLE CX3333FF CX00FFFF CX00FF00 ORANGE CXFFCC66 CXFFFF00 );
pie Rank_Product_Sales_Percent / otherpercent=0
  response=Sales
  sliceorder=respdesc direction=clockwise
  startangle=90 startpos=edge
  datalabeldisplay=none;
keylegend / noborder title=''
  across=1 position=right
  valueattrs=(size=9pt)
  fillaspect=golden fillheight=9pt;
run;
```

A Tour of What You Can Do with Donut Charts

A donut chart should be ordered and include categories (descriptions), values, and percents. A donut chart is simply a pie chart with a hole in the middle.

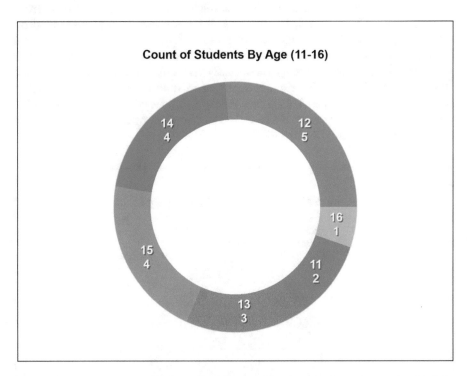

Figure 5-16. Donut chart defaults except slicing and label color white—better than black for readability

Listing 5-16. Code used to create Figure 5-16, changes from Figure 5-1 in bold

```
ods listing style=GraphFontArial11ptBold gpath="C:\temp" dpi=300;
title1 'Count of Students By Age (11-16)';
title2 color=white 'INVISIBLE Text to create white space';
ods graphics / reset=all noscale width=5.7in height=4.3in
  imagename=
  'Fig5-16_DefaultDonutChart_ExceptSlicingAndDataLabelColor';
proc sgpie data=sashelp.class;
/* No STYLEATTRS. Taking default colors */
donut age / otherpercent=0
  sliceorder=respdesc direction=counterclockwise
```

```
startangle=0 startpos=edge
datalabelattrs=(color=white); /* needed for contrast
          with default colors to maximize readability */
run;
```

As of the time of writing for this book, PROC SGPIE was in Preproduction status. The Production version's output might differ in some respects from what is shown here. It might cure the phenomenon of unrequested drop shadows on data labels, which you can see in Figure 5-16 which uses white data labels and where some of the area fills are light enough to show the drop shadows. The drop shadows are most easily discernible on the light green area fill for age 16. With black data labels, the drop shadow is hidden as a thicker contour for the character. This drop shadow anomaly, which is not present for other ODS Graphics graphs, is a needless decoration, often not apparent, and never an asset to visual communication.

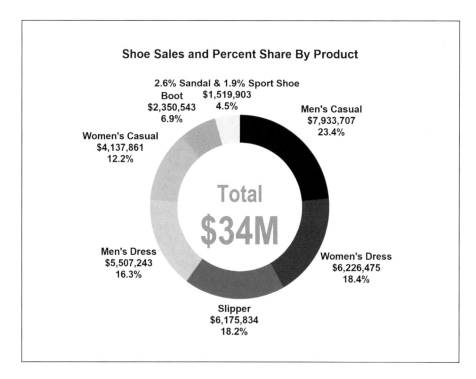

Figure 5-17. Donut chart analogue of Figure 5-11 pie chart

In the donut chart hole, you can display text with the HOLELABEL option and any numeric variable with the HOLEVALUE option, but there is no font size control for the hole label and hole value.

To control the text characteristics of that information, there are the HOLELABELATTRS and HOLEVALUEATTRS options, but with the unexpected limitation of no access to the SIZE control. The software automatically sizes the text based on space available and length of the text. Furthermore, the software also does automatic abbreviation of large numbers and large dollar values. This comes with a loss in precision, but approximate information is better than no information. An abbreviated value is easier to read, more quickly read, and easier to remember—all of which are assets for communication-effective visual communication.

To try to prevent truncation of precision for numbers, you can create the number as a symbolic variable of characters, not numbers (as in the code for Figure 5-22, but there customized brevity was chosen). The symbolic variable is used with HOLELABEL="&YourSymVarName". If the resolved string of characters is too long for the hole size, it will be unprettily truncated. Your next step would be to define a custom-truncated symbol to see whether that might fit. If that fails, there are the reliable alternatives of a subtitle or footnote, or maybe the use of the INSET statement, but none of those options will put the number in the donut hole. Donut hole displays are a gimmick, not a communication necessity, and not necessarily a communication enhancer. With subtitle, footnote, or INSET statement, you regain control of text size for the number or text value.

When a hole value is present, the font size for a hole label is limited to 60% of the font size chosen by the software for the hole value. If no hole value is present, then the hole size determines the font size chosen for the hole label by the software.

Listing 5-17. *Code used to create Figure 5-17, changes from Figure 5-11 in bold*

```
proc summary data=sashelp.shoes;
class Product;
var Sales;
output out=work.FromSUMMARY sum=;
run;

data _null_; /* Provide the grand total for the hole value */
set work.FromSUMMARY;
where _type_ EQ 0;
call symput('GrandTotalSales',trim(left(Sales)));
run;
```

```
ods listing style=GraphFontArial11ptBold gpath="C:\temp" dpi=300;
ods graphics / reset=all scale=off width=5.7in height=4.3in
  imagename=
  'Fig5-17_DonutOutsideCatRespPct_HoleInfo_InformativeOTHER';
title1 'Shoe Sales and Percent Share By Product';
title2 color=white 'INVISIBLE Text to create white space';
proc sgpie data=sashelp.shoes;
styleattrs datacolors=(
BLACK PURPLE CX3333FF CX00FFFF CX00FF00 ORANGE CXFFCC66 CXFFFF00);
donut Product / response=Sales
  sliceorder=respdesc direction=clockwise
  startangle=90 startpos=edge
  otherpercent=5
  otherlabel='2.6% Sandal & 1.9% Sport Shoe'
  datalabeldisplay=all
  datalabelattrs=(size=9pt)
  datalabelloc=outside
  holelabel='Total'
  holelabelattrs=(family='Arial Narrow' color=CX009900)
  holevalue=&GrandTotalSales
  holevalueattrs=(family='Arial Narrow' color=CX009900);
run;
```

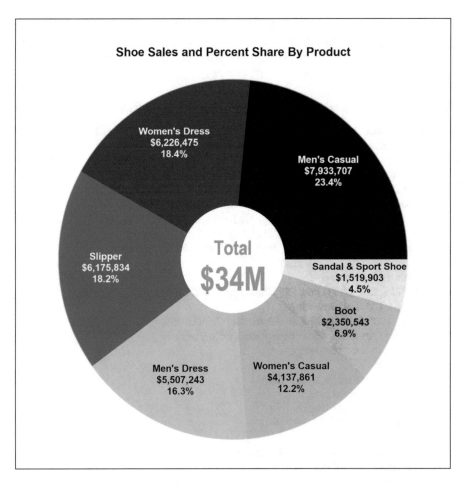

Figure 5-18. Similar to Figure 5-17, but with labels inside of a thicker donut (RINGSIZE=0.7), and different slice start angle and rotation direction

The RINGSIZE option is unique to the donut chart and specifies how much of the radius is used for the donut. With a default of 0.3, it ranges from 0 for an unusable donut chart to, nominally, 1. One might expect RINGSIZE=1 to cause reversion to a pie chart. However, the practical maximum value is 0.85. A donut chart with RINGSIZE greater than 0.85 will be created exactly the same way as the donut chart for RINGSIZE=0.85.

Increasing the RINGSIZE is essential when you need to fit INSIDE labels as in Figure 5-18. Decreasing RINGSIZE can accommodate more text in the donut hole.

The choice of the word RINGSIZE for this option is interesting and telling. To my eye, a default donut chart looks like a ring, not a donut. I speak with the advantage of a long acquaintance with, and authority of experience of enjoyment of, real donuts.

Listing 5-18. *Code used to create Figure 5-18, changes from Figure 5-17 in bold*

```
/* requires the data preprocessing from Listing 5-17 to have been
   done to create the GrandTotalSales macro variable */

ods listing style=GraphFontArial11ptBold gpath="C:\temp" dpi=300;
ods graphics / reset=all scale=off width=5.7in height=5.7in
  imagename=
  'Fig5-18_DonutInsideCatRespPct_HoleInfo_LessInformativeOTHER';
title1 'Shoe Sales and Percent Share By Product';
title2 color=white 'INVISIBLE Text to create white space';
proc sgpie data=sashelp.shoes;
styleattrs datacolors=(
BLACK PURPLE CX3333FF CX00FFFF CX00FF00 ORANGE CXFFCC66 CXFFFF00);
donut Product / response=Sales
  ringsize=0.7 /* make space for inside labels */
  sliceorder=respdesc direction=counterclockwise
  startangle=0 startpos=edge
  otherpercent=5
  otherlabel='Sandal & Sport Shoe'
  datalabeldisplay=all
  datalabelattrs=(size=9pt)
  datalabelloc=inside
  holelabel='Total'
  holelabelattrs=(family='Arial Narrow' color=CX009900)
  holevalue=&GrandTotalSales
  holevalueattrs=(family='Arial Narrow' color=CX009900);
run;
```

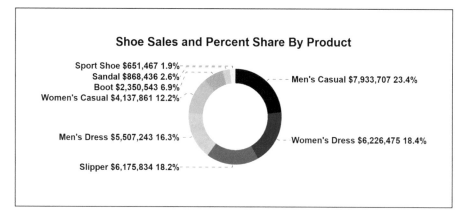

Figure 5-19. Donut chart analogue of Figure 5-12 pie chart with CALLOUT labels

Figure 5-19 is created by changing the IMAGENAME value and replacing PIE with DONUT in the PIE statement in the code for Figure 5-12.

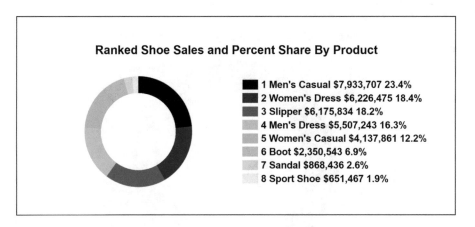

Figure 5-20. Donut chart analogue of Figure 5-15 pie chart with legend

Figure 5-20 is created by changing the IMAGENAME value and replacing PIE with DONUT in the PIE statement in the code for Figure 5-15. But it requires that the code for data preprocessing used in Listing 5-13 be run so that the input data set work.Rank_Product_Sales_Percent is available.

What Was Really My First Donut Chart

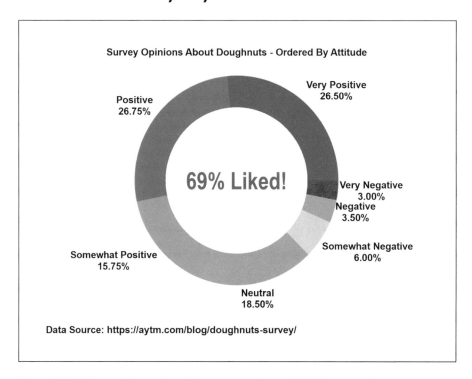

Figure 5-21. Donut chart ordered by category color-coded relative significance

When searching the Internet in a quest to find out who invented the donut chart, when, and how it was used, I never found the answers to those questions, but I stumbled across an article about people's preferences with respect to donuts. It included a two-part graphic (not a donut chart) concerning the information in Figure 5-21, but presented in a manner that I decided needed a different solution. Since the data was about donuts, a donut chart was the obvious solution. In this case, rather than order the slices by size, which is my usual recommendation, I decided to order them by comparative meaning, with color coding to visually signal that comparison.

Listing 5-21. *Code used to create Figure 5-21*

```
data work.ForChart;
length RankedOpinion $ 19;
infile cards;
input @1 Percent 5.2 @7 Opinion $17. @25 RankByAttitude 1.;
PercentAsDecimalPartOfOne = Percent/ 100;
RankedOpinion = put(RankByAttitude,1.) || ':' || Opinion;
```

```
cards;
03.00 Very Negative      7
03.50 Negative           6
06.00 Somewhat Negative 5
18.50 Neutral            4
15.75 Somewhat Positive 3
26.75 Positive           2
26.50 Very Positive      1
; run;

data work.ToFormat;
retain fmtname 'OpinionFORMAT' type 'C';
set work.ForChart
  (rename=(RankedOpinion=START Opinion=LABEL));
run;
proc format cntlin=work.ToFormat; run;

proc sort data=work.ForChart(drop=Opinion);
by RankedOpinion; run;

ods listing style=GraphFontArial9ptBold gpath="C:\temp" dpi=300;
ods graphics / reset=all noscale width=5.7in height=4.3in
  imagename='Fig5-21_DonutChart_For_Opinions_About_DoughNuts';
title1 'Survey Opinions About Doughnuts - Ordered By Attitude';
title2 color=white 'INVISIBLE Text to create white space';
footnote1 color=white 'INVISIBLE Text to create white space';
footnote2 justify=left
  'Data Source: https://aytm.com/blog/doughnuts-survey/';
proc sgpie data=work.ForChart;
STYLEATTRS DATACOLORS=(CX0000FF CX6666FF CX9999FF CX999999
                       CXFFCCCC CXFF9999 CXFF0000);
donut RankedOpinion / response=PercentAsDecimalPartOfOne
  otherpercent=0
  sliceorder=UNFORMATTED direction=counterclockwise
  startangle=0 startpos=edge
  holelabel='69% Liked!'
  holelabelattrs=
    (family='Arial Narrow' weight=Bold color=blue)
  datalabeldisplay=(category response)
  datalabelloc=outside;
format RankedOpinion $OpinionFORMAT.;
format PercentAsDecimalPartOfOne percent6.2;
run;
footnote; /* Prevent footnotes from being inherited by later
  code submissions during the same session. Alternatively,
  starting later programs with FOOTNOTE; can prevent that. */
```

My Latest Donut Charts

On the day that I was finishing this chapter, I opened a hardcopy 2020 Annual Report from the Bank of America. (To find it online, search with "Bank of America 2020 annual report." When the report is accessed online, your viewing tool might count the front and inside cover as page numbers 1 and 2. Page numbers cited here are those physically printed on the pages.) I'm always curious to see how corporations present information graphically. A few years after I first touted the simplicity and power of The Pac-Man Pie Chart, I had the satisfaction of seeing the concept used in the annual report of the corporation that owned my employer, Miller Brewing Company.

On page 4 of the report are two bar charts for financial data. There are no pie charts in the report. Donut charts are now the fashionable alternative, of course. And, as I mentioned earlier as the distinguishing feature of donut charts, each of the report's donut charts includes a big number in the donut hole.

More interesting in the report are the donut charts on page 31. They are about human resources data. Their layout is different from that of the donut charts in Figure 5-22. Their important segment is dark blue and in all cases starts at 12 o'clock (90 degrees), sweeping in the clockwise direction. Each chart has a big percent in the donut hole, but there are no labels or values on the perimeter of the donuts. Instead, below each donut and therefore below that big percent is text. The unlabeled "Other" pieces are minimally conspicuous white, which is visible on the light blue background for the images. So, each illustration is, in effect, a sentence that starts with a donut bite, continues with a big percent as a hole label, and finishes with words. In Chapter 1, I recommended using TITLE1 as a headline for the graph. For these donut charts, the entire composite of "concatenated" image, percent number, and words is a headline.

The utter simplicity and focused design of those four donut charts reminded me of the Pac-Man pie charts in Figure 1-15 in Chapter 1. So, I decided to create the donut charts in Figure 5-22. There are two noteworthy points about these charts.

First, since, as of the time of writing this book, the Preproduction version of PROC SGPIE does not support the use of a discrete attribute map to specify the color of the data labels, it is impossible to make the label for the Other slice disappear by assigning white as its color.

Second, this is the first instance where it was necessary for me to use the STARTPOS=CENTER option, where CENTER is actually the default (which I usually override with EDGE). I can describe what happens with a starting position of EDGE for donut chunks that are located at 90 degrees, but I encourage the reader to perform that experiment to see the results. In that case, each donut is a different size, and the two labels for each donut occur at different locations around the perimeter. The "parallel" layout for the three images in Figure 5-22 is part of their visual charm. Interpretation of a set of graphs is facilitated by not having to "recalibrate your perception" from image to image. Consistency is always a communication asset.

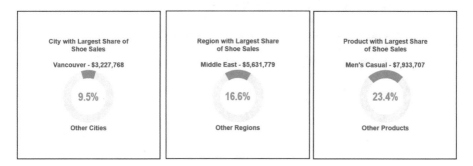

Figure 5-22. Donut charts that focus on a single not-Other slice, a conceptual analogue of The Pac-Man Pie Chart (shown in Figure 1-15 in Chapter 1)

For the code for the Region and Product charts, see Listing A5-22 in Appendix A, which also includes the code from Listing 5-22.

Listing 5-22. *Code used to create Figure 5-22 (only the Cities chart)*

```
ods listing style=GraphFontArial6ptBold gpath="C:\temp" dpi=300;

proc summary data=sashelp.shoes;
class Region Subsidiary Product;
var Sales;
output out=work.FromSUMMARY sum=;
run;

data work.Cities work.Regions work.Products;
set work.FromSummary;
if _type_ EQ 0
then call symput('GrandTotalSales',trim(left(Sales)));
else if _type_ EQ 1 then output work.Products;
else if _type_ EQ 2 then output work.Cities;
else if _type_ EQ 4 then output work.Regions;
run;

proc sort data=work.Cities;
by descending Sales;
run;

data work.MaxSalesCityAndOthers;
set work.Cities;
```

```
if _N_ EQ 1;
call symput('PctMaxCity',
  trim(left(put(Sales/&GrandTotalSales,percent6.1))));
  /* it is necessary to use the percent6.1 format, to allocate
     enough width for (N.N%), where parenthesis is for negative,
     even though the value is positive */
  /* in DATA steps for MaxSalesRegionAndOthers
     and MaxSalesProductAndOthers, use percent7.1 */
CityLabel = trim(left(Subsidiary)) || ' - ' ||
          trim(left(put(Sales,dollar10.)));
output;
Sales = &GrandTotalSales - Sales;
CityLabel = 'Other Cities';
output;
stop;
run;

ods graphics / reset=all scale=off width=1.85in height=1.85in
  imagename='Fig5-22_Left_Donut_HoleInfo_MaxSalesPct_City';
title1 color=blue 'City with Largest Share of Shoe Sales';
title2 height=3pt color=white 'INVISIBLE Text for white space';
proc sgpie data=work.MaxSalesCityAndOthers;
styleattrs datacolors=(CX009900 CXEEEEEE);
donut CityLabel / response=Sales
  sliceorder=respasc /* start with the smallest donut bite */
  holelabel="&PctMaxCity"
  holelabelattrs=(family='Arial Narrow' color=CX009900)
  startangle=90 /* accepting the default STARTPOS=CENTER */
  datalabelattrs=(color=blue)
  datalabeldisplay=(category)
datalabelloc=outside;
run;
```

Summary

A donut chart is simply a pie chart with a hole in the middle. All of the syntax and capabilities for a pie chart apply to a donut chart. To convert a pie chart to a donut chart, simply substitute DONUT for PIE in the PIE statement. The remaining remarks, for brevity, only mention pie charts, but they also apply to donut charts.

Displaying precise numbers has always been a part of pie charts. Since it's always automatically computable by the software and therefore available, be sure to include Percent, not just the Response. However, because Percent is not an input variable for the PROC step, the FORMAT statement cannot be used to get more precision than the software-selected format with only one decimal position, tenths. The only way to overcome that is to create a Category variable that includes the percent to the precision that you prefer. You can suppress the display of the software-computed percent as a label with

DATALABELDISPLAY=(CATEGORY RESPONSE). The use of an even more information-rich Category variable is the key to the legend design for Figures 5-13, 5-14, 5-15, and 5-20.

The default slice order is the unformatted value of the Category. So, to show the viewer what's important, use the RESPDESC option to order the slices by descending size (unless smallness is better than largeness). To avoid creating questions, rather than answering them, it is best to specify OTHER=0 to suppress creation of an "Other" slice. If you *must* create an Other slice, whenever possible give it an at least partially informative label such as that in Figures 5-11, 5-17, and 5-18.

Ordering the slices by size collects all of the smaller ones adjacent to each other, which increases the likelihood of collisions between the slice labels. As long as readability is not sacrificed, the problem might be cured by using smaller labels. A better alternative can be the use of CALLOUT labels as in Figures 5-12 and 5-19. That solution keeps the labels connected to the slices with a line.

An always successful solution is a Fully Informative Legend, such as that in Figures 5-13, 5-14, 5-15, and 5-20. With a legend, an Other slice is never necessary. Even multiple slices of vanishing size are successfully represented with full information as to Category, Response, Percent, and, if provided, Rank. To assure easy and reliable visual association between slices and legend entries, use FILLASPECT=GOLDEN to get legend color samples that are rectangles (with more area than the default squares) and sufficient FILLHEIGHT (always matched to the SIZE of the legend values—when looking at examples here I recently noticed fills are a bit larger than values, so that fills 1 pt size smaller might be sufficient). In any case, when using a legend, I recommend arranging the (descending size) pie slices to correspond to the arrangement of the legend.

For a legend at the right side, arrange the slices to be read from the top, starting the first slice at 180 degrees (9 o'clock), and clockwise around the pie, as in Figure 5-5. In the case of the data for Figure 5-5, the first slice fills the entire top half of the pie and more. In the more general case, where that first slice might not exceed one half of the pie, the starting position must be 90 degrees (12 o'clock), so that it is at the top of the pie and next to the legend.

For a legend at the bottom that is read left to right, you can arrange the slices to be read from the left, starting the first slice at 90 degrees (12 o'clock) if the slice is larger than one half of the pie, and counterclockwise around the pie, as in Figure 5-3. In the more general case, where that first slice might not exceed one half of the pie, the starting position must be 180 degrees (9 o'clock), so that it is at the bottom of the pie and immediately above the legend.

For ODS Graphics, pie charts are implemented with a special, new arrangement as the defaults, as shown in Figure 5-6 (which has one exception to the defaults, namely, its use of DIRECTION=CLOCKWISE). The arrangement defaults are STARTANGLE=0, DIRECTION=COUNTERCLOCKWISE, and STARTPOS=CENTER. For a more customary pie chart, use STARTPOS=EDGE.

An option not demonstrated here is DATASKIN, which is a decoration feature meant to provide a pseudo-3D effect, which has no communication benefits. There are six choices for DATASKIN, for which the best choice is NONE. Though not shown here, I found that the SHEEN dataskin can adversely affect readability for WHITE inside labels. The visual effect of this dataskin relies on a spot of brightness in one area of the pie, with a gradient of decreasing brightness around it. The brightness decreases the contrast of the slice color fill with a white data label, to the detriment of readability.

Whenever using INSIDE labels, it's important to assure readability of the text colors on the slice fill colors. ODS Graphics will, by default, automatically choose black or white for INSIDE labels, slice by slice. In one or more cases, it might not make what you deem to be the best decision for slice-specific label color versus the background fill color, from the standpoint of readability. DATALABELATTRS permits you to only select one color for the labels. If one color is not readable across all of the slice colors used, whether the colors are default or custom, then you must use the STYLEATTRS statement to produce a color palette for which whatever is your *selected* label color is readable on all slices. In Figure 5-9, the software's automatic choice of black text on the shade of gray detracts from readability of the label. For Figure 5-10, all of the slice colors assigned with the STYLEATTRS statement were chosen to assure readability with white labels. If you want to be sure of INSIDE label readability, for that situation, you need to establish a color palette that works with all white labels or all black labels, whichever is your preference.

As of the time of writing for this book, PROC SGPIE was in Preproduction status. The Production version's output might differ in some respects from what is shown here. Please see my remarks earlier in this chapter, in regard to Figure 5-16, about the drop shadow for text anomaly. Drop shadows are a needless decoration and never an asset to visual communication.

Pie charts and donut charts are easy-to-use, popular data visualization tools that deliver image and precise numbers, with graphic elements that can be ordered by importance, all in a universally familiar and unambiguously interpreted format. Unless you use a legend, which is an optional design, the graphic image elements and their precise numbers are immediate to each other or, in the case of callout labels, connected by a line. This distinguishes pie charts and donut charts from the rest of graphs—they always, by structure and tradition, can deliver what's needed for visual inference, both image and precise numbers.

In closing, let me remind you that the simplest possible pie chart or donut chart can be a very effective visual communication. See Figure 1-15 in Chapter 1 for a real-life pie chart example, and see Figure 5-22 for donut chart examples inspired by real-life corporate communication.

Heat Maps

In 1873, Toussaint Loua created a heat map. A heat map is a matrix of color-coded cells for a response variable, typically numeric, using X and Y variables to label the columns and rows. If the X and/or Y data is continuous numeric, those values will be "binned." The full range of the values is divided into subranges or bins. In that case, the bins, when identified by axis values, are represented by midpoints of the subranges, if ODS Graphics presents the axis values, or by the average of the variables' values within each subrange *if using the custom macro provided in this book*. For binned X and Y pairs, the numeric response value for each cell in the matrix can only be some statistic (average, sum, frequency, etc.) for observations with that pair of X and Y values. See examples in Figure 6-1.

© LeRoy Bessler 2023
LeR. Bessler, *Visual Data Insights Using SAS ODS Graphics*,
https://doi.org/10.1007/978-1-4842-8609-8_6

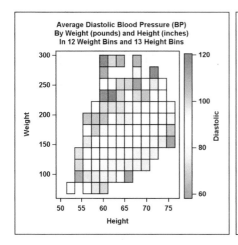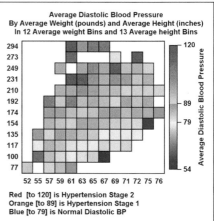

Figure 6-1. Heat map examples: at the left, default axis values, which align with no bins, and default legend; at the right, using a macro, custom bins, aligned axis values, custom legend

---

■ **Note**   The example at the right is a smaller version of Figure 6-15, but without annotation and without that example's explanatory titles and footnotes. No code is provided here.

The X and Y variables can be (a) one or both continuous numeric; (b) one or both discrete numeric; or (c) one or both character, which is always discrete. It can sometimes be convenient to convert continuous numeric data into categories, which are inherently discrete character data. Even binned numeric data is, in effect, a set of categories. Normally, for presentation of categorical data, I urge that it be presented in order of importance, but when there are two categorical keys, one along each axis, there is no way to present the data in order of importance for BOTH keys. A heat map "orders" the cells via color coding, not physically. The ordering via color coding requires a gradient legend with ordered colors from the lowest value at the bottom to the highest value at the top. Unless the response values are discrete, each color used in the legend (sometimes, there is only one color) is presented as a gradient of continuously changing lightness to darkness (or darkness to lightness).

The response variable that is visually delivered in a heat map is often a frequency count, but it can be any variable that is associated with the X and Y variables. Figure 6-1 is for average diastolic blood pressure by weight and height in a population of 5199 persons from the SASHELP.HEART. This data set will be used again later in the chapter to deliver much more informative and useful heat maps.

It is impossible to deliver precise numbers with a gradient legend, except when it can be a strip of solid color blocks, not a gradient. (The characteristics of the heat map legend are specified with a GRADLEGEND statement, even when the legend is not a color gradient. The legend is a three-color gradient by default.) The solid color blocks must be long enough to be easily distinguishable, as in Figure 6-18. The associated COLORRESPONSE variable, which is the HEATMAP statement option used to identify which variable is to be reflected in the legend, must have discrete values. The combination of the number of values and the height of the image must be just right to permit long enough color blocks.

More likely to be feasible as a way to deliver precise numbers is to annotate the cells of the matrix, as will be presented in several examples. For annotation, the response variable for the heat map can be continuous or discrete numeric.

Figure 6-1 is clearly unsatisfactory, and the second example is inadequate. This kind of heat map will be addressed, starting with Figure 6-15, after we explore other examples, but of satisfactory heat maps. Despite the fact that it's not a good example, see the code for the left-hand-side heat map in Listing 6-1 to get acquainted with some elements of coding for a heat map.

Listing 6-1. *Code used to create left-hand-side heat map in Figure 6-1*

```
ods listing gpath="C:\temp" dpi=300 style=GraphFontArial6ptBold;
ods graphics / reset=all scale=off width=2.8in height=2.8in
  imagename="Fig6-1_LeftSide_HeatMapForMean_13Xby12YwithGrid";
title1 justify=center "Average Diastolic Blood Pressure (BP)";
title2 justify=center "By Weight (pounds) and Height (inches)";
title3 justify=center "In 12 Weight Bins and 13 Height Bins";
proc sgplot data=sashelp.heart;
where height NE . AND weight NE . AND Diastolic NE .;
/* eliminates 6 observations with missing height & weight */
/* omit null values of the response variable (none actually
   present), which would have no useful value */
heatmap x=height y=weight / colorresponse=Diastolic
  colorstat=mean
  nxbins=13 nybins=12
  outline; /* between cells */
xaxis grid;
yaxis grid;
run;
```

General Remarks About Code Used

Several examples have %INCLUDE statements for code or macros from folder C:\SharedCode, which could instead be any folder or location of your choice.

The following framing code has been more expansively discussed in Chapter 3 in the section "Outer Structure of ODS Graphics Code in Examples." The framing code for all examples in this chapter and others is

```
ods results off; /* verify results by opening the image file,
                    rather than using the SAS Output window */
ods _all_ close; /* avoid unintended consequences
                    and superfluous concurrent output */
< ODS LISTING statement here >
< example-specific code here >
ods listing close; /* ALWAYS Best Practice */
```

For brevity, the example code in listings omits the first two lines and the last one. It is best to add them back at your runtime. (Source code files include them.)

The ODS LISTING statement can vary. All of the examples in this chapter use a statement of the following form, either explicitly in the code listing or generated by a macro, to specify the text characteristics:

```
ods listing style=GraphFontArial10ptBold gpath="C:\temp" dpi=300;
```

but usually with font sizes other than 10pt. The statement assumes that the ODS style GraphFontArial10ptBold has been created. To assure that all of the styles needed in this chapter are available, use this code:

```
%include "C:\SharedCode\AllGraphTextSetup.sas";
%AllGraphTextSetup(5);
%AllGraphTextSetup(6);
%AllGraphTextSetup(7);
%AllGraphTextSetup(8);
%AllGraphTextSetup(10);
%AllGraphTextSetup(12);
```

For more information about ODS custom styles, as well as the source code for the AllGraphTextSetup macro, see the section "Control of Text Attributes with a Custom ODS Style" in Chapter 3. For information about options for direct control of text attributes, which can override the default text attributes that are set up by an ODS style, see the section "Text Attributes Control in ODS Graphics" in Chapter 3.

If your heat map includes a gradient legend, and you wish to control legend values' text characteristics, you *must* use an ODS style. The GRADLEGEND statement does not support the VALUEATTRS option.

In closing this section, here is a simple tip. For heat maps, never use the NOBORDER option on PROC SGPLOT. It can sometimes cause one of the four sides of the heat map matrix to be suppressed. (That has been my experience.) A border on the matrix of cells is the default. I can think of no harm, functional or aesthetic, that the border does.

Types of Heat Maps

When the X and Y variables are continuous numeric, the total range of the data for each axis is divided into bins or subranges. This must be the case when those variables are, for example, height and weight, as in Figure 6-1, or MilesPerGallon and horsepower.

The axes can instead be for character variables, like region and product, in which case the bins are discrete categorical values. Discrete categories can be character or numeric values.

A third situation possible is for one axis as discrete categories and the other as continuous numeric.

There are two other situations that can arise.

You can convert a numeric range into subranges to each of which you assign a character categorical label, such as high, medium, and low.

When the count of numeric values is reasonably small, you can convert them to character values, so that you end up with bins of one X or Y value each.

Heat Maps with Character Variables for X and Y

Using the SASHELP.CARS data set, let's first create a heat map, using Type (Sedan, SUV, etc.) and Origin (place of manufacture: USA, Europe, or Asia). See Figure 6-2 for a simple example.

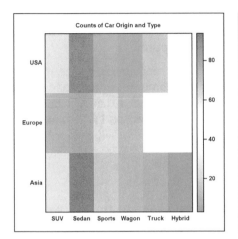 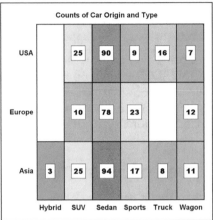

Figure 6-2 and 6-3. Left is a default heat map. Right is annotated and has no legend.

Axis values in Figure 6-3 can be larger because no horizontal space is used for a legend. With a quick inspection of this small heat map, the viewer can readily infer that darker blue is much smaller and darker red is much larger. The color gradient legend provided as a default in Figure 6-2 makes it impossible to determine any precise values. Also, for me, the lack of outlines between the colored cells is visually disturbing. The annotated cells in truly usable Figure 6-3 include a white backfill to make the precise values easily readable. The default legend that is used in Figure 6-1 and the color coding in both Figures 6-2 and 6-3 are, in ODS Graphics, called the ThreeColorRamp.

Listing 6-2. *Code used to create Figure 6-2*

```
ods listing gpath="C:\temp" dpi=300 style=GraphFontArial5ptBold;
ods graphics / reset=all scale=off width=2.8in height=2.8in
  imagename="Fig6-2_HeatMapDefaultLegendNoOutlines";
title1 justify=center "Counts of Car Origin and Type";
proc sgplot data=sashelp.cars;
heatmap x=type y=origin;
  /* When COLORRESPONSE is not specified,
     default processing determines the frequency count,
     and uses that to color the heat map.
     If you DO specify COLORRESPONSE,
     then that variable's values are used to color the heat map.
     Default frequency counts and in-step-computed statistics
     are not available to be used to annotate the cells.
     Any variable to be used for annotation,
     as discussed in Listing 6-3,
     must be in the input to this PROC. */
```

```
xaxis display=(nolabel noticks);
yaxis display=(nolabel noticks);
gradlegend / notitle;
run;
```

Listing 6-3. *Code used to create Figure 6-3*

```
/* Make the frequency counts available as input to PROC SGPLOT
   for use in both the HEATMAP statement and the TEXT statement */
proc freq data=sashelp.cars noprint;
tables type*origin /
  out=sasuser.CarsFREQout; /* data set persists for other use */
run;

ods listing gpath="C:\temp" dpi=300 style=GraphFontArial6ptBold;
ods graphics / reset=all scale=off width=2.8in height=2.8in
  imagename="Fig6-3_AnnotatedHeatMap";
title1 justify=center "Counts of Car Origin and Type";
proc sgplot data=sasuser.CarsFREQout noautolegend;
heatmap x=type y=origin /
  colorresponse=count /* from PROC FREQ */
  outline; /* outline is between the heat map cells
             (there is an OUTLINECOLOR option) */
text x=type y=origin text=count /
  strip /* remove any leading or trailing blanks on the text */
  backfill /* in a box around the text,
             overlay the cell fill color,
             so that text is easily readable */
  fillattrs=(color=white) /* IMPORTANT since the default
                            BackFill color is NOT white */
  outline  /* around the BackFill */
  textattrs=(family='Arial Black');
  /* using Arial Black, which is thicker than Arial,
     for maximum readability */
xaxis display=(noticks nolabel);
  /* Omitting the legend makes more horizontal space available
     to accommodate the larger 6pt font for the X axis values.
     The Y axis value size matches. Figure 6-2 uses 5pt. */
yaxis display=(noticks nolabel);
run;
```

Another option is the use of any two color gradient model, such as ColorModel=(LightGreen DarkGreen), which is shown in Figure 6-4. If you instead use an ODS Graphics range attribute map, you can break up the data range into subranges with distinct, more easily and reliably distinguished colors, as shown in Figure 6-5. The legends for these two annotated heat maps are superfluous, but are included so that you can see how color is used in, and to create, a gradient legend. The legends are easily suppressed by including NOAUTOLEGEND on the PROC SGPLOT statement and omitting the GRADLEGEND statement in the PROC step.

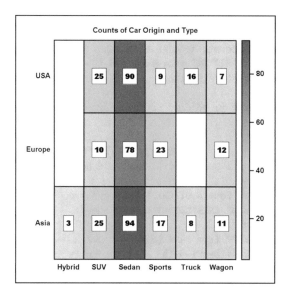

Figure 6-4. Heat map with two color model continuous color gradient using colors LightGreen to DarkGreen

Listing 6-4. Code used to create Figure 6-4

```
ods listing gpath="C:\temp" dpi=300 style=GraphFontArial5ptBold;
ods graphics / reset=all scale=off width=2.8in height=2.8in
  imagename="Fig6-4_AnnotatedHeatMap_WithLightDarkGreenGradient";
title1 justify=center "Counts of Car Origin and Type";
proc sgplot data=sasuser.CarsFREQout;
  /* noautolegend; allow legend UNLIKE Figure 6-3 */
  /* input data was created for Figure 6-3 */
heatmap x=type y=origin / outline
  colormodel=(LightGreen DarkGreen)
  /* light to dark green color gradient for legend */
  colorresponse=count;
text x=type y=origin text=count / textattrs=(family='Arial Black')
  strip backfill fillattrs=(color=white) outline;
xaxis display=(noticks nolabel)
  fitpolicy=none; /* force display of values without tilting */
yaxis display=(noticks nolabel);
gradlegend / notitle;
run;
```

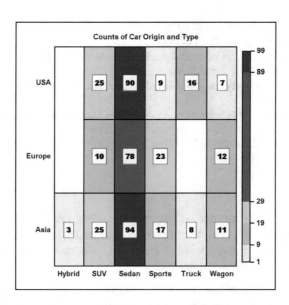

Figure 6-5. Annotated heat map with five distinct colors for area fill and using a range attribute map

Figure 6-5 uses five easily distinguished colors. My initial choice of color palette was five shades of green, but two of them were not easy to distinguish. The choice of distinct hues was more quickly accomplished than experimenting with shades of green would have found a good combination.

Listing 6-5. *Code used to create Figure 6-5*

```
/* Create a Range Attribute map */
data work.RattrMap_FiveColors;
retain id "RangeID";
length min   max $ 2 color $ 8;
input  min $ max $   color $;
/* INPUT statement ignores everything after the color.
   You can use that area for notes. */
datalines;
1   9 CXFFFF00 Yellow
9  19 CX00FF00 Green
19 29 CX00FFFF Cyan (aka Aqua or Turquoise)
29 89 CX0000FF Blue
89 99 Purple
run;

ods listing gpath="C:\temp" dpi=300 style=GraphFontArial5ptBold;
ods graphics / reset=all scale=off width=2.8in height=2.8in
  imagename="Fig6-5_AnnotatedHeatMap_LegendFiveColors";
title1 justify=center "Counts of Car Origin and Type";
```

```
proc sgplot data=sasuser.CarsFREQout
  rattrmap=work.RattrMap_FiveColors;
  /* use this range attribute map instead of a colormodel */
heatmap x=type y=origin / outline
  rattrid=RangeID /* key to relevant information in RattrMap */
  colorresponse=count;
text x=type y=origin text=count / textattrs=(family='Arial Black')
  strip backfill fillattrs=(color=white) outline;
xaxis display=(noticks nolabel) fitpolicy=none;
yaxis display=(noticks nolabel);
gradlegend / notitle;
run;
```

There is an RATTRID variable since a range attribute map can contain multiple range attribute definitions for different purposes, each range and color definition set being distinguishable from the others by the value of the ID variable in the RATTRMAP data set.

So far, the readability of annotation in heat maps has been assured by using backfill of white (with an outline—not essential to readability). An alternative that requires more work is to omit the backfill, but assure that the text color has sufficient contrast with the cell area fill. A benefit of this alternative is that more of the area fill color shows. If the annotation is large, and the cell area is not substantially larger, when using BACKFILL, very little of the area fill will be visible. That situation defeats the purpose of color coding by making it difficult to associate the area fill color with its, admittedly very approximately ascertainable, location on the gradient legend. Even if color association with the legend is of no use for precise knowledge, the color differences DO serve the purpose of visual comparison of relative magnitude of the measure of interest. It should be noted that there is a BACKLIGHT option for the TEXT statement, which takes up much, much less of the cell area. It creates a halo of contrasting color around the text. Its use will be shown in a later example. For the example of Figure 6-6, I prefer a different alternative to BACKFILL and BACKLIGHT. If you experiment with those options for this particular heat map, you will understand my choice.

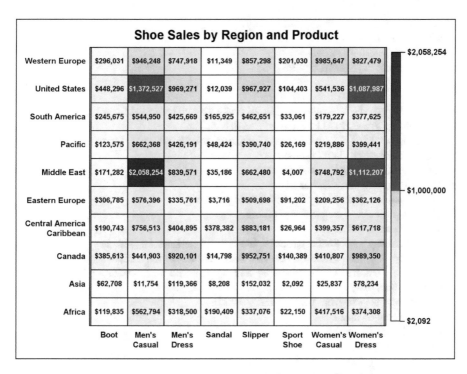

Shoe Sales by Region and Product								
Western Europe	$296,031	$946,248	$747,918	$11,349	$857,298	$201,030	$985,647	$827,479
United States	$448,296	$1,372,527	$969,271	$12,039	$967,927	$104,403	$541,536	$1,087,987
South America	$245,675	$544,950	$425,669	$165,925	$462,651	$33,061	$179,227	$377,625
Pacific	$123,575	$662,368	$426,191	$48,424	$390,740	$26,169	$219,886	$399,441
Middle East	$171,282	$2,058,254	$839,571	$35,186	$662,480	$4,007	$748,792	$1,112,207
Eastern Europe	$306,785	$576,396	$335,761	$3,716	$509,698	$91,202	$209,256	$362,126
Central America Caribbean	$190,743	$756,513	$404,895	$378,382	$883,181	$26,964	$399,357	$617,718
Canada	$385,613	$441,903	$920,101	$14,798	$952,751	$140,389	$410,807	$989,350
Asia	$62,708	$11,754	$119,366	$8,208	$152,032	$2,092	$25,837	$78,234
Africa	$119,835	$562,794	$318,500	$190,409	$337,076	$22,150	$417,516	$374,308
	Boot	Men's Casual	Men's Dress	Sandal	Slipper	Sport Shoe	Women's Casual	Women's Dress

Color scale: $2,058,254 — $1,000,000 — $2,092

Figure 6-6. Annotated heat map with two continuous color gradient ranges. Text and area fill color contrast assures annotation readability

Using a range attribute map with the ALTCOLOR variable can deliver color contrast between text and area fill to assure annotation readability.

Listing 6-6. *Code used to create Figure 6-6*

```
data work.RattrMap_BlueGradients_BWtext;
retain id "RangeID";
length min    max $ 7 color    altcolor
  colormodel1    colormodel2 $ 18;
input  min $ max $    color $ altcolor $
  colormodel1 $ colormodel2 $;
/* altcolor controls the text color */
/* colormodel1 and colormodel2 specify
   start and end of color gradient ranges
   (here, the two subranges) */
datalines;
_min_ 1000000 . Black White LightBlue
1000000 _max_ . White Blue DarkBlue
run;
```

```
proc summary data=sashelp.shoes nway;
class region product;
var sales;
output out=work.ToHeatMap sum=;
run;

ods listing gpath="C:\temp" dpi=300 style=GraphFontArial7ptBold;
ods graphics / reset=all scale=off width=5.7in
   imagename=" Fig6-6_AnnoHeatMapBlueGrads_AnnoVsCellColorContrast";
title1 height=11pt justify=center
   'Shoe Sales by Region and Product';
proc sgplot data=work.ToHeatMap
   rattrmap=work.RattrMap_BlueGradients_BWtext;
heatmap x=product y=region / outline
   colorresponse=sales
   name='heatmap' /* NAME= assures that the Gradient Legend is
                associated with the heat map area fill color.
            Otherwise it would be set up for the text color. */
   rattrid=RangeID;
text x=product y=region text=sales / strip
   colorresponse=sales
   textattrs=(size=6pt)
   rattrid=RangeID;
yaxis display=(noline noticks nolabel)
   fitpolicy=splitalways splitchar='/';
xaxis display=(noline noticks nolabel)
   fitpolicy=splitalways splitchar=' ';
gradlegend 'heatmap' / notitle;
run;
```

Heat Map with Multifunction Annotation and a Categorical Response Variable

In a heat map, you can annotate the cells with any data elements available in the input data set. The only limit is on space and readability. A heat map can use color coding for more than frequency counts. The SASHELP.HEART data set contains a variety of numeric and character data elements. To color-code Blood Pressure Status (Optimal, Normal, and High) in a heat map requires it to be converted to a number (in this case, I have chosen 1, 2, and 3). Figure 6-7 shows BP Status and frequency count using Cholesterol Status and Weight Status as the categorical character variables for Y and X.

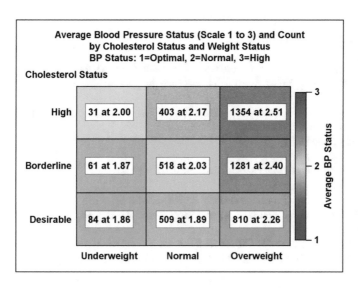

Figure 6-7. Heat map with multifunction annotation and a two-color gradient legend

The default legend for the heat map in Figure 6-7 would be the ThreeColorRamp of blue, white, and red. When that color model for the legend was used, the cell with Average BP Status equal to 2.03, a bit above normal, was color-coded light blue. That happened because the color range was applied to the data range in the input, which is 1.86 to 2.51, and 2.03 was below the midpoint.

Listing 6-7. *Code used to create Figure 6-7*

```
data work.ToSummary;
set sashelp.heart(keep=weight_status chol_status bp_status);
where bp_status NE ' '
  AND chol_status NE ' '
  AND weight_status NE ' ';
if bp_status EQ 'Optimal'
then bp_measure = 1;
else
if bp_status EQ 'Normal'
then bp_measure = 2;
else bp_measure = 3; /* 'High' is the only other value */
run;

proc summary data=work.ToSummary nway;
class weight_status chol_status;
var bp_measure;
output out=work.Summary
       mean=avg_bp_measure; /* to be the COLORRESPONSE variable
                               AND part of the TEXT variable */
run;
```

```
data work.ToHeatMap;
length CountAndAvgBPstatus $ 12;
set work.Summary;
CountAndAvgBPstatus = /* to be the TEXT (annotation) variable */
  trim(left(_freq_)) || ' at ' || put(avg_bp_measure,4.2);
run;

data work.RattrNap_BlueRed;
retain id "RangeID";
length min max $ 1
  color altcolor colormodel1 colormodel2 $ 18;
input id $ min $ max $
  color $ altcolor $ colormodel1 $ colormodel2 $;
  /* INPUT statement ignores everything after COLORMODEL2 */
datalines;
RangeID 1 2 . . CX0000FF CXCCCCFF Blue to Very Light Blue
RangeID 2 3 . . CXFFCCCC CXFF0000 Very Light Red to Red
run;

ods listing gpath="C:\temp" dpi=300 style=GraphFontArial8ptBold;
ods graphics / reset=index scale=off width=4in
  imagename=
  "Fig6-7_AvgBPmeasureAndCountByCholStatusAndWgtStatus";
title1 justify=center
  'Average Blood Pressure Status (Scale 1 to 3) and Count';
title2 justify=center 'by Cholesterol Status and Weight Status';
title3 justify=center 'BP Status: 1=Optimal, 2=Normal, 3=High';proc sgplot
data=work.ToHeatMap rattrmap=work.RattrNap_BlueRed;
heatmap x=weight_status y=chol_status /
  colorresponse=avg_bp_measure
  rattrid=RangeID
  outline;
text x=weight_status y=chol_status text=CountAndAvgBPstatus /
  strip /* remove any leading or trailing blanks */
  backfill fillattrs=(color=white) outline
  splitchar=' ';
xaxis display=(noticks nolabel)
  values=('Underweight' 'Normal' 'Overweight');
yaxis display=(noticks)
  labelpos=top /* prevents vertical label */
  values=('Desirable' 'Borderline' 'High');
gradlegend / title='Average BP Status';
  /* There is no way to move the legend title
     to the top and make it horizontal.
     If there were, it would also be best
     to split the title between Average & BP. */
run;
```

Heat Maps with a Character Variable for Y and a Numeric Variable for X

Now let's look at an interesting situation of a heat map for one variable that is character data and the other variable is ostensibly a continuous numeric variable. The heat map is shown in Figure 6-8.

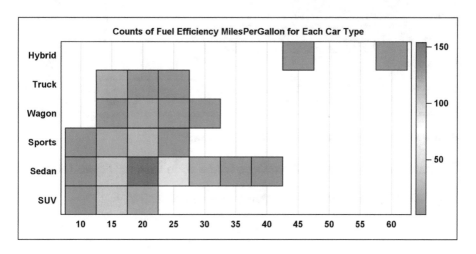

Figure 6-8. The SHOWBINS option displays and labels 11 bins

Listing 6-8. *Code used to create Figure 6-8*

```
ods listing gpath="C:\temp" dpi=300 style=GraphFontArial8ptBold;
ods graphics / reset=all scale=off width=5.7in height=2.8in
  imagename="Fig6-8_SHOWXbins_HeatMap_CharacterY_NumericX";
title1 justify=center
  "Counts of Fuel Efficiency MilesPerGallon for Each Car Type";
proc sgplot data=sashelp.cars;
heatmap y=type x=MPG_City / outline
   showxbins; /* without this there would be only three X axis values
               despite eleven bins created */
yaxis display=(noticks nolabel);
xaxis display=(noticks nolabel)
  grid; /* useful to connect cells for Hybrid with X axis values */
gradlegend / notitle;
run;
```

More granularity can be provided by using NXBINS=20, but SHOWXBINS would not work. The X axis values must be hardcoded. See the result in Figure 6-9.

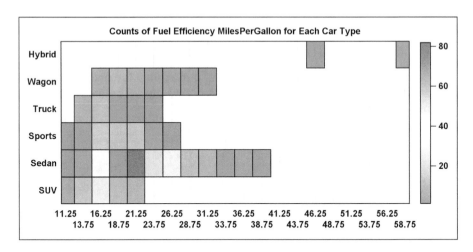

Figure 6-9. Using NXBINS=20 and a VALUES statement

To create Figure 6-9, the only changes to the code used for Figure 6-8 are

```
imagename="Fig6-9_NXbinsEQ20_HeatMap_CharacterY_NumericX"
```

and these HEATMAP and XAXIS statements:

```
heatmap y=type x=MPG_City / outline
  nxbins=20;

xaxis display=(noticks nolabel) grid
  fitpolicy=stagger /* display X axis values in two rows */
  values=(11.25 to 58.75 by 2.5);
```

Heat Map with Character Y Values and Numeric X Values Converted to Character

Though the two prior examples show what can be done with bins, bin labels, and a legend, they fail to provide precise counts associated with the cells. For this particular data, the numeric variable does not have a huge number of values. There are only 28 distinct values for MPG. They can be converted to character values, and PROC FREQ can deliver counts for each possible cell in the heat map. The convenient and very informative result is shown in Figure 6-10.

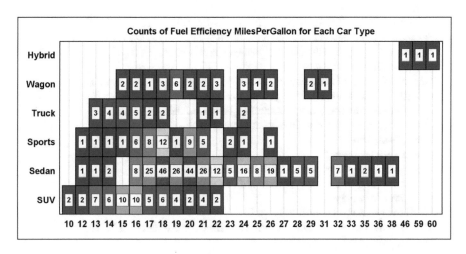

Figure 6-10. Most communication-effective heat map for MPG by car type

Listing 6-10. *Code used to create Figure 6-10*

```
data work.MPG_As_Character_Data;
set sashelp.cars;
MPG_City_Characters = put(MPG_City,2.);
run;

proc freq data=work.MPG_As_Character_Data noprint;
tables type*MPG_City_Characters / out=work.FREQout_MPGasCharData;
run;

proc sort data=work.FREQout_MPGasCharData
  out=work.FREQout_MPGasCharData_Sorted;
by MPG_City_Characters;
run;

data work.RattrMap_DarkBlueRed;
retain id "RangeID";
length min max $ 2
  color altcolor colormodel1 colormodel2 $ 18;
input id $ min $ max $
  color $ altcolor $ colormodel1 $ colormodel2 $;
  /* INPUT statement ignores everything after second color */
datalines;
RangeID 1  12  . . CX0000CC CXCCCCFF DarkBlue to Very Light Blue
RangeID 12 46  . . CXFFCCCC CXFF0000 Very Light Red to Red
run;
```

```
ods listing gpath="C:\temp" dpi=300 style=GraphFontArial8ptBold;
ods graphics / reset=all scale=off width=5.7in height=2.8in
  imagename="Fig6-10_AnnoHeatMap_MPGasCharacterData_Sorted";
title1 justify=center
  "Counts of Fuel Efficiency MilesPerGallon for Each Car Type";
proc sgplot data=work.FREQout_MPGasCharData_Sorted
  noautolegend rattrmap=work.RattrMap_DarkBlueRed;
heatmap y=type x=MPG_City_Characters / outline
  rattrid=RangeID
  colorresponse=count;
text y=type x=MPG_City_Characters text=count /
  strip backfill fillattrs=(color=white) outline
  textattrs=(size=6pt);
xaxis display=(noticks nolabel) grid
  fitpolicy=none; /* so all values are displayed without tilting */
yaxis display=(noticks nolabel);
run;
```

Heat Maps with Both X and Y As Numeric Data

For the case where both X and Y are numeric, in Figure 6-11 are shown a scatter plot of weight versus height and three heat maps, of decreasing granularity. These graphs use the SASHELP.HEART data set.

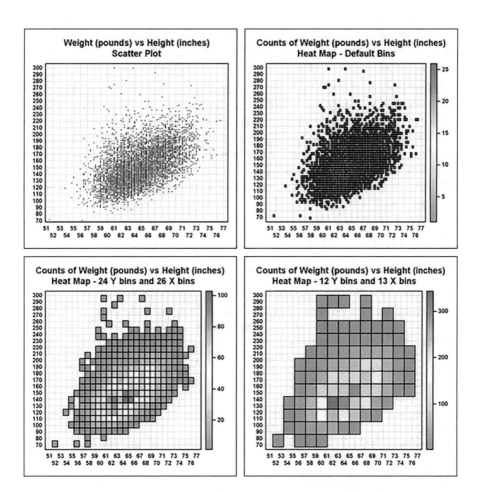

Figure 6-11. A scatter plot of weight versus height and three heat maps of frequency counts of weight-height. One heat map with default bins and two heat maps for bin levels of decreasing granularity

When both X and Y are numeric, a heat map of frequency count, in effect, simply collects the presence of the scatter plot points into rectangular cell segments of the plot area, and counts them, with the level of granularity depending on the number of bins and cells. As the cells get bigger when bin counts are smaller, the maximum cell frequency count gets bigger. Compare the counts on the legends for the preceding three heat maps.

For alternative insight into the data, even if not so granular as the scatter plot or the default heat map in the upper right of Figure 6-11, you can specify the numbers of bins as in the code used for the two lower heat maps in Figure 6-11. The heat map gathers near-together data points and consolidates them into one cell, where they are collectively represented by color coding for a count (or statistic or other response values) that is "spread across" the cell. The values are not shown. The legend enables, at best, a vague guess. Any "binning" level you choose is arbitrary.

Let's first look at the code for the examples in Figure 6-11. The number of X and Y bins in the default heat map can only be determined by counting them. The axis values in all four cases of Figure 6-11 are specified in the code, not automatically provided. They do not align with the bins. You cannot specify the bin X and Y values for the AXIS statements since you don't know the bin midpoints, only the numbers of bins for the two cases when NXBINS and NYBINS are used. The default axis values would be sparse, and they would not align with the bins either.

Listing 6-11. *Code used to create the four graphs in Figure 6-11*

```
ods listing gpath="C:\temp" dpi=300 style=GraphFontArial5ptBold;

ods graphics / reset=all scale=off width=2.8in height=2.8in
  ANTIALIASMAX=5300 /* recommended in the SAS log for this plot
                      due to the large number of points */
  imagename="Fig6-11_UpperLeft_ScatterPlot";
title1 height=8pt 'Weight (pounds) vs Height (inches)';
title2 height=8pt 'Scatter Plot';
proc sgplot data=sashelp.heart;
scatter y=weight x=height /
  markerattrs=(symbol=CircleFilled size=1px);
xaxis display=(noline nolabel noticks) grid
  fitpolicy=stagger /* so that X axis values specified can fit */
  values=(51 to 77 by 1);
yaxis display=(noline nolabel noticks) grid
  fitpolicy=none values=(70 to 300 by 10);
run;

/* Common TITLE1 statement for all three next heat maps */
title1 height=8pt 'Counts of Weight (pounds) vs Height (inches)';

ods graphics / imagename="Fig6-11_UpperRight_HeatMap_DefaultBins";
/* Other ODS GRAPHICS options settings are inherited. */
/* RESET=INDEX assures that code can be rerun,
   if desired during the same SAS session, without SAS adding an
   index number suffix to image file names with each rerun */
title2 height=8pt 'Heat Map - Default Bins';
proc sgplot data=sashelp.heart;
heatmap y=weight x=height / outline; /* default bins accepted */
xaxis display=(noline nolabel noticks) grid
  fitpolicy=stagger values=(51 to 77 by 1);
yaxis display=(noline nolabel noticks) grid
```

```
  fitpolicy=none values=(70 to 300 by 10);
gradlegend / notitle;
run;

ods graphics /
  imagename="Fig6-11_LowerLeft_HeatMap_24YbinsBy26Xbins";
title2 height=8pt 'Heat Map - 24 Y bins and 26 X bins';;
proc sgplot data=sashelp.heart;
heatmap y=weight x=height / outline nybins=24 nxbins=26;
xaxis display=(noline nolabel noticks) grid
  fitpolicy=stagger values=(51 to 77 by 1);
yaxis display=(noline nolabel noticks) grid
  fitpolicy=none values=(70 to 300 by 10);
gradlegend / notitle;
run;

ods graphics /
  imagename="Fig6-11_LowerRight_HeatMap_12YbinsBy13Xbins";
title2 height=8pt 'Heat Map - 12 Y bins and 13 X bins';
proc sgplot data=sashelp.heart;
heatmap y=weight x=height / outline nybins=12 nxbins=13;
xaxis display=(noline nolabel noticks) grid
  fitpolicy=stagger values=(51 to 77 by 1);
yaxis display=(noline nolabel noticks) grid
  fitpolicy=none values=(70 to 300 by 10);
gradlegend / notitle;
run;
```

See Figure 6-12, which is similar to the first heat map in Figure 6-1, but with different titles and without axis labels. If you look at the grid, it is clear that the axis values do not line up with any of the bins. In pursuit of alignment between axis values and bins, see Figure 6-13, which uses the SHOWXBINS and SHOWYBINS instead of NXBINS and NYBINS options.

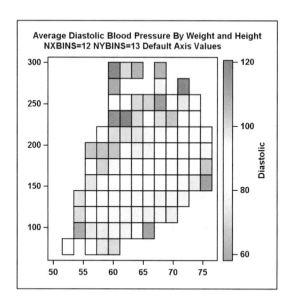

Figure 6-12. NYBINS=13, NXBINS=12. No alignment between axis values and bins

To create Figure 6-12, the only changes to the code used for Figure 6-1 are

```
imagename="Fig6-12_HeatMapUsingNbinsOption";
```

```
title1 justify=center
  'Average Diastolic Blood Pressure By Weight and Height';
title2 justify=center 'NXBINS=12 NYBINS=13 Default Axis Values';
/* title3 IS NOT USED */
```

```
/* in the XAXIS and YAXIS statements, adding: */
```

```
  display=(nolabel)
```

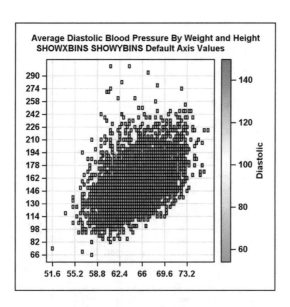

Figure 6-13. With SHOWYBINS SHOWXBINS, default values do align with bins

As you can see, SHOWXBINS and SHOWYBINS create more bins using some undisclosed default algorithm, but do not label *all* of the bins with axis values. Only 7 X bins and 15 Y bins are labeled. At the specified font size of 6pt, it is clearly impossible to label all of the bins. In the next example, Figure 6-14, we try to address that problem.

To create Figure 6-13, the only changes to the code used for Figure 6-12 are

```
imagename= "Fig6-13_HeatMapUsingSHOWbinsOption";

title2 justify=center 'SHOWXBINS SHOWYBINS Default Axis Values';
```

/* In the PROC SGPLOT step replacing nxbins=13 nybins=12 with: */
showxbins showybins

Confronted by an incomplete set of bin labels with the axis values in Figure 6-13, I decided to see what I could do by decreasing the axis value font sizes. Not as a surprise, in Figure 6-14, with a large enough image, a heat map with an axis value for every bin *is* possible, but at the expense of readability.

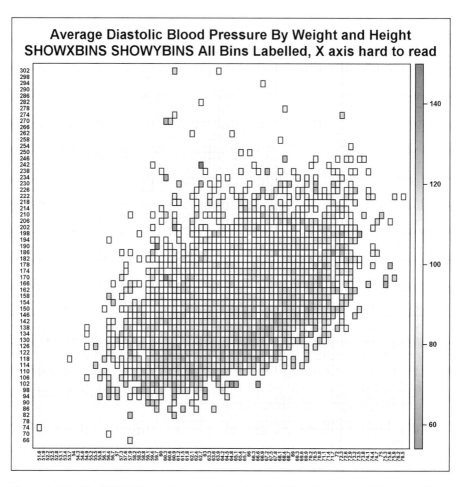

Figure 6-14. The SHOWbins option now does align all of the axis values and bins, but all bins can be labeled only by reducing the font sizes

A remaining and fundamental problem is that, as in the case of Figure 6-13, the default bins deliver an array of unusable color patches. They are too small to be able to match any of them to a corresponding point on the legend. The only way to determine response value and coordinates for a random cell in this heat map would be to deliver it as an HTML web page with mouseover text to *temporarily* display the cell-specific information: X, Y, and response value.

To create Figure 6-14, the only changes to the code used for Figure 6-13 are

```
ods listing gpath="C:\temp" dpi=300 style=GraphFontArial12ptBold;

ods graphics / reset=all scale=off width=5.7in height=5.7in
  imagename="Fig6-14_SHOWbinsAndTinyAxisValuesAllBinsLabelled";
```

```
title2 justify=center
  'SHOWXBINS SHOWYBINS All Bins Labelled, X axis hard to read';

xaxis grid display=(nolabel noticks) valueattrs=(size=3pt)
  fitpolicy=rotate valuesrotate=vertical;
yaxis grid display=(nolabel noticks) valueattrs=(size=5pt)
  fitpolicy=none;

gradlegend / notitle; /* reduce horizontal space for legend,
                          providing more for X axis values */
```

So, How Can We Get Some Insight *Visually* into This Data?

In principle, an obvious way to deliver axis values that are both readable and bin-aligned would be to reduce the number of bins with the SHOWXBINS and SHOWYBINS options in effect so that a readable font could be used and still label *all* of them in alignment. And, perhaps the cells might be big enough to get a good sense of their colors. Unfortunately, NXBINS and NYBINS options are needed to control the bin counts, and, as of this publication date, the two different sets of options, SHOW_BINS and N_BINS where _ can be X or Y, are incompatible.

However, there *is* a solution. It is delivered by another solution, the one needed to provide precise numbers for the response variable by annotating the heat map. It involves the use of custom macros that I developed. Listing 6-15 shows you the code that I found necessary and effective. The code is macros based, except for a preliminary DATA step to create the range attribute map.

The BinsForHeatMap macro creates the bins, assigns observations to each bin, and assigns axis values to the "binned" observations. The bins are subranges of the full ranges of the X and Y variables. The axis values assigned are not the bin midpoints, but instead the macro computes and uses the average X and average Y for each bin. It might look peculiar to see axis values that do not have equal increments. However, it is more meaningful and representative to show the viewer what is reflective of the X and Y values found for the contents of each bin.

The "binned" data set created by the macro can be input to PROC FREQ, PROC SUMMARY, PROC UNIVARIATE, etc. to prepare whatever is the statistic of interest to be displayed via color-coded cells with the heat map generated by PROC SGPLOT and a HEATMAP statement. The PROC FREQ output COUNT variable can be used by the TEXT statement for annotation of a frequency heat map. PROC SUMMARY always includes a _FREQ_ variable along with whatever statistics are requested. PROC UNIVARIATE also includes counts with its output. You will see examples that take advantage of counts being available as *accessory* information.

To use the binning macro is simple. You identify the input and output data sets, the X and Y variables, and how many bins for X and Y. There are two internally used parameters that you can choose to leave at the defaults.

Besides preparing a binned data set for the heat map creation step, the binning macro puts the values of the Average X and Average Y values for the bins as macro variables that are stored in your SAS session's global symbol table. The graph creation step retrieves those macro variables from the global symbol table to initialize the axis VALUES= lists in the XAXIS and YAXIS statements. If you use OPTION MPRINT as shown in the example code, your SAS log will show the macro magic at work when you look at the "resolved" XAXIS and YAXIS statements for the PROC SGPLOT step.

The HeatMapAnnoColorLegendRefTicks macro uses the binned data and macro variables to create the heat map with annotation and a color legend. As currently written, it is designed to determine the average of the response variable in each of the cells. It has numerous features and controls that are demonstrated in the code listings that use it for Figures 6-15 through 6-18.

Figure 6-15 is an annotated version of the custom heat maps shown in Figure 6-1, but with more information in the title lines. Numbers in the third and fourth title lines are dynamically delivered by the HeatMapAnnoColorLegendRefTicks macro at runtime, not hardcoded.

Besides any explanation here in the chapter text, each of the three macros used for Figures 6-15 through 6-18 has an explanatory introduction/self-description at the head of the macro source code.

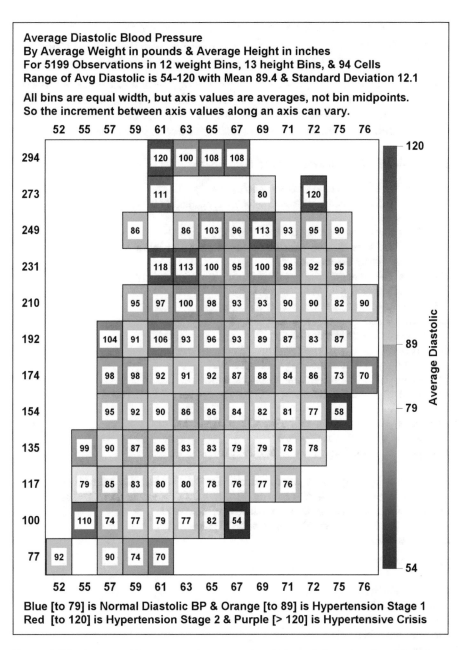

Figure 6-15. Annotated heat map with macro-created bins and dynamic titles and a custom data-appropriate gradient legend using a range attribute map

Just as the X values are repeated at the top of the heat map so that they are closer to the cells in the upper half of the heat map, so, too, one can optionally use macro option RefTicksForY=YES, which is not done here.

The code in Listing 6-15 (as well as that in Listings 6-16 and 6-17) uses macros. The macros have been validated for successfully creating examples in this book and for a few other cases. However, they cannot be guaranteed to work for absolutely any data set or with conditions not tested by these examples.

Listing 6-15. *Code used to create Figure 6-15*

```
%include "C:\SharedCode\BinsForHeatMap.sas";
%include "C:\SharedCode\HeatMapAnnoColorLegendRefTicks.sas";

data work.RattrMap_ForDiastolicBP_Max120;
/* A data-interpretative standards-based Range Attribute Map.
   See the image footnotes. */
retain id "BP_ranges";
length  min max $ 5 color    altcolor
  colormodel1   colormodel2 $ 18;
input min $ max $    color $ altcolor $
  colormodel1 $ colormodel2 $;
datalines;
_min_   79   . . DarkBlue        LightBlue
79      89   . . VeryLightOrange DarkOrange
89     120   . . CXFFCCCC        CXCC0000   (very light red & dark red)
run;
/* maximum in THIS data is below the mininum 121
   for the not relevant range:
120 _max_ . . VeryLightPurple DarkPurple */

/* to get a listing, without the usual SAS log prefix for each line,
of the code generated by the macros (but not OTHER code in the SAS log) include
these two statements (with your preferred folder):
filename mprint "C:\temp\YourChoiceOfFileName.txt";
options mfile; */

options mprint;

%BinsForHeatMap(
data=sashelp.heart
,out=work.WgtVsHgtBins
,ResponseVar=Diastolic
,Xvar=height
,nXbins=13
,Yvar=weight
,nYbins=12);

ods results off;
ods _all_ close;
```

```
%HeatMapAnnoColorLegendRefTicks(
data=work.WgtVsHgtBins
,Xvar=height
,Yvar=weight
,ResponseVar=Diastolic
,AnnoVar=AvgDiastolic
,ColorVar=AvgDiastolic
,ImageFileName=
Fig6-15_HeatMap_NumericXandY_RespVarForAnnoAndColor
,ImageFolder=C:\temp
,ImageWidth=5.7in
,ImageHeight=7.75in
,DPI=300
,GraphFontSize=10pt
,AnnotateFontSize=8pt
/* LegendTitleText= (letting the macro generate it) */
,Xgrid=NO /* same as default */
,Ygrid=NO /* same as default */
,RefTicksForX=YES /* NO is the default */
,RefTicksForY=NO /* YES: duplicate YAXIS values at right side */
,RattrMap=work.RattrMap_ForDiastolicBP_Max120
,RattrID=BP_ranges
,DoAnnotate=YES
,BackFill=YES
,TitleAndFootnoteJustify=left
,Title1=Average Diastolic Blood Pressure
,Title2=By Average Weight in pounds & Average Height in inches
,FootNote1=Blue [to 79] is Normal Diastolic BP & Orange [to 89] is
Hypertension Stage 1
,FootNote2=Red   [to 120] is Hypertension Stage 2 & Purple [> 120] is
Hypertensive Crisis
);

footnote; /* Prevent footnotes from being inherited by later
  code submissions during the same session. Alternatively,
  starting later programs with FOOTNOTE; can prevent that. */
```

Notice the use of square brackets, instead of parentheses, in the FOOTNOTE1 and FOOTNOTE2 text. When assigning text strings to macro parameters, inside the string do not use parentheses or commas.

The HeatMapAnnoColorLegendRefTicks macro has more capabilities. There are five to be discussed here.

First, instead of using both annotation and the legend for the average of the response variable, it can use annotation to display the frequency count for observations in each cell and the legend to compare the average response value for observations in the cells, or vice versa. When either of these dual-reporting options is used, TITLE5 can be used, with user-provided text (automatically highlighted in blue to get the viewer's attention) to explain what has been annotated versus what is available from the legend.

When TITLE5 is NOT used, but TITLE6 and TITLE7 ARE used, as in the case of Figure 6-15, a gap appears in the title line stack. That could be remedied with a macro enhancement, but I leave that as an option for the interested reader. If the macro is not used with TITLE6 and TITLE7, the gap due to a possibly absent TITLE5 will be unnoticed. This macro also provides automatically delivered information in TITLE3 and TITLE4. Some users might not want to provide all of it. It is easier to simplify the macro with code changes to suit one's preferences than to enhance the macro to add a function.

Second, instead of using white BackFill, as in Figure 6-15, to improve readability of text in the cells, the macro can use the BackLight option, as in Figures 6-16 and 6-17, which not only can improve readability (but perhaps not as much, and not necessarily satisfactorily in every situation—you need to verify the consequences of using BackLight versus BackFill) but also leaves more cell color fill uncovered to make it easier to match cell fill color with the color gradient legend.

Third, if desired, you can turn on grid lines for X and/or Y by including Xgrid=YES and/or Ygrid=YES when you invoke the HeatMapAnnoColorLegendRefTicks. If there is a lot of white space between some of the axis values and the color-coded cells, grid lines can be useful.

Fourth, another option is to get X axis values duplicated at the top of the heat map, which can be a usability convenience when a heat map is very tall. It requires the use of RefTicksForX=YES upon invocation of the HeatMapAnnoColorLegendRefTicks macro. There is a RefTicksForY=YES option as well, but it creates an awkward situation with a list of Y values next to the list of legend values on the other side of the legend color strip. In Figure 6-18, which is tall and has several lonely cells near the top, far from the X axis values at the bottom, it is useful to repeat them at the top.

Fifth, if used with input data that has only one X value in each X bin, and one Y value in each bin, it provides optional TITLE6 and TITLE7 lines to explain that to the viewer—but with text that must be provided with invocation of the macro. Alternatively, as is the case for Figure 6-15, when the X and Y values are averages of multiple values of X and Y in each bin, those optional TITLE6 and TITLE7 lines can be used to explain that—as is shown in that illustration.

Complementary demonstrations of the two alternative ways to use annotation and the legend to present two different variables are presented on the same page for easy comparison. To fit them, Figures 6-16 and 6-17 have only four Y bins. A minor option used for these two examples suppresses the legend title. The legend significance can be identified instead, as shown, with TITLE5.

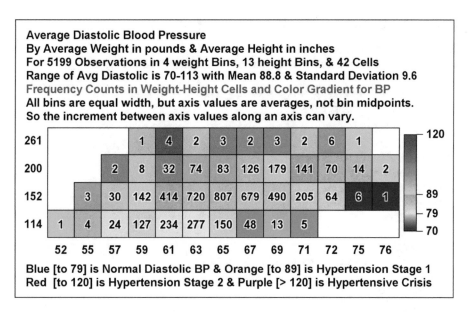

Figure 6-16. Supplying one piece of information with annotation, another with the legend. Fewer Y bins to save display space. Using BackLight for readability and maximum color fill

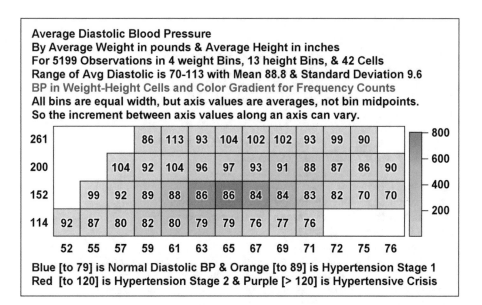

Figure 6-17. Supplying one piece of information with annotation, another with the legend, conversely to what was done for Figure 6-16. Here, too, four Y bins and BackLight

Listing 6-16. *Code used to create Figure 6-16*

```
%include "C:\SharedCode\BinsForHeatMap.sas";
%include "C:\SharedCode\HeatMapAnnoColorLegendRefTicks.sas";

< code for work.RattrMap_ForDiastolicBP_Max120 DATA step here,
  copied from Listing 6-15 >

options mprint;

%BinsForHeatMap(
data=sashelp.heart
,out=work.WgtVsHgtBins
,ResponseVar=Diastolic
,Xvar=height
,nXbins=13
,Yvar=weight
,nYbins=4); /* change from Listing 6-15 */

ods results off;
ods _all_ close;

%HeatMapAnnoColorLegendRefTicks(
data=work.WgtVsHgtBins
,Xvar=height
,Yvar=weight
,ResponseVar=Diastolic
,AnnoVar=_freq_          /* change from Listing 6-15 */
,ColorVar=AvgDiastolic  /* change from Listing 6-15 */
,ImageFileName=          /* change from Listing 6-15 */
Fig6-16_HeatMap_NumericXandY_FreqForAnno_RespVarForColor
,ImageFolder=C:\temp
,ImageWidth=5.7in
,ImageHeight=3.5in      /* change from Listing 6-15 */
,DPI=300 /* this can be null or smaller
            (text strings will be less wide) */
,GraphFontSize=10pt
,AnnotateFontSize=10pt /* change from Listing 6-15 */
,LegendTitle=NO          /* change from Listing 6-15 */
,Xgrid=NO /* same as default */
,Ygrid=NO /* same as default */
,RefTicksForX=NO /* All cells are very close to X axis values,
                   unlike the situation for Figure 6-15 */
,RefTicksForY=NO /* YES: duplicate YAXIS values at right side */
,RattrMap=work.RattrMap_ForDiastolicBP_Max120
,RattrID=BP_ranges
,DoAnnotate=YES
```

```
/* ,BackFill=YES NOT USED change from Listing 6-15 */
,BackLight=YES          /* change from Listing 6-15 */
,TitleAndFootnoteJustify=left
,Title1=Average Diastolic Blood Pressure
,Title2=By Average Weight in pounds & Average Height in inches
,FootNote1=Blue [to 79] is Normal Diastolic BP & Orange [to 89] is
Hypertension Stage 1
,FootNote2=Red   [to 120] is Hypertension Stage 2 & Purple [> 120] is
Hypertensive Crisis
,Title5=                /* change from Listing 6-15 */
Frequency Counts in Weight-Height Cells and Color Gradient for BP
);
footnote;
```

Listing 6-17. *Code used to create Figure 6-17, changes from Figure 6-16 in bold*

```
%include "C:\SharedCode\BinsForHeatMap.sas";
%include "C:\SharedCode\HeatMapAnnoColorLegendRefTicks.sas";

/* work.RattrMap_ForDiastolicBP_Max120 DATA step is not needed */

options mprint;

%BinsForHeatMap(
data=sashelp.heart
,out=work.WgtVsHgtBins
,ResponseVar=Diastolic
,Xvar=height
,nXbins=13
,Yvar=weight
,nYbins=4);

ods results off;
ods _all_ close;

%HeatMapAnnoColorLegendRefTicks(
data=work.WgtVsHgtBins
,Xvar=height
,Yvar=weight
,ResponseVar=Diastolic
,AnnoVar=AvgDiastolic    /* change from Listing 6-16 */
,ColorVar=_freq_         /* change from Listing 6-16 */
,ImageFileName=          /* change from Listing 6-16 */
Fig6-17_HeatMap_NumericXandY_RespVarForAnno_FreqForColor
,ImageFolder=C:\temp
,ImageWidth=5.7in
,ImageHeight=3.5in
```

```
,DPI=300 /* this can be null or smaller
            (text strings will be less wide) */
,GraphFontSize=10pt
,AnnotateFontSize=10pt
,LegendTitle=NO
,Xgrid=NO /* same as default */
,Ygrid=NO /* same as default */
,RefTicksForX=NO /* YES: duplicate XAXIS values at top */
,RefTicksForY=NO /* YES: duplicate YAXIS values at right side */
,RattrMap= /* RattrMap  NOT USED change from Listing 6-16 */
,RattrID=  /* BP_ranges NOT USED change from Listing 6-16 */
,ColorModel=
VeryLightGreen VeryDarkGreen /* change from Listing 6-16 */
,DoAnnotate=YES
,BackLight=YES
,TitleAndFootnoteJustify=left
,Title1=Average Diastolic Blood Pressure
,Title2=By Average Weight in pounds & Average Height in inches
,FootNote1=Blue [to 79] is Normal Diastolic BP & Orange [to 89] is
Hypertension Stage 1
,FootNote2=Red   [to 120] is Hypertension Stage 2 & Purple [> 120] is
Hypertensive Crisis
,Title5=                /* change from Listing 6-16 */
BP in Weight-Height Cells and Color Gradient for Frequency Counts
);
footnote;
```

For numeric X and Y variables, all of the heat maps so far have involved binning that collected usually, and always potentially, multiple X-Y pairs of response data in each cell. One can take, as was done, the average of all of the X-Y pairs' response values and depict that with color and/or with annotation. The X-Y pair associated with each cell is, with the algorithm used for Figures 6-15, 6-16, and 6-17, the average X and the average Y for all of the observations in the cell. So, you obtain visually a display of an approximate or "average" relationship between X, Y, and the response variable in each cell.

The ultimate precise insight would be achievable with data where there is only one response value for each X-Y pair. Less insightful than that, but nevertheless more insightful than the foregoing heat maps, is one where for each cell there is only one X-Y pair.

To bin the input data for the HeatMapAnnoColorLegendRefTicks macro when there is only one X value and one Y value for each X bin and Y bin requires the use of the macro OneXYperCellForHeatMap.

For a demonstration, there was no data set suitable, as is, in the SASHELP data library. Data preprocessing code in Listing 6-18 creates a subset of raw observations from SASHELP.HEART which are spread uniformly over all values of Weight (to be used as Y), but limited to 12 distinct values. For each Weight value, there can be multiple Height values (to be used as X). For the source data set, the Y values (Weight) are integer. In any case, the OneXYperCellForHeatMap rounds X and Y to integers. Across the 12 Y values, there are 18 integer X values.

The interplay between OneXYperCellForHeatMap and the HeatMapAnnoColorLegendRefTicks macro is analogous to that for the BinsForHeatMap macro. The binning macro prepares the input data set for the heat map creation macro. The global symbol table here, too, carries the information to initialize the VALUES lists for the XAXIS and YAXIS statements.

Figure 6-18 demonstrates the result from these tools. However, it uses a legend that is solid color blocks, rather than color gradients as in many prior examples. With a small enough number of distinct values to match, it was feasible to select a palette of easily distinguishable colors. The image had to be presented at full page height so that there would be enough color fill in each cell to easily distinguish the color. So that the BackFill box, for the longer strings of digits, 100 and above, would not overlay the cell side boundaries with white, the ImageWidth was set to 6.2 inches. When inserted for publication, the image was shrunk to fit, with no detriment to readability. (ImageHeight was increased commensurately, so that when the image was shrunk to fit the page width, its height was the same as that of Figure 6-15.) For this image, the use of BackLight instead of BackFill was not a satisfactory alternative to deliver readability of the annotation. You could modify the code and verify that.

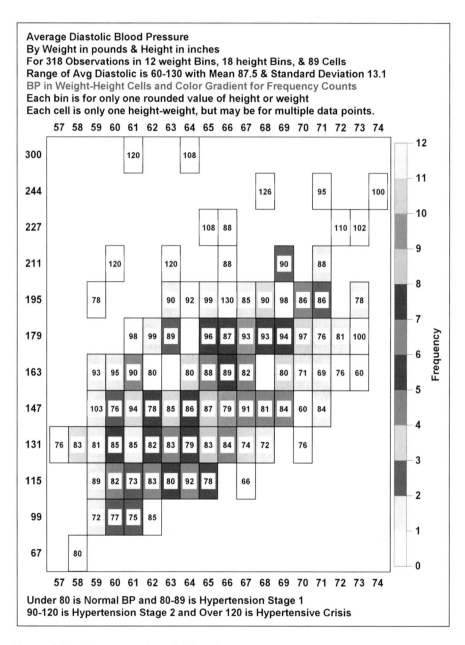

Figure 6-18. Heat map with one X-Y pair (but multiple observations) per cell and with X axis values repeated at the top of the heat map

This heat map is unlike the typical heat maps that have bins where an X value (a Y value) represents a span of X values (Y values).

Listing 6-18. *Code used to create Figure 6-18*

```
%include "C:\SharedCode\OneXYperCellForHeatMap.sas";
%include "C:\SharedCode\HeatMapAnnoColorLegendRefTicks.sas";

data work.ToSelect;
set sashelp.heart;
where height NE . and weight NE .;
run;

proc sort data=work.ToSelect out=work.DistinctWeights nodupkey;
by weight;
run;

data work.SelectedWeights(keep=weight);
retain InputSoFar 0 Selected 0 NextOneToSelect 1;
set work.DistinctWeights end=LastOne;
InputSoFar + 1;
if Selected LT 12;
if _N_ EQ NextOneToSelect
then do;
  output;
  Selected + 1;
  NextOneToSelect + 16;
end;
if LastOne
then put InputSofar= Selected=;
run;

proc sort data=work.ToSelect;
by weight;
run;

data work.HeatMapRawInput;
merge work.ToSelect work.SelectedWeights(in=Selected);
by weight;
if Selected;
run;

options mprint;

%OneXYperCellForHeatMap(
data=work.HeatMapRawInput
,out=work.ToHeatMap
,ResponseVar=Diastolic
,Xvar=height
```

```
,Xformat=2.
,Yvar=weight
,Yformat=3.);

data work.RattrMap_ForIntegers1to12;
retain id "Integers1to12";
length  min max $ 2 color $ 18;
input min $ max $ color $;
datalines;
0  1  white
1  2  lightblue
2  3  blue
3  4  lightgreen
4  5  green
5  6  brown
6  7  lightpurple
7  8  purple
8  9  lightorange
9  10 darkorange
10 11 turquoise
11 12 yellow
run;

ods results off;
ods _all_ close;

%HeatMapAnnoColorLegendRefTicks(
data=work.ToHeatMap
,OneXYperCell=YES
,Xvar=height
,Yvar=weight
,ResponseVar=Diastolic
,AnnoVar=AvgDiastolic
,ColorVar=_freq_
,ImageFileName=
  Fig6-18_OneXYperCell_AnnoHeatMap_RespVarForAnnoAndFreqForColor
,ImageFolder=C:\temp
,ImageWidth=6.2in /* Extra width needed so that backfill boxes
are not be wider than cell width.
When that happens at ImageWidth=5.7in,
cell side boundaries are overlaid with white. */
,ImageHeight=8.36in /* When width shrinks to fit in the page,
this shrinks to the same height as Figure 6-15 */
,DPI=300
,GraphFontSize=10pt
,AnnotateFontSize=8pt
,LegendTitle=YES
,RefTicksForX=YES /* duplicate XAXIS values at top, NO is default */
,RattrMap=work.RattrMap_ForIntegers1to12
```

```
,RattrID=Integers1to12
,DoAnnotate=YES
,BackFill=YES
,Title1=Average Diastolic Blood Pressure
,Title2=By Weight in pounds & Height in inches
,Title5=
 BP in Weight-Height Cells and Color Gradient for Frequency Counts
,FootNote1=Under 80 is Normal BP and 80-89 is Hypertension Stage 1
,FootNote2=90-120 is Hypertension Stage 2 and Over 120 is Hypertensive
Crisis);
footnote;
```

If you would like to create the companion heat map to that earlier, with AnnoVar=_freq_ and ColorVar=AvgDiastolic, you need to add one DATALINE to the range attribute map creation DATA step that was used for Figure 6-15:

```
120 _max_ . . VeryLightPurple DarkPurple
```

Not shown here is a heat map to visually show the relationship between the Body Mass Index and height and weight. The BMI formula is available on the Internet, as are the recommended standards. As an exercise, the reader could adapt the code furnished here to create BMI heat maps analogous to Figures 6-15, 6-16, and 6-17.

When assigning values as text strings, as in the case of titles and footnotes, the value assigned is recognized to begin at the first non-blank character and to end at the last non-blank character, or at the comma for the next macro parameter assignment, or at the closing parenthesis of the macro invocation. So, as an example, in the macro invocation for Figure 6-18, the value assigned to TITLE5 is on the next line after TITLE5=.

Warnings About Assigning Text Strings to Macro Parameters (e.g., as in the case of TITLE5): (a) include no commas; (b) include no parentheses. If you need an exception to these warnings, there are ways to deal with that, but the how-to is outside the scope of this book. You need to consult the SAS Macro Language documentation.

Summary

The heat map is a data visualization tool to present response values for two "key" variables, X and Y, in a color-coded matrix. A challenge posed by most, but not all, heat maps is knowing what is the precise response value for each cell in the color-coded matrix.

To interpret the display, using ODS Graphics, by default a gradient legend using the so-called ThreeColorRamp of continuous tones of blue and red with white in the middle is provided. A slightly better continuous-tone gradient legend omits the white and is demonstrated with an image and code for Figure 6-7. (When the lightest red and the lightest blue meet at legend value 2, it looks like white. It is not white.)

Knowing precisely where a cell's fill color is on a continuous-tone gradient is impossible. The ambiguity is exacerbated by the skimpy number of values displayed by default along the gradient legend. You can force more values and/ or control the values along the legend by use of a range attribute map.

See Figure 6-5 (with solid color subranges), Figure 6-6 (with gradients of light shades of blue and dark shades of blue, with a boundary between them at "target" value for Sales by Product within a Region), Figure 6-7 (mentioned earlier, with shades of blue and shades of red, separated at boundary between Normal Blood Pressure Status and High Blood Pressure Status), and Figures 6-1, 6-15, and 6-16 (shades of blue, orange, and red for three categories of Diastolic Blood Pressure).

The best gradient legend involves no gradients and eliminates all of the guessing as to the value for a color-coded cell. The solid color blocks of Figure 6-18, with one value per color, decode the color fill with absolute precision. This was feasible because the number of distinct values was not very large, so that the color blocks could be big enough to be easily distinguishable.

Despite the lack of precision, continuous-tone color gradient legends do allow the use of color coding to make a quick and easy assessment of *relative magnitude* of the response value in the various cells of the heat map. Figures 6-4 and 6-17 relied on the use of the ColorModel option on the HEATMAP statement to specify a color gradient between two extreme shades of green, as a substitute for the default ThreeColorRamp of blue, white, and red, which appears in all of the figures where no range attribute map was used.

However, to get the *precise value* for a cell, the only solution is annotation. When X and Y are character variables, or can be converted to character variables, annotation is easy, as shown in the cases of Figures 6-3, 6-4, 6-5, 6-6, 6-7, and 6-10. With the aid of macros, annotation for cases of X and Y as numeric variables was accomplished for Figures 6-15 through 6-18.

You have seen how the NXBINS and NYBINS options can be used and how the SHOWXBINS and SHOWYBINS options underdeliver communication value. And it has been explained that the present incompatibility of these options is a problem, for which a software modification is uncertain. The problem was overcome with custom macros.

The readability effects of the use of the TEXT statement options BACKFILL and BACKLIGHT were shown in Figures 6-15 and 6-18 (BACKFILL) and Figures 6-16 and 6-17 (BACKLIGHT). BACKLIGHT may usually be satisfactory when text is large, but as suggested earlier, verify.

By using a range attribute map to not only control fill color but also the TEXT annotation color, Figure 6-6 presents another way to assure readability of text on a colored background, which is always a potential problem without BACKFILL or BACKLIGHT. The benefit of using this range attribute map solution is that the result, presuming that all colors used are wisely selected, the text is always readable, and none of the cell color is sacrificed, assuring maximum color distinguishability. In Figure 6-6, cells with dark fill color have white text, and cells with light fill color have black text.

Three ways of dual-purpose information delivery were shown. In Figure 6-7, the annotation in the wide cells includes for each cell not only the response value of Blood Pressure Status but also the count of observations. A different route to that objective for Figures 6-16 and 6-17 is to offer complementary heat maps, where one uses the color code for response value and the annotation for counts, while the other uses the color code for counts and the annotation for response value. For this last method, a convenience (though not a necessity) is that when PROC SUMMARY is used to determine the average response value in each cell, the output from it also includes the frequency count for each cell. The count is also always available when extracting statistics with PROC UNIVARIATE. In Figure 6-18, the third solution annotates each cell with the response, but color-codes each cell with its frequency count which is decoded by the discrete legend.

This chapter offers you a variety of ways to get the best out of ODS Graphics heat maps. I encourage you to see what, and what else, *you* can do with heat maps. Other chapters provide other ways to use color coding as a visual communication aid for response variables with two key variables.

Bubble Plots

A bubble plot is an internal boundary–free matrix of (optionally) color-filled circles for the response variable, which is called the SIZE variable. The values of the X and Y variables provide the column labels and row labels for the matrix. X and Y are variables with discrete values, and the bubble plot is an excellent alternative to a bar chart for two categorical variables, where commonly used alternatives are a stacked bar chart and a clustered bar chart. By color-coding the bubbles and using a legend, it is possible to visually present a second response variable on the bubble plot.

General Remarks About Code Used

The following framing code has been more expansively discussed in Chapter 3 in the section "Outer Structure of ODS Graphics Code in Examples." The framing code for all examples in this chapter and others is

```
ods results off; /* verify results by opening the image file,
                    rather than using the SAS Output window */
ods _all_ close; /* avoid unintended consequences
                    and superfluous concurrent output */
< ODS LISTING statement here >
< example-specific code here >
ods listing close; /* ALWAYS Best Practice */
```

For brevity, the example code in listings omits the first two lines and the last one. It is best to add them back at your runtime. (Source code files include them.)

© LeRoy Bessler 2023
LeR. Bessler, *Visual Data Insights Using SAS ODS Graphics*,
https://doi.org/10.1007/978-1-4842-8609-8_7

The ODS LISTING statement can vary. All of the examples in this chapter use a statement of the following form to specify the text characteristics:

```
ods listing style=GraphFontArial11ptBold gpath="C:\temp" dpi=300;
```

but often with font sizes other than 11pt. The statement assumes that the ODS style GraphFontArial11ptBold has been created. To assure that all of the styles needed in this chapter are available, use this code:

```
%include "C:\SharedCode\AllGraphTextSetup.sas";
%AllGraphTextSetup(7);
%AllGraphTextSetup(9);
%AllGraphTextSetup(10);
%AllGraphTextSetup(11);
```

For more information about ODS custom styles, as well as the source code for the AllGraphTextSetup macro, see the section "Control of Text Attributes with a Custom ODS Style" in Chapter 3. For information about options for direct control of text attributes, which can override the default text attributes that are set up by an ODS style, see the section "Text Attributes Control in ODS Graphics" in Chapter 3.

Examples and Methods

Rather than starting with the more powerful capabilities of bubble plots, let's start simple. Figure 7-1 displays *two* examples, at an artificially restricted width. The size limitation causes bubble overlap since they are sized to fit the annotation inside, rather than, say, at the top of the bubbles. Overlap causes no loss in communication. The viewer can still observe the relative sizes, and the annotation delivers the precise numbers. The FITPOLICY=STAGGER option is used for the X axis to prevent value overlap, without sacrificing text size. In a real situation, the image size would be bigger, and no bubble overlap would occur, and in other situations if axis labels are very long.

Annotation is not the default, but is easily done with the DATALABELS option. The left-hand-side bubble plot demonstrates the readability benefit of overriding the default fill color with yellow.

A key concern for bubble plots is assuring that the bubble areas are proportional to the SIZE variable values that they represent. The PROPORTIONAL option must be specified on the BUBBLE statement. It is not the default.

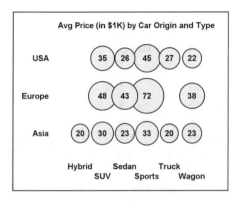 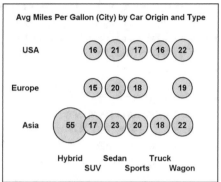

Figure 7-1. Annotated bubble plots for two categorical variables and one response variable

Listing 7-1. *Code used to create bubble plots in Figure 7-1*

```
proc summary data=sashelp.cars nway;
class type origin;
var MPG_City MSRP;
output out=work.SUMMARYout mean=;
run;

data work.ToPlot; /* used for all Figures except 7-4 and 7-9 */
set SUMMARYout;
MPG_City = round(MPG_City,1);
MSRPinThousands = round(MSRP / 1000,1); /* MSRP alternative */
run;

ods listing gpath="C:\temp" dpi=300 style=GraphFontArial7ptBold;
ods graphics / reset=all scale=off width=2.8in height=2.25in
  imagename="Fig7-1Left_SimpleAnnotatedBubblePlot";
title1 "Avg Price (in $1K) by Car Origin and Type";
proc sgplot data=work.ToPlot noborder;
bubble x=type y=origin size=MSRPinThousands / proportional
  fillattrs=(color=yellow)
  datalabel=MSRPinThousands datalabelpos=center;
xaxis display=(noline noticks nolabel) fitpolicy=stagger;
yaxis display=(noline noticks nolabel);
run;

ods graphics / reset=all scale=off width=2.8in height=2.25in
  imagename="Fig7-1Right_SimpleAnnotatedBubblePlot";
title1 "Avg Miles Per Gallon (City) by Car Origin and Type";
proc sgplot data=work.ToPlot noborder;
bubble x=type y=origin size=MPG_City / proportional
```

```
/* fillattrs=(color=yellow) taking the default */
 datalabel=MPG_City datalabelpos=center;
xaxis display=(noline noticks nolabel) fitpolicy=stagger;
yaxis display=(noline noticks nolabel);
run;
```

Always use the PROPORTIONAL option. It assures that bubbles for different X-Y combinations have areas that are proportional to the relative magnitude of the SIZE values. An X-Y pair with a SIZE value that is twice the SIZE value of the second X-Y pair will have an area that is twice the area for that second pair. The documentation states that LINEAR is the default alternative, but you cannot code that option. To see the consequences of taking the default, see the example in Figure 7-9. If you want to use circles as a measure of relative size, proportional areas compare the measure of interest, fairly, accurately, and meaningfully.

As previously mentioned, the left-hand-side bubble plot in Figure 7-1 demonstrates the readability benefit of overriding the default fill color with yellow. Both of the bubble plots in Figure 7-1 would be *equally* communication-effective and would have eminently easy-to-read data labels *if the bubbles were left undecorated with color*. To turn off the bubble color fill, it is simply necessary to include the OUTLINE option on the BUBBLE statement. When OUTLINE is requested, no FILL is provided. Conversely, when FILL is requested on the BUBBLE statement, no OUTLINE is provided. However, the default, of both FILL and OUTLINE, was accepted. When both FILL and OUTLINE are (unnecessarily) requested on the BUBBLE statement, neither is omitted.

In a situation where a bubble completely, or nearly completely, overlays an adjacent bubble and/or its data label, transparency can be a solution. There are two ways to use it, as explained in the section "Options Available but Not Used Here." If you care about the order in which overlapping bubbles are drawn (i.e., which bubble overlays which bubble), see the discussion of the DRAWORDER option for the BUBBLE statement in the *SAS ODS Graphics Procedures Guide*.

ODS Graphics bubble plots can deliver more. With color coding and a legend, optionally supported by an attribute map to customize the color palette, you can visually deliver information with color for a second measurement variable while using bubble areas and annotation for the SIZE variable. Figures 7-2 and 7-3 show you everything that a bubble plot can deliver, without using axis tables (which are used for Figure 7-4).

When the bubbles are color-coded and a legend is used, the default color of data label text and the default color of bubble outlines are not what you might expect. I would expect black, which is the default color for everything else in ODS Graphics. To get black, you must use two options on the BUBBLE statement. For black data labels, you must specify

DATALABELATTRS=(COLOR=BLACK). For black bubble outlines, you must specify LINEATTRS=(COLOR=BLACK). This control for outline color is required only when using a Key Legend (KEYLEGEND statement) for a second response variable with discrete values. When using a Gradient Legend (GRADLEGEND statement) for a second response variable with continuous values, the default color for bubble outlines is black.

The default color schemes for data labels and bubble outlines serve no communication purpose and could cause confusion as to their intended significance—of which there is none, except perhaps decoration. Black text is always most readable. Black bubble outlines are neutral and a does-no-harm choice. The default colors will surprise you if you accept them. To see the defaults, you need to do that coding yourself. Here, you will see only how to do what is recommended.

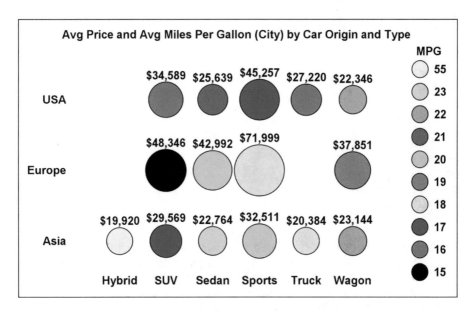

Figure 7-2. Annotated bubble plot with custom color coding and a KeyLegend, visually presents two response variables for two categorical variables

Custom color coding for discrete numeric values requires the creation and use of a discrete attribute map. The variable to be color-coded is assigned with the GROUP option on the BUBBLE statement. Customization of the legend requires a KEYLEGEND statement.

Listing 7-2. *Code used to create Figure 7-2*

```
proc summary data=sashelp.cars nway;
class type origin;
var MPG_City MSRP;
output out=work.SUMMARYout mean=;
run;

data work.ToPlot; /* used for all Figures except 7-4 and 7-9 */
set SUMMARYout;
MPG_City = round(MPG_City,1);
MSRPinThousands = round(MSRP / 1000,1); /* MSRP alternative
                                   used in some other figures */
run;

data work.DattrMap_TenColors;
retain id "DiscreteID";
length value $ 2 fillcolor $ 18;
input value $ fillcolor $;
datalines;
15 black
16 gray
17 blue
18 lightblue
19 green
20 turquoise
21 magenta
22 darkorange
23 lightorange
55 yellow
run;

ods listing gpath="C:\temp" dpi=300 style=GraphFontArial10ptBold;
ods graphics / reset=all scale=off width=5.7in height=3.5in
  /* comments below about bubble collisions and legend
     disappearance are in the context of these dimensions */
  imagename="Fig7-2_AnnoColorCodedBubblePlotKeyLegendDattrMap";
title1
"Avg Price and Avg Miles Per Gallon (City) by Car Origin and Type";
title2 " ";
  /* white space between TITLE1 and the legend title */
proc sgplot data=work.ToPlot noborder
  dattrmap=work.DattrMap_TenColors;
bubble x=type y=origin size=MSRP /
  group=MPG_City
  attrid=DiscreteID
  proportional
  bradiusmax=31 /* larger radius causes bubble collisions */
  lineattrs=(color=black) /* mandatory if you want black bubble
                              outlines, black is not the default */
```

```
    datalabel=MSRP
    datalabelattrs=(color=black) /* mandatory if you want black text,
                                    black is not the default */
    datalabelpos=top;
xaxis display=(noline noticks nolabel);
yaxis display=(noline noticks nolabel);
keylegend / noborder /* default is BORDER */
  position=right /* default is BOTTOM */
  sortorder=descending
  title='MPG'
  fillheight=17pt; /* larger makes the legend disappear */
run;
```

Before proceeding with more examples, there are several points to explain that are unique to bubble plots when using ODS Graphics.

When bubble plots are annotated with the DATALABEL option, location is controlled with the DATALABELPOS option, which supports nine different locations. The undocumented default for DATALABELPOS is TOPRIGHT. My experiments with TOPRIGHT, RIGHT, BOTTOMRIGHT, BOTTOMLEFT, LEFT, and TOPLEFT all led to overlaps between labels and adjacent (not relevant) bubbles. Of course, a larger image area and/or a smaller font size for labels could eliminate the overlap. For the examples in this chapter, the TOP position was satisfactory. The BOTTOM position puts the annotation for the bottom row of bubbles close to the X axis values, which have no exclusive relationship with that row of annotated response values. Except for the CENTER position discussed later, TOP is the best position for annotation.

If the smallest circle is sufficiently large and your longest annotation value is sufficiently small, then you can use DATALABELPOS=CENTER, but you must assure sufficient color contrast between annotation and fill color.

If you are not satisfied with the default bubble sizes, you can control the maximum bubble radius with the BRADIUSMAX option on the BUBBLE statement. When using the PROPORTIONAL option, as recommended, do not also specify BRADIUSMIN, since you can unwittingly encounter unwanted results. The software, at your request, will *want* to maintain proportionality of the bubbles for the smallest and largest values of the SIZE variable. Its final decision about physical sizing of the bubbles must respect the radius limits, if both are specified. If they are incompatible with proportionality, the bubble areas delivered will not be proportional.

Using a KeyLegend and a discrete attribute map, you can color-code the bubbles for any discrete numeric variable in the input data set, as in Figure 7-2, where GROUP=MPG_City.

Using a GradLegend and a range attribute map, you can color-code the bubbles for any continuous numeric variable in the input data set, as in Figure 7-3, where COLORRESPONSE=MSRP.

It is easy to invert the presentation methods for MSRP and MPG_City, as shown in Figure 7-3.

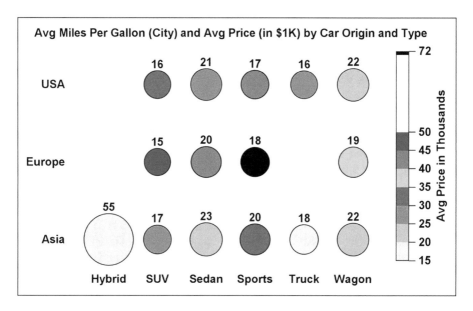

Figure 7-3. Annotated bubble plot with custom color coding and a distinct color gradient legend, visually presents two response variables for two categorical variables

Custom color coding for continuous numeric values requires the creation and use of a range attribute map. The variable to be color-coded is assigned with the COLORRESPONSE option on the BUBBLE statement. Customization of the legend requires a GRADLEGEND statement.

Note that this easy-to-use color gradient legend is a sequence of solid color subranges. Rather than try to match a bubble's color fill with a color somewhere along a smear of gradient colors, here the viewer can know with certainty in which subrange the vehicle selling price lies. It is not knowledge of a *precise* number, but it is better than the typical color gradient alternative.

Listing 7-3. *Code used to create Figure 7-3, changes from Figure 7-2 in bold*

```
/* replace the DATA step for work.DattrMap_TenColors with: */
data work.RattrMap_NineColors; /* Range Attribute Map */
retain id "RangeID";
length min   max $ 5 color $ 32;
input  min $ max $    color $;
datalines;
15 20 yellow
```

```
20 25 lightorange
25 30 darkorange
30 35 magenta
35 40 turquoise
40 45 green
45 50 blue
50 71 white
71 72 black
run;

ods listing gpath="C:\temp" dpi=300 style=GraphFontArial10ptBold;
ods graphics / reset=all scale=off width=5.7in height=3.5in
   imagename="Fig7-3_AnnoColorCodedBubblePlotGradLegendRattrMap";
title1 "Avg Miles Per Gallon (City) and Avg Price (in $1K) by Car Origin
and Type";
/* No TITLE2 statement */
proc sgplot data=work.ToPlot noborder
  rattrmap=work.RattrMap_NineColors;
bubble x=type y=origin size=MPG_City /
  colorresponse=MSRPinThousands
  rattrid=RangeID
  proportional
  bradiusmax=31
  /* lineattrs=(color=black) BLACK is default when color-coding
     for a continuous var, and a RattrMap & GRADLEGEND are used */
  datalabel=MPG_City
  datalabelattrs=(color=black) /* mandatory if you want black text
                                  black is not the default */
  datalabelpos=top;
xaxis display=(noline noticks nolabel);
yaxis display=(noline noticks nolabel);
gradlegend / title='Avg Price in Thousands';
run;
```

We have seen the scope of communication-effective possibilities with basic bubble plots. Figure 7-4 uses axis tables to *add* information. Blue and red as text and number colors in Figure 7-4 draws attention to the axis tables' content and ties it to the title where the identity of the values in the axis tables is specified. The purple color for subtitle and legend title and values draws attention and connects the subtitle to the delivered information. The code for this example is lengthy, but conceptually straightforward.

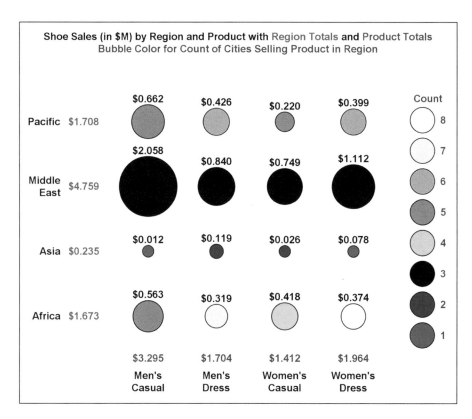

Figure 7-4. Annotated bubble plot with custom color coding and a KeyLegend, visually presents two response variables, but with axis tables for one response variable

Listing 7-4. *Code used to create Figure 7-4*

```
proc summary data=sashelp.shoes nway;
where Region IN ('Africa' 'Asia' 'Middle East' 'Pacific')
AND  (Product =: "Men's" OR Product =: "Women's");
class Region Product;
var Sales;
output out=work.ToRescale(rename=(_freq_ = CountOfCities)) sum=Sales;
run;
data work.ToChart;
set work.ToRescale;
Sales = Sales / 1000000;
run;

data work.DattrMap_EightColors;
retain id "DiscreteID";
length value $ 1 fillcolor $ 9;
input value $ fillcolor $;
datalines;
```

```
1 blue
2 purple
3 black
4 turquoise
5 green
6 orange
7 yellow
8 white
run;

ods listing gpath="C:\temp" dpi=300 style=GraphFontArial9ptBold;
ods graphics on / reset=all scale=off width=5.7in height=4.8in
  imagename="Fig7-4_AnnoColorCodedBubblePlotWithRowAndColumnTotals";
title1 font='Arial/Bold' height=9pt justify=center
  'Shoe Sales (in $M) by Region and Product with ' color=blue
  'Region Totals' color=black ' and ' color=red 'Product Totals';
title2 font='Arial/Bold' height=9pt justify=center color=purple
  'Bubble Color for Count of Cities Selling Product in Region';
proc sgplot data=work.ToChart noborder
  dattrmap=work.DattrMap_EightColors;
bubble x=Product y=Region size=Sales / proportional
  bradiusmax=36 /* For this example the default left the bubbles
                widely separated. Too much empty space was wasted. */
  lineattrs=(color=black)
  group=CountOfCities attrid=DiscreteID
  datalabel=Sales datalabelattrs=(color=black) datalabelpos=top;
xaxistable Sales / x=Product stat=sum label=' '
  location=inside position=bottom
  valueattrs=(color=red);
yaxis display=(nolabel noline noticks)
  fitpolicy=splitalways splitchar=' ';
yaxistable Sales / y=Region stat=sum label=' '
  location=inside position=left
  valueattrs=(color=blue);
xaxis display=(nolabel noline noticks)
  fitpolicy=splitalways splitchar=' ';
format Sales dollar6.3;
keylegend / noborder position=right
  sortorder=descending
  title='Count' titleattrs=(color=purple)
  valueattrs=(color=purple)
  fillheight=24pt;
run;
```

Figure 7-4 uses the axis tables for totals of the SIZE variable. Depending on the nature of the second response variable that is being delivered via color coding and a legend, one might find it useful to add a second set of axis tables for a statistic for that variable as well. For example, for this data, one could add axis tables for the mean Count of Cities, where the Y axis table values would be the mean number of cities where the four products are sold in each region, and the X axis table values would be the mean number of regions where each product is sold.

Having explored increasing the information that can be delivered with bubble plots, let's look at what happens to the two bubble plots in Figures 7-2 and 7-3 when the code used is simplified. There are two steps in code simplification for each of the bubble plots. The first step is to eliminate the attribute map for custom color coding, and the second step is to eliminate the legend statement. Figure 7-5 shows the result of the first step applied to what had been Figure 7-2.

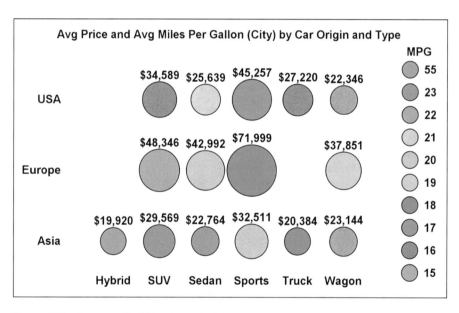

Figure 7-5. Annotated bubble plot with default color coding and a KeyLegend

You might prefer this default color palette instead of the custom color palette for Figure 7-2. To create this bubble plot, you must omit the discrete attribute map creation code step.

Listing 7-5. *Changes to code used for Figure 7-2 needed to create Figure 7-5*

```
/* DATA step  beginning with data work.DattrMap_TenColors; is removed */

  imagename="Fig7-5_AnnoColorCodedBubblePlotKeyLegendNoDattrMap"

proc sgplot data=work.ToPlot noborder;
/* dattrmap=work.DattrMap_TenColors is removed from PROC statement */
```

```
/* On the BUBBLE statement,
   attrid=DiscreteID is removed */
```

Figure 7-6 shows the result of giving up the custom color coding used in Figure 7-3 by omitting the range attribute map creation and use. The default color gradient legend in ODS Graphics is called the Three Color Model and uses blue, white, and red. The default gradient legend is less informative than the custom legend in Figure 7-3. For the next step in Figure 7-8, there is a different gradient legend that uses a gradient of shades of only one hue.

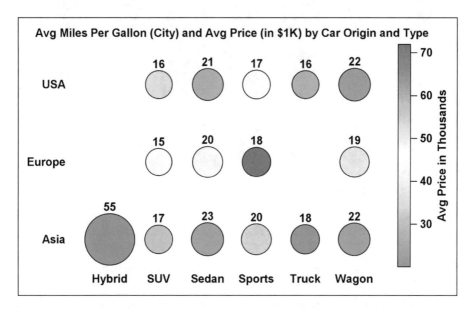

Figure 7-6. Annotated bubble plot with a default color model and a color gradient legend

To create this bubble plot, you must omit the range attribute map creation code step.

Listing 7-6. *Changes to code used for Figure 7-3 needed to create Figure 7-6*

```
/* DATA step  beginning with data work.RattrMap_NineColors; is removed */
imagename="Fig7-6_AnnoColorCodedBubblePlotGradLegendNoRattrMap"

proc sgplot data=work.ToPlot noborder;
/* rattrmap=work.RattrMap_NineColors
   is removed from PROC statement */

/* On the BUBBLE statement,
   attrid=RangeID is removed */
```

Figure 7-7 shows the result of not only removing the use of a discrete attribute map but also removing the KEYLEGEND statement for a customized legend. The default legend is located at the bottom, not at the side, and is displayed in a box.

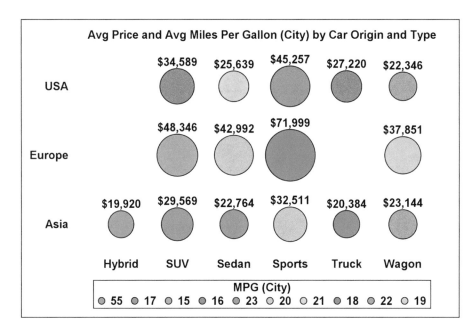

Figure 7-7. Annotated bubble plot with default color coding and a default KeyLegend

To create Figure 7-7 by changing the code for Figure 7-5 requires only three changes: omit the KEYLEGEND statement, omit the TITLE2 white space statement, and use this image filename:

```
Fig7-7_AnnoColorBubblePlotDiscreteNumGroup_DefaultLegend
```

Figure 7-8 uses a two-color model color gradient, but omits the GRADLEGEND statement, from which the only effect on the legend is substitution of the COLORRESPONSE variable name in place of the custom title that was used in Figure 7-6. Because the COLORMODEL option is added to the code, it is not the absolute simplest coding solution, but to retain the less-added-value default color gradient would not have been a better choice. The default ThreeColorModel legend with blue, white, and red can carry an intended or unintended difference in significance of blue values versus red values, but with white in the middle, and the added uncertainty of whether a bubble is white OR very light blue OR very light red. In this gradient color domain, uncertainty as to match between bubble and legend value reigns, and a not very populous list of legend values is provided. Even when the GRADLEGEND statement is retained, there is no option to control the list of legend values for a bubble plot. Only a range attribute map makes that possible.

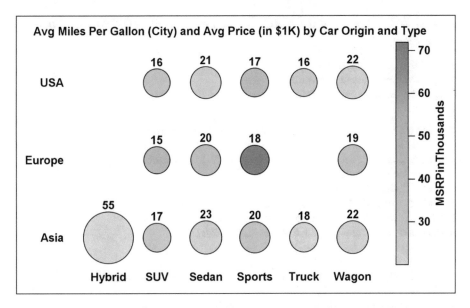

Figure 7-8. Annotated bubble plot with a custom color model and a default GradLegend

To create Figure 7-8 by changing the code used for Figure 7-6 requires only three changes: omit the GRADLEGEND statement, use this image filename:

`Fig7-8_AnnoTwoColorModelBubblePlotDefaultGradLegend`

and on the BUBBLE statement, insert this option:

`colormodel=(verylightgreen verydarkgreen)`

Figure 7-9 is a demonstration of the difference in results between using the BUBBLE statement PROPORTIONAL option as recommended here and accepting the LINEAR sizing default.

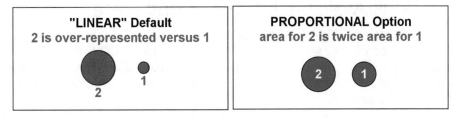

Figure 7-9. Default sizing of bubbles without and with the PROPORTIONAL option

For the LINEAR example, based on my physically measuring the bubbles and doing the math, my estimate is that the area for SIZE=2 is approximately NINE times area for SIZE=1.

Listing 7-9. *Code using the BUBBLE statement with PROPORTIONAL option and without*

```
data work.ForComparison;
X=1; Y=1; Response=2; output;
X=2; Y=1; Response=1; output;
run;

ods listing gpath="C:\temp" dpi=300 style=GraphFontArial11ptBold;

ods graphics / reset=all scale=off width=2.8in height=1.3in
   imagename="Fig7-9Left_LINEAR";
title1 '"LINEAR" Default';
title2 color=red "2 is over-represented versus 1";
proc sgplot data=work.ForComparison noborder;
bubble x=X y=Y size=Response / datalabel=Response
   datalabelattrs=(color=red)
   datalabelpos=bottom
   /* omit PROPORTIONAL as only way to access default alternative */
   fillattrs=(color=red);
xaxis display=none values=(0 1 2 3); yaxis display=none;
run;

ods graphics / reset=all scale=off width=2.8in height=1.3in
   imagename="Fig7-9Right_PROPORTIONAL";
title1 "PROPORTIONAL Option";
title2 color=blue "area for 2 is twice area for 1";
proc sgplot data=work.ForComparison noborder;
bubble x=X y=Y size=Response / datalabel=Response
   datalabelattrs=(color=white)
   datalabelpos=center
   PROPORTIONAL /* as recommended */
   fillattrs=(color=blue);
xaxis display=none values=(0 1 2 3); yaxis display=none;
run;
```

Options Available but Not Used Here

For a heat map, REFTICKS can be used to replicate X and Y axis values on the opposite side of the heat map. For a bubble plot, the XAXIS2 statement, if used, *moves* the X axis to the top of the bubble plot, but unlike REFTICKS does not leave a complementary X axis at the bottom. The YAXIS2 statement function is analogous.

If you like the effect, DATASKIN=PRESSED on the BUBBLE statement makes the bubble fill look like a button. Other bubble decoration options include CRISP, GLOSS, MATTE, and SHEEN. My favorite choice is the no-choice-necessary default of NONE. For your information, the DATASKIN feature is *also* available for bar charts and other ODS Graphics deliverables that involve area fills. If the feature will have some benefit for your application, even if it does not make it more communication-effective, it might do no harm. However, if you are embedding a data label or text in the filled area, it is essential to verify that the superfluous dataskin has no negative effect on readability of the text. The dataskin effect is not a plain solid fill color. The best "skin" for communication-effectiveness (and which requires no additional coding) is a plain solid fill color. Actually, if no color coding is involved, an empty fill is sufficient and offers the benefit of reliable contrast for readability when the area is annotated.

Transparency options are available in ODS Graphics for situations where there might be overlap of graphic elements. Depending on the size of the bubbles, your plot might create some overlap, as shown, for example, in Figure 7-1. There are two transparency options for bubble plots: (1) TRANSPARENCY=YourValue directly on the BUBBLE statement, which affects both the bubble fill and the bubble outline; and (2) FILLATTRS=(TRANSPARENCY=YourOtherValue) which affects only bubble fill.

The value for transparency ranges from 0 for none to 1 for everything white (erasure of all communication). A good use of transparency was shown in Figure 2-9, which is not a bubble plot.

There are other options available that are not discussed in this section, and not used in this chapter, which you can find in the documentation for the ODS Graphics BUBBLE statement in the *SAS ODS Graphics Procedures Guide*.

Summary

Let me start with three reminders.

If you follow the recommendation that bubble areas should be proportional, it is essential to include PROPORTIONAL on the BUBBLE statement since the default is LINEAR, with consequences like that shown in Figure 7-9.

If you are color-coding the bubbles, with either a custom palette by using an attribute map or a default color palette without an attribute map, and you are also using data labels for the bubbles (typically, as is done here, to annotate the value of the SIZE variable—which is used to determine bubble sizes), for black text you must specify DATALABELATTRS=(COLOR=BLACK) on the BUBBLE statement. (Other text characteristics controls can also be included.) With color coding in effect, the default color for the data labels is the color of the fill used for the bubble. The color of the bubble is used to represent the value of the GROUP or COLORRESPONSE variable, not the value of the SIZE variable. This default situation is confusing, not communication-effective.

If you are color-coding the bubbles using the GROUP option (for a variable with discrete values), black outlines for the bubbles are NOT the default. What happens depends on whether the color coding is custom or default. In any case, to get black outlines on the bubbles, on the BUBBLE statement you must specify LINEATTRS=(COLOR=BLACK).

A bubble plot is like a heat map that has escaped from the prison of that grid of cells. Despite that escape advantage, when feasible, the best place to annotate is inside the bubbles. It imposes no additional space needs to fit the annotation, and there is no possible ambiguity as to which bubble the annotation pertains. However, the combination of minimum bubble size and font size desired for readability might prohibit that.

The next best choice is above the bubbles. By making the image tall enough, it is always easy to annotate the bubbles with the DATALABELPOS=TOP option.

Rather than use an all-in-one bubble plot, with bubbles and annotation for a SIZE variable, and color coding and a legend for a second variable, a good alternative can be a complementary pair of bubble plots with annotated bubbles for only a SIZE variable, as demonstrated by the bubble plots in Figure 7-1. The benefit is absolute certainty and precision for the values of both variables. Yes, the viewer must look in two places, but the all-in-one solution of annotation and color coding with legend also requires looking in two places. And if the color-coded variable is continuous numeric, the legend is a gradient which makes knowledge of the precise numbers impossible. The coding for the pair is the simplest. With no need for color coding, you can suppress the color fill (by use of the OUTLINE option, which really means outline-only). The benefits of no color fill are (1) the possibility of annotation inside the bubbles, subject to compatibility between minimum bubble size and needed annotation font size, and (2) an image that can be, if needed, printed (reproduced) on a black-and-white printer (copier).

With axis tables, you can go in the opposite direction as in Figure 7-4 and be maximally informative. When your bubble values in rows and columns are additive, you can present a more complex image with axis tables for row and column totals. You could, if interested and it's appropriate, use axis tables for more than totals. The choices for the STAT option on an XAXISTABLE or YAXISTABLE statement are FREQ, MEAN, MEDIAN, PERCENT, and SUM, where SUM is the default. You can present multiple axis tables for each axis.

Also, though you always have the option to assert control over bubble sizes with the BRADIUSMAX option on the BUBBLE statement, never also use the BRADIUSMIN option. Top and bottom limits on the bubble radius can create a situation where they are in contradiction with the intention of proportionality. Whenever there is such a contradiction, proportionality loses the battle. The default maximum bubble size, which depends on space available and software estimation, may usually turn out to be to your satisfaction. In any case, BRADIUSMAX is available to use however you choose, until you find an acceptable visual outcome.

The ODS Graphics bubble plot is a powerful and communication-effective tool to easily deliver, for the X and Y categorical keys, the combination of image and precise numbers for the SIZE variable. When the bubbles are color-coded by assigning a second variable to the GROUP (COLORRESPONSE) option and using a discrete (range) attribute map, as was done for Figure 7-2 (Figure 7-3), the bubble plot can carry out a twofold communication mission. The GROUP option is for a variable with discrete values, and the COLORRESPONSE option is for a variable with continuous numeric values. With an attribute map, you can control the color palette. Without one, you get a default color palette, and in the case of the COLORRESPONSE option, no control over the values listed on the gradient legend.

Time Series Plots and Trend Lines

A business enterprise, organization, or government entity has essential data that includes variables that are dates, times, or datetimes, also known as time series data, trend data, or temporal data.

William Playfair invented the time series plot (and the pie chart). His first 43 time series plots were in the book *The Commercial and Political Atlas*, which was published in London in 1786.

A key design principle of my book is that graphs, in addition to a visual representation of the data for quick and easy inference, must also deliver precise numbers for inferences that are accurate and reliable. The challenges of time series graphs are (a) the frequent high density of plot points, (b) the common use of overlay plots, and (c) the possible confluence of both situations. Data labels are prone to collisions, whether label with label or label with line. Overlay plots are even more prone to collisions due to the presence of more points to collide with each other and of more lines to collide with points.

© LeRoy Bessler 2023
LeR. Bessler, *Visual Data Insights Using SAS ODS Graphics*,
https://doi.org/10.1007/978-1-4842-8609-8_8

Workarounds for these obstacles will be presented. And a variety of ways to present time series data will be shown.

Though this is the introduction to Chapter 8, it should be noted that other ways to present time series and trend data are provided in Chapters 9, 10, and 14, and with vertical bar charts in Chapter 4.

General Remarks About Code Used

Several examples have %INCLUDE statements for code or macros from folder C:\SharedCode, which could instead be any folder or location of your choice.

The following framing code has been more expansively discussed in Chapter 3 in the section "Outer Structure of ODS Graphics Code in Examples." The framing code for all examples in this chapter and others is

```
ods results off; /* verify results by opening the image file,
                    rather than using the SAS Output window */
ods _all_ close; /* avoid unintended consequences
                    and superfluous concurrent output */
< ODS LISTING statement here >
< example-specific code here >
ods listing close; /* ALWAYS Best Practice */
```

For brevity, the example code in listings omits the first two lines and the last one. It is best to add them back at your runtime. (Source code files include them.)

The ODS LISTING statement can vary. All of the examples in this chapter use a statement of the following form to specify the text characteristics:

```
ods listing style=GraphFontArial11ptBold gpath="C:\temp" dpi=300;
```

but often with font sizes other than 11pt. The statement assumes that the ODS style GraphFontArial11ptBold has been created. To assure that all of the styles needed in this chapter are available, use this code:

```
%include "C:\SharedCode\AllGraphTextSetup.sas";
%AllGraphTextSetup(8);
%AllGraphTextSetup(10);
%AllGraphTextSetup(11);
```

For more information about ODS custom styles, as well as the source code for the AllGraphTextSetup macro, see the section "Control of Text Attributes with a Custom ODS Style" in Chapter 3. For information about options for direct control of text attributes, which can override the default text attributes that are set up by an ODS style, see the section "Text Attributes Control in ODS Graphics" in Chapter 3.

Key Concerns and Methods for Time Series Plots

In a graph context where plot point density can be high, how one allocates the space available is important.

For a multi-line overlay plot, you can put the line identity in a legend at the bottom, or you can put it in curve labels at the ends (or starts) of the lines. One solution compresses the lines displayed vertically; the other does it horizontally. The best choice is image specific, which is really data specific. In this chapter, curve labels are used for an example for which the purpose is to simply *demonstrate* the CURVELABEL option or for situations where curve labels fit without detriment and are deemed to be the better choice than a legend. Their benefit is their immediate attachment to the lines, so that the viewer's eye need not hunt for the line identity in a legend at the bottom of the image.

Another concern with time series plots as regards space use is the range allocation for the Y axis. The software default lays out the axis with the Y value minimum and maximum at each end. This maximizes the granularity of the plot and, for a multi-line overlay plot, reduces the probability of data label collisions, both label-label and label-line. Whether the plot is single-line or multi-line, if neither data labels nor an X axis table is feasible, then a more granular Y axis can reduce the amount of error in estimating where a plot point's value lies along the Y axis. Both grid lines and minor grid lines can help with that.

The disadvantage of the default is magnification of change—that is, maximizing the slope from point to point on the line. Whenever possible without detriment to the usability and interpretability of the plot, I steadfastly recommend starting the Y axis at zero. This policy prevents unjustified elation and needless anxiety about what might really be a modest change that is artificially visually magnified by increasing the slope between points. Significance of change is best determined based on numeric change in value or percent change in value, or by meeting or exceeding a goal, or by crossing a threshold of significance.

In Chapter 4 on graphs for categorical data, the recommendation "Show Them What's Important" was implemented with ranking and subsetting. Those principles and methods are not applicable for time series data. However, for temporal data, not all dates are necessarily equally important.

A point where a significant event or environmental change occurred can be identified with a reference line along the X axis. A point where the measure of interest has met (or exceeded) a goal, or crossed a threshold, can be identified with a reference line along the Y axis. If there is a special zone of values for Y (X), that entire subrange of the Y (X) axis can be identified with a band of a light shade of a preferred color or perhaps of a color with special significance.

Furthermore, when tracking some measure of interest, the most interesting points during the time period displayed are the starting value, the ending value, any intermediate maximum or minimum, and any point where the rate of change has persistently changed, from slow to fast or vice versa.

Empowering the viewer to identify these points of significance is achieved by my decades old principle of sparse annotation of the time series plot line, and now by my recent reinvention of that idea with the Sparse Line (a vast improvement over, and concept different from, the so-called Sparkline). With my characteristic propensity for understatement, I like to call this concept "The Ineffable Incontrovertible Insightful Power of Simplicity of the Annotated Sparse Line." The Sparse Line omits all axes and includes an additional annotation (below the plot point) at the end of the plot line to report the change since the second last plot point. I call this graph interchangeably Sparse Line and Annotated Sparse Line. A sparse plot line without annotation would be useless. So, "Annotated" should always be understood if referring to a Sparse Line.

Fitting data labels for those points of significance is not a problem for a single-line plot. You will also see it done for a multi-line plot.

More typical time series plots, whether multi-line or single-line, have numerous points and providing data labels for all of them can be difficult, if not impossible. How to deal with that will be addressed.

Though the graphs usually rendered to present time series data or trend data are plot lines, this chapter also presents other graphic alternatives, including the counterintuitive solution of delivering precise numbers and trend, the temporal pattern, by using only a graphic display of the Y and X coordinate values, Y over X, at each plot point, with no marker. By using text only, with no visible axes and no plot line, one can provide the viewer a clear and fair graphic visual presentation of both the temporal change and the precise numbers of Y and X, together in pairs, with the two values concatenated or stacked.

Tools for Time Series Graphs

The ODS Graphics procedure used in this chapter is SGPLOT.

PROC SGPANEL can be used to assemble and display an array or matrix of individual time series graphs. That is covered in Chapter 9.

ODS HTML5 enables the web deployment of graphs, singly, with several interlinked views (entire or subsetted), or with same-page or linked-to and back-from tables. ODS HTML5, ODS EXCEL, ODS POWERPOINT, ODS WORD, and ODS PDF are ways to package graphs with companion lookup tables or collections of related graphs. ODS HTML5 offers the advantage of displaying a temporary data label with the mouse. That data tip can be as fancy and information-rich as the programmer is willing to make it.

Examples created here use PROC SGPLOT and the ODS LISTING. The LISTING destination delivers static graphs to disk or some other storage location.

PROC SGPLOT supports several statements usable for time series graphs:

> NEEDLE
>
> HIGHLOW
>
> SCATTER
>
> SERIES
>
> STEP
>
> TEXT
>
> VBAR
>
> VLINE (not shown in this chapter)

Accessory statements used here with PROC SGPLOT:

> BAND
>
> DROPTO
>
> REFLINE
>
> STYLEATTRS
>
> XAXISTABLE
>
> Y2AXIS (YAXIS is the norm, Y2AXIS can be used in addition or instead.)

Options for Lines and Markers

To customize the plot line, use LINEATTRS=(with suboptions here), where the suboptions are

COLOR

THICKNESS (default unit is pixels, abbreviated as px, if not omitted)

PATTERN (there are 46 choices, but I use only Solid, or Dot, or ThinDot, where thinness means wider separation between dots, not smaller dots)

There is no way to turn off the plot lines for the SERIES statement. In cases where you want to suppress the plot line, the only solution is to use COLOR=WHITE. A good reason to do this is to prevent collisions between data labels and lines. The lines are drawn first, so there is no risk of white lines crossing data labels or markers.

When not hidden with COLOR=WHITE, most of the lines in the examples are Solid. PATTERN=Dot is used in Figures 8-16, 8-25, and 8-30. PATTERN=ThinDot is used, in order to minimize the impact of collisions with data labels, in Figures 8-3, 8-4, and 8-10.

The lines in this chapter's examples are drawn either at default thickness (which is 1 pixel or 1px) or at some wider thickness, which can be necessary for color distinguishability on a multi-line overlay plot which is color-coded and relies on matching colors in a legend, in an X axis table, or on curve labels. (Color matching is less of a concern for curve labels which are located at an end of each line.) For color-coding examples where line thickness is important for color matching, see Figures 8-21, 8-22, 8-25, 8-30, and 8-31. In Figure 8-21, the first title line also serves as a legend to identify the plot lines.

When needing to match a line color to text, the text must also be thick enough. Throughout all examples in this chapter, all text is drawn Bold. (In a situation where you need something thicker than Bold, use Arial Black as the font.) In Figures 8-17 to 8-21, color-coded titles serve as legends to identify data labels. In Figure 8-17, the markers also match the identifying part of the title text.

It should be noted that the LINEATTRS option is also available for the REFLINE, BAND, DROPLINE, HIGHLOW, STEP, and many other statements that result in drawing of lines. There are examples of such uses in this chapter.

For the SERIES statement (the most frequently used ODS Graphics statement in this chapter), markers are omitted by default. To turn them on, use the MARKERS option.

To customize markers, use MARKERATTRS=(with suboptions here), where the suboptions are

> COLOR
>
> SIZE (default unit is pixels, abbreviated as px, if not omitted)
>
> SYMBOL (there are 30 choices, default is a Circle, I prefer CircleFilled)

In addition to customization with MARKERATTRS, the option FILLEDOUTLINEMARKERS can be specified to turn on the capability to specify different colors for fill and outline using two options:

> MARKERFILLATTRS (used for COLOR of the marker fill)
>
> MARKEROUTLINEATTRS (used for COLOR and for THICKNESS of the marker outline, with default units of pixels)

Before presenting code from an example, let me explain the context. Figure 8-26 is an overlay plot for a monthly measurement variable for five different years. Each year's plot line and plot markers are a distinctive color by default. Color for the lines and the markers can be customized with a STYLEATTRS statement in the PROC SGPLOT code block. The lines and basic markers for Figure 8-26 are drawn by a SERIES statement with these options:

```
lineattrs=(pattern=Solid)
markers markerattrs=(symbol=CircleFilled size=7)
```

The markers are selectively overlaid at the minimum and maximum points in each year with SCATTER statements with these options:

```
/* on the SCATTER statement for the yearly maxima */
markerattrs=(symbol=CircleFilled size=7)
markerfillattrs=(color=LightGray)
markeroutlineattrs=(color=Black thickness=1)

/* on the SCATTER statement for the yearly minima */
markerattrs=(symbol=CircleFilled size=7)
markerfillattrs=(color=White)
markeroutlineattrs=(color=Black thickness=1)
```

Special Data Sets Used for Some Time Series Graphs

There are five data sets for daily, weekly, monthly, quarterly, and yearly financial data that are provided as members of the SASHELP data library, but only if the site has a license for the SAS/ETS product. However, readers without a SAS/ETS license must download the zip file CitiData.zip from https://github.com/Apress/Visual-Data-Insights-Using-SAS-ODS-Graphics and store the five unzipped files in any location that is preferred, such as C:\CitiData.

The data set names are citiday, citiwk, citimon, citiqtr, and citiyr, for daily, weekly, monthly, quarterly, and yearly data, respectively. The examples in this book use only citiday and citimon.

Information about all SASHELP data sets is provided at

https://support.sas.com/documentation/tools/sashelpug.pdf

If you have SAS/ETS license, you can reference the needed data sets as sashelp. citiday and sashelp.citimon. If not, before referencing the data, your code must run a LIBNAME statement such as this:

```
libname citilib "C:\CitiData";
```

where the presumption is that you have stored the zip file contents in that folder. Thereafter, during the same SAS session, you can reference the needed data sets as citilib.citiday and citilib.citimon.

Of course, the LIBREF need not be CitiLib, but code for this book assumes that. To simplify the task of accessing the CITIDAY and CITIMON data sets, macros were created for use in this chapter, as well as Chapters 9 and 14. Listing 8-0 prepares two data sets from CITIMON and CITIDAY for use in this chapter as well as elsewhere.

Listing 8-0. *Extract S and P index by month and Dow Jones index by day*

```
/* To prepare sasuser.SandPbyMonth1980to1991
   and subset sasuser.SandPbyMonth1987to1991 */
%include "C:\SharedCode\ExtractSandPbyMonthTwoRanges.sas";
options mprint;
%ExtractSandPbyMonthTwoRanges
(SASETSsiteUseSASHELPDataLib=NO,
OtherSiteFolderForCitiData=C:\CitiData,
OutLib=SASUSER);

/* To prepare sasuser.DowJonesByDayIn1990 */
%include "C:\SharedCode\ExtractDowJonesByDayIn1990.sas";
options mprint;
```

```
%ExtractDowJonesByDayIn1990
(SASETSsiteUseSASHELPDataLib=NO,
OtherSiteFolderForCitiData=C:\CitiData,
OutLib=SASUSER);
```

/* To prepare WORK.DowJonesByDayInJan1991
which is DELETED at end of the SAS session */
```
%include "C:\SharedCode\ExtractDowJonesByDayInJan1991.sas";
options mprint;
%ExtractDowJonesByDayInJan1991
(SASETSsiteUseSASHELPDataLib=NO,
OtherSiteFolderForCitiData=C:\CitiData,
OutLib=WORK);
```

Inspecting and Managing the SASUSER Data Library

If you wish to create a list of what you have accumulated in SASUSER, for any purpose, the needed code is

```
options linesize=max pagesize=max nocenter nodate nonumber;
title;
ods noproctitle;
ods results off;
ods _all_ close;
ods listing
  file="C:\temp\DirectoryListingForSASUSERdataLibrary.txt";
proc datasets library=sasuser;
contents data=_all_ nods;
run;
ods listing close;
```

You can omit all of the framing in the preceding code if you only want to see the contents in the SAS log. To inspect a data set called Whatever that is in SASUSER, the needed code is

```
ods listing file="C:\temp\ContentsOfDataSetNamedWhatever.txt";
proc datasets library=sasuser;
contents data=Whatever;
run;
ods listing close;
```

To remove a no longer needed data set in SASUSER, use this code:

```
proc datasets library=sasuser;
delete Whatever;
run;
```

and look for this NOTE in the SAS log:

```
NOTE: Deleting SASUSER.WHATEVER (memtype=DATA).
```

Time Series One-Line Plots

Getting Started

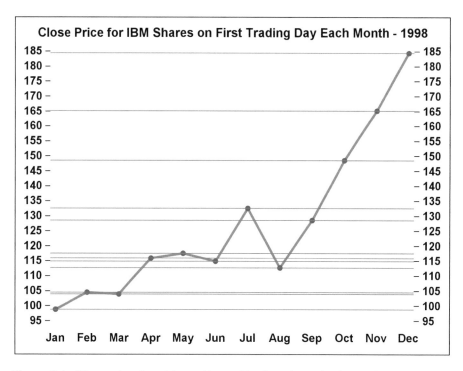

Figure 8-1. Time series plot with two Y axes, Y tick marks, and reference lines (where the reference lines serve, in effect, as drop lines to both Y axes)

Figure 8-1 is a best effort solution that tries to provide as much as possible to make estimating easier, even though the result inevitably is NOT precise values. Though I usually recommend starting the Y axis for a trend at zero, when relying on estimating Y values it is best to have the range of the Y variable use all of the available vertical space. The combination of reference lines (as a surrogate for drop lines) and tick marks enables a more nearly accurate guess as to the precise values of the Y values. Two Y axes allow the viewer to choose the shortest visual trip from any plot point to its Y value on the nearer Y axis.

Listing 8-1. *Code used to create Figure 8-1*

```
ods listing style=GraphFontArial11ptBold gpath="C:\temp" dpi=300;
ods graphics on / reset=all scale=off width=5.7in
  imagename="Fig8-1_SeriesClose_TwoYaxes_RefLines";
title1 justify=center
'Close Price for IBM Shares on First Trading Day Each Month - 1998';
proc sgplot data=sashelp.stocks noborder
  noautolegend; /* because two lines are drawn (one for Y axis,
  other for Y2 axis, a useless legend would appear by default. */
where year(Date) EQ 1998 and Stock EQ 'IBM';
series x=Date y=Close /
  markers /* In a SERIES plot, markers are ABSENT by default */
  markerattrs=(symbol=CircleFilled color=blue size=6)
  /* The default SYMBOL is an OPEN circle.
    The default unit for SIZE is pixels, as in 6px
    The default size is 7px */
  lineattrs=(pattern=Solid color=green thickness=3px);
  /* The default PATTERN is NOT Solid.
    The default COLOR is NOT Black.
    The default unit for THICKNESS is pixels, as in 3px
    The default thickness is 1px
    In color-coded line plot, much thicker is better
    to assure color distinguishability. */
series x=Date y=Close / y2axis /* extra Y axis on the right side */
  markers markerattrs=(symbol=CircleFilled color=blue size=6)
  lineattrs=(pattern=Solid color=green thickness=3);
refline Close; /* A reference line at every value of Close.
  It acts as a bi-directional drop line.
  The DROPLINE statement can create drop lines only to
  a left-hand-side Y axis (and/or to the X axis),
  not to both the Y axis and the Y2 axis. */
yaxis  display=(noline nolabel) fitpolicy=none
  values=(95 to 185 by 5) valueattrs=(size=10pt);
y2axis display=(noline nolabel) fitpolicy=none
  values=(95 to 185 by 5) valueattrs=(size=10pt);
xaxis  display=(noline noticks nolabel) valueattrs=(size=10pt)
  type=discrete; /* suppresses display of 1998 below Jan */
format Date monname3. Close 3.;
run;
```

Using the ODS Graphics SERIES Statement for a Single-Line Time Series Plot

An X axis table, as in Figure 8-2, is an always reliable way to deliver the precise numbers, unless the Y values are too wide to fit in the image width at a readable font size.

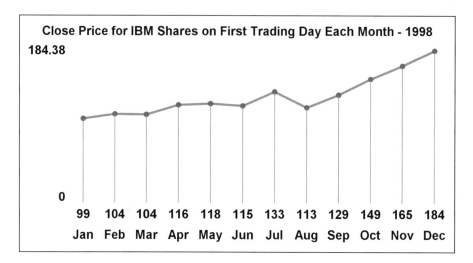

Figure 8-2. An X axis table delivers the precise Y values adjacent to X values. The Y axis starts at zero. Drop lines probably not really needed for so few points, but do no harm

There is no X-Y association uncertainty in Figure 8-2 since the X and Y values are immediately adjacent, but those values are remote from the plot points. Drop lines are included as demonstration of capability, not due to compelling visual communication need, despite the remoteness. Various ways to deal with remoteness are presented later in this chapter.

In Figure 8-2, and in many of the remaining examples in this chapter, the Y axis starts at zero. As previously explained, this policy presents the slope of change in a more representative fashion and prevents unjustified optimism and needless anxiety about changes that would otherwise be artificially visually magnified if all of the available vertical space were devoted only to the range between minimum and maximum Y values. A change is best evaluated by using the raw magnitude or the percent change or by whether or not it crosses some desired goal or to-be-avoided threshold. Chapter examples where the Y axis does *not* start at zero either minimize collisions for data labels or better present the image in other respects.

There are two disadvantages when using zero, one insignificant. Starting the Y axis at zero squashes the spread of Y values for the points. This is a problem only when there are no data labels or X axis table to deliver precise Y values, and the viewer is guessing where a point lies along the tick marks and values on the Y axis. The other concern is not for the viewer. Starting the Y axis at zero (until ODS Graphics is someday enhanced to support an analogue of the easy-to-use VZERO option in SAS/GRAPH) requires data preprocessing to find the maximum Y value and a little more other coding to get it into the YAXIS statement. It is not difficult, but is extra work for the programmer, as shown in Listing 8-2.

Listing 8-2. *Code used to create Figure 8-2*

```
/* The macro variables
   (MaxClose, MaxCloseDisplay, and MaxCloseRoundedUp)
   disappear at end of SAS session.
   So, any examples that reference them must either be run
   during the same session as the run to create Figure 8-3,
   or this DATA step must be rerun. */
data work.IBM1998Close;
retain MaxClose 0;
set sashelp.Stocks end=LastOne;
where year(Date) EQ 1998 and Stock EQ 'IBM';
MaxClose = max(MaxClose,Close);
Output;
if LastOne;
call symput('MaxClose',MaxClose);
call symput('MaxCloseDisplay',trim(left(put(MaxClose,6.2))));
call symput('MaxCloseRoundedUp',ceil(MaxClose));
         /* round up to next integer */
run;
/* The above DATA step code is stored in C:\SharedCode as
   IBM1998CloseAndMaxCloseMacroVariable.sas;
   for %INCLUDE in other examples. */

ods listing style=GraphFontArial11ptBold gpath="C:\temp" dpi=300;
ods graphics on / reset=all scale=off width=5.7in height=3in
   imagename="Fig8-2_SeriesClose_YstartAtZero_DropLines_XaxisTable";
title1 justify=center
'Close Price for IBM Shares on First Trading Day Each Month - 1998';
proc sgplot data=work.IBM1998Close noborder;
series x=Date y=Close /
   markers markerattrs=(symbol=CircleFilled color=blue size=6)
   lineattrs=(pattern=Solid color=green thickness=3);
dropline x=Date y=Close / dropto=x;
xaxistable Close /
   label=' ' /* if LABEL='' (i.e., a null, not a blank),
   or if the LABEL option is not used,
   then the data set label for the CLOSE variable will be displayed
   if a label exists. If no label exists,
   then the variable name itself will be displayed. */
   title='' /* If TITLE=' ' (i.e., a blank, not the null),
   a useless blank line will be created above the axis table. */
   location=inside; /* INSIDE means above the X axis values */
yaxis display=(noline noticks nolabel)
   values=(0 &MaxClose) /* start the axis at zero,
                         end the axis at the maximum value */
   valuesdisplay=('0' "&MaxCloseDisplay");
```

```
/* Five choices for VALUESDISPLAY option:
    1. Omit VALUESDISPLAY for ZERO as 0.00
       and Max Y value as 184.38
    2. VALUESDISPLAY=("0" "&MaxCloseDisplay") for 0 and 184.38
    3. VALUESDISPLAY=("0" "&MaxCloseRoundUp") for 0 and 185
    4. VALUESDISPLAY=("0" " ") for 0 and no Max Y value
    5. VALUESDISPLAY=(" " " ") for no Y axis values */
xaxis display=(noline noticks nolabel) type=discrete;
format Date monname3. Close 3.;
run;
```

In Figure 8-3, the drop lines are omitted, and with only 12 pairs of plot points and X axis values, the eye can reliably associate any plot point with its X value. So, there is no uncertainty or ambiguity without the drop lines, but their omission for some viewers might be annoying. To make them less impactful, one can use the LINEATTRS option on the DROPLINE statement. Rather than present the alternatives here, I encourage the reader, if interested, to experiment with LINEATTRS to establish a preferred design. Of the possibilities, I prefer COLOR=LightGray. For me, COLOR=Gray did not look noticeably different from the default color (Black). PATTERN=Dot is OK, but I find PATTERN=ThinDot visually irritating when used for drop lines. You can verify that the default is the same as THICKNESS=1px (1 pixel). So it is impossible to make the drop lines thinner.

Figure 8-3 provides precise values with Y value data labels at the plot points. The Y values are the default data label variable, but you can use *any* variable, or *multiple* variables concatenated horizontally or stacked, for the data labels, as will be shown.

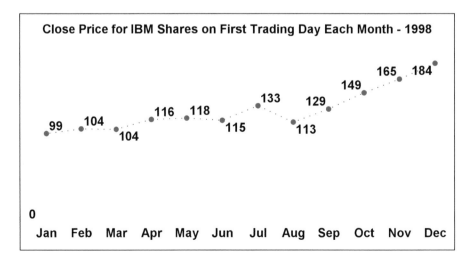

Figure 8-3. Collision of label and plot line is harmless when using the option LINEATTRS PATTERN=ThinDot. The only Y value displayed is zero to prevent magnifying the line slope

As to freedom from collisions, it should be noted that if values are very long, or a stack of value elements, they are more likely to collide with the line, the point, or each other.

After my first run for Figure 8-3, I did not like the coziness between the December data label of 184 and the 1998 at the end of the title line. When I added the TITLE2 statement with COLOR=White to provide white space, the data label for December collided with the plot line. The adverse effect on readability is eliminated by using PATTERN=ThinDot in the LINEATTRS option for the SERIES statement. In Figure 8-3, eliminating the distance between plot points and their Y values is achieved by replacing the X axis table with data labels, but there remains the distance between the plot points and their X values. The better solution is Figure 8-4.

Listing 8-3. *Code used to create Figure 8-3*

```
%include "C:\SharedCode\IBM1998CloseAndMaxCloseMacroVariable.sas";

ods listing style=GraphFontArial11ptBold gpath="C:\temp" dpi=300;
ods graphics on / reset=all scale=off width=5.7in height=3in
  imagename="Fig8-3_SeriesClose_DataLabelsForYvalues";
title1 justify=center
'Close Price for IBM Shares on First Trading Day Each Month - 1998';
title2 color=white 'White Space';
proc sgplot data=work.IBM1998Close noborder;
series x=Date y=Close / datalabel lineattrs=(pattern=ThinDot)
  markers markerattrs=(symbol=CircleFilled color=blue size=6);
yaxis display=(noline noticks nolabel) values=(0 &MaxClose)
  valuesdisplay=("0" " "); /* Identify the Y=0 point of the axis.
  Hide the maximum Y axis value. The end value is the maximum,
  and is identified by the data label. */
xaxis display=(noline noticks nolabel) type=discrete;
format Date monname3. Close 3.;
run;
```

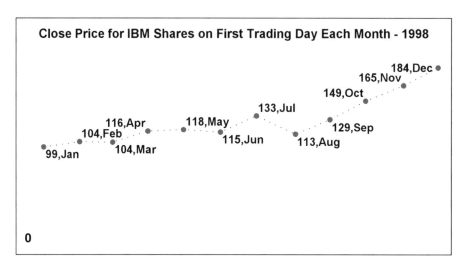

Figure 8-4. Data labels with Y and X values concatenated provide the most communication-effective and communication-efficient image

Figure 8-4 eliminates any uncertainty or ambiguity about Y and X value association and their association with their plot point. The visual behavior of the curve requires no axis values, and starting the Y axis at zero provides a truly representative vision of the trend.

If you look closely at Figure 8-4, you will see that the data labels, which, based on the custom ODS style specified on the ODS LISTING statement, should be the same size as the TITLE text, but are not. Equality in sizing *is* true for Figure 8-5. For Figure 8-4, the software dynamically adjusted the size in an effort to reduce or prevent the possibility of the collisions between labels (notice how close they are for February and April). The possibility that specifications may be overridden is mentioned in the *SAS ODS Graphics Procedures Guide*, where it says:

> For some data and curve labels, font sizes might be automatically reduced in order to achieve less overlapping. This behavior affects all data labels with non-fixed positions, and curve labels for which you have specified a curve label position of MIN or MAX.

Listing 8-4. *Code used to create Figure 8-4*

```
%include "C:\SharedCode\IBM1998CloseAndMaxCloseMacroVariable.sas";

data work.IBM1998Close_CustomDataLabels;
length DataLabelForYandX $ 7;
set work.IBM1998Close;
```

```
DataLabelForYandX = put(Close,3.) || ',' ||
  put(Date,monname3.);
run;

/* The above DATA step code is stored as
"C:\SharedCode\AddCustomDataLabelsToIBM1998Close.sas";
for %INCLUDE in other examples. */

ods listing style=GraphFontArial11ptBold gpath="C:\temp" dpi=300;
ods graphics on / reset=all scale=off width=5.7in height=3in
  imagename="Fig8-4_SeriesClose_DataLabelsForYandXConcatenated";
title1 justify=center
'Close Price for IBM Shares on First Trading Day Each Month - 1998';
title2 color=white 'White Space';
proc sgplot data=work.IBM1998Close_CustomDataLabels noborder;
series x=Date y=Close / datalabel=DataLabelForYandX
  markers markerattrs=(symbol=CircleFilled color=blue size=6)
  lineattrs=(pattern=ThinDot); /* mitigate the readability
                                  effect of collisions */
yaxis display=(noline noticks nolabel) values=(0 &MaxClose)
  valuesdisplay=("0" " "); /* Hide the maximum Y axis value.
  The labelled ending value is the maximum Y value. */
xaxis display=none;
format Close 3.;
run;
```

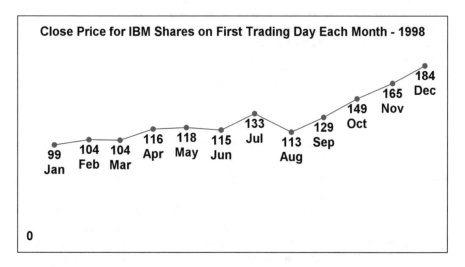

Figure 8-5. The stacked concatenation of Y and X prevents label-line collisions

Stacking the Y and X values (rather than concatenating them as in Figure 8-4) eliminates any possibility of collisions (or the near collisions and the software's shrinking of the font—which occurred for Figure 8-4).

Listing 8-5. *Code used to create Figure 8-5*

```
%include "C:\SharedCode\IBM1998CloseAndMaxCloseMacroVariable.sas";
%include "C:\SharedCode\AddCustomDataLabelsToIBM1998Close.sas";

ods listing style=GraphFontArial11ptBold gpath="C:\temp" dpi=300;
ods graphics on / reset=all scale=off width=5.7in height=3in
  imagename="Fig8-5_SeriesClose_DataLabelsForYandXvaluesStacked";
title1 justify=center
'Close Price for IBM Shares on First Trading Day Each Month - 1998';
title2 color=white 'White Space';
proc sgplot data=work.IBM1998Close_CustomDataLabels noborder;
series x=Date y=Close / datalabel=DataLabelForYandX
  datalabelpos=bottom /* DATALABELPOS=TOP causes collisions.
    Default DATALABELPOS causes more and worse collisions. */
  splitchar=',' /* stack the two parts of the label */
  splitjustify=center lineattrs=(pattern=Solid color=blue)
  markers markerattrs=(symbol=CircleFilled color=blue size=6);
yaxis display=(noline noticks nolabel)
  offsetmin=0 /* DATALABELPOS=BOTTOM by default causes Y=0
  to be raised from its usual position (which is shown here)
  in order to prevent POSSIBLE very low Y values
  from having data labels that extend below the Y=0 point.
  For this data that would not happen,
  but the software prepares for the worst case.
  OFFSETMIN=0 overrides the unnecessary default action. */
  values=(0 &MaxClose) valuesdisplay=("0" " ");
xaxis display=none;
format Close 3.;
run;
```

Since a monthly plot inherently cannot show any intermediate points, the plot line serves no bona fide communication purpose. Figure 8-6 delivers a "virtual line" of plot points. The eye only needs to follow the points. A line just gets in the way. DATALABELPOS=TOP causes Data Label with Line collision problems, but the plot line is hidden with COLOR=WHITE in the LINEATTRS option. The only function that a visible plot line could serve in this case would be to provide something to look at, but which is irrelevant and has no significance. With the data labels at the top, OFFSETMIN=0 can be omitted on the YAXIS statement because there is no need to override the software's no longer relevant caution about the lowest of the formerly bottom data labels possibly extending below the X axis.

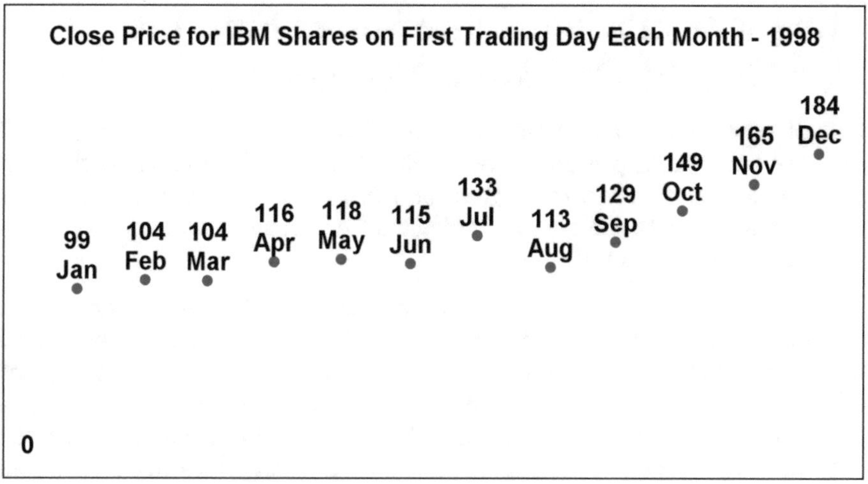

Figure 8-6. Hiding the plot line "erases" any line-label collisions. The eye has a pleasant visual journey along the nonline

Listing 8-6. Code used to create Figure 8-6

```
%include "C:\SharedCode\IBM1998CloseAndMaxCloseMacroVariable.sas";
%include "C:\SharedCode\AddCustomDataLabelsToIBM1998Close.sas";

ods listing style=GraphFontArial11ptBold gpath="C:\temp" dpi=300;
ods graphics on / reset=all scale=off width=5.7in height=3in
   imagename="Fig8-6_SeriesClose_TopDataLabelsStack_HiddenPlotLine";
title1 justify=center
'Close Price for IBM Shares on First Trading Day Each Month - 1998';
title2 color=white 'White Space';
proc sgplot data=work.IBM1998Close_CustomDataLabels noborder;
series x=Date y=Close / datalabel=DataLabelForYandX
   datalabelpos=top /* causes collisions of labels and line */
   splitchar=',' splitjustify=center
   markers markerattrs=(symbol=CircleFilled color=blue size=6)
   lineattrs=(pattern=Solid color=white); /* Hide the line.
      Data labels are drawn after the line.
      So the white line cannot overlay them. */
yaxis display=(noline noticks nolabel)
   values=(0 &MaxClose) valuesdisplay=("0" " ");
xaxis display=none;
format Close 3.;
run;
```

The Most Efficient Time Series Plot: No Plot Line, No Markers, No Axis Lines

Out of context for this section on the SERIES statement is using a TEXT statement to visually present Y and X with their trend. However, its design is the next logical step in the progression from Figure 8-1 to Figure 8-6. The series of Y-over-X text blocks is, in effect, a "virtual line," and the text blocks serve as "virtual markers."

The assertion of "No Axis Lines" in the section title can be regarded as misleading. To present the zero point of the Y axis in Figure 8-7 does require the definition of a Y axis, but the line itself is suppressed. This interesting and useful graph could have been rendered without starting the axis at zero. The image would be simpler, and the slope of the missing line segments (the slope between text blocks) would be steeper. Its rendering does make its layout similar to that of other plots for the same data in this chapter for comparison.

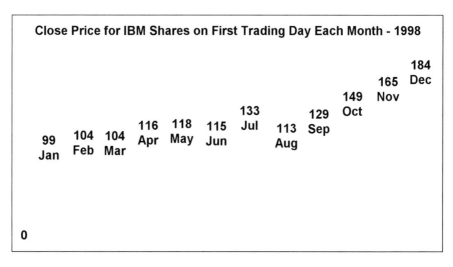

Figure 8-7. The sparse time series plot. Using the TEXT statement to create a truly minimal graph. No plot line is created, real or hidden, and no markers/plot points

One can see the trend without markers and a line. The essential information of exactly what (the precise Y values) and when (the precise X values) is delivered, and the trend is shown at the same time. The TEXT blocks become the markers/plot points, with the association between Y value, X value, and absent marker being immediate and certain. This is the most visually efficient way to achieve our key design objective of image (here, text) for quick, easy inference and precise numbers for correct, reliable inference.

Listing 8-7. *Code used to create Figure 8-7*

```
%include "C:\SharedCode\IBM1998CloseAndMaxCloseMacroVariable.sas";
%include "C:\SharedCode\AddCustomDataLabelsToIBM1998Close.sas";

ods listing style=GraphFontArial11ptBold gpath="C:\temp" dpi=300;
ods graphics on / reset=all scale=off width=5.7in height=3in
  imagename="Fig8-7_TextChartForStackOfCloseOverDate_NoPlotLine";
title1 justify=center
'Close Price for IBM Shares on First Trading Day Each Month - 1998';
title2 color=white 'White Space';
proc sgplot data=work.IBM1998Close_CustomDataLabels noborder;
text x=Date y=Close text=DataLabelForYandX /
  contributeoffsets=(xmax xmin ymax)
  /* These three values are actually PART OF the default.
     The option is specified to turn off the default YMIN.
     When YMIN is in effect, the Y=0 point of the Y axis is,
     for this data, unnecessarily raised
     from where the viewer would expect it to be.
     The purpose of the offsets is to protect displayed values
     that are near the ends of the axes from being clipped.
     To see a demonstration of these these remarks,
     run this code with YMIN added to the list,
     and then run this code with CONTRIBUTEOFFSETS=NONE.
     CONTRIBUTEOFFSETS=ALL (or the full list) is the default. */
  splitchar=',' splitjustify=center splitpolicy=splitalways;
  /* If SPLITPOLICY=SPLITALWAYS is omitted,
     the TEXT values are presented concatenated,
     rather than stacked, with collisions for many cases. */
yaxis display=(noline noticks nolabel)
  values=(0 &MaxClose) valuesdisplay=("0" " ");
xaxis display=none;
format Date monname3. Close 3.;
run;
```

Now back to the SERIES statement, but for a maximally informative and minimally simple deliverable.

The Simplest, Yet Most Importantly Informative, Time Series Plot

In Chapter 1, Figures 1-16 and 1-17 demonstrated my earliest efforts to deliver the simplest possible time series chart, but at the same time to deliver the most important information for the time series data. The description that I coined for the design and construction concept was "Sparse Line Annotation." Graphs like that in Figure 1-16 would identify only the start and end points and points at any intermediate maximum or minimum. Graphs like that in

Figure 1-17 would identify only the start and end points, no intermediate minimum or maximum. Instead, it would identify any intermediate point which where the trend permanently changes in any of these ways:

1. From rapidly increasing to slowly increasing

2. From slowly increasing to rapidly increasing

3. From rapidly decreasing to slowly decreasing

4. From slowly decreasing to rapidly decreasing

Of course, one could consider or encounter more complicated possibilities that combine permanent slope change after an intermediate maximum or minimum. That is out of scope here. In Figure 8-8, but reduced, are those Chapter 1 examples.

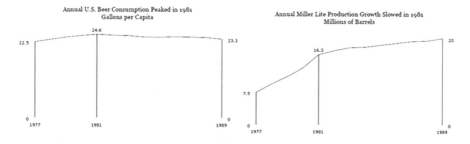

Figure 8-8. Copies of Figures 1-16 and 1-17 (reduced size and harder to read here). Sparse Line Annotation two types: left is start, end, intermediate maximum. Right is start, end, persistent change in slope (rapid increase to slow increase)

I revisited this concept and have reinvented it as what I call a Sparse Line, not to be confused with sparklines, which are less informative and different. Also, I realized that the end point should also be annotated with the change since the second last plot point, since that is almost always of interest, not just highlights of past history.

I want to clarify the difference between a Sparse Line and a sparkline. I developed Sparse Line Annotation (as shown in Figure 8-8) in 1990. The sparklines of today are similar to their first appearance in 1998, when a feature called "inline charts" was implemented in the personal computer trading platform Medved QuoteTracker by interface designer Peter Zelchenko. That was the first real-world example of what has become known as the sparkline. To see what his sparklines look like, examine the screenshot at https://upload. wikimedia.org/wikipedia/commons/9/95/Screenshot_of_Sparklines_ in_Medved_QuoteTracker%2C_1998.png. The sparklines appear in the Chart column of the table of stock information. They are squiggly lines with no stock values and no dates. They are, indeed, summary pictures of the historical trend for each stock in the Medved QuoteTracker. The label "sparkline" is due to Edward Tufte.

The Sparse Line shown in Figure 8-9 delivers both the image of the trend and the values and dates for essential, always-of-interest points in the trend (and its latest change) in one self-sufficient package: both image and precise numbers, which are required for both quick, easy inference and correct, reliable inference.

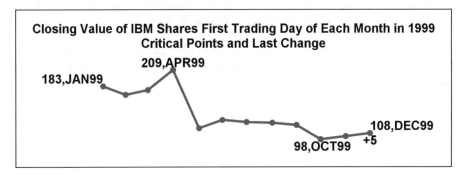

Figure 8-9. The Sparse Line: minimum essentials that the viewer is likely to want to know

Listing 8-9. Code used to create Figure 8-9

```
/* When you run the macro,
    the SAS log will contain the NOTE pasted in below.
    The NOTE has no material signficance.
    It concerns the date format used for the X axis,
    but the X axis is suppressed.
    The DateDisplayFormat, which IS used, is indeed honored.
    You can ignore this:
    "NOTE: The column format DATE7
    is replaced by an auto-generated format on the axis." */

%include "C:\SharedCode\SparseLine.sas";
options mprint;

%SparseLine(
Data=sashelp.stocks,
Filter=%str(where Stock EQ 'IBM' and year(Date) EQ 1999),
Var=Close,
Format=3.,
DateDisplayFormat=MONYY5., /* for monthly data */
    /* default is DATE7.
        use YEAR4. for yearly data
        use YYQ4.  for quarterly data
        etc. */
```

```
Font=Arial,       /* same as default */
FontSize=11pt,    /* same as default */
FontWeight=Bold, /* same as default */
  /* TITLEs are forced to be Bold */
TargetFolder=C:\temp, /* same as default */
ImageName=Fig8-9_SparseLine,
ImageWidth=5.7in,  /* default is 6.5in */
ImageHeight=2.0in, /* same as default */
DPI=300,           /* same as default */
TitleText=Closing Value of IBM Shares First Trading Day of Each Month in 1999);
/* TITLE2 is ALWAYS "Critical Points and Last Change" */
```

All preceding macro parameters, except FILTER and those for which there is a default in the macro definition, are mandatory. It should be noted that the Sparse Line can be generated with whatever image height and image width that you deem appropriate and readable.

Using a Reference Line in the Time Series Plot

Figure 8-10. Using the REFLINE statement and a thin dotted plot line

Reference lines can be used en masse for every value of Y (or X) as in Figure 8-1 or singly for a significant X value as in Figure 8-10. Multiple reference lines can be specified, either with separate REFLINE statements or with one, as in this example:

```
refline 'Mar' 'Aug' / axis=X
  label=('Post January Minimum' 'Start Steady Increase')
  splitchar=' ' labelattrs=(color=green);
```

You can, of course, specify reference lines for both X and Y values if desired. You can also use the LINEATTRS option to customize the lines. The defaults for the reference line are thickness of 1 pixel and a color that appears to be gray. Though you can specify multiple line labels with LABEL=('label 1' 'label 2') in one REFLINE statement as shown, if you want different colors for the labels and/or the lines, two separate REFLINE statements are required. If the reference line is conspicuously different or has been specified thicker with LINEATTRS and THICKNESS=, and the REFLINE statement appears after the SERIES statement in the SGPLOT procedure step, its overlay on a marker can be noticed. One should always place the REFLINE statement(s) before the SERIES statement, so that the reference line is drawn first and any possibly coinciding marker or data label will overlap the line. Since the line extends above and below the overlap, line location and presence will still be clear.

Listing 8-10. Code used to create Figure 8-10

```
%include "C:\SharedCode\IBM1998CloseAndMaxCloseMacroVariable.sas";

ods listing style=GraphFontArial11ptBold gpath="C:\temp" dpi=300;
ods graphics on / reset=all scale=off width=5.7in height=3in
   imagename="Fig8-10_SeriesClose_DataLabelsReflineThinDotPlotLine";
title1 justify=center
'Close Price for IBM Shares on First Trading Day Each Month - 1998';
proc sgplot data=work.IBM1998Close noborder;
refline 'Aug' / axis=X splitchar=' '
   label='Start Steady Increase' labelattrs=(color=blue);
series x=Date y=Close / datalabel lineattrs=(pattern=ThinDot)
   markers markerattrs=(symbol=CircleFilled color=blue size=6);
yaxis display=(noline noticks nolabel)
   values=(0 &MaxClose) valuesdisplay=("0" " ");
xaxis display=(noline noticks nolabel) type=discrete;
format Date monname3. Close 3.;
run;
```

Time Series Graphs Can Be Created *Without* the SERIES Statement

Though time series data is usually presented as a series of markers connected by line segments or a curve, there are three other ways, besides the TEXT statement, to present it: a vertical bar chart, a needle plot (in effect, just a different shape for a bar chart), and a step plot. Let's take them up, in turn.

Vertical Bar Charts for Time Series Data

The earliest bar chart ever created (see the discussion of the work of Philippe Buache earlier in the chapter) was a vertical bar chart for time series data, but it was a bar chart overlay where low water level bars always overlaid, but left exposed, the high water level bars.

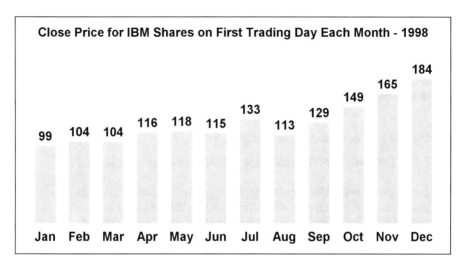

Figure 8-11. A vertical bar chart for time series: more visually impactful than dots and a line. You can "rest" the eye on bar ends to carry the trend, rather than being required to follow a plot line and points

In my experience, vertical bar charts are the commonest image used to present time series data in corporate annual reports. "Just show me what happened." That's the question to be answered.

I go so far as to suggest that any time series data for which the available image width can accommodate the bar widths and readable data label widths is better presented with a vertical bar chart than by a series plot for which a plot line has no real data Y value significance. The connectors between time series markers are just lines, not additional in-between plots for Y values corresponding to invisible X values between the X axis tick mark values.

Listing 8-11. *Code used to create Figure 8-11*

```
ods listing style=GraphFontArial11ptBold gpath="C:\temp" dpi=300;
ods graphics on / reset=all scale=off width=5.7in height=3in
  imagename="Fig8-11_VbarCloseWithDataLabelsForYvalues";
title1 justify=center
'Close Price for IBM Shares on First Trading Day Each Month - 1998';
```

```
title2 color=white 'White Space';
proc sgplot data=sashelp.stocks noborder;
where year(Date) EQ 1998 and Stock EQ 'IBM';
vbar Date / response=Close datalabel
    displaybaseline=off /* default is a baseline, which appears even
                           when there is no X axis line. */
    barwidth=0.6 nooutline;
yaxis display=none;
xaxis display=(noline noticks nolabel);
    /* XAXIS TYPE=DISCRETE is not needed.
       VBAR statement EXPECTS to be handling categorical data,
       which would entail discrete X axis values. */
format Date monname3. Close 3.;
run;
```

With a vertical bar chart, it is impossible to use the REFLINE statement to insert a described separator between July and August to emphasize that start of steady increase in the value of Close. Figure 8-12 provides this function by color-coding the rising bars. (An analogous design was used in Figure 4-39 to highlight the latest report year in a four-year bar chart of Total Annual Profit using the SASHELP.ORSALES data set. In that chart, there is no attempt to explain the purpose of highlighting. The presumption in that case is that the viewer will understand that the purpose is to focus on the latest news.)

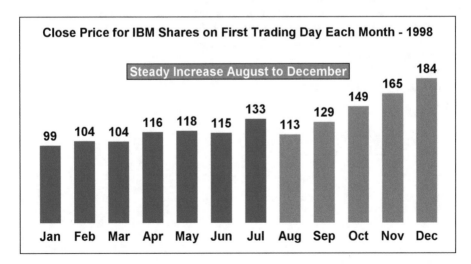

Figure 8-12. Color-coded vertical bar chart for time series data. Color-coded bars and color-matched explanation draw attention to the significant trend feature demonstrated by the bars

Listing 8-12. *Code used to create Figure 8-12*

```
data work.ColorMap;
retain ID 'Colors';
length Value $ 3 FillColor $ 5;
set sashelp.stocks;
where year(Date) EQ 1998 and Stock EQ 'IBM';
Value = put(Date,monname3.); /* It is necessary to use
  the FORMATTED value of Date. If Date is used instead,
  the attribute map will have no effect. */
if month(Date) LT 8 then FillColor = 'Blue';
else FillColor = 'Green';
run;


ods listing style=GraphFontArial11ptBold gpath="C:\temp" dpi=300;
ods graphics on / reset=all scale=off width=5.7in height=3in
  imagename="Fig8-12_VbarCloseWithDataLabelsForYvalues_ColorCoded";
title1 justify=center
'Close Price for IBM Shares on First Trading Day Each Month - 1998';
title2 color=white 'White Space';
proc sgplot data=sashelp.Stocks noborder
  noautolegend /* use of GROUP would trigger an unneeded legend */
  DattrMap=work.ColorMap;
where year(Date) EQ 1998 and Stock EQ 'IBM';
inset 'Steady Increase August to December' /
  position=Top border backcolor=green textattrs=(color=white);
vbar Date / response=Close group=Date attrid=Colors datalabel
    displaybaseline=off barwidth=0.6 nooutline;
yaxis display=none;
xaxis display=(noline noticks nolabel);
format Date monname3. Close 3.;
run;
```

Needle Plot for Time Series Data

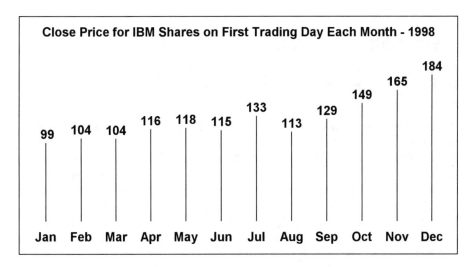

Figure 8-13. Needle plot without the MARKERS option: thinnest possible vertical bar chart for time series data

A needle plot offers no advantage over vertical bar charts except for looking like a bar chart that is starved. A vertical bar chart, though usable for time series data, is really expected to be used for categorical data, with discrete values for the X axis variable. A needle plot, designed to be used for a numeric X variable, can be used for an X variable with discrete values, but that use must be identified on the XAXIS statement, if you want its appearance to match that of a vertical bar chart. The default position of data labels on a needle plot is UpperRight. It is better to instead use DATALABELPOS=TOP to match the default position of data labels on a vertical bar chart. UpperRight data labels unnecessarily use up more of the available horizontal space.

Listing 8-13. *Code used to create Figure 8-13*

```
ods listing style=GraphFontArial11ptBold gpath="C:\temp" dpi=300;
ods graphics on / reset=all scale=off width=5.7in height=3in
  imagename="Fig8-13_NeedleCloseWithDataLabelsForYvalues";
title1 justify=center
'Close Price for IBM Shares on First Trading Day Each Month - 1998';
title2 color=white 'White Space';
proc sgplot data=sashelp.stocks noborder;
where year(Date) EQ 1998 and Stock EQ 'IBM';
needle x=Date y=Close / datalabel displaybaseline=off
  datalabelpos=top; /* default is UpperRight */
yaxis display=none;
```

```
xaxis display=(noline noticks nolabel) type=discrete;
format Date monname3. Close 3.;
run;
```

Step Plots for Time Series Data

A step plot shows a step, up or down, at every date point of time series data, as shown in the default example in Figure 8-14, which is not a recommended solution.

My own experience with practical use of a step plot was different from what is shown in this section. In real life, if one is tracking demand on a resource versus available capacity over time, the demand is continuously changing, probably increasing, at least over long enough time. However, the capacity available is almost always constant over segments of time, with "steps" where capacity is incrementally, not continually, added from time to time. Unfortunately, I don't have sample data to show you such an overlay plot. For such an example, the demand would be rendered with a SERIES statement and the capacity with a STEP statement.

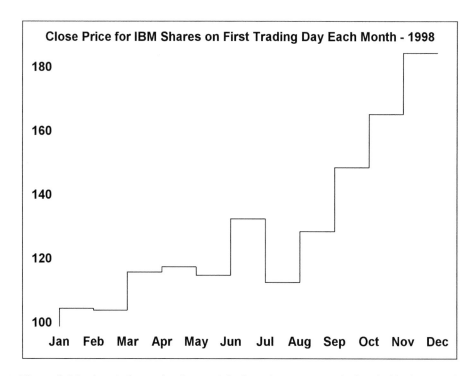

Figure 8-14. A typical step plot. For me, it looks ambiguous as to which is the Y value at each X value, except for December

Listing 8-14. *Code used to create Figure 8-14*

```
ods listing style=GraphFontArial11ptBold gpath="C:\temp" dpi=300;
ods graphics on / reset=all scale=off width=5.7in
   imagename="Fig8-14_StepPlotCloseWithDefaultsExceptYvarFormat";
title1 justify=center
'Close Price for IBM Shares on First Trading Day Each Month - 1998';
proc sgplot data=sashelp.stocks noborder;
where year(Date) EQ 1998 and Stock EQ 'IBM';
step x=Date y=Close;
xaxis display=(noline noticks nolabel) type=discrete;
yaxis display=(noline noticks nolabel);
format Date monname3. Close 3.;
run;
```

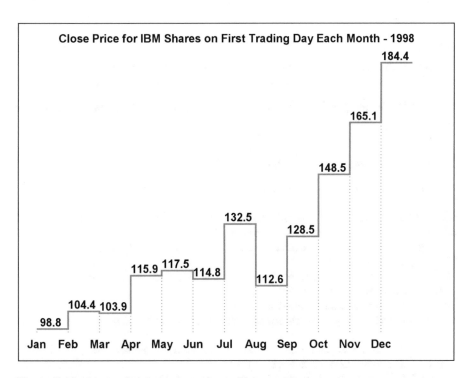

Figure 8-15. Maximally informative and unambiguous step plot

The Y values could have been supplied via an X axis table, but here you find the Y value by visually "taking the step." For a reason that I cannot guess, my eye felt the need for the drop lines, even though there are not a lot of X values, and they are well separated. Since it takes some extra data preprocessing to be able to create them, it would be easy for the reader to eliminate them, if desired. Regardless of the inclusion or exclusion of that drop line feature, the code for this step plot is very complex and can be found in Listing A8-15 in Appendix A.

Applying Bands to Time Series Plots

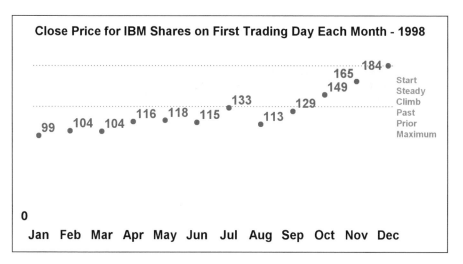

Figure 8-16. Scatter plot where the band with constant upper and lower values serves as an alternative to reference lines

---

Listing 8-16. Code used to create Figure 8-16

```
%include "C:\SharedCode\IBM1998CloseAndMaxCloseMacroVariable.sas";

ods listing style=GraphFontArial11ptBold gpath="C:\temp" dpi=300;
ods graphics on / reset=all scale=off width=5.7in height=3in
  imagename="Fig8-16_BandForConstantHighLow_SeriesClose_DataLabels";
title1 justify=center
'Close Price for IBM Shares on First Trading Day Each Month - 1998';
title2 color=white 'White Space';
proc sgplot data=work.IBM1998Close noborder
  noautolegend; /* statements would trigger an unneeded legend. */

band x=Date upper=184 lower=134 / outline lineattrs=(pattern=Dot)
  fill fillattrs=(color=CXEEEEEE) splitchar=' '
  curvelabellower='Start Steady Climb Past Prior Maximum'
  curvelabelloc=outside curvelabelpos=max
  curvelabelattrs=(family=Arial size=8pt weight=Bold color=green);
scatter x=Date y=Close / datalabel datalabelattrs=(color=blue)
  markerattrs=(color=blue symbol=CircleFilled size=6);
yaxis display=(noline noticks nolabel)
  values=(0 &MaxClose) valuesdisplay=("0" " ");
xaxis display=(noline noticks nolabel) type=discrete;
format Date monname3. Close 3.;
run;
```

High, Low, Open, and Close Price for IBM Shares
On First Trading Day of Each Month in 1998

	Jan	Feb	Mar	Apr	May	Jun	Jul	Aug	Sep	Oct	Nov	Dec
High	108	106	107	120	129	120	138	135	136	150	171	190
Open	105	100	104	104	116	117	116	134	113	125	148	164
Low	96	98	96	103	116	106	113	113	111	117	146	162

Figure 8-17. Scatter plot and data label for close share value with band overlay for high and low values. X axis tables provide precise values for high, low, and open values

Listing 8-17. Code used to create Figure 8-17

```
%include "C:\SharedCode\IBM1998CloseAndMaxCloseMacroVariable.sas";

ods listing style=GraphFontArial11ptBold gpath="C:\temp" dpi=300;
ods graphics on / reset=all scale=off width=5.7in height=3.6in
   imagename=
   "Fig8-17_BandHighLow_ScatterPlotClose_AxisTablesHighOpenLow";
title1 justify=center 'High, Low, '
   color=red 'Open'
   color=black ', and '
   color=blue 'Close'
   color=black ' Price for IBM Shares';
title2 justify=center 'On First Trading Day of Each Month in 1998';
proc sgplot data=work.IBM1998Close noautolegend noborder;
band x=Date upper=High lower=Low / type=series
   fill fillattrs=(color=CXEEEEEE);
scatter x=Date y=Close / datalabel datalabelattrs=(color=blue)
   markerattrs=(color=blue symbol=CircleFilled size=6);
xaxistable High / label='High' location=inside title='';
xaxistable Open / label='Open' location=inside title=''
   labelattrs=(color=red) valueattrs=(color=red);
xaxistable Low  / label='Low'  location=inside title='';
yaxis display=(noline noticks nolabel)
```

```
     values=(0 &MaxClose) valuesdisplay=("0" " ");
xaxis display=(noline noticks nolabel) type=discrete;
format Date monname3. High Low Open Close 3.;
run;
```

Time Series Plots Using the HIGHLOW Statement

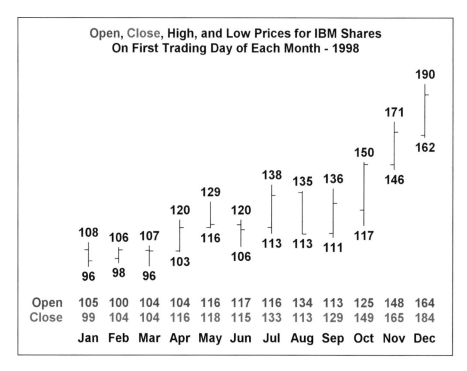

Figure 8-18. HIGHLOW statement with labels, but open and close axis tables. The small left (right) "bar" on the high-low connector is for the Y value of open (close)

A graph that requires an explanation is never a satisfactory deliverable.

For me, this result is an image awaiting completion. Those little horizontal bars on each side of the vertical line connecting high and low are just a tease. What *are* the values there? Did the graph creator really want me to compare their location with axis values if they had been optionally provided? At least there is a limited courtesy of axis table values that are aligned with, but disconnected from, those little tease bars. The incompletely labeled high-low chart visual elements might be cute, but I prefer information and useful function over cuteness. See Figure 8-19 instead.

Listing 8-18. Code used to create Figure 8-18

```
ods listing style=GraphFontArial11ptBold gpath="C:\temp" dpi=300;
ods graphics on / reset=all scale=off width=5.7in
  imagename="Fig8-18_HighLowOpenClose_LabelsAndAxisTables";
title1 justify=center color=red 'Open' color=black ', ' color=blue
  'Close' color=black ', High, and Low Prices for IBM Shares';
title2 justify=center 'On First Trading Day of Each Month - 1998';
proc sgplot data=sashelp.Stocks noautolegend noborder;
where year(Date) EQ 1998 and Stock EQ 'IBM';
highlow x=Date high=high low=low /
  highlabel=high lowlabel=low open=open close=close;
xaxistable Open / label='Open' location=inside title=''
  labelattrs=(color=red) valueattrs=(color=red);
xaxistable Close / label='Close' location=inside title=''
  labelattrs=(color=blue) valueattrs=(color=blue);
yaxis display=none;
xaxis display=(noline noticks nolabel) type=discrete;
format Date monname3. High Low Open Close 3.;
run;
```

The use of the TEXT statement (twice) in Figure 8-19 to display the OPEN and CLOSE values replaces the tick marks on the vertical lines with usable precise information. If the image in Figure 8-19 were created for a more typical page size, or especially for a full computer screen width web page, a larger font could be used to enhance the readability.

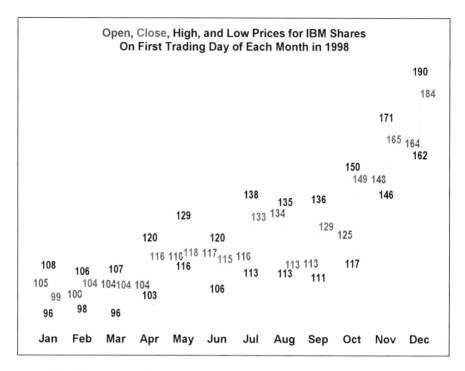

Figure 8-19. The most informative, most convenient, most immediate visual communication with the HIGHLOW statement, supplemented with TEXT statements: a color-coded high-low plot with all available measures as labels. The high-low connector is light gray for de-emphasis. The trend is shown, but emphasis is on all of the precise numbers

This graph would be more visually pleasing if it were not so compact and congested. A wider image, not possible here, is the only way to decongest it.

The HIGHLOW statement for PROC SGPLOT is designed, but not limited, to plot the High, Low, Open, and Close values of financial instruments such as stocks. It can produce "clipped" vertical bar charts (i.e., ones with no bottom bar area between the low value for the Y variable and zero). Here, the default of vertical lines is used since the width of bar fill would add no communication value, but would consume more of the already limited horizontal space.

Listing 8-19. *Code used to create Figure 8-19*

```
ods listing style=GraphFontArial10ptBold gpath="C:\temp" dpi=300;
ods graphics on / reset=all scale=off width=5.7in
   imagename=
  "Fig8-19_HighLowOpenClose_HIGHLOWandTEXTstatements_NarrowLabels";
title1 justify=center color=red 'Open' color=black ', ' color=blue
   'Close' color=black ', High, and Low Prices for IBM Shares';
title2 justify=center 'On First Trading Day of Each Month in 1998';
proc sgplot data=sashelp.stocks noautolegend noborder;
```

```
where year(Date) EQ 1998 and Stock EQ 'IBM';
text x=Date y=Open text=Open / position=left
  textattrs=(color=red family='Arial Narrow');
highlow x=Date high=high low=low / highlabel=high lowlabel=low
    labelattrs=(family='Arial Narrow') lineattrs=(color=LightGray)
  open=open close=close;
text x=Date y=Close text=Close / position=right
  textattrs=(color=blue family='Arial Narrow');
yaxis display=none;
xaxis display=(noline noticks nolabel) type=discrete;
format Date monname3. High Low Open Close 3.;
run;
```

The closing price for stock shares is always the most important measure. The range of the price over the course of the day is also interesting. So the image can be simplified with no great diminution in value as in Figure 8-20.

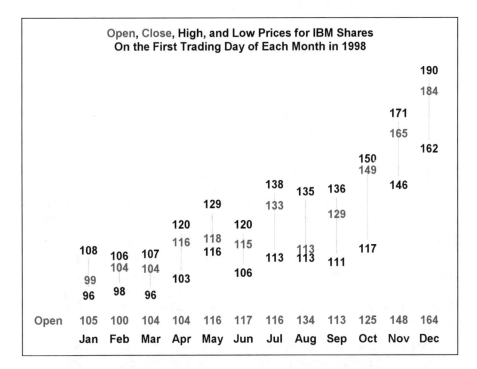

Figure 8-20. HIGHLOW statement for high and low with SERIES statement for close and X axis table for open. Labels for high and low. Data label for close. Hidden plot line

Not requiring both Open and Close to be adjacent to the high-low connector relieves the congestion of Figure 8-19, without serious detriment. The Close value is usually of more interest than Open, and the Open value is available in the axis table.

Listing 8-20. *Code used to create Figure 8-20*

```
ods listing style=GraphFontArial10ptBold gpath="C:\temp" dpi=300;
ods graphics on / reset=all scale=off width=5.7in
  imagename="Fig8-20_HighLowLabels_CloseLabels_AxisTableForOpen";
title1 justify=center color=red 'Open' color=black ', ' color=blue
  'Close' color=black ', High, and Low Prices for IBM Shares';
title2 justify=center
  'On the First Trading Day of Each Month in 1998';
proc sgplot data=sashelp.Stocks noautolegend noborder;
where year(Date) EQ 1998 and Stock EQ 'IBM';
highlow x=Date high=high low=low / highlabel=high lowlabel=low
  lineattrs=(color=LightGray);
series x=Date y=Close /
  datalabel datalabelattrs=(color=blue) datalabelpos=center
  lineattrs=(color=white);
xaxistable Open / label='Open' location=inside title=''
  labelattrs=(color=red) Valueattrs=(color=red);
yaxis display=none;
xaxis display=(noline noticks nolabel) type=discrete;
format Date monname3. High Low Open Close 3.;
run;
```

In Figure 8-20, the OPEN values are moved to the X axis table. With one-fourth fewer labels to be displayed inside the plot area, a larger font can be used for HIGH, LOW, and CLOSE values.

Multi-line Time Series Plots

The last four graphs served as alternatives to multi-line time series plots. There are three kinds of multi-line time series plots that are overlay plots.

One kind has multiple lines for one key variable, but multiple measurement variables with the same units. An example could be series plots for Daily Open, Close, High, and Low values over time for the price of shares of a particular corporation. It would be functionally equivalent to plots in Figures 8-17 to 8-20, but created with different software machinery. It will not be presented here.

A second kind has multiple lines, one for each value of a category variable, but all lines for the same response variable. An example could be the Daily Close value for the price of shares for IBM, Intel, and Microsoft.

A third kind, with a limit of two lines, has one line using the left-hand axis for one response variable and the other line using the right-hand axis for a second response variable. Both response variables have the same set of X axis time values. An example could be the Daily Close value for the price of IBM shares and the Daily Volume of IBM shares traded, on the first trading day of each month in one year.

Overlay Plots of Two Response Variables with Different Units by Date

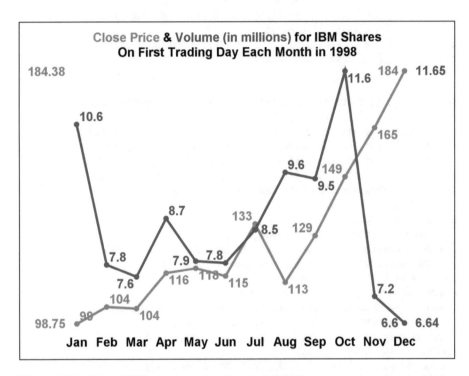

Figure 8-21. Using SERIES statement for Close and SERIES statement for volume, with data labels, and minimum and maximum Y axis values for both responses. Color-coded TITLE1 serves as a legend to identify the plot lines. Note the unwanted collisions between data labels and a plot line

Listing 8-21. Code used to create Figure 8-21

```
/* data set and macro variables used for Figures 8-21 and 8-22 */
data work.IBM1998WithVolumeInMillions;
retain MinClose MinVolume 999999999999 MaxClose MaxVolume 0;
set sashelp.Stocks end=LastOne;
where year(Date) EQ 1998 and Stock EQ 'IBM';
Volume = Volume / 1000000;
output;
MinVolume = min(MinVolume,Volume);
MaxVolume = max(MaxVolume,Volume);
MinClose = min(MinClose,Close);
MaxClose = max(MaxClose,Close);
if LastOne;
```

```
call symput('MaxCloseDisplay',trim(left(put(MaxClose,6.2))));
call symput('MaxClose',MaxClose);
call symput('MaxVolumeDisplay',trim(left(put(MaxVolume,6.2))));
call symput('MaxVolume',MaxVolume);
call symput('MinCloseDisplay',trim(left(put(MinClose,6.2))));
call symput('MinClose',MinClose);
call symput('MinVolumeDisplay',trim(left(put(MinVolume,6.2))));
call symput('MinVolume',MinVolume);
run;


ods listing style=GraphFontArial11ptBold gpath="C:\temp" dpi=300;
ods graphics on / reset=all scale=off width=5.7in
  imagename="Fig8-21_SeriesClose_SeriesVolume_DataLabels_TwoYaxes";
title1 justify=center   color=green 'Close Price' color=black ' & '
  color=blue 'Volume (in millions)' color=black ' for IBM Shares';
title2 justify=center 'On First Trading Day Each Month in 1998';
proc sgplot data=work.IBM1998WithVolumeInMillions
  noautolegend noborder;
series x=Date y=Close /
  datalabel datalabelattrs=(color=green)
  markers markerattrs=(symbol=CircleFilled color=green size=6)
  lineattrs=(pattern=Solid color=green thickness=3);
series x=Date y=Volume / y2axis
  datalabel datalabelattrs=(color=blue)
  markers markerattrs=(symbol=CircleFilled color=blue size=6)
  lineattrs=(pattern=Solid color=blue thickness=3);
yaxis display=(noline noticks nolabel) valueattrs=(color=green)
  values = (&MinClose &MaxClose)
  valuesdisplay = ("&MinCloseDisplay" "&MaxCloseDisplay");
y2axis display=(noline noticks nolabel) valueattrs=(color=blue)
  values = (&MinVolume &MaxVolume)
  valuesdisplay = ("&MinVolumeDisplay" "&MaxVolumeDisplay");
xaxis display=(noline noticks nolabel) type=discrete;
format Date monname3. Close 3. Volume 4.1;
run;
```

In Figure 8-21, there are some collisions between data labels and plot lines. Those collisions could be mitigated by making the lines lighter and thinner. An alternative is the use of X axis tables as in Figure 8-22.

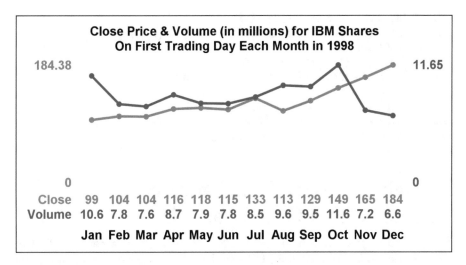

Figure 8-22. Color-coded lines and X axis tables unambiguously deliver precise numbers with no chance of collisions, but the numbers are remote from their plot points.

Absence of data labels that could suffer collisions allows the image height to be reduced and the Y axes to start at zero, rather than at Y variable minimum values.

Listing 8-22. *Code used to create Figure 8-22, changes from Figure 8-21 in bold*

```
ods listing style=GraphFontArial11ptBold gpath="C:\temp" dpi=300;
ods graphics on / reset=all scale=off width=5.7in height=3in
  imagename="Fig8-22_SeriesClose_SeriesVolume_XaxisTables_TwoYaxes";
title1 justify=center
  'Close Price & Volume (in millions) for IBM Shares';
title2 justify=center 'On First Trading Day Each Month in 1998';
proc sgplot noautolegend noborder
  data=work.IBM1998WithVolumeInMillions; /* Listing 8-21 created
  this input data set, and the macro variables that are used
  in the AXIS statements. */
series x=Date y=Close /
  markers markerattrs=(symbol=CircleFilled color=green size=6)
  lineattrs=(pattern=Solid color=green thickness=3);
series x=Date y=Close /
  markers markerattrs=(symbol=CircleFilled color=green size=6)
  lineattrs=(pattern=Solid color=green thickness=3);
series x=Date y=Volume / y2axis
  markers markerattrs=(symbol=CircleFilled color=blue size=6)
  lineattrs=(pattern=Solid color=blue thickness=3);
xaxistable Close / valueattrs=(color=green) labelattrs=(color=green)
  label='Close'  location=inside title='';
xaxistable Volume / valueattrs=(color=blue) labelattrs=(color=blue)
```

```
  label='Volume' location=inside title='';
yaxis display=(noline noticks nolabel) valueattrs=(color=green)
  values = (0 &MaxClose)
  valuesdisplay = ("0" "&MaxCloseDisplay");
y2axis display=(noline noticks nolabel) valueattrs=(color=blue)
  values = (0 &MaxVolume)
  valuesdisplay = ("0" "&MaxVolumeDisplay");
xaxis display=(noline noticks nolabel) type=discrete;
format Date monname3. Close 3. Volume 4.1;
run;
```

Multi-line Overlay Time Series Plots for Data with a Group Variable

The GROUP option assigns a variable for which there is a separate SERIES line for each value of that GROUP variable. Also, a legend is automatically generated to identify the plot lines.

In cases where color coding can be explained without a legend, for example, when a color-coded X axis table is present, the legend can be suppressed with the NOAUTOLEGEND option on the PROC SGPLOT statement.

The plot line color coding is either default or controlled with a STYLEATTRS statement with a list of preferred colors in the DATACONTRASTCOLORS option of that statement.

If present, markers, data labels, and curve labels automatically inherit that same color list which is used for the plot lines.

For the XAXISTABLE statement, there are options COLORGROUP, CLASS, and CLASSORDER demonstrated in Figures 8-25 and 8-26. The color coding is that from the STYLEATTRS DATACONTRASTCOLORS color list.

The SCATTER statement can be used to selectively override the color of markers and data labels for certain X values as in Figures 8-26, 8-27, and 8-28.

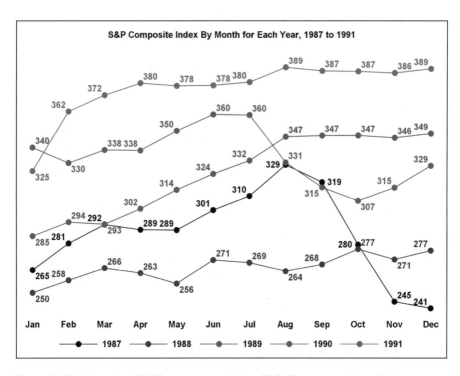

Figure 8-23. Using the SERIES statement with the GROUP option and data labels

Listing 8-23. Code used to create Figure 8-23

```
/* requires a prior run of Listing 8-0 to create input data */

ods listing style=GraphFontArial8ptBold gpath="C:\temp" dpi=300;
ods graphics on / reset=all scale=off width=5.7in
  imagename="Fig8-23_FiveLineOverlay_DataLabels";
title1 justify=center
  'S&P Composite Index By Month for Each Year, 1987 to 1991';
proc sgplot data=sasuser.SandPbyMonth1987to1991 noborder;
StyleAttrs datacontrastcolors=(Black Purple Blue Red CXFF00FF);
series x=Date y=FSPCOM / group=Year /* one line for each year */
  datalabel lineattrs=(pattern=Solid)
  markers markerattrs=(symbol=CircleFilled size=7);
yaxis display=none;
xaxis display=(noline noticks nolabel) type=discrete;
keylegend / title='' noborder;
format Date monname3. FSPCOM 3.;
run;
```

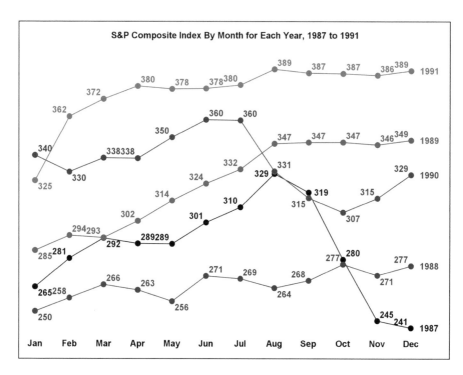

Figure 8-24. Using the SERIES statement with the GROUP option and data labels, but curve labels rather than a legend

Curve labels cost horizontal space for the sake of more vertical space. Which space is more precious is likely to be situation dependent.

Listing 8-24. *Code used to create Figure 8-24*

```
/* requires a prior run of Listing 8-0 to create input data */

ods listing style=GraphFontArial8ptBold gpath="C:\temp" dpi=300;
ods graphics on / reset=all scale=off width=5.7in
  imagename="Fig8-24_ FiveLineOverlay_DataLabels_CurveLabels";
title1 justify=center
  'S&P Composite Index By Month for Each Year, 1987 to 1991';
proc sgplot data=sasuser.SandPbyMonth1987to1991
  noautolegend /* curve labels replace the legend */
  noborder;
StyleAttrs datacontrastcolors=(Black Purple Blue Red CXFF00FF);
series x=Date y=FSPCOM / group=Year /* one line for each year */
  datalabel lineattrs=(pattern=Solid)
  markers markerattrs=(symbol=CircleFilled size=7)
  curvelabel curvelabelloc=outside curvelabelpos=max;
```

```
yaxis display=none;
xaxis display=(noline noticks nolabel) type=discrete;
format Date monname3. FSPCOM 3.;
run;
```

With a color-coded X axis table used instead of data labels in Figure 8-25, no
legend is necessary. Since there is no risk of data label collisions, the use of
vertical space can be converted to presenting the plot lines and the data more
realistically by starting the Y axis at zero. Value-labeled reference lines for the
five-year minimum and maximum Y values eliminate the need for the viewer
to discover them by examining all 60 values in the axis table.

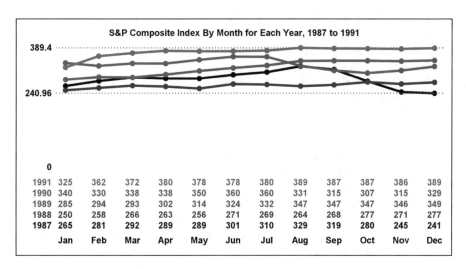

Figure 8-25. Using the SERIES statement with the GROUP option and X axis table instead
of data labels. Color-coded axis table labels serve as a legend. Starting the Y axis at zero
removes the magnified apparent variation caused when spreading out the lines in Figures 8-23
and 8-24 to prevent data label collisions

The squashed character of this image is not pleasant, but it does make it
easier to assess the similarity or dissimilarity of the plot line variations
over time.

Listing 8-25. Code used to create Figure 8-25

```
/* requires a prior run of Listing 8-0 to create input data */

proc sql noprint; /* pass the data bounds as macro variables */
select max(FSPCOM),min(FSPCOM) into :FSPCOM_max,:FSPCOM_min
  from sasuser.SandPbyMonth1987to1991;
quit;
```

```
ods listing style=GraphFontArial8ptBold gpath="C:\temp" dpi=300;
ods graphics on / reset=all scale=off width=5.7in height=3in
  imagename="Fig8-25_FiveLineOverlay_XaxesTable_RefLines";
title1 justify=center
 'S&P Composite Index By Month for Each Year, 1987 to 1991';
proc sgplot data=sasuser.SandPbyMonth1987to1991
  noborder noautolegend; /* color in axis table acts as a legend */
StyleAttrs datacontrastcolors=(Black Purple Blue Red CXFF00FF);
series x=Date y=FSPCOM / group=Year /* one line for each year */
  lineattrs=(thickness=3 pattern=Solid)
  markers markerattrs=(symbol=CircleFilled size=6px);
refline &FSPCOM_min &FSPCOM_max / axis=Y /* show the data extrema */
  lineattrs=(pattern=Dot thickness=2px);
xaxistable FSPCOM / colorgroup=Year class=Year classorder=descending
  location=inside title='';
yaxis display=(noline noticks nolabel)
  values=(0 &FSPCOM_min &FSPCOM_max)
  valuesdisplay=("0" "&FSPCOM_min" "&FSPCOM_max");
xaxis display=(noline noticks nolabel) type=discrete;
format Date monname3. FSPCOM 3.;
run;
```

The next three examples have some of the features of a Sparse Line and might serve as a Sparse Line Table alternative, but they omit annotation of the last change for each line, and they have added information (an X axis table in Figure 8-26, curve labels in Figure 8-27, and all of the X axis values in all three examples). Compare them with the bona fide Sparse Line Table in Figures 9-9 and 9-12. They differ from a Sparse Line Table since their lines overlay and are not presented in separate rows.

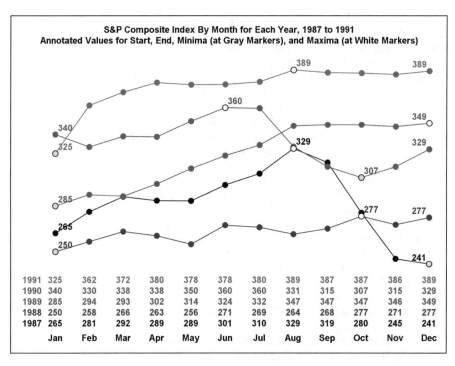

Figure 8-26. Using the SERIES statement with the GROUP option and an X axis table. All Y values are in the axis table. Color-coded axis table labels serve as a legend. Yearly maximum and minimum values have color-coded markers. Start, end, maximum, and minimum values are annotated. Maximum and minimum values have color-coded markers

Listing 8-26. Code used to create Figure 8-26

```
/* requires a prior run of Listing 8-0 to create input data */

%include "C:\SharedCode\MonthlyDataForMultiLinePlot.sas";
options mprint;
%MonthlyDataForMultiLinePlot(
Data=sasuser.SandPbyMonth1987to1991,
Out=work.ToPlot_26,
ClassVar=Year,
ResponseVar=FSPCOM,
DateVar=Date,
MinMaxWithMonthLabels=NO);
/* NO is the default. In THIS example,
   the months are identifiable from the X axis values. */

ods listing style=GraphFontArial8ptBold gpath="C:\temp" dpi=300;
ods graphics on / reset=all scale=off width=5.7in
   imagename="Fig8-26_FiveLineOverlay_SparseAnno_XaxisTableForAllY";
title1 justify=center
```

```
'S&P Composite Index By Month for Each Year, 1987 to 1991';
title2 justify=center 'Annotated Values for Start, End, Minima (at Gray
Markers), and Maxima (at White Markers)';
proc sgplot data=work.ToPlot_26 noautolegend noborder;
StyleAttrs datacontrastcolors=(Black Purple Blue Red CXFF00FF);
series x=Date y=FSPCOM / group=Year lineattrs=(pattern=Solid)
  /* draw the basic plot lines and markers, both color-coded */
  markers markerattrs=(symbol=CircleFilled size=7);
scatter x=Date y=FSPCOMFirstInYear / group=Year datalabel
  /* provide data labels and color coding for each January */
  markerattrs=(symbol=CircleFilled size=7);
scatter x=Date y=FSPCOMLastInYear / group=Year datalabel
/* provide data labels and color coding for each December */
  markerattrs=(symbol=CircleFilled size=7);
scatter x=Date y=MinFSPCOM / group=Year datalabel
  /* Provide data label and color-coding for each minimum.
     If minimum is a First or Last X value,
     the original marker color is replaced.
     The color of the data label is that of the Year. */
  FilledOutlinedMarkers
  markerattrs=(symbol=CircleFilled size=7)
  markerfillattrs=(color=LightGray)
  markeroutlineattrs=(color=black thickness=1px);
scatter x=Date y=MaxFSPCOM / group=Year datalabel
  /* Provide data label and color-coding for each maximum.
     If maximum is a First or Last X value,
     the original marker color is replaced.
     The color of the data label is that of the Year. */
  FilledOutlinedMarkers
  markerattrs=(symbol=CircleFilled size=7)
  markerfillattrs=(color=white)
  markeroutlineattrs=(color=black thickness=1px);
xaxistable FSPCOM / /* provide precise Y values for all points */
  colorgroup=Year class=Year classorder=descending
  location=inside title='';
yaxis display=none;
xaxis display=(noline noticks nolabel) type=discrete;
format Date monname3.
  FSPCOM FSPCOMFirstInYear FSPCOMLastInYear MinFSPCOM MaxFSPCOM 3.;
run;
```

Overlay Plots for Nearly Sparse Lines

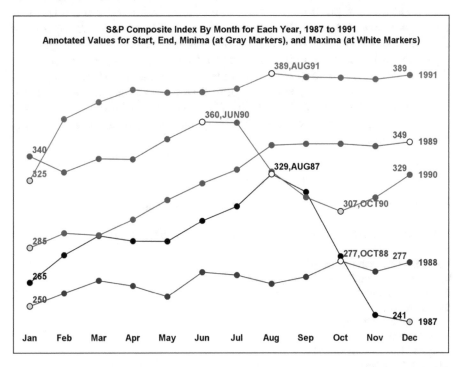

Figure 8-27. Using the SERIES statement with the GROUP option and curve labels. Data labels, including month values, are provided for yearly maximum and minimum values. Start and end values are annotated. Maximum and minimum values have color-coded markers

If curve labels could also be provided at the start of the lines, the year identity for any January value that is a yearly minimum would be immediately apparent without having to annotate the date as well as the value. Intermediate minimum and maximum values do have the date included as part of the annotation. One *could* enhance the code to include year in the annotation of any January values that are the yearly minimum. Of course, the year *is* available at the other end of the line.

Figure 8-27 is similar to Figure 8-26 except for

- The omission of the X axis table
- The use of curve labels (the X axis table had provided year identification)
- The inclusion of X values in the annotation for minima and maxima

Compare these grouped Sparse Lines with the single Sparse Line in Figure 8-9. The single Sparse Line has the year included in the annotation of each critical point, and the end point has an extra line of annotation for the change since the second last plot point. In Figures 8-26 and 8-27, the markers for minima and maxima are color-coded. With a single line in Figure 8-9, identifying the minimum and maximum is visually immediate with no extra lines and points in the field of view, and each of its extreme values does have a data label. For Figure 8-9, where the fact that it is only data for 1999 is announced in the title, including the year in the data labels is really superfluous. However, the SparseLine macro was developed for the general case, where the data range might span multiple years.

Listing 8-27. *Code used to create Figure 8-27*

```
/* requires a prior run of Listing 8-0 to create input data */

%include "C:\SharedCode\MonthlyDataForMultiLinePlot.sas";
options mprint;
%MonthlyDataForMultiLinePlot(
Data=sasuser.SandPbyMonth1987to1991,
Out=work.ToPlot_27,
ClassVar=Year,
ResponseVar=FSPCOM,
DateVar=Date,
MinMaxWithMonthLabels=YES,
ResponseVarFormat=3.,
MonthFormat=monyy5.,
DataLabelLength=9);
/* For length, use 3 + 5 + 1 (for comma) */

ods listing style=GraphFontArial8ptBold gpath="C:\temp" dpi=300;
ods graphics on / reset=all scale=off width=5.7in
   imagename="Fig8-27_FiveLineOverlay_SparseAnnoForMinMaxStartEnd";
title1 justify=center
  'S&P Composite Index By Month for Each Year, 1987 to 1991';
title2 justify=center 'Annotated Values for Start, End, Minima (at Gray
Markers), and Maxima (at White Markers)';
proc sgplot data=work.ToPlot_27
  noautolegend noborder;
StyleAttrs datacontrastcolors=(Black Purple Blue Red CXFF00FF);
series x=Date y=FSPCOM / group=Year lineattrs=(pattern=Solid)
  /* NO use of DATALABEL option */
  markers markerattrs=(symbol=CircleFilled size=7)
  curvelabel curvelabelloc=outside curvelabelpos=max;
scatter x=Date y=FSPCOMFirstInYear / group=Year datalabel
  markerattrs=(symbol=CircleFilled size=7);
scatter x=Date y=FSPCOMLastInYear  / group=Year datalabel
```

```
  markerattrs=(symbol=CircleFilled size=7);
scatter x=Date y=MinFSPCOM / group=Year datalabel=Min
  FilledOutlinedMarkers
  markerattrs=(symbol=CircleFilled size=7)
  markerfillattrs=(color=LightGray)
  markeroutlineattrs=(color=black thickness=1px);
scatter x=Date y=MaxFSPCOM / group=Year datalabel=Max
  FilledOutlinedMarkers
  markerattrs=(symbol=CircleFilled size=7)
  markerfillattrs=(color=white)
  markeroutlineattrs=(color=black thickness=1px);
yaxis display=none;
xaxis display=(noline noticks nolabel) type=discrete;
format Date monname3.
  FSPCOM FSPCOMFirstInYear FSPCOMLastInYear MinFSPCOM MaxFSPCOM 3.;
run;
```

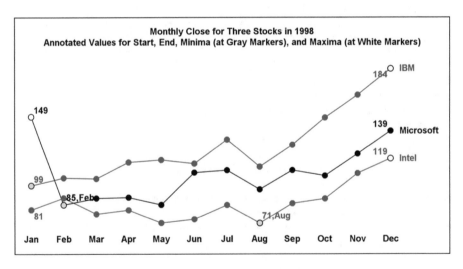

Figure 8-28. Sparsely annotated overlay plot of share prices

Figure 8-28 differs from the content of the web-enabled Sparse Line Table in
Figure 14-15. It is not only a difference in the date range for this data, but also
the last change for each line is not annotated and the X axis values are
retained. Furthermore, here the lines are overlaid, whereas in the Sparse Line
Table each line is in a separate row.

Listing 8-28. *Code used to create Figure 8-28*

```
%include "C:\SharedCode\MonthlyDataForMultiLinePlot.sas";
options mprint;
%MonthlyDataForMultiLinePlot(
Data=sashelp.stocks,
Out=work.ThreeStocksIn1998,
Filter=%str(where Year(Date) EQ 1998),
ClassVar=Stock,
ResponseVar=Close,
DateVar=Date,
MinMaxWithMonthLabels=YES,
ResponseVarFormat=3.,
MonthFormat=monname3.,
DataLabelLength=7);


ods listing style=GraphFontArial8ptBold gpath="C:\temp" dpi=300;
ods graphics on / reset=all scale=off width=5.7in height=3in
  imagename="Fig8-28_ThreeLineOverlay_SparseAnnoForMinMaxStartEnd";
title1 justify=center "Monthly Close for Three Stocks in 1998";
title2 justify=center 'Annotated Values for Start, End, Minima (at Gray
Markers), and Maxima (at White Markers)';
title3 color=white 'White Space';
proc sgplot data=work.ThreeStocksIn1998 noautolegend noborder;
StyleAttrs datacontrastcolors=(Blue Red Black);
series x=Date y=Close / group=Stock lineattrs=(pattern=Solid)
  markers markerattrs=(symbol=CircleFilled size=7)
  curvelabel curvelabelloc=outside curvelabelpos=max;;
scatter x=Date y=CloseFirstInStock / group=Stock datalabel
  markerattrs=(symbol=CircleFilled size=7);
scatter x=Date y=CloseLastInStock  / group=Stock datalabel
  markerattrs=(symbol=CircleFilled size=7);
scatter x=Date y=MinClose / group=Stock datalabel=Min
  FilledOutlinedMarkers
  markerattrs=(symbol=CircleFilled size=7)
  markerfillattrs=(color=LightGray)
  markeroutlineattrs=(color=black thickness=1px);
scatter x=Date y=MaxClose / group=Stock datalabel=Max
  FilledOutlinedMarkers
  markerattrs=(symbol=CircleFilled size=7)
  markerfillattrs=(color=white)
  markeroutlineattrs=(color=black thickness=1px);
yaxis display=none;
xaxis display=(noline noticks nolabel) type=discrete;
format Date monname3.
  Close CLOSEFirstInStock CLOSELastInStock MinCLOSE MaxCLOSE 3.;
run;
```

Very Long Time Series Plot of Monthly Data

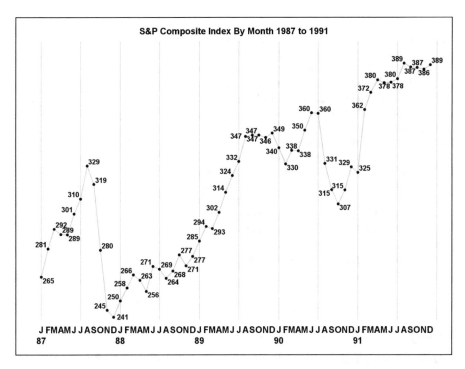

Figure 8-29. Using the SERIES statement without the GROUP option to concatenate the five yearly plots from Figure 8-23. Like the design for that figure, the Y axis does not start at zero, so that data label collisions are less likely

Despite the plot point density, the data labels are readable. Getting the years on a line below the months uses the trick of two X axis tables, rather than an XAXIS statement option—there is none. How to present long time series data, among other things, will be explored further in later chapters in two other ways: (a) with PROC SGPANEL and (b) ODS HTML5. This applies also to the examples in Figures 8-31, 8-32, and 8-33.

Listing 8-29. *Code used to create Figure 8-29*

```
/* requires a prior run of Listing 8-0 to create input data */

data work.CitiMonWithYYandMonthInitial;
length YY $ 2 MonthInitial $ 1;
set sasuser.SandPbyMonth1987to1991;
MonthInitial = substr(put(Date,monyy7.),1,1);
```

```
if month(Date) EQ 1 then YY = substr(Year,3,2);
else YY = ' ';
run;

ods listing style=GraphFontArial8ptBold gpath="C:\temp" dpi=300;
ods graphics on / reset=all scale=off width=5.7in
   imagename="Fig8-29_SandPfiveYearsByMonth_DataLabels";
title1 justify=center 'S&P Composite Index By Month 1987 to 1991';
proc sgplot data=work.CitiMonWithYYandMonthInitial noborder;
series x=Date y=FSPCOM / datalabel datalabelattrs=(size=6pt)
  markers markerattrs=(symbol=CircleFilled size=3)
  lineattrs=(color=LightGray);
/* LightGray plot line makes colliding data labels easier to read */
/* To get a grid only at January of each year,
   remove GRID option the from XAXIS statement and use statement:
   REFLINE 'Jan1987' 'Jan1988' 'Jan1989' 'Jan1990' 'Jan1991' /
     axis=X lineattrs=(color=LightGray); */
xaxistable MonthInitial YY / location=inside title='' label=' ';
yaxis display=none;
xaxis display=(noline noticks nolabel novalues) grid;
format Date monyy7. FSPCOM 3.;
run;
```

Daily Time Series Plots

The first example is for one month of days. The remaining are for a full year of days. All of the examples are for stock trading: with no data for weekends and holidays.

One Month of Time Series Data

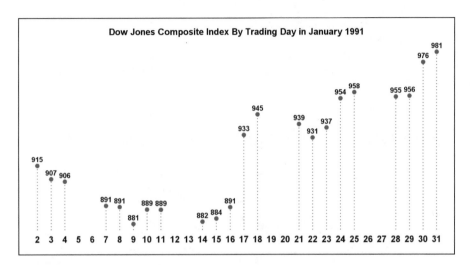

Figure 8-30. Using SERIES statement with data labels and a hidden plot line (which would add no value). Dotted-line drop lines make identification of date easy, quick, and certain

Figure 8-30 is analogous, visually and functionally, to a needle plot, but with markers. See, for example, Figure 8-13. However, a needle plot by default starts the Y axis at zero. To emulate this image, the input data would need to be preprocessed to determine the minimum and maximum Y values and to feed them to the SGPLOT PROC step as macro variables retrieved by a dynamic YAXIS statement. Of course, Figure 8-30 could have instead been created with Y=0, but the result would be a plot where there the plot points do not show much variation. Y=0 is my usual recommendation, but Figure 8-30 is an exception to provide a more interesting plot, and not a demonstration of best practice.

Listing 8-30. Code used to create Figure 8-30

```
/* requires a prior run of Listing 8-0 in THIS SAS SESSION
   to create input data */

ods listing style=GraphFontArial8ptBold gpath="C:\temp" dpi=300;
ods graphics on / reset=all scale=off width=5.7in height=3in
   imagename="Fig8-30_DowByDayJan1991_DataLabels_DropLines_Markers";
title1 justify=center
   'Dow Jones Composite Index By Trading Day in January 1991';
proc sgplot data=work. DowJonesByDayInJan1991 noborder;
series x=Day y=DailyDJ /
   datalabel datalabelattrs=(size=6pt) datalabelpos=top
```

```
  markers markerattrs=(symbol=CircleFilled color=blue size=5)
    lineattrs=(color=white); /* hide the plot line */
  dropline x=Day y=DailyDJ / dropto=x
    lineattrs=(color=blue pattern=Dot);
  yaxis display=none;
  xaxis display=(noline noticks nolabel) fitpolicy=none
    values=(2 to 31 by 1); /* January 1st is never a trading day */
  format DailyDJ 3.;
run;
```

Single-Line Daily Time Series Plot for a Year

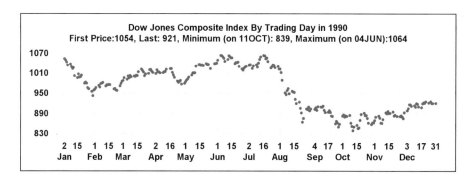

Figure 8-31. Single-line plot custom X axis, displaying essential values in the title

Sparse data labels are replaced in function by the subtitle, but the markers for minimum and maximum are not automatically discoverable with color coding. (With some additional coding, the reader could color-code those two points if desired.)

The helpful, but odd-looking, X axis values are a necessity imposed by the absence of days when there is no trading: weekends and holidays. For a full year of days, the mid-month axis values provided could all be 15, and all months would start with Day 1.

Listing 8-31. *Code used to create Figure 8-31*

```
/* requires a prior run of Listing 8-0 to create input data */

proc sort data=sasuser.DowJonesByDayIn1990 out=work.DowJonesIn1990ByMonthByDay;
by Month Day;
run;

data work.DowJonesWithMonAndDayForAxis;
retain MidMonthTradingDayFound 'N'
  MinDJ 999999999 MaxDJ MinDate MaxDate 0;
```

```
length Mon $ 3 DayForAxis $ 2; /* added to input for plot step */
set work.DowJonesIn1990ByMonthByDay end=LastOne;
by Month;
if DailyDJ LT MinDJ then do;
  MinDJ = DailyDJ;
  MinDate = Date;
end;
else if DailyDJ GT MaxDJ then do;
  MaxDJ = DailyDJ;
  MaxDate = Date;
end;
if _N_ EQ 1
then call symput('FirstDJ',put(DailyDJ,4.)); /* for use in title */
if LastOne
then do;
  call symput('LastDJ',put(DailyDJ,4.));     /* for use in title */
  call symput('MinDJ',put(MinDJ,4.));        /* for use in title */
  call symput('MaxDJ',put(MaxDJ,4.));        /* for use in title */
  call symput('MinDate',put(MinDate,date5.)); /* for use in title */
  call symput('MaxDate',put(MaxDate,date5.)); /* for use in title */
end;
if first.Month
then DayForAxis = Day;
else
if Day IN (15 16 17 18)
  AND
    MidMonthTradingDayFound EQ 'N'
then do;
  DayForAxis = Day;
  MidMonthTradingDayFound = 'Y';
end;
else
if last.Month then do;
  if Month EQ 12
  then DayForAxis = Day;
  MidMonthTradingDayFound = 'N';
end;
else DayForAxis = ' ';
if first.Month then Mon = put(Date,monname3.);
else Mon = ' ';
run;

ods listing style=GraphFontArial8ptBold gpath="C:\temp" dpi=300;
ods graphics on / reset=all scale=off width=5.7in height=2in
  imagename="Fig8-31_DowByDayIn1990_SingleLinePlot";
title1 justify=center
  "Dow Jones Composite Index By Trading Day in 1990";
title2 justify=center
  "First Price:&FirstDJ, Last:&LastDJ, Minimum (on &MinDate):&MinDJ, Maximum
```

```
(on &MaxDate):&MaxDJ";
proc sgplot data=work.DowJonesWithMonAndDayForAxis noborder;
series x=Date y=DailyDJ /
  markers markerattrs=(symbol=CircleFilled size=3px color=blue)
  lineattrs=(color=lightgray);
xaxistable DayForAxis Mon / /* as X axis tick mark values */
  location=inside title='' label=' ';
yaxis display=(noline noticks nolabel) grid
  values=(830 to 1070 by 60);
xaxis display=(noline noticks nolabel novalues) grid;
format DailyDJ 4.;
run;
```

Multi-line Monthly Plot for Daily Time Series Data of One Year

To get more visual insight into 252 data points, without looking at a much wider plot on a sufficiently wide monitor screen, the only solution is to break the range into pieces. Those pieces can be simultaneously displayed in a panel as is shown in Chapter 9. Figure 8-32 is a way to present the pieces all in one image, not in an array of images. This overlay makes it easier to detect a common pattern, from month to month, if there is any.

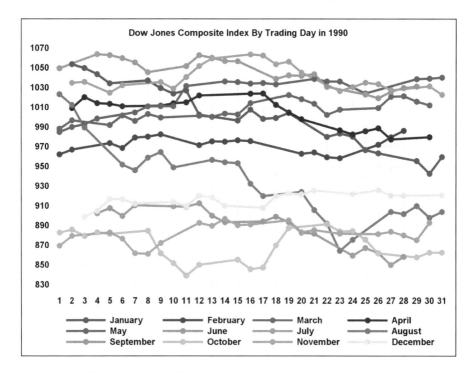

Figure 8-32. Thick lines assure distinguishable color coding

The density of markers and lines makes data labels infeasible for this data. The number of axis values and the widths of the Y values that would be there make an X axis table infeasible as well.

Listing 8-32. *Code used to create Figure 8-32*

```
proc format;
value MonthNm
    1 = 'January'   2 = 'February'   3 = 'March'
    4 = 'April'     5 = 'May'        6 = 'June'
    7 = 'July'      8 = 'August'     9 = 'September'
   10 = 'October'  11 = 'November'  12 = 'December';
run;

/* requires a prior run of Listing 8-0 to create input data: */

ods listing style=GraphFontArial8ptBold gpath="C:\temp" dpi=300;
ods graphics on / reset=all scale=off width=5.7in
   imagename="Fig8-32_DowByDayEachMonth1990_MultiLine_SimpleLegend";
title1 justify=center
    'Dow Jones Composite Index By Trading Day in 1990';
proc sgplot data=sasuser.DowJonesByDayIn1990 noborder;
series y=DAILYDJ x=Day / group=Month /* one plot line for each */
   markers markerattrs=(size=7 symbol=CircleFilled)
   lineattrs=(thickness=3 pattern=Solid);
yaxis display=(nolabel noticks noline) grid minorgrid minorcount=1
   values=(830 to 1080 by 20);
xaxis display=(nolabel noticks noline) grid
   fitpolicy=none /* prevents thinning of the axis values */
   values=(1 TO 31 BY 1);
keylegend / title='' noborder across=4;
format DAILYDJ 4. Month monthnm9.;
run;
```

Adding Value to the Multi-line Plot When Data Labels Are Impossible

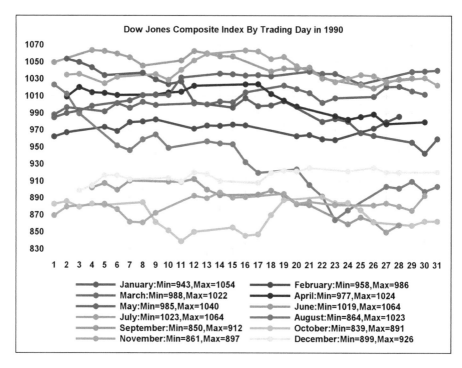

Figure 8-33. Legend enhanced with monthly minimum and maximum values, but lacking the monthly start and end values

The informative legend is a substitute for (infeasible) data labels, but the information is not adjacent to the 24 plot points. In a single-line plot, or a less dense multi-line plot where they might be accommodated without collisions, data labels for extreme values, and Start and End, are the better solution.

Listing 8-33. *Code used to create Figure 8-33*

```
/* requires a prior run of Listing 8-0 to create input data */

proc summary data=sasuser.DowJonesByDayIn1990 nway;
class Month;
var DAILYDJ;
output out=work.MinMaxByMonth min=MinDJ max=MaxDJ;
run;
```

```sas
proc format;
value MonthNm
    1 = 'January'   2 = 'February'   3 = 'March'
    4 = 'April'     5 = 'May'        6 = 'June'
    7 = 'July'      8 = 'August'     9 = 'September'
   10 = 'October'  11 = 'November'  12 = 'December';
run;

/* Prepare the MonthStats format to be used for the legend. */
data work.ToFormat;
keep fmtname type start label;
retain fmtname 'MonthStats' type 'N';
length start 3 label $ 64;
set work.MinMaxByMonth;
start = Month;
label = compress(put(Month,MonthNm9.) || ': Min=' ||
  put(MinDJ,4.) || ',Max=' || put(MaxDJ,4.));
run;
proc format library=work cntlin=work.ToFormat;
run;

ods listing style=GraphFontArial8ptBold gpath="C:\temp" dpi=300;
ods graphics on / reset=all scale=off width=5.7in
   imagename=
   "Fig8-33_DowByDayEachMonth1990_MultiLine_LegendStatistics";
title1 justify=center
   'Dow Jones Composite Index By Trading Day in 1990';
proc sgplot data=sasuser.DowJonesByDayIn1990 noborder;
series y=DAILYDJ x=Day / group=Month
  markers markerattrs=(size=7 symbol=CircleFilled)
  lineattrs=(thickness=3 pattern=Solid);
yaxis display=(nolabel noticks noline) grid minorgrid minorcount=1
  values=(830 to 1080 by 20);
xaxis display=(nolabel noticks noline) grid fitpolicy=none
  values=(1 TO 31 BY 1);
keylegend / title='' noborder across=2;
format DAILYDJ 4. Month MonthStats.; /* statistics in the legend */
run;
```

Adding More Value to the Multi-line Plot

With data preprocessing of the input, one can put almost anything into the legend. For Figure 8-34, this stratagem is used to deliver not only the monthly minimum and maximum values but also the monthly median, start, and end values, for each month in its legend entry. The blocks of white (at each monthly maximum) and black (at each monthly minimum) are an alternative to annotation, which is impractical on a plot with so much density of points and lines.

With appropriate coding, you can use the legend to deliver any statistics that you prefer and even line-specific comments. Going in an alternative direction, you could omit the median values from the legend or highlight their plot points with blocks of gray.

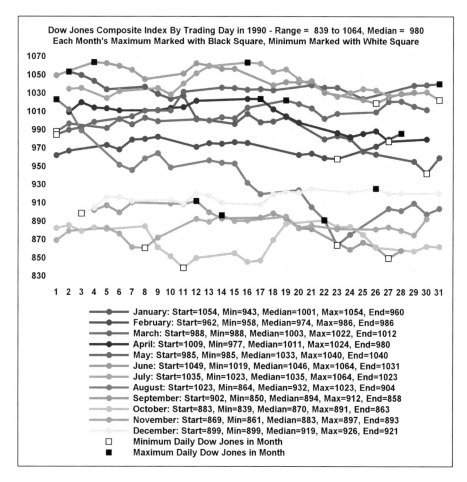

Figure 8-34. Legend enhanced with even more information. Color-coded maxima and minima

Listing 8-34. Code used to create Figure 8-34

```
/* Code below between START and END is stored as
   C:\SharedCode\CommonCodeForFig8_34AndFig14_16.sas */

/* START of Common Code used to create Figure 8-34 & Figure 14-16 */
/* requires a prior run of Listing 8-0 or 14-0 to create input data */
```

```
proc summary data=sasuser.DowJonesByDayIn1990;
class Month;
var DailyDJ;
output out=work.MinMedianMaxDJandMinMaxDay
  (drop=_freq_)
  min=MinDJ minid(DailyDJ(day))=MinDay
  median=MedDJ
  max=MaxDJ maxid(DailyDJ(day))=MaxDay;
run;

data work.MinMedianMaxDJandMinMaxDay
     work.MinDJandDay(keep=Month MinDj MinDay rename=(MinDay=Day))
     work.MaxDJandDay(keep=Month MaxDj MaxDay rename=(MaxDay=Day));
drop _type_;
length Month MinDay MinDJ MedDJ MaxDJ MaxDay 8;
label MinDJ='Minimum Daily Dow Jones in Month';
label MedDJ='Median Daily Dow Jones in Month';
label MaxDJ='Maximum Daily Dow Jones in Month';
set work.MinMedianMaxDJandMinMaxDay;
if _type_ EQ 0 then do; /* for statistics in TITLE1 */
  call symput('MinDJ1990',put(MinDJ,4.));
  call symput('MedDJ1990',put(MedDJ,4.));
  call symput('MaxDJ1990',put(MaxDJ,4.));
  delete;
end;
run;

data work.DowJonesByDayIn1990MonthlyMinMax;
set sasuser.DowJonesByDayIn1990 work.MinDJandDay work.MaxDJandDay;
run;

data work.DJ_MonthlyStartAndEnd;
retain StartDJ 0;
set sasuser.DowJonesByDayIn1990;
by Month;
if First.Month then StartDJ=DailyDJ;
if Last.Month;
EndDJ = DailyDJ;
run;

proc format library=work;
value MonthNm
  1 = 'January'  2 = 'February'  3 = 'March'
  4 = 'April'    5 = 'May'       6 = 'June'
  7 = 'July'     8 = 'August'    9 = 'September'
 10 = 'October' 11 = 'November' 12 = 'December';
run;
```

```
data work.ToFormat;
keep fmtname type start label;
retain fmtname 'MonthStats' type 'N';
length start 3 label $ 64;
merge work.MinMedianMaxDJandMinMaxDay work.DJ_MonthlyStartAndEnd;
by Month;
start = Month;
label = compress(put(Month,MonthNm9.))       ||
  ': Start='  || compress(put(StartDJ,4.)) ||
  ', Min='    || compress(put(MinDJ,4.))   ||
  ', Median=' || compress(put(MedDJ,4.))   ||
  ', Max='    || compress(put(MaxDJ,4.))   ||
  ', End='    || compress(put(EndDJ,4.));
run;
proc format library=work cntlin=work.ToFormat;
run;
```

/* END of Common Code used to create Figures 8-34 and 14-16 */

```
ods listing style=GraphFontArial8ptBold gpath="C:\temp" dpi=300;
ods graphics on / reset=all scale=off width=5.7in height=5.7in
  maxlegendarea=30 /* with the default 20,
                      the legend would be omitted */
  imagename=
" Fig8-34_DowByDayEachMonth1990_MultiLine_MostInfo_MinMaxMarkers";
title1 justify=center
  "Dow Jones Composite Index By Trading Day in 1990 - Range = &MinDJ1990 to
  &MaxDJ1990, Median = &MedDJ1990";
title2 justify=center
  "Each Month's Maximum Marked with Black Square, Minimum Marked with White
  Square";
proc sgplot data=work.DowJonesByDayIn1990MonthlyMinMax noborder;
series y=DAILYDJ x=Day / group=Month
  markers markerattrs=(size=7 symbol=CircleFilled)
  lineattrs=(thickness=3 pattern=Solid);
scatter x=Day y=MinDJ /
  FilledOutlinedMarkers
  markerattrs=(symbol=SquareFilled size=7px)
  markerfillattrs=(color=white)
  markeroutlineattrs=(color=black thickness=1px);
scatter x=Day y=MaxDJ /
  markerattrs=(symbol=SquareFilled size=7px color=black);
yaxis display=(nolabel noticks noline) grid minorgrid minorcount=1
  values=(830 to 1080 by 20);
xaxis display=(nolabel noticks noline) grid fitpolicy=none
  values=(1 TO 31 BY 1);
keylegend / title='' noborder across=1;
format DailyDJ 4. Month MonthStats.;
run;
```

Seeing the Big Picture, Seeing It Better in Pieces, Seeing It Differently

In later chapters, other alternatives for complex time series situations are presented.

PROC SGPANEL can deliver an array of plots, each of which is a segment of the total reporting time period. The array can be cells all in one column, cells all in one row, or cells in a matrix. (PROC SGPANEL is not limited to presenting time series plots.) The content of the panels must be from one data set, with each cell being for different values of one or more class variables. (Year, Month, or Week can be a class variable.)

The ODS LAYOUT destination is more versatile. A target image area is laid out as you choose, and each area is filled by any ODS Graphics procedure step needed, using any data set needed.

Also, there are a variety of other ODS destinations that offer the opportunity to package graphs, and optionally tables, in useful ways, combining them on one page or interlinking them on separate pages (or worksheets). ODS HTML5 provides the distinctive, but temporary, advantage of "mouseover text" for the plot points in web pages where plot points are too dense for permanent data labels. In this chapter, the focus is on the LISTING destination which routes a static image file to disk or another location.

More ways to present time series and trend data are provided in Chapters 9, 10, and 14, and with vertical bar charts in Chapter 4.

Summary

Examples in this chapter are guided by the key design principle of providing precise numbers. Time series plots can make that difficult. Most of the examples are simply graphs of 12 months. That makes it easier than it typically might be. With few enough plot points, and if a single line, data labels can be provided without suffering collisions with each other or with the line. If collisions between data labels and the line do occur, they can be eliminated by coloring the line white or mitigated by using a thinly dotted line. A white line does not make the plot points disappear. They are more important than a line to connect them, and a connecting line is not necessarily representative of the Y values for intervening X values, and for many, if not most, time series, there are no intervening X values. A line to connect points in a time series is more a matter of convention, and not a communication necessity.

As in the case for *all* graphs, one should present the precise numbers unless it is physically impossible to do so with readability assured. This chapter's main mission is finding the ways, the most effective ways, and some very efficient ways to accomplish that.

Data labels and the X axis table alternative are infeasible when there are too many X values. Though it is not really necessary in this case with so few data points, Figure 8-1 presents a suboptimal solution, but better than no solution. It can be used when there is no better alternative. Because it has both a Y axis at the left and a "mirrored" Y2 axis at the right, Figure 8-1 uses reference lines for each of the Y values. For the case of a single vertical axis, drop lines to the Y axis would be the only choice. Drop lines to the X axis are also always available, if needed, to make identification of X values easy, quick, and certain.

Though not really needed, Figure 8-2 demonstrates the use of drop lines to the X axis. For Figure 8-30, drop lines are helpful.

Though drop lines take the eye to precise points on an axis, they often land *between* axis values, *not on* axis values. Those locations are not precise numbers, but the estimating then required is based on visual knowledge of *where* the numbers are in the range. Even when drop lines fail to deliver the precise numbers, they are helpful visual assistants to guide the eye in the viewer's pursuit of precise numbers.

For Figure 8-29, with five years of twelve months each, reference lines are provided at each January and July to make it easier to determine the month for any of the 60 plot points.

The usual function of reference lines is to mark some significant point in the time series, as in Figure 8-10, or the time when some influencing or affected event occurred, or a goal to be achieved or a threshold for concern. A very different use of reference lines is in Figure 8-25, where a pair of lines with labels for the Y values at the upper and lower bounds on all of the data (60 data points) provides information that would otherwise be clumsy and time-consuming to discover from the graph. Data visualization is intended to accelerate and facilitate discovery about the data, and this is another way to do that. The pair of lines serves, in effect, as a band.

The BAND statement can be used in two ways. The band with constant upper and lower bounds in Figure 8-16 is analogous to the two reference lines used in Figure 8-25, but with very light area fill between the bounds. (You can also create vertical bands between two X values, or both a vertical and a horizontal band, or multiple bands in the same or both directions.)

In Figure 8-17, the band has variable bounds to display the monthly high and low share prices above and below the monthly closing share price. The precise values for those high and low prices are displayed in X axis tables. This is an alternative to the data-labeled plots of the information in Figures 8-18 to 8-20.

Those three plots in Figures 8-18 to 8-20 use the HIGHLOW statement as an alternative to multi-line plots with a SERIES statement and a GROUP variable. The HIGHLOW statement was designed to present the opening, closing, high, and low values of a stock over time, but it can be used, if desired, for *any* four variables, two of which are the minimum and maximum values related to the other variables.

Figures 8-23 to 8-28 are examples of multi-line plots delivered with a SERIES statement in which X and Y variables have a GROUP variable companion. There is one plot line for each value of the GROUP variable. The lines are color-coded, and a legend for finding the identity of each (the GROUP value) is automatically produced. There is a default color list, but colors can be customized with the DATACONTRASTCOLORS option of the STYLEATTRS statement. The color list, default or custom, is applied to the plot lines and, if present, also automatically to markers, data labels, and (color-coded) axis table. To make the axis table color-coded requires extra options as demonstrated in Listings 8-25 and 8-26.

The collection of six multi-line plots includes two fully data-labeled versions, one with a legend in Figure 8-23 and another with curve labels instead of a legend in Figure 8-24, which saves the viewer the extra visual work of discovering line identity in a legend. Curve labels are adjacent to the end (or start) of each time series line, which accelerates and facilitates the viewer's determination of line identity.

Figures 8-25 and 8-26 are for situations where the quest for a multi-line plot with precise numbers might be infeasible due to data label collisions. Both examples use an X axis table to present all of the Y values for all the lines.

Figure 8-25 starts the Y axis at zero, which squashes the plot lines together making any annotation (data labels) impossible, but it provides a fair comparison of the historical behavior of the five plot lines (five years of monthly data). There is no magnification of month-to-month changes that is caused when the vertical space available is devoted only the minimum-to-maximum range of the five years of data.

Throughout the examples in this chapter, starting the Y axis at zero is pursued as a norm. The exceptions are usually cases where starting Y at zero would increase data label collisions. Other cases include the Sparse Line, which would become boringly flat, with the same being true for Figure 8-30. The collection of 12 already clashing lines in the overlay plot of Figures 8-32, 8-33, and 8-34 would become an unhelpful mishmash of lines, markers, and color—a useless and annoying vision, not a communication-effective data visualization.

Figure 8-26 uses the vertical space available to instead provide maximum granularity in the time series plots and provides enough open space to present data labels for all of the essential points: start, end, any intermediate minimum, and any intermediate maximum for each line. These sparsely annotated lines are further enhanced by color-coding the markers for minima with light gray and the markers for maxima with white. All of those markers for extrema have black outlines.

Figures 8-27 and 8-28 are also sparsely annotated like Figure 8-26, but the axis table is omitted, and what is presented is part of what might be provided in a Sparse Line Table. Here, the history lines are overlaid, not stacked in a column as in a Sparse Line Table. For Sparse Line Tables, see Figures 9-9 and 9-12, and see Figure 14-15 for a web-enabled example. For Sparse Line Panels, see Figures 9-11 and 9-13.

As mentioned in context, the plots in Figures 8-26, 8-27, and 8-28 are only "nearly Sparse Lines" since they omit annotation of the last change, and they include extra content.

The true Sparse Line (a reinvention of Sparse Line Annotation) in Figure 8-9 does the best possible job of delivering the key things that one would likely want to know and see for a one-line time series: the picture of every data point, with precise numbers and dates for all four essential data points, as well as the change from second last date to the ending date. It includes only the line and its annotation, unlike "the nearly Sparse Lines."

But when you want to show the viewer *all* of the precise numbers for Y and X for each data point in a one-line time series, a visually illuminating, precise knowledge–providing, and most efficient solution possible is the example shown in Figure 8-7. It uses a TEXT statement to display, centered at each marker-free data point, a stack of the Y value over the X value. Visual knowledge of the precise location of the data points is unnecessary. The precise coordinates Y and X for each data point are provided instead in the text blocks. The axes are eliminated. The shape of the trend is apparent from the collection of text blocks. A physical line would add no communication value, but could collide with the text information which is what the image is all about. Figure 8-7 is the sparse time series plot.

If one wants to present a line, Figures 8-2 through 8-5 provide ways to do that, *and* to provide precise numbers. Figure 8-6 is functionally equivalent to the text-only method of Figure 8-7, but with the text blocks sitting above a string of markers, which *are* precise indicators of the plot point locations. Figure 8-7 has each stack of Y and X values centered around its invisible plot point. Figure 8-2, which uses an axis table, does stack the Y values above the X values, but the plot line is sitting far above them, connected to those Y-X coordinate text blocks by drop lines.

If one is going to create a step plot, an example of the most communication-effective solution is shown in Figure 8-15, but the code is only in Listing A8-15 in Appendix A.

Before closing with the only other graph types not reviewed here yet, I want to discuss the Y2AXIS statement. Its use is essential to create Figures 8-21 and 8-22, which present two different response variables in overlaid time series plots. In Figure 8-1, it is used to provide duplicate Y axes at the left and right of the plot, to provide a shortest visual distance from any point to its value on an axis. In situations where data labels and an axis table are unavailable for precise values, getting to their Y value locations on an axis deserves to be facilitated and expedited. Visual assistance is always useful when interpreting a graph.

Figure 8-30 is a departure from the monthly plots. It is a daily plot for one month. The SERIES statement is used with markers, but the plot line is hidden with COLOR=WHITE in the LINEATTRS option. The markers have data labels. Drop lines are used to connect the markers to their X values. This image looks like a needle plot, but the Y axis does not start at zero. A needle plot by default starts its Y axis at zero.

Figure 8-13 is a needle plot. The needle plot default location for data labels is TopRight. The TopRight position adds no communication value and can be, and should be, overridden with the option POSITION=TOP on the NEEDLE statement. TopRight requires extra space between the needles. With limited horizontal space, there is no benefit in wasting it.

A needle plot is functionally a very thin vertical bar chart. The vertical bar chart examples in Figures 8-11 and 8-12 are, in effect, wide versions of the needle plot in Figure 8-13. Figure 8-12 is the same vertical bar chart as Figure 8-11, but with color coding of the bars to deliver a comment visually and tacitly and with a companion color-coded INSET statement to make that comment explicit. The REFLINE statement was used with the SERIES statement for Figure 8-10 to visually locate a persistent trend change and to comment about it. The REFLINE statement is not available for a bar chart. Figure 8-12 overcomes this problem by coloring the bars differently before and after the trend change and putting the comment about the change with an INSET statement. That comment is rendered with white text over background color that matches the color of the post-trend-change vertical bars.

In a time series plot with markers and a line, the line segments between markers have no information significance. What the Y values might be for time points between those that are displayed (if there actually are any intermediate time points) is unknown, and there is no reason to expect that they would lie on a line segment, or artificially smoothed curve, between those markers. A SCATTER statement plot of Y versus X would serve just as well as a SERIES statement plot. However, a vertical bar chart also serves equally well and is more visually interesting and impactful than a collection of markers. An always visually pleasant design is that of Figure 8-11, where the width of the data labels matches that of the bars. The only constraint on feasibility is image width versus the combined width of the bars and spaces. When space constraints make a bar chart infeasible, the advantage of a SERIES statement with a hidden line is that the software will adjust data label positions to try to prevent collisions, including label-label collisions which remain a risk even when label-line collisions "disappear" by hiding the line.

Figure 8-29 presents five years of data "linearly," rather than stacked in an overlay plot of the individual five years. Despite consisting of 60 data points, it is successfully data labeled, collision-free, and readable. The code makes no attempt at assigning a position for the data labels, and a smart internal algorithm in ODS Graphics does a good job of dynamically finding collision-free label locations.

With 60 tick mark positions for the months of 1987 through 1991, it is infeasible to use X axis values such as 87JAN, 87FEB, ..., 91DEC. The XAXIS statement provides no option to deal with this. The X axis was suppressed with the DISPLAY=NONE option on the XAXIS statement, and an XAXISTABLE statement creates two rows, with month initials in the top row and two-digit year in the bottom row, but only under each January (the first J initial in each year).

Figures 8-30 through 8-34 provide a variety of ways to present daily data, but Figure 8-30 is devoted to just one month of days. In that situation, the plot points can be data-labeled. The other examples present the best that one can do without data labels. In those situations where data labels are infeasible, an axis table is likewise.

Figures 8-32, 8-33, and 8-34 present a twelve-line overlay of one plot line for the days of each month in 1990 for the Dow Jones Composite Index Closing Value. Data labels are clearly infeasible. A 12-row axis table might be feasible if the image width were wide enough to provide space for 31 columns for the Y values in a readable font for up to four-digit numbers. A web page on a wide screen monitor might be a suitable display, but this book's page width is not.

The three examples use a grid and the default color palette for the plot lines, markers, and legend. Plot lines are assigned sufficient thickness to assure color distinguishability. Figure 8-32 has the default legend.

Figures 8-33 and 8-34, on the other hand, use the legend to deliver essential value information in this case, where even Sparse Line Annotation is impossible. The custom legend not only identifies the lines but also reports the minimum and maximum values for each month. In Figure 8-34, the medians are added to the legend entries, each month's markers for maximum and minimum are color-coded, and the year's minimum, maximum, and median are included in the title.

More ways to present time series and trend data are provided in Chapters 9, 10, and 14, and with vertical bar charts in Chapter 4.

That concludes this retrospective review of the chapter.

Here is an incomplete closing list of tips that were illustrated in this chapter:

- To hide the lines that come with the SERIES statement, but cannot be turned off, use LINEATTRS=(COLOR=White).

- To soften the effect of collisions between SERIES statement plot lines, use LINEATTRS=(PATTERN=ThinDot).

- To turn on markers at data points with the SERIES statement, use the option MARKERS, which then makes the MARKERATTRS option (and other markers-related options) available for marker customization.

- If the top of the graph is too close to the last title line, use (for the case only one title line)

  ```
  TITLE2 COLOR=WHITE 'White Space or any other text here';
  ```

- There are cases where it is necessary to add the option TYPE=DISCRETE to the XAXIS statement. They are best understood by studying the cases in this chapter where used.

- Instead of a legend, variable names in a title can be color-coded to identify lines and/or markers and/or data labels. (See Figures and Listings 8-17 through 8-21.) This does require extra coding, but viewer convenience is more important than programmer convenience. For *every* graph, the first thing that is *always* read by the viewer is the title. A color-coded title eliminates the extra step for the viewer of looking down into a legend to determine the identity of graphic elements.

Other Features

Graphic Composites with PROC SGPANEL

PROC SGPANEL (and PROC SGSCATTER) makes it possible to display different views of a data set in a composite of images in one column, one row, or an array of M rows and N columns.

Since a composite consists of multiple images, presenting readable precise numbers as data labels is likely to often be difficult and in some cases impossible. How to cope with that challenge is explored somewhat here and also in Chapter 14 using ODS HTML5.

© LeRoy Bessler 2023
LeR. Bessler, *Visual Data Insights Using SAS ODS Graphics*,
https://doi.org/10.1007/978-1-4842-8609-8_9

Shown here are composites for time series plots, for categorical data charts, and for scatter plots. Scatter plots are taken up further in Chapter 10, both in standalone format and in composites.

PROC SGPANEL can be used with almost all of the ODS Graphics statements that are used in the earlier chapters. There are some substitutions: in PROC SGPANEL, the XAXIS, YAXIS, XAXISTABLE, and YAXISTABLE statements are replaced by COLAXIS, ROWAXIS, COLAXISTABLE, and ROWAXISTABLE statements. Waterfall charts, a niche application for a narrow purpose, are not supported by PROC SGPANEL. To the best of my knowledge, all of the other PROC SGPLOT graph, plot, and chart statements should also work with PROC SGPANEL.

What follows in this section is a lot of description *about* what PROC SGPANEL does. You might skip ahead to the next section, read this section later, and get to *seeing* what it *does* sooner.

PROC SGPANEL tries to make best use of the space available to display multiple related images in an array. Its PANELBY statement is used to identify one or more class variables for which the values identify the individual images that are displayed in cells of the array. In addition to the PROC SGPANEL statement and the PANELBY statement, the PROC step must include one or more statements to specify the graphic content of the cells in the array, such as an HBAR statement for horizontal bar charts. The LAYOUT option on the PANELBY statement can be PANEL (the default), LATTICE, COLUMNLATTICE, or ROWLATTICE.

The result from LAYOUT=ROWLATTICE is one column of rows and looks the same as LAYOUT=PANEL COLUMNS=1, except the cell headings are displayed at the side of each cell in a lattice, rather than above each cell in a panel. The result from LAYOUT=COLUMNLATTICE is one row of columns and is identical to the result from LAYOUT=PANEL ROWS=1, with the cell headings in both cases displayed at the top of each cell.

In the case of one class variable for PANELBY, the choice between one row and one column for the composite is best made based on your judgment as to which is better for viewing and interpretation. Test both options, unless there is some basis for an a priori choice.

The LATTICE layout can be used only with two class variables. The PANEL layout can be used with any number of class variables. For a lattice, the number of rows and columns is determined by the number of distinct values for the two class variables. The array is defined by assigning the columns, in alphabetical order, to values of the first specified class variable and assigning the rows to values of the second specified class variable. Any combinations of values of the two class variables that are not present in the input data are represented by an empty cell.

With the PANEL layout for one, two, or more class variables, the user can specify the numbers of rows and columns or let the software decide. In either case, the cells are filled from top to bottom (by default—an override is possible for bottom to top) in the rows and left to right in the columns within each row. When there is only one class variable, the filling process is easy to understand. See, for example, Figure 9-2. In this chapter, all examples with two class variables are for the LATTICE layout. If you examine Figure 9-33 for the case of a PANEL layout with three class variables, you can infer, I think, how the fill process works for two class variables. If not, it should be straightforward to adapt its code by omitting one of the class variables.

Unlike the case of a LATTICE layout where ClassVar1 ClassVar2 combinations without data are represented by an empty cell, the PANEL fill process just proceeds to the next available combination of values in the input to fill the next cell (left to right, top to bottom). If the product of row count and column count exceeds the number of class variable value combinations in the input, enough empty cells are displayed at the bottom right of the panel to complete a rectangular array. (The process will complete a currently incomplete row, but will not create additional fully empty rows.) For the panel in Figure 9-33, the SKIPEMPTYCELLS option is used on the PANELBY statement. So, blank space appears instead of empty cells.

Why Axis Offsets Are Important in PROC SGPANEL Applications

Axis offsets are also available for AXIS statements used with PROC SGPLOT. OFFSETMIN can be used to adjust where the first axis value occurs along an axis, and OFFSETMAX can be used for the last axis value. In my experience, using what the software assigns as defaults for these offsets in PROC SGPLOT applications is *usually* acceptable (though not always). Needs to override them can be infrequent, but are sometimes necessary. The need is not always obvious, but is important.

For the 33 PROC SGPANEL examples in this chapter, there are frequent overrides of the defaults. Some of them are intended to improve the appearance of the result and/or to make better use of the space available. However, in four examples, limited to bar charts with data labels, overrides are mandatory to prevent misleading graphs. These situations, more precisely described later, are the only conditions in which I found the problem.

Misleading graphs arise when the default offsets are not uniform across all of the cells in a panel or lattice. If they are not uniform, then a bar chart bar length, for example, that represents value 3 in one cell of the composite might be greater than the bar chart bar length that represents value 4 in another cell. This is easily solved by overriding the defaults by assigning the OFFSETMAX to a satisfactory value in the ROWAXIS or COLAXIS statement, depending on which axis is involved in the problem. That OFFSETMAX is the same across all cells, replacing any varying default offsets. The four bar charts in this chapter vulnerable to the problem were fixed. The listings for those figures show the solution. (To instead see the problem, you can reuse the code, but with tick marks and values turned on and with the offsets removed.)

Problems for bar charts with data labels were prevented in these vulnerable cases (and examples):

> HBAR charts for LAYOUT=COLUMNLATTICE (Figure 9-19)
>
> VBAR charts for LAYOUT=ROWLATTICE (Figure 9-20)
>
> VBAR charts for LAYOUT=LATTICE or LAYOUT=PANEL and, in either case, more than one row of cells (Figure 9-22)
>
> HBAR charts for LAYOUT=LATTICE or LAYOUT=PANEL and, in either case, more than one column of cells (Figure 9-33)

Figure 9-18, which uses code that accepts the default offsets, demonstrates the problem of misleading output.

Note   The HBAR chart problem for LAYOUT=COLUMNLATTICE also affects LAYOUT=PANEL ROWS=1. The VBAR chart problem for LAYOUT=ROWLATTICE also affects LAYOUT=PANEL COLUMNS=1.

How PROC SGPANEL Can Affect Image Dimensions

A distinctive feature of PROC SGPANEL as compared to, for example, PROC SGPLOT (and all other ODS Graphics procedures) is how the image height is assigned when only the image width is specified. First, let me describe what happens when neither dimension is specified on the ODS GRAPHICS statement. The software decides, presumably based on the rows by columns arrangement that the user picks or that the software chooses, whether the image should be landscape, portrait, or a square. Regardless of shape, the maximum default dimension of the image is 6.67 inches. If a rectangle, the smaller dimension is 5 inches. If a square, both dimensions are 6.67 inches.

The aspect ratio of width to height is 4:3 if landscape, 3:4 if portrait, or 1:1 if square. For procedures other than SGPANEL, the default width is always 6.67 inches and default height is 5 inches, with an aspect ratio of 4:3.

With other procedures, if only the image width is specified, the image height is always three-fourths of the image width. With SGPANEL, if only the image width is specified, the software will decide which shape of the image it will create and will use one of the three aspect ratios described earlier to compute the height that it uses for the image.

So, if you have a preference as to image dimensions, use both the WIDTH and the HEIGHT options on the ODS GRAPHICS statement.

General Remarks About Code Used

Several examples have %INCLUDE statements for code or macros from folder C:\SharedCode, which could instead be any folder or location of your choice.

The following framing code has been more expansively discussed in Chapter 3 in the section "Outer Structure of ODS Graphics Code in Examples." The framing code for all examples in this chapter and others is

```
ods results off; /* verify results by opening the image file,
                      rather than using the SAS Output window */
ods _all_ close; /* avoid unintended consequences
                      and superfluous concurrent output */
< ODS LISTING statement here >
< example-specific code here >
ods listing close; /* ALWAYS Best Practice */
```

For brevity, the example code in listings omits the first two lines and the last one. It is best to add them back at your runtime. (Source code files include them.)

The ODS LISTING statement can vary. All of the examples in this chapter use a statement of the following form to specify the text characteristics:

```
ods listing style=GraphFontArial11ptBold gpath="C:\temp" dpi=300;
```

but usually with font sizes other than 11pt. The statement assumes that the ODS style GraphFontArial11ptBold has been created. To assure that all of the styles needed in this chapter are available, use this code:

```
%include "C:\SharedCode\AllGraphTextSetup.sas";
%AllGraphTextSetup(7);
%AllGraphTextSetup(8);
```

```
%AllGraphTextSetup(9);
%AllGraphTextSetup(10);
%AllGraphTextSetup(11);
```

For more information about ODS custom styles, as well as the source code for the AllGraphTextSetup macro, see the section "Control of Text Attributes with a Custom ODS Style" in Chapter 3. For information about options for direct control of text attributes, which can override the default text attributes that are set up by an ODS style, see the section "Text Attributes Control in ODS Graphics" in Chapter 3.

Input Data for the Examples

For some examples, a custom data set is built with a DATA step. For other examples, the input data is either SASHELP.CARS or SASHELP.CLASS. In some examples, that source data is preprocessed for the SGPANEL PROC step.

With one-time setup processing in Listing 9-0, you can avoid running the same code over and over. This non-graphics code need not be repeated in every example that needs its output for input.

This chapter includes several time series graphs. For background information about the input data required, in Chapter 8, please see section "Special Data Sets Used for Some Time Series Graphs." If your site does not have SAS/ETS, you must download the zip file CitiData.zip from https://github.com/Apress/Visual-Data-Insights-Using-SAS-ODS-Graphics and store the five unzipped files in folder C:\CitiData.

Whichever is the case, the next step is to prepare data that is used in this chapter for several examples. My SAS site does *not* have SAS/ETS.

Listing 9-0. *Create persisting data sets for use in Chapter 9*

```
/* To prepare sasuser.SandPbyMonth1987to1991
   (this macro also harmlessly prepares
   sasuser.SandPbyMonth1980to1991, which is not used here) */
%include "C:\SharedCode\CreateSandPbyMonthTwoRanges.sas";
options mprint;
%CreateSandPbyMonthTwoRanges
(SASETSsiteUseSASHELPDataLib=NO,
OtherSiteFolderForCitiData=C:\CitiData,
OutLib=SASUSER);

/* To prepare sasuser.DowJonesByDayIn1990 */
%include "C:\SharedCode\CreateDowJonesByDayIn1990.sas";
options mprint;
%CreateDowJonesByDayIn1990
(SASETSsiteUseSASHELPDataLib=NO,
OtherSiteFolderForCitiData=C:\CitiData,
OutLib=SASUSER);
```

```
data sasuser.CarsWithMSRPinThousands;
set sashelp.cars;
MSRP = MSRP / 1000;
run;
```

Included Code

Macros and other code that are used in multiple examples are %INCLUDEd at the top of the affected listings. The examples assume that the code files are stored in folder C:\SharedCode, which, of course, could instead be whatever is your preferred location. Their source code is, in some cases, first shown in an example.

Composites of Time Series Plots

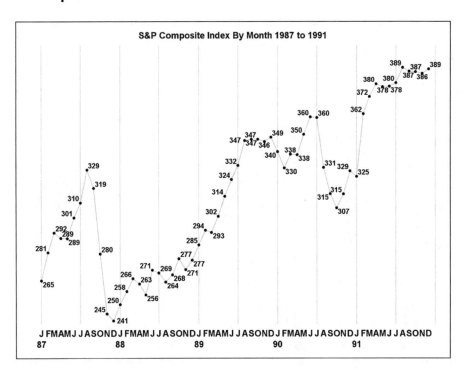

Figure 9-1. Not a composite (a redisplay of Figure 8-29). A complete all-in-one presentation of the data that is presented with panels and lattices in this chapter

Figure 9-1 is a plot of 60 points for five years of monthly data. Due to the fewness of plot points, it is actually possible to use data labels to deliver all of the precise values. The CitiMon data set, the ultimate source of the data used for Figure 9-1, actually contains 12 years of monthly economic data.

This chapter's examples provide other ways to show what Figure 9-1 already shows satisfactorily. Later examples will show daily data, either by day within month, for 12 months, or by day within week, for a full year of weeks.

Panels of Monthly Data

Figure 9-2 is a non-overlaid alternative to an overlay plot of the five years. It undoes the overlay, presenting the yearly plots side by side. It is not a better solution, it is a different solution. For data with denser plot points, separating the cycles can make data labels which in overlay are infeasible become possible. An overlay makes it easy to look for seasonality. An alternate view can make precise values displayable, as in Figure 9-7, which covers a 12-year range and provides data labels—which would be impossible for a single-line plot if it were to fit in this page width.

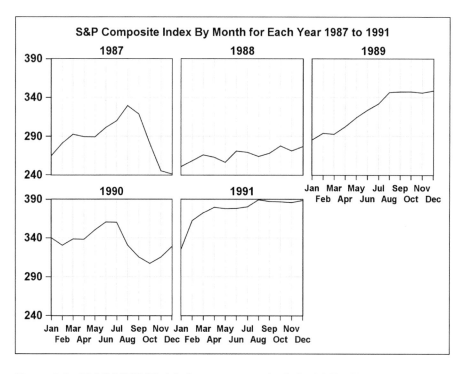

Figure 9-2. PROC SGPANEL default arrangement of cells for LAYOUT=PANEL

It is a panel, rectangular when it is too long to fit in one row.

The empty cell is due to the SKIPEMPTYCELLS option on the PANELBY statement. Without it, a useless box for an empty cell appears.

The comments in Listing 9-2 are a helpful description of many aspects of syntax for the PANELBY statement and associated statements for PROC SGPANEL.

Listing 9-2. Code used to create Figure 9-2

```
proc format;
value NumberToMonthAbbrev
    1 = 'Jan'  2 = 'Feb'  3 = 'Mar'  4 = 'Apr'
    5 = 'May'  6 = 'Jun'  7 = 'Jul'  8 = 'Aug'
    9 = 'Sep' 10 = 'Oct' 11 = 'Nov' 12 = 'Dec';
quit;

/* The PROC FORMAT step code above can be filed as, e.g.,
   C:\SharedCode\CreateMonthNumberToThreeCharsFormat.sas */
/* Code for later examples includes (and runs) the code with:
   %include
   "C:\SharedCode\CreateMonthNumberToThreeCharsFormat.sas"; */

/* requires a prior run of Listing 9-0 to create input data: */

ods listing style=GraphFontArial10ptBold gpath="C:\temp" dpi=300;
ods graphics on / reset=all scale=off width=5.7in
  /* default height assigned by software is 4.28 inches,
     With a 4:3 aspect ratio */
  imagename="Fig9-2_Panel_MonthlyData_Customized";
title1 justify=center
  'S&P Composite Index By Month for Each Year 1987 to 1991';
proc sgpanel data=sasuser.SandPbyMonth1987to1991;
panelby Year /
  /* layout=panel is the default */
  onepanel /* Usually Best Practice, unless you are willing to risk
  having the software decide to split the panel or lattice into
  multiple images of one or more cells each, which would be a
  Decomposed Composite. Such splitting is unpredictable. However,
  for some content, with too many cells for the space available in a
  single image file, a single panel can result in an unreadable
  result. In that case, the ONEPANEL option is inappropriate.*/
  skipemptycells /* omit this, if you wish, to see poor result */
  novarname /* omit superfluous nonlabel FSPCOM from cell headers */
  spacing=10 /* Eliminates possible confusion as to whether
    header label belongs to cell above or below. Also, prevents
    collisions between ending value (Dec) and starting value (Jan)
    for axes of adjacent cells. */
  noheaderborder; /* This eliminates the top and sides of headers,
  but more important is that this eliminates
  a needless thickened boundary between cell header
  and top edge of cell content. If data labels are used,
  that boundary can be subject to collisions with data labels
```

```
  near the maximum Y value in the cell. */
series x=Month y=FSPCOM;
rowaxis values=(240 to 390 by 50)
  offsetmin=0 offsetmax=0 /* No data labels are present,
  and the SERIES statement provides no markers as a default,
  so top and bottom plot points can be at the edges.
  No space for data labels or markers is needed. */
  grid minorgrid minorcount=4
  display=(nolabel noline); /* omit unneeded */
colaxis
  display=(nolabel noline)
  grid
  offsetmin=0 offsetmax=0 /* No data labels are present,
  so first and last plot points can be at the edges.
  No markers are being used. No space for them is needed. */
  valueattrs=(size=8pt)
  fitpolicy=stagger /* values won't fit in a single line */
  values=(1 to 12 by 1);
  /* It is necessary to explicitly specify values to get the desired
  result when Values are displayed using the Month format below. */
format Month NumberToMonthAbbrev.;
run;
```

With a sufficiently informative title or subtitle, axis labels are superfluous. In most cases, that is also the case for tick marks. If using a grid, the tick marks can be visually useful, attention-drawing, connectors between axis values and grid lines. In a case where data labels are used for the response value in a graph, values along the relevant axis would have no value, in which case the NOVALUES option is appropriate for DISPLAY=. However, I have found that in such a case, the best choice is DISPLAY=NONE. This automatically includes, in effect, the NOLINE option, as well as NOLABEL, NOTICKS, and NOVALUES.

With a panel or lattice, the line at issue is actually hidden by the border of the cells nearest to that axis. Despite the fact that the line is hidden, for some graphs its hidden presence reserves white space along that margin of the image. This wasted space reduces the space available for real content. The only way to see the line is to use the NOBORDER option on the PANELBY statement to turn off all of the cell borders in the panel or lattice. However, as I mentioned, the usually hidden line reserves space to its left or bottom only for some graphs, not in the case of Figure 9-2.

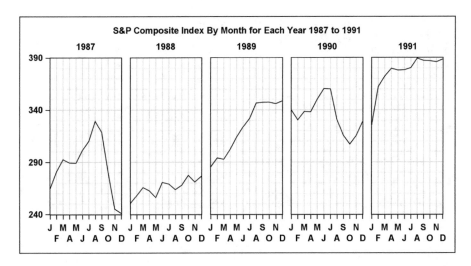

Figure 9-3. Using LAYOUT=COLUMNLATTICE. This is a demonstration of a column lattice, not a better alternative than a single five-year image

---

■ **Note** Unless you are willing to accept a possibly unexpected result of having your output panel or lattice being split into separate pieces of one or more cells each, it is best practice to *always* include the ONEPANEL option on the PANELBY statement. However, if the content is too much for the image space available, the cell content can be unusable, in which case the ONEPANEL option should not be used.

Listing 9-3. *Code used to create Figure 9-3*

/* requires a prior run of Listing 9-0 to create input data */

```
ods listing style=GraphFontArial8ptBold gpath="C:\temp" dpi=300;
ods graphics on / reset=all scale=off width=5.7in
  height=3.0in /* larger default height would be superfluous */
  imagename="Fig9-3_ColumnLattice_MonthlyData_Customized";
title1 justify=center
  'S&P Composite Index By Month for Each Year 1987 to 1991';
proc sgpanel data=sasuser.SandPbyMonth1987to1991;
panelby Year / layout=columnlattice
  spacing=10 onepanel novarname noheaderborder;
series x=Month y=FSPCOM;
rowaxis values=(240 to 390 by 50) offsetmin=0 offsetmax=0
  grid minorgrid minorcount=4 display=(nolabel noline);
colaxis grid display=(nolabel noline) fitpolicy=stagger
```

```
values=(1 to 12 by 1) offsetmin=0 offsetmax=0
/* No space for anything longer than one character */
valuesdisplay=('J' 'F' 'M' 'A' 'M' 'J' 'J' 'A' 'S' 'O' 'N' 'D');
run;
```

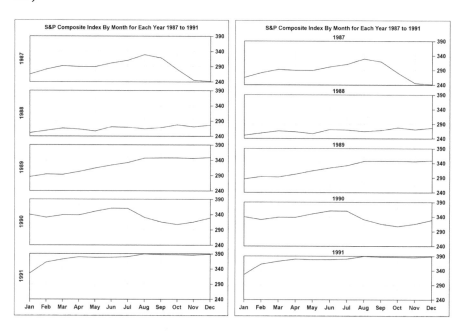

Figures 9-4 and 9-5. Left is LAYOUT=ROWLATTICE. Right is LAYOUT=PANEL COLUMNS=1

The software chose image height, using 7.6 inches for an aspect ratio of 3:4.

Listing 9-4. Code used to create Figure 9-4

```
%include "C:\SharedCode\CreateMonthNumberToThreeCharsFormat.sas";

/* requires a prior run of Listing 9-0 to create input data: */

ods listing style=GraphFontArial10ptBold gpath="C:\temp" dpi=300;
ods graphics on / reset=all scale=off width=5.7in
  imagename="Fig9-4_RowLattice_MonthlyData_Customized";
title1 justify=center
 'S&P Composite Index By Month for Each Year 1987 to 1991';
proc sgpanel data=sasuser.SandPbyMonth1987to1991;
panelby Year / layout=rowlattice
  spacing=20 /* separate last and first row axis values
                of consecutive rows */
  rowheaderpos=left /* text is easier to read at the left */
  onepanel novarname noheaderborder;
```

```
series x=Month y=FSPCOM;
rowaxis display=none
  refticks=(values) /* move the values to the right side,
    to prevent their visually clashing with the row labels */
  values=(240 to 390 by 50) offsetmin=0 offsetmax=0
  grid minorgrid minorcount=4 ;
colaxis grid display=(nolabel noline) /* valueattrs=(size=9pt) */
  offsetmin=0 offsetmax=0
  values=(1 to 12 by 1); /* mandatory when using the format below */
format Month NumberToMonthAbbrev.;
run;
```

The assembled code for Listing 9-5 also requires a prior run of Listing 9-0 to create input data.

Listing 9-5.   *Code used to create Figure 9-5 (changes to code for Figure 9-4)*

```
ods graphics on / reset=all scale=off width=5.7in
  imagename="Fig9-5_OneColumnPanel_MonthlyData_Customized";

panelby Year / layout=panel columns=1
  spacing=5 /* separate cell bottom and header of next cell */
  /* rowheaderpos=left not relevant for LAYOUT=PANEL */
  onepanel novarname noheaderborder;
```

Not demonstrated here, but just as a panel with one column is the equivalent of LAYOUT=ROWLATTICE, so, too, a panel with one row is the equivalent of a LAYOUT=COLUMNLATTICE. The only difference between a panel of one column and a row lattice is the location of the cell label.

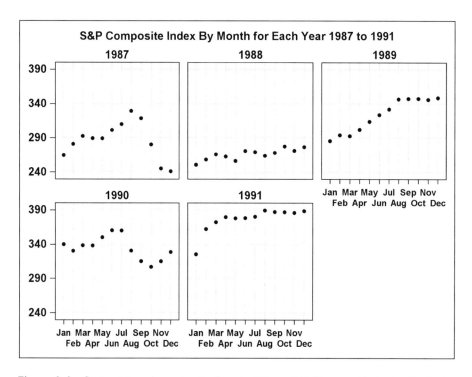

Figure 9-6. Customizing when using the layout of Figure 9-2. The no-added-value line in that figure has been omitted

The plot line in Figure 9-2 which has no markers is a liability. In that figure, when the slope change at a month is either too small or absent, it is impossible to know where the point is for that month and therefore its Y value.

The preceding result could have been rendered by using the SCATTER statement instead of the SERIES statement. The SCATTER statement by default provides no line. The SERIES statement by default provides no markers. To create Figure 9-6 requires three bits of extra work: hiding the line with LINEATTRS=(COLOR=WHITE), turning on markers with the option MARKERS, and then optionally customizing the markers with the MARKERSATTRS option.

Listing 9-6. *Code used to create Figure 9-6 (highlighting is for differences from the code used for Figure 9-2)*

```
%include "C:\SharedCode\CreateMonthNumberToThreeCharsFormat.sas";

/* requires a prior run of Listing 9-0 to create input data: */

ods listing style=GraphFontArial10ptBold gpath="C:\temp" dpi=300;
ods graphics on / reset=all scale=off width=5.7in
   imagename=
   "Fig9-6_Panel_MonthlyData_Customized_ButDefaultAxisOffsets";
title1 justify=center
   'S&P Composite Index By Month for Each Year 1987 to 1991';
proc sgpanel data=sasuser.SandPbyMonth1987to1991;
panelby Year /
   spacing=10 onepanel skipemptycells novarname noheaderborder;
series x=Month y=FSPCOM /
   lineattrs=(color=white) /* Hide the useless line. This leaves the
   visual emphasis on plot points, which are where the data is. */
   markers /* for the SERIES statement, markers are not automatic */
   markerattrs=(symbol=CircleFilled size=6px color=black);
rowaxis values=(240 to 390 by 50)
   /* offsetmin=0 offsetmax=0 Accept default offsets.
      Markers would be clipped if at an edge of the image. */
   grid minorgrid minorcount=4 display=(nolabel noline);
colaxis grid display=(nolabel noline) valueattrs=(size=8pt)
   /* offsetmin=0 offsetmax=0 Accept default offsets.
      Markers would be clipped if at an edge of the image. */
   fitpolicy=stagger
   values=(1 to 12 by 1); /* mandatory when using the format below */
format Month NumberToMonthAbbrev.;
run;
```

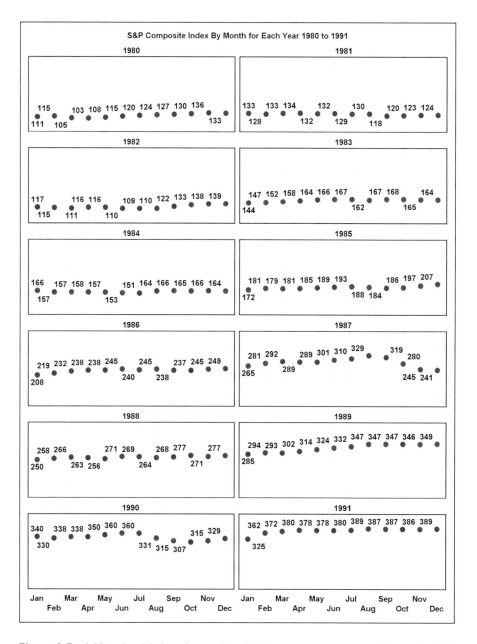

Figure 9-7. Adding data labels and expanding the date range, suppressing values and grid for the RowAxis, and letting software choose the image height (7.6 inches with X:Y aspect ratio 3:4)

Reducing the column count to two provides more horizontal space available for data labels. Increased image height provides more vertical space available for data labels.

Red dots are used for the markers to make them stand out from the black mass of data labels.

Listing 9-7. *Code used to create Figure 9-7*

```
%include "C:\SharedCode\CreateMonthNumberToThreeCharsFormat.sas";

/* requires a prior run of Listing 9-0 to create input data: */

ods listing style=GraphFontArial7ptBold gpath="C:\temp" dpi=300;
ods graphics on / reset=all scale=off width=5.7in
    /* accepting the software decision
       to set height to 7.6 inches (3 to 4 aspect ratio) */
    imagename="Fig9-7_TwoColumnPanelWithDataLabels_TwelveYearsMonthly
Data_Customized";
title1 justify=center
    'S&P Composite Index By Month for Each Year 1980 to 1991';
proc sgpanel data=sasuser.SandPbyMonth1980to1991;
panelby Year /
    columns=2 /* provide more width for data labels */
    onepanel skipemptycells novarname noheaderborder spacing=5;
series x=Month y=FSPCOM / lineattrs=(color=white)
    markers markerattrs=(symbol=CircleFilled
    size=11px color=red) /* more conspicuous markers amid
                            all of the black for data labels */
    datalabel;
rowaxis display=none offsetmin=0.17 offsetmax=0.17;
colaxis display=(noline noticks nolabel) grid
    fitpolicy=stagger
    values=(1 to 12 by 1); /* mandatory when using the format below */
format Month NumberToMonthAbbrev.;
format FSPCOM 3.; /* for data labels, otherwise .NN is retained */
run;
```

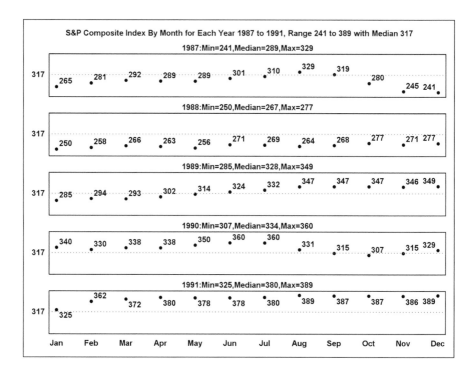

Figure 9-8. One-column panel with statistics (year specific) in cell headers and for all of the data in the title. Providing a reference line at the five-year median

Letting the software impose a 3:4 aspect ratio for width to height would produce more Y variation in the plot lines over the range of X.

Listing 9-8. *Code used to create Figure 9-8*

```
%include "C:\SharedCode\CreateMonthNumberToThreeCharsFormat.sas";
```

/* requires a prior run of Listing 9-0 to create input data: */

```
proc summary data=sasuser.SandPbyMonth1987to1991;
class Year;
var FSPCOM;
output out=work.MinMaxByYear min=MinSandP median=MedianSandP max=MaxSandP;
run;

data _null_;
set work.MinMaxByYear;
where _type_ EQ 0; /* stats for entire five-year period */
call symput('MinY',MinSandP);
call symput('MedianY',MedianSandP);
call symput('MaxY',MaxSandP);
```

```
call symput('MinYdisplay',compress(put(MinSandP,4.)));
call symput('MedianYdisplay',compress(round(MedianSandP,1),4.));
call symput('MaxYdisplay',compress(put(MaxSandP,4.)));
run;

data work.ToFormat;
keep fmtname type start label;
retain fmtname ' YearMinMedianMax' type 'N';
length start 3 label $ 64;
set work.MinMaxByYear;
where _type_ EQ 1; /* stats by year */
start = Year;
label = compress(put(Year,4.) || ': ' ||
        'Min=' || put(MinSandP,3.) ||
        ',Median=' || put(round(MedianSandP,1),3.) ||
        ',Max=' || put(MaxSandP,3.));
run;
proc format library=work cntlin=work.ToFormat;
run;

ods listing style=GraphFontArial7ptBold gpath="C:\temp" dpi=300;
ods graphics on / reset=all scale=off width=5.7in
   height=4.28in /* Forcing height to be usual default of 0.75 times width,
when no height is specified. Prevent the software from picking the height,
which here would be 7.6 inches. */
   imagename="Fig9-8_PanelWithMinMedianMaxInTitleAndCellHeaders";
title1 justify=center
   'S&P Composite Index By Month for Each Year 1987 to 1991, '
   "Range &MinYdisplay to &MaxYdisplay with Median &MedianYDisplay";
/* Double-quoted part of title to resolve macro variables,
   but single-quoted first part to prevent attempt to resolve &P */
proc sgpanel data=sasuser.SandPbyMonth1987to1991 noautolegend;
panelby Year / columns=1 /* A rectangular panel with only one PANELBY variable
serves no special purpose,
but using a single column for it eases looking for seasonality. */
   onepanel spacing=5 novarname noheaderborder;
series x=Month y=FSPCOM / datalabel lineattrs=(color=white)
   markers markerattrs=(symbol=CircleFilled size=6px color=black);
refline &MedianY / axis=y lineattrs=(pattern=Dot);
rowaxis display=(noline noticks nolabel)
   values = (&MinY &MedianY &MaxY)
   valuesdisplay = (" "  "&MedianYdisplay"  " ")
   offsetmin=0.1 offsetmax=0.1;
   /* with software's choice of offsetmax instead,
      one data label appears to be touching a cell border */
colaxis display=(noline noticks nolabel) values=(1 to 12 by 1);
format FSPCOM 3. Year YearMinMedianMax. Month NumberToMonthAbbrev.;
run;
```

Sparse Line Tables and Sparse Line Panels

It is possible to add colored highlights to the minimum and maximum Y values in a panel. Each example in Figure 9-9 does more, and less, than a typical panel, as a Sparse Line Table.

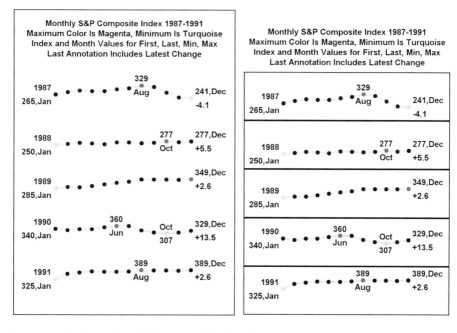

Figure 9-9. Sparse Line Tables using PROC SGPANEL LAYOUT=ROWLATTICE for five years of monthly data. At the left, cell borders are absent, but an image border is present. At the right, the reverse

The S&P Index value data label wanders between top and bottom along the plot line. The first data label must be at the bottom in order to display the Year value at the top, which is an appropriate place for the plot line label. The last data label must be at the top so that the lesser bit of information, the change since the second last plot point, can be at the bottom. With this inherent inconsistency already in effect, being consistent with data label location for intermediate minimum and maximum would have no value. Instead, the index value which is more important than the month value is symbolically at the top for the maximum and at the bottom for the minimum. By splitting the index value from the month value, the lesser width requirement to label the point means that there is less likelihood of data label collisions. When an intermediate maximum or minimum is at the point next to either the starting point or ending point, a wider one-line data label for index value and month value might collide with a data label for the adjacent start point or end point.

Listing 9-9. *Code used to create Figure 9-9*

```
%include "C:\SharedCode\CreateMonthNumberToThreeCharsFormat.sas";
%include "C:\SharedCode\PrepareInputForSparseLines.sas";
%include "C:\SharedCode\DisplaySparseData.sas";
options mprint;

/* requires a prior run of Listing 9-0 to create input data: */

%PrepareInputForSparseLines(
Data=sasuser.SandPbyMonth1987to1991,
out=work.ForSparseLines,
ClassVar=Year,
ClassVarFormat=4.,
Yvar=FSPCOM,
YvarFormat=3.,
Xvar=Month,
XvarFormat=NumberToMonthAbbrev.,
LastChangePosCount=5);


/* &MinYdisplay and &MaxYdisplay created above could be used
   in a title line to report the five-year range */

ods listing style=GraphFontArial7ptBold gpath="C:\temp" dpi=300;

ods graphics on / reset=all scale=off
   width=2.8in /* making it wider would reduce curves' variation */
   noborder /* eliminate border next to table border */
   imagename=
   "Fig9-9Right_SparseLines_5YrsMonthly_CellBordersNoImageBorder";
title1 justify=center 'Monthly S&P Composite Index 1987-1991';
/* use single quotes above to prevent software's attempt to resolve
   what it would otherwise think is a macro variable reference &P */
title2 justify=center
   "Maximum Color Is Magenta, Minimum Is Turquoise";
title3 justify=center
   "Index and Month Values for First, Last, Min, Max";
title4 justify=center "Last Annotation Includes Latest Change";
proc sgpanel data=work.ForSparseLines
   noautolegend; /* prevent a legend caused by multiple plots: */
   from a SERIES statement and ten SCATTER statements */
panelby Year / layout=RowLattice onepanel novarname
   noheader /* instead, use the value of the Class Var
   (here Year), as the top data label, at each first plot point */
   spacing=0; /* compact the table entries */
%DisplaySparseData(xVar=Month,yVar=FSPCOM);
   /* The above macro contains a SERIES statement to draw the line
      and ten SCATTER statements to annotate and color code it. */
rowaxis display=none values=(&MinY &MaxY);
colaxis display=none offsetmin=0.19 offsetmax=0.17;
```

```
/* If default offsets are not overridden as done here,
   data labels at ends of the colaxis cause the software
   to excessively offset the axis ends to prevent its
   estimated collisions of data labels with cell boundaries. */
/* The offsets must be done iteratively, until you find
   the values at the best distance from the cell boundaries.
   For this case, experimentation found 0.19 and 0.17 offsets. */
run;

ods graphics on / border
  reset=index /* leave everything else the same */
  imagename=
  "Fig9-9Left_SparseLines_5YrsMonthly_ImageBorderNoCellBorders";
/* inherit the titles already in effect */
proc sgpanel data=work.ForSparseLines noautolegend;
panelby Year / layout=RowLattice
  noborder /* no borders around each cell in the panel */
  onepanel novarname noheader spacing=0;
%DisplaySparseData(xVar=Month,yVar=FSPCOM);
rowaxis display=none values=(&MinY &MaxY);
colaxis display=none offsetmin=0.16 offsetmax=0.14;
run;
```

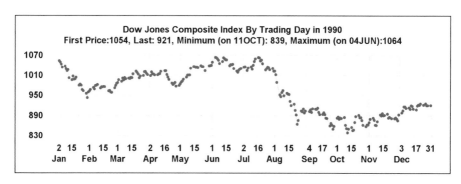

Figure 9-10. Not a composite (a redisplay of Figure 8-31). A complete all-in-one presentation of the data that is presented with panels and lattices in later figures

With 252 trading days in the year (the New York Stock Exchange is closed on weekends and holidays), it is impossible to provide data labels. In Chapter 8, there are three examples of various ways to present data with variations of a 12-month, 12-line overlap plot. None of them involve data labels—12 clashing lines make data labels impossible. Two examples use custom legends, where the entries include the minimum and maximum values for each month, not just the name of the month with the color-coding artifact—which is the functional limit of a typical legend. The plot for one of those custom legend examples makes each line's minimum and maximum identifiable with a color-coded marker.

PROC SGPANEL makes it possible to break up the single line of Figure 9-10 and the overlay plots of Chapter 8 into a panel or lattice of 12 individual single-month plots. Figure 9-11 is a panel of 12 cells, with cell headers that include the values for monthly minimum and maximum and with plots that have those critical points color-coded.

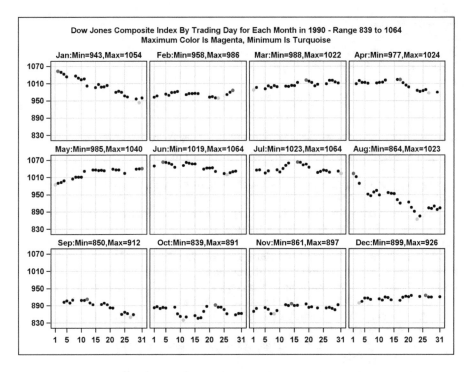

Figure 9-11. A Sparse Line Panel. Decomposing the overlay in Figure 8-33 to create a composite that visually locates minima and maxima and lists them

Listing 9-11. *Code used to create Figure 9-11*

```
%include "C:\SharedCode\CreateMonthNumberToThreeCharsFormat.sas";
%include "C:\SharedCode\PrepInputWithMinMaxIdentified.sas";
options mprint;

/* requires a prior run of Listing 9-0 to create input data: */

%PrepInputWithMinMaxIdentified(
Data=sasuser.DowJonesByDayIn1990,
OutForPlot=work.ToPlot,
OutForMinMaxByClass=work.ForMonthMinMax,
ClassVar=Month,
Yvar=DailyDJ,
YvarFormat=4.,
Xvar=Day);
```

```
/* prepare the MonthMinMax format to be used for cell headers
   that identify the minimum and maximum Y values */

data work.ToFormat;
keep fmtname type start label;
retain fmtname 'MonthMinMax' type 'N';
length start 3 label $ 64;
set work.ForMonthMinMax;
start = Month;
label = compress(put(Month,NumberToMonthAbbrev.) || ': Min=' ||
  put(MinY,4.) || ',Max=' || put(MaxY,4.));
run;
proc format library=work cntlin=work.ToFormat;
run;

ods listing style=GraphFontArial7ptBold gpath="C:\temp" dpi=300;
ods graphics on / reset=all scale=off width=5.7in
  imagename=
  "Fig9-11_PanelWithMinMaxInCellHeadersAndColorCodedInPlots";
title1 justify=center
  'Dow Jones Composite Index By Trading Day for Each Month in 1990'
  " - Range &MinYdisplay to &MaxYdisplay";
title2 justify=center
  "Maximum Color Is Magenta, Minimum Is Turquoise";
proc sgpanel data=work.ToPlot noautolegend;
panelby Month / rows=3 columns=4 spacing=3 novarname noheaderborder;
series x=Day y=DailyDJ / lineattrs=(color=white)
  markers markerattrs=(symbol=CircleFilled size=4px color=black);
scatter x=Day y=MinY /
  markerattrs=(symbol=CircleFilled size=5px color=CX00FFFF);
scatter x=Day y=MaxY /
  markerattrs=(symbol=CircleFilled size=5px color=CXFF00FF);
rowaxis display=(noline nolabel) grid values=(830 to 1070 by 60);
colaxis display=(noline nolabel) grid values=(1 5 10 15 20 25 31);
format DailyDJ 4. Month MonthMinMax.;
run;
```

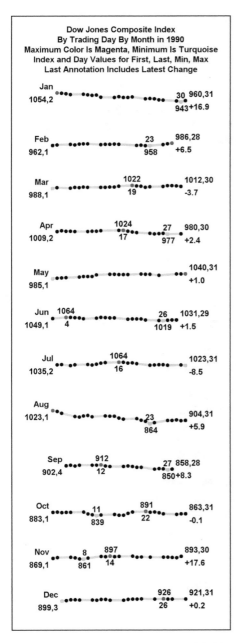

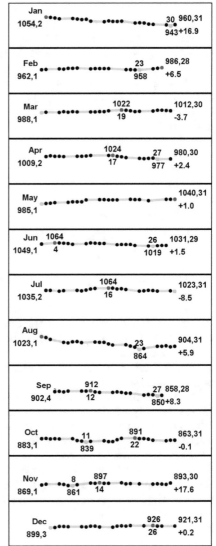

Figure 9-12. Sparse Line Tables using PROC SGPANEL LAYOUT=ROWLATTICE for 12 months of daily data. At the left, cell borders are absent, but an image border is present. At the right, the reverse

Listing 9-12. *Code used to create Figure 9-12*

```
%include "C:\SharedCode\CreateMonthNumberToThreeCharsFormat.sas";
%include "C:\SharedCode\PrepareInputForSparseLines.sas";
%include "C:\SharedCode\DisplaySparseData.sas";
options mprint;
/* requires a prior run of Listing 9-0 to create input data: */
/* NOTE: Except for the LABELMAX option used here, all comments about the code
for Listing 9-9 also apply to this code. */

%PrepareInputForSparseLines(
Data=sasuser.DowJonesByDayIn1990,
Out=work.ForSparseLines,
ClassVar=Month,
ClassVarFormat=NumberToMonthAbbrev.,
Yvar=DailyDJ,
YvarFormat=4.,
Xvar=Day,
XvarFormat=2.,
LastChangePosCount=5);

ods listing style=GraphFontArial7ptBold gpath="C:\temp" dpi=300;

ods graphics on / reset=all scale=off width=2.8in height=7.6in
  labelmax=300 /* Suggested in SAS log. It suppresses WARNINGs. */
  noborder imagename=
"Fig9-12Right_SparseLines_12MonthsDaily_CellBordersNoImageBorder";
title1 justify=center "Dow Jones Composite Index";
title2 justify=center "By Trading Day By Month in 1990";
title3 justify=center
  "Maximum Color Is Magenta, Minimum Is Turquoise";
title4 justify=center
  "Index and Day Values for First, Last, Min, Max";
title5 justify=center "Last Annotation Includes Latest Change";
proc sgpanel data=work.ForSparseLines noautolegend;
panelby Month / layout=RowLattice
  onepanel novarname noheader spacing=0;
%DisplaySparseData(xVar=Day,yVar=DailyDJ);
rowaxis display=none values=(&MinY &MaxY);
colaxis display=none offsetmin=0.16 offsetmax=0.18
  values=(1 to 31 by 1);
run;

ods graphics on / border reset=index imagename=
  "Fig9-12Left_SparseLines_12MonthsDaily_ImageBorderNoCellBorders";
proc sgpanel data=work.ForSparseLines noautolegend;
panelby Month / layout=RowLattice
  noborder onepanel novarname noheader spacing=0;
```

```
%DisplaySparseData(xVar=Day,yVar=DailyDJ);
rowaxis display=none values=(&MinY &MaxY);
colaxis display=none offsetmin=0.16 offsetmax=0.18
  values=(1 to 31 by 1);
run;
```

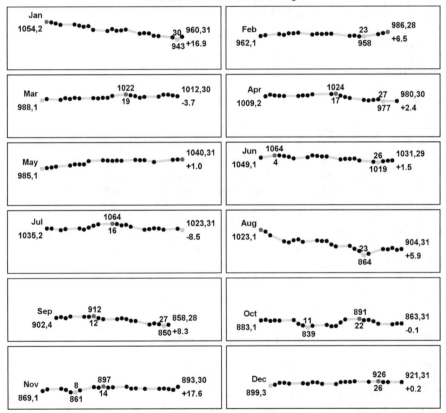

Figure 9-13. Converting the right side of Figure 9-12 to a two-column Sparse Line Panel. Less convenient if looking for "seasonality," but vertically more compact. More vertical space within cells produces plot lines with more variation (less "flat")

Listing 9-13. *Code used to create Figure 9-13*

```
%include "C:\SharedCode\CreateMonthNumberToThreeCharsFormat.sas";
%include "C:\SharedCode\PrepareInputForSparseLines.sas";
%include "C:\SharedCode\DisplaySparseData.sas";
/* requires a prior run of Listing 9-0 to create input data: */

options mprint;
%PrepareInputForSparseLines(
Data=sasuser.DowJonesByDayIn1990,
Out=work.ForSparseLines,
ClassVar=Month,
ClassVarFormat=NumberToMonthAbbrev.,
Yvar=DailyDJ,
YvarFormat=4.,
Xvar=Day,
XvarFormat=2.,
LastChangePosCount=5);

ods listing style=GraphFontArial7ptBold gpath="C:\temp" dpi=300;
ods graphics on / reset=all scale=off width=5.7in height=5.7in
  labelmax=300 /* Suggested in SAS log. It suppresses WARNINGs. */
  noborder imagename=
  "Fig9-13_SparseLines_Panel6Rows2Columns_1YearOfDaysMonthly";
title1 justify=center
  "Dow Jones Composite Index By Trading Day By Month in 1990";
title2 justify=center
  "Maximum Color Is Magenta, Minimum Is Turquoise";
title3 justify=center
  "Index and Day Values for First, Last, Min, Max";
title4 justify=center "Last Annotation Includes Latest Change";
proc sgpanel data=work.ForSparseLines noautolegend;
panelby Month / columns=2
  onepanel novarname noheader spacing=5;
%DisplaySparseData(xVar=Day,yVar=DailyDJ);
rowaxis display=none values=(&MinY &MaxY);
colaxis display=none offsetmin=0.16 offsetmax=0.18
  values=(1 to 31 by 1);
run;
```

Panels for a Year of Days by Week

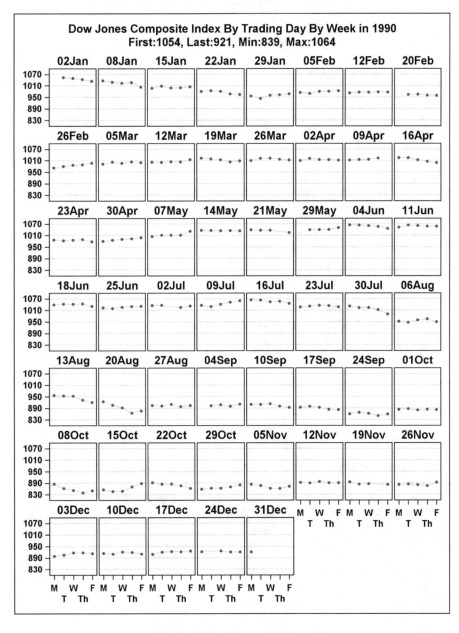

Figure 9-14. Presenting the year of trading days by week

Listing 9-14. *Code used to create Figure 9-14*

```
/* requires a prior run of Listing 9-0 to create input data */

data work.DowJonesByWeekByDayIn1990;
set sasuser.DowJonesByDayIn1990;
Week = WEEK(Date);
DayOfWeek = WEEKDAY(Date);
run;

proc sort data=work.DowJonesByWeekByDayIn1990;
by Week DayOfWeek;
run;

data sasuser.DowJonesByWeekByDay; /* data will persist */
retain WeekDate FirstDJ MaxDJ 0 MinDJ 999999999;
set work.DowJonesByWeekByDayIn1990 end=LastOne;
by Week;
if First.Week then WeekDate = Date;
if _N_ EQ 1 then FirstDJ = DailyDJ;
MaxDJ = max(DailyDJ,MaxDJ);
MinDJ = min(DailyDJ,MinDJ);
if LastOne then do;
  call symput('FirstDJ',trim(left(put(FirstDJ,4.))));
  call symput('LastDJ',trim(left(put(DailyDJ,4.))));
  call symput('MinDJ',trim(left(put(MinDJ,4.))));
  call symput('MaxDJ',trim(left(put(MaxDJ,4.))));
end;
run;

ods listing style=GraphFontArial10ptBold gpath="C:\temp" dpi=300;
ods graphics on / reset=all scale=off width=5.7in height=7.6in
  imagename="Fig9-14_Panel_7Rows8Columns_OneYearOfDaysWeekly";
title1 justify=center
  "Dow Jones Composite Index By Trading Day By Week in 1990";
title2 justify=center
  "First:&FirstDJ, Last:&LastDJ, Min:&MinDJ, Max:&MaxDJ";
proc sgpanel data=sasuser.DowJonesByWeekByDay;
panelby WeekDate / rows=7 columns=8
  spacing=2 novarname noheaderborder skipemptycells;
series y=DailyDJ x=DayOfWeek / lineattrs=(color=red)
  markers markerattrs=(symbol=CircleFilled size=5px color=blue)
  lineattrs=(color=LightGray);
rowaxis display=(nolabel noline) grid
  values=(830 to 1070 by 60) valueattrs=(size=8pt)
  fitpolicy=none; /* prevent thinning of axis values */
colaxis display=(nolabel noline) valueattrs=(size=8pt)
```

```
values=(2 to 6 by 1) valuesdisplay=('M' 'T' 'W' 'Th' 'F')
   fitpolicy=stagger; /* prevent thinning of axis values */
format DailyDJ 4. WeekDate Date5.;
run;
```

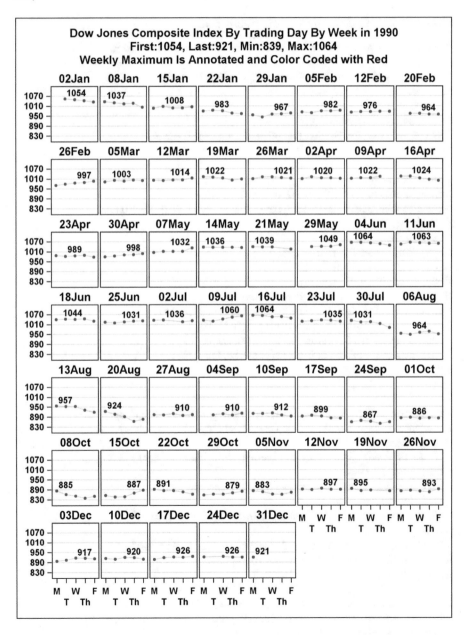

Figure 9-15. The year of trading days by week with each weekly maximum identified and located

The input for this graph is data that was preprocessed for Figure 9-14. Adding color coding and data labels in this way is a model that could be adapted elsewhere.

Listing 9-15. *Code used to create Figure 9-15*

```
/* requires a prior run of Listing 9-0 to create input data */

proc summary data=sasuser.DowJonesByWeekByDay nway;
class Week;
var DailyDJ;
output out=work.WeeklyMax(drop=_type_ _freq_)
  maxid(DailyDJ(DayOfWeek))=DayOfWeek max=WeeklyMaxDJ;
run;

data work.ToPlot;
retain WeekDate FirstDJ MaxDJ 0 MinDJ 999999999;
merge sasuser.DowJonesByWeekByDay(in=BaseInfo) work.WeeklyMax;
by Week DayOfWeek;
if BaseInfo;
if _N_ EQ 1 then FirstDJ = DailyDJ;
MaxDJ = max(DailyDJ,MaxDJ);
MinDJ = min(DailyDJ,MinDJ);
if Last.Week and Last.DayOfWeek then do;
  call symput('FirstDJ',trim(left(put(FirstDJ,4.))));
  call symput('LastDJ',trim(left(put(DailyDJ,4.))));
  call symput('MinDJ',trim(left(put(MinDJ,4.))));
  call symput('MaxDJ',trim(left(put(MaxDJ,4.))));
end;
run;

ods listing style=GraphFontArial10ptBold gpath="C:\temp" dpi=300;
ods graphics on / reset=all scale=off width=5.7in height=7.6in
  imagename=
  "Fig9-15_Panel_7Rows8Columns_OneYearOfDaysWeekly_WeeklyMaxShown";
title1 justify=center
  "Dow Jones Composite Index By Trading Day By Week in 1990";
title2 justify=center
  "First:&FirstDJ, Last:&LastDJ, Min:&MinDJ, Max:&MaxDJ";
title3 justify=center
  "Weekly Maximum Is Annotated and Color Coded with Red";
proc sgpanel data=work.ToPlot noautolegend;
panelby WeekDate / rows=7 columns=8
  spacing=2 novarname noheaderborder skipemptycells;
series y=DailyDJ x=DayOfWeek / lineattrs=(color=red)
  markers markerattrs=(symbol=CircleFilled size=5px color=blue)
  lineattrs=(color=LightGray);
scatter y=WeeklyMaxDJ x=DayOfWeek /
```

```
    markerattrs=(symbol=CircleFilled size=5px color=red)
    datalabel=WeeklyMaxDJ datalabelattrs=(size=8pt);
rowaxis display=(nolabel noline) grid
    offsetmax=0.17
    values=(830 to 1070 by 60) valueattrs=(size=8pt)
    fitpolicy=none; /* prevent thinning of axis values */
colaxis display=(nolabel noline) valueattrs=(size=8pt)
    values=(2 to 6 by 1) valuesdisplay=('M' 'T' 'W' 'Th' 'F')
    fitpolicy=stagger; /* prevent thinning of axis values */
format DailyDJ WeeklyMaxDJ 4. WeekDate Date5.;
run;
```

This is the end of an exploration of how PROC SGPANEL can be used to deliver as much precise information and visual help for time series as possible. Depending on the size of the target area and the size of the components, one can use ODS LAYOUT to assemble multiple views of the data in a composite of composites and/or simple "unpanelled" graphs, as will be shown in Chapter 13. The most effective way to provide precise numbers for very dense time series is with a web graph, using ODS HTML5, which is the subject of Chapter 14. The only disadvantage is that the precise numbers are temporary, lasting only as long as you keep the mouse over each point, and, of course, you can only reveal one precise number at a time. Of course, the cumbersome option of a static table can always deliver everything permanently. A table and a graph can be inter-linked with ODS HTML5. When a table is small enough, it can be packaged together with a graph on the same web page.

Composites of Categorical Data

This section includes horizontal and vertical bar charts and their alternatives with less mass for the visual elements, namely, dot plots and needle plots.

In this section, the OFFSETMIN and OFFSETMAX are used often. In some cases, you (and perhaps I) might like the defaults. In most cases, I think not.

In several cases, the default offsets cause bars, needles, or dot plot lines to be unnecessary squashed together in the space available. It must be emphasized that misleading bar lengths occur by default only when data labels are used.

In four cases described in an earlier section of this chapter, the default for OFFSETMAX produces a misleading result. All of the cases involve bar charts with data labels. Figure 9-18 shows the problem for one case, and Figure 9-19 shows its correction and how to do it. Figures 9-20, 9-22, and 9-33 are examples where the problem is prevented. (As noted there, two more vulnerable cases exist, for which no examples are provided, but in each case, the configuration of the composite is identical to one already being shown, but created using LAYOUT=PANEL with ROWS=1 or COLUMNS=1, instead of LAYOUT=COLUMNLATTICE or LAYOUT=ROWLATTICE.)

In many cases, the result of default offsets is not misleading, but poor use of the space available. Each example in this section strives to use offsets that present the best results. In some cases, the default offsets are satisfactory. The outcome from default offsets varies based on whether the graphs are bar charts, dot plots, or needle plots. Some problems stem from the presence of data labels—which are an essential.

If you have a situation where you want to override the default offsets, it is always an iterative task. An efficient procedure, during this tuning/development phase, is to use OFFSETMIN=&OSmin OFFSETMAX=&OSmax on the ROWAXIS or COLAXIS statement with %LET statements at the top of your code to assign the values to the macro variables OSmin and OSmax. Of course, if you prefer, making the changes in place with "hard coding" in the ROWAXIS or COLAXIS statement will always work. Here, you will see finished products of my exercises with this process. The objective is always to make maximum use of the space available, without any collisions of graph elements (markers, bars, dots, or needles) with the cell boundaries and without collisions of data labels with the cell boundaries.

Composites of Horizontal Bar Charts

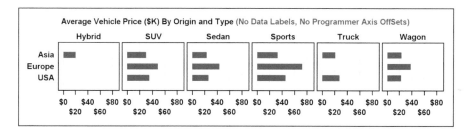

Figure 9-16. LAYOUT=COLUMNLATTICE without data labels and without programmer axis offsets

Though it is not obviously the case for Figure 9-16, a common suboptimal outcome from the default axis offsets is squashing bars, dot plot lines, or needle plot lines unnecessarily close together. This is aesthetically detrimental and provides absolutely no practical benefit. When there is space in the image, *use* it, with the best design possible.

Figure 9-16 wastes horizontal space with needless minimum ColAxis offsets as defaults. However, it may be that the purpose of the offsets is to prevent collisions between the end and start axis values of adjacent cells. A better solution is to increase the spacing between cells. The maximum offset used does make room for the last axis value to be displayed. If you wish to assume that the viewer will infer the value from the succession of preceding values and the sameness of the intervalue distance, the maximum offset can be set to zero, and the last axis value can be suppressed, as in Figure 9-17.

Figure 9-16 is not as extreme a case of needless compression of the bars in the vertical space available as I have seen in other situations. A prospective viewer might not even notice. Figure 9-17 has the offsets adjusted to my preference.

Listing 9-16. *Code used to create Figure 9-16*

```
ods listing style=GraphFontArial7ptBold gpath="C:\temp" dpi=300;
ods graphics on / reset=all scale=off width=5.7in height=1.5in
   imagename="Fig9-16_ColumnLatticeHBars_NoDataLabels_NoUserOffSets";
title1 justify=center
   "Average Vehicle Price ($K) By Origin and Type"
  color=blue " (No Data Labels, No Programmer Axis OffSets)";
proc sgpanel data=sashelp.cars;
panelby Type / layout=columnlattice
   onepanel novarname noheaderborder spacing=3;
hbar Origin / response=MSRP stat=mean displaybaseline=off
   nooutline barwidth=0.5 fillattrs=(color=blue);
rowaxis display=(noticks nolabel noline) fitpolicy=none;
colaxis display=(nolabel noline) grid minorgrid minorcount=1
   values=(0 to 80000 by 20000) fitpolicy=stagger
   valuesdisplay=('$0' '$20' '$40' '$60' '$80');
run;
```

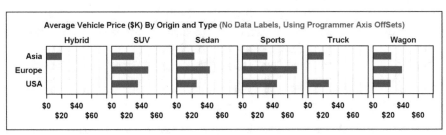

Figure 9-17. The column lattice of Figure 9-16 with minimum and maximum offsets adjusted for RowAxis and ColAxis

The axis offsets needed tuning. Rather than hardcode them in the program itself, it's more convenient to pass them to it as macro variables that are easily adjusted until a satisfactory outcome is achieved.

Listing 9-17. *Code used to create Figure 9-17*

```
%let ColAxisOffSets = 0;
%let RowAxisOffSets = 0.21;

ods listing style=GraphFontArial7ptBold gpath="C:\temp" dpi=300;
ods graphics on / reset=all scale=off width=5.7in height=1.5in
  imagename=
  "Fig9-17_ColumnLatticeHBars_NoDataLabels_UserAxisOffSets";
title1 justify=center
  "Average Vehicle Price ($K) By Origin and Type"
  color=blue " (No Data Labels, Using Programmer Axis OffSets)";
proc sgpanel data=sashelp.cars;
panelby Type / layout=columnlattice
  onepanel novarname noheaderborder spacing=5;
hbar Origin / response=MSRP stat=mean displaybaseline=off
  nooutline barwidth=0.5 fillattrs=(color=blue);
rowaxis display=(noticks nolabel noline) fitpolicy=none
  OffSetMin=&RowAxisOffSets OffSetMax=&RowAxisOffSets;
colaxis display=(nolabel noline) grid minorgrid minorcount=1
  OffSetMin=&ColAxisOffSets OffSetMax=&ColAxisOffSets
  values=(0 to 80000 by 20000) fitpolicy=stagger
  valuesdisplay=('$0' '$20' '$40' '$60' ' '); /* Note the blank */
run;
```

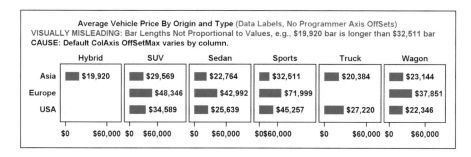

Figure 9-18. If data labels are present, bar lengths can be misleading. Despite contradictory comparative bar lengths, Asia Hybrid price is less than Asia Sports

This demonstration example makes it clear that there is a problem. The key to exposing it is the display of tick marks and axis values, which shows there is inherently an inconsistency or disproportionality in bar lengths. In other cases, without these normally superfluous graphic features that are unnecessary when there are data labels, the lurking problem could go overlooked. I only discovered it in a first draft of this output *without* tick marks and axis values by noticing the situation that is described in the red subtitle. In a different example, the discrepancy, if not prevented, is much smaller, less pervasive, and easily overlooked. If I had not done a check by running the code with tick marks and values turned on, I would not have noticed the problem.

A graph with precise numbers (i.e., data labels) always delivers accurate information. However, when visual elements are present, they inevitably cause the viewer to focus on one of more parts based on visual comparison. Let me find the maximum (or minimum) quickly. Ah, the longest (shortest) bar has the number that I care about. I'm not going to bother to compare it with the other numbers. That can be a viewer's thought process and graph use procedure. Similarly, a graph viewer might be interested only in comparing the bars for two categories. Whichever is of interest, the longer or the shorter, that alone might drive the conclusion regardless of the precise number. Misleading bar lengths are defects.

The software chooses a different maximum offset in each column, evidently to make maximum use of the space available, with adverse consequences. This problem is solved in Figure 9-19.

Listing 9-18. *Code used to create Figure 9-18*

```
ods listing style=GraphFontArial7ptBold gpath="C:\temp" dpi=300;
ods graphics on / reset=all scale=off width=5.7in height=1.75in
   imagename=
   "Fig9-18_ColumnLatticeHBars_DataLabels_BadDefaultAxisOffSets";
title1 justify=center "Average Vehicle Price By Origin and Type"
   color=blue " (Data Labels, No Programmer Axis OffSets)";
title2 justify=left color=red "VISUALLY MISLEADING:"
   " Bar Lengths Not Proportional to Values,"
   " e.g., $19,920 bar is longer than $32,511 bar";
title3 justify=left
   "CAUSE: Default ColAxis OffSetMax varies by column.";
proc sgpanel data=sashelp.cars;
panelby Type / layout=columnlattice
   onepanel novarname noheaderborder spacing=3;
hbar Origin / response=MSRP stat=mean
   datalabel datalabelfitpolicy=none
   nooutline barwidth=0.5 fillattrs=(color=blue)
   displaybaseline=off datalabel;
rowaxis display=(noticks nolabel noline) fitpolicy=none
   offsetmin=0.21 offsetmax=0.21;
colaxis display=(nolabel noline) grid; /* accepting the offsetmin
                                           and offsetmax defaults */
run;
```

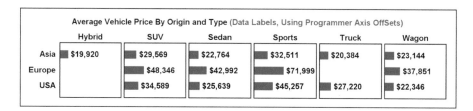

Figure 9-19. Figure 9-18 corrected. COLAXIS OFFSETMAX prevents misleading comparative bar lengths between different cells. RowAxis offsets spread the bars optimally in the vertical space

Listing 9-19. *Code used to create Figure 9-19*

```
%let RowAxisOffSets = 0.21;
%let ColAxisOffSetMin = 0;
%let ColAxisOffSetMax = 0.52; /* prevent misleading bar lengths */

ods listing style=GraphFontArial7ptBold gpath="C:\temp" dpi=300;
ods graphics on / reset=all scale=off width=5.7in height=1.25in
  imagename=
  "Fig9-19_ColumnLatticeHBars_DataLabels_UserAxisOffSets";
title1 justify=center
  "Average Vehicle Price By Origin and Type"
  color=blue " (Data Labels, Using Programmer Axis OffSets)";
proc sgpanel data=sashelp.cars;
panelby Type / layout=columnlattice
  onepanel novarname noheaderborder spacing=3;
hbar Origin / response=MSRP stat=mean displaybaseline=off
  nooutline barwidth=0.5 fillattrs=(color=blue) datalabel;
rowaxis display=(noticks nolabel noline) fitpolicy=none
  offsetmin=&RowAxisOffSets offsetmax=&RowAxisOffSets;
colaxis display=(noticks nolabel noline novalues)
  offsetmin=&ColAxisOffSetMin offsetmax=&ColAxisOffSetMax;
run;
```

Composites of Vertical Bar Charts

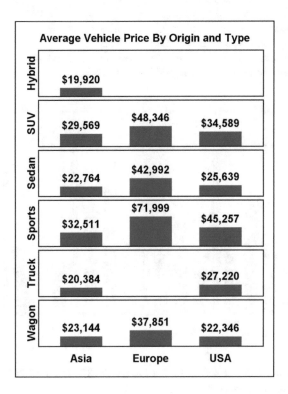

Figure 9-20. For same data as Figure 9-19, using LAYOUT=COLUMNLATTICE with ROWAXIS OFFSETMIN=0 and OFFSETMAX=0.35

▨ Note   With the ROWAXIS defaults for OFFSETMAX, the bar lengths **would be misleading**, as in Figure 9-18.

Listing 9-20. *Code used to create Figure 9-20*

```
%let RowAxisOffSetMin = 0;
%let RowAxisOffSetMax = 0.35; /* prevent misleading bar lengths */

ods listing style=GraphFontArial8ptBold gpath="C:\temp" dpi=300;
ods graphics on / reset=all scale=off width=2.8in
  imagename="Fig9-20_RowLatticeVBars_DataLabels_UserAxisOffSets";
title1 justify=center "Average Vehicle Price By Origin and Type";
proc sgpanel data=sashelp.cars;
panelby Type / layout=rowlattice
```

```
rowheaderpos=left /* text is easier to read at the left */
  onepanel novarname noheaderborder spacing=3;
vbar Origin / response=MSRP stat=mean displaybaseline=off
  nooutline barwidth=0.6 fillattrs=(color=blue) datalabel;
rowaxis display=(noticks nolabel noline novalues)
  offsetmin=&RowAxisOffSetMin offsetmax=&RowAxisOffSetMax;
colaxis display=(noticks nolabel noline noticks);
run;
```

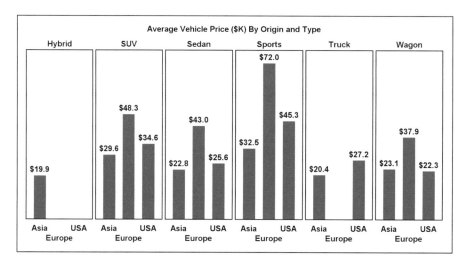

Figure 9-21. Same data as Figure 9-20, but LAYOUT=COLUMNLATTICE. Appropriate bar lengths from default RowAxis offsets

ColAxis offsets are used only to adjust spacing of bars in the cells.

In a column lattice of vertical bar charts, there is only one set of tick marks and values (displayed or suppressed) in the RowAxis that controls all of the cells. So there is no possibility of bar length discrepancies. The same is true for a row lattice of horizontal bar charts with one set of tick marks and values in the ColAxis.

Listing 9-21. *Code used to create Figure 9-21*

%let ColAxisOffSets = 0.20;

```
ods listing style=GraphFontArial7ptBold gpath="C:\temp" dpi=300;
ods graphics on / reset=all scale=off width=5.7in height=3in
  imagename=
  "Fig9-21_ColumnLatticeVBars_DataLabels_UserColAxisOffSets";
title1 justify=center
  "Average Vehicle Price ($K) By Origin and Type";
proc sgpanel data=sasuser.CarsWithMSRPinThousands;
```

```
panelby Type / layout=columnlattice
  onepanel novarname noheaderborder spacing=3;
vbar Origin / response=MSRP stat=mean displaybaseline=off
  nooutline barwidth=0.6 fillattrs=(color=blue) datalabel;
rowaxis display=none;
colaxis display=(nolabel noline noticks) fitpolicy=stagger
  offsetmin=&ColAxisOffSets offsetmax=&ColAxisOffSets;
format MSRP dollar5.1;
run;
```

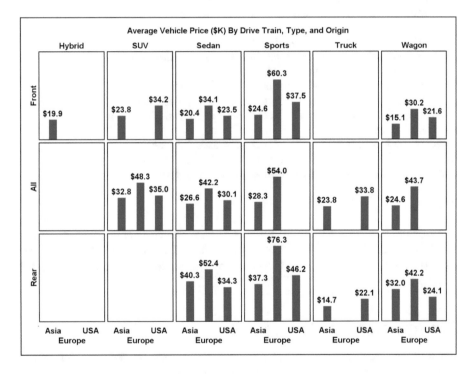

Figure 9-22. LAYOUT=LATTICE and PANELBY with two class variables. ROWAXIS OFFSETMIN=0 and OFFSETMAX=0.1

Note If accepting the ROWAXIS default OFFSETMAX, the bar lengths would be misleading, as in Figure 9-18.

ColAxis offsets are used here only to adjust spacing of bars in the cells. For the BARWIDTH and ColAxis offsets used here during development of the example, the data labels were initially displayed vertically. Adding the option DATALABELFITPOLICY=NONE to the VBAR statement solved the problem.

Listing 9-22. *Code used to create Figure 9-22*

```
%let RowAxisOffSetMin = 0;
%let RowAxisOffSetMax = 0.1; /* prevent misleading bar lengths */
%let ColAxisOffSets = 0.21;

ods listing style=GraphFontArial7ptBold gpath="C:\temp" dpi=300;
ods graphics on / reset=all scale=off width=5.7in
  imagename="Fig9-22_LatticeVBars_DataLabels_UserColAxisOffSets";
title1 justify=center
  "Average Vehicle Price ($K) By Drive Train, Type, and Origin";
proc sgpanel data=sasuser.CarsWithMSRPinThousands;
panelby Type Drivetrain / layout=lattice
  rowheaderpos=left /* text is easier to read at the left */
  onepanel novarname noheaderborder spacing=3;
vbar Origin / response=MSRP stat=mean displaybaseline=off
  nooutline barwidth=0.4 fillattrs=(color=blue) datalabel
  datalabelfitpolicy=none; /* needed for horizontal data labels */
rowaxis display=none
  offsetmin=&RowAxisOffSetMin offsetmax=&RowAxisOffSetMax;
colaxis display=(nolabel noline noticks) fitpolicy=stagger
  offsetmin=&ColAxisOffSets offsetmax=&ColAxisOffSets;
format MSRP dollar5.1;
run;
```

The default RowAxis OFFSETMIN was zero when the OFFSETMAX option was not used. When OFFSETMAX was adjusted to prevent misleading bar lengths, the OFFSETMIN was increased by the software. The offset was set back to zero using the OFFSETMIN option.

Composites of Dot Plots

Using PROC SGPANEL with dot plots and data labels incurs no problems as to the proportionality of dot location. However, the first try to create Figure 9-23 with default offsets for the ColAxis suffered severe compression of the dot locations. The dots occupied less than one-sixth of the available horizontal space. Examples in Figures 9-23 to 9-25 solve that problem and show three different ways to display the data labels: three different locations and, for one location, the dollar amount *not* in thousands. All three examples have the RowAxis offsets customized to improve the vertical spacing of the dot plot lines in the image height available.

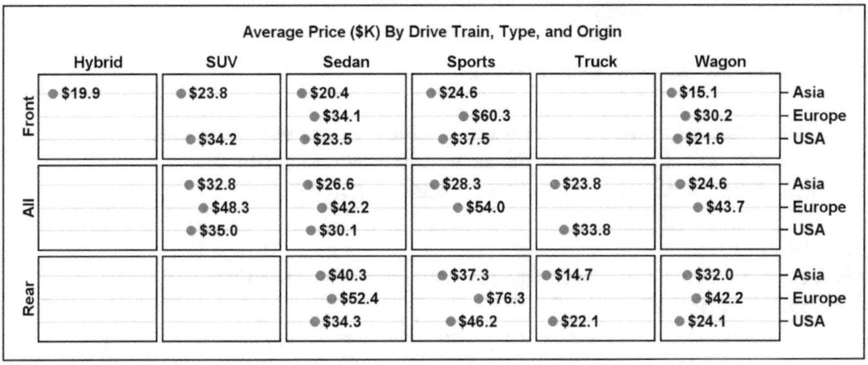

Average Price ($K) By Drive Train, Type, and Origin						
	Hybrid	SUV	Sedan	Sports	Truck	Wagon	

Front
	●$19.9	●$23.8	●$20.4	●$24.6		●$15.1	– Asia
			●$34.1	●$60.3		●$30.2	– Europe
		●$34.2	●$23.5	●$37.5		●$21.6	– USA

All
	●$32.8	●$26.6	●$28.3	●$23.8	●$24.6	– Asia
	●$48.3	●$42.2	●$54.0		●$43.7	– Europe
	●$35.0	●$30.1		●$33.8		– USA

Rear
	●$40.3	●$37.3	●$14.7	●$32.0	– Asia
	●$52.4	●$76.3		●$42.2	– Europe
	●$34.3	●$46.2	●$22.1	●$24.1	– USA

Figure 9-23. Lattice of dot plots with data labels at the right of the dots

Listing 9-23. *Code used to create Figure 9-23*

```
/* Macro source could be filed in your equivalent of C:\SharedCode
   as LatticeDotPlotWithDataLabels.sas */

%macro LatticeDotPlotWithDataLabels(
imagename=,
imageheight=,
data=,
title=,
datalabelformat=,
datalabelpos=,
rowaxisoffsetmin=,
rowaxisoffsetmax=,
colaxisoffsetmin=,
colaxisoffsetmax=);
ods graphics on / reset=all scale=off imagename="&imagename"
  width=5.7in height=&imageheight;
title1 justify=center "&title";
proc sgpanel data=&data;
panelby Type Drivetrain / layout=lattice
  rowheaderpos=left /* text is easier to read at the left */
  onepanel novarname noheaderborder spacing=3;
dot Origin / response=MSRP stat=mean
  datalabel datalabelpos=&datalabelpos
  markerattrs=(color=Green symbol=CircleFilled size=7pt);
rowaxis display=(nolabel noline noticks) fitpolicy=none
  offsetmin=&rowaxisoffsetmin offsetmax=&rowaxisoffsetmax;
rowaxis display=none fitpolicy=none
  refticks=(values) /* move the values to the right side,
    to prevent their visually clashing with the row labels */
  offsetmin=&rowaxisoffsetmin offsetmax=&rowaxisoffsetmax;
colaxis display=none
  offsetmin=&colaxisoffsetmin offsetmax=&colaxisoffsetmax;
```

```
format MSRP &datalabelformat;
run;
%mend  LatticeDotPlotWithDataLabels;

/* If the macro source code is not in-line, as above, then use:
   %include "C:\SharedCode\LatticeDotPlotWithDataLabels.sas";
   as is done in Listing 9-24 and Listing 9-25. */

options mprint;
ods listing style=GraphFontArial7ptBold gpath="C:\temp" dpi=300;
%LatticeDotPlotWithDataLabels(
imagename=Fig9-23_LatticeDotPlot_DataLabelPosEqualRight_DollarsInK,
imageheight=2.25in,
title=%str(Average Price ($K) By Drive Train, Type, and Origin),
data=sasuser.CarsWithMSRPinThousands,
datalabelformat=dollar5.1,
datalabelpos=right,
rowaxisoffsetmin=0.22,
rowaxisoffsetmax=0.22,
colaxisoffsetmin=0.08,
colaxisoffsetmax=0.40);
```

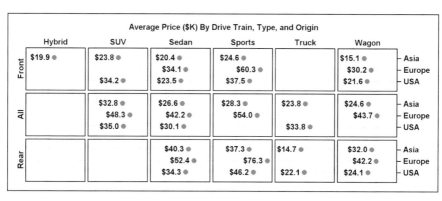

Figure 9-24. Lattice of dot plots with data labels at the left of the dots

Listing 9-24. *Code used to create Figure 9-24*

```
%include "C:\SharedCode\LatticeDotPlotWithDataLabels.sas";
options mprint;

ods listing style=GraphFontArial7ptBold gpath="C:\temp" dpi=300;
%LatticeDotPlotWithDataLabels(
imagename=Fig9-24_LatticeDotPlot_DataLabelPosEqualLeft_DollarsInK,
imageheight=2.25in,
title=%str(Average Price ($K) By Drive Train, Type, and Origin),
data=sasuser.CarsWithMSRPinThousands,
datalabelformat=dollar5.1,
```

```
datalabelpos=left,
rowaxisoffsetmin=0.22,
rowaxisoffsetmax=0.22,
colaxisoffsetmin=0.43,
colaxisoffsetmax=0.05);
```

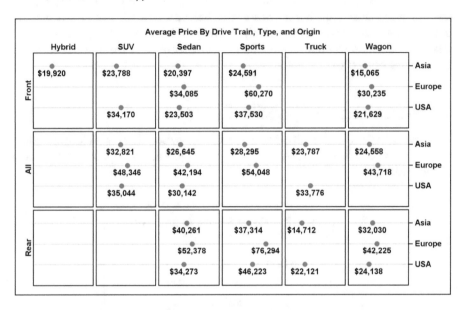

Figure 9-25. Lattice of dot plots with data labels at the bottom of the dots, using dollars rather than thousands of dollars

Displaying dollars rather than thousands of dollars is feasible with DATALABELPOS=BOTTOM.

Listing 9-25. Code used to create Figure 9-25

```
%include "C:\SharedCode\LatticeDotPlotWithDataLabels.sas";
options mprint;

ods listing style=GraphFontArial7ptBold gpath="C:\temp" dpi=300;
%LatticeDotPlotWithDataLabels(
imagename=Fig9-25_LatticeDotPlot_DataLabelPosEqualBottom_Dollars,
imageheight=3.5in,
title=%str(Average Price By Drive Train, Type, and Origin),
data=sashelp.Cars,
datalabelformat=dollar7.,
datalabelpos=bottom,
rowaxisoffsetmin=0.17,
rowaxisoffsetmax=0.27,
colaxisoffsetmin=0.27,
colaxisoffsetmax=0.24);
```

The lattices of dot plots are included to assure that all of ways of presenting categorical data presented in Chapter 4 are included here. Horizontal bar charts are probably a better choice. When data labels are present, panels or lattices of horizontal bar charts always require tuning of the ColAxis offsets to prevent a visually misleading image. (Exceptions to that problem prevention task for horizontal bar charts with data labels are row lattices and panels or lattices where all of the cells are only in one row.) For dot plots, the tuning of offsets is required to undo the excessive horizontal compression of the range of the dots due to the defaults.

Composites of Needle Plots

In all cases here, the default offsets for the RowAxis do not yield misleading lengths for the needles. ColAxis offsets are adjusted to improve the spacing of the needles.

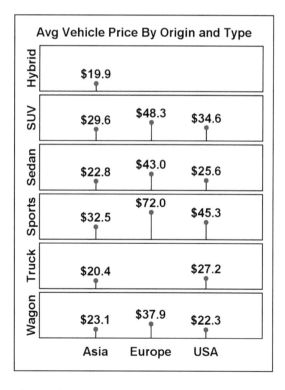

Figure 9-26. Row lattice of needle plots with RowAxis OffSetMin set to zero and ColAxis OffSets adjusted for spacing

Listing 9-26. *Code used to create Figure 9-26*

```
proc summary data=sasuser.CarsWithMSRPinThousands nway;
class Origin Type;
var MSRP;
output out=sasuser.CarsAvgMSRPK_byOriginbyType mean=AvgMSRP;
/* Data set persists, and is also used for Figure 9-27. */
run;

%let ColAxisOffSets = 0.25;

ods listing style=GraphFontArial9ptBold gpath="C:\temp" dpi=300;
ods graphics on / reset=all scale=off width=2.8in
   imagename=
   "Fig9-26_RowLatticeNeedlePlot_DataLabels_UserAxisOffSets";
title1 justify=center "Avg Vehicle Price By Origin and Type";
proc sgpanel data=sasuser.CarsAvgMSRPK_byOriginbyType;
panelby Type / layout=rowlattice
   rowheaderpos=left /* text is easier to read at the left */
   onepanel novarname noheaderborder spacing=3;
needle x=Origin y=AvgMSRP /
   markers markerattrs=(symbol=CircleFilled color=blue)
   displaybaseline=off datalabel datalabelpos=top;
rowaxis display=none offsetmin=0; /* this is not the default */
colaxis display=(nolabel noline noticks)
   offsetmin=&ColAxisOffsets offsetmax=&ColAxisOffsets;
format AvgMSRP dollar5.1;
run;
```

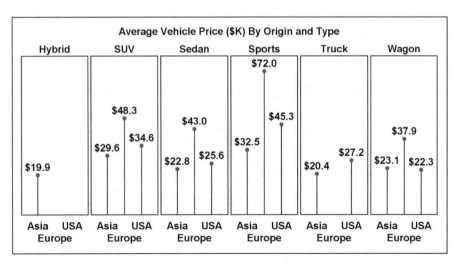

Figure 9-27. Column lattice of needle plots with RowAxis OffSetMin set to zero and ColAxis OffSets adjusted for spacing

Listing 9-27. *Code used to create Figure 9-27*

```
%let ColAxisOffSets = 0.24;

ods listing style=GraphFontArial9ptBold gpath="C:\temp" dpi=300;
ods graphics on / reset=all scale=off width=5.7in height=3in
imagename=
  "Fig9-27_ColumnLatticeNeedlePlot_DataLabels_UserColAxisOffSets";
title1 justify=center
  "Average Vehicle Price ($K) By Origin and Type";
proc sgpanel data=sasuser.CarsAvgMSRPK_byOriginbyType;
panelby Type / layout=columnlattice
  onepanel novarname noheaderborder spacing=3;
needle x=Origin y=AvgMSRP /
  markers markerattrs=(symbol=CircleFilled color=blue)
  displaybaseline=off datalabel datalabelpos=top;
rowaxis display=none offsetmin=0;
colaxis display=(nolabel noline noticks) fitpolicy=stagger
  offsetmin=&ColAxisOffsets offsetmax=&ColAxisOffsets;
format AvgMSRP dollar5.1;
run;
```

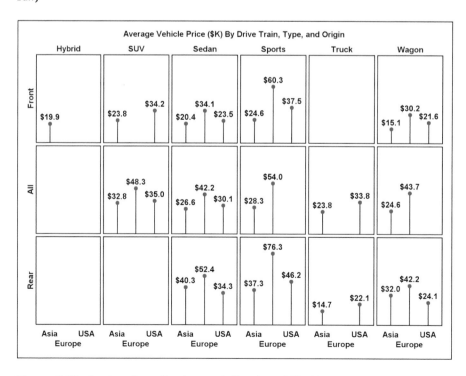

Figure 9-28. Lattice of needle plots with RowAxis OffSetMin set to zero and ColAxis OffSets adjusted for spacing

Listing 9-28. *Code used to create Figure 9-28*

```
proc summary data=sasuser.CarsWithMSRPinThousands nway;
class Origin Type Drivetrain;
var MSRP;
output out=work.CarsAvgMSRP_OriginTypeDrivetrain mean=AvgMSRP;
run;

%let ColAxisOffSets = 0.21;

ods listing style=GraphFontArial7ptBold gpath="C:\temp" dpi=300;
ods graphics on / reset=all scale=off width=5.7in
imagename="Fig9-28_LatticeNeedlePlot_DataLabels_UserColAxisOffSets";
title1 justify=center
  "Average Vehicle Price ($K) By Drive Train, Type, and Origin";
proc sgpanel data=work.CarsAvgMSRP_OriginTypeDrivetrain;
panelby Type Drivetrain / layout=lattice
  rowheaderpos=left /* text is easier to read at the left */
  onepanel novarname noheaderborder spacing=3;
needle x=Origin y=AvgMSRP /
  markers markerattrs=(symbol=CircleFilled color=blue)
  displaybaseline=off datalabel datalabelpos=top;
rowaxis display=none offsetmin=0;
colaxis display=(nolabel noline noticks) fitpolicy=stagger
  offsetmin=&ColAxisOffsets offsetmax=&ColAxisOffsets;
format AvgMSRP dollar5.1;
run;
```

Composites of Scatter Plots

PROC SGSCATTER with its PLOT statement has its own, more versatile, way to create composites of multiple scatter plots. In this section are composites created using PROC SGPANEL and the same SCATTER statement as is supported by PROC SGPLOT. One of the examples is a helpful, but nonstandard, way to get more out of PROC SGPANEL for scatter plots. As is sometimes the case, it requires a bit of data preprocessing to be able to use the software to do more than the usual.

The first two examples show the typical consequence of creating a high-density scatter plot, namely, the infeasibility of data labels. The remaining examples use a data label–friendly data set, which might be representative of some real-world situations that one could encounter. Whenever one can present the precise numbers, one should do so.

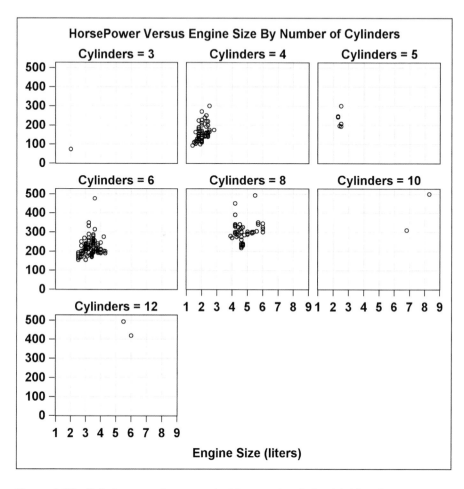

Figure 9-29. Default rows-columns panel with somewhat distinguishable points

Two columns would be better for point distinguishability, but the software chosen height would fill up the page. Experiments with a column lattice, a row lattice, or a two-row panel instead squashed the plot points either horizontally or vertically into a blob.

The VARNAME option was retained for the cell headers for which the variable values are undescriptive integers. This might be unnecessary for most, or perhaps all, viewers, but clarity and information can do no harm.

When only the image width is specified, the software usually chooses a height with a width-to-height aspect ratio of either 4:3 (horizontal rectangle) or 3:4 (vertical rectangle, which is what happens for a two-column panel for this data). Here, the software chooses a square with an aspect ratio of 1:1.

I had previously verified that EngineSize would not have markers at the minimum and maximum axis values, that minimum HorsePower is sufficiently above the minimum axis value, and that maximum HorsePower is 500. The axis offsets are set accordingly.

Listing 9-29. *Code used to create Figure 9-29*

```
ods listing style=GraphFontArial11ptBold gpath="C:\temp" dpi=300;
ods graphics on / reset=all scale=off width=5.7in
  imagename=
  "Fig9-29_PanelWithDefaultRowAndColumnCounts_ScatterPlots";
title1 justify=center "HorsePower Versus Engine Size By Number of Cylinders";
proc sgpanel data=sashelp.cars;
panelby Cylinders /
  skipemptycells onepanel noheaderborder spacing=10;
scatter x=EngineSize y=HorsePower;
rowaxis display=(nolabel) grid
  values=(0 to 500 by 100) fitpolicy=none
  offsetmin=0 offsetmax=0.05; /* a marker is at y=500 */
colaxis grid minorgrid minorcount=1
  values=(1 to 9 by 1) fitpolicy=stagger
  offsetmin=0 offsetmax=0; /* no markers near boundaries */
format HorsePower 3. EngineSize 4.2 Cylinders 2.;
label EngineSize='Engine Size (liters)';
run;
```

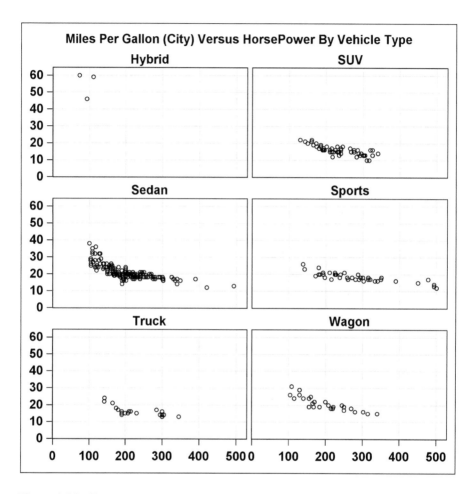

Figure 9-30. Two-column panel with programmer-assigned square image height. Plot points are somewhat distinguishable

The default markers for the SCATTER statement are open circles. The consequence is less opportunity to create a blob with overlapping markers. That is why Figure 9-30 has plot points that are somewhat distinguishable. Perhaps that consequence was the intent of the software design decision for the default markers.

If image height is not assigned, the software chooses image height that is 4/3 times the image width, which spreads the points in the vertical direction. (That result is not shown here.) A square was chosen only to save page space. A row lattice, a column lattice, and LAYOUT=PANEL without any specification as to rows or columns would give results that are not better than what is delivered in Figure 9-30. (For the third case, the software would choose three columns and an image height that is 3/4 times the image width—shorter than the preceding image.) A better way to expose the granularity of a scatter plot is with standalone scatter plots on interlinked web pages (with the option of mouseover text for X and Y values). The trade-off is the loss of simultaneous comparability. The solution then is to present a panel as one of the interlinked web pages. ODS HTML5 is the subject of Chapter 14.

Listing 9-30. *Code used to create Figure 9-30*

```
ods listing style=GraphFontArial11ptBold gpath="C:\temp" dpi=300;
ods graphics on / reset=all scale=off width=5.7in height=5.7in
   imagename="Fig9-30_PanelWithTwoColumnsSquareImage_ScatterPlots";
title1 justify=center
   "Miles Per Gallon (City) Versus HorsePower By Vehicle Type";
proc sgpanel data=sashelp.cars;
panelby Type / columns=2
   onepanel novarname noheaderborder spacing=5;
scatter x=horsepower y=mpg_city;
rowaxis display=(nolabel noline) grid
   values=(0 to 60 by 10)
   offsetmin=0; /* does not clip any markers */
colaxis display=(nolabel noline) grid
   values=(0 to 500 by 100)
   offsetmin=0; /* does not clip any markers */
format HorsePower 3. mpg_city 2.;
run;
```

If your knowledge of the data assures you that setting the minimum axis offset to zero will not clip part of a marker (or a data label), then that will maximize the use of then available image height and/or width.

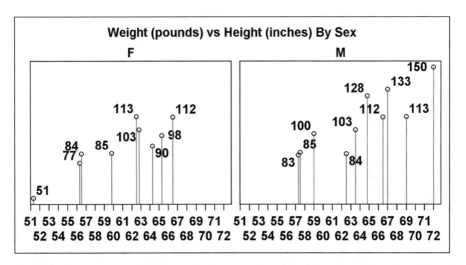

Figure 9-31. One-row panel, data labels for Y, drop lines for X

Figure 9-31 is a tolerable compromise, but does not deliver all of the precise numbers. It still requires guessing for the X values. Figure 9-32 does much better.

Listing 9-31. *Code used to create Figure 9-31*

```
ods listing style=GraphFontArial11ptBold gpath="C:\temp" dpi=300;
ods graphics on / reset=all scale=off width=5.7in height=3in
  imagename="Fig9-31_PanelOneRow_DataLabelsForY_DropLinesForX";
title1 justify=center "Weight (pounds) vs Height (inches) By Sex";
proc sgpanel data=sashelp.class;
panelby Sex / rows=1 onepanel novarname noheaderborder spacing=10;
scatter x=height y=weight / datalabel;
dropline x=height y=weight / dropto=x;
rowaxis display=none;
colaxis display=(noline nolabel)
  offsetmin=0 /* does not clip any markers */
  values=(51 to 72 by 1) fitpolicy=stagger;
format Weight 3. Height 2.;
run;
```

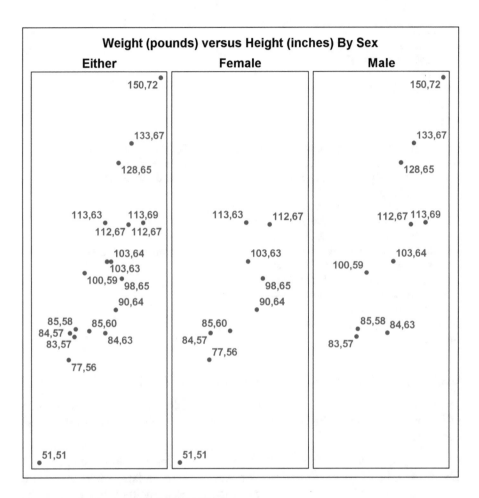

Figure 9-32. Getting PROC SGPANEL to show more

It was easy to add X values to the data labels, but I also wanted to show Female data alone, Male data alone, and both of them together, all in one composite. The way to achieve this requires (a) data preprocessing to create a class variable that covers all three cases and (b) the use of the single-sex Sex variable as a Group variable so that the SCATTER statement color-codes the markers.

Listing 9-32. *Code used to create Figure 9-32*

```
data work.ToPlot;
length YandX $ 8 Gender $ 6;;
set sashelp.class;
YandX = compress(put(weight,3.) || ',' || put(height,2.));
```

```
if Sex EQ 'F'
then Gender = 'Female';
else Gender = 'Male';
output;
Gender='Either';
output;
run;

ods listing style=GraphFontArial11ptBold gpath="C:\temp" dpi=300;
ods graphics on / reset=all scale=off width=5.7in height=5.7in
  imagename="Fig9-32_OneRowPanel_ScatterPlots_DataLabelsForYandX";
title1 justify=center
  "Weight (pounds) versus Height (inches) By Sex";
proc sgpanel data=work.ToPlot noautolegend;
styleattrs datacontrastcolors=(red blue);
panelby Gender / rows=1 onepanel novarname noheaderborder spacing=5;
scatter x=height y=weight / group=Sex
  markerattrs=(symbol=circlefilled)
  datalabel=YandX datalabelattrs=(size=9pt);
rowaxis display=none;
colaxis display=none values=(51 to 72 by 21);
run;
```

Composites with Three Class Variables

There is no limit on the number of class variables that can be listed on a PANELBY statement. Perhaps there is, but it is not mentioned in the documentation.

Already at three class variables, although the panel delivers all of the ClassVar1 ClassVar2 ClassVar3 combinations for which there is data, I find the result clumsy to use. That is, if you wish to compare one combination with another, it is not easy, unless both combinations have the same value for the topmost class variable. However, if the value of a comprehensive delivery of "the whole enchilada" is more important than convenience in its use, then the result achieves that objective.

The only composite with more than one class variable where comparing combinations of values of class variables is always easy is LAYOUT=LATTICE, which only applies to two class variables.

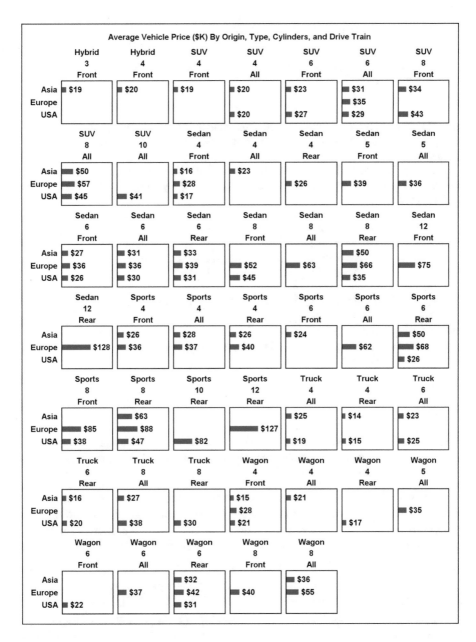

Figure 9-33. A panel with three class variables: PANELBY Type, (Number of) Cylinders, Drivetrain

Listing 9-33. *Code used to create Figure 9-33*

```
data work.ToPlot;
set sashelp.cars(keep=Type Cylinders Drivetrain Origin MSRP);
MSRP = MSRP / 1000;
run;

ods listing style=GraphFontArial7ptBold gpath="C:\temp" dpi=300;
ods graphics on / reset=all scale=off width=5.7in height=7.6in
   imagename=
   "Fig9-33_PanelWithThreeClassVariablesForHbarsWithDataLabels";
title1 justify=center 'Average Vehicle Price ($K) By Origin, Type, Cylinders,
and Drive Train';
proc sgpanel data=work.ToPlot;
panelby Type Cylinders Drivetrain / layout=panel
   onepanel novarname noheaderborder spacing=5 skipemptycells;
hbar Origin / response=MSRP stat=mean displaybaseline=off
   nooutline barwidth=0.4 fillattrs=(color=blue)
   datalabel datalabelfitpolicy=none;
rowaxis display=(noticks noline nolabel) fitpolicy=none
   offsetmin=0.2 offsetmax=0.2;
colaxis display=none offsetmin=0
   offsetmax=0.43; /* prevent misleading bar lengths */
format MSRP dollar4.;
run;
```

Summary

There are several ways to communication-effectively present composite images and, whenever possible, their precise numbers. In some cases, data labels are possible.

In others, such as time series plots where the points are too dense to permit data labels, it is useful at least to present the maximum, or the maximum and minimum, and, if desired, even the median or some other statistics for week, month, or year and for the total range of time being presented by cycle. The critical points within each cell can be highlighted with color coding.

In the remarks that follow, the options mentioned pertain to the PANELBY statement. There are also options for the PROC SGPANEL statement, none of which are discussed here. The only procedure statement options used in the examples are DATA= and, to suppress a legend if it is unnecessary for use or clarity, NOAUTOLEGEND.

Categorical data is most easily annotated with data labels. Scatter plots, unless for atypical data sets with few observations, are the most difficult to annotate, due to not only the volume of plot points but also the fact that points often cluster into what is inelegantly, but aptly, called "a blob."

When there are two class variables for the composite, a lattice offers a clearly organized structure where the values of Class Variable 1 are column headers and the values of Class Variable 2 are the row headers. Combinations of values of the two class variables for which there is no data are represented by empty cells at their row-value, column-value locations in the lattice. The cells are identified by row and column labels at the top and right side of the lattice. The ROWHEADERPOS and COLHEADERPOS options permit the labels to be switched to the opposite location from what is the default, or to put row headers on both sides of the lattice and column headers at both the top and the bottom of the lattice.

A panel instead simply wraps the string of combinations in cells, proceeding from left to right within in rows, proceeding through rows from top to bottom in the panel. The class variable values are displayed at the top of each cell. It uses only as many cells as there are non-missing combinations of values for the class variables. There is no cell reserved for each missing combination. If the product of row count and column count exceeds the number of class variable value combinations with data, empty cells are created at the lower right of the panel. This compaction makes it less convenient to compare different, but related, combinations of values.

Looking back at the examples after writing the body of this chapter, I noticed that I predominantly used the lattice layout. This was undoubtedly the result of preference for how the lattice presents the combinations of values for two class variables. The only composite with more than one class variable where comparing combinations of values of class variables is always easy is LAYOUT=LATTICE, which only applies to two class variables.

However, a lattice comes with the disappointing consequence of vertical text for the row headers. (For decades, and again in this book, I have advocated abstention from unnatural vertical text. For example, you can instead put the Y axis label in the title or subtitle of your graph.) Those row headers are doubly disappointing. They are not only vertical but at the right side of the image and the page. Vertical labels at the left side are less unwelcome to read. At the right side, they are nearly insufferable. There *is* the option ROWHEADERPOS=LEFT (not the default) to display them at the left side of the lattice, to the left of the RowAxis values, but then the row headers get into a visual fight with the RowAxis values. There is no option to create an array that uses Class Variable 1 values for the columns' content, and Class Variable 2 values for the rows' content, as is the case for LAYOUT=LATTICE, but stacks the two class variables' values for each cell in a header above the cell, as is the case for LAYOUT=PANEL. The solution to this quandary is to use ROWHEADERPOS=LEFT to move the row labels to the left side of the lattice and to move the RowAxis values to the right side of the lattice with the REFTICKS option. See Figures 9-4 and 9-5 and Figures 9-23 through 9-25.

You can force a panel layout to display blank cells for the missing combinations with the SPARSE option of the PANELBY statement.

For both lattices and panels, the variable names are displayed, not just the variable values, in the labels used for rows, columns, and cells. They can be removed with the NOVARNAME option. In most cases, they are superfluous.

By default, for both panels and lattices, the cell, row, and column headers have borders, with no communication value. They can be turned off with the NOHEADERBORDER option.

The SKIPEMPTYCELLS option can be used to erase the empty cells that can appear at the lower right of a panel as previously explained. If present, they have no communication value.

The SPACING option is useful for at least two practical purposes, in addition to controlling the spacing between cells to suit the programmer's preference. Increasing the spacing in a panel makes it clearer that a cell header belongs to the cell below, not the cell above. Also, sometimes the axis values at the bottom of a lattice or panel (i.e., the last value for one cell and the first value for the next cell to its right) are so close together that they collide. Increasing the spacing sufficiently can prevent collisions or remediate what you might deem to be peculiar closeness.

An option that one might wish to always code (as I do), since it is not a default, is ONEPANEL. It prevents the software from splitting the panel or lattice into separate images. However, there can be instances where the number of cells required is so large within the image dimensions that the cells become too small. In that case, ONEPANEL should be omitted so that the software can create images that are readable subset composites.

When there is only one class variable, there are three choices: LAYOUT= ROWLATTICE for columns all in one row, LAYOUT=COLUMNLATTICE for rows all in one column, and LAYOUT=PANEL for which the user or the software can determine the number of rows and columns. A panel can be more compact, but clumsier to use for comparison. Whether a row lattice or column lattice is the better "one-dimensional" layout depends on the data. One can test both options to decide which is the better result for viewers of the composite.

There is a SORT option, which was not used in any of the examples. For information about it, or other options for the PANELBY statement, or for options of the PROC SGPANEL statement, see the *SAS ODS Graphics Procedures Guide*.

In a one-column panel, a composite of Sparse Lines becomes a Sparse Line Table. See examples in Figures 9-9 and 9-12. The composites of Sparse Lines in Figures 9-11 and 9-13 are Sparse Line Panels, with multiple columns of cells, not just one column.

Using a "manufactured" Group variable as in Figure 9-32 can provide a directly comparable picture of the data from two or more cells of a composite in an extra cell as a companion to the standalone pictures of the data in those "contributing" cells. The benefit of this innovative use of PROC SGPANEL for what might be called a two-level composite is that it delivers both of the relevant views of the data, by sex and all sexes, in one image.

Though a lattice is limited to two class variables, the panel layout has no maximum. However, the panel, with its wrapped array of cells, is more difficult to use for finding and/or comparing combinations of class variable values. Of course, if the objective is only to present all of the data, regardless of the difficulty in finding a particular cell, that result is always deliverable with a panel.

A composite can also be used as an overview of, and index to, all of the combinations of the class variables. It could be web linked to standalone fully annotated images of each cell, using the ODS HTML5 destination. Here and heretofore, the book relies on the LISTING destination.

Scatter Plots in Composites Using PROC SGSCATTER

Chapter 9 presented four ways to create composites of scatter plots using PROC SGPANEL and the SCATTER statement. In Chapter 3, eight of its eleven examples were standalone scatter plots, using PROC SGPLOT and the SCATTER statement.

The focus of this chapter is composites of scatter plots created with PROC SGSCATTER and its PLOT, COMPARE, and MATRIX statements and time series plots created with the PLOT statement (using its JOIN option to connect the dots).

The first example is not a composite. Figure 10-1 compares PROC SGSCATTER and its PLOT statement with PROC SGPLOT and its SCATTER statement. For a single, standalone scatter plot, PROC SGPLOT is usually better.

© LeRoy Bessler 2023
LeR. Bessler, *Visual Data Insights Using SAS ODS Graphics*,
https://doi.org/10.1007/978-1-4842-8609-8_10

But SGSCATTER can do composites of scatter plots that neither SGPLOT nor SGPANEL can do. Unlike the PROC SGPLOT SCATTER statement, which is limited to X=Xvar y=Yvar, the PROC SGSCATTER PLOT and COMPARE statements support creation of a panel of scatter plots for all combinations of a set of (one or more) X variables and a set of (one or more) Y variables.

The PLOT statement and the COMPARE statement do essentially the same thing as each other except for two important features. (There are other differences, but they are comparatively minor.) The PLOT statement has optional ROWS and COLUMNS controls (counts), whereas the COMPARE statement makes its own row and column decisions that are not subject to possible change.

The PLOT statement provides axis labels and tick mark values at the left side of and bottom of each cell in the panel, but the COMPARE statement provides shared axis labels and tick mark values at the left side and bottom of the panel, so that all cells in a row share the same Y axis values and all cells in a column share the same X axis values. See Figure 10-5 for a PLOT panel and Figure 10-6 for a COMPARE panel, both for the same set of X and Y variables. With respect to axis information, both the PLOT statement and the COMPARE statement have a REFTICKS option that is demonstrated and discussed further later.

The MATRIX statement uses a single list of variables that serve as X-Y pairs. The panel is a matrix where each variable in the list is presented in one cell as the X variable and in a cell on the other side of the diagonal as the Y variable. See Figure 10-7. In this case, too, like the COMPARE panel, the axis information is at the edges of the panel. All three panel types can display a confidence or prediction ellipse for each scatter plot. The MATRIX statement can display a histogram and/or normal distribution and/or kernel density estimate in the diagonal cells. There is one diagonal cell for each of the variables being plotted. See Figure 10-8. Since the diagonal cells and the off-diagonal scatter plots have incompatible axis information, none can be displayed. How to deal with that problem is discussed in the Summary.

The PLOT and COMPARE statements also have options for REG, LOESS, and PBSPLINE fits. Details about them, all other available features and options, and complete information about syntax are provided in the *SAS ODS Graphics Procedures Guide*.

Image Size Determination

Like PROC SGPANEL, when only one dimension is specified on the ODS GRAPHICS statement, PROC SGSCATTER chooses the value for the other image dimension, based on the image content. The image dimensions then will have a width-to-height aspect ratio of 4:3 (landscape), 3:4 (portrait), or 1:1 (square).

If you have a preference as to the aspect ratio and/or the precise dimensions in the image result, it's necessary to specify WIDTH and HEIGHT on the ODS GRAPHICS statement.

General Remarks About Code Used

The following framing code has been more expansively discussed in Chapter 3 in the section "Outer Structure of ODS Graphics Code in Examples." The framing code for all examples in this chapter and others is

```
ods results off; /* verify results by opening the image file,
                    rather than using the SAS Output window */
ods _all_ close; /* avoid unintended consequences
                    and superfluous concurrent output */
< ODS LISTING statement here >
< example-specific code here >
ods listing close; /* ALWAYS Best Practice */
```

For brevity, the example code in listings omits the first two lines and the last one. It is best to add them back at your runtime. (Source code files include them.)

The ODS LISTING statement can vary. All of the examples in this chapter use a statement of the following form to specify the text characteristics:

```
ods listing style=GraphFontArial11ptBold gpath="C:\temp" dpi=300;
```

but often with font sizes other than 11pt. The statement assumes that the ODS style GraphFontArial11ptBold has been created. To assure that all of the styles needed in this chapter are available, use this code:

```
%include "C:\SharedCode\AllGraphTextSetup.sas";
%AllGraphTextSetup(8);
%AllGraphTextSetup(9);
%AllGraphTextSetup(10);
%AllGraphTextSetup(11);
```

For more information about ODS custom styles, as well as the source code for the AllGraphTextSetup macro, see the section "Control of Text Attributes with a Custom ODS Style" in Chapter 3. For information about options for direct control of text attributes, which can override the default text attributes that are set up by an ODS style, see the section "Text Attributes Control in ODS Graphics" in Chapter 3.

Special Data Requirement for This Chapter

Some examples in this chapter use real economic data. For background information about the input data required, please see in Chapter 8 the section "Special Data Sets Used for Some Time Series Graphs." If your site does not have SAS/ETS, you must download the zip file CitiData.zip from https://github.com/Apress/Visual-Data-Insights-Using-SAS-ODS-Graphics and store the five unzipped files in folder C:\CitiData.

Whichever is the case, the next step is to prepare data used in this chapter for several examples. My SAS site does *not* have SAS/ETS.

Listing 10-0. *Create a persisting data set for use in Listings 10-12 to 10-15*

```
/* To prepare sasuser.EconomicData */
%include "C:\SharedCode\ExtractEconomicData.sas";
options mprint;
%ExtractEconomicData
(SASETSsiteUseSASHELPDataLib=NO,
OtherSiteFolderForCitiData=C:\CitiData,
OutLib=SASUSER);
```

PROC SGSCATTER PLOT Versus PROC SGPLOT SCATTER

One can use PROC SGSCATTER to create a paneled image of scatter plots for multiple combinations of variables, using the PLOT statement, the COMPARE statement, or the MATRIX statement.

The PLOT statement can create

1. A single scatter plot of one Y variable versus one X variable (see Figure 10-1)

2. A panel of plots of one Y variable versus each of multiple X variables (see Figures 10-2 and 10-3)

3. A panel of plots of each of multiple Y variables versus one X variable (see Figure 10-4)

4. A panel of plots of each of multiple Y variables versus each of multiple X variables (see Figure 10-5)

PROC SGPLOT with the SCATTER statement can create only a SINGLE scatter plot.

PROC SGPANEL with the SCATTER statement can create four different types of arrays of scatter plots of one Y variable versus one X variable, where the cells are identified by the value of one or more class variables.

The first example is a comparison of SGSCATTER PLOT and SGPLOT SCATTER for a single scatter plot. Scatter plots, unless they are very scanty on plot points like this example, are prone to data label collisions and/or having many data labels totally or largely obscured by the mass of plot points.

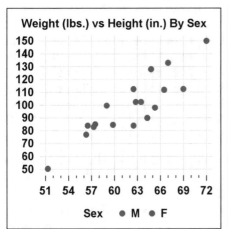 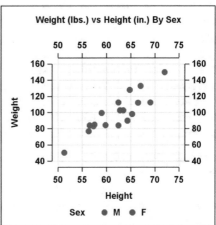

Figure 10-1. PROC SGPLOT and SCATTER statement (left) versus PROC SGSCATTER and PLOT statement (right)

The only advantage of using PROC SGSCATTER for a single standalone scatter plot is the REFTICKS option which can be used to duplicate axis values, and also labels if desired, on both the left and right sides as well as above and below. Duplication of only the X axis or only the Y axis is not an option. To do this, optionally for only the X axis or only the Y axis or both axes, is possible using PROC SGPLOT, but the code is complicated. If you are interested, see Listing A10-1 in Appendix A, which includes an illustration of the result.

PROC SGSCATTER provides no choice of axis values. The software selects them based on variable values available, dimensions of the image, and font size. Both PROC SGPLOT and PROC SGSCATTER sometimes "thin" axis values (i.e., selectively omit them) if displaying more of them would be a tight fit. The XAXIS and YAXIS statements available for PROC SGPLOT have a FITPOLICY option with possible values of "NONE" (which says "Do it anyway.") or STAGGER (which instructs the software to display the values in two rows, alternating values from upper to lower row and back, continuing to alternate). The FITPOLICY option is not available with PROC SGSCATTER. The only way to eliminate or reduce the thinning is to increase the relevant image dimension and/or reduce the font size.

For both PROC SGPLOT and PROC SGSCATTER, there are GRID and MINORGRID options and GRIDATTRS and MINORGRIDATTRS options to control their attributes (color, thickness, and line pattern), but with PROC SGSCATTER, there is no control on the PLOT or COMPARE statements for the number of minor grid lines between major grid line pairs. No minor tick marks can be turned on. With no control of the number of minor grid lines, the result of using the MINORGRID option can vary between one and, in some cases, so many as to be unusable. (For example, if MINORGRID were used for Figure 10-6, there would be 12 minor grid lines for each axis, where the X value increments between major grid lines are 100 and Y value increments are 10. Who wants to take on the mental math challenge of trying to determine the minor grid line value when the sub-increment is one-thirteenth of 10 or 100? The lesson is that, when using the MINORGRID option, evaluate the result for its usefulness.)

With PROC SGSCATTER, there is no way to turn off the axis labels, a limitation that wastes space and makes the plot area smaller. (The label information can be provided in the graph title, as is the case for Figure 10-1, or a graph subtitle.) This, along with the choice to use the REFTICKS option, requires that the font be three points smaller than the font used with PROC SGPLOT.

The AXISEXTENT option is unique to the PLOT statement. The choice of AXISEXTENT=DATA used in Listing 10-1 is, in my judgment, better than the default. There is a NOBORDER option for the PLOT statement, but it has visible effect only if the AXISEXTENT default is accepted, and the REFTICKS option has not been used. The choice of AXISEXTENT=DATA automatically turns off the border. The REFTICKS option, when it duplicates X and Y axis labels and tick mark values, also turns on axis lines above and at the right side, which create a border. (The NOBORDER option is available on the PROC SGPLOT statement, not the SCATTER statement.)

Both the PLOT statement and the SCATTER statement have DATALABEL and DATALABELPOS options, but the PLOT statement does not have the DATALABELATTRS option—the control of the color is via the PROC SGSCATTER DATACONTRASTCOLORS option.

PROC SGPLOT can create axis tables for scatter plots, but PROC SGSCATTER cannot.

PROC SGSCATTER with its PLOT statement has some deficiencies. Nevertheless, its PLOT, COMPARE, and MATRIX statements have important composite-building capabilities, shown in the remaining examples of this chapter, that are not available with PROC SGPLOT or PROC SGPANEL.

Listing 10-1. *Code used to create the two images in Figure 10-1*

/* For image at left: */

```
ods listing style=GraphFontArial10ptBold gpath="C:\temp" dpi=300;
ods graphics on / reset=all scale=off width=2.8in height=2.8in
  imagename="Fig10-1Left_SGPLOT_ScatterPlot";
title1 justify=center 'Weight (lbs.) vs Height (in.) By Sex';
proc sgplot data=sashelp.class noborder;
```
styleattrs datacontrastcolors=(red blue);
   /* Colors are applied to markers and legend color swatches
      in the order of the values of the group variable
      in the input data set. For this data, M is first value. */
```
scatter y=weight x=height / group=sex
```
   markerattrs=(symbol=CircleFilled);
   /* default markers would have less evident color */
```
yaxis display=(noline nolabel noticks)
   values=(50 to 150 by 10) grid
```
   fitpolicy=none; /* prevent thinning of Y axis values */
```
xaxis display=(noline nolabel) values=(51 to 72 by 3) grid
```
   /* display tick marks to draw attention to minor tick marks */
```
   minor minorcount=2 minorgrid;
```
keylegend / noborder;
```
run;
```

/* For image at right: */

%let ASPECTvalue = 0.8; /* Tune this to your satisfaction.
   This is the ratio of plot area height to the plot area width.
   It can be any number greater than 0.
   For ASPECT=1, the plot area is a square.
   If ASPECT is not used, the plot area height
   is the same as that for ASPECT=1, but the plot area is wider.
   It affects the space between the X axis label and the legend.
   0.8 is my preference as to optimal spacing.
   Regrettably, it also inserts needless extra space
   below the title and compresses the plotting area.
   Values greater than 1 squash the plotting area horisontally.
   Only values less than 1 can increase space between
   the X axis label and the legend.
   If ASPECT is not assigned, the plotting area is shaped and
   sized to make best use of the image area available.
   By default, the X axis label is (too) close to the legend.
   If no legend is present, ASPECT is probably best omitted. */
```
ods listing style=GraphFontArial8ptBold gpath="C:\temp" dpi=300;
```
   /* 9pt and 10pt fonts reduce the size of the plot area, and
      put X axis label closer to the legend than to the axis.
      11pt, besides the above, causes thinning of values
      on both axes, and a line break in the title. */

```
ods graphics on / reset=all scale=off width=2.8in height=2.8in
  imagename="Fig10-1Right_SGSCATTER_ScatterPlot";
title1 justify=center 'Weight (lbs.) vs Height (in.) By Sex';
proc sgscatter data=sashelp.class
  datacontrastcolors=(red blue); /* for markers, etc. */
  /* NOTE: If using FILLEDOUTLINEDMARKERS option,
     marker color is controlled by DATACOLORS */
plot weight*height / group=sex
  grid
  minorgrid /* with fewer axis values, turn on some extra help, even
    if not ideally located for X axis (non-integer locations) */
  aspect=&ASPECTvalue
  legend=(noborder) /* If the aspect option is not used,
  omit this. The X axis label will be too close
  to the legend, possibly causing confusion. */
  axisextent=data /* better axis layout than the default */
  refticks=(values) /* duplicate tick marks & values
                        on the right side and on the top */
  markerattrs=(symbol=CircleFilled);
  /* default markers would have less evident color */
run;
```

Creating Composites with PROC SGSCATTER

The distinctive strength of the PLOT, COMPARE, and MATRIX statements of PROC SGSCATTER versus using a SCATTER statement with PROC SGPLOT or PROC SGPANEL is their ability to create an array of cells to plot various combinations of Y and X variables. Let's begin a journey through the possibilities.

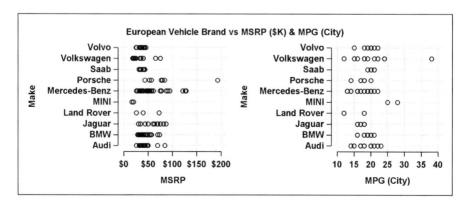

Figure 10-2. Using PLOT statement with one Y variable and two X variables

There is no technical limit on the number of X variables, but readability, given the size of image target area and the font size, what is practical is the determining limit. With more than two X variables, the panel wraps into a two-dimensional array unless a code override is used. Cell sizes, as well as the software's choice of number of rows and columns, are determined by the image dimensions and the number of cells. The ROWS and COLUMNS options can be used to control the shape of the array.

Listing 10-2. Code used to create Figure 10-2

```
data sasuser.EuropeanCarsDollarsInK; /* data set will persist */
set sashelp.cars;
where Origin EQ 'Europe';
MSRPinThousands = MSRP / 1000;
run;

ods listing style=GraphFontArial8ptBold gpath="C:\temp" dpi=300;
ods graphics on / reset=all scale=off width=5.7in height=2.3in
  imagename="Fig10-2_OneYvar_MulipleXvars_ScatterPlots";
title1 justify=center
  'European Vehicle Brand vs MSRP ($K) & MPG (City)';
proc sgscatter data=sasuser.EuropeanCarsDollarsInK;
plot (Make) * (MSRPinThousands MPG_City) /
  axisextent=data grid minorgrid;
format MSRPinThousands dollar4.;
label MSRPinThousands='MSRP';
run;
```

The vertical or "portrait" alternative in Figure 10-3 is rendered by using COLUMNS=1 in the PLOT statement. With HEIGHT=4.3in in the ODS GRAPHICS statement and no WIDTH specified, the software automatically chooses a width of 3.23 inches, which is three-fourths of the height. Recall that when only one dimension is chosen, the software will select the other dimension, based on cell content, with an aspect ratio for width to height of either 4:3 (landscape), 3:4 (portrait, as in Figure 10-3), or 1:1 (square).

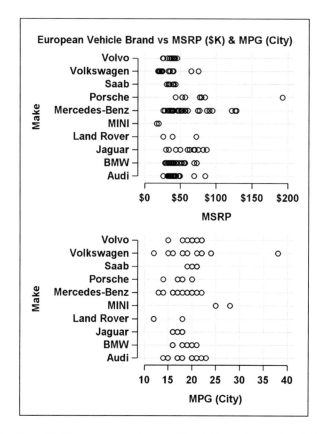

Figure 10-3. Using PLOT statement with one Y variable and two X variables and option COLUMNS=1

Listing 10-3. Code used to create Figure 10-3

```
ods listing style=GraphFontArial8ptBold gpath="C:\temp" dpi=300;
ods graphics on / reset=all scale=off
  height=4.3in /* minimum height that avoids thinning values */
  imagename="Fig10-3_OneYvar_MulipleXvars_ScatterPlots_OneColumn";
title1 justify=center
  'European Vehicle Brand vs MSRP ($K) & MPG (City)';
proc sgscatter data=sasuser.EuropeanCarsDollarsInK;
                 /* input created in Listing 10-2 */
plot (Make) * (MSRPinThousands MPG_City) / columns=1
  axisextent=data grid minorgrid;
format MSRPinThousands dollar4.;
label MSRPinThousands='MSRP';
run;
```

A larger font size for Figure 10-3 would cause thinning of the X axis values. A smaller font size would leave a bit more space for the plotting area, but with no significant improvement in distinguishability of individual plot markers. At 8pt, there are no additional axis values or grid lines. There are minor grid lines already. They could be made more easily seen, if desired, by using the MINORGRIDATTRS option. (There is also a GRIDATTRS option for the major grid lines.)

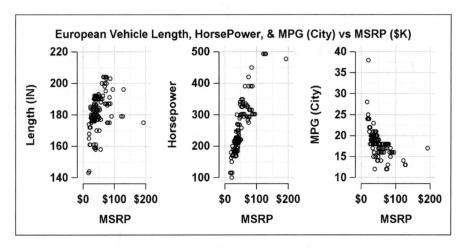

Figure 10-4. Using PLOT statement with three Y variables and one X variable

Listing 10-4. Code used to create Figure 10-4

```
ods listing style=GraphFontArial10ptBold gpath="C:\temp" dpi=300;
   /* a larger font size would thin the X axis to two values */
ods graphics on / reset=all scale=off width=5.7in height=2.8in
   imagename="Fig10-4_MultipleYvars_OneXvar_ScatterPlots";
title1 justify=center
   'European Vehicle Length, HorsePower, & MPG (City) vs MSRP ($K)';
proc sgscatter data=sasuser.EuropeanCarsDollarsInK;
                  /* input created in Listing 10-2 */
plot (Length HorsePower MPG_City) * (MSRPinThousands) / rows=1
   /* Without ROWS=1 the result would be two rows
      of vertically squashed cells, two in row 1, one in row 2. */
   axisextent=data grid minorgrid;
format MSRPinThousands dollar4.;
label MSRPinThousands='MSRP';
run;
```

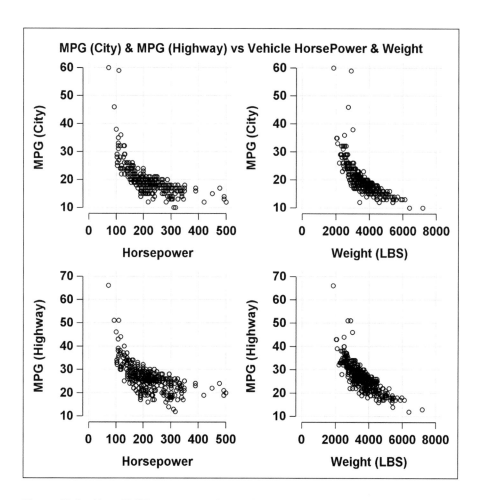

Figure 10-5. Using PLOT statement with two Y variables and two X variables

The ODS GRAPHICS statement in Listing 10-5 specifies only the image width. The software chose the image height to match the width for a 1:1 aspect ratio.

Listing 10-5. *Code used to create Figure 10-5*

```
ods listing style=GraphFontArial11ptBold gpath="C:\temp" dpi=300;
ods graphics on / reset=all scale=off width=5.7in
  imagename="Fig10-5_MultipleYvars_MultipleXvars_ScatterPlots";
title1 justify=center
  'MPG (City) & MPG (Highway) vs Vehicle HorsePower & Weight';
proc sgscatter data=sashelp.cars;
plot (MPG_City MPG_Highway)*(HorsePower Weight) /
  axisextent=data grid;
run;
```

Figure 10-6 renders an alternative configuration for the preceding graph composite, using the COMPARE statement instead of the PLOT statement. It uses the REFTICKS option which puts the tick marks and values also at the right and top edges of the panel. The same option for a PLOT statement panel would have put them at the top and right edges of every cell. The COMPARE statement uses less space in the image for axis information, with or without the REFTICKS option.

■ **Note**   The COMPARE statement has no ROWS and COLUMNS options. For a custom row count or column count layout of the cells, the PLOT statement is required. Examples of such use are in Figures 10-3, 10-4, 10-12, and 10-14.

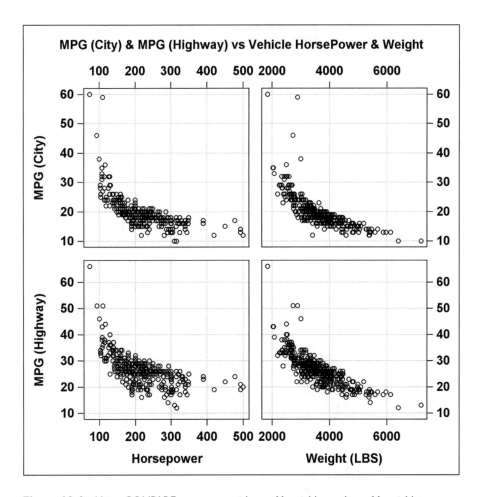

Figure 10-6. Using COMPARE statement with two Y variables and two X variables

Listing 10-6. *Code used to create Figure 10-6*

```
ods listing style=GraphFontArial11ptBold gpath="C:\temp" dpi=300;
ods graphics on / reset=all scale=off width=5.7in
  imagename=
  "Fig10-6_MultipleYvars_MultipleXvars_CompareScatterPlots";
title1 justify=center
  'MPG (City) & MPG (Highway) vs Vehicle HorsePower & Weight';
title2 height=4pt color=white
  'White Space (Adjust as desired, or eliminate it';
  /* Without it, proximity of axis values & title looks peculiar. */
proc sgscatter data=sashelp.cars;
compare y=(MPG_City MPG_Highway) x=(HorsePower Weight) /
  refticks=(values) /* tick marks and values duplicated
                       at top and at right side */
  spacing=15 /* Default is 0,
                which lets 500 and 2000 for the X axes collide.
                Default for PLOT statement is 10. */
  /* AXISEXTENT option is not relevant for COMPARE statement */
  grid;
run;
```

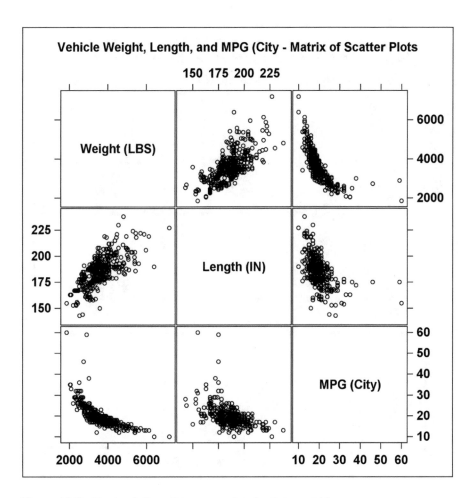

Figure 10-7. Matrix of all possible scatter plots for three variables

Listing 10-7. Code used to create Figure 10-7

```
ods listing style=GraphFontArial11ptBold gpath="C:\temp" dpi=300;
ods graphics on / reset=all scale=off width=5.7in
  imagename="Fig10-7_3Vars_MatrixOfScatterPlots";
title1 justify=center
  'Vehicle Weight, Length, and MPG (City - Matrix of Scatter Plots';
title2 height=4pt color=white
  'White Space (Adjust as desired, or eliminate it';
  /* Without it, proximity of axis values & title looks peculiar. */
proc sgscatter data=sashelp.cars;
matrix Weight Length MPG_City;
run;
```

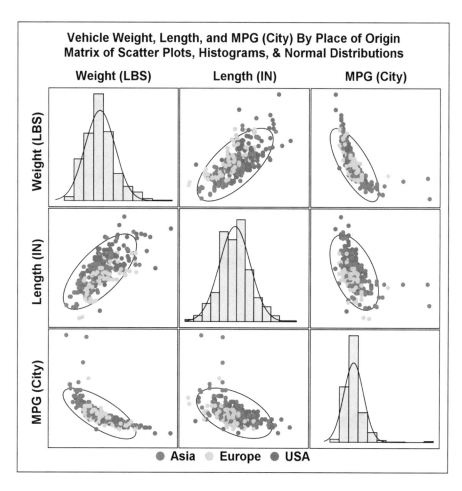

Figure 10-8. Matrix for three variables with scatter plots, predicted ellipses, histograms, and normal distributions

Axis values are impossible due to incompatible ranges for the diagonal plots versus those of the scatter plots.

Why create a graph with no precise numbers and not even axis values to guess what they might approximately be? A *practical* alternative to this would be to use ODS HTML5 (the subject of Chapter 14) to create a web-enabled graph with mouseover text to present precise numbers for the scatter plots, histograms, and distributions.

You can produce a usable version of a matrix panel with a GROUP variable and a legend with ODS LISTING by simply turning off the DIAGONAL option. The result will include the axis values that are in Figure 10-7. The code in Listing 10-8 shows how to control the color palette with the DATACONTRASTCOLORS option.

Listing 10-8. *Code used to create Figure 10-8*

```
ods listing style=GraphFontArial11ptBold gpath="C:\temp" dpi=300;
ods graphics on / reset=all scale=off width=5.7in
  imagename=
  "Fig10-8_3VarsGroupVar_MatrixOfScatterPlots_WithDiagonalContent";
title1 justify=center
  'Vehicle Weight, Length, and MPG (City) By Place of Origin';
title2 justify=center
  'Matrix of Scatter Plots, Histograms, & Normal Distributions';
proc sgscatter data=sashelp.cars
  datacontrastcolors=(gray turquoise magenta);
matrix Weight Length MPG_City / group=Origin
  legend=(notitle
    autoitemsize /* make the color swatches bigger
      based on legend values' font size */
    noborder)
  markerattrs=(symbol=CircleFilled) /* to see color well,
    markers need more mass than an open circles */
  diagonal=(histogram normal) /* delete DIAGONAL=
    to get the axis values as in Figure 10-7 */
  ellipse=(type=predicted);
run;
```

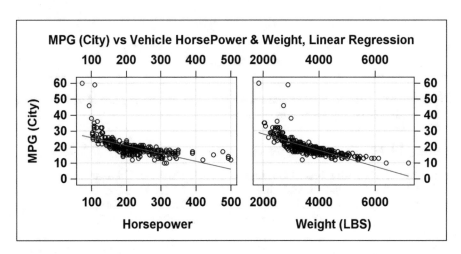

Figure 10-9. Using COMPARE statement with one Y variable and two X variables and linear regression

A smaller font than the 11pt used would leave a bit more space for the plotting area, but with no significant improvement in the distinguishability of individual plot markers. At 8pt, there would be no additional axis values or grid lines.

Listing 10-9. *Code used to create Figure 10-9*

```
ods listing style=GraphFontArial11ptBold gpath="C:\temp" dpi=300;
ods graphics on / reset=all scale=off width=5.7in height=2.8in
  imagename="Fig10-9_1Yvar2Xvars_Reg_COMPARE";
title1 justify=center
  'MPG (City) vs Vehicle HorsePower & Weight, Linear Regression';
proc sgscatter data=sashelp.cars;
compare y=MPG_City x=(HorsePower Weight) /
  reg=(degree=1 lineattrs=(color=red thickness=1px))
  spacing=10 refticks=(values) grid;
run;
```

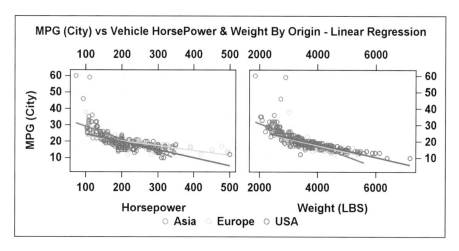

Figure 10-10. Using COMPARE statement with one Y variable and two X variables and a group variable. Linear regression is by group values

Listing 10-10. *Code used to create Figure 10-10*

```
ods listing style=GraphFontArial10ptBold gpath="C:\temp" dpi=300;
  /* a larger font size would thin the Y axis to three values */
ods graphics on / reset=all scale=off width=5.7in height=2.8in
  imagename="Fig10-10_1Yvar2Xvars_GroupVarUsedForReg_COMPARE";
title1 justify=center
  'MPG (City) vs Vehicle HorsePower & Weight By Origin - Linear Regression';
proc sgscatter data=sashelp.cars
  datacontrastcolors=(gray turquoise magenta); /* for markers */
compare y=MPG_City x=(HorsePower Weight) / group=Origin
  legend=(noborder notitle)
  markerattrs=(symbol=Circle) /* With a GROUP variable,
    the default symbol would vary by GROUP value.
    All Circles is a better choice. Color distinguishes. */
  reg=(degree=1
```

```
  lineattrs=(pattern=Solid) /* With a GROUP variable,
  the default line pattern would vary by GROUP value.
  All Circles is a better choice. Color distinguishes. */
  )
spacing=10 refticks=(values) grid;
run;
```

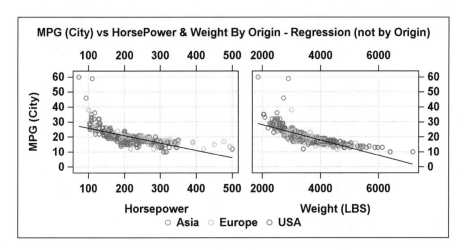

Figure 10-11. Using COMPARE statement with one Y variable and two X variables and group variable. Linear regression ignores the group variable. Same regression as Figure 10-9

Listing 10-11. *Code used to create Figure 10-11, changes from Figure 10-10 in bold*

```
ods listing style=GraphFontArial10ptBold gpath="C:\temp" dpi=300;
  /* a larger font size would cause a title line break,
     and thin the Y axis to four values */
ods graphics on / reset=all scale=off width=5.7in height=2.8in
  imagename="Fig10-11_1Yvar2Xvars_GroupVarIgnoredForReg_COMPARE";
title1 justify=center
  'MPG (City) vs HorsePower & Weight By Origin - Regression (not by Origin)';
proc sgscatter data=sashelp.cars
  datacontrastcolors=(gray turquoise magenta);
compare y=MPG_City x=(HorsePower Weight) / group=Origin
  legend=(noborder notitle)
  markerattrs=(symbol=Circle)
  reg=(degree=1
    nogroup /* ignore group for regression */
    lineattrs=(
      color=black /* otherwise, first color in palette (gray) */
      thickness=1px))
  spacing=10 refticks=(values) grid;
run;
```

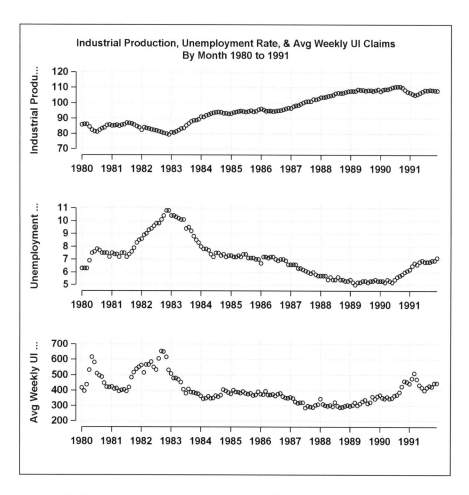

Figure 10-12. Monthly time series plot for three different measures over 12 years using PROC SGSCATTER with the PLOT statement

Though PROC SGSCATTER is lacking in some graphic controls, Figure 10-12 shows it as a visual tool to discover correlations. That said, it should be mentioned that Figures 8-21 and 8-22 provide that capability, with a different format and tool, but limited to two Y variables. Another way to provide the ability to look for correlations by date for three Y variables is shown in Figure 10-13, as a side-by-side comparison with a reduced copy of Figure 10-12. The two alternatives shown in Figure 10-13 can be extended to any number of plot lines.

Listing 10-12. *Code used to create Figure 10-12*

```
/* requires a prior run of Listing 10-0 to create input data */

ods listing style=GraphFontArial9ptBold gpath="C:\temp" dpi=300;
   /* larger font would cause thinning of Y axis values */
ods graphics on / reset=all scale=off width=5.7in height=5.7in
   imagename="Fig10-12_TimeSeriesPlotsOneColumn3Yvars144Months";
title1 justify=center
   'Industrial Production, Unemployment Rate, & Avg Weekly UI Claims';
title2 justify=center 'By Month 1980 to 1991';
proc sgscatter data=sasuser.EconomicData;
plot (IP LHUR LUINC)*Date / columns=1
   axisextent=data grid minorgrid;
label Date='00'X; /* only way to make the label invisible */
run;
```

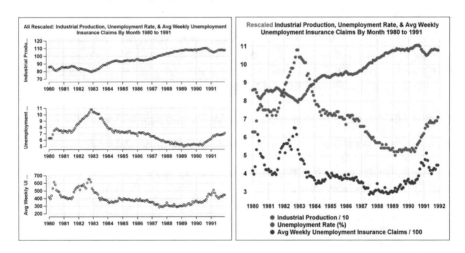

Figure 10-13. Left: Reduced copy of Figure 10-12 (data using PROC SGSCATTER with the PLOT statement). Right: Same data (rescaled) using PROC SGPLOT with the SCATTER statement

---

Note   Both images were created at full-page width, but shrunk to fit after insertion into the page.

The overlay plot in the right-hand-side image in Figure 10-13, using PROC SGPLOT with the SCATTER statement, provides a more direct visual comparison of the Y value for any date (year-month) than do the three separate panels created with PROC SGSCATTER and the PLOT statement. And estimating the Y values involves using only one axis list of values. However, to create the overlay plot requires more coding and rescaling two of the variables to be able to display all data points on the same Y axis. For *this* data, the PROC SGSCATTER method does require the use of a smaller font, but at full size in Figure 10-12, the font size is not a readability obstacle.

The overlay displayed in Figure 10-12 is for an X variable which is a date. Of course, it could be any data type. For example, the overlay method with PROC SGPLOT and the SCATTER statement can produce an alternative to a one-column version of Figure 10-4 for European Vehicle Length, HorsePower, and MPG (City) versus MSRP. The Length and HorsePower variables would need to be rescaled with division by ten to be able to share the Y axis with MPG (City).

PROC SGSCATTER and the PLOT or COMPARE statement are nevertheless indispensable to create a panel of one Y variable versus multiple X variables, or a panel of multiple Y variables versus multiple X variables. And the MATRIX statement is the only available ODS Graphics tool to do what it does.

Listing 10-13. *Code used to create an image at the right in Figure 10-13*

```
/* requires a prior run of Listing 10-0 to create input data */

data work.IPtoMerge work.LHURtoMerge work.LUINCtoMerge;
keep CitiVar CitiValue Date;
length CitiVar $ 5  CitiValue 8;
set sasuser.EconomicData;
CitiVar = 'IP';
CitiValue = IP / 10;
output work.IPtoMerge;
CitiVar = 'LHUR';
CitiValue = LHUR;
output work.LHURtoMerge;
CitiVar = 'LUINC';
CitiValue = LUINC / 100;
output work.LUINCtoMerge;
run;

data work.ToPlot;
set work.IPtoMerge work.LHURtoMerge  work.LUINCtoMerge;
run;
```

```
proc format;
value $CitiVarName
  'IP' = 'Industrial Production / 10'
  'LHUR' = 'Unemployment Rate (%)'
  'LUINC' = 'Avg Weekly Unemployment Insurance Claims / 100';
quit;

ods listing style=GraphFontArial11ptBold gpath="C:\temp" dpi=300;
ods graphics on / reset=all scale=off width=5.7in height=5.7in
  imagename=
  "Fig10-13Right_TimeSeriesOverlayPlotFor3GroupValuesOver144Months";
title1 justify=center color=magenta 'Rescaled ' color=black
    'Industrial Production, Unemployment Rate, & Avg Weekly Unemployment
Insurance Claims By Month 1980 to 1991';
proc sgplot data=work.ToPlot noborder;
where 1980 LE YEAR(Date) LE 1991;
styleattrs datacontrastcolors=(blue red purple);
scatter y=CitiValue x=Date / Group=CitiVar
  markerattrs=(symbol=CircleFilled);
yaxis display=(nolabel noline noticks)
  grid minorgrid minorcount=9
  values=(3 to 11 by 1)
  offsetmin=0.05 offsetmax=0.05;
xaxis display=(nolabel noline noticks) grid
  valueattrs=(size=10pt);
keylegend / title='' noborder autoitemsize;
format CitiVar $CitiVarName.;
run;
```

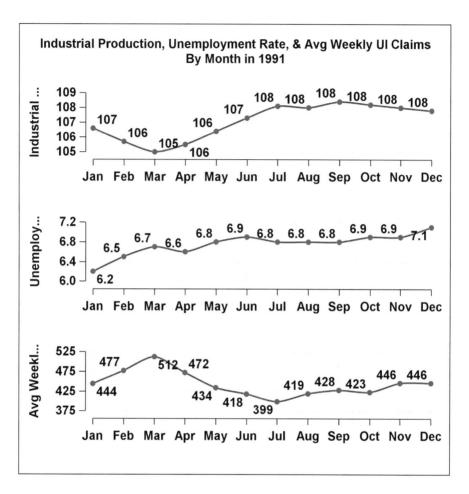

Figure 10-14. Twelve-month time series plot for three measures with data labels using PROC SGSCATTER with the PLOT statement

As could be expected, limiting the number of months makes data labels feasible. It is likely that they are also feasible for a few years, rather than just one year, especially if the image width were increased. Though it adds no communication value, and there are no between-month numbers with plot points represented by the connecting curve, the curve demonstrates the effect of using the SMOOTHCONNECT suboption of the JOIN option that connects the dots.

Listing 10-14. Code used to create Figure 10-14

```
/* requires a prior run of Listing 10-0 to create input data */

ods listing style=GraphFontArial11ptBold gpath="C:\temp" dpi=300;
ods graphics on / reset=all scale=off width=5.7in height=5.7in
  imagename=
  "Fig10-14_TimeSeriesPlotsOneColumn3Yvars12MonthsDataLabels";
title1 justify=center
  'Industrial Production, Unemployment Rate, & Avg Weekly UI Claims';
title2 justify=center 'By Month in 1991';
title3 color=white 'white space';
proc sgscatter data=sasuser.EconomicData;
where YEAR(Date) EQ 1991;
plot (IP LHUR LUINC)*Month /
  columns=1
  join=(smoothconnect /* not jagged */
        lineattrs=(color=red thickness=2px))
  markerattrs=(symbol=CircleFilled color=blue size=9px)
  datalabel axisextent=data grid;
label Month='00'X; /* Using a blank instead yields the VarName */
format IP 3.; /* keep IP data labels shorter, but sufficient */
run;
```

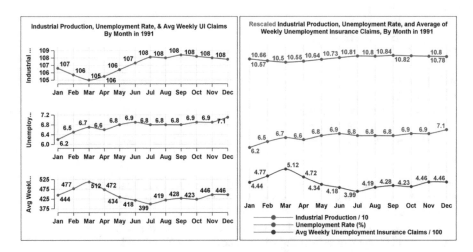

Figure 10-15. Left: Reduced copy of Figure 10-14 (data using PROC SGSCATTER with the PLOT statement). Right: Same data (rescaled) using PROC SGPLOT with the SERIES statement

Note   Both images were created at full-page width, but shrunk to fit after insertion into the page.

The overlay using PROC SGPLOT with the SERIES statement provides more direct visual comparison for any month. Creating the overlay requires more coding and rescaling two of the variables to be able to display all data points on the same Y axis. Unlike the case of Figure 10-12 for a plot of 144 months, the font for the PROC SGSCATTER method is the same as that for the PROC SGPLOT method. So there is no readability difference, but only the difference of three separate plots stacked in an image versus a three-line overlay plot as the image.

In the case of *this* overlay, the lines are sufficiently separated due to the distance in the data values, so that there is no chance of data label collisions. In the general case, especially if there were no need to rescale any of the variables to get all of the variables' plot points into the same Y axis range, data label collisions between lines might be a problem—to which the PROC SGSCATTER solution is always immune due to its physically separated plotting areas.

Listing 10-15. *Code used to create an image at the right in Figure 10-15*

```
/* requires a prior run of Listing 10-13
   to create the input data set work.ToPlot */

data work.ToPlot1991;
set work.ToPlot;
where YEAR(Date) EQ 1991;
Month=put(Date,monname3.);
run;

proc format;
value $CitiVarName
  'IP' = 'Industrial Production / 10'
  'LHUR' = 'Unemployment Rate (%)'
  'LUINC' = 'Avg Weekly Unemployment Insurance Claims / 100';
quit;

ods listing style=GraphFontArial11ptBold gpath="C:\temp" dpi=300;
ods graphics on / reset=all scale=off width=5.7in height=5.7in
  imagename=
"Fig10-15Right_TimeSeriesOverlayPlotDataLabelsGroupValues12Months";
title1 justify=center color=magenta 'Rescaled ' color=black
  'Industrial Production, Unemployment Rate, and Average of Weekly Unemployment
Insurance Claims, By Month in 1991';
title2 color=white 'white space';
proc sgplot data=work.ToPlot1991 noborder;
styleattrs datacontrastcolors=(blue red purple);
series y=CitiValue x=Month / Group=CitiVar
  datalabel markers
  markerattrs=(symbol=CircleFilled size=7px)
  lineattrs=(pattern=solid thickness=2px)
```

```
  smoothconnect; /* not jagged */
yaxis display=none values=(4 to 11 by 1)
  offsetmin=0.05 offsetmax=0.05;
xaxis display=(nolabel noline noticks) grid;
keylegend / title='' noborder autoitemsize;
format CitiVar $CitiVarName.;
run;
```

Summary

For a single, standalone scatter plot, use PROC SGPLOT and the SCATTER statement, unless you need the REFTICKS option and are willing to accept the limitations of PROC SGSCATTER and the PLOT statement. However, see Listing A10-1 in Appendix A for code to emulate REFTICKS when using PROC SGPLOT and the SCATTER statement.

To construct a composite of multiple scatter plots, PROC SGSCATTER and its PLOT or COMPARE statements can deliver a panel of plots for (a) one Y variable versus multiple X variables (Figures 10-2 and 10-3), (b) multiple Y variables versus one X variable (Figure 10-4), or (c) all of the combinations of multiple Y variables versus multiple X variables (Figures 10-5 and 10-6). The MATRIX statement can take any number of variables, such as A, B, and C, and display scatter plots for A versus B, B versus A, A versus C, C versus A, B versus C, and C versus B in a matrix (Figure 10-7). The MATRIX statement can display distributions of each of the variables in the diagonal cells of the matrix, but with a loss of the axis values (Figure 10-8). The scatter plots and the diagonal cell plots require different axis values. The only single panel solution to this quandary is to web-enable the matrix with ODS HTML5, which can at least serve up the precise numbers as data tips (mouseover text). ODS HTML5 is the subject of Chapter 14.

The options of the PLOT and COMPARE statements are mostly the same, but the PLOT statement has some extra ones. It permits control of the shape of the panel with ROWS= and COLUMNS= options. For this reason, each cell in a PLOT panel is independent, and each cell carries its own axis labels and tick mark values, as in Figure 10-5. The COMPARE panel is always laid out as an NY by NX matrix, where NY is the number of rows which is the number of Y variables and NX is the number of columns which is the number of X variables. See, for comparison, the COMPARE panel in Figure 10-6. For a COMPARE panel, there are Y variable labels and tick mark values only at the left side of the panel, and X variable labels and tick mark values only at the bottom of the panel. Both PLOT and COMPARE support the REFTICKS option, but for a PLOT panel, that takes up a lot of space inside the panel, whereas for a COMPARE panel, the duplication only occurs at the right and top edges of the panel. Even without REFTICKS present, in a PLOT panel there is less plot drawing space in each cell than a COMPARE panel. With REFTICKS, that difference is greater.

Figures 10-12 to 10-15 demonstrate that the function of a one-column PLOT panel for scatter plots of multiple Y variables versus one X variable can also be served by a PROC SGPLOT overlay plot. An SGPLOT solution always requires more coding and will usually require scaling some of the Y variables to assure that all Y variables can use the same Y axis range of values. The advantage of this alternative is that the plot points are more directly comparable. However, if data labels are to be used, with an overlay there is possibility of collisions, label-with-label and/or label-with-line. These examples were time series plots, but the method is feasible for any type of X variable.

There are features and options for PROC SGSCATTER and its three statements that were not used in this chapter. For complete information, see the *SAS ODS Graphics Procedures Guide*.

CHAPTER

11

Fits and Confidence Plots

Fits and confidence plots are intended to provide visual insights into the relationship between X and Y variables.

ODS Graphics PROC SGPLOT and PROC SGPANEL provide tools for fit and confidence plots with these statements: ELLIPSE, REG, LOESS, PBSPLINE, and SPLINE.

ELLIPSE produces a confidence ellipse for the mean and a prediction ellipse derived from the input data.

REG produces a regression line or curve (of degree 1, 2, or 3) overlaid on its own scatter plot.

LOESS produces a nonlinear fit line overlaid on its own scatter plot of the data. It supports locally weighted polynomial regression and smoothing.

PBSPLINE produces a penalized B-spline curve overlaid on its own scatter plot of the data.

© LeRoy Bessler 2023
LeR. Bessler, *Visual Data Insights Using SAS ODS Graphics*,
https://doi.org/10.1007/978-1-4842-8609-8_11

■ Note   It is important to realize that, though the REG, LOESS, and PBSPLINE statements can display the plot points and data labels, some markers and/or some data labels can get overwritten by the lines that are drawn by these three statements. So, the best approach is to use the NOMARKERS option and to omit using the DATALABEL option and to include a SCATTER statement as the last drawing statement in the PROC step to draw the markers and data labels last, so that they overlay any lines that pass through the same space.

SPLINE creates a smooth curve using a quadratic Bézier spline interpolation. The creation process first connects all of the points, each pair a straight line. This jagged start is then smoothed into a curve. (If you create an overlay of a SERIES plot and a SPLINE plot, you can see the relationship between process start and end.)

(For PROC SGSCATTER, the PLOT and COMPARE statements have options for ELLIPSE, REG, LOESS, and PBSPLINE, which produce similar results (but with some feature differences not to be discussed here) as the statements with those names for PROC SGPLOT and PROC SGPANEL.)

REG and PBSPLINE statements have confidence options, CLI and CLM, for individual value confidence limits and mean value confidence limits. LOESS has only a mean value confidence limits option. SPLINE has no confidence limits.

Both LOESS and PBSPLINE provide options to specify the degree of local polynomials for the regression and to specify a custom smoothing technique to override the default smoothing.

Unlike the REG, LOESS, and PBSPLINE statements, ELLIPSE and SPLINE do not display the input data points. For them, data point markers can be added to the results with a SCATTER statement in the PROC step. The REG, LOESS, and PBSPLINE statements can add data labels. When using ELLIPSE and SPLINE, the SCATTER statement can be used to add data labels.

Only SGPLOT statement–based methods are shown in this chapter.

Details about all of these SG procedures, statements, and options for fits and confidence plots, and complete information about syntax, are provided in the *SAS ODS Graphics Procedures Guide*.

General Remarks About Code Used

The following framing code has been more expansively discussed in Chapter 3 in the section "Outer Structure of ODS Graphics Code in Examples." The framing code for all examples in this chapter and others is

```
ods results off; /* verify results by opening the image file,
                    rather than using the SAS Output window */
ods _all_ close; /* avoid unintended consequences
                    and superfluous concurrent output */
< ODS LISTING statement here >
< example-specific code here >
ods listing close; /* ALWAYS Best Practice */
```

For brevity, the example code in listings omits the first two lines and the last one. It is best to add them back at your runtime. (Source code files include them.)

The ODS LISTING statement can vary. All of the examples in this chapter use a statement of the following form to specify the text characteristics:

```
ods listing style=GraphFontArial11ptBold gpath="C:\temp" dpi=300;
```

but sometimes with a font size other than 11pt. The statement assumes that the ODS style GraphFontArial11ptBold has been created. To assure that all of the styles needed in this chapter are available, use this code:

```
%include "C:\SharedCode\AllGraphTextSetup.sas";
%AllGraphTextSetup(8);
%AllGraphTextSetup(11);
```

For more information about ODS custom styles, as well as the source code for the AllGraphTextSetup macro, see the section "Control of Text Attributes with a Custom ODS Style" in Chapter 3. For information about options for direct control of text attributes, which can override the default text attributes that are set up by an ODS style, see the section "Text Attributes Control in ODS Graphics" in Chapter 3.

ELLIPSE

For the ELLIPSE statement, TYPE=MEAN creates a confidence ellipse for the population mean, and TYPE=PREDICTED (which is the default) creates a confidence ellipse for a new observation not already in the input data set. It is assumed that both X and Y have a normal distribution. The default value of ALPHA is 0.05, for a 95% confidence level.

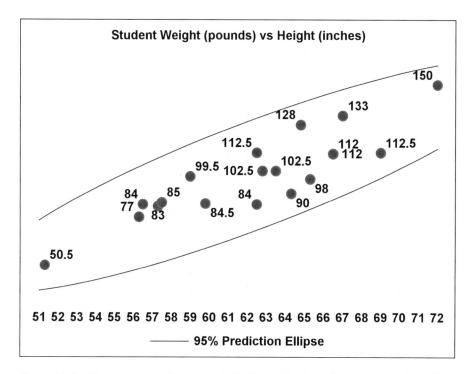

Figure 11-1. Custom scatter plot with default ellipse. (The legend's description of the ellipse is supplied by software based on the choice of ellipse type and the value of alpha.)

In a graph with only one plot line color in use, the line need not be thickened to assure color distinguishability. The blue outline of the red markers could be thickened to make their outline color more conspicuous, but, even at 1 pixel, the outline color is distinguishable from the black of the 1 pixel thick ellipse boundary.

In this example, all of the markers are inside the ellipse. For a smaller confidence level (larger ALPHA value), the ellipse is smaller and would be more likely to overlay some markers and/or data labels. With this 95% confidence level, a different input data set might incur overlays. Overlays can be avoided by always locating the SCATTER statement after any ELLIPSE statement(s) in the PROC SGPLOT step. Such placement is *not* used in Listing 11-1.

Listing 11-1. *Code used to create Figure 11-1*

```
ods listing style=GraphFontArial11ptBold gpath="C:\temp" dpi=300;
ods graphics on / reset=all scale=off width=5.7in
  imagename="Fig11-1_CustomScatterPlotwithELLIPSEdefaults";
title1 'Student Weight (pounds) vs Height (inches)';
proc sgplot data=sashelp.class noborder;
scatter x=height y=weight /
  datalabel
  FilledOutlinedMarkers
  markerfillattrs=(color=red)
  markerattrs=(symbol=CircleFilled size=9pt)
  markeroutlineattrs=(color=blue thickness=1px);
ellipse x=height y=weight /
  name='EllipsePlot' /* to be able to limit the scope
    of the legend to a line and description of the ellipse.
    Otherwise the legend would also display a marker
    and its explanation. */
  /* CLIP option can be used to assure that
     the range of the ellipse is ignored
     when software chooses the axis ranges.
     Clipping is always in effect for PROC SGPANEL.
     In THIS example,
     ranges are set with XAXIS & YAXIS statements.
     So, the ellipse is forcibly clipped. */
  type=PREDICTED /* This is the default.
    MEAN is the alternative. */
  alpha=.05; /* This is the default.
    Specifies 95% confidence level for the ellipse. */
yaxis display=none;
xaxis display=(noline noticks nolabel) grid
  values=(51 to 72 by 1);
keylegend 'EllipsePlot' / title='' noborder;
run;
```

Rather than create a standalone confidence ellipse or experiment with other values for Alpha, next is a scatter plot with both ellipse types. (If interested, you can modify the code in Listing 11-1 and verify that increasing the value of ALPHA will cause the size of the ellipse to decrease. When fewer data points are included in the ellipse, the confidence level decreases.

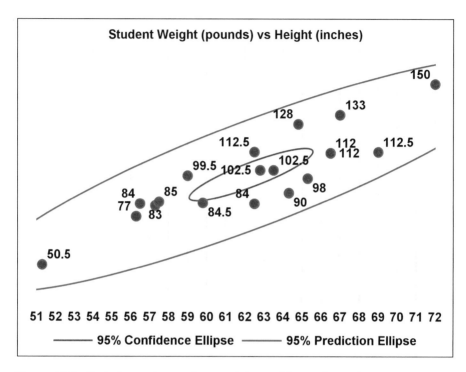

Figure 11-2. Both the prediction ellipse and the confidence ellipse. (See comment in the code listing for how data labels avoided being obscured by the confidence line.)

Listing 11-2. *Code used to create Figure 11-2*

```
ods listing style=GraphFontArial11ptBold gpath="C:\temp" dpi=300;
ods graphics on / reset=all scale=off width=5.7in
  imagename=
"Fig11-2_CustomScatterPlotAndConfidenceAnePredictionEllipses";
title1 'Student Weight (pounds) vs Height (inches)';
proc sgplot data=sashelp.class noborder;
ellipse x=height y=weight /
  name='EllipseForMean' type=MEAN
  lineattrs=(color=red thickness=2px); /* for first ELLIPSE statement in the
PROC step, the default line pattern is solid */
ellipse x=height y=weight /
  name='EllipseForPredicted' type=PREDICTED
  lineattrs=(color=blue thickness=2px
             pattern=Solid); /* presence of first ellipse
    triggers a dashed line without this PATTERN override. */
/* NOTE: Run the SCATTER statement AFTER the ELLIPSE statements
    to assure that the data labels overlay the ellipse lines
    for easy readability of the numbers. */
scatter x=height y=weight /
  datalabel
```

```
FilledOutlinedMarkers
markerfillattrs=(color=red)
markerattrs=(symbol=CircleFilled size=9pt)
markeroutlineattrs=(color=blue thickness=1px);
yaxis display=none;
xaxis display=(noline noticks nolabel) grid
  values=(51 to 72 by 1);
keylegend 'EllipseForMean' 'EllipseForPredicted' /
  title='' noborder;
run;
```

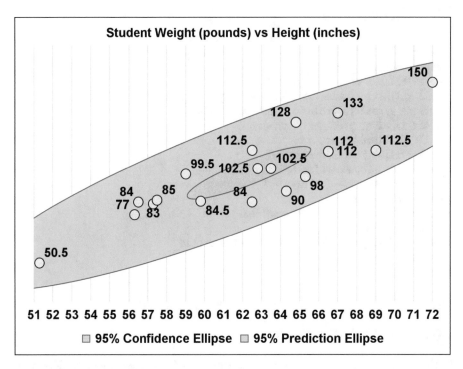

Figure 11-3. Ellipses with interior color fill. (See comments in the code listing about the importance of the order of statements.)

If you feel it is not obvious from the title that data labels are Weight values, the LEGEND statement can omit the two NAME values for the ELLIPSE statements, and the legend will also include a yellow marker with the identifier "Weight."

Listing 11-3.　*Code used to create Figure 11-3*

```
ods listing style=GraphFontArial11ptBold gpath="C:\temp" dpi=300;
ods graphics on / reset=all scale=off width=5.7in
  imagename="Fig11-3_CustomScatterPlotBothEllipsesWithFills";
title1 'Student Weight (pounds) vs Height (inches)';
proc sgplot data=sashelp.class noborder;
/* NOTE: The two ELLIPSE statements and the SCATTER statement
   must run in the order as below. This assures that
   the inner ellipse overlays fill for the outer ellipse, and
   markers and data labels overlay fill for the inner ellipse. */
ellipse x=height y=weight /
  name='EllipseForPredicted' type=PREDICTED
  fill fillattrs=(color=CXCCCCFF) /* very light blue */
  outline lineattrs=(color=blue pattern=Solid);
ellipse x=height y=weight /
  name='EllipseForMean' type=MEAN
  fill fillattrs=(color=CXFFCCCC) /* light very red */
  outline lineattrs=(color=red pattern=Solid);
scatter x=height y=weight / datalabel
  FilledOutlinedMarkers
  markerfillattrs=(color=yellow)
  markerattrs=(symbol=CircleFilled size=9pt)
  markeroutlineattrs=(color=black thickness=1px);
yaxis display=none;
xaxis display=(noline noticks nolabel) grid
  values=(51 to 72 by 1);
keylegend 'EllipseForMean' 'EllipseForPredicted'
  / title='' noborder;
run;
```

Fit Statements for PROC SGPLOT (and PROC SGPANEL)

In this section, the focus is on using statements for fits with PROC SGPLOT.

There are four fit statements: REG, LOESS, PBSPLINE, and SPLINE. The first three will draw not only the fit line or curve, and any associated confidence lines and confidence area fills, but also markers and data labels. Since their fit line or curve, etc. might overwrite markers and/or data labels, it is best to use a SCATTER statement at the bottom of the PROC step to draw markers and data labels last, after all of the lines have been drawn. The markers from the fit statement can be declined with the NOMARKERS option, and the DATALABEL option can be omitted on the fit statement. For the SPLINE statement, such an end-of-PROC-step SCATTER statement is the only way to get markers and optionally data labels.

Figure 11-4 is an overlay of all four fits, using their defaults, except for line color and pattern control used in pursuit of distinguishability in this plot that is rather crowded. No options that change the shape of the fit from the default fit are used.

For the SPLINE statement, there are no options. For REG, the only choices are DEGREE equal to 2 or 3 for a quadratic or cubic fit. LOESS and PBSPLINE offer more controls for the fit, but they will not be explored here. The SPLINE process first connects the dots in pairs with line segments and then smooths that result. For a simulation of what that first step looks like, in the code for Figure 11-4, remove the REG, LOESS, and PBSPLINE statements and insert this statement:

```
series x=height y=weight / lineattrs=(color=red);
    name='series' legendlabel='Simulatedf Spline First Step'
    markers markerattrs=(symbol=CircleFilled color=red);
```

and change the KEYLEGEND statement thus:

```
keylegend 'series' 'spline' / noborder;
```

In the result for a SPLINE fit, of course, that starting series line is omitted, as is the case in Figure 11-4.

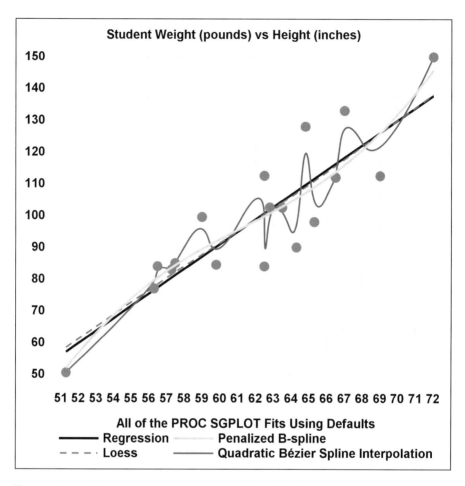

Figure 11-4. All fits that can be created with PROC SGPLOT, using defaults

Listing 11-4. *Code used to create Figure 11-4*

```
proc sort data=sashelp.class out=work.SortedForSPLINE;
by height; run; /* NOTE: The SORT is essential
                   to avoid a chaotic result for the SPLINE fit. */

/* NOTE: It is more generally the case that three PROC SGPLOT statements,
SERIES, SPLINE, and STEP, all must have their input data sorted by the X
variable to deliver the result as expected. */

ods listing style=GraphFontArial11ptBold gpath="C:\temp" dpi=300;
ods graphics on / reset=all scale=off width=5.7in height=5.7in
imagename=
```

```
  "Fig11-4_SGPLOT_OverlayOfAllFourFitOptionsWithDefaults";
title1 justify=center 'Student Weight (pounds) vs Height (inches)';
proc sgplot data=work.SortedForSPLINE noborder;
reg x=height y=weight / name='reg' nomarkers
  lineattrs=(color=black thickness=3px)
  /* Default PATTERN is Solid. Any additional lines drawn
     in the PROC step will default to non-Solid patterns. */
  /* Thickness of this line is largest
     bacause the LOESS curve will coincide with it
     at the higher X values. */
  degree=1; /* Linear Regression. This the default.
                Alternatives are 2 (Quadratic) & 3 (Cubic). */
loess x=height y=weight / name='loess' nomarkers
  lineattrs=(color=CXFF00FF thickness=2px pattern=Dash)
  /* Using PATTERN=DASH so that the LOESS curve is more easily
     seen when it is very near or on the REG line. */
  degree=1 /* The degree of the local polynomials
                 to use for each local regression.
                 This the default. Alternative is 2. */
  interpolation=linear; /* The degree of the
              interpolating polynomials that are used for blending
              local polynomial fits at the kd tree vertices.
              Default is LINEAR. Alternative is CUBIC. */
spline x=height y=weight / name='spline'
  legendlabel='Quadratic Bézier Spline Interpolation'
  /* default label is the name (or label) of the Y variable */
  lineattrs=(color=blue thickness=2px pattern=Solid);
/* run PBSPLINE with markers last in PROC step
   to assure that markers overlay any fit lines */
pbspline x=height y=weight / name='pbspline'
  markerattrs=(color=gray symbol=CircleFilled size=9pt)
  lineattrs=(color=CX00FFFF thickness=3px pattern=Solid)
  degree=3; /* Specifies the degree of the spline transformation
                Default is 3. Range is 0 to 10. */
keylegend 'reg' 'loess' 'pbspline' 'spline' / noborder down=2
  title='All of the PROC SGPLOT Fits Using Defaults' noborder;
yaxis grid display=(noline noticks nolabel)
  values=(50 to 150 by 10);
xaxis grid display=(noline noticks nolabel)
  values=(51 to 72 by 1) fitpolicy=none;
run;
```

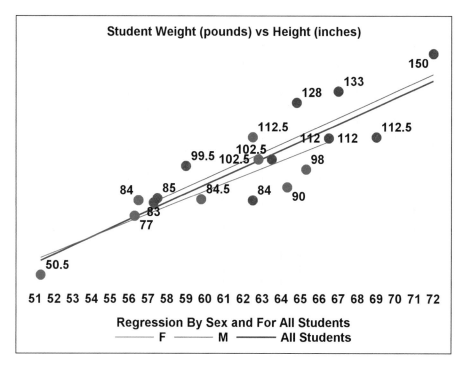

Figure 11-5. Regression by group and regression for all

Listing 11-5. *Code used to create Figure 11-5*

```
ods listing style=GraphFontArial11ptBold gpath="C:\temp" dpi=300;
ods graphics on / reset=all scale=off width=5.7in
  imagename="Fig11-5_RegressionByGroupVarAndRegressionForAll";
title1 'Student Weight (pounds) vs Height (inches)';
proc sgplot data=sashelp.class noborder;
styleattrs datacontrastcolors=(blue red);
reg x=height y=weight /
  name='RegOfAll' legendlabel='All Students'
  nomarkers /* Let the SCATTER statement display them. */
  lineattrs=(thickness=2px pattern=Solid color=purple)
  /* Solid line is default for first REG statement. */
  degree=1;
reg x=height y=weight / group=Sex
  name='RegByGroup' /* Any LEGENDLABEL would be disregarded. */
  nomarkers /* Let the SCATTER statement display them. */
  lineattrs=(thickness=1px pattern=Solid)
  /* Let GROUP processing and
     STYLEATTRS DATACONTRASTCOLORS determine line colors. */
  /* By default, second line drawn would not be DASHED. */
  degree=1;
/* By running SCATTER statement last in the PROC step,
```

```
  no markers and no data labels can be overwritten
  by the regression lines. */
scatter x=height y=weight / group=Sex
  datalabel datalabelattrs=(color=black)
  markerattrs=(symbol=CircleFilled size=9pt);
yaxis display=none;
xaxis display=(noline noticks nolabel) grid
  values=(51 to 72 by 1);
keylegend 'RegByGroup' 'RegOfAll' /
  title='Regression By Sex and For All Students'
  noborder fillheight=11pt fillaspect=GOLDEN;
run;
```

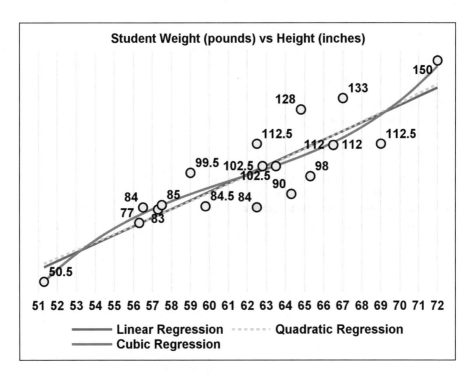

Figure 11-6. Regression for degree equal to 1, 2, and 3

Listing 11-6. *Code used to create Figure 11-6*

```
ods listing style=GraphFontArial11ptBold gpath="C:\temp" dpi=300;
ods graphics on / reset=all scale=off width=5.7in
  imagename="Fig11-6_LinearAndQuadraticAndCubicRegression";
title1 'Student Weight (pounds) vs Height (inches)';
proc sgplot data=sashelp.class noborder;
reg x=height y=weight /
  name='linear' legendlabel='Linear Regression'
```

```
      nomarkers
      lineattrs=(color=CXFF00FF thickness=3px) /* Solid by default */
      degree=1;
    reg x=height y=weight /
      name='quadratic' legendlabel='Quadratic Regression'
      nomarkers
      lineattrs=(color=CX00FFFF thickness=3px pattern=ShortDash)
      /* For this data, the degree=2 fit in many places
         partially or fully overlays the degree=1 fit.
         Using a high contrast color and a ShortDash pattern
         makes it easier to see both of the fits. */
      degree=2;
    reg x=height y=weight /
      nomarkers
      name='cubic' legendlabel='Cubic Regression'
      lineattrs=(color=gray thickness=3px pattern=Solid)
      degree=3;
    scatter x=height y=weight /
      datalabel
      FilledOutlinedMarkers
      markerattrs=(symbol=CircleFilled size=9pt)
      markerfillattrs=(color=yellow)
      markeroutlineattrs=(color=black thickness=2px);
    yaxis display=none;
    xaxis display=(noline noticks nolabel) grid
      values=(51 to 72 by 1);
    keylegend 'linear' 'quadratic' 'cubic' /
      noborder fillheight=11pt fillaspect=GOLDEN;
    run;
```

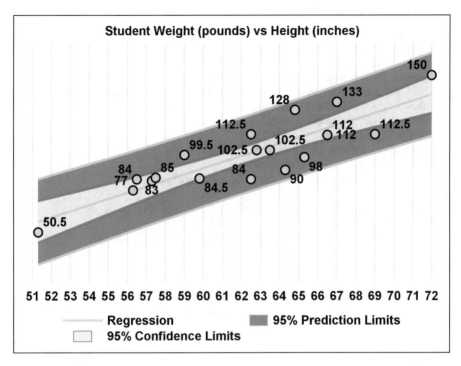

Figure 11-7. Regression using both of the confidence options, and with maximum, but effective, use of color

Listing 11-7. *Code used to create Figure 11-7*

```
ods listing style=GraphFontArial11ptBold gpath="C:\temp" dpi=300;
                /* All text is 11pt. */
ods graphics on / reset=all scale=off width=5.7in
  imagename="Fig11-7_LinearRegressionWithCLMandCLI";
title1 'Student Weight (pounds) vs Height (inches)';
proc sgplot data=sashelp.class noborder;
reg x=height y=weight /
  name='reg' /* So the legend can be limited to REG. It needs
    nothing to explain markers from the SCATTER statement. */
  nomarkers /* The REG statement runs. Then the SCATTER statement
    runs. The markers & data labels from the SCATTER statement
    cannot be overwritten by lines from the REG statement. It could
    overwrite its the markers if it created them. */
lineattrs=(color=LightGray thickness=3px)
  /* The regression line is overlaid by Black data labels.
    Light Gray instead of, say, Black, avoida
    a visual clash with the data labels.
    Since the regression is a focus of the graph,
    no viewer is in danger of not noticing it
    despite its being Light Gray. */
```

```
clm clmattrs=(fill clmfillattrs=(color=Yellow)
      outline clmlineattrs=(color=Green thickness=3px))
Cli cliattrs=(fill clifillattrs=(color=CXFF66FF)
      outline clilineattrs=(color=CX00FFFF thickness=3px))
degree=1 /* The degree of the polynomial fit. 1 is the default.
  This is a straight line. Other possible values are 2-10. */
alpha=.05; /* This is the default. */
scatter x=height y=weight / datalabel
  FilledOutlinedMarkers
  markerattrs=(symbol=CircleFilled size=9pt)
  markerfillattrs=(color=LightGray)
  markeroutlineattrs=(color=black thickness=2px);
yaxis display=none;
xaxis display=(noline noticks nolabel) grid values=(51 to 72 by 1);
keylegend 'reg' / noborder fillaspect=GOLDEN
  fillheight=11pt; /* match the height of the descriptions */
run;
```

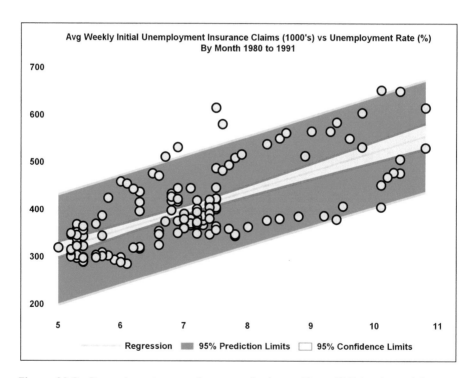

Figure 11-8. Regression using same features and colors as Figure 11-7, but for real data

For background information about the input data used here, in Chapter 8 please see the section "Special Data Sets Used for Some Time Series Graphs." If your site does not have SAS/ETS, you must download the zip file CitiData.zip from https://github.com/Apress/Visual-Data-Insights-Using-SAS-ODS-Graphics and store the five unzipped files in folder C:\CitiData. Whichever is the case, the first step in Listing 11-8 is to extract the data that is used here. My SAS site does *not* have SAS/ETS.

Listing 11-8. *Code used to create Figure 11-8, changes from Figure 11-7 in bold*

```
/* To prepare sasuser.EconomicData */
%include "C:\SharedCode\ExtractEconomicData.sas";
options mprint;
%ExtractEconomicData
(SASETSsiteUseSASHELPDataLib=NO,
OtherSiteFolderForCitiData=C:\CitiData,
OutLib=SASUSER);

ods listing style=GraphFontArial8ptBold gpath="C:\temp" dpi=300;
                  /* All text is 8pt. */
ods graphics on / reset=all scale=off width=5.7in
   imagename="Fig11-8_LinearRegressionUsingRealData";
title1 "Avg Weekly Initial Unemployment Insurance Claims (1000's) vs
Unemployment Rate (%)";
title2 'By Month 1980 to 1991';
proc sgplot data=sasuser.EconomicData noborder;
reg x=LHUR y=LUINC / name='reg' nomarkers
lineattrs=(color=LightGray thickness=3px)
  clm clmattrs=(fill clmfillattrs=(color=Yellow)
       outline clmlineattrs=(color=Green thickness=3px))
  Cli cliattrs=(fill clifillattrs=(color=CXFF66FF)
       outline clilineattrs=(color=CX00FFFF thickness=3px))
  degree=1 alpha=.05;
scatter x=LHUR y=LUINC / /* DATALABEL not used. Points too dense */
  FilledOutlinedMarkers
  markerattrs=(symbol=CircleFilled size=9pt)
  markerfillattrs=(color=LightGray)
  markeroutlineattrs=(color=black thickness=2px);
yaxis display=(noline noticks nolabel);
xaxis display=(noline noticks nolabel); /* No GRID, No VALUES= */
keylegend 'reg' / noborder fillaspect=GOLDEN
  fillheight=8pt; /* match the height of the descriptions */
run;
```

Summary

ODS Graphics provides several ways, ELLIPSE, REG, LOESS, PBSPLINE, and SPLINE statements, to try to show the possible relationship between two numeric variables in a data set. All of the PROC SGPLOT/PROC SGPANEL statements, except SPLINE, have confidence limit options.

Though the REG, LOESS, and PBSPLINE statements can display markers for the data points and support the DATALABEL option, if you wish to prevent overlay of markers and/or data labels, it is best to use the NOMARKERS option and omit using the DATALABEL option. Instead, create markers and data labels with a SCATTER statement after the fit statement in the PROC step.

The ELLIPSE and SPLINE statements do not create markers, and, therefore, have no DATALABEL option. With those statements also, create markers and data labels with a SCATTER statement after the ELLIPSE or SPLINE statement in the PROC step.

Distributions, Histograms, Box Plots, and Alternative Tools

Distributions of a response variable can be created with ODS Graphics PROC SGPLOT and PROC SGPANEL, using HISTOGRAM, HBOX, VBOX, and DENSITY statements. This chapter also shows several ways to do that, and to do it more informatively, with NEEDLE, SERIES, SCATTER, and FRINGE statements. Besides the obvious use of those statements, this chapter relies on several macros, which use NEEDLE, SERIES, and SCATTER statements "under the covers" to create solutions that are otherwise unavailable from ODS Graphics. In addition, the PDF function and SERIES statement are used to create a Normal Distribution.

© LeRoy Bessler 2023
LeR. Bessler, *Visual Data Insights Using SAS ODS Graphics*,
https://doi.org/10.1007/978-1-4842-8609-8_12

As always, an important objective here is to present precise numbers, not just a visual. But with usually a high density of data points in the image, the precise numbers cannot be displayed for the points.

Histograms are widely used visual tools. They are, in effect, vertical bar charts with the horizontal axis used for subranges of a numeric variable, which are called bins, rather than for categories. The bins serve as the categories, but the HISTOGRAM statement, not the VBAR statement, is used to draw the chart. When the number of distinct values is small enough, the bins can be assigned one value each (including any multiple instances of that value), but that is neither a typical use of a histogram nor the default outcome from HISTOGRAM statement use. There is no fixed default when none of the bin controls of the HISTOGRAM are used. The default selected is a function of the characteristics of the data. Getting a desired configuration when bin controls are specified is not a guaranteed outcome.

Four macros are provided and demonstrated which *do* provide dependable histogram outcomes. Three other macros are also provided and demonstrated. One is for the Informative Box Plot, which is for horizontal box plots. Another is for an alternative to vertical box plots. The third delivers the Actual Distribution, with or without a normal distribution overlay, and, in both cases, with precise values for statistics as well as visual markers of where those statistics are located on the Actual Distribution plot.

The macros are offered as black boxes to do the work without their user needing to see or know the code details, just like the purpose of SAS procedures and SAS functions. They can be adapted to data sets other than those from the SASHELP data library that are used in the examples, and using the macro options differently if desired.

Box plots, drawn with the HBOX (horizontal box plot) or VBOX (vertical box plot) statement, are a compact way to visually present the *location* of statistics (mean, median, etc.). More informative than the standard output is the Informative Box Plot.

A fringe plot is a simple, but useful, tool that shows you *where the data is really distributed*, with short vertical lines along the X axis. Values with multiple occurrences in the data set are represented by the same fringe. The fringe plot shows you where the data is, but it is not a frequency plot.

The DENSITY statement is available, but it is not used in this chapter.

If one wishes to draw a Normal Distribution curve for a data set, the PDF function can create the list of Y values for the input X values, using as added input the mean and standard deviation. After sorting the output by X, the SERIES statement can draw the curve, either in a standalone plot or as an overlay, but not as an overlay with output from the HISTOGRAM statement.

The most informative tool to present and understand the distribution of a variable provided in this chapter is a macro to create the Actual Distribution with visuals and statistics. It can optionally draw a Normal Distribution overlay. Rather than try to summarize or enumerate what all the macro delivers, the results themselves in Figures 12-16 and 12-19 are the best description. The images show and tell the viewer anything that is likely to be of interest, with precision, clarity, and visuals.

General Remarks About Code Used

Several examples have %INCLUDE statements for code or macros from folder C:\SharedCode, which could instead be any folder or location of your choice.

The following framing code has been more expansively discussed in Chapter 3 in the section "Outer Structure of ODS Graphics Code in Examples." The framing code for all examples in this chapter and others is

```
ods results off; /* verify results by opening the image file,
                    rather than using the SAS Output window */
ods _all_ close; /* avoid unintended consequences
                    and superfluous concurrent output */
< ODS LISTING statement here >
< example-specific code here >
ods listing close; /* ALWAYS Best Practice */
```

For brevity, the example code in listings omits the first two lines and the last one. It is best to add them back at your runtime. (Source code files include them.)

The ODS LISTING statement can vary. All of the examples in this chapter use a statement of the following form to specify the text characteristics:

```
ods listing style=GraphFontArial11ptBold gpath="C:\temp" dpi=300;
```

but often with font sizes other than 11pt. The statement assumes that the ODS style GraphFontArial11ptBold has been created. To assure that all of the styles needed in this chapter are available, use this code:

```
%include "C:\SharedCode\AllGraphTextSetup.sas";
%AllGraphTextSetup(7);
%AllGraphTextSetup(8);
%AllGraphTextSetup(9);
%AllGraphTextSetup(10);
%AllGraphTextSetup(11);
```

For more information about ODS custom styles, as well as the source code for the AllGraphTextSetup macro, see the section "Control of Text Attributes with a Custom ODS Style" in Chapter 3. For information about options for direct control of text attributes, which can override the default text attributes that are set up by an ODS style, see the section "Text Attributes Control in ODS Graphics" in Chapter 3.

Box Plots and the HBOX and VBOX Statements

Box plots are a very compact way of showing the distribution of the data introduced by John Tukey in 1970. They are also known as box and whisker plots or box and whiskers plots.

Box plots are often used, but they are a tool for the initiated. For the SAS programmer, the documentation for the HBOX and VBOX statements comes with a diagram and detailed explanation of how to interpret the box plot. The viewer of a traditional box plot only gets the, for me, *inscrutable* box plot. What does it all *mean*?

There is a DISPLAYSTATS option for the box plot statements. In principle, it can deliver up to 13 statistics, but the default is only 3. For a horizontal box plot, the horizontal table of 13 statistics squashes the box plot into unusability. Also, the software may decide that it cannot fit all of the statistics requested and, if so, delivers a truncated table next to the unusable box plot. A vertical box plot, with a tall enough image, will deliver all 13 statistics in a vertical table, with a vertically compressed box plot. The box plot statistics table contains the underinforming presence of the pairs DataMin and Min, and DataMax and Max, as descriptions.

Furthermore, when outliers are included in the display and the DATALABEL option is used, if one does not use the OFFSETMAX and OFFSETMIN options on the XAXIS statement, the data labels for the most extreme outliers might be clipped off and/or some of the less extreme data labels might be overlaid.

The code in this section addresses the clipping and overlay problems. Basic horizontal box plots are presented, followed by the Informative Box Plot as an alternative. The remainder of the discussion will let the images speak for themselves, which is what I contend that they always should do. Two of box plots do not have much to say. The Informative Box Plot is self-explanatory. It answers every relevant question, inaudibly.

See Figure 12-20 for an alternative to the VBOX statement.

The Basic Box Plot

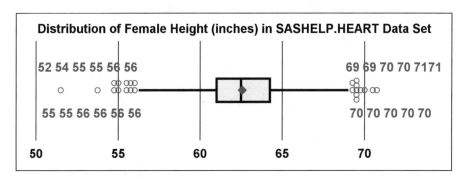

Figure 12-1. Basic box plot with outliers (automatic), data labels requested, offset for X axis max, optional grid, thickened lines, optional red and yellow

Except for outliers, this plot, without an explanation, is notably uninformative. The right end of the X axis is offset so that the data labels equal to 71 are permitted to appear and so that overlays of data labels equal to 70 are eliminated.

Listing 12-1. Code used to create Figure 12-1

```
ods listing style=GraphFontArial11ptBold gpath="C:\temp" dpi=300;
ods graphics on / reset=all scale=off width=5.7in height=2in
  imagename="Fig12-1_BasicBoxPlotIncludingOutliersAndDataLabels";
title1
'Distribution of Female Height (inches) in SASHELP.HEART Data Set';
proc sgplot data=sashelp.heart noborder;
where Sex EQ 'Female' AND Height NE .;
hbox Height /
  datalabel datalabelattrs=(color=blue)
  /* data labels are provided only for the outliers */
  spread /* not always really needed,
    only has effect if there are duplicate outlier values */
  fillattrs=(color=yellow)
  medianattrs=(color=black thickness=3px) /* Make this thicker
    if too hidden when overlaid by the mean red diamond.
    With this image height, enough of the median line is exposed
    above and below the mean diamond */
  meanattrs=(color=red symbol=DiamondFilled)
  lineattrs=(thickness=3px)
  whiskerattrs=(thickness=3px)
  nocaps /* no bars at the ends of the whiskers */
  outlierattrs=(color=blue symbol=Circle); /* open circles are more
    distiguishable when overlaid */
```

```
xaxis display=(noline noticks nolabel)
  offsetmax=0.16 /* needed to reveal missing data labels
                     and to eliminate data label overlays */
  grid gridattrs=(color=black); /* black to increase visibility */
format Height 2.; /* rounded from 5.2 (format in the source data)
  to reduce data label collisions */
run;
```

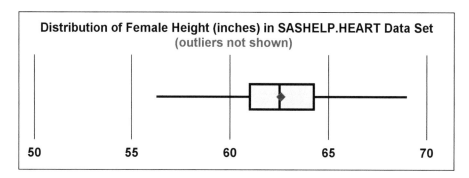

Figure 12-2. Same box plot as Figure 12-1, but without outliers

Without outliers displayed, the minimum and maximum values are unknown.

Listing 12-2. Code used to create Figure 12-2

```
ods listing style=GraphFontArial11ptBold gpath="C:\temp" dpi=300;
ods graphics on / reset=all scale=off width=5.7in height=2in
  imagename="Fig12-2_BasicBoxPlotWithOutliersSuppressed";
title1
  'Distribution of Female Height (inches) in SASHELP.HEART Data Set'
  color=blue ' (outliers not shown)';
proc sgplot data=sashelp.heart noborder;
where Sex EQ 'Female' AND Height NE .;
hbox Height / nooutliers
  fillattrs=(color=yellow)
  medianattrs=(color=black thickness=3px)
  meanattrs=(color=red symbol=DiamondFilled)
  lineattrs=(thickness=3px)
  whiskerattrs=(thickness=3px)
  nocaps;
xaxis display=(noline noticks nolabel)
  grid gridattrs=(color=black);
run;
```

It is possible to do box plots more informatively, with and without outliers.

Building an Informative Box Plot

There are two ways to enhance, decode, and add utility to a box plot, using a macro to put everything needed all together in a self-explanatory image, an image that talks to the viewer, though inaudibly.

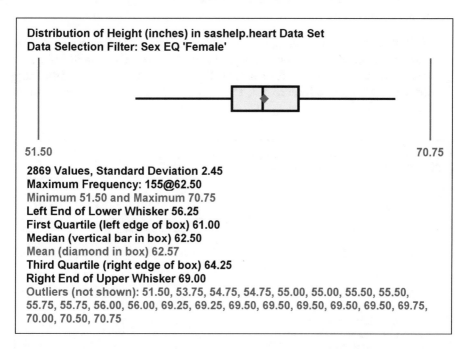

Figure 12-3. The Informative Box Plot, with outliers listed but not displayed

Listing 12-3. Code used to create Figure 12-3

```
/* The macro creates all of the macro variables to dynamically
   complete the subtitle and the footnotes. */

%include "C:\SharedCode\InformativeBoxPlot.sas";
options mprint;

ods listing style=GraphFontArial10ptBold gpath="C:\temp" dpi=300;
%InformativeBoxPlot(
subtitle=%str(), /* not used here */
data=sashelp.heart,
where=%str(Sex EQ 'Female'),
var=height,
varlabel=%str(Height (inches)),
format=5.2, /* format in the source data */
ShowOutliers=N, /* Y is the default.
```

If using Y, be sure to read the discussion in the code
for Figure 12-4, or inside the macro source code. */
imagename=Fig12-3_InformativeBoxPlotWithOutliersSuppressed,
imagewidth=5.7in,
/* the image height is set so that black median line
is less obscured by the red mean diamond */
imageheight=4in);

Figure 12-4 shows the outliers and all of the statistics, but with less precision. Less precision reduces data label collisions. In any case, with the list of every (precise) outlier value in the footnote of Figure 12-3, there is no compelling reason to show the outliers, but the option is available and is used in Figure 12-4.

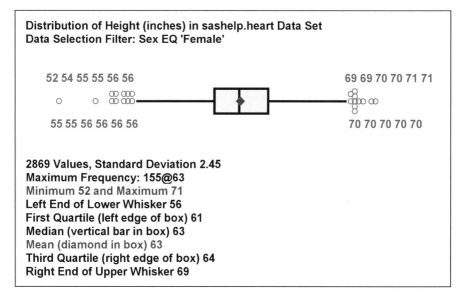

Figure 12-4. Informative Box Plot, but instead of listing precise outliers, showing the outliers and with less precision in the numbers to reduce data label collisions

NOTE The macro invocation for the first run to create Figure 12-4 omitted the use of the Xaxisoffsetmax option. The result suffered clipping of the rightmost data labels and overlay of rightmost data labels that were not clipped. Even if you have no interest using the outliers-suppressed version of the box plot in an image like Figure 12-3, that image's complete list of outliers provides evidence as to whether or not your outliers-shown version of the box plot is in fact complete. So, if creating a box plot with outliers and data labels, it is best to first create it with the outliers turned off to be able to verify the integrity of your ultimate result.

Listing 12-4. *Code used to create Figure 12-4*

```
%include "C:\SharedCode\InformativeBoxPlot.sas";
options mprint;

ods listing style=GraphFontArial10ptBold gpath="C:\temp" dpi=300;
%InformativeBoxPlot(
subtitle=%str(),
data=sashelp.heart,
where=%str(Sex EQ 'Female'),
var=height,
varlabel=%str(Height (inches)),
format=2., /* rounded from 5.2 (format in the source data)
   to reduce data label collisions */
ShowOutliers=Y, /* If Y, one or both offsets might be needed,
   to prevent clipping of the most extreme outlier data labels.
   A prior run of this macro with N will present a complete
   list of all of the outliers in FOOTNOTE10 of the image.
   That list can be compared with the output from this run.
   Increasing the offset can also eliminate data label overlays. */
Xaxisoffsetmax=0.16, /* needed to reveal missing data labels
                        and to eliminate data label overlays */
Xaxisoffsetmin=, /* not needed for this example */
imagename=Fig12-4_InformativeBoxPlotIncludingOutliersAndDataLabels,
imagewidth=5.7in,
/* need less vertical space without the outliers footnote */
imageheight=3.5in);
```

Comparing the Informative Box Plot, with and Without Outliers

The Informative Box Plot created here is equally communication-effective, in terms of image and numbers, with and without outliers displayed in the plot. It is a matter of preference. Seeing the outliers visually does offer the advantage of visual comparison, unlike just listing them. The listing option avoids any possible problem of collisions for the data labels or crowding of the markers.

A long list of outliers can cause the footnote to wrap. That is not a real problem. There is a limit of 256 characters on the length of the footnote, but when that limit is reached, the alternative of data labels for the outliers might be a worse problem. To cope with this perhaps improbable situation of a string of outliers longer than 256 characters, there is the option to modify the macro source code to move the outliers to subtitles, where statements TITLE3 through TITLE10 are available. Of course, there might be situations where the number and individual character lengths of the outliers exceed the capacity to list them in 2048 characters. In that case, ignoring and suppressing the outliers eliminates the problem. They can be listed in a tabular report instead.

Effective Use of the Basic Box Plot

Figure 12-5 does not deliver any precise numbers, but is useful for a quick, easy visual comparison of distributions for different values of a category variable (presuming that the viewer has already been initiated into how to interpret it). One could provide a companion tabular listing of the statistics, but a composite of box plots and table must be constructed with an ODS destination other than LISTING.

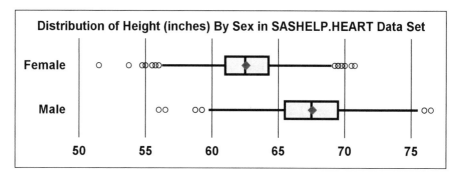

Figure 12-5. Box plots by category. No precise numbers, but an easy, quick visual comparison that can be applied to any number of category values

No data labels are provided for the outliers, but precise knowledge of them is perhaps less important than being able to visually compare the box and whiskers for the categories in the box plot stack.

Listing 12-5. Code used to create Figure 12-5

```
ods listing style=GraphFontArial11ptBold gpath="C:\temp" dpi=300;
ods graphics on / reset=all scale=off width=5.7in height=2in
  imagename=
  "Fig12-5_BasicBoxPlotByCategory_WithOutliersButUnlabeled";
title1
'Distribution of Height (inches) By Sex in SASHELP.HEART Data Set';
proc sgplot data=sashelp.heart noborder;
where Height NE .;
hbox Height / category=Sex
  fillattrs=(color=yellow)
  medianattrs=(color=black thickness=3px) /* Make this thicker
    if too hidden when overlaid by the mean red diamond.
    With this image height, enough of the median line is exposed
    above and below the mean diamond */
  meanattrs=(color=red symbol=DiamondFilled)
  lineattrs=(thickness=3px)
  whiskerattrs=(thickness=3px)
  nocaps; /* no bars at the ends of the whiskers */
```

```
xaxis display=(noline noticks nolabel)
  grid gridattrs=(color=black); /* black to increase visibility */
yaxis display=(noline noticks nolabel);
format Height 5.2; /* format in the source data */
run;
```

Histograms

Histograms offer the charm of being inherently and immediately comprehensible to their viewers and easily constructed to show precise numbers using ODS Graphics. They are the opposite of box plots that require either prior explanation and experience or a companion diagram and definitions to decode and understand them.

The histogram was introduced in the 1890s by Karl Pearson, a mathematician and biostatistician and the founder of mathematical statistics. The concept of grouping data into what histogrammers (my neologism for histogram creators) call bins was explored, but only for tabular reporting, by early demographer and epidemiologist John Graunt already in the seventeenth century.

ODS Graphics provides the HISTOGRAM statement. It has options to specify the layout of the histogram: NBINS option for the number of bins, BINWIDTH for the width of the bins, and BINSTART for the X value of the first bin. All can be omitted, or one or a combination of the options can be specified. For all three options, the default is determined by the system based on the data it finds. The net result is that the output might not be what is expected. The software has a reason for what it does. In the case of NBINS, the documentation contains an explicit warning that the bin count might not be as specified. However, using a value list on the XAXIS statement might help the software deliver what is desired by the histogrammer.

In any case, an arbitrary choice of bin layout might conceal some interesting aspects of the distribution that the delivered bins conceal. Later in the chapter, an unequivocally helpful way to show the distribution of the data will be shown. Before this recommended tool is shown, four innovative histogram solutions, not using the HISTOGRAM statement, are demonstrated.

But first is what can be done with the HISTOGRAM statement itself.

The Basic Histogram

The HISTOGRAM statement has three SCALE options: COUNT (number of observations in the bin), PERCENT, and PROPORTION (count for the bin divided by total count, which is the same as percent divided by 100). The default is PERCENT.

The HISTOGRAM statement has four DATALABEL options: COUNT, PERCENT, PROPORTION, and DENSITY. If a specific value for DATALABEL is not specified, then whatever was assigned for the SCALE is used. The DENSITY data label value is "proportion per unit," calculated as proportion divided by the bin width.

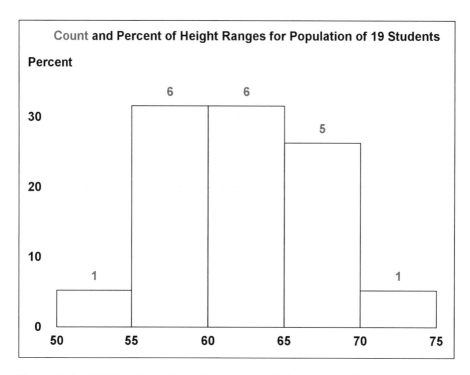

Figure 12-6. *A slightly enhanced basic histogram with default scale and with data labels. It includes color-coded identification for the data labels and a grid*

The histogram reveals the unsurprising relationship between SCALE=PERCENT and DATALABEL=COUNT. The roles of SCALE and DATALABEL can be reversed.

Listing 12-6. *Code used to create Figure 12-6*

```
ods listing style=GraphFontArial11ptBold gpath="C:\temp" dpi=300;
ods graphics on / reset=all scale=off width=5.7in
imagename=
  "Fig12-6_HistogramWithPercentAsScaleAndCountsAsDataLabels";
title1 color=blue "Count" color=black
  " and Percent of Height Ranges for Population of 19 Students";
title2 color=white height=4pt
```

```
"white space: Y axis label would be too close to the title";
proc sgplot data=sashelp.class noborder;
histogram height /
  outline /* This is not reliably the default.
    The default depends on the ODS style in effect.
    OUTLINE turns off the FILL option,
    unless FILL is specified on the HISTOGRAM statement. */
  scale=percent /* SCALE is for the Y axis.
                  PERCENT is the default.
    Other options are COUNT and PROPORTION.
    PROPORTION is the percent divided by 100 */
  datalabelattrs=(color=blue) /* to match reference in title */
  datalabel=count; /* If no value is assigned,
    the data label will be whatever is assigned to SCALE.
    Other options are PERCENT, PROPORTION, DENSITY, AUTO.
    AUTO uses whatever option is used for SCALE. */
xaxis display=(nolabel noline noticks);
yaxis display=(noline noticks) grid
  minorgrid minorcount=9 /* specifying this only because
  knowing values are multiples of ten from a prior run */
  labelpos=top; /* readable without head tilting */
run;
```

Usually, my design preference is to suppress axis labels as superfluous. In this example, numeric measures for the histogram are present in two places, on the Y axis and at the bar ends. The significance of the data labels is identified with a color-coded tie to part of the title. It seems appropriate to be equally explicit as to the significance of the axis values, especially since there are a variety of choices for what can be used as the axis scale and as the data labels.

In Figure 12-7, a straightforward enhancement to the traditional histogram is the use of the ODS Graphics accessory of the FRINGE statement. The fringe plot is a welcome, genuinely informative, visually precise tool, much needed to deliver helpful added information for the clumpy histogram.

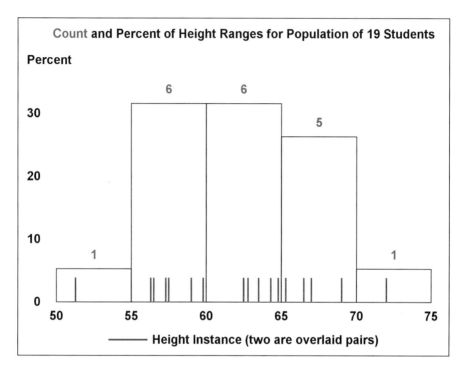

Figure 12-7. The fringe plot overlay shows all of the actual values. A minor grid is provided for the Y values

A suboptimal reality of the fringe plot is that any duplicate values overlay each other and that values which are very close can appear as one value. This is regrettable, but it is useful to see *where the data really is*, rather just a set of clumps that are the standard deliverable of limited information from a traditional histogram. The fringe plot is not a frequency plot.

Listing 12-7. *Changes to code in Listing 12-6 to create Figure 12-7. Replace the image name assignment with*

```
imagename="Fig12-7_HistogramWithFringePlot";
```

After the HISTOGRAM statement, insert two statements:

```
fringe height /
  legendlabel='Height Instance (two are overlaid pairs)'
  height=30px lineattrs=(color=red thickness=2);
keylegend / noborder;
```

For Figures 12-6 and 12-7, the software chose the bin count and boundaries as it deemed best.

A Histogram to Look Deeper

One can *try* to decrease or increase the granularity of the histogram with the NBINS option. Experiments with higher numbers can merely deliver *different* collections of clumps of the values, with no apparent superior choice among results. For *this* data, given the non-huge range of the values, it is reasonable and intuitively appropriate to maximize the granularity, short of getting into fractional inches for the heights. Maximizing histogram granularity for a range of integer values is always a sensible choice when the image width and a readable font make it feasible to display all of the X axis values for the bins. The FITPOLICY=STAGGER option for the XAXIS statement can increase bin count possibilities without thinning the axis values. Of course, thinning the X axis values does not necessarily make the bins without labels impossible to identify. However, counting the unlabeled bins and doing mental arithmetic to determine their identity is not a viewer-desired exercise.

A small number of bins as in Figures 12-6 and 12-7 present less for the viewer to consider, but it can hide important aspects of the distribution-significant finer-grained concentrations that might be important to know about.

Figure 12-8 goes to the finer granularity extreme for this data, but still with bin values that are integers. (The input data is actually to tenths of the inch. That it is not integer inches is apparent from the fringe plot in Figure 12-7.)

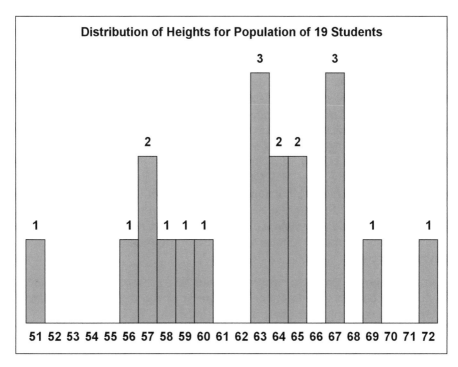

Figure 12-8. The maximally informative histogram for integer values, a histogram with ultimate fine grain

Listing 12-8. Code used to create Figure 12-8

```
ods listing style=GraphFontArial11ptBold gpath="C:\temp" dpi=300;
ods graphics on / reset=all scale=off width=5.7in
  imagename=
  "Fig12-8_HistogramWithOneBinPerIntegerResponseValueOrValueGap";
title "Distribution of Heights for Population of 19 Students";
proc sgplot data=sashelp.class noborder;
histogram height / nbins=22 /* includes empty bins */
  outline /* if omitted, FILL option turns off the outlines */
  fill fillattrs=(color=CX9999FF)
  /* OUTLINE option would cause FILLATTRS to be ignored.
     FILL turns it on.
     Fill is needed to prevent confusion
     between unfilled bars snd spaces
     (e.g., space at height=66) */
  scale=count datalabel=count;
xaxis display=(nolabel noline noticks)
  values=(51 to 72 by 1);
yaxis display=none;
run;
```

By comparing Figure 12-8 with Figure 12-6 (or Figure 12-7), it is clear that the default bin assignment process collected bins 56 to 60 into one bin of six observations, collected bins 63 and 64 and two observations from bin 65 into another bin of six observations, and used the leftover observation in bin 65 to combine with bins 67 and 69 into a third bin, but of five observations. In this data, one *might* want to present six clusters of bins, but they cannot be presented as six bins because bins must be equal width.

The Ultimate Histogram: A Bin for Each (Integer) Value

In many, if not most, cases, rounding the response variable for a histogram to integers is acceptable, and much data is inherently integer as is. The ultimate histogram in Figure 12-9 is created with the OneBinPerIntegerValueInRange macro. The macro's histogram output has a used or empty bin for every integer in the input data range. An empty bin is not an abnormality. There is no data for such a bin.

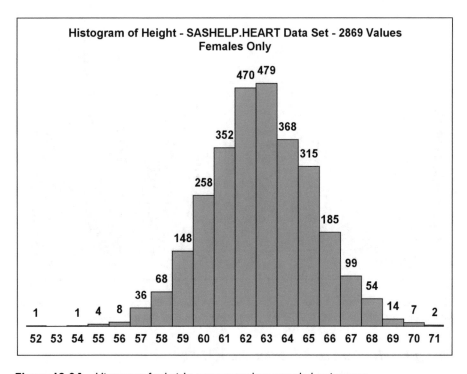

Figure 12-9A. Histogram for height response values rounded to integers

Listing 12-9A. *Code used to create Figure 12-9A*

```
%include "C:\SharedCode\OneBinPerIntegerValueInRange.sas";
options mprint;

ods listing style=GraphFontArial10ptBold gpath="C:\temp" dpi=300;
%OneBinPerIntegerValueInRange(
data=SASHELP.HEART,
where=%str(Sex EQ 'Female'),
var=Height,
RoundedFormat=2.,
stagger=N,
imagewidth=5.7in, imageheight=,
imagename=Fig12-9A_HistogramOneBinPerIntegerResponseValueOrValueGap,
    subtitle=Females Only);
```

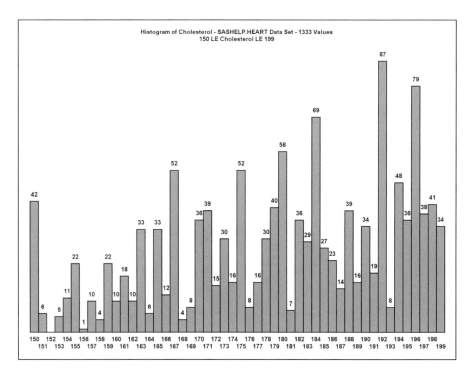

Figure 12-9B. Histogram with 50 bins for response values rounded to integers(5pt font fits data labels and axis values, STAGGER=Y prevents squashing of the axis values)

Listing 12-9B. *Code used to create Figure 12-9B*

```
ods listing style=GraphFontArial5ptBold gpath="C:\temp" dpi=300;
%OneBinPerIntegerValueInRange(
data=SASHELP.HEART,
```

```
where=%str(150 LE Cholesterol LE 199),
var=Cholesterol,
RoundedFormat=3.,
stagger=Y,
imagewidth=5.7in,
imageheight=, imagename=
  Fig12-9B_HistogramOneBinPerIntegerResponseValueOrValueGap,
subtitle=%str(150 LE Cholesterol LE 199));
```

The Significance-Based Histogram: Binning Based on a Rationale

The best way to analyze and display the distribution of the data is not inherently based on bin count, or a choice of bin start and width, or the ultimate histogram.

An intuitively practical way to use a distribution is based on the significance or impact of response values in certain subranges of the total data range: Safe, At Risk, Dangerous; Good and Bad; Low, Medium, High; Short, Typical, Tall. The Significance-based histogram has no limit on the number of bins to be specified.

The creation of such a histogram is supported with the general-purpose HistogramBinsPerBoundaryList macro. For the macro, subranges are described by their upper boundaries. The macro uses a comma-separated list of upper boundaries and a text string of the bin descriptions. Figure 12-10 is a histogram of only three bins, but the macro can support *any* number of bins. The bins are not a fixed width since the bin boundaries are dictated by the boundary definitions, which are determined by significance, not a meaningless, arbitrary bin definition decision.

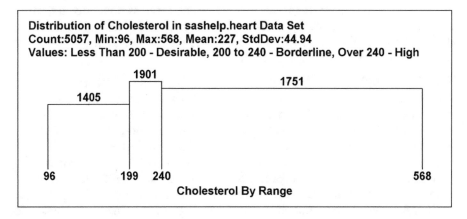

Figure 12-10. Histogram with bins determined by significance and with data labels

Listing 12-10. *Code used to create Figure 12-10*

```
%include "C:\SharedCode\HistogramBinsPerBoundaryList.sas";
options mprint;

ods listing style=GraphFontArial10ptBold gpath="C:\temp" dpi=300;
  /* 11pt font would cause line break in SubRange Descriptions */
%HistogramBinsPerBoundaryList(
BoundaryList=%str(199,240),
SubRangesDescriptions=
  %str(Less Than 200 - Desirable, 200 to 240 - Borderline, Over 240 - High),
Data=sashelp.heart,
Where=,
Var=Cholesterol,
Label=%str(Cholesterol By Range),
XaxisValueFormat=3.,
Format=6.2,
XaxisMinAndMaxOffSets=0.05, /* this is the default */
  /* Make larger if X axis value clipping,
     smaller if too much white space at sides. */
SubTitle=,
Imagename=Fig12-10_HistogramWithSubRangesAsBins,
ImageWidth=5.7in,
ImageHeight=2.5in);
```

The Normality Test Histogram: Seven Bins for Values Within One, Two, and Three Standard Deviations and the Minimum and Maximum

A variation on the significance-based histogram concept is a histogram of seven bins whose boundaries are the minimum and maximum (inevitable boundaries) and boundaries above and below the mean at one, two, and three standard deviations from the mean. If data follows the Normal Distribution, then 68.27%, 95.45%, and 99.73% of the values should be within one, two, and three standard deviations from the mean.

The HistogramBinsBySTDranges macro not only creates a histogram with its intermediate boundaries at those standard deviation–based points but also reports out how many values are within those boundaries. It also reports the value of the standard deviation, the mean, the median, and the most frequent value (the mode). Another characteristic of a Normal Distribution is that the mean, median, and mode should be identical. This straight-on visual and precise number–based investigation of the data is a more reliable alternative than overlaying a histogram with a normal distribution curve. The goodness of fit of a curve to the stepped chart of a histogram's bin bars is *impossible to assess with certainty.*

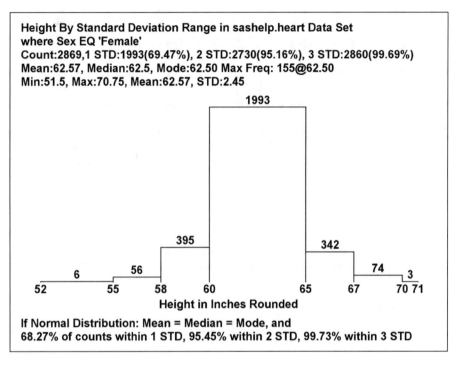

Figure 12-11. Histogram with bins based on standard deviation ranges, with data labels, with all relevant statistics reported, and with explanatory footnotes

Listing 12-11. Code used to create Figure 12-11

```
%include "C:\SharedCode\HistogramBinsBySTDranges.sas";
options mprint;

ods listing style=GraphFontArial10ptBold gpath="C:\temp" dpi=300;
%HistogramBinsBySTDranges(
Data=sashelp.heart,
Where=%str(Sex EQ 'Female'),
Var=Height,
Label=%str(Height in Inches Rounded),
XaxisValueFormat=2.,
Format=5.2,
XaxisMinAndMaxOffSets=0.05, /* the default */
  /* make larger if X axis value clipping,
     smaller if too much white space at sides. */
SubTitle=,
Imagename=Fig12-11_HistogramBinsByStandardDeviationRanges,
ImageWidth=5.7in,
ImageHeight=); /* accepting the default */
```

The Quantiles Histogram: N Bins with All the Same Number of Observations

The title is only sometimes correct. If the total number of observations divided by the number of quantiles (with that quotient rounded up) leaves a remainder, then the last quantile must contain less than the other quantiles.

While the standard histogram consists of bins of equal width with varying observation counts, the quantiles histogram has variable-width bins with equal observation counts. It's a picture of data concentration, showing where the values are closer together (perhaps more frequently repeated) versus where the values are more widely separated.

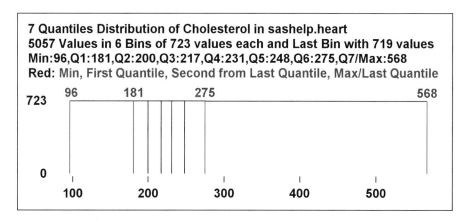

Figure 12-12. Quantiles-based histogram with default axis values

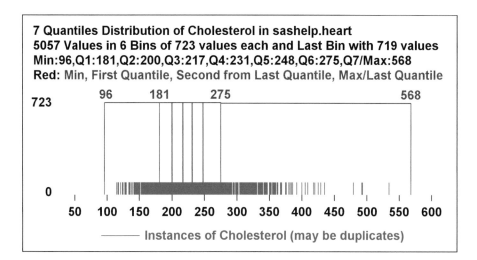

Figure 12-13. Quantiles-based histogram with a fringe plot and custom X axis

The fringe does not show the frequency of each value, only the *presence* of each value with undisclosed multiplicity.

Listings 12-12 and 12-13. *Code used to create Figures 12-12 and 12-13*

```
%include "C:\SharedCode\HistogramWithQuantilesAsBins.sas";
options mprint;

ods listing style=GraphFontArial11ptBold gpath="C:\temp" dpi=300;

%HistogramWithQuantilesAsBins(
Data=sashelp.heart,
Var=Cholesterol,
Format=3.,
QuantileCount=7,
ImageName=Fig12-12_UnFringedSevenQuantilesHistogramWithDefaultXaxis,
ImageWidth=5.7in,
ImageHeight=2.5in);

%HistogramWithQuantilesAsBins(
Data=sashelp.heart,Var=Cholesterol,Format=3.,
QuantileCount=7,
Fringe=Y,
XaxisCustom=Y,
XaxisMin=50,
XaxisMax=600,
XaxisIncrement=50,
XaxisStagger=N, /* (default) If using 75 to 575 by 25,
  XaxisStagger=Y prevents thinning of the axis values. */
ImageName=Fig12-13_FringedSevenQuantilesHistogramWithCustomXaxis,
ImageWidth=5.7in,
ImageHeight=3in);
```

Though the quantiles histogram shows you where the data is stretched or compressed based on quantile bin width, all but one of the remaining examples show you where the data really is, exactly where it is, and how much is there.

How to Display the Actual Distribution

SAS has a PDF statement that can be used to provide an input to the SERIES statement to draw the curve for any one of twenty-five (25) different probability distributions, from Bernoulli to Weibull. They are curves based on formulas.

Though these distributions have their purposes, an Actual Distribution is always of value. A histogram of counts of the contents of bins when the range of the response variable is divided into bins gives a result that is *arbitrary*. Arbitrary might be better than nothing, but an Actual Distribution provides knowledge, understanding, and unambiguity.

My formula (no Greek letter and no mathematical operation symbols necessary) for the Actual Distribution is this:

Y = Frequency(X)

The ActualDist_VisualsAndStatistics macro, in effect, uses *that* mathematical function to create the Actual Distribution shown in Figure 12-16.

Though Figure 12-16 provides more value and information, it is worth using a simple, straightforward alternative, shown in Figure 12-14, to get started in the quest to see clearly the real distribution of the data without underinforming box plots, histograms, or distribution curves that are based on formulas and assumptions about data, which might *not* be relevant. Not all data is normally distributed. (The *not* normal might be the real normal, in terms of relative frequency of occurrence.)

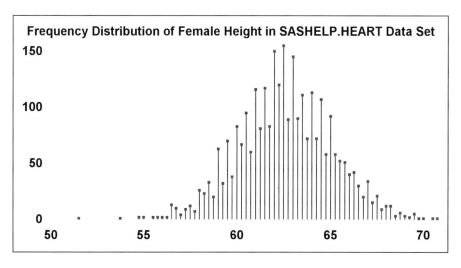

Figure 12-14. The Actual Distribution of female height in the SASHELP.HEART data set, a nearly all-default example

The maximum X axis and Y axis values are beyond the last axis values. This situation and how to amend it are discussed after the next example.

Since very small frequencies (such as the always possible value 1) could be nearly undiscernible, markers are added to the needles.

Listing 12-14. *Code used to create Figure 12-14*

```
data work.Extract(keep=Height);
set sashelp.heart(where=(Sex EQ 'Female' AND Height NE .));
run;

proc summary data=work.Extract nway;
class Height;
var Height;
output out=work.ToPlot(keep=Height _freq_) N=Unused;
run;

/* NOTE: PROC SUMMARY automatically outputs the data in ascending order of
CLASS. If preparing the input the NEEDLE statement by some other method, it
is necessary to sort it, to have it plotted by ascending X. */

ods listing style=GraphFontArial11ptBold gpath="C:\temp" dpi=300;
ods graphics on / reset=all scale=off width=5.7in height=3in
  imagename="Fig12-14_FrequencyDistribution_NearlyDefault";
title
"Frequency Distribution of Female Height in SASHELP.HEART Data Set";
proc sgplot data=work.ToPlot noborder noautolegend;
needle x=Height y=_freq_ / displaybaseline=off
   /* without markers, very small frequencies are barely visible */
   markers markerattrs=(symbol=SquareFilled color=red size=3px);
xaxis display=(noline noticks nolabel);
yaxis display=(noline noticks nolabel);
run;
```

It is easy to do better than Figure 12-14, by making the image taller to fit more Y axis values, displaying them on both sides to decrease the distance between half of the needles to Y axis values, adding Y axis grid lines, and providing more useful X axis values. Though estimating the frequency for a value is still necessary (data labels cannot be fit and be readable), the enhancements help the viewer make a better estimate. Figure 12-15 is a helpful improvement.

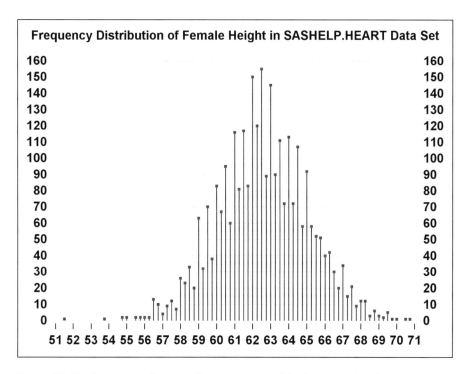

Figure 12-15. Maximizing the ease of interpretation of the frequency distribution, but stopping short of including minor grid lines (which is an additional option)

This chart, unlike all, or almost all, of the prior examples in this book, displays tick marks for the X axis. Given the density of the needles in the chart, tick marks make it easier to estimate the X value for a needle.

The custom axis definitions guarantee that the plot points are "framed" with axis values. Using default axes for Figure 12-14 yields a graph where the last X axis value is outside of the provided axis values in the default range (50 to 70 by 5), and where the highest frequency is beyond the provided Y axis values in the default range (0 to 150 by 50), but these "unframed" needles are displayed. There are unused THRESHOLDAXISMAX=1 and THRESHOLDAXISMIN=1 options for the XAXIS and YAXIS statements, which force any "missing" axis values to be displayed.

If one knows the range of the axis values, then a custom value list can prevent missing axis values. If not, then THRESHOLDAXISMAX=1 and THRESHOLDAXISMIN=1 can be used on the axis statement(s) preemptively. For Figure 12-14, THRESHOLDAXISMAX=1 would have displayed axis value 75 past the maximum value which is unenclosed there, but that would have added a lot of unused width. The better choice is the axis values list used in Figure 12-15.

Listing 12-15. *Code used to create Figure 12-15*

```
data work.Extract(keep=Height);
set sashelp.heart(where=(Sex EQ 'Female' AND Height NE .));
run;

proc summary data=work.Extract nway;
class Height; var Height;
output out=work.ToPlot(keep=Height _freq_) N=Unused;
run;

ods listing style=GraphFontArial11ptBold gpath="C:\temp" dpi=300;
ods graphics on / reset=all scale=off width=5.7in
   /* height=3in
      turn off short height to make more space for Y axis values */
   imagename=
   "Fig12-15_FrequencyDistributionTallerWithMarkersAndCustomAxes";
title1
"Frequency Distribution of Female Height in SASHELP.HEART Data Set";
title2 height=4pt color=white "White Space";
proc sgplot data=work.ToPlot noborder noautolegend;
needle x=Height y=_freq_ / displaybaseline=off;
   /* let the SCATTER statement for the  Y2 axis draw the markers */
scatter x=Height y=_freq_ / y2axis
   markerattrs=(symbol=SquareFilled color=red size=3px);
xaxis display=(noline nolabel) /* display tick marks */
   values=(51 to 71 by 1);
yaxis display=(noline noticks nolabel)
   grid /* with grid lines, ticks are superfluous */
/* NOT USED: minorgrid minorcount=N
   N could be 1 for minor grid lines at 5, 15, . . ., 155
   or N could be 9 for minor grid lines at each integer */
   values=(0 to 160 by 10) fitpolicy=none;
y2axis display=(noline noticks nolabel)
   values=(0 to 160 by 10) fitpolicy=none;
run;
```

Image and Precise Numbers: Showing the Actual Distribution and Its Statistics—with Their Locations

With a little (no, a lot of) help from macros, a much enhanced distribution plot takes the viewer's picture and understanding of the Actual Distribution to a higher level.

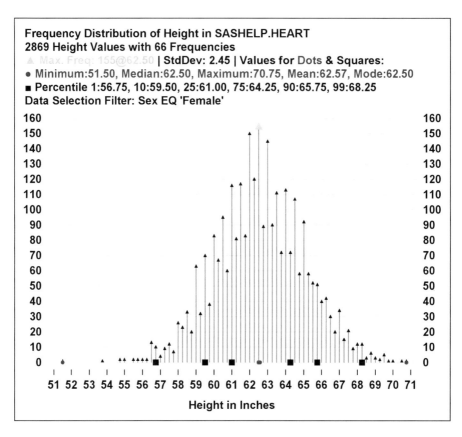

Figure 12-16. Actual Distribution, statistics, and statistics' locations. A maximally self-explanatory deliverable for the viewer

Listing 12-16. *Code used to create Figure 12-16*

```
%include "C:\SharedCode\GetEssentialValues.sas"; /* used inside
                    the ActualDistWithOptionalNormalDist macro */
%include "C:\SharedCode\ActualDistWithOptionalNormalDist.sas";
options mprint;

ods listing style=GraphFontArial10ptBold gpath="C:\temp" dpi=300;
%ActualDistWithOptionalNormalDist(
NormalDistOverlay=N, /* this is the default */
DuplicateYaxisAtRightSide=Y, /* Y is IGNORED if NormalDistOverlay=Y
                    because the Normal Distribution uses that axis. */
Data=SASHELP.HEART,
Where=%str(Sex EQ 'Female'),
Var=Height,
VarLabel=Height in Inches,
Format=F5.2,
```

```
ImageWidth=5.7in,
ImageHeight=5.1in,
XaxisCustom=Y, /* N is the default */
XaxisMin=51,
XaxisMax=71,
XaxisIncrement=1,
XaxisStagger=N, /* this is the default */
YaxisCustom=Y, /* N is the default */
YaxisMax=160,
YaxisIncrement=10,
YaxisGrid=Y, /* N is the default */
ForceYaxisThresholdMax=N, /* this is the default */
ForceXaxisThresholdMin=N, /* this is the default */
ForceXaxisThresholdMax=N, /* this is the default */
   /* If accepting the default X axis with YaxisCustom=N,
      there might not be an X axis value before (after) the first
      (last) needle. It would happen in
      this case for the last axis value.
      To force a missing X axis value to be drawn,
      use ForceXaxisThresholdMin=Y or ForceXaxisThresholdMax=Y
      for the first or last axis value. If the Y axis
      had not been customized, the end of the maximum frequency
      needle would extend beyond the default maximum Y axis value.
      That could be undone with ForceYaxisThresholdMax=Y. */
SubTitle=%str(), /* fill the parentheses when needed */
ImageName=Fig12-16_ActualDistributionAndStatistics);
```

Density Plots

I experimented with the ODS Graphics DENSITY statement, but did not find it satisfactory for my purposes. No examples are provided here.

The Normal Distribution and the PDF Function

A dependable and inherently appropriate tool for drawing a Normal Distribution plot is the combination of the PDF function to prepare the probability density values and a SERIES statement with PROC SGPLOT to draw the curve with X for the response values and Y for the probability density values, as in Figure 12-17.

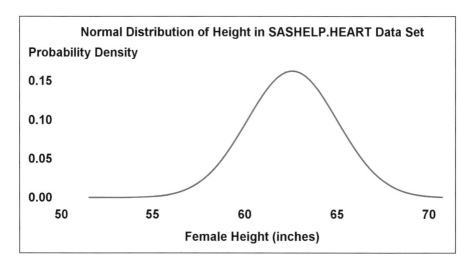

Figure 12-17. Standalone Normal Distribution curve. Density values are created by the PDF function and the PROC SGPLOT SERIES statement draws the curve

Listing 12-17. *Code used to create Figure 12-17*

```
data work.Extract(keep=Height);
set sashelp.heart(where=(Sex EQ 'Female' AND Height NE .));
run;

proc sql noprint;
select mean(Height),std(Height) into :Mean,:STD from work.Extract;
quit;

data work.FromPDF(keep=PDF_Y Height);
set work.Extract;
format PDF_Y best20.;
PDF_Y = pdf("Normal", /* PDF can create 24 other distributions */
            Height, /* the X variable for the subsequent plot */
            &Mean, &STD);
run;

proc sort data=work.FromPDF; /* data must be sorted for the */
by Height;          /* SERIES statement to plot it as desired */
run;

ods listing style=GraphFontArial11ptBold gpath="C:\temp" dpi=300;
ods graphics on / reset=all scale=off width=5.7in height=3in
  imagename="Fig12-17_StandAloneNormalDistribution";
title "Normal Distribution of Height in SASHELP.HEART Data Set";
proc sgplot data=work.FromPDF noborder;
series x=Height y=PDF_Y / smoothconnect
```

```
    lineattrs=(color=blue thickness=2px pattern=Solid);
xaxis display=(noline noticks)
    label='Female Height (inches)';
yaxis display=(noline noticks)
    labelpos=Top /* no head tilting required to read the label */
    label='Probability Density';
run;
```

The Normal Distribution As an Overlay to the Real Distribution

When I created Figure 12-16, I noticed, as shown in the statistics in the subtitles, that the mean, the median, and the mode (the value with the highest frequency) are nearly equal. Equality of those three statistics is a characteristic of a normal distribution.

So I decided that I wanted to see an overlay of the Actual Distribution and a Normal Distribution. Rather than immediately demonstrate such an overlay on the image from Figure 12-16, it can be kept simple as in Figure 12-18.

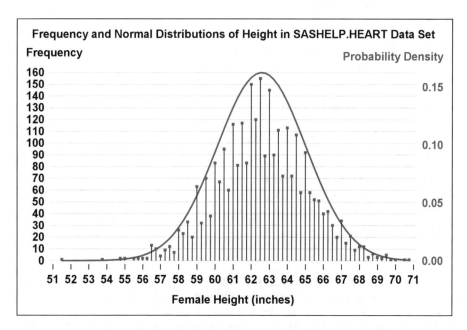

Figure 12-18. Overlay of frequency distribution and normal distribution using a NEEDLE statement for the frequency data and PDF function–created input to a SERIES statement for the normal distribution

To keep it simpler than the code in Listing 12-18, one might have thought that it is possible to overlay the frequency plot with a DENSITY TYPE=NORMAL plot. That yields in the SAS log this message: "ERROR: Attempting to overlay incompatible plot or chart types." The DENSITY statement can be used standalone, that is, not as an overlay. Alternatively, it can be used in an overlay only with a HISTOGRAM statement. A histogram is less helpful, less precise, and less informative than the output of a needle for every distinct value of the X variable.

Listing 12-18. *Code used to create Figure 12-18*

```
/* start code from Listing 12-17 */
data work.Extract(keep=Height);
set sashelp.heart(where=(Sex EQ 'Female' AND Height NE .));
run;

proc sql noprint;
select mean(Height),std(Height) into :Mean,:STD from work.Extract;
quit;

data work.FromPDF(keep=PDF_Y Height);
set work.Extract;
format PDF_Y best20.;
PDF_Y = pdf("Normal", Height, &Mean, &STD);
run;

proc sort data=work.FromPDF; by Height; run;
/* end code from Listing 12-17 */

proc summary data=work.Extract nway;
class Height;
var Height;
output out=work.FreqOut(keep=Height _freq_) N=Unused;
run;

data work.ToPlot;
set work.FromPDF work.FreqOut;
run;

ods listing style=GraphFontArial11ptBold gpath="C:\temp" dpi=300;
ods graphics on / reset=all scale=off width=5.7in height=3.76in
  imagename="Fig12-18_FrequencyAndNormalDistributions";
title "Frequency and Normal Distributions of Height in SASHELP.HEART Data Set";
proc sgplot data=work.ToPlot noborder noautolegend;
series x=Height y=PDF_Y / y2axis smoothconnect
  lineattrs=(color=blue thickness=2px pattern=Solid);
needle x=Height y=_freq_ / displaybaseline=off
  markers markerattrs=(symbol=SquareFilled color=red size=3px);
```

```
xaxis display=(noline) label='Female Height (inches)'
  values=(51 to 71 by 1);
yaxis display=(noline noticks) label='Frequency' labelpos=Top
  values=(0 to 160 by 10) fitpolicy=none grid;
y2axis display=(noline noticks) valueattrs=(color=blue)
  labelattrs=(color=blue)
  label='Probability Density' labelpos=Top;
run;
```

Putting It All Together: Frequency Distribution, Normal Distribution, and Statistics

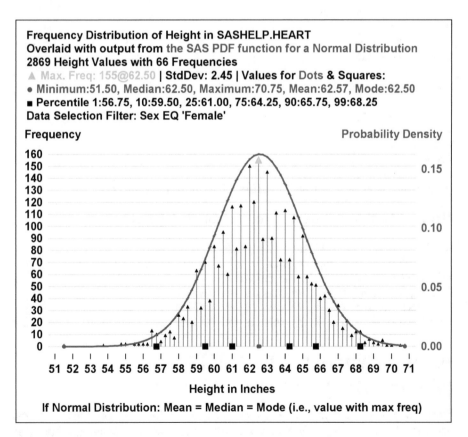

Figure 12-19. Actual Distribution of female height in SASHELP.HEART data set with Normal Distribution overlay

This is Figure 12-16 with the normal distribution curve overlay.

Listing 12-19. *Code used to create Figure 12-19*

```
%include "C:\SharedCode\GetEssentialValues.sas"; /* used inside
                      the ActualDistWithOptionalNormalDist macro */
%include "C:\SharedCode\ActualDistWithOptionalNormalDist.sas";
options mprint;

ods listing style=GraphFontArial10ptBold gpath="C:\temp" dpi=300;
%ActualDistWithOptionalNormalDist(
NormalDistOverlay=Y, /* N is the default */
Data=SASHELP.HEART,
Where=%str(Sex EQ 'Female'),
Var=Height,
VarLabel=Height in Inches,
Format=F5.2,
ImageWidth=5.7in,
ImageHeight=5.1in,
XaxisCustom=Y,
XaxisMin=51,
XaxisMax=71,
XaxisIncrement=1,
YaxisCustom=Y,
YaxisMax=160,
YaxisIncrement=10,
YaxisGrid=Y,
ImageName=Fig12-19_ActualAndNormalDistributionsAndStatistics);
```

Not used for this example, but also available in the macro are

```
SubTitle=%str(), /* fill the parentheses when needed */
YaxisGrid=Y, /* N is the default */
XaxisStagger=N, /* this is the default */
ForceYaxisThresholdMax=N, /* this is the default */
ForceXaxisThresholdMin=N, /* this is the default */
ForceXaxisThresholdMax=N, /* this is the default */
```

An Alternative to the VBOX (Vertical Box) Plot

Please see the section on box plots, which is focused on HBOX plots, horizontal box plots. The VBOX statement was discussed, but not demonstrated. There is no good way to enhance its output similar to what can be done with the InformativeBoxPlot macro for horizontal box plots, as an alternative to the standard HBOX statement output.

Figure 12-20 is offered as an alternative for a vertical presentation of the statistics (without a box, the width of which would have had no significance).

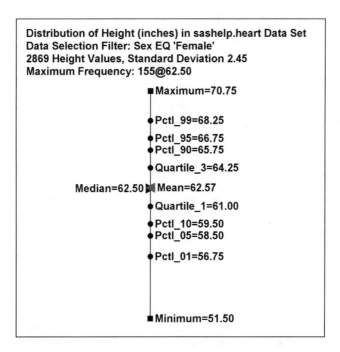

Figure 12-20. An alternative to the VBOX statement's vertical box plot

The macro used does not support the display of outliers. However, it does deliver the maximum frequency and mode (the location of the maximum frequency) in a subtitle, the minimum and maximum, and percentiles 1, 5, 10, 90, 95, and 99, visually and numerically, with the option to suppress any of them other than 10 and 90. Percentiles 10 and 90 are both reliably distant from both the minimum and maximum, and the first and third quartiles, so it is unlikely that there would be a need to suppress them to avoid collisions.

For a wider image, and with font size reduced if needed, the AlternativeToVboxPlot macro could be enhanced to display plots for two (or possibly three) values of category variable, such as Female and Male.

Listing 12-20. *Code used to create Figure 12-20*

```
%include "C:\SharedCode\AlternativeToVboxPlot.sas";
options mprint;

ods listing style=GraphFontArial10ptBold gpath="C:\temp" dpi=300;
%AlternativeToVboxPlot(
subtitle=%str(), /* not used here */
```

```
data=sashelp.heart,
where=%str(Sex EQ 'Female'),
var=Height,
varlabel=%str(Height (inches)),
format=5.2, /* format in the source data */
showP1=Y, /* the default */
showP5=Y, /* the default */
showP95=Y, /* the default */
showP99=Y, /* the default */
imagename=Fig12-20_AlternativeToVboxPlot,
imagewidth=4.275in,
imageheight=4.275in);
```

Summary

This chapter is the result of the exploration and evaluation of the tools in ODS Graphics that are intended to provide insight into how a single variable's values are distributed.

Solutions provided here that require the use of macros make it easy to emulate the examples with your data, not just the SAS sample data sets in the SASHELP data library.

The tools typically used to show the distribution of a single variable are the HISTOGRAM, HBOX, VBOX, and DENSITY statements (no use here of the last one). This chapter makes interesting use of the NEEDLE, SERIES, and SCATTER statements and the PDF function to do more than the standard tools. The FRINGE statement is a helpful accessory for two examples.

The standard box plot is really a visual tool for an already initiated viewer. For the first-time viewer to decode it requires documentation that includes an annotated diagram and descriptions of each feature of the plot. The viewer of a box plot is not referring to the documentation. A communication-effective graph should require no explanation outside of the image.

As a replacement for the conventional horizontal box plot, the Informative Box Plot is as informative as possible, whether the outliers are plotted or not. Compare Figures 12-3 and 12-4 with Figures 12-1 and 12-2. When not plotted, outliers are serially listed in a footnote.

The standard box plot is as a quick easy tool to compare multiple distributions in a stack, as in Figure 12-5.

As an alternative to the vertical box plot, Figure 12-20 provides a slimmer, but very informative, vertical statistical plot.

Histograms never show the real distribution of the data. Instead, there is a tool to show the Actual Distribution, its associated statistics, and their precise location. See Figure 12-16.

A standard histogram is better than nothing, but is underinformative. See Figure 12-6. It can be easily enhanced with a fringe plot (Figure 12-7), to show exactly where the data is, but that accessory overlay cannot reveal the frequency of each fringe's value.

One can improve the insight from a histogram by increasing the granularity, but that eventually prevents annotating the bars with readable data labels.

Figure 12-8 is a feasible annotated example, with 22 bins some of which are empty, that can be created with the HISTOGRAM statement. When feasible, one value per bin is unequivocally informative and can deliver precise numbers. It is precise both visually and numerically. However, the user cannot in general be sure that the NBINS, BINSTART, and BINWIDTH will deliver what is expected, and the HISTOGRAM statement is limited in what it can do.

With the HISTOGRAM statement, one has a choice of accepting the default or picking some arbitrary alternative. Whether N bins or K bins is the better choice is a priori unknowable.

Though my conclusion is that the Actual Distribution is a better data visualization tool than the standard histogram, there are some interesting nonstandard histogram possibilities. Four types of histograms rely on macros with capabilities beyond that of the HISTOGRAM statement.

The ultimate histogram reliably provides a bin for each integer value (see Figure 12-9).

The significance-based histogram does its binning based on a rationale (see Figure 12-10).

The quantiles histogram delivers N bins all for the same number of observations, but with bin width varying as needed according to the subrange of observation values needed to amount to the desired 1/N of the total observations in each bin (see Figures 12-12 and 12-13).

The normality test histogram is a tool to evaluate whether data follows the Normal Distribution (see Figure 12-11).

The normal distribution curve in Figure 12-17 is created with the PDF function to deliver the probability density values using the response data and its mean and standard deviation, with the output used by PROC SGPLOT and the SERIES statement to draw the curve.

Figures 12-14 and 12-15 are, respectively, a basic frequency distribution and a version that is more helpful to the viewer. Both of them are ultra-lean versions of the macro-created Figure 12-16, which has been previously described and is the most widely usable tool in the whole kit.

Figure 12-18 is an overlay of the simple frequency distribution of Figure 12-14 with the normal distribution curve of Figure 12-17. The more information-rich version of that overlay is Figure 12-19, created with the same macro as the standalone, but equally highly informative, frequency distribution that is shown in Figure 12-16.

Two ways are shown that allow one to determine how close to the normal distribution a data set might be (Figures 12-11 and 12-19). For the normal distribution, a better alternative than the DENSITY statement is given (Figures 12-17, 12-18, and 12-19).

That completes the reprise of this chapter's value. Some of the coding is neither concise nor easy, but that code is provided in macros that are as easy to use as any SAS procedure, statement, or function. In any case, what matters is the ease and effectiveness of use of the end product by the viewer, not the complexity of the tool that even the programmer need not see unless interested, or desiring to change and/or enhance it.

Creating Composites of Graphs, Tables, and Text with ODS LAYOUT

The advantages of composites include the ability to present

(a) Alternative graphs for the same data set

(b) A graph with a companion table of precise values which could not be included inside the graph with data labels or an axis table

(c) Any collection of graphs and tables and text

© LeRoy Bessler 2023
LeR. Bessler, *Visual Data Insights Using SAS ODS Graphics*,
https://doi.org/10.1007/978-1-4842-8609-8_13

Item (c) could qualify as what has become called an infographic (not to be confused with what I called an InfoGeographic in 1996—an annotated choropleth map created with PROC GMAP or, if created now using ODS Graphics, with PROC SGMAP).

An infographic is a collection of any mixture of text, tables, graphs, diagrams, and other images in one visual package, often featuring at least one BIG number. The BIG number offers the advantage of offering at least one simple element in the package to let the viewer's eye easily discover something of interest to focus on and for the viewer's mind to instantly understand. The big number is eye comfort, providing visual communication therapy for what might be information overload. You can build an infographic with ODS LAYOUT. This chapter features composite images that are simpler than typical infographics.

To assemble a composite that includes one or more tables, any table can be easily deployed if first packaged as an image. ODS Graphics users can use the ODS PRINTER destination to create a table as an image file.

The combination of ODS LAYOUT and ODS PRINTER is used to assemble a composite of images and to output that composite as an image. The constituent images in the composite can be images created from tables and/or images created with any ODS Graphics SG procedure. For title or footnote text that cannot be embedded with a TITLE or FOOTNOTE statement in a procedure step that creates a graph or table, PROC ODSTEXT and the P statement can be used in the composite building process. Since the composite is an assembly of multiple images, a side-by-side pair of them, for example, might need a common title and/or footnote. A complex composite might need section titles. PROC ODSTEXT and the P statement are the tools to embed them.

Before demonstrating the use of ODS LAYOUT, the first step in this chapter is to create tables as images with ODS PRINTER and PROC PRINT.

The other two SAS report writing procedures, PROC REPORT and PROC TABULATE, can also be used with ODS PRINTER to produce tabular output as an image file.

Many of the SAS procedures that are not explicitly intended as general-purpose report writing tools also produce tables of information. For these procedures, there may be *multiple* tables that are output. They comprise ODS Output Objects. For PROC UNIVARIATE, there are five. How to capture two and display them as an image is shown at the end of this chapter.

For now, the focus is on the old workhorse of SAS software for reporting, PROC PRINT, which is adequate for any simple tabular reporting needs.

For graphs, the ODS GRAPHICS statement has the BORDER/NOBORDER option, where BORDER is the default. When a table is created as an image, the process cannot provide a border. A second step is required to apply the border. (It actually uses PROC GSLIDE from SAS/GRAPH.)

With exceptions only when needed (accomplished with direct text controls), it is always best to use the same font for *everything* in a composite. Bold Arial is suitable for everything—Bold for maximum readability, not for emphasis. Anything in the image that is unimportant is best omitted, not de-emphasized. Omission is the ultimate in de-emphasis of the unimportant. If some part of an image desperately needs emphasis, that can be accomplished with a distinguishing color, rather than a thicker font. Using a bold font for color, as explained in Chapter 2, assures distinguishability of the color and, therefore, the color's effectiveness as a tool for visual emphasis.

If Arial Bold is not sufficient, consider using Arial Black instead.

Just as prior chapters used an ODS style to specify the text characteristics for graphs, this chapter uses an ODS style to control *all* of the text with respect to font family, font size, and font weight. The chapter also uses three derivative styles to (a) assure that all text (backgrounds) of the table contents is black (are white), (b) turn off the table grid, and (c) reduce the height of rows in the table if the grid has been turned off. By "derivative" it means that these additional styles not only include the basic style controls for text characteristics (font family, font size, and font weight) but also add other needed functions.

Progressive Customization of a Table Created As an Image with ODS PRINTER

Male Student Information

Name	Age	Height
Alfred	14	69.0
Henry	14	63.5
James	12	57.3
Jeffrey	13	62.5
John	12	59.0
Philip	16	72.0
Robert	12	64.8
Ronald	15	67.0
Thomas	11	57.5
William	15	66.5

Figure 13-1. Table created as an image, but background for headers is unwanted

To create a table as an image requires the ODS PRINTER destination. For that destination, the default style is PRINTER. In the PROC TEMPLATE code used to customize the table fonts, the PRINTER style is used as the PARENT style. That style applies background colors as shown. They are removed in Figure 13-2.

Though the ODS Graphics statement has a default of BORDER to provide a border around the image created with any ODS Graphics procedure, here no such option is available. The border was added with the Border option of Microsoft Word, after the image was inserted into the manuscript for this chapter. For Figure 13-5, a border is applied to the image with coding.

The source code for the AllTextSetup macro is an expansion of the AllGraphTextSetup macro introduced in the "Control of Text Attributes with a Custom ODS Style" section of Chapter 3 with its source code in Listing 3-13. In Listing 13-1, the text controls for tables are added with the CLASS FONTS statement.

Listing 13-1. Code used to create Figure 13-1

```
%macro AllTextSetup(Size,Family=Arial,Weight=Bold,Parent=PRINTER);
/* this macro can be stored as "C:\SharedCode\AllTextSetup.sas" */
%let FamilyForStyle = %sysfunc(compress(&Family,' '));
/* For example, this compresses Times New Roman into TimesNewRoman
   Style name cannot have blanks. */
proc template;
  define style AllTextFont&FamilyForStyle.&Size.pt&Weight;
  parent=styles.&Parent;
  class GraphFonts /
     'GraphValueFont' = ("&Family",&Size.pt,&Weight)
     'GraphLabelFont' = ("&Family",&Size.pt,&Weight)
     'GraphDataFont'  = ("&Family",&Size.pt,&Weight)
     'GraphTitleFont' = ("&Family",&Size.pt,&Weight)
     'GraphFootnoteFont' = ("&Family",&Size.pt,&Weight);
/* All below are for non-graph output */
  class Fonts /
     'TitleFont'   = ("&Family",&Size.pt,&Weight)  /* table titles
                                                       and footnotes */
     'headingFont' = ("&Family",&Size.pt,&Weight)  /* column headers
                                                       and row headers */
     'docFont'     = ("&Family",&Size.pt,&Weight); /* table cells   */
end;
run;
%mend AllTextSetup;

/* Since it is in-stream above, it is not necessary to use
   %include "C:\SharedCode\AllTextSetup.sas"; */

%AllTextSetup(11); /* create style AllTextFontArial11ptBold */

footnote1; /* erase any unerased footnote(s)
              previously used in this session */
options nonumber; /* SAS default is NUMBER */
options nodate;   /* SAS default is DATE */
options center;   /* Same as SAS default */
options papersize=(2.13in 3.84in); /* image dimensions */
  /* Optimum image size was determined by using output
  from a prior run with dimensions 5in X 5in, inserting the image
  into Microsoft Word, using the Format > Crop tool to trim
  the image to what I liked, and using the Size option to see
  what the result was. It was 2.13in wide and 3.84in high.
  The height is suitable to fit 10 rows for Male students.
  Of course, such fussy and minimal sizing of the table image is
  not mandatory, but since this table will ultimately be embedded
  in a composite image, avoiding wasted space is an advantage. */
```

```
ods results off;
ods _all_ close;
ods printer style=AllTextFontArial11ptBold
  file="C:\temp\Fig13-1_TableAsImage_NotOK.png"
  printer=PNG300 dpi=300;
title1 height=8pt color=white "White Space";
title2 "Male Student Information";
proc print data=sashelp.class;
where Sex EQ 'M';
id Name;
var Age Height;
run;
ods printer close;
```

Male Student Information		
Name	Age	Height
Alfred	14	69.0
Henry	14	63.5
James	12	57.3
Jeffrey	13	62.5
John	12	59.0
Philip	16	72.0
Robert	12	64.8
Ronald	15	67.0
Thomas	11	57.5
William	15	66.5

Figure 13-2. Black and white table as an image

Listing 13-2. *Code used to create Figure 13-2*

```
%include "C:\SharedCode\AllTextSetup_BlackWhiteTable.sas";
%include "C:\SharedCode\AllTextSetup.sas";

options mprint;
ods results off;
ods _all_ close;
options nodate nonumber;
options papersize=(2.13in 3.84in);
title1 height=8pt color=white "White Space";
title2 "Male Student Information";
```

```
%AllTextSetup_BlackWhiteTable(11,Family=Arial,Weight=Bold);
ods printer style=AllTextFontArial11ptBold_BlackWhiteTable
   file="C:\temp\Fig13-2_BlackWhiteTableAsImage.png"
   printer=PNG300 dpi=300;
proc print data=sashelp.class(where=(Sex EQ 'M'));
id Name; var Age Height;
run;
ods printer close;

/* Using a macro only for the text controls, but STYLE() options for color
controls: */

%AllTextSetup(11);
/* OPTIONS and TITLE statements from above persist */
ods printer style=AllTextFontArial11ptBold
   file="C:\temp\Fig13-2_Duplicate.png" printer=PNG300 dpi=300;
proc print data=sashelp.class(where=(Sex EQ 'M'))
   style(header)    = [color=black backgroundcolor=white]
   style(obsheader) = [color=black backgroundcolor=white]
   style(obs)       = [color=black backgroundcolor=white]
   style(data)      = [color=black backgroundcolor=white];
id Name; var Age Height;
run;
ods printer close;
```

Male Student Information		
Name	Age	Height
Alfred	14	69.0
Henry	14	63.5
James	12	57.3
Jeffrey	13	62.5
John	12	59.0
Philip	16	72.0
Robert	12	64.8
Ronald	15	67.0
Thomas	11	57.5
William	15	66.5

Figure 13-3. Table without a grid

Listing 13-3. *Code used to create Figure 13-3*

```
%include "C:\SharedCode\AllTextSetup_BlackWhiteTblNoGrid.sas";
%include "C:\SharedCode\AllTextSetup.sas";
options mprint;

ods results off;
ods _all_ close;
options nodate nonumber;
options papersize=(2.13in 3.84in);
title1 height=8pt color=white "White Space";
title2 "Male Student Information";

%AllTextSetup_BlackWhiteTblNoGrid(11,Family=Arial,Weight=Bold);
ods printer style=AllTextFontArial11ptBold_BlackWhiteTblNoGrid
  file="C:\temp\Fig13-3_BlackWhiteTableNoGridAsImage.png"
  printer=PNG300 dpi=300;
proc print data=sashelp.class(where=(Sex EQ 'M'));
id Name; var Age Height;
run;
ods printer close;

/* Using a macro only for the text controls, but STYLE() options for color
controls and table grid removal: */

%AllTextSetup(11);
/* OPTIONS and TITLE statements from above persist */
ods printer style=AllTextFontArial11ptBold
  file="C:\temp\Fig13-3_Duplicate.png" printer=PNG300 dpi=300;
proc print data=sashelp.class(where=(Sex EQ 'M'))
  style(header)   = [color=black backgroundcolor=white]
  style(obsheader) = [color=black backgroundcolor=white]
  style(obs)      = [color=black backgroundcolor=white]
  style(data)     = [color=black backgroundcolor=white]
  style(table) = [rules=none frame=void];
id Name; var Age Height;
run;
ods printer close;
```

Since the white space between the rows serves no communication value, it is best removed as in Figure 13-4.

Male Student Information		
Name	Age	Height
Alfred	14	69.0
Henry	14	63.5
James	12	57.3
Jeffrey	13	62.5
John	12	59.0
Philip	16	72.0
Robert	12	64.8
Ronald	15	67.0
Thomas	11	57.5
William	15	66.5

Figure 13-4. Compact table as an image

Listing 13-4. Code used to create Figure 13-4

```
%include "C:\SharedCode\AllTextSetup_CompactBlkWhtTable.sas";
%include "C:\SharedCode\AllTextSetup.sas";
options mprint;

ods results off;
ods _all_ close;
options nodate nonumber;
options papersize=(2.13in 2.5in);
        /* 2.5in would be 3.84in if not compacted */
title1 height=8pt color=white "White Space";
title2 "Male Student Information";

%AllTextSetup_CompactBlkWhtTable(
   11,CellHeight=8pt,Family=Arial,Weight=Bold);
ods printer style=AllTextFontArial11ptBold_CompactBlkWhtTable
   file="C:\temp\Fig13-4_CompactBlackWhiteTableAsImage.png"
   printer=PNG300 dpi=300;
proc print data=sashelp.class(where=(Sex EQ 'M'));
id Name; var Age Height;
run;
ods printer close;

/* Using a macro only for the text controls, but STYLE() options for color
controls, turning off the grid, and compacting the rows: */

%AllTextSetup(11);
/* OPTIONS and TITLE statements from above persist */
ods printer style=AllTextFontArial11ptBold
   file="C:\temp\Fig13-4_Duplicate.png" printer=PNG300 dpi=300;
proc print data=sashelp.class(where=(Sex EQ 'M'))
   style(header)    = [color=black backgroundcolor=white]
   style(obsheader) = [color=black backgroundcolor=white]
   style(obs)       = [color=black backgroundcolor=white]
```

```
style(data)      = [color=black backgroundcolor=white]
  style(table) = [rules=none frame=void];
/* Table grid must be absent if compressing the rows. */
id Name          / style(column)=[cellheight=8pt];
var Age Height / style(column)=[cellheight=8pt];
run;
ods printer close;
```

Direct Customization Without Customized Styles

The examples in Figures 13-2, 13-3, and 13-4 rely on further customization of the style that was developed to control the text characteristics of both graphs and tables. The objectives accomplished by each macro were duplicated by direct customization of the PROC PRINT code with STYLE() options. Such direct customization of PROC PRINT when building a table allows you to do *anything* on an ad hoc basis, without needing a previously built ODS style, or when applying overrides to an otherwise controlling style. The three macros for those examples can be stored once and for all in a folder like C:\SharedCode, to serve as a definite convenience and as an alternative to directly customizing the various parts of a table. Each of the three listings showed both the enhanced-function macro solution and the alternate solution of using the STYLE() options in PROC PRINT.

It should be noted that even Figure 13-1 can have its text customized to 11pt Arial Bold *without* the use of the style, but direct customization must then be applied to the TITLE2 statement, and the assignments for fontfamily, fontsize, and fontweight must be coded for the options STYLE(OBSHEADER) for the ID column header, STYLE(OBS) for the ID column values, STYLE(HEADER) for the VAR column headers, and STYLE(DATA) for the VAR values. Direct control of text characteristics for PROC PRINT is most useful only when applying *exception* controls to specific parts of the PROC PRINT output while allowing an ODS style to control everything else. Demonstrating the full range of what can be done with STYLE() options in PROC PRINT is beyond the scope and needs of this chapter.

Borders for Tables As Images: Using a Tool That Will Apply a Border to *Any* Image

The macro used for Figure 13-5 can apply a border not just to a table image but any image file (such as a logo, photograph, diagram, etc.), if desired.

Male Student Information		
Name	Age	Height
Alfred	14	69.0
Henry	14	63.5
James	12	57.3
Jeffrey	13	62.5
John	12	59.0
Philip	16	72.0
Robert	12	64.8
Ronald	15	67.0
Thomas	11	57.5
William	15	66.5

Figure 13-5. Table as an image with programmatically applied border

Listing 13-5. *Code used to create Figure 13-5*

```
/* code in Listing 13-4 must be run first to create input file
   Fig13-4_CompactBlackWhiteTableAsImage.png */

%include "C:\SharedCode\ApplyBorderToAnyImage.sas";
options mprint;
%ApplyBorderToAnyImage(
in=C:\temp\Fig13-4_CompactBlackWhiteTableAsImage.png,
out=C:\temp\Fig13-5_CompactTableAsImageWithBorder.png,
width=2.13in,
height=2.5in);
```

General-Purpose Macro to Create a Table As an Image

The objective is to make it easy to create a PROC PRINT table from *any* data set, *with a variety of options*, such as grid or no grid for the table, and, if no grid, whether to compress the rows to make a shorter image, suppressing the needless empty space, which provides no communication value. The table can include one or more ID variable columns.

```
Student Information
where Name =: 'J'

Name     Age  Sex
James     12   M
Jane      12   F
Janet     15   F
Jeffrey   13   M
John      12   M
Joyce     11   F
Judy      14   F
```

Figure 13-6. Custom table as an image, created by using the CustomTableAsImage macro and using the ApplyBorderToAnyImage macro to apply the border

The macro assures that table text is black and table background is white.

As noted in the comment in the code listing, image width that is too narrow will have unpredictable consequences.

It the image height is too short, one or more rows at the bottom will be omitted. However, unless you know how many rows there *should* be, you might, unwittingly, provide the recipient or viewer an incomplete report. So, unless you instead prefer to create tables as oversized images, minimizing size requires care.

As I previously mentioned, the image from my first run for any trimmed example was inserted into Microsoft Word, where I used the Format ➤ Crop function and Size to determine the safe minimum size for the image dimensions. Minimizing the size and avoiding wasted space is a personal preference, not mandatory.

Listing 13-6. *Macro invocation code used to create Figure 13-6*

```
%include "C:\SharedCode\CustomTableAsImage.sas";
%include "C:\SharedCode\ApplyBorderToAnyImage.sas";
options mprint;

/* NOTE: The macro assures that table text is black,
         and table background is white. */

%CustomTableAsImage(
parent=PRINTER, /* same as macro default */
Family=Georgia, /* default is Arial */
Size=12pt,      /* default is 11pt */
```

```
Weight=Normal,   /* default is Bold */
tablegridoff=YES, /* macro default is null (=NO) */
NonDefaultCellHeight=9pt, /* macro default is null
                              (i.e, no row compaction) */
dpi=300, /* same as macro default */
title=%str(Student Information),
title_justify=left, /* same as macro default */
title_color=blue, /* macro default is black */
whitespaceabovetitleInPts=, /* macro default is null */
center=NO, /* same as macro default */
date=NO, /* same as macro default */
imagefolder=C:\temp,
imagefilename=Fig13-6_CustomTableAsImage,
data=sashelp.class,
where=%str(Name =: 'J'),
ShowWhere=YES, /* (i.e., as subtitle) same as macro default */
idlist=Name, /* optional to use */
varlist=Age Sex, /* if unaasigned, PROC PRINT lists
              all variables, except ID var(s), if any */
width_inches=1.53, /* if too narrow, results are unpredictable */
height_inches=2.18); /* if too short, bottom rows are omitted */

%ApplyBorderToAnyImage(
in=C:\temp\Fig13-6_CustomTableAsImage.png,
out=C:\temp\Fig13-6_CompactTableAsImageWithBorder.png,
width=1.53in,
height=2.18in);
```

Building a Composite with ODS LAYOUT and ODS PRINTER

Every ODS destination except LAYOUT is limited on how you can arrange content in the output entity that it delivers. ODS LAYOUT is the great enabler. With ODS LAYOUT and ODS PRINTER, you can assemble whatever composite you wish and output it as an image. That image can be embedded in the output for another ODS destination, such as a web page, PDF page, etc.

Having emphasized the ability to embed a composite in one's document type of choice, the immediate order of business is to demonstrate how to *build* a composite. As you will see, the coding can be lengthy, but conceptually it is very straightforward, requiring no abstruse folderol.

Figure 13-7 is not the most elaborate composite that one could contrive, but it is a good learning tool. It was *my* learning tool.

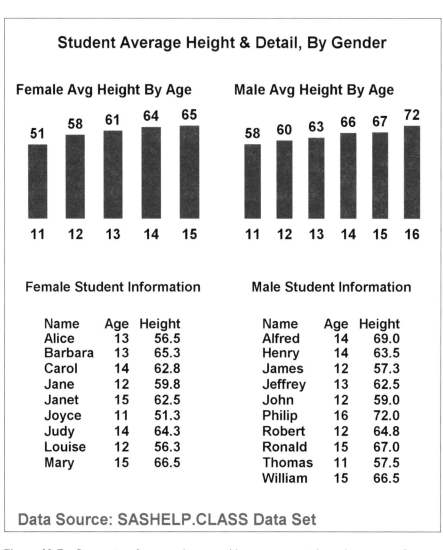

Figure 13-7. Composite of two graphs, two tables, a common title, and a common footnote in six regions of ODS LAYOUT

This example of using ODS LAYOUT for a composite assembles a two-by-two array with a row of two graphs above a row of two tables. The array can consist of any number of rows and columns. The collection of regions inside the layout need not be an array, matrix, grid, or whatever you might call this configuration. That is clear from the presence of an overall title and overall footnote outside the array. The regions can be any rectangular or square shape. Areas of the overall layout can be unallocated and unused. Those spaces are voids. From row to row, the number of columns can vary. Content need not be organized in *any* rows or columns. The total area can be broken up into *any* arrangement of internal regions. The only limit on region size, region shape, or total number of regions is readability. Any ODS destination allows you to stack content, but arranging the content in *arbitrary* way is possible *only* with ODS LAYOUT.

The macros used in this example are CustomTableAsImage (previously demonstrated for Figure 13-6) and ApplyBorderToAnyImage (previously demonstrated for Figure 13-5).

Listing 13-7. *Code used to create Figure 13-7*

```
%include "C:\SharedCode\CustomTableAsImage.sas";
%include "C:\SharedCode\ApplyBorderToAnyImage.sas";

/* NOTE: Since the image might require tuning to get to a satisfactory result,
it is convenient to gather controls that are likely to need change up here to
the top of the code. */

%let TitleFootnoteTextAttrs =
  %str(fontfamily='Arial' font_size=13pt font_weight=Bold);
%let CommonTitleAttrs =
  &TitleFootnoteTextAttrs just=center color=black;
%let CommonFootnoteAttrs =
  &TitleFootnoteTextAttrs just=left color=blue;

%let CommonTitle = %str(Student Average Height & Detail, By Gender);
%let CommonFootnote = %str(Data Source: SASHELP.CLASS Data Set);
* let CommonTitle = %str( );   /* omit common title */
* let CommonFootnote = %str(); /* omit common footnote */
/* The common title and/or common footnote can be omitted without detriment
to the body of the image, but unused white space would be reserved at the top
and/or bottom of the composite image,
unless the layout is changed accordingly. */

%let GeneralFontSize = 11pt;
%let WhiteSpace = 0.225in; /* between graphs row and tables row */

ods results off;
ods _all_ close;

/* Prepare the two tables as image files */

%CustomTableAsImage(
imagefolder=C:\temp,
imagefilename=RightTable,
Family=Arial,
Size=&GeneralFontSize,
Weight=Bold,
tablegridoff=YES,
NonDefaultCellHeight=8pt,
```

```
dpi=300,
center=YES,
title=%str(Male Student Information),
title_justify=center,
data=SASHELP.CLASS,
where=%str(Sex EQ 'M'),
ShowWhere=NO,
idlist=Name, /* optional to use */
varlist=Age Height,
width_inches=2.11,
height_inches=2.4);
/* optimum image size was determined
by using output from a prior ODS LISTING run,
OUTSIDE of this ODS LAYOUT ODS PRINTER code block,
with dimensions 5in X 5in
(ODS GRAPHICS / WIDTH=5in HEIGHT=5in),
inserting the output image into Microsoft Word,
using the Word Format > Crop tool
to trim the image to what I liked,
and using the MS Word Size option
to see what those dimensions were. */

/* macro invocation same as for Male, except as highlighted */
%CustomTableAsImage(
imagefolder=C:\temp,imagefilename=LeftTable,
Family=Arial,Size=&GeneralFontSize,Weight=Bold,
tablegridoff=YES,NonDefaultCellHeight=8pt,
dpi=300,center=YES,
title=%str(Female Student Information),
title_justify=center,
data=SASHELP.CLASS,where=%str(Sex EQ 'F'),ShowWhere=NO,
idlist=Name,varlist=Age Height,
width_inches=2.11,height_inches=2.4);
/* These dimensions match those for the Male table,
for symmetry, and they accommodate the content well. */

/* Defaults are DATE NUMBER CENTER */
options nodate nonumber;

options papersize=("5in" "5.69in"); /* composite width & height */

ods results off;
ods _all_ close;
ods printer printer=PNG dpi=300
  file="C:\temp\Fig13-7_Composite.png";

/* ODS PRINTER creates the composite image */
/* ODS LAYOUT places the right items in the right places */

ods layout absolute;
```

```
title; footnote; /* nullify any leftover
  TITLE or FOOTNOTE statements from earlier in the SAS session. */

/* Inlay a common title. If none set up above with %LET, then blank space
occurs */
ods region x=0in y=0in width=5in height=0.6in;
proc odstext;
p ' ' / style={font_size=0.1in}; /* white space */
p "&CommonTitle" / style={&CommonTitleAttrs};
run;

/* set up for BOTH images: */
ods graphics on / reset=all
  scale=off width=2.5in height=2in noborder;

ods region x=0in y=0.6in width=2.5in height=2in;
ods graphics / reset=index imagename="LeftGraph";
title justify=left font=Arial Bold height=&GeneralFontSize
  'Female Avg Height By Age';
proc sgplot data=sashelp.class noborder;
where Sex='F';
vbar age / response=height stat=mean
  displaybaseline=off datalabel
  datalabelattrs=(family=Arial size=&GeneralFontSize weight=Bold)
  nooutline fillattrs=(color=red) barwidth=0.5;
yaxis display=none;
xaxis display=(nolabel noline noticks)
  valueattrs=(family=Arial size=&GeneralFontSize weight=Bold);
format age 2. height 2.;
run;

/* same code as for Female, except as highlighted */
ods region x=2.5in y=0.6in width=2.5in height=2in;
ods graphics / reset=index imagename="RightGraph";
title justify=left font=Arial Bold height=&GeneralFontSize
  'Male Avg Height By Age';
proc sgplot data=sashelp.class noborder;
where Sex='M';
vbar age / response=height stat=mean
  displaybaseline=off datalabel
  datalabelattrs=(family=Arial size=&GeneralFontSize weight=Bold)
  nooutline fillattrs=(color=red) barwidth=0.5;
yaxis display=none;
xaxis display=(nolabel noline noticks)
  valueattrs=(family=Arial size=&GeneralFontSize weight=Bold);
format age 2. height 2.;
run;

/* insert the images of the two tables, below white space */
ods region x=0in y=2.6in width=2.5in height=2.84in;
```

```
proc odstext; p ' ' /  style={font_size=&WhiteSpace}; run;
data _null_;
dcl odsout obj();
obj.image(file: "C:\temp\LeftTable.png");
run;

ods region x=2.5in y=2.6in width=2.5in height=2.84in;
proc odstext; p ' ' /  style={font_size=&WhiteSpace}; run;
data _null_;
dcl odsout obj();
obj.image(file: "C:\temp\RightTable.png");
run;

/* Inlay a common footnote. If none set up above with %LET, then blank space
occurs */
ods region x=0in y=5.44in width=5in height=0.25in;
proc odstext; p "   &CommonFootnote" /
  style={asis=on &CommonFootnoteAttrs};
/* ASIS=ON preserves the three leading blanks for an indent */
run;

ods layout end;
ods printer close;

%ApplyBorderToAnyImage(
in=C:\temp\Fig13-7_Composite.png,
out=C:\temp\Fig13-7_CompositeWithBorder.png,
width=5in,
height=5.69in);
```

Capturing ODS Objects from SAS Procedure Output As Images

If any SAS procedure generates a table as part of its function, then you can substitute its invocation for the PROC PRINT procedure step when using ODS PRINTER to output a table as an image. Some SAS procedures generate multiple tables, in which case you can optionally select only the table or tables that you want to present. The first step is to discover the name of the tables as ODS Output Objects to be used on an ODS SELECT statement. This selectable output object concept can also be applied for output as a listing, a PDF, or any output format, not just when packaging that output as an image.

To use the output of a SAS procedure selectively, you need to know the names of the ODS Output Objects. To find them, you must use the ODS TRACE statement as in Listing 13-8. The LISTING option displays the trace information in the LISTING output before each section/ODS Output Object of the report.

ODS Trace of ODS Output Objects for PROC UNIVARIATE
Variable: Height
Output Added:

Name:	**Moments**	
Label:	**Moments**	
Template:	**base.univariate.Moments**	
Path:	**Univariate.Height.Moments**	

```
                                 Moments
N                          19   Sum Weights                 19
Mean                62.3368421   Sum Observations        1184.4
Std Deviation       5.12707525   Variance            26.2869006
Skewness           -0.2596696    Kurtosis            -0.1389692
Uncorrected SS        74304.92   Corrected SS        473.164211
Coeff Variation     8.22479143   Std Error Mean      1.17623173
```

Figure 13-8. Excerpt of the beginning of the PROC UNIVARIATE output

(Blank lines were manually deleted. Bold face was manually applied to title and to trace information block.)

The Name in the trace is what is used in an ODS SELECT or ODS EXCLUDE statement to generate a partial report. The SELECT or EXCLUDE may include multiple Names.

Listing 13-8. Code to find the name of ODS Output Objects

```
ods results off;
ods _all_ close;
options nodate nonumber;
title;
ods noproctitle;
ods trace on / listing;
ods listing
  file="C:\temp\Listing13-8_ODSoutputObjectsInPROCunivariate.txt";
proc univariate data=sashelp.class;
var Height;
run;
ods listing close;
ods trace off;
```

Figure 13-9 delivers two output objects from PROC UNIVARIATE.

```
Basic Statistics and Quantiles for Female Student Height

Variable: Height

                Basic Statistical Measures

        Location                  Variability
   Mean      60.58889   Std Deviation        5.01833
   Median    62.50000   Variance            25.18361
   Mode          .      Range               15.20000
                        Interquartile Range  7.80000



   Quantiles (Definition 5)

   Level           Quantile
   100% Max          66.5
   99%               66.5
   95%               66.5
   90%               66.5
   75% Q3            64.3
   50% Median        62.5
   25% Q1            56.5
   10%               51.3
   5%                51.3
   1%                51.3
   0% Min            51.3
```

Figure 13-9. Two ODS Output Objects from PROC UNIVARIATE as an image, using 9pt Arial Bold font for compact black and white tables with no grids

Creating the two tables separately and using ODS LAYOUT could have permitted displaying the two tables side by side rather than stacked. The image width was deliberately set to available width on this page to demonstrate the possibility for improvement. The one capability absent from the macro to create the ODS style used for this image of selected parts of PROC UNIVARIATE output is control of the text used to display "Variable: Height".

Listing 13-9. *Code used to create Figure 13-9*

```
%include "C:\SharedCode\AllTextSetup_CompactBlkWhtTable.sas";
%include "C:\SharedCode\ApplyBorderToAnyImage.sas";

%AllTextSetup_CompactBlkWhtTable(
  9,CellHeight=6pt,Family=Arial,Weight=Bold);

ods results off;
ods _all_ close;
ods noproctitle;
options nocenter nodate nonumber;
```

```
options papersize=(5.7in 4.2in);
ods select BasicMeasures Quantiles;
title1 "Basic Statistics and Quantiles for Female Student Height";
ods printer printer=PNG300 dpi=300
  style=AllTextFontArial9ptBold_CompactBlkWhtTable
  file="C:\temp\Fig13-9_PartialUnivariateAsCompactImage.png";
proc univariate data=sashelp.class(where=(Sex EQ 'F'));
var Height;
run;
ods printer close;

%ApplyBorderToAnyImage(
in=C:\temp\Fig13-9_PartialUnivariateAsCompactImage.png,
out=C:\temp\Fig13-9_PartialUnivariateAsCompactImage_WithBorder.png,
width=5.7in,
height=4.2in);
```

Summary

The scope of this chapter is small, but the power of the tools and methods presented is huge. It shows how to create tables as images and how to create image files that are composites of any combination and arrangement of graphs, tables, text strings, and, though not demonstrated, even non-graphic images. Chapter 14 demonstrates how to embed a composite in a web page.

The ODS PRINTER destination and PROC PRINT were used to output tables as image files. To assemble a composite of tables as image files and graphs (which are always image files), ODS PRINTER and ODS LAYOUT were used.

The ODS Report Writing Interface statements

```
dcl odsout obj();
obj.image(file: "C:\temp\FileName.png");
```

were used in a DATA _NULL_ step to embed table images in regions of a layout. As is shown in Chapter 14, that same type of DATA step can be used to embed images in web pages with ODS HTML5. Running PROC SGPLOT in regions of the layout displayed the graph images where desired. ODS PRINTER and ODS LAYOUT delivered an image of images.

A general-purpose macro was provided and used to create tables as images. It not only allows control of the text characteristics in the table (font family, font size, and font weight) but also whether the table grid is used or omitted, and, when the grid is omitted, whether the cell height in the table should be reduced to remove the superfluous white space between the rows. The macro forces table text to be black and table backgrounds to be white. The macro allows specification of the PARENT style to be used by PROC

TEMPLATE when it builds the custom style used for the table. The default is PRINTER. It must be noted that the effect of other possible parent style choices *has not been tested.*

The ApplyBorderToAnyImage macro was provided and used to apply a border to a table as an image file because there is no BORDER/NOBORDER option for the code used to create the table image. As its name says, the macro can be used to apply a border to *any* image (e.g., photograph, diagram, etc.).

PROC TEMPLATE was used in macros to enable the generation of ODS styles to not only format the text, both for graphs and tables, but also to assure that the table is black and white, to turn off the table grid, and to reduce the table cell height to compact the table and eliminate wasted vertical space that has no communication value. For the non-text customization options, example code was provided that accomplishes the same objective as the custom style by directly coding STYLE controls in PROC PRINT code.

To provide a common title and a common footnote for a composite, PROC ODSTEXT and the P statement were used. The TITLE and FOOTNOTE statements that are available for the composite's constituent graph and table procedures cannot be used to create an overall title and footnote for the composite content.

The tabular output from *any* SAS procedure can be converted to an image, not just the output from PROC PRINT, PROC REPORT, and PROC TABULATE. Some of those other tabular output procedures create *multiple* tables. The tables can be identified as ODS Output Objects using the ODS TRACE statement. The relevant code to create an image with one of those procedures can include an ODS SELECT or ODS EXCLUDE statement to limit what goes into the image. However, when creating an image file from one of those procedures, whether in full or subsetted with SELECT or EXCLUDE, if the image height is too short, one or more sections at the end of the report will be omitted. Though here the ODS Output Objects are being packaged as an image file with ODS PRINTER, this selective output technique can also be applied when using the procedure for any other ODS destination.

Delivering Precise Numbers and Alternative Views for Graphs Using SAS ODS HTML5

A companion table of the precise values that are input to a graph can be below the graph, or next to the graph, or can be on a separate web page (especially if lengthy) that is interlinked with the graph web page. Some composites in this chapter are more complex than graph-table or graph-graph pairs. The most familiar features of HTML are that you can link any web to any web page and go from one to another via a variety of clickable links and you can provide "data tips" containing any information that you wish that pop up when the mouse rests on a graphic element (point, bar, pie slice, etc.)

© LeRoy Bessler 2023
LeR. Bessler, *Visual Data Insights Using SAS ODS Graphics*,
https://doi.org/10.1007/978-1-4842-8609-8_14

You can create a network of interlinked graphs and include tables in the network. To exit from a graph to another, the link can be on a line of text or a graphic element such as a bar, a pie slice, a plot point, or a unit geographic area that can be clickable.

A web graph can also be interlinked with an Excel worksheet of the input data. That worksheet can be reformatted or reused by the user/recipient however desired. Almost any computer user can be expected to have and know how to use Excel. (NOTE: Changing the worksheet will not change the web graph.)

SAS ODS web support initially was not HTML5. The distinctive advantage of HTML5 is that the graph image file is embedded in the output HTML file. So, if a web page is to be shared via, say, email, there is no need to also send an image file for which a pre-HTML5 web page was, in effect, merely a picture frame.

However, if using the SAS Report Writing Interface facility and the ODS.IMAGE statement to insert an image in ODS HTML5, then OPTIONS(BITMAP_MODE='INLINE') must be used on the ODS HTML5 statement to assure that the image file is indeed embedded. If not, then the HTML file serves only as a picture frame.

There are three examples where ODS PRINTER is used to create a composite image which is inserted in ODS HTML5. It can be embedded in the HTML file with the preceding option, and that source image file for the embed can be deleted at the end of processing. In more typical cases, graphs (and tables) are created directly inside an ODS HTML5 code block, and the embed of any graph images occurs without any explicit insertion processing. The reason for creating the composite outside of the ODS HTML5 code block will become clear at the point of doing it.

A key advantage of web graphs is the ability to provide data tips that display when the mouse is rested on a plot point, bar chart bar, pie chart slice, etc. The data tips can be customized to display not only values of the variables that drive the graph but also the values of any variables in the input data set.

Furthermore, not only can a web graph have a link to a companion table or another web graph that can provide either an alternative view of the same data, or a graph of related data, but also the graphic elements (plot points, bar chart bars, pie slices, etc.) can serve as clickable hot links to related information, graphic or tabular.

For a static composite image of a collection of graphs and/or tables, the best tool is the ODS PRINTER destination. It can be used with the ODS LAYOUT ABSOLUTE statement, which, with its REGION statements, allows the best possible control of the layout. That image file can be embedded in an HTML5 web page as explained earlier.

ODS HTML5 Code Basics

```
title; footnote; /* prevent inheriting titles/footnotes */
ods results off;
ods _all_ close;
ods html5 path="C:\temp" body="FileName.html"
  /* NOGTITLE NOGFOOTNOTE */
  /* The defaults are GTITLE GFOOTNOTE, in which case the titles and
     footnotes ae drawn in the graph image.
     Otherwise, they are created as web page text.
     If creating a hyperlink with the LINK= option in a TITLE or
     FOOTNOTE statement, then NOGTITLE or NOGFOOTNOTE is used. */
  style=Styles.HTMLEncore; /* This default can be omitted. */
< your example code goes here >
Ods html5 close;
```

The ODS HTML5 statement also offers options and features that are outside the scope of this chapter. A Google search for "ODS HTML5 statement" can take you to the latest information.

See comments in the code, as well as the reprise in the "Summary" section, of special coding practices that are unique to the examples in this chapter.

Custom ODS Styles Used in This Chapter

Prior to Chapter 13, in the chapters that were limited to graphs, the most commonly used custom style was GraphFontArial11ptBold. In Chapter 13, four macros were introduced and used to extend font customization with ODS styles to table text and table titles and to implement certain table customization options (all black and white tables, tables without a grid, or gridless tables with the rows compressed).

This chapter includes code to create a style that removes page breaks (horizontal black lines) between parts of certain web pages. It also shows you how to control the background of the web page. Previously used styles are built from the parent style PRINTER, which provides a white background for the web page. In other cases, STYLE=STYLES.PEARL replaces the ODS HTML5 default background color with white.

Custom styles used in this chapter include those in this list:

GraphFontArial8ptBold

AllTextFontArial11ptBold

AllTextFontArial12ptBold

AllTextFontArial12ptBold_BlackWhiteTable

AllTextFontArial11ptBold_BlackWhiteTblNoGrid

AllTextFontArial12ptBold_BlackWhiteTblNoGrid

To assure that they are available, run the following code:

```
%include "C:\SharedCode\AllGraphTextSetup.sas";
%AllGraphTextSetup(8);

%include "C:\SharedCode\AllTextSetup.sas";
%AllTextSetup(11);
%AllTextSetup(12);

%include "C:\SharedCode\AllTextSetup_BlackWhiteTable.sas";
%AllTextSetup_BlackWhiteTable(12);

%include "C:\SharedCode\AllTextSetup_BlackWhiteTblNoGrid.sas";
%AllTextSetup_BlackWhiteTblNoGrid(11);
%AllTextSetup_BlackWhiteTblNoGrid(12);
```

Time Series Data Used in This Chapter

For background information, please see the section "Special Data Sets Used for Some Time Series Graphs" in Chapter 8. If your site does not have SAS/ETS, you must download the zip file CitiData.zip from https://github.com/Apress/Visual-Data-Insights-Using-SAS-ODS-Graphics and store the five unzipped files in folder C:\CitiData.

Whichever is the case, the next step is prepare data that is used for Figures 14-1 and 14-16 by using Listing 14-0. My SAS site does *not* have SAS/ETS.

Listing 14-0. *Extract the Dow Jones index by day*

```
/* To prepare sasuser.DowJonesByDayIn1990 */
%include "C:\SharedCode\CreateDowJonesByDayIn1990.sas";
options mprint;
%CreateDowJonesByDayIn1990
(SASETSsiteUseSASHELPDataLib=NO,
OtherSiteFolderForCitiData=C:\CitiData,
OutLib=SASUSER);
```

Examples

A convincing case for the value of ODS HTML5 with data tips is Figure 14-1, where data labels and an X axis table are clearly infeasible.

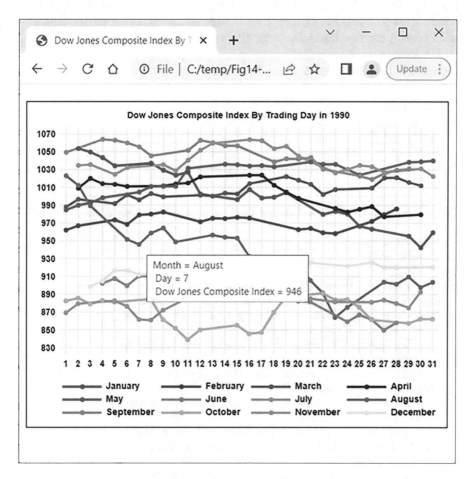

Figure 14-1. A graph for which data tips are essential

Having demonstrated the case for data tips with this complex example of clashing plot lines and plot points, the remaining examples will be simpler. Their focus is on the various ways to deliver composites of graphs or graphs and tables. Since most of the example graphs used have data labels, only three examples have data tips. This proportion is not meant to be representative of the general situation. The need for data tips depends on the application.

The code in Listing 14-1 is a simple adaptation of the ODS LISTING code in Listing 8-32 that is used to create a static image file. The ODS HTML5 statements replace the ODS LISTING statements. The TIP, TIPFORMAT, and TIPLABEL options are used to select the tip variables and customize the data tips. The image width is reduced to allow for the presence, within this page width, of web browser framing that is part of the screen capture that was used to prepare the illustrations for this chapter.

Listing 14-1. *Code used to create Figure 14-1*

```
proc format;
value MonthNm
   1 = 'January'   2 = 'February'   3 = 'March'
   4 = 'April'     5 = 'May'        6 = 'June'
   7 = 'July'      8 = 'August'     9 = 'September'
  10 = 'October'  11 = 'November'  12 = 'December';
run;

/* requires a prior run of Listing 14-0 to create input data: */

title; footnote;
ods results off;
ods _all_ close;
ods html5 path="C:\temp" style=GraphFontArial8ptBold
  body="Fig14-1_DowByDayEachMonth1990_WithDataTips.html"
  (title='Dow Jones Composite Index By Trading Day in 1990');
  /* the optional TITLE= text appears
     in the upper left corner of the web browser window */
ods graphics on / reset=all scale=off width=5.56in
  /* smaller image width would cause the legend to not fit */
   imagemap=on /* needed for data tips */
   outputfmt=SVG; /* In principle the default, but in certain
   circumstances that can be unwittingly overridden.
   It does no harm to ensure SVG as OUTPUTFMT the default,
   which can be expected to deliver satisfactory results. */
title1 justify=center
  'Dow Jones Composite Index By Trading Day in 1990';
proc sgplot data=sasuser.DowJonesByDayIn1990 noborder
  description=' '; /* prevent mouseover pop-up of
                       "The SGPLOT Procedure", which is a distraction
                       when trying to raise data tips. */
series y=DailyDJ x=Day / group=Month /* one plot line for each */
  tip=(Month Day DailyDJ)
  tipformat=(monthnm9. F2. F4.)
  tiplabel=('Month' 'Day' 'Dow Jones Composite Index')
  markers markerattrs=(size=7 symbol=CircleFilled)
  lineattrs=(thickness=3 pattern=Solid);
yaxis display=(nolabel noticks noline) grid minorgrid minorcount=1
  values=(830 to 1080 by 20);
```

```
xaxis display=(nolabel noticks noline) grid
  fitpolicy=none /* prevents thinning of the axis values */
  values=(1 TO 31 BY 1);
keylegend / title='' noborder across=4;
format DailyDJ 4. Month monthnm9.;
run;
ods html5 close;
```

Remaining examples show ways to present multiple graphs, a graph and companion table, and other combinations of graphs and tables.

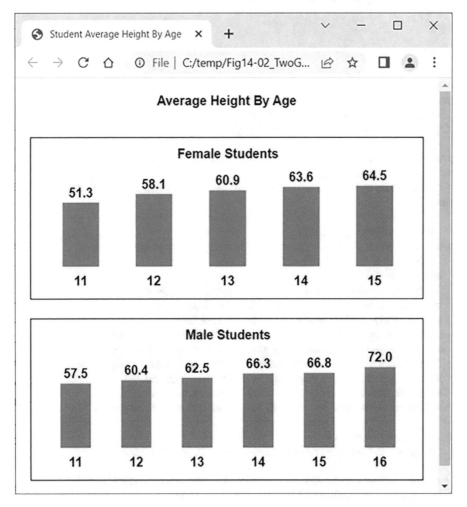

Figure 14-2. Two graphs stacked in one HTML5 web page (with page breaks removed by use of a custom style)

If the code in Listing 14-2 is used with either the default style or style AllTextFontArial12ptBold, Figure 14-2 will have a horizontal line after the title and between the two graphs.

Listing 14-2. *Code used to create Figure 14-2*

```
proc template;
  /* prevent horizontal lines between parts of the web page */
  define style AllTextFontArial12ptBoldNoPageBrks;
    parent=AllTextFontArial12ptBold;
      class pagebreak / display=none;
  end;
run;

title; footnote;
ods results off;
ods _all_ close;
ods html5 path="C:\temp" style=AllTextFontArial12ptBoldNoPageBrks
  body="Fig14-2_TwoGraphsStacked.html"
  (title='Student Average Height By Age');

proc odstext; /* create a common title for both graphs */
p "Average Height By Age" /
  style=[just=c font_face="Arial" font_size=12pt font_weight=Bold];
run;

/* setup for both graphs */
ods graphics on / reset=all scale=off width=500px height=200px
  /* Default size in pixels is 640 by 480. */
  outputfmt=SVG
  imagemap; /* Unnecessary with data labels available,
  but this prevents strange mouse-triggered pop-ups of:
  (1) an empty bubble where "The SGPLOT Procedure"
  would have appeared if description=' ' were not specified;
  and (2) a pop-up to unnecessarily display graph title lines.
  This option also is unexpectedly used in other HTML5 code,
  also to prevent those pop-ups. Even if data tips emerge
  when not really needed, they do no harm and are not odd.
  Phenomena described in (1) and (2) above are definitely odd. */

title 'Female Students';
proc sgplot data=sashelp.class(where=(sex EQ 'F')) noborder
  description=' ';
vbar age / response=height stat=mean datalabel displaybaseline=off
  barwidth=0.5 nooutline fillattrs=(color=green);
yaxis display=none;
xaxis display=(nolabel noline noticks);
format height 4.1 age 2.;
run;
```

```
title 'Male Students';
proc sgplot data=sashelp.class(where=(sex EQ 'M')) noborder
  description=' ';
vbar age / response=height stat=mean datalabel displaybaseline=off
  barwidth=0.5 nooutline fillattrs=(color=green);
yaxis display=none;
xaxis display=(nolabel noline noticks);
format height 4.1 age 2.;
run;

ods html5 close;
```

A common footnote for the two graphs would require the use of PROC ODSTEXT and a P statement analogous to that used for the common title.

The code to display two graphs is essentially the same as that to display three or more or only one. The only difference between the code for one graph and the code for a stack of graphs is that a common title is created for a stack of graphs.

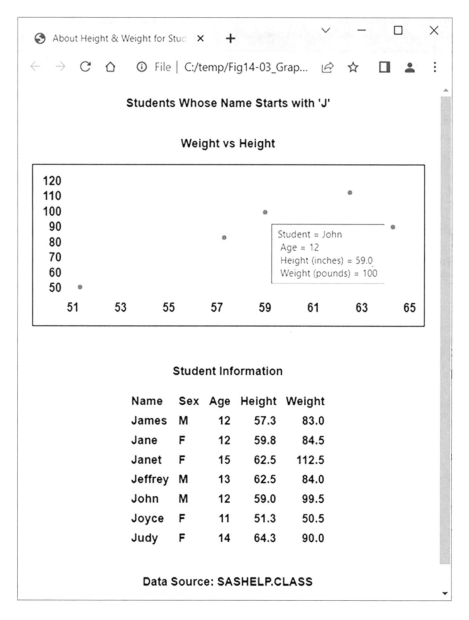

Figure 14-3. Graph with data tips and with a companion table to provide permanent information

In Listing 14-3, the use of PROC ODSTEXT and its P statement does more than was done for Figure 14-2. They provide a common title and a common footnote for the graph and table, as well as extra white space between the graph and table, which otherwise would be closer together. Without the extra white space, the title for the table would be closer to the graph above than to the table below.

Listing 14-3. *Code used to create Figure 14-3*

```
proc template;
  define style AllTextFontArial11ptBold_BlackWhiteTblNoGridNoPageBrks;
    parent=AllTextFontArial11ptBold_BlackWhiteTblNoGrid;
      class pagebreak / display=none;
  end;
run;

title; footnote;
ods results off;
ods _all_ close;
options center;
ods html5 path="C:\temp" nogtitle nogfootnote
  body="Fig14-3_GraphAboveTable.html"
  (title=
   "About Height & Weight for Students Whose Name Starts with 'J'")
  style=AllTextFontArial11ptBold_BlackWhiteTblNoGridNoPageBrks;

proc odstext;
p "Students Whose Name Starts with 'J'" /
  style=[just=c font_face="Arial" font_size=11pt font_weight=Bold];
run;

ods graphics on / reset=all scale=off width=500px height=200px
  outputfmt=SVG
  imagemap=on; /* turn on data tips */
title justify=center 'Weight vs Height';
proc sgplot data=sashelp.class(where=(name =: 'J')) noborder
  description=' ';
scatter x=height y=weight /
  tip=(name age height weight)
  tipformat=(auto auto F4.1 F3.)
  tiplabel=('Student' 'Age' 'Height (inches)' 'Weight (pounds)')
  markerattrs=(symbol=CircleFilled color=green);
xaxis display=(noline noticks nolabel) values=(51 to 65 by 2);
yaxis display=(noline noticks nolabel) values=(50 to 120 by 10);
run;
```

```
proc odstext;
p "Extra White Space" / style=[font_size=2pt color=white];
                    /* default font_size is too large */
run;

title justify=center 'Student Information';
proc print data=sashelp.class(where=(name =: 'J')) noobs;
run;

proc odstext;
p "Data Source: SASHELP.CLASS" /
  style=[just=c font_face="Arial" font_size=11pt font_weight=Bold];
run;

ods html5 close;
```

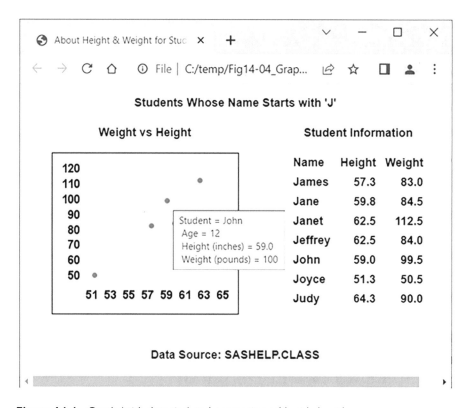

Figure 14-4. Graph (with data tips) and companion table side by side

The ODS LAYOUT facility is embedded in the ODS HTML5 code block to enable display of procedure outputs side by side. Without the ODS LAYOUT and REGION statements, the table would appear below the graph as in Figure 14-3.

If a companion table is small enough to be seen in the web browser window without scrolling left-right and without scrolling up-down, it is best presented at the side of the graph for viewer convenience.

The method used to display the table at the right could be used to instead display a second graph there. Also, the gridded layout can be extended to any number of columns. Whether requiring the viewer to scroll left-right or up-down to view more than two graphs is a matter of programmer choice.

Listing 14-4. Code used to create Figure 14-4

```
title; footnote;
ods results off;
ods _all_ close;
title "Students Whose Name Starts with 'J'";
footnote "Data Source: SASHELP.CLASS";
ods html5 path="C:\temp" nogtitle nogfootnote
  body="Fig14-4_GraphWithTableAtItsRight.html"
  (title=
   "About Height & Weight for Students Whose Name Starts with 'J'")
  style=AllTextFontArial11ptBold_BlackWhiteTblNoGrid;

ods layout gridded
  columns=2 column_widths=(240px 240px) column_gutter=20px;

ods region column=1;
ods graphics on / reset=all scale=off width=240px height=200px
  outputfmt=SVG
  imagemap=on; /* needed for data tips */
title justify=center 'Weight vs Height';
proc sgplot data=sashelp.class(where=(name =: 'J')) noborder
  description=' '; /* prevent mouseover pop-up of
                      "The SGPLOT Procedure", which is a distraction
                      when trying to raise data tips. */
scatter x=height y=weight /
  tip=(name age height weight)
  tipformat=(auto auto F4.1 F3.)
  tiplabel=('Student' 'Age' 'Height (inches)' 'Weight (pounds)')
  markerattrs=(symbol=CircleFilled color=green);
xaxis display=(noline noticks nolabel) values=(51 to 63 by 2);
yaxis display=(noline noticks nolabel) values=(50 to 120 by 10);
run;
```

```
ods region column=2;
title justify=center 'Student Information';
proc print data=sashelp.class(where=(name =: 'J')) noobs;
var name height weight;
run;

ods layout end;
ods html5 close;
```

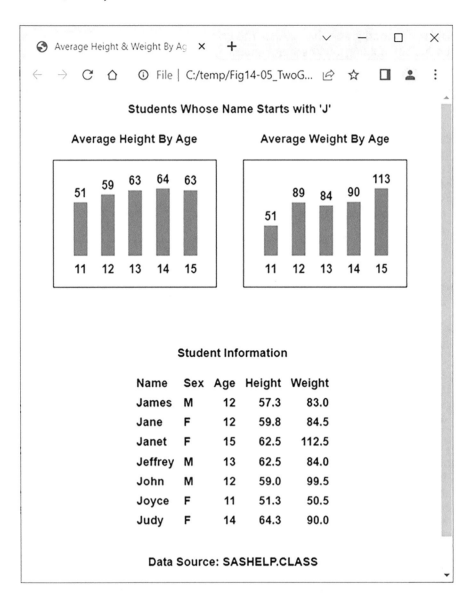

Figure 14-5. Two graphs above one table, using a gridded layout

The space between the graphs and the table is larger than needed, but it cannot be reduced using a gridded layout.

Listing 14-5. Code used to create Figure 14-5

```
title; footnote;
ods results off;
ods _all_ close;
title "Students Whose Name Starts with 'J'";

ods html5 path="C:\temp" nogtitle nogfootnote
  body="Fig14-5_TwoGraphsAboveOneTable.html"
  (title="Average Height & Weight By Age And All Information about Students
Whose Names Start with 'J'")
    style=AllTextFontArial11ptBold_BlackWhiteTblNoGrid;

ods layout gridded columns=2
  column_widths=(210px 210px) column_gutter=20px;

ods graphics on / reset=all scale=off width=210px
  outputfmt=SVG imagemap=on;

ods region column=1;
title justify=center 'Average Height By Age';
proc sgplot data=sashelp.class(where=(name =: 'J')) noborder
  description=' ';
vbar age / response=height stat=mean datalabel displaybaseline=off
  barwidth=0.5 nooutline fillattrs=(color=green);
yaxis display=none;
xaxis display=(noline noticks nolabel);
format height 2.;
run;

ods region column=2;
title justify=center 'Average Weight By Age';;
proc sgplot data=sashelp.class(where=(name =: 'J')) noborder
  description=' ';
vbar age / response=weight stat=mean datalabel displaybaseline=off
  barwidth=0.5 nooutline fillattrs=(color=green);
yaxis display=none;
xaxis display=(noline noticks nolabel);
format weight 3.;
run;

ods layout end; /* end first grid (two columns) */

ods layout gridded columns=1 column_widths=(440px);

ods region column=1;
```

```
title justify=center 'Student Information';
footnote "Data Source: SASHELP.CLASS";
proc print data=sashelp.class(where=(name =: 'J')) noobs;
var name sex age height weight;
run;

ods layout end; /* end second grid (one column) */

ods html5 close;
```

With ODS LAYOUT GRIDDED, Figure 14-5 uses two grids, each of one row, but the first with two columns and the second with one column.

ODS LAYOUT ABSOLUTE allows complete control of spacing in the layout, but it is not supported when using ODS HTML5. It does not rely on a grid concept of columns and rows. Regions can be created anywhere on the "page" with any dimensions that fit. Any areas not "covered" by a region are white space.

ODS LAYOUT ABSOLUTE is only supported with ODS PRINTER and ODS PDF. The next two examples use ODS PRINTER to create an image file with ODS LAYOUT ABSOLUTE, and the image file is embedded in an ODS HTML5 web page with a DATA _NULL_ step and the OBJ.IMAGE statement from the SAS Report Writing Interface facility.

The disadvantage of this solution is that any graphs inside the composite image file cannot have data tips provided.

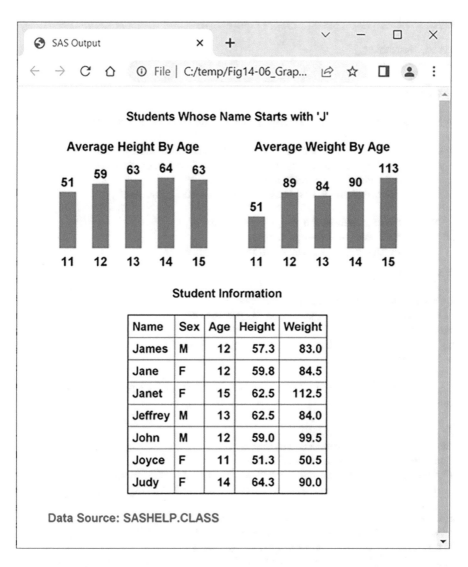

Figure 14-6. Two graphs above one table (with grid), using an absolute layout

The code to build the table is inside the ODS LAYOUT code block. If the code in Listing 14-6 were to use the style AllTextFontArial11ptBold_ BlackWhiteTblNoGrid that was used in Listing 14-5 for Figure 14-5, it would have no effect due to the use of ODS LAYOUT.

Listing 14-6. Code used to create Figure 14-6

```
title; footnote;
ods results off;
ods _all_ close;
options nodate nonumber;

options papersize=("5in" "5.58in"); /* composite width & height */

ods printer printer=PNG dpi=300 style=AllTextFontArial11ptBold
  /* this style affects text from PROC SGPLOT and PROC PRINT,
     but not output from PROC ODSTEXT. */
  file="C:\temp\Fig14-6_GraphsAboveTableBuiltInLayout.png";

/* ODS PRINTER creates the composite image */
/* ODS LAYOUT and REGION statements put
   items in the right places of allocated sizes */

ods layout absolute;

/* inlay the common title for the content */
ods region x=0in y=0in width=5in height=0.6in;
proc odstext;
p ' ' / style={font_size=0.1in}; /* white space */
p "Students Whose Name Starts with 'J'" /
  style={just=center
         fontfamily='Arial' font_size=11pt font_weight=Bold};
run;

/* set up for both graphs */
ods graphics on / reset=all scale=off
  width=2.5in height=1.88in noborder;
/* The output format is set to PNG on the ODS PRINTER statement.
   The situation is the same in Listing 14-7 and Listing 14-11. */

ods region x=0in y=0.45in width=2.5in height=1.88in;
/* overlay bottom of first region which is at 0.6in */
title justify=center 'Average Height By Age';
proc sgplot data=sashelp.class(where=(Name =: 'J')) noborder;
/* description=' ' is not needed to block an unwanted pop-up. This
is ODS PRINTER static image output, not web-enabled output from ODS
HTML5. The static image gets embedded in ODS HTML5 with code that
runs after ODS PRINTER. The situation is the same in Listing 14-7
and Listing 14-11, and for the PROC SGPLOT step below and there. */
vbar age / response=height stat=mean
  displaybaseline=off datalabel
  nooutline fillattrs=(color=green) barwidth=0.5;
yaxis display=none;
xaxis display=(nolabel noline noticks);
format height 2.;
run;
```

```
ods region x=2.5in y=0.45in width=2.5in height=1.88in;
/* overlay bottom of first region which is at 0.6in */
title justify=center 'Average Weight By Age';
proc sgplot data=sashelp.class(where=(Name =: 'J')) noborder;
vbar age / response=weight stat=mean
  displaybaseline=off datalabel
  nooutline fillattrs=(color=green) barwidth=0.5;
yaxis display=none;
xaxis display=(nolabel noline noticks);
format weight 3.;
run;

/* create the table */
ods region x=0in y=2.43in /* adding white space:
            bottom of second region is at 2.33in */
  width=5in height=2.9in;
title 'Student Information';
proc print data=sashelp.class(where=(Name =: 'J')) noobs
/* style(rowheader) = [background=white]
   needed if ID var used or NOT noobs */
  style(header) = [background=white];
run;
title; /* prevent table title inheritance by the ODS HTML5 step */

ods region x=0in y=5.33in   /* bottom of region 3 is at 5.23in */
  width=5in height=0.25in; /* bottom of page     is at 5.58in */
proc odstext; p "    Data Source: SASHELP.CLASS" /
  style={asis=on just=left color=blue
        /* ASIS=ON preserves the three leading blanks for indent */
          fontfamily='Arial' font_size=11pt font_weight=Bold};
run;

ods layout end;
ods printer close;

/* After the code below runs, the PNG file remains distinct in
the C:\temp folder. However, it is physically embedded in the HTML file, and
can be deleted manually or programmatically without creating a void in the web
browser display of the HTML file.
The situation is the same for Listing 14-7 and Listing 14-11. */

title; footnote;
ods html5 style=Styles.Pearl path="C:\temp"
    /* default style has light blue web page background */
  options(bitmap_mode='inline') /* embed the image in HTML file */
  body="Fig14-6_GraphsAboveTableBuiltInLayout.html";
data _null_;
declare odsout obj();
```

```
obj.image(file:
  'C:\temp\Fig14-6_GraphsAboveTableBuiltInLayout.png');
run;
ods html5 close;

/* The file Fig14-6_GraphsAboveTableBuiltInLayout.png
   can be deleted after this code has run. */
```

The image file is not embedded in the HTML file unless the BITMAP_MODE option is used as before. After the code has run, the file can be deleted, manually or programmatically, from the C:\temp folder.

In Listing 14-6, the title of the table, if not erased when no longer needed, would appear also at the top of the web page. The code has an erasure statement (TITLE;) in two places, which is redundant. It is a reminder to me and to the reader to prevent the same initial mystification that I suffered when creating this example without either of the erasure statements. Best practice, in principle, is to code TITLE; FOOTNOTE; at the bottom of every PROC step that includes a TITLE and/or FOOTNOTE statement. One or both might be unnecessary, but neither does any harm, and sometimes one or both prevent confusing inheritance of a title or footnote. The programmer need not wonder, "Where did that title/footnote come from?"

In this chapter, the policy has been to code TITLE; FOOTNOTE; at the *top* of every example to protect its processing from inheriting titles and/or footnotes from any processing that might occur earlier during the same SAS session. In a few cases, the TITLE;FOOTNOTE; erasure is also done in the middle of a program to protect later processing from title or footnote inheritance from earlier processing in the same program.

In Figure 14-7, an alternative way to use ODS LAYOUT ABSOLUTE creates the table with no grid and with its rows compacted.

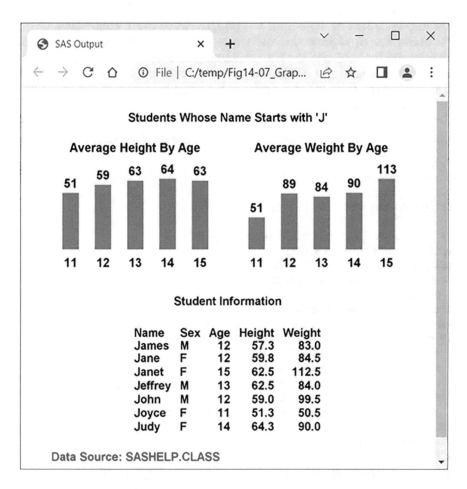

Figure 14-7. Two graphs above one table (compacted), using an absolute layout

The table is created as an image file in code at the beginning of the program. That image file is inserted using a Report Writing Interface DATA _NULL_ step in the ODS LAYOUT code block. That makes removing the table grid and compacting the rows possible, unlike the case for Figure 14-6, for which the table is created *inside* the ODS LAYOUT code block.

The code in Listing 14-7 is a derivative of that in Listing 14-6. The key differences are these: (a) an ODS PRINTER step, near the top of the code, to build the table as an image file, before the layout assembly begins; (b) replacement of the PROC PRINT step in the main ODS PRINTER/ODS LAYOUT code block with a DATA _NULL_ step to insert the table image file in the third region of the layout; and (c) changes to the Y coordinates of the third and fourth regions (for table and common footnote). Other minor changes are the names of the composite image file and the web page filename and the placement of a TITLE statement to turn off a title that could be inherited by the ODS HTML5 code—the turnoff is located at the end of the last PROC SGPLOT step.

Listing 14-7. *Code used to create Figure 14-7, changes from Figure 14-6 in bold*

```
title; footnote;
ods results off;
ods _all_ close;
options nodate nonumber;

/* Prepare the compacted table as an image file */
options papersize=(5in 2.0in);
ods printer printer=PNG dpi=300
  style=AllTextFontArial11ptBold
  file="C:\temp\Table.png";
title1 'Student Information';
proc print data=sashelp.class(where=(Name =: 'J')) noobs
/* style(rowheader) = [background=white]
   needed if ID var used or NOT noobs */
  style(header) = [background=white]
  style(table) = [rules=none frame=void]; /* remove the grid */
var Name Sex Age Height Weight /
  style(column)=[cellheight=9pt]; /* compact the rows */
run;
ods printer close;
title; footnote;

options papersize=("5in" "4.78in"); /* the table is smaller */

/* create the composite as an image file */
ods printer printer=PNG dpi=300 style=AllTextFontArial11ptBold
  file="C:\temp\Fig14-7_GraphsAboveTablePreBuiltAsImage.png";

ods layout absolute;

/* inlay the common title for the content */
ods region x=0in y=0in width=5in height=0.6in;
proc odstext;
p ' ' / style={font_size=0.1in}; /* white space */
p "Students Whose Name Starts with 'J'" /
  style={just=center
         fontfamily='Arial' font_size=11pt font_weight=Bold};
run;
```

```
/* set up for both graphs */
ods graphics on / reset=all scale=off
  width=2.5in height=1.88in noborder;
/* the output format is set to PNG on the ODS PRINTER statement */

ods region x=0in y=0.45in width=2.5in height=1.88in;
/* overlay bottom of first region which is at 0.6in */
title justify=center 'Average Height By Age';
proc sgplot data=sashelp.class(where=(Name =: 'J')) noborder;
vbar age / response=height stat=mean
  displaybaseline=off datalabel
  nooutline fillattrs=(color=green) barwidth=0.5;
yaxis display=none;
xaxis display=(nolabel noline noticks);
format height 2.;
run;

ods region x=2.5in y=0.45in width=2.5in height=1.88in;
/* overlay bottom of first region which is at 0.6in */
title justify=center 'Average Weight By Age';
proc sgplot data=sashelp.class(where=(Name =: 'J')) noborder;
vbar age / response=weight stat=mean
  displaybaseline=off datalabel
  nooutline fillattrs=(color=green) barwidth=0.5;
yaxis display=none;
xaxis display=(nolabel noline noticks);
format weight 3.;
run;
title; /* prevent inheritance by ODS HTML5 step */

/* insert the prebuilt image of the table */
ods region x=0in y=2.53in /* adding white space:
           bottom of second region is at 2.33in */
  width=5in height=2.0in; /* the table rows are compacted */
data _null_;
dcl odsout obj();
obj.image(file: "C:\temp\Table.png");
run;

/* inlay the common footnote for the content */
ods region x=0in y=4.53in  /* bottom of region 3 is at 4.53in */
  width=5in height=0.25in; /* bottom of page      is at 4.78in */
proc odstext;
p "   Data Source: SASHELP.CLASS" /
  style={asis=on just=left color=blue
      /* ASIS=ON preserves the three leading blanks for indent */
        fontfamily='Arial' font_size=11pt font_weight=Bold};
run;
```

```
ods layout end;
ods printer close;

title; footnote;
/* insert the composite image file in the ODS HTML5 web page */
ods html5 style=Styles.Pearl path="C:\temp"
  options(bitmap_mode='inline') /* embed the image in HTML file */
  body="Fig14-7_GraphsAboveTablePreBuiltAsImage.html";
data _null_;
declare odsout obj();
obj.image(file:
  'C:\temp\Fig14-7_GraphsAboveTablePreBuiltAsImage.png');
run;

ods html5 close;

/* The files Fig14-7_GraphsAboveTablePreBuiltAsImage.png
   and table.png can be deleted after this code has run. */
```

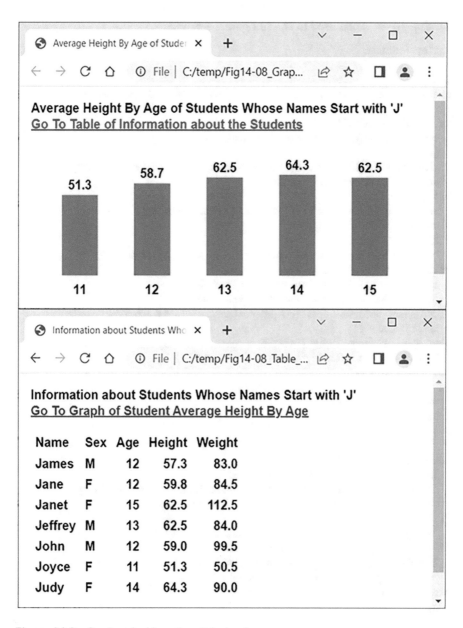

Figure 14-8. Graph and table on interlinked web pages

Listing 14-8. *Code used to create Figure 14-8*

```
title; footnote;
ods results off;
ods _all_ close;
options nocenter; /* THIS CAN PERSIST AFTER THIS CODE HAS RUN */

ods html5 path="C:\temp" nogtitle
  body="Fig14-8_GraphLinkedToTable.html"
  (title=
    "Average Height By Age of Students Whose Names Start with 'J'")
  style=AllTextFontArial12ptBold;
ods graphics on /
  reset=all scale=off width=500px height=200px noborder
  outputfmt=SVG imagemap;
title1 justify=left
  "Average Height By Age of Students Whose Names Start with 'J'";
title2 justify=left color=blue underline=1
  link="C:\temp\Fig14-8_TableLinkedToGraph.html"
  'Go To Table of Information about the Students';
proc sgplot data=sashelp.class(where=(name =: 'J')) noborder
  description=' ';
vbar age / response=height stat=mean datalabel displaybaseline=off
  barwidth=0.5 nooutline fillattrs=(color=green);
yaxis display=none;
xaxis display=(nolabel noline noticks);
format height 4.1 age 2.;
run;
ods html5 close;

ods html5 path="C:\temp"
  body="Fig14-8_TableLinkedToGraph.html"
  (title="Information about Students Whose Names Start with 'J'")
  style=AllTextFontArial12ptBold_BlackWhiteTblNoGrid;
title1 justify=left
  "Information about Students Whose Names Start with 'J'";
title2 justify=left color=blue underlin=1
  link="C:\temp\Fig14-8_GraphLinkedToTable.html"
  "Go To Graph of Student Average Height By Age";
proc print data=sashelp.class(where=(name =: 'J')) noobs;
run;
ods html5 close;

options center; /* undo OPTIONS NOCENTER which would persist
    after this code has run, and potentially cause unwanted
      effects for other code run during the same SAS session */
```

A companion table can be provided as an Excel worksheet, rather than a web table. A web table is view-only. An Excel worksheet, if desired, can be reformatted or adapted to any purpose that suits the user's needs. Any changes to the worksheet leave the web graph unchanged. To make the worksheet changes permanent, it must be saved with a new filename.

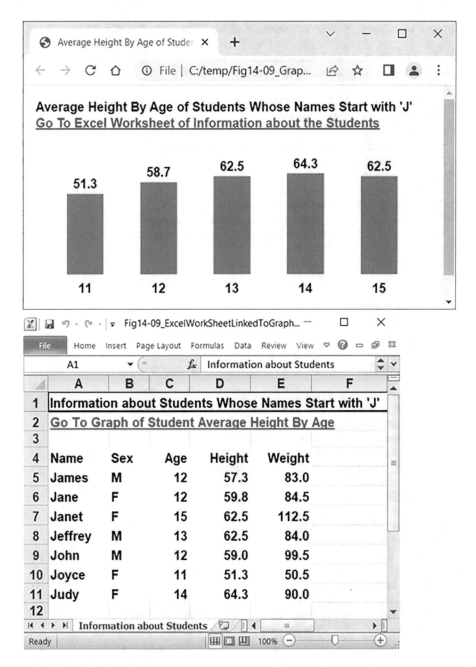

Figure 14-9. Web graph and Excel worksheet interlinked

Listing 14-9. Code used to create Figure 14-9

```
title; footnote;
ods results off;
ods _all_ close;
options nocenter; /* THIS CAN PERSIST AFTER THIS CODE HAS RUN */

ods html5 path="C:\temp" nogtitle
  body="Fig14-9_GraphLinkedToExcelWorkSheet.html"
  (title=
    "Average Height By Age of Students Whose Names Start with 'J'")
  style=AllTextFontArial12ptBold;
ods graphics on /
  reset=all scale=off width=500px height=200px noborder
  outputfmt=SVG imagemap;
title1 justify=left
  "Average Height By Age of Students Whose Names Start with 'J'";
title2 justify=left color=blue underline=1
  link="C:\temp\Fig14-9_ExcelWorkSheetLinkedToGraph.xlsx"
  'Go To Excel Worksheet of Information about the Students';
proc sgplot data=sashelp.class(where=(name =: 'J')) noborder
  description=' ';
vbar age / response=height stat=mean datalabel displaybaseline=off
  barwidth=0.5 nooutline fillattrs=(color=green);
yaxis display=none;
xaxis display=(nolabel noline noticks);
format height 4.1 age 2.;
run;
ods html5 close;

ods excel style=AllTextFontArial12ptBold_BlackWhiteTable
  file= "C:\temp\Fig14-9_ExcelWorkSheetLinkedToGraph.xlsx"
  options(embedded_titles='yes'
          title_footnote_nobreak='yes'
          sheet_name='Information about Students');
          /* sheet_name limit is 24 characters */
title1 justify=left
  "Information about Students Whose Names Start with 'J'";
title2 justify=left color=blue underlin=1
  link="C:\temp\Fig14-9_GraphLinkedToExcelWorkSheet.html"
  "Go To Graph of Student Average Height By Age";
proc print data=sashelp.class(where=(name =: 'J')) noobs;
run;
ods excel close;
options center; /* undo OPTIONS NOCENTER which would persist
      after this code has run, and potentially cause unwanted
      effects for other code run during the same SAS session */
```

More Complex Composites, Using Gridded Versus Absolute Layouts

The next two examples are two different ways to deliver a more complex composite. One uses a gridded layout and provides data tips; the other uses an absolute layout for better control of the layout but cannot provide data tips.

The second example also demonstrates how to apply a border to the composite. The ApplyBorderToAnyImage can be used to create a border for any image file, but the output is always a PNG file. (I also tested the macro with image file formats JPEG, JPG, and GIF. For me, the quality of the output PNG file with a border was acceptable, but I cannot guarantee your satisfaction.)

The first example builds everything directly inside the ODS HTML5 code block. There is no way to provide a border for that composite. The second example builds the composite as an image file with ODS PRINTER. That image file, after its build, can have a border applied with postprocessing. The file for the bordered image is then inserted in an ODS HTML5 web page.

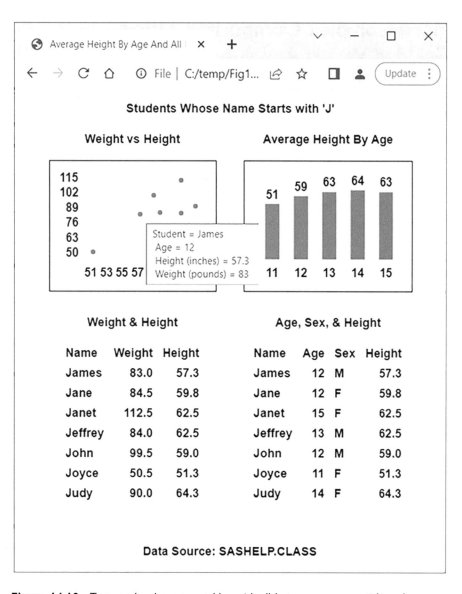

Figure 14-10. Two graphs above two tables with all between common title and common footnote, using a gridded layout

Data tips are available, but there is less control of the layout when using ODS LAYOUT GRIDDED. Note the big gap between the tables and the footnote. The use of ODS LAYOUT ABSOLUTE for Figure 14-11 is the solution.

Listing 14-10. *Code used to create Figure 14-10*

```
ods results off;
ods _all_ close;
title "Students Whose Name Starts with 'J'";
footnote "Data Source: SASHELP.CLASS";

ods html5 path="C:\temp" nogtitle nogfootnote
  body="Fig14-10_TwoGraphsAboveTwoTables_GriddedLayout.html"
  (title="Average Height By Age And All Information about Students Whose Names
Start with 'J'")
  style=AllTextFontArial11ptBold_BlackWhiteTblNoGrid;

ods layout gridded rows=2 columns=2 column_widths=(210px 210px)
  column_gutter=20px;

/* setup for both graphs */
ods graphics on / reset=all scale=off width=210px
  outputfmt=SVG
  imagemap=on; /* needed for data tips */

ods region row=1 column=1;
title justify=center 'Weight vs Height';
proc sgplot data=sashelp.class(where=(name =: 'J')) noborder
  description=' ';
scatter x=height y=weight /
  tip=(name age height weight)
  tipformat=(auto auto F4.1 F3.)
  tiplabel=('Student' 'Age' 'Height (inches)' 'Weight (pounds)')
  markerattrs=(symbol=CircleFilled color=green);
xaxis display=(noline noticks nolabel)
      values=(51 to 65 by 2) fitpolicy=none;
yaxis display=(noline noticks nolabel)
      values=(50 to 115 by 13) fitpolicy=none;
run;

ods region row=1 column=2;
title justify=center 'Average Height By Age';
proc sgplot data=sashelp.class(where=(name =: 'J')) noborder
  description=' ';
vbar age / response=height stat=mean datalabel
  displaybaseline=off
  barwidth=0.5 nooutline fillattrs=(color=green);
yaxis display=none;
xaxis display=(noline noticks nolabel);
format height 2.;
run;
```

```
ods region row=2 column=1;
title justify=center 'Weight & Height';
proc print data=sashelp.class(where=(name =: 'J')) noobs;
var name weight height;
run;

ods region row=2 column=2;
title justify=center 'Age, Sex, & Height';
proc print data=sashelp.class(where=(name =: 'J')) noobs;
var name age sex height;
run;

ods layout end;
ods html5 close;
```

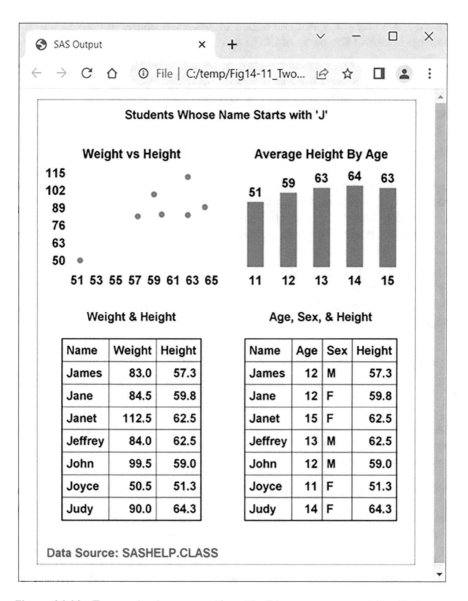

Figure 14-11. Two graphs above two tables with all between common title and common footnote, using an absolute layout, with a border applied to the composite and the result inserted in an HTML5 web page

There are no data tips, but the data is immediately below the tables, and the *absolute* layout of the parts of the image is *exactly* as I prefer it to be.

The absolute layout cannot be used in an ODS HTML5 code block. ODS PRINTER can be used instead to create an image file that is inserted in an ODS HTML5 code block. With the absolute layout, the vertical spacing can be controlled, but the disadvantage is that no data tips can be supplied with the imagemap option.

The net conclusion from Figures 14-10 and 14-11 and their associated Listings 14-10 and 14-11 is that you have a choice between maximum control of the layout versus data tips and simpler coding. Of course, it could be possible that you can find a way to get a more compact gridded layout that is to your satisfaction. However, since the detail numbers for the scatter plot are available in the table below it, the unavailability of data tips is not a denial of access to the precise numbers.

The situation where data tips are most helpful is on a high-density time series or trend plot, as in Figures 14-1 and 14-15. A companion lookup table, if desired, can be adequately provided below the plot or on an interlinked web page or Excel worksheet, as demonstrated in Figures 14-8 and 14-9.

Listing 14-11. *Code used to create Figure 14-11*

```
%include "C:\SharedCode\ApplyBorderToAnyImage.sas";

title; footnote;
ods results off;
ods _all_ close;
options nodate nonumber;

options papersize=("5in" "5.9in"); /* composite width & height */

ods printer printer=PNG dpi=300 style=AllTextFontArial11ptBold
  /* this style affects text from PROC SGPLOT and PROC PRINT,
     but not output from PROC ODSTEXT. */
  file=
    "C:\temp\Fig14-11_TwoGraphsAboveTwoTables_AbsoluteLayout.png";

ods layout absolute;

/* create the common title 0.1in below the top of the image */
ods region x=0in y=0.1in width=5in height=0.6in;
proc odstext;
p "Students Whose Name Starts with 'J'" /
  style={just=center
         fontfamily='Arial' font_size=11pt font_weight=Bold};
run;

/* create the graphs side-by-side */
```

```
/* setup for both graphs */
ods graphics on /
  reset=all scale=off width=2.5in height=2.0in noborder;
/* the output format is set to PNG on the ODS PRINTER statement */

ods region x=0in y=0.5in width=2.5in height=2.0in;
title justify=center 'Weight vs Height';
proc sgplot data=sashelp.class(where=(name =: 'J')) noborder;
scatter x=height y=weight /
  markerattrs=(symbol=CircleFilled color=green);
xaxis display=(noline noticks nolabel)
      values=(51 to 65 by 2);
yaxis display=(noline noticks nolabel)
      values=(50 to 115 by 13) fitpolicy=none;
run;

ods region x=2.5in y=0.5in width=2.5in height=2.0in;
title justify=center 'Average Height By Age';
proc sgplot data=sashelp.class(where=(name =: 'J')) noborder;
vbar age / response=height stat=mean datalabel
  displaybaseline=off
  barwidth=0.5 nooutline fillattrs=(color=green);
yaxis display=none;
xaxis display=(noline noticks nolabel);
format height 2.;
run;

/* create the tables side-by-side */

ods region x=0in y=2.65in /* adding white space:
            bottom of second region is at 2.5in */
  width=2.5in height=2.7in;
title justify=center 'Weight & Height';
proc print data=sashelp.class(where=(name =: 'J')) noobs
/* style(rowheader) = [background=white]
   needed if ID var used or NOT noobs */
  style(header) = [background=white];
var name weight height;
run;

ods region x=2.5in y=2.65in /* adding white space:
            bottom of second region is at 2.5in */
  width=2.5in height=2.7in;
title justify=center 'Age, Sex, & Height';
proc print data=sashelp.class(where=(name =: 'J')) noobs
/* style(rowheader) = [background=white]
   needed if ID var used or NOT noobs */
  style(header) = [background=white];
var name age sex height;
```

```
run;
title; /* prevent inheritance by ODS HTML5 step */

/* create the common footnote, leaving some white between it and the bottom
of the image */
ods region x=0in y=5.65in  /* bottom of region 3 is at 5.35in */
  width=5in height=0.25in; /* bottom of page    is at 5.9in */
proc odstext; p "   Data Source: SASHELP.CLASS" /
  style={asis=on just=left color=blue
      /* ASIS=ON preserves the three leading blanks for indent */
         fontfamily='Arial' font_size=11pt font_weight=Bold};
run;

ods layout end;
ods printer close;

%ApplyBorderToAnyImage(
in=C:\temp\Fig14-11_TwoGraphsAboveTwoTables_AbsoluteLayout.png,
out=C:\temp\Fig14-11_TwoGraphsAboveTwoTables_WithOuterBorder.png,
height=5.9in,width=5in);

/* insert the composite image with border into the web page */
title; footnote;
ods html5 style=Styles.Pearl path="C:\temp"
     /* default style has light blue web page background */
  options(bitmap_mode='inline') /* embed the image in HTML file */
  body="Fig14-11_TwoGraphsAboveTwoTables_AbsoluteLayout.html";
data _null_;
declare odsout obj();
obj.image(file:
  'C:\temp\Fig14-11_TwoGraphsAboveTwoTables_WithOuterBorder.png');
run;
ods html5 close;

/* Both PNG files can be deleted after this code has run */
```

Drill-Down Links to Other Web Pages from Elements of a Web Graph

Any of the graph elements (plot point, bar, pie slice, etc.) on a web page can be a hot link to another web page. That web page can be another graph or a table instead.

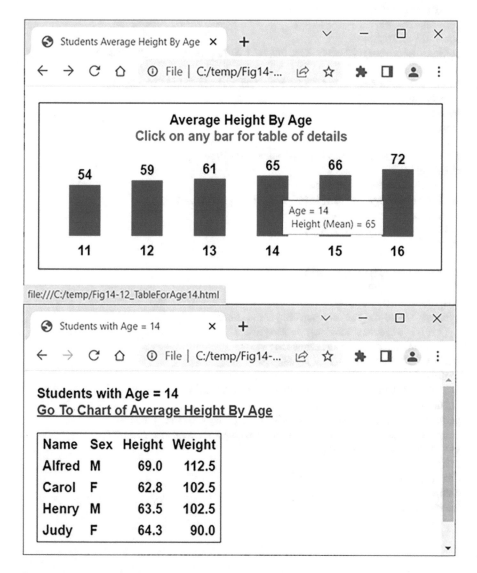

Figure 14-12. In the graph web page, the mouse resting on the bar for age 14 not only raises the data tip for the bar but also causes the display of the hot link at lower left. In the table web page for age 14, there is a link back to the graph

Any data tips in the graph are not needed when data labels are present, but the IMAGEMAP option is required for the hot links to work. When the IMAGEMAP option is used, the data tip, wanted or not, is illuminated when the mouse hovers over a bar to exercise the hot link.

Listing 14-12. *Code used to create Figure 14-12*

```
title; footnote;
ods results off;
ods _all_ close;
options nocenter; /* THIS CAN PERSIST AFTER THIS CODE HAS RUN */

proc sort data=sashelp.class(keep=Age) out=work.DistinctAges
  nodupkey;
by Age;
run;

/* create a macro variable for each distinct age */
data _null_;
set work.DistinctAges end=LastOne;
call symput('Age'||trim(left(_N_)),trim(left(Age)));
if LastOne;
call symput('HowMany',_N_);
run;

%macro TableByAge(AgeCount);
%do i = 1 %to &AgeCount %by 1;
ods html5 path="C:\temp"
  body="Fig14-12_TableForAge&&Age&i...html"
  (title="Students with Age = &&Age&i")
  style=AllTextFontArial12ptBold;
title1 "Students with Age = &&Age&i";
title2 justify=left color=blue underline=1
  link="C:\temp\Fig14-12_AverageHeightByAge.html"
  'Go To Chart of Average Height By Age';
proc print data=sashelp.class(where=(Age EQ &&Age&i)) noobs
  style(header) = [backgroundcolor=white]; /* replace gray */
var Name Sex Height Weight;
run;
ods html5 close;
%end;
%mend  TableByAge;
```

```
/* create a tabular web page for each age value */
options mprint;
%TableByAge(&HowMany);

data work.ClassWithLinks;
length LinkVar $ 27;
set sashelp.class;
LinkVar = "Fig14-12_TableForAge" || trim(left(Age)) || ".html";
run;

/* create the web graph with hot link at each bar */
ods html5 path="C:\temp"
  body="Fig14-12_AverageHeightByAge.html"
  (title="Students Average Height By Age")
  style=AllTextFontArial12ptBold;
ods graphics on / reset=all scale=off width=500px height=200px
  outputfmt=SVG
  imagemap; /* needed for hot links */
title1 justify=center 'Average Height By Age';
title2 justify=center color=blue 'Click on any bar for table of details';
proc sgplot data=work.ClassWithLinks noborder
  description=' ';
vbar age / response=height stat=mean datalabel
  url=LinkVar /* makes each bar a hot link */
  displaybaseline=off
  barwidth=0.5 nooutline fillattrs=(color=blue);
yaxis display=none;
xaxis display=(noline noticks nolabel);
format height 2.;
run;
ods html5 close;
options center; /* undo OPTIONS NOCENTER which would persist
     after this code has run, and potentially cause unwanted
     effects for other code run during the same SAS session */
```

Control of the Web Page Background Color and Graph Transparency (Pink Is *Not* Recommended)

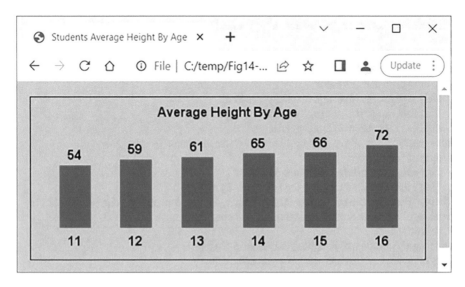

Figure 14-13. Pink web page background for a transparent graph

The color was chosen for demonstration only. I don't see any visual hazard, but it is an improbable color choice. If the graph is not made transparent as shown in the code, then it would be drawn in an island of white (the default background color for ODS Graphics graphs), which would undercut the purpose of the pink background, converting it to a "surroundground." The choice of parent style is whatever you prefer. The consequences of a different choice are a priori unknown.

Listing 14-13. *Code used to create Figure 14-13*

```
proc template;
  define style PinkBackground;
    parent=AllTextFontArial12ptBold;
      class body / backgroundcolor=pink;
  end;
run;

title; footnote;
ods results off;
ods _all_ close;
ods html5 path="C:\temp"
```

```
  body="Fig14-13_TransparentGraphOnPinkBackground.html"
  (title="Students Average Height By Age")
  style=PinkBackground;
ods graphics on / reset=all scale=off width=500px height=200px
  outputfmt=SVG imagemap;
title justify=center 'Average Height By Age';
proc sgplot data=sashelp.class noborder
  description=' '
  noopaque nowall; /* make the graph transparent */
vbar age / response=height stat=mean datalabel
  displaybaseline=off
  barwidth=0.5 nooutline fillattrs=(color=blue);
yaxis display=none;
xaxis display=(noline noticks nolabel);
format height 2.;
run;
ods html5 close;
```

The focus of this book is graphic output, not tabular output. However, since companion tables are included, it is appropriate to show that the web page background for a table can be customized. In fact, since the parent style chosen imposes a gray background in the header cells for the custom style, it is important to provide this cautionary example of how to deal with that hazard to intended design. This table is not a companion for Figure 14-13.

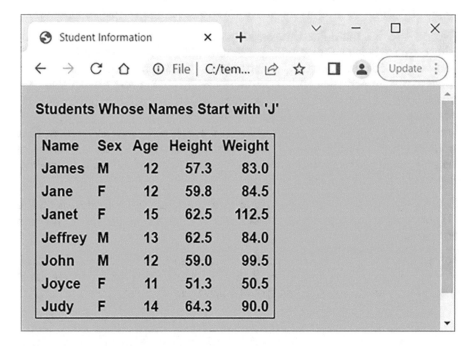

Figure 14-14. Pink web page background for a table

Listing 14-14. *Code used to create Figure 14-14*

```
title; footnote;
ods results off;
ods _all_ close;
options nocenter; /* THIS CAN PERSIST AFTER THIS CODE HAS RUN */

ods html5 path="C:\temp"
  body="Fig14-14_TableOnPinkBackground.html"
  (title="Student Information")
  style=PinkBackground; /* created in Listing 14-13 */
title justify=left "Students Whose Names Start with 'J'";
proc print data=sashelp.class(where=(name =: 'J')) noobs
  style(header) = [background=Pink];
  /* The parent style used for the PinkBackground style
     has a different background color in the header cells. */
run;
ods html5 close;
options center; /* undo OPTIONS NOCENTER which would persist
      after this code has run, and potentially cause unwanted
      effects for other code run during the same SAS session */
```

The Web-Enabled Sparse Line Table

In 1990, I introduced the concept of Sparse Line Annotation, an effective way to present the most important information about time series/trend history.

Figure 14-15 is a multi-line time series plot where data tips are essential, but where data labels are used with maximum utility. The critical values, Start, End, Intermediate Minimum, Intermediate Maximum, and Most Recent Change, are immediately and permanently available, but any other values are available as data tips. If desired, this web-enabled Sparse Line Table could be interlinked with a static table of *all* of the values, as in Figure 14-8 or 14-9, preferably with date as a row header and stock as a column header. That would be the ultimate package for presenting time series data with visual insight as to comparative performance and trends, plus the certainty, convenience, and printability of detail.

Figure 14-15 is a web-enabled upgrade to, and a valuable enhancement of, the original version of Sparse Line Annotation. See Figures 1-16 and 1-17 for that first edition.

For static versions of Sparse Line Tables, see Figures 9-9 and 9-12. For static versions of Sparse Line Panels, see Figures 9-11 and 9-13. A Sparse Line Panel is a multi-column, multi-row matrix of Sparse Lines.

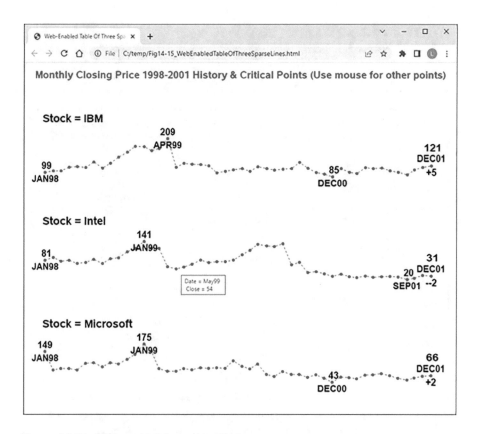

Figure 14-15. Web-enabled Sparse Line Table

The code for this example is too long, even for this comparatively code-verbose chapter. Please see Listing A14-15 in Appendix A.

In a case where a Sparse Line Table might be longer than you like, then Figure 14-16 can serve as a web-enabled enhancement for Figure 14-1.

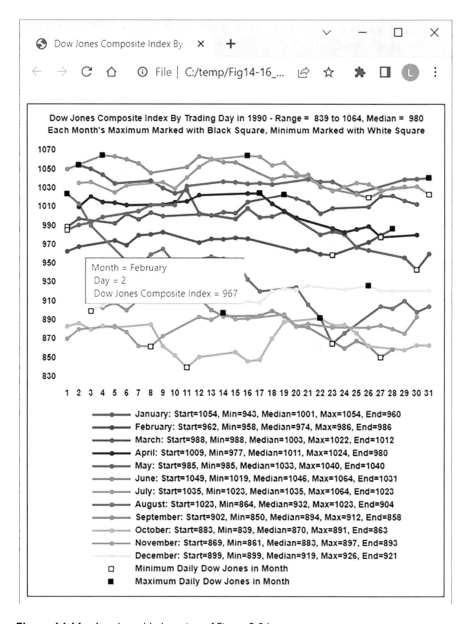

Figure 14-16. A web-enabled version of Figure 8-34

Listing 14-16. *Code used to create Figure 14-16*

```
/* requires a prior run of Listing 14-0 to create input data */
%include "C:\SharedCode\CommonCodeForFig8_34AndFig14_16.sas";

title; footnote;
ods results off;
ods _all_ close;
ods html5 path="C:\temp" style=GraphFontArial8ptBold
  body=
"Fig14-16_DowByDayEachMonth1990_Overlay_MostInfo_MinMaxMarkers.html"
  (title='Dow Jones Composite Index By Trading Day in 1990');
  /* the optional TITLE= text appears
     in the upper left corner of the web browser window */
ods graphics on / reset=all scale=off width=5.56in height=6.4in
  maxlegendarea=30 /* with the default 20, the legend would be omitted */
  imagemap=on /* needed for data tips */
  outputfmt=SVG; /* In principle the default, but in certain
  circumstances that can be unwittingly overridden.
  It does no harm to ensure SVG as OUTPUTFMT the default,
  which can be expected to deliver satisfactory results. */
title1 justify=center
  "Dow Jones Composite Index By Trading Day in 1990 - Range = &MinDJ1990 to
&MaxDJ1990, Median = &MedDJ1990";
title2 justify=center
  "Each Month's Maximum Marked with Black Square, Minimum Marked with White
Square";
proc sgplot data=work.DowJonesByDayIn1990MonthlyMinMax noborder
/* this input data created by CommonCodeForFig8_34AndFig14_16.sas */
  description=' '; /* prevent mouseover pop-up of
                      "The SGPLOT Procedure", which is a distraction
                      when trying to raise data tips. */
series y=DAILYDJ x=Day / group=Month
  tip=(Month Day DailyDJ)
  tipformat=(monthnm9. F2. F4.)
  tiplabel=('Month' 'Day' 'Dow Jones Composite Index')
  markers markerattrs=(size=7 symbol=CircleFilled)
  lineattrs=(thickness=3 pattern=Solid);
scatter x=Day y=MinDJ /
  FilledOutlinedMarkers
  markerattrs=(symbol=SquareFilled size=7px)
  markerfillattrs=(color=white)
  markeroutlineattrs=(color=black thickness=1px);
scatter x=Day y=MaxDJ /
  markerattrs=(symbol=SquareFilled
    size=9px /* to make drawn size close to that of white markers */
    color=black);
yaxis display=(nolabel noticks noline) grid minorgrid minorcount=1
```

```
   values=(830 to 1080 by 20);
xaxis display=(nolabel noticks noline) grid fitpolicy=none
   values=(1 TO 31 BY 1);
keylegend / title='' noborder across=1;
format DailyDJ 4. Month MonthStats.;
/* MonthStats format created by CommonCodeForFig8_34AndFig14_16 */
run;
ods html5 close;
```

Summary

This summary section includes important reminders and explanations about coding practices that are unique to this chapter. But first is the summary.

This chapter is not an expansive exposition of what you can do with ODS HTML5. Here, the focus has been on its utility in getting graph viewers access to precise numbers which cannot be made available via data labels and axis tables.

ODS HTML5 is the tool to provide a viewer access to precise values for any plot point or other graphic elements in situations where high density makes data labels and an X axis table impractical as ways to display those values. The data tips are transitory. So a companion table on the same web page below the graph or on an interlinked web page is still necessary if the viewer wants static, permanent, and printable access to the precise values. The table can alternatively be an Excel worksheet which is linked back to the web graph.

Data tips can include values of *any* variables available in the input data, and the SAS formats and labels for those data tip variables can be customized.

In addition to the possibility of a companion table on the same or a linked web page, a web graph can, via hot links on its graphic elements (plot points, bars, pie slices, etc.), take the user of the web browser to any related information for a graphic element.

ODS HTML5 is an important improvement on ODS HTML in that all of the images used in web pages are embedded in the web page's HTML file. With ODS HTML, the web page is, in effect, a picture frame only. The ODS HTML frame's contents are loose files that must be moved with the HTML file, whether to a different storage location, or sent in an email. If not, the picture frame will be empty.

A few coding practices in this chapter deserve a mention/reminder.

Since OPTIONS NOCENTER is used for some examples, such code should end with OPTIONS CENTER to reset to the default so that other code run during the same SAS session does not deliver output that is unexpectedly left-justified.

There are two options that are used in every ODS GRAPHICS statement in this chapter.

Though OUTPUTFMT=SVG is the nominal default for ODS HTML5, during a multi-run SAS session with other graphic activity going on, in certain circumstances, PNG might become the default. It does no harm to specify an option that in most cases would be the default. SVG is the superior graph image file format.

While most of the examples don't use data tips or provide drill-down, the IMAGEMAP option is always turned on. This prevents unusual phenomena in the web browser, which are described in a comment in Listing 14-2. IMAGEMAP is *required* not only for data tips (default or custom) but also for the drill-down that is implemented in Figure 14-12. In the chapter examples that use data labels, the imagemap being turned on also provides (unneeded) default data tips. Of course, if the viewer never moves the mouse around the web page, the fact that they are unnecessarily present will not be apparent. If discovered, they will not contradict data labels and can do no harm. The alternative of two strange pop-ups without the data tips is not a better construction choice and is not by programmer design or intent.

In a few examples, OPTIONS NODATE NONUMBER is used. The SAS defaults are DATE and NUMBER. Since *none* of the examples are intended to display the SAS session start date and page numbers, the lack of any default restoration code at the end of code for examples that require the options to be turned off cannot lead to adverse consequences for other examples in this chapter. The turnoff is done only for three examples, Figures 14-6, 14-7, and 14-11. They use ODS PRINTER to create image files which are programmatically inserted into ODS HTML5. All other examples create their output directly in ODS HTML5, and the code is inherently immune to the DATE and NUMBER options that are the SAS defaults. Of course, if you should run the code for any of these three examples in a SAS session where subsequent processing of other code is *expected* to produce output with DATE and/or NUMBER in effect, then either your version of this code must restore the option(s) as its last action, or the subsequent processing must explicitly turn the needed option(s) back on.

■ **Note**   In examples where the composite is created as an image with ODS PRINTER and then inserted into ODS HTML5 (Figures 14-6, 14-7, and 14-11), the composite image file remains in the folder used. It is physically embedded in the HTML file and can be deleted, unlike the case for the ODS HTML predecessor to ODS HTML5. The same deletability applies to the Table.png file that is created for Figure 14-7. In its case, it is physically embedded in the composite image file. As previously explained, the three images that are inserted in ODS HTML5 require specification of OPTIONS(BITMAP_MODE='INLINE') on the ODS HTML5 statement to assure that they are indeed embedded and can be deleted, or simply ignored, after the code has run.

Delivering Precise Numbers When Using PROC SGMAP

The first choropleth map was created in 1826 by Baron Charles Dupin. It was a gray-shaded map concerning primary school education across France. Choropleth maps are also called thematic maps.

My first encounter with choropleth maps was to assist a SAS/GRAPH project by Steven J. Subichin in the Market Research Department at Miller Brewing Company in the 1980s. To create output at faster rates, they were printed with gray shades on a laser printer, rather than being output in color with a pen plotter. The states were annotated with three lines of information. To assure readability, the annotation process not only laid down the information but created islands of white behind the information. The ability to produce

© LeRoy Bessler 2023

LeR. Bessler, *Visual Data Insights Using SAS ODS Graphics*,
https://doi.org/10.1007/978-1-4842-8609-8_15

what ODS Graphics PROC SGMAP TEXT statement calls BACKFILL (white rectangles as background for annotation) only came later as a feature for PROC GMAP.

Using ODS Graphics PROC SGMAP here and selecting sufficiently light shades of area fill, no BACKFILL is required for readability. Always a decision for choropleth maps is how the categories are defined, which determines the size of the color palette for shading.

For a later mapping project unrelated to that described earlier, I faced a problem caused by what was the default behavior of SAS/GRAPH PROC GMAP. The upshot was my exploration of the various ways to specify categories, which led me to what I called Rationale-Based Response Range Assignment, and ways to accomplish that dynamically at runtime based on the data. Figure 15-1 demonstrates one way.

Figure 15-1 is an ODS Graphics PROC SGMAP update and enhancement and adaption to color of Subichin's original creation. It is actually created at a size suitable for use in a standard-width (i.e., 10 inches by 7.5 inches) PowerPoint slide, but remains readable even when shrunk to fit in this available page width. When I experimented with using the actual page width and adjusting the font size so that labels would fit in the states, the image quality was not as good. That phenomenon is interesting and might have application in other situations when trying to get the best image in a constrained space. "Build bigger than needed for better image quality at smaller size." I can't guarantee how often and when that is the case, however.

Figure 15-1. Choropleth map for top ten, remainder above median, median, bottom ten, and remainder below median, with annotation of state abbreviation, population, and population rank

The only apparent imperfection in this result is the collision of the bottom of annotation for Tennessee (State Code "TN") with boundary with the lower boundary. The population (in millions) is still readable. Position adjustments like those made for other states cannot solve the problem for this state. If the text stack were moved left or right, there would be no increase in the available vertical space.

Producing an annotated map such as this can also be done for other geographic entities.

Not available in the M7 maintenance level, nor the forthcoming M8 maintenance level, of SAS ODS Graphics used are

> FILLHEIGHT option for KEYLEGEND statement
>
> FILLASPECT option for KEYLEGEND statement
>
> NOBORDER option for KEYLEGEND statement

These options might be in the M9 maintenance level.

FILLASPECT=GOLDEN with FILLHEIGHT set equal to the font height of legend values is always preferred. As explained in Chapter 2, legend color samples must be large enough to assure color distinguishability.

Listing 15-1. *Code used to create Figure 15-1*

```
ods results=off;
ods _all_ close;

proc sort data=sashelp.us_data(keep=state statecode statename population_2010)
out=ToCntlinPrep;
where statecode NE 'PR';
by population_2010;
run;

data ToFormat;
retain fmtname 'popfmt' type 'N' Start 0;
length Start End 8 Label $ 64;
set ToCntlInPrep;
if _N_ EQ 1 then Start = population_2010;
if _N_ LT 10 then return;
if _N_ EQ 10 then do;
  End = population_2010;
  Label = trim(left(put(Start,comma10.))) || ' - ' ||
    trim(left(put(population_2010,comma10.))) || ' (ten lowest)';
  output;
end;
if _N_ EQ 11 then Start = population_2010;
else
if _N_ LT 25 then return;
else
if _N_ EQ 25 then do;
  End = population_2010;
  Label = trim(left(put(Start,comma10.))) || ' - ' ||
    trim(left(put(population_2010,comma10.))) || ' (below median)';
  output;
end;
else
if _N_ EQ 26
then do;
  Start = population_2010;
  End = population_2010;
  Label = trim(left(put(Start,comma10.))) || ' - ' ||
    trim(left(put(End,comma10.))) || ' (median)';
  output;
end;
else
```

```
if _N_ EQ 27 then Start = population_2010;
if _N_ LT 41 then return;
else
if _N_ EQ 41 then do;
  End = population_2010;
  Label = trim(left(put(Start,comma10.))) || ' - ' ||
    trim(left(put(population_2010,comma10.))) || ' (above median)';
  output;
end;
else
if _N_ EQ 42 then Start = population_2010;
if _N_ LT 51 then return;
else
if _N_ EQ 51 then do;
  End = population_2010;
  Label = trim(left(put(Start,comma10.))) || ' - ' || trim(left(put(populati
on_2010,comma10.))) || ' (ten highest)';
  output;
end;
run;

proc format cntlin=ToFormat library=work;
run;

/* turn on the LISTING destination to see output from:
proc format fmtlib;
run; */

proc sort  data=sashelp.us_data(keep=statecode  statename  population_2010)
out=ToRank;
where statecode NE 'PR';
by descending population_2010;
run;

data Ranked;
length Rank $ 2 /* NOT USED: PopDisplay $ 5 PopShort $ 4 */;
set ToRank;
Rank = left(put(_N_,2.));
run;

proc sort data=Ranked out=RankedToMerge;
by statecode;
run;

proc  sort  data=mapsgfk.uscenter(keep=x  y  state  statecode  ocean)
out=StateCentersToMerge;
by statecode;
run;
```

```
data population_plus_statecenter;
merge StateCentersToMerge(in=StateCenter) RankedToMerge(in=Ranked);
by statecode;
if StateCenter and Ranked;
if ocean EQ 'Y' AND statecode EQ 'VT'
then delete;
else
if ocean EQ 'N' AND statecode NE 'VT'
then delete;
run;

data statelabels;
set population_plus_statecenter;
length label $15;
label=statecode;
if label='FL'
then x = x + 0.005;
if label='HI'
then y = y + 0.025;
if label='ME'
then y = y + 0.01;
if ocean EQ 'Y'
then do;
  if statecode IN ('NH')
  then x = x + 0.03;
  else
  if statecode IN ('MA' 'CT' 'RI')
  then x = x + 0.04;
  else
  if statecode EQ 'MD'
  then x = x + 0.02;
  else
  if statecode EQ 'DC'
  then x = x + 0.01;
  else
  if statecode IN ('NJ' 'DE')
  then x = x + 0.03;
  label = trim(Rank) || ' - ' || statecode || ' - ' ||
          put(population_2010 / 1000000,5.2);
  output;
end;
else do;
  if statecode EQ 'VT'
  then do;
    y = y + 0.025;
  x = x - 0.005;
  end;
  y = y + 0.01;
  label = Rank;
```

```
   output;
   y = y - 0.01;
   label = statecode;
   output;
   y = y - 0.01;
   label = put(population_2010 / 1000000,5.2);
   output;
end;
 /* NOT USED:
PopDiaplay = put(population_2010 / 1000000,5.2);
PopShort = put(population_2010 / 1000000,4.1);
 */
run;

proc template;
define style styles.LeRB_FiveColorMap_POGCB;
 parent=styles.htmlblue;
/* NOT USED:
   style graphbackground / color=cxfafae6;
    If dark palette, make background black
    all text for title, anno, legend white.
*/
class graphcolors /
   'gdata1'=pink
   'gdata2'=verylightorange
   'gdata3'=lightgray
   'gdata4'=CXCCFFFF
   'gdata5'=lightblue
   ;
 end;
run;

proc sort data=sashelp.us_data(keep=state statecode population_2010)
   out=ForLegendEntriesInDesiredOrder;
where statecode NE 'PR';
by population_2010;
run;

ods listing style=styles.LeRB_FiveColorMap_POGCB gpath="C:\temp";
ods graphics / reset=all noscale
   width=10in /* default height=7.5in */
   imagename=
'Fig15-1_FiveColorMap_RationaleRanges_AnnoRankStateCodePopulation';
title height=16pt
      "Categorized and Ranked State Populations for United States of America -
Year 2010";
proc sgmap
   maprespdata=ForLegendEntriesInDesiredOrder
   mapdata=mapsgfk.us
```

```
  plotdata=statelabels;
format population_2010 popfmt.;
/* This WARNING message, with no practical significance,
   will appear in the SAS log:
WARNING: Variable POPULATION_2010 not found in data set
         MAPSGFK.US. */
choromap population_2010 / mapid=statecode discrete
  lineattrs=(thickness=1 color=black)
  name='FiveColorMap_AutoRespRanges_ThreeLineAnno';
text x=x y=y text=label /
  textattrs=(color=black family=Arial size=8pt weight=bold);
keylegend 'FiveColorMap_AutoRespRanges_ThreeLineAnno' / title=''
  valueattrs=(family=Arial size=12pt weight=bold) autoitemsize;
run;
ods listing close;
title; footnote;
```

Summary

This chapter on choropleth maps is limited to showing a useful way to display multiple precise numbers, not just geographic area identity, on a color-coded map. Producing an annotated map such as this can be done for other geographic entities.

Appendix A

All of the code in Appendix A, as well as the macros and code blocks that are %INCLUDEd here, can be downloaded by readers at https://github.com/Apress/Visual-Data-Insights-Using-SAS-ODS-Graphics.

Listing A2-5. Code to create an Excel worksheet to display samples of the SAS Predefined Colors, without and with text (one column black text embedded, the other column white text embedded), and a column for their SAS RGB color codes. The workbook also includes a second worksheet to display samples of 360 HLS colors, without and with embedded text, and a column for their SAS HLS color codes.

```
proc registry
export="C:\temp\colornames.txt"
  usesashelp
  startat="COLORNAMES";
run;

data work.SASpredefinecColorList(keep=ColorName RGBcode);
retain FirstColorFound 'N' MaxLength 0;
length RGBsource $ 8 RGBcode $ 8;
infile " C:\temp\colornames.txt " pad end=LastOne;
input @1 Line $60.;
if Line =: '"AliceBlue'
then FirstColorFound = 'Y' ;
if FirstColorFound EQ 'N' then delete;
AfterColor = index(substr(Line,2,59),'"' );
ColorName = substr(Line,2,AfterColor-1);
if length(ColorName) GT 2;
if ColorName EQ 'Cornsilk'  then  ColorName = 'CornSilk';
if ColorName EQ 'lightGray' then  ColorName = 'LightGray';
```

```
if ColorName EQ 'Oldlace'  then  ColorName = 'OldLace';
if ColorName EQ 'Peachpuff' then  ColorName = 'PeachPuff';
if ColorName EQ 'Seashell'  then  ColorName = 'SeaShell';
MaxLength = max(MaxLength,length(ColorName));
RGBsource = substr(Line,index(Line,':') + 2,8);
RGBcode = 'CX' || compress(RGBsource,',');
if LastOne
then call symput('MaxLengthOfColorNames' ,MaxLength);
run;

data work.HLScolorCodes(keep=HLScode);
retain hhh 0;
length HLScode $ 8;
do hhh = 0 to 360 by 1;
  HLScode = 'H' || put(hhh,hex3.) || '80FF';
  output;
end;
run;

footnote;
ods results off;
ods _all_ close;
ods excel file=
  "C:\temp\Fig2-5_SAS_PredefinedColors_AND_No_Figure_HLScolors.xlsx"
    options( embedded_titles='yes'
             title_footnote_nobreak='yes'
             sheet_interval='proc'
             zoom='200' /* adjust as preferred, or omit, or keep */
          );

ods excel options(sheet_name='Predefined Colors');
title1 justify=left font='Arial/Bold' height=10pt
  "SAS PreDefined Color Names";
title2 justify=left font='Arial/Bold' height=10pt
  "Consider clearing any cell with hard-to-read text" ;
title3 justify=left font='Arial/Bold' height=10pt
  "and saving this Excel spreadsheet with a new filename" ;
proc report data=work.SASpredefinecColorList nowd;
column ColorName colorname=clr colorname=clrBlackText colorname=clrWhiteText
RGBcode=clrRGBcolorCode;
define ColorName / 'Color Name' ;
define clr / 'Color' ;
compute clr /char length=35;
  call define(_col_,'style',
    'style={background='||ColorName||'      foreground='||ColorName||' } ');
endcomp;
```

```
define clrBlackText / 'With Black Text';
compute clrBlackText /char length=35;
  call define(_col_,'style',
    'style={background='||ColorName||' foreground=Black}');
endcomp;
define clrWhiteText / 'With White Text';
compute clrWhiteText /char length=35;
  call define(_col_,'style',
    'style={background='||ColorName||' foreground=White}');
endcomp;
run;

ods excel options(sheet_name='HLS Colors');
title1 justify=left font='Arial/Bold' height=10pt
  "HLS Colors and SAS HLS Color Codes";
proc report data=work.HLScolorCodes nowd;
column HLScode HLScode=clr HLScode=clrBlackText HLScode=clrWhiteText;
define HLScode / 'HLS Code' ;
define clr / 'Color' ;
compute clr /char length=8;
  call define(_col_,'style',
    'style={background='||HLScode||' foreground='||HLScode||' } ');
endcomp;
define clrBlackText / 'With Black Text';
compute clrBlackText /char length=8;
  call define(_col_,'style',
    'style={background='||HLScode||' foreground=Black}');
endcomp;
define clrWhiteText / 'With White Text';
compute clrWhiteText /char length=8;
  call define(_col_,'style',
    'style={background='||HLScode||' foreground=White}');
endcomp;
run;

ods excel close;
title;
```

Listing A3-1. *Code to create Figure 3-1*

```
ods results=off;
ods _all_ close;
ods listing style=listing gpath='C:\temp' dpi=300;

ods graphics on / reset=all noscale
  width=5.7in /* Available page width in this book */
             /* Accepting the default height */
  imagename='Fig3-1_INSETandTEXTstatementsAndTitlesAndFootnotes';
```

```
title1 font='Arial/Bold' height=10pt justify=CENTER
  'Scatter Plot of Height versus Age for Two Students in SASHELP.CLASS';
/* leading spaces in remaining titles to align them with TITLE1 */
title2 font='Arial/Bold' height=10pt justify=LEFT
  'Text locations using ' color=blue
  'INSET Statements';
title3 font='Arial/Bold' height=10pt justify=LEFT
  'Name values placed at Height-Age locations using the ' color=red 'TEXT
Statement';
footnote1 font='Arial/Bold' height=10pt
  justify=left 'JUSTIFY=LEFT'
  justify=center 'JUSTIFY=CENTER (the default)'
  justify=right 'JUSTIFY=RIGHT';
footnote2 font='Arial/Bold' height=10pt justify=left
  'Up to 10 FOOTNOTE statements, FOOTNOTE1 to FOOTNOTE10.';
footnote3 font='Arial/Bold' height=10pt justify=left
  'FOOTNOTE is a synonym for FOOTNOTE1.';
footnote3 font='Arial/Bold' height=10pt justify=left
  'The default color is black.';
footnote4 font='Arial/Bold' height=10pt justify=left
  'Rules are the same for TITLE statements.';
proc sgplot data=sashelp.class noborder noautolegend;
where name IN ('Carol' 'Mary');
text x=age y=height text=name / position=Top
  textattrs=(color=red  family=Arial size=10pt weight=Bold);
inset 'Top Left'     / position=TopLeft
  textattrs=(color=blue family=Arial size=10pt weight=Bold);
inset 'Top'          / position=Top
  textattrs=(color=blue family=Arial size=10pt weight=Bold);
inset 'Top Right'    / position=TopRight
  textattrs=(color=blue family=Arial size=10pt weight=Bold);
inset 'Right'        / position=Right
  textattrs=(color=blue family=Arial size=10pt weight=Bold);
inset 'Bottom Right' / position=BottomRight
  textattrs=(color=blue family=Arial size=10pt weight=Bold);
inset 'Bottom'       / position=Bottom
  textattrs=(color=blue family=Arial size=10pt weight=Bold);
inset 'Bottom Left'  / position=BottomLeft
  textattrs=(color=blue family=Arial size=10pt weight=Bold);
  /* separating the assigned INSET string into quoted pieces
     produces a line break in between each quoted piece */
inset 'Left' 'with line breaks,' 'border, and' 'background color' /
  position=Left
  border
  backcolor=yellow
  textattrs=(color=blue family=Arial size=10pt weight=Bold);
yaxis display=(noline noticks)
  values=(62 to 67 by 1)
  valueattrs=(family=Arial size=10pt weight=Bold)
```

```
  labelattrs=(family=Arial size=10pt weight=Bold)
  labelpos=top; /* PREVENT vertical text for vertical axis */
xaxis display=(noline noticks)
  values=(11 to 16 by 1)
  valueattrs=(family=Arial size=10pt weight=Bold)
  labelattrs=(family=Arial size=10pt weight=Bold);
run;

ods listing close;
title; footnote;
```

Listing A3-11. *Code to create Figure 3-11*

```
proc sort data=sashelp.class(keep=age height)
          out=ByAgeHeight;
by age descending height;
run;

data ToPlot;
retain LineAndRowNumber 0;
set ByAgeHeight;
by age;
if First.Age
then LineAndRowNumber = 1;
else LineAndRowNumber + 1;
run;

proc summary data=sashelp.class nway;
class age;
var height;
output out=AvgHgt(keep=age AvgHgt) mean=AvgHgt;
run;

data ToPlot;
merge ToPlot AvgHgt;
by age;
run;

footnote;
ods results=off;
ods _all_ close;
ods listing style=listing gpath="C:\temp";

ods graphics on / reset=all scale=off width=5.7in height=5.7in
  imagename=" Fig3-11_XaxisTablesReplacePlotPointDataLabels";
```

```
title1 font='Arial/Bold' height=11pt justify=center
  'Height (inches) vs Age (years)';
title2 font='Arial/Bold' height=11pt justify=center
  'With Plot of ' color=red 'Average Height ' color=black 'vs Age';
proc sgplot data=ToPlot
  noborder
  noautolegend;
styleattrs
  datacontrastcolors=(indigo gray blue magenta saddlebrown)
  datacolors=(indigo gray blue magenta saddlebrown);
scatter x=age y=height /
  group=LineAndRowNumber
  markerattrs=(symbol=CircleFilled size=11pt);
series x=age y=AvgHgt / lineattrs=(color=red thickness=2);
yaxis display=(noline noticks)
  label='Height'
  labelpos=top
  labelattrs=(family=Arial size=11pt weight=Bold)
  values=(51 to 72 by 21)
  valueattrs=(family=Arial size=11pt weight=Bold);
xaxis display=(noline noticks)
  label='Age'
  labelpos=left
  labelattrs=(family=Arial size=11pt weight=Bold)
  values=(11 to 16 by 1)
  valueattrs=(family=Arial size=11pt weight=Bold);
xaxistable height /
  class=LineAndRowNumber
  colorgroup=LineAndRowNumber
  location=inside
  position=bottom
  title=''
  nolabel
  valueattrs=(family=Arial size=11pt weight=Bold);
xaxistable height / stat=mean
  location=inside
  position=bottom
  title=''
  label='Avg '
  labelpos=left
  labelattrs=(family=Arial size=11pt weight=Bold color=red)
  valueattrs=(family=Arial size=11pt weight=Bold color=red);
format AvgHgt height 4.1;
run;

ods listing close;
title; footnote;
```

Listing A4-7. *Code to create the three images in Figure 4-7*

```
/* Code to Create the Three Images in Figure 4-7,
   with highlighting for:
   the ODS GRAPHICS statement,
   the three TITLE statements, and
   the DATA step that are unique to the image */

/* HEIGHT in the ODS GRAPHICS statement differs for each case,
   since the number of horizontal bars varies between examples,
   and I want the bar widths and spacing to look
   approximately the same for all three cases. */

/* Data selection criterion and image height for the top image */
%let TopN = 10;
%let HeightForTopImage = 2.54in;

/* Data selection criterion and image height for the middle image */
%let Minimum = 1000000;
%let HeightForMiddleImage = 2.30in;

/* Data selection criterion and image height for the bottom image */
%let SubtotalPercentSelected = 60;
%let HeightForBottomImage = 3.14in;

/* Pre-processing of input data for all three cases,
   to capture all totals needed as macro or symbolic variables,
   and to present totals by city in rank order
   for use in the image creation steps */

proc summary data=sashelp.shoes;
class Subsidiary;
var Sales;
output out=work.Totals sum=;
run;

data _null_;
set work.Totals nobs=CityCountPlusOne;
where _type_ EQ 0;
call symput('TotalSales',Sales);
call symput('TotalDollars',trim(left(put(Sales,dollar11.))));
call symput('CityCount',trim(left(CityCountPlusOne - 1)));
run;

proc sort data=work.Totals out=work.CityTotals;
where _type_ NE 0;
by descending Sales;
run;
```

```
footnote;
ods results=off;
ods _all_ close;
ods listing style=GraphFontArial8ptBold gpath="C:\temp" dpi=300;

/* ODS GRAPHICS settings for ALL three images: */
ods graphics on / reset=all scale=off width=5.7in;

/* Figure 4-7 Top Image for Ranked Subset Hbar Charts
   Subset is Top N Responses */

data work.ToTopChart;
retain SubTotalSales 0;
set work.CityTotals;
Rank = _N_;
Percent = 100 * (Sales / &TotalSales);
Share = trim(left(put(Percent,4.1))) || '%';
SubTotalSales + Sales;
output;
if _N_ EQ &TopN then do;
  call symput('SubTotalSales',
             trim(left(put(SubTotalSales,dollar12.))));
  SubTotalPercent = 100 * (SubTotalSales / &TotalSales);
  call symput('SubTotalPercent',
             trim(left(put(SubTotalPercent,4.1))) || '%');;
  stop;
end;
run;

ods graphics / height=&HeightForTopImage
  imagename="Fig4-7Top_RankedSubsetHBarChart_SelectingTopN";
title1 height=10pt justify=center
  "Top &TopN Ranked Shoes Sales By City";
title2 height=10pt justify=center
  "Selecting Only Top &TopN";
title3 height=10pt justify=center
  "SubTotal Sales &SubTotalSales is &SubTotalPercent of Total";
title4 height=10pt justify=center
  "All &CityCount Cities had Total Sales &TotalDollars";
proc sgplot data=work.ToTopChart noborder;
hbar Subsidiary / response=Sales categoryorder=respdesc
  fillattrs=(color=Green)
  displaybaseline=off nooutline barwidth=0.7;
yaxistable Rank  / location=outside position=left label='Rank';
yaxistable Sales / location=inside  position=left stat=sum label='Sales';
yaxistable Share / location=inside  position=left label='Share';
yaxis display=(nolabel noline noticks) fitpolicy=none;
xaxis display=none;
run;
title; footnote;
```

```
/* Figure 4-7 Middle Image for Ranked Subset Hbar Charts
   Subset is Responses Above a Minimum */

data work.ToMiddleChart;
retain SubTotalSales 0;
set work.CityTotals;
if Sales GE &Minimum
then do;
  Rank = _N_;
  Percent = 100 * (Sales / &TotalSales);
  Share = trim(left(put(Percent,4.1))) || '%';
  SubTotalSales + Sales;
  /* When the first non-qualifying input category
     will occur cannot be foreseen.
     So, do this for every qualifying category: */
  call symput('CutOffCount',trim(left(_N_)));
  call symput('SubTotalSales',
              trim(left(put(SubTotalSales,dollar12.))));
  SubTotalPercent = 100 * (SubTotalSales / &TotalSales);
  call symput('SubTotalPercent',
              trim(left(put(SubTotalPercent,4.1))) || '%');
  output;
end;
else delete;
run;

ods graphics / height=&HeightForMiddleImage
  imagename="Fig4-7Middle_RankedSubsetHBarChart_UsingMinimum";
title1 height=10pt justify=center
  "Top &CutOffCount Ranked Shoes Sales By City";
title2 height=10pt justify=center
  "Selecting Only Cities with Sales At Least $&Minimum";
title3 height=10pt justify=center
  "SubTotal Sales &SubTotalSales is &SubTotalPercent of Total";
title4 height=10pt justify=center
  "All &CityCount Cities had Total Sales &TotalDollars";
proc sgplot data=work.ToMiddleChart noborder;
hbar Subsidiary / response=Sales categoryorder=respdesc
  fillattrs=(color=Green)
  displaybaseline=off nooutline barwidth=0.7;
yaxistable Rank  / location=outside position=left label='Rank';
yaxistable Sales / location=inside  position=left stat=sum label='Sales';
yaxistable Share / location=inside  position=left label='Share';
yaxis display=(nolabel noline noticks) fitpolicy=none;
xaxis display=none;
run;
title; footnote;
```

```
/* Figure 4-7 Bottom Image for Ranked Subset Hbar Charts
   Subset is Subtotal Percent */

data work.ToBottomChart;
retain SubTotalSales SubTotalPercent 0;
set work.CityTotals;
Rank = _N_;
Percent = 100 * (Sales / &TotalSales);
Share = trim(left(put(Percent,4.1))) || '%';
SubTotalSales + Sales;
SubTotalPercent + Percent;
output;
if SubTotalPercent GE &SubtotalPercentSelected
then do;
  call symput('TopPercentCount',trim(left(_N_)));
  call symput('SubTotalSales',
              trim(left(put(SubTotalSales,dollar12.))));
  call symput('SubTotalPercent',
              trim(left(put(SubTotalPercent,4.1))) || '%');
  stop;
end;
run;

ods graphics / height=&HeightForBottomImage
  imagename="Fig4-7Bottom_RankedSubsetHBarChart_SubtotalPercent";
title1 font='Arial/Bold' height=10pt justify=center
  "Top &TopPercentCount Ranked Shoes Sales By City";
title2 font='Arial/Bold' height=10pt justify=center
    "Selecting Only Enough for At Least &SubtotalPercentSelected.% of
Total Sales";
title3 height=10pt justify=center
  "SubTotal Sales &SubTotalSales is &SubTotalPercent of Total";
title4 height=10pt justify=center
  "All &CityCount Cities had Total Sales &TotalDollars";
proc sgplot data=work.ToBottomChart noborder;
hbar Subsidiary / response=Sales categoryorder=respdesc
  fillattrs=(color=Green)
  displaybaseline=off nooutline barwidth=0.7;
yaxistable Rank  / location=outside position=left label='Rank';
yaxistable Sales / location=inside  position=left stat=sum label='Sales';
yaxistable Share / location=inside  position=left label='Share';
yaxis display=(nolabel noline noticks) fitpolicy=none;
xaxis display=none;
run;
title; footnote;

ods listing close;
```

About These Three Images

HEIGHT in the ODS GRAPHICS statement differs in the code for each case, since the number of horizontal bars varies between examples, and I want the bar widths and spacing to look approximately the same for all three cases. A follow-up fancy bit of coding can allow you to automate the height determination so that your graph looks similar, though shorter or longer, for any number of bars, without your having to manually change the HEIGHT value. The algorithm, however, is specific to the font sizes and font used in these example cases. Back in 1991, I first wrote about what I called Intelligent Graphics—making graph creation code adapt to the data (and/or date) situation or other runtime differences, making the code auto-customize itself.

In a typical graph design and construction situation, you might first take the image height default. Recall that the default is always three-fourths of (or 0.75 times) the image width. If the results are unsatisfactory, you adjust the height until the result is to your satisfaction. If your graph creation process is one-time or any other situation where you will see the result before it is delivered or made available to its audience, then you can adjust the code if needed.

Algorithmic control of the dimensions of your image is necessary only if you care about the appearance and format of your graph in a situation where its delivery is automatic, such as an online interactive response, or via a computer's periodically scheduled run of your program. If delivery is not automatic, you can view the result and iteratively adjust the height of the image until you are satisfied.

To implement automated height specification for this particular graph design and data, the code changes are simple.

These statements must be inserted in the work.ToChart DATA step:

```
ImageHeightInches = 1.35 + (_N_ * 0.119);
call symput('ImageHeightInches',trim(left(ImageHeightInches)));
```

where _N_ is the number of bars which is the same as the number of categories that are selected. For the Top N and Top Percent cases, the statements must be inserted before the STOP statement. For the CutOff case, they must be inserted before the OUTPUT statement.

The ODS Graphics statement must be changed thus:

```
ods graphics on / reset=all scale=off
  width=5.7in height=&ImageHeightInches.in imagename="Whatever";
```

Listing A4-57. *Macro source code and common prep code to create Figures 4-57 to 4-61*

```
/* Both code items below are %INCLUDEd in Listings 4-57 to 4-61. */

/* The following macro source code can be stored as, e.g.,
   C:\SharedCode\Modified_genAreaBarDataBasic.sas */

/*******************************************************************
The original macro genAreaBarDataBasic by Dan Heath is found at
 https://blogs.sas.com/content/graphicallyspeaking/2022/04/30/area-
bar-charts-using-sgplot
Any lines of code added or changed here for this derivative macro
are marked with: LeRB mod
*******************************************************************/

/************************************************/
/*  Basic area bar chart                      */
/*  notes:                                    */
/*  - The values for the response and width   */
/*    input variables are summed.             */
/*  - The response output column contains the */
/*    response values for labeling.           */
/*  - The width output column contains the width */
/*    values for labeling.                    */
/*                                            */
/*  args:                                     */
/*  input - input data set name               */
/*  output - output data set name             */
/*  category - category variable for each bar */
/*  response - variable for the length of each bar */
/*  width - variable for the width of each bar */
/*  datalabel - variable for bar datalabel         */ /* LeRB mod */
/************************************************/

/*  %macro genAreaBarDataBasic(input, output, category, response,
width); Original Code COMMENTED OUT HERE AS LeRB mod */

%macro Modified_genAreaBarDataBasic(
  input, output, category, response, width
  , datalabel   /* LeRB mod */
  );

proc summary data=&input nway;
%if %length(&datalabel) NE 0 %then %do; /* LeRB mod */
id &datalabel; /* LeRB mod */
%end; /* LeRB mod */
class &category;
var &response &width;
output out=_out_totals_ sum=;
run;
```

```
data &output;
retain x 0;
label x="&width" y="&response" ID="&category";
set _out_totals_;
ID=&category;
response=&response;
width=&width;
y=0;
x=x;
output;
y=&response;
output;
x = x + &width;
output;
y=0;
output;
run;
```

%mend Modified_genAreaBarDataBasic;

/* The following prep code can be stored as
   C:\SharedCode\CommonPrepForFigures4-57to4-61.sas

/* The prep code below must be run for each example. Even if the output data
set were stored in the SASUSER data library to assure persistence after the
SAS session ends, there are four macro variables needed in every example that
disappear at the end of the SAS session. Unless the post-prep parts of each
example's code were all concatenated in the same code submission for a single
SAS session, the macro variables need to be created for each SAS session, if
each example is run in a separate session. So, a practical solution is to
store the prep code in a folder and %INCLUDE it for each example. */

```
data totals;
input Site $ Quarter Sales Salespersons;
format Sales dollar12.2;
datalines;
Lima 1   4043.97   4
NY    1  8225.26  12
Rome 1   3543.97   6
Lima 2   3723.44   5
NY    2  8595.07  18
Rome 2   5558.29  10
Lima 3   4437.96   8
NY    3  9847.91  24
Rome 3   6789.85  14
Lima 4   6065.57  10
NY    4 11388.51  26
Rome 4   8509.08  16
;
run;
```

```
proc summary data=totals;
class Site;
var Sales Salespersons;
output out=SiteTotals sum=SiteTotalSales SiteSalespersons;
run;
```

```
data work.SiteTotalsAndAreasAndYperX;
retain MaxSiteTotalSales 0;
length NumbersForSite $ 8 SiteWithNumbers $ 13;
set SiteTotals end=LastOne;
if _type_ EQ 0
then do;
  call symput('GrandTotalSales',
    trim(left(put(SiteTotalSales,dollar7.))));
  call symput('GrandTotalSalespersons',
    trim(left(put(SiteSalespersons,3.))));
  delete;
end; /* macro variables disappear at end of SAS session */
NumbersForSite =
  trim(left(SiteSalesPersons)) || '-' ||
  trim(left(put((SiteTotalSales / 1000),dollar5.1)));
SiteWithNumbers =
  trim(left(Site)) || '-' || trim(left(NumbersForSite));
Area = SiteTotalSales * SiteSalespersons;
YperX = SiteTotalSales / SiteSalespersons;
MaxSiteTotalSales = max(MaxSiteTotalSales,SiteTotalSales);
if LastOne then do;
  call symput('MaxSiteTotalSales',MaxSiteTotalSales);
  call symput('MaxSiteTotalSalesDisplay',
    trim(left(put((MaxSiteTotalSales / 1000),dollar5.1))));
end; /* macro variables disappear at end of SAS session */
run;
/* End of Prep Code for Area Bar Chart Examples */
```

Listing A5-22. *Code to create the three donut charts in Figure 5-22 (analogues of what I call The Pac-Man Pie Chart)*

```
ods results off;
ods _all_ close;

ods listing style=GraphFontArial6ptBold gpath="C:\temp" dpi=300;

proc summary data=sashelp.shoes;
class Region Subsidiary Product;
var Sales;
output out=work.FromSUMMARY sum=;
run;
```

```
data work.Cities work.Regions work.Products;
set work.FromSummary;
if _type_ EQ 0
then call symput('GrandTotalSales',trim(left(Sales)));
else if _type_ EQ 1 then output work.Products;
else if _type_ EQ 2 then output work.Cities;
else if _type_ EQ 4 then output work.Regions;
run;

proc sort data=work.Cities;
by descending Sales; run;

data work.MaxSalesCityAndOthers;
set work.Cities;
if _N_ EQ 1;
call symput('PctMaxCity',
  trim(left(put(Sales/&GrandTotalSales,percent6.1))));
  /* it is necessary to use the percent6.1 format, to allocate
     enough width for (N.N%), where parenthesis is for negative,
     even though the value is positive */
  /* in DATA steps for MaxSalesRegionAndOthers
     and MaxSalesProductAndOthers, use percent7.1 */
CityLabel = trim(left(Subsidiary)) || ' - ' ||
            trim(left(put(Sales,dollar10.)));
output;
Sales = &GrandTotalSales - Sales;
CityLabel = 'Other Cities';
output;
stop; run;

ods graphics / reset=all scale=off width=1.85in height=1.85in
  imagename='Fig5-22_Left_Donut_HoleInfo_MaxSalesPct_City';
title1 color=blue 'City with Largest Share of Shoe Sales';
title2 height=3pt color=white 'INVISIBLE Text for white space';
proc sgpie data=work.MaxSalesCityAndOthers;
styleattrs datacolors=(CX009900 CXEEEEEE);
donut CityLabel / response=Sales
  sliceorder=respasc /* start with the smallest donut bite */
  holelabel="&PctMaxCity"
  holelabelattrs=(family='Arial Narrow' color=CX009900)
  startangle=90  /* accepting the default STARTPOS=CENTER */
  datalabelattrs=(color=blue)
  datalabeldisplay=(category) datalabelloc=outside;
run;

proc sort data=work.Regions;
by descending Sales;
run;
```

```
data work.MaxSalesRegionAndOthers;
set work.Regions;
if _N_ EQ 1;
call symput('PctMaxRegion',
  trim(left(put(Sales/&GrandTotalSales,percent7.1))));;;
  /* enough width for (NN.N%), where parenthesis is for negative) */
RegionLabel = trim(left(Region)) || ' - ' || trim(left(put(Sales,dollar10.)));
output;
Sales = &GrandTotalSales - Sales;
RegionLabel = 'Other Regions';
output;
stop; run;

ods graphics / reset=all scale=off width=1.85in height=1.85in
  imagename='Fig5-22_Center_Donut_HoleInfo_MaxSalesPct_Region';
title1 color=blue 'Region with Largest Share of Shoe Sales';
title2 height=3pt color=white 'INVISIBLE Text for white space';
proc sgpie data=work.MaxSalesRegionAndOthers;
styleattrs datacolors=(CX009900 CXEEEEEE);
donut RegionLabel / response=Sales
  sliceorder=respasc
  holelabel="&PctMaxRegion"
  holelabelattrs=(family='Arial Narrow' color=CX009900)
  startangle=90
  datalabelattrs=(color=blue)
  datalabeldisplay=(category)
  datalabelloc=outside;
run;

proc sort data=work.Products;
by descending Sales;
run;

data work.MaxSalesProductAndOthers;
set work.Products;
if _N_ EQ 1;
call symput('PctMaxProduct',
  trim(left(put(Sales/&GrandTotalSales,percent7.1))));
  /* enough width for (NN.N%), where parenthesis is for negative) */
ProductLabel = trim(left(Product)) || ' - ' || trim(left(put(Sales,dol
lar10.)));
output;
Sales = &GrandTotalSales - Sales;
ProductLabel = 'Other Products';
output;
stop; run;

ods graphics / reset=all scale=off width=1.85in height=1.85in
  imagename='Fig5-22_Right_Donut_HoleInfo_MaxSalesPct_Product';
title1 color=blue 'Product with Largest Share of Shoe Sales';
```

```
title2 height=3pt color=white 'INVISIBLE Text for white space';
proc sgpie data=work.MaxSalesProductAndOthers;
styleattrs datacolors=(CX009900 CXEEEEEE);
donut ProductLabel / response=Sales
  sliceorder=respasc
  holelabel="&PctMaxProduct"
  holelabelattrs=(family='Arial Narrow' color=CX009900)
  startangle=90
  datalabelattrs=(color=blue)
  datalabeldisplay=(category)
  datalabelloc=outside;
run;

ods listing close;
title;
```

Listing A8-15. *Code to create Figure 8-15 (maximally informative and unambiguous step plot)*

```
%macro StepDataByDate(
data=
,out=
,DateVar=
,Yvar=
,YvarRescaleDivisor=
,DataLabelVar=DataLabelValue
,DataLabelLength=
,DataLabelFormat=
,StepInterval=
,Filter=);

proc sort data=&data
  out=work.ToPrep
      (keep=&DateVar &Yvar);
%if %length(&Filter) NE 0 %then %do;
&Filter;
%end;
by Date;
run;

data work.ToPlot_&Yvar
  (keep=&DateVar &Yvar &DataLabelVar DropLineYvar);
%if %length(&DataLabelVar) NE 0 AND %length(&DataLabelLength) NE 0 %then %do;
length &DataLabelVar $ &DataLabelLength;
%end;
retain YvalueForPreviousDate TempSaveYvar 0 Seq 0;
set work.ToPrep end=LastOne;
DropLineYvar=&Yvar;
```

```
%if %length(&YvarRescaleDivisor) NE 0 %then %do;
&Yvar = &Yvar / &YvarRescaleDivisor;
%end;
Seq + 1;
if _N_ EQ 1 then do;
%if %length(&DataLabelVar) NE 0 AND %length(&DataLabelFormat) NE 0
%then %do;
  &DataLabelVar = put(&Yvar,&DataLabelFormat);
%end;
  DropLineYvar=&Yvar;
  output;
  YvalueForPreviousDate = &Yvar;
end;
else do;
  TempSaveYvar = &Yvar;
  &Yvar = YvalueForPreviousDate;
  &DataLabelVar = ' ';;
  DropLineYvar=&Yvar;
  output;
  Seq + 1;
  &Yvar = TempSaveYvar;
%if %length(&DataLabelVar) NE 0 AND %length(&DataLabelFormat) NE 0
%then %do;
  &DataLabelVar = put(TempSaveYvar,&DataLabelFormat);
%end;
  DropLineYvar=&Yvar;
  output;
  YvalueForPreviousDate = &Yvar;
  if LastOne
  then do;
    Seq + 1;
    &DateVar=intnx("&StepInterval",&DateVar,1);
    &DataLabelVar = ' ';;
    DropLineYvar=.;
    output;
  end;
end;
run;

%mend StepDataByDate;

options mprint;

%StepDataByDate(
data=sashelp.stocks
,out=work.ToPlot
,DateVar=Date
,Yvar=Close
,YvarRescaleDivisor=1
```

```
,DataLabelVar=DataLabelValue
,DataLabelLength=5
,DataLabelFormat=5.1
,StepInterval=Quarter
,filter=%str(where year(Date) EQ 1998 and Stock EQ 'IBM';)
);

data _null_;
retain MonthCount 0;
set work.ToPlot_Close end=LastOne;
where DataLabelValue NE ' ';
MonthCount + 1;
call symput('Date'||trim(left(put(MonthCount,3.))),Date);
if LastOne;
Date + 31;
call symput('Date13',Date);
run;

%macro GetDates;
%do i = 1 %to 13 %by 1;
  &&Date&i
%end;
%mend GetDates;

options mprint;

footnote;
ods results off;
ods _all_ close;
ods listing style=GraphFontArial10ptBold gpath="C:\temp" dpi=300;
ods graphics on / reset=all scale=off width=5.7in
  imagename="Fig8-15_UnambiguousMaximallyInformativeStepPlot";
title1 justify=center
'Close Price for IBM Shares on First Trading Day Each Month - 1998';
proc sgplot data=work.ToPlot_Close noautolegend noborder;
series x=Date y=Close /
  lineattrs=(pattern=solid color=green thickness=2);
dropline x=Date y=DropLineYvar /
  dropto=x lineattrs=(pattern=Dot);
text x=Date y=Close text=DataLabelValue /
  TextAttrs=(family='Arial' size=10pt)
  Position=TopRight;
xaxis display=(noline noticks nolabel) type=discrete
  values=(%GetDates)
  valuesdisplay=('Jan' 'Feb' 'Mar' 'Apr' 'May' 'Jun'
                 'Jul' 'Aug' 'Sep' 'Oct' 'Nov' 'Dec' ' ');
yaxis display=none;
run;
ods listing close;
title;
```

Listing A10-1. *Emulation of the PROC SGSCATTER PLOT statement's REFTICKS option using PROC SGPLOT and the SCATTER statement*

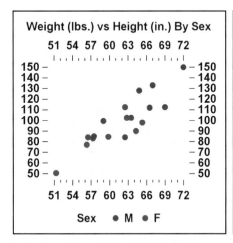 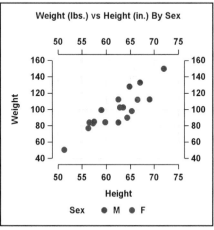

Left: Emulation SGPLOT SCATTER   Right: REFTICKS SGSCATTER PLOT

Left: Emulation SGPLOT SCATTER. Right: REFTICKS SGSCATTER PLOT (from the right-hand side of Figure 10-1)

```
footnote;
ods results=off;
ods _all_ close;
ods listing style=GraphFontArial10ptBold gpath="C:\temp" dpi=300;
   /* 11pt font would case aa title line break */
ods graphics on / reset=all scale=off width=2.8in height=2.8in
   imagename="AppendixA10-1_RefTicksEmulationForSGPLOTwithSCATTER";
title1 justify=center 'Weight (lbs.) vs Height (in.) By Sex';
proc sgplot data=sashelp.class noborder;
styleattrs datacontrastcolors=(red blue);
scatter y=weight x=height /
  name='ScatterPlotWithGroupVar'
  group=sex
  markerattrs=(symbol=CircleFilled);
scatter y=weight x=height /
  y2axis x2axis
  markerattrs=(size=0);
yaxis
  display=(noline nolabel)
  values=(50 to 150 by 10)
  fitpolicy=none
  grid;
xaxis
```

```
  minor minorcount=2
  display=(noline nolabel)
  values=(51 to 72 by 3)
  fitpolicy=none
  grid minorgrid minorcount=2;
y2axis
  display=(noline nolabel)
  values=(50 to 150 by 10)
  fitpolicy=none;
x2axis
  minor minorcount=2
  display=(noline nolabel)
  values=(51 to 72 by 3)
  fitpolicy=none;
keylegend 'ScatterPlotWithGroupVar'
 /* This legend ID assures that the
    legend is only for that scatter plot.
    Without NAME= a second legend is created
    for the second SCATTER statement */
 / title='Sex' /* When using NAME=, this title
   is not automatic as it normally would be. */
  noborder;
run;
ods listing close;
title;
```

Listing A14-15. *Code to create Figure 14-15*

/* select, prepare, and sort the input data */

```
data work.CloseByStockByMon;
  format Date 5.;
  format Close 3.;
  set SASHELP.STOCKS
    (keep=Stock Date Close);
  if 1998 LE year(Date) LE 2001;
  Close=round(Close); /* eliminate pennies */
run;

proc sort data=work.CloseByStockByMon;
by Stock Date; /* in case input
  is in reverse chronological order,
  which happens to be true for SASHELP.STOCKS */
run;
```

%macro PrepareAnno(
```
yvar=,
yvarformat=,
yvarlabelsize=,
```

```
xvar=,
xvarformat=,
xvarlabelsize=);
  label = put(&yvar,&yvarformat);
  textsize = &yvarlabelsize;
  anchor = 'bottom';
  output anno;
  label = put(&xvar,&xvarformat);
  textsize = &xvarlabelsize;
  anchor = 'top';
  output anno;
%mend  PrepareAnno;

%macro DoAnno; /* used for REPEATED CONCISE invocations */
  %PrepareAnno(
    yvar=Close,yvarformat=3.,yvarlabelsize=14,
    xvar=Date,xvarformat=monyy5.,xvarlabelsize=13);
%mend  DoAnno;

%macro SparseLineForCategory(Category=,Value=);

data work.CloseByMon;
set work.CloseByStockByMon;
WHERE &Category EQ "&Value";
run;

proc means data=work.CloseByMon min max noprint;
  var Close;
  output out=MinMax;
run;

data _null_;
set MinMax end=LastOne;
retain MinY MaxY;
if _STAT_ EQ 'MIN'
then do;
  MinY = Close;
  call symput('MinYvalue',Close);
end;
else
if _STAT_ EQ 'MAX'
then do;
  MaxY = Close;
  call symput('MaxYvalue',Close);
end;
if LastOne;
call symput('YvalueRange',MaxY - MinY);
run;
```

```
data anno(keep=
  x1 y1 label anchor function x1space y1space
  border
  justify
  layer
  rotate
  textcolor
  textfont
  textsize
  textstyle
  textweight
  transparency);
length
  label $ 16
  anchor $ 11;
/* ANCHOR values:
   'TOPLEFT' | 'TOP' | 'TOPRIGHT' | 'RIGHT' | 'BOTTOMRIGHT' |
   'BOTTOM' | 'BOTTOMLEFT' | 'LEFT' | 'CENTER'
   specify the anchor position of the annotation.
   This point is placed on the specified X1 and Y1 positions. */
retain
  PredecessorToLastY
  function 'text'
  x1space 'datavalue'
  y1space 'datavalue'
  border 'false'
  justify 'CENTER'
  layer 'FRONT' /* in front of the graph */
  rotate 0 /* Bessler: NEVER ROTATE */
  textcolor 'Black'
  textfont 'Arial'
  /* textsize 10  Actual value supplied in the DoAnno macro */
  textstyle 'Normal' /* Italic */
  textweight 'Bold' /* Normal */
  transparency 0; /* opaque max tranaparency is 1.0 */
set work.CloseByMon end=LastOne nobs=ObsCount;
x1 = Date;
y1 = Close;
if _N_ EQ 1
then do;
  %DoAnno;
end;
else
if _N_ EQ ObsCount - 1
then do;
  PredecessorToLastY = Close;
end;
else
if LastOne
```

```
then do;
  label = put(Close,3.);
  label = trim(left(label)) || ' ' || put(Date,monyy5.);
  textsize = 14;
  anchor = 'bottom';
  output anno;
  change = Close - PredecessorToLastY;
  if change GE 0
  then label = '+' || trim(left(put(change,3.)));
  else label = '-' || trim(left(put(change,3.)));
  textsize = 14;
  anchor = 'top';
  output anno;
end;
else
if put(Close,12.8) EQ &MinYvalue
then do;
  %DoAnno;
end;
else
if put(Close,12.8) EQ &MaxYvalue
then do;
  %DoAnno;
end;
run;

/* NOTE: In some situations, I have found it necessary to add
    footnote1 height=1pt ' ';
    to provide white space below the lowest annotation
    so that its bottom is not truncated. */

%macro SGPLOTstep(PadPercent=5);

proc sgplot data=work.CloseByMon sganno=anno noautolegend
      description=' ' /* turn off "The SGPLOT Procedure" pop-up */
      noborder /* turn off border around plot area */
      pad=&PadPercent%;
  series x=Date y=Close /
    markers
    markerattrs=(color=Blue symbol=CircleFilled)
    /* default symbol is an open Circle */
    lineattrs=(color=Red pattern=ShortDash);
  yaxis DISPLAY=(NOVALUES NOLINE NOTICKS NOLABEL);
  xaxis DISPLAY=(NOVALUES NOLINE NOTICKS NOLABEL);
  format Date monyy5.;
run;

%mend   SGPLOTstep;
```

```
ods graphics / reset=all scale=off
  noborder /* turn off border around each image */
  imagemap tipmax=2500
  outputfmt=SVG
  imagename="SparseLineHistoryTableEntryFor_&Value"
  width=9.5in height=2in; /* adjust this later if desired */

title1 height=16pt justify=left "&Category = &Value";
title2 height=4pt /* 28pt */ ' ';
footnote1;
%SGPLOTstep; /* using macro default for PadPercent */

%mend SparseLineForCategory;

options mprint;

/* If using a Parent style that does pagebraaks
proc template;
  define style styles.PARENT_nobreak;
    parent=styles.PARENT;
    style body from body /
    pagebreakhtml=_undef_;
  end;
run;
IF using this, reference it below with STYLE=. */

/* the remainder uses everything above to do the job */

footnote;
ods results=off;
ods _all_ close;

ods html5 path="C:\temp"
  style=styles.Pearl
  gtitle gfootnote
  body="Fig14-15_WebEnabledTableOfThreeSparseLines.html"
 (title="Web-Enabled Table Of Three Sparse Lines");

ods startpage=no;

title; /* suppress default title "The SAS System"
  Suppression needed when first PROC run is ODSTEXT,
  not a graph or table. */

proc odstext;
  p "Monthly Closing Price 1998-2001 History & Critical Points (Use mouse for
  other points)"
    / style={fontsize=16pt fontweight=bold just=center color=blue};
run;
```

```
%SparseLineForCategory(Category=Stock,Value=IBM);
%SparseLineForCategory(Category=Stock,Value=Intel);
%SparseLineForCategory(Category=Stock,Value=Microsoft);

ods html5 close;
title; footnote;
```

For Further Information on SAS ODS Graphics

This book cannot cover all of the options available. SAS ODS Graphics is Options SuperRich. The reference for more and *complete* information is the SAS ODS Graphics Procedures Guide. It is accessible online and will always be the up-to-date resource on ODS Graphics syntax, procedures, statements, and options. Graph Template Language is included in some references below. The fact is mentioned, but that topic is out of scope of, and unneeded for, this book.

If you want to create data visualizations that comply with the Section 508 amendment to the United States Workforce Rehabilitation Act, with the Web Content Accessibility Guidelines (WCAG), and with other accessibility standards, see the paper:
Accessibility and ODS Graphics:
Seven Simple Steps to Section 508 Compliance Using SAS 9.4M5
By Ed Summers, Julianna Langston, and Dan Heath
Found at: https://www.sas.com/content/dam/SAS/support/en/sas-global-forum-proceedings/2018/1980-2018.pdf

A book especially useful for first-time users of SAS ODS Graphics is:
Statistical Graphics Procedures by Example: Effective Graphs Using SAS
By Sanjay Matange and Dan Heath

© LeRoy Bessler 2023
LeR. Bessler, *Visual Data Insights Using SAS ODS Graphics*,
https://doi.org/10.1007/978-1-4842-8609-8

For topics not covered by me, see Chapter 9 for Annotation, Chapter 2 for Health and Life Sciences Graphs, Chapter 13 for Business Graphs, and Chapter 16 for Tips.

A book that applies SAS ODS Graphics (and Graph Template Language) is:
"Clinical Graphs using SAS"
By Sanjay Matange

An online book for SAS ODS Graphics is:
Advanced ODS Graphics Examples (contains some Graph Template Language)
By Warren F. Kuhfeld
Found at: https://support.sas.com/documentation/prod-p/grstat/9.4/en/PDF/odsadvg.pdf

An online book on PROC SGPLOT and Graph Template Language is:
Basic ODS Graphics Examples
By Warren F. Kuhfeld
Found at: https://support.sas.com/documentation/prod-p/grstat/9.4/en/PDF/odsbasicg.pdf

An abundant and diverse source of SAS ODS Graphics examples are web postings
By Robert Allison
Found at: https://robslink.com/SAS/ods1/aaaindex.htm

A Year 2017 paper on Styles is:
Diving Deep into SAS® ODS Graphics Styles
By Dan Heath
Found at: https://support.sas.com/resources/papers/proceedings17/SAS0675-2017.pdf

A Year 2014 paper on Styles is:
Putting on the Ritz: New Ways to Style Your ODS Graphics to the Max
By Dan Heath
Found at: https://support.sas.com/resources/papers/proceedings14/SAS156-2014.pdf

For extended coverage of PROC SGPANEL see:
Using SAS ODS Graphics
By Chuck Kincaid
Found at: https://support.sas.com/resources/papers/proceedings12/154-2012.pdf

For ODS Graphics Annotation and for using Style Attributes to control colors, markers, and line patterns, see:
Intermediate SAS ODS Graphics
By Chuck Kincaid
Found at: https://analytics.ncsu.edu/sesug/2015/HOW-99.pdf

A paper devoted in full to ODS Graphics Annotation is:
Controlling the Drawing Space in ODS Graphics by Example

By Max Cherny
Found at: https://www.lexjansen.com/phuse-us/2018/ct/CT07.pdf

If you are a SAS/GRAPH user and would like a tutorial to assist the transition, see:
Something for Nothing! Converting Plots from SAS/GRAPH to ODS Graphics
By Philip R. Holland
Found at https://support.sas.com/resources/papers/proceedings14/1610-2014.pdf

Another SAS/GRAPH-to-ODS-Graphics conversion resource is:
Converting Annotate to ODS Graphics. Is It Possible?
By Philip R. Holland
Found at https://support.sas.com/resources/papers/proceedings15/2686-2015.pdf

An eBook of Course Notes for Converting Plots from SAS/GRAPH to ODS Graphics and for Converting Annotate to ODS Graphics is:
Practical ODS Graphics Course Notes
By Philip R. Holland

An updated tutorial for ODS Graphics newcomers is:
Introduction to ODS Graphics for the Non-Statistician
By Mike Kalt and Cynthia Zender
Found at: https://www.misug.org/uploads/8/1/9/1/8191072/czender_ods_graphics.zip

A tutorial (with links to 46 extra examples, and a link to all code used to prepare the paper) is:
Keeping Up to Date with ODS Graphics
By Warren F. Kuhfeld and Dan Heath
Found at: https://www.lexjansen.com/mwsug/2018/SP/MWSUG-2018-SP-139-SAS.pdf

The first paper about ODS Graphics by SAS users, rather than SAS employees, was:
Using PROC SGPLOT for Quick High Quality Graphs
By Lora D. Delwiche & Susan J. Slaughter
Found at https://www.lexjansen.com/wuss/2008/how/how05.pdf
This paper was written based on an earlier version (9.2). Nevertheless, it contains four helpful tables, even if not up-to-date and complete for the current version of SAS ODS Graphics. One shows, for PROC SGPLOT, which ODS Graphics graph types can be used with each other, which options can be used with which graph types. The other table that displays skeleton syntax and selected options for each of fifteen PROC SGPLOT statements (e.g., SCATTER, SERIES, STEP, etc.). See the paper for what the other tables include.

An example of using a Bubble Plot overlay with PROC SGMAP is included in:
Creating Great Maps in ODS Graphics using PROC SGMAP
By Kelly Mills
Found at: https://www.sas.com/content/dam/SAS/support/en/sas-global-forum-proceedings/2019/3314-2019.pdf

An interesting use of PROC SGMAP to present numeric measures by geographic location is:
Spatial Analysis of Humanitarian OpenStreetMap Team Data Using SAS ODS Graphics Procedures
By Michael Matthews
Found at: https://www.sas.com/content/dam/SAS/support/en/sas-global-forum-proceedings/2019/3102-2019.pdf
To read the maps you will need to use the zoom feature in whatever is your PDF reader.

I

Index

© LeRoy Bessler 2023
LeR. Bessler, *Visual Data Insights Using SAS ODS Graphics*,
https://doi.org/10.1007/978-1-4842-8609-8

Printed in the United States
by Baker & Taylor Publisher Services